Building Products Buyer's Guide

13,000 Products from 2,800 Manufacturers

A Desktop Reference from

The Editors of *Builder*

The Magazine of The National Association of Home Builders

HOME PLANNERS
A Division of Hanley-Wood, Inc.
Tucson, Arizona

Published by Home Planners
A Division of Hanley-Wood, Inc.
Editorial and Corporate Offices:
3275 West Ina Road, Suite 110
Tucson, Arizona 85741

Distribution Center:
29333 Lorie Lane
Wixom, Michigan 48393

Rickard D. Bailey, CEO and Publisher
Cindy Coatsworth Lewis, Publications Manager
Paulette Mulvin, Special Projects and Acquisitions Editor
Kathleen M. Hart, Project Coordinator
Jan Prideaux, Senior Editor
Sara Lisa-Rappaport, Production Coordinator
Sarah P. Smith, Copy Editor
Paul Fitzgerald, Senior Graphic Designer
Michael Shanahan, Project Designer

and

The Editors of *Builder*

First Printing: October 1997

10 9 8 7 6 5 4 3 2 1

Printed in the United States of America

Library of Congress Catalog Card Number: 97-074041

ISBN: 1-881955-39-7

How to Use the
Buyer's Guide

Shopping for building products can be an overwhelming task. You can search through literature you've collected, rummage through old magazines you've saved, even roam the aisles of your favorite home center, and eventually you'll find the information you need. But there's a better, more efficient way.

Start with *Building Products Buyer's Guide*, the one-stop reference that includes building product manufacturers and their latest products. You'll find information about more than 2,800 companies and close to 13,000 building products, all in this one handy volume!

The guide is easy to use. Products are organized into twenty-nine main categories and then further defined by more specific products within those categories. Looking for laminate countertops? Turn to the countertops section and look under laminate to find a list of manufacturers.

Many manufacturers offer product literature that can be sent directly to you if you fill out the order card inserted in this book. Simply check the circle numbers beside those manufacturers' names in the product section and circle the corresponding numbers on the card to receive detailed information about their products. Special product listings at the end of each section give details about some interesting products in that section. Those manufacturers who include these special listings have a page number shown in the product box to refer you to the page where that listing is found.

Want even more information about a manufacturer's product? Turn to the Manufacturer Index (page 206) and you'll find their address and phone number, and, in some cases, a FAX number, or an E-mail and Internet address, too. We've even included a handy Product Index (page 200) with cross references to give you the best, most complete sourcebook for building products.

But that's not all! Turn to page 172 for a bonus section of some of Home Planners' best-selling home plans. This collection of 44 designs represents the most popular and finest homes from our portfolio of over 3,000 homes. You'll find a variety of styles and sizes—one that just might be the perfect home for you and your family.

Manufacturer Index: Here you'll find addresses, phone numbers (many toll free), FAX numbers and more for over 2,800 companies. See page 206.

Product Index: Refer to this index if you're looking for a specific product and don't know where to find it. See page 200.

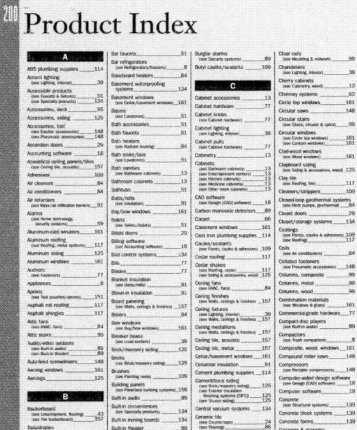

Manufacturer	Products							Sales		Circle No.
	Ceramic tile	Cultured marble	Laminate	Marble/granite/slate/stone	Solid surfacing	Stainless steel	Wood	Local dealer/distributor	Factory-direct	
AB Cushing Mills							■			
Advanced Technology			■					■	■	
American Marazzi Tile	■							■		
American Marble Industries/Kephaco Corp.	27							■	■	337
American Olean Tile	■		■					■		
Ampco Products			■	■				■		
Amsterdam Corp.	■							■	■	
Arctic Metal Products		■	■			■		■		
Arius Tile Co.	■							■	■	
Avonite					■			■		
Bally Block/Michigan Maple							■	■	■	
Bangkok Intl.							■	■	■	

Products: Read across to see what products a company offers. Products that are featured in the section (usually at the back of the section) will show a page number in their box. Notice that there is also a handy circle number included for those manufacturers that offer product literature through our mail-in program. See insert card to order product literature.

Smarter home building decisions

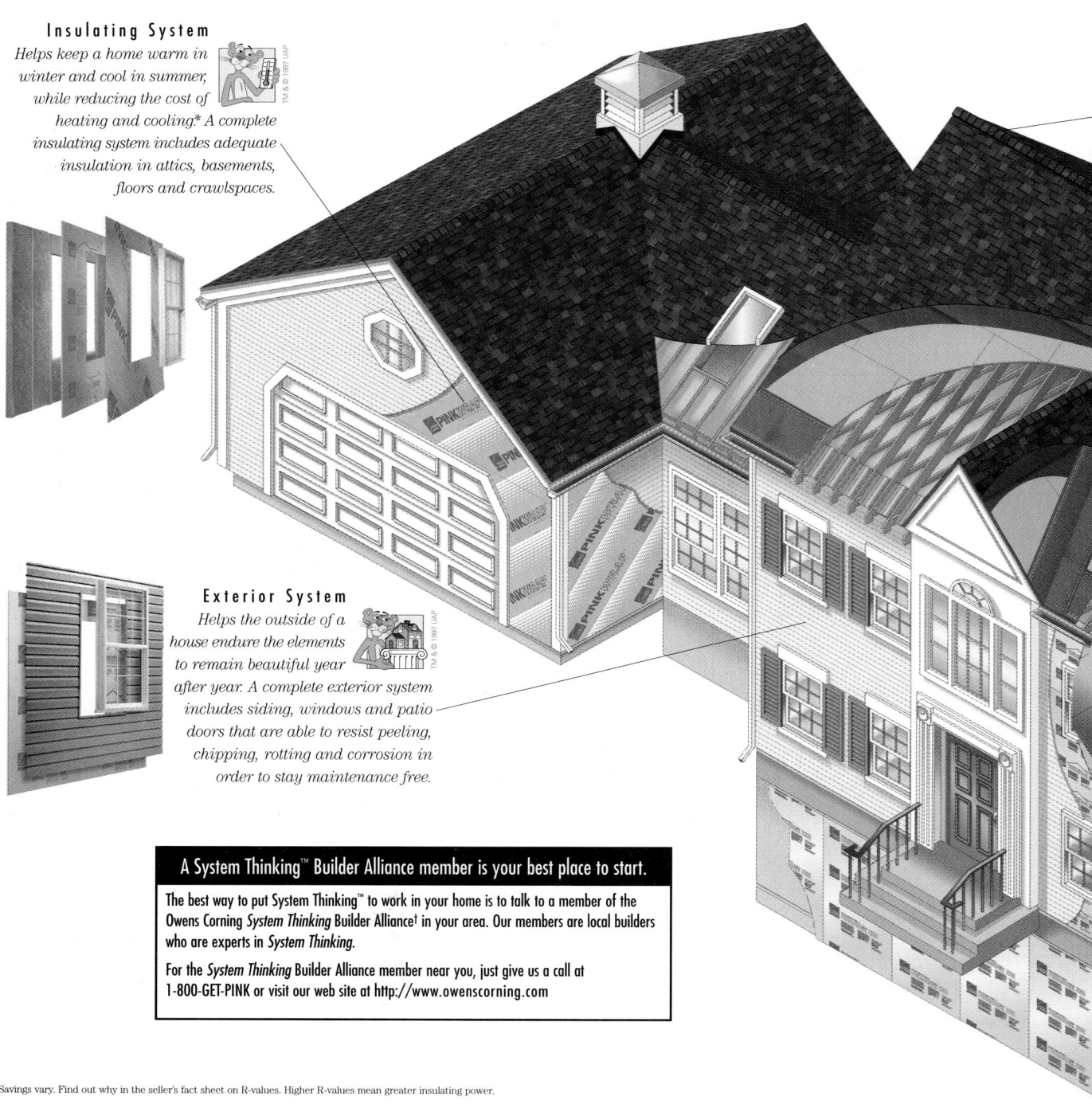

Insulating System
Helps keep a home warm in winter and cool in summer, while reducing the cost of heating and cooling.* A complete insulating system includes adequate insulation in attics, basements, floors and crawlspaces.

Exterior System
Helps the outside of a house endure the elements to remain beautiful year after year. A complete exterior system includes siding, windows and patio doors that are able to resist peeling, chipping, rotting and corrosion in order to stay maintenance free.

A System Thinking™ Builder Alliance member is your best place to start.

The best way to put System Thinking™ to work in your home is to talk to a member of the Owens Corning *System Thinking* Builder Alliance† in your area. Our members are local builders who are experts in *System Thinking*.

For the *System Thinking* Builder Alliance member near you, just give us a call at 1-800-GET-PINK or visit our web site at http://www.owenscorning.com

*Savings vary. Find out why in the seller's fact sheet on R-values. Higher R-values mean greater insulating power.

†Builders participating in the Owens Corning *System Thinking* Builder Alliance program are independently owned and operated. Therefore, participation by a builder in this program does not imply an endorsement by Owens Corning of the builder's workmanship, quality, performance, integrity or financial strength. This assessment rests with the homebuyer.

begin with System Thinking.™

Roofing System

Much more than just shingles, a complete roofing system protects a home from the damaging effects of wind, rain, snow and sun. The roofing system includes shingles, underlayment and proper ventilation, which work together for a healthier roof.

Sound Control System

Helps reduce the transmission of noise from adjoining rooms. By utilizing acoustic batts in interior walls, a Fiberglas® duct system that absorbs sound waves, and recommended construction techniques, noise levels in active rooms can be managed to help provide peace and quiet in the room next door. With proper customizing, even home offices and media rooms can coexist peacefully.

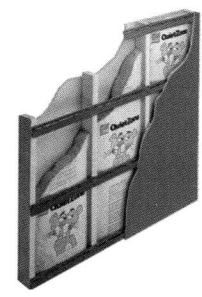

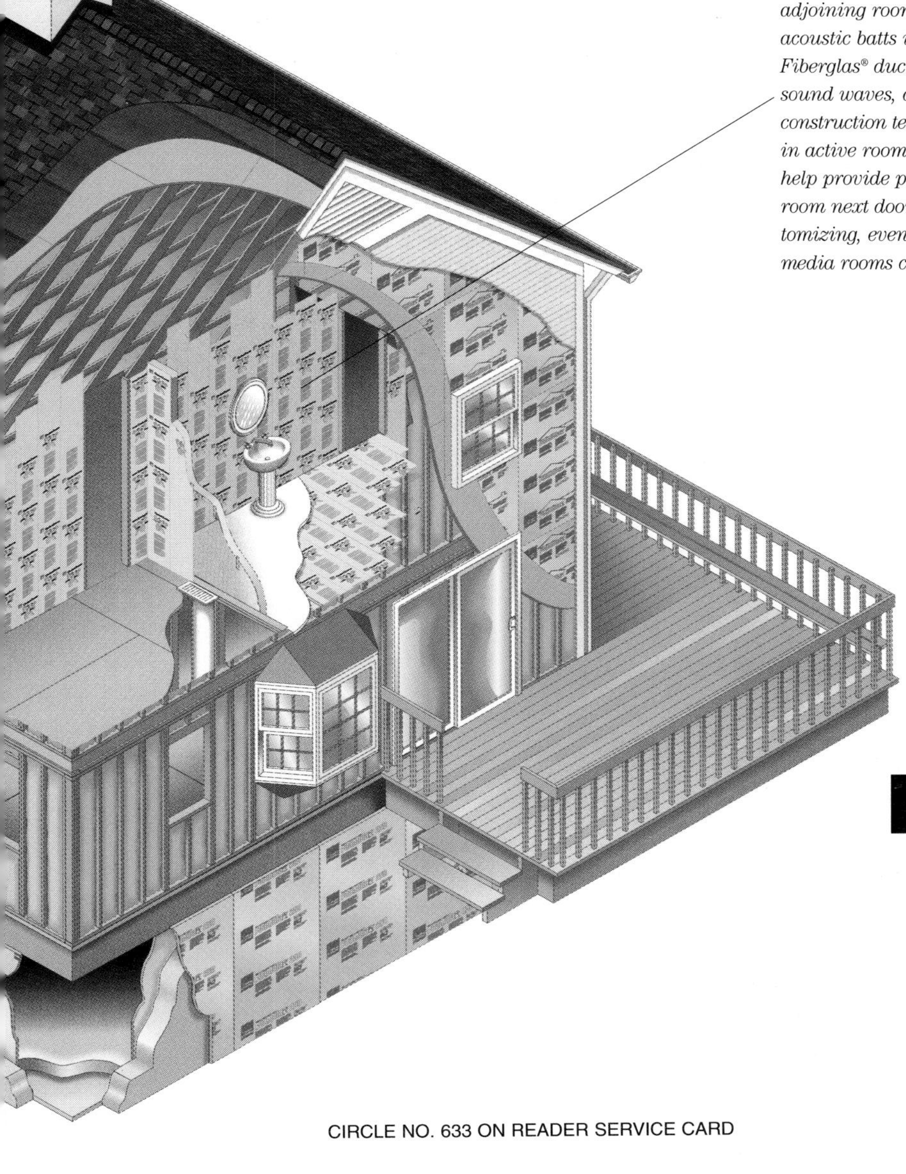

Your home is basically a series of systems. At Owens Corning, we want to help you understand how those systems work and how simple it is to make them work better. That's what System Thinking for the Home™ is all about.

If you're building or remodeling, ask us for free information on the Owens Corning Roofing, Exterior, Insulating or Sound Control Systems.

1-800-GET-PINK

http://www.owenscorning.com

OWENS CORNING

SYSTEM THINKING
for the Home™

BUILDING PRODUCTS BUYER'S GUIDE

13,000 Products from 2,800 Manufacturers

THE BUILDING PRODUCTS BUYER'S GUIDE

features almost 13,000 products. It includes:

TWENTY-NINE PRODUCT SECTIONS
in color-coded blocks.

FORTY-FOUR HOME DESIGNS
in a special bonus section starting on page 172.

PRODUCT INDEX
on page 200.

MANUFACTURER INDEX
on page 206.

HOW TO USE THE BUYER'S GUIDE
on page 3.

ILLUSTRATIONS BY
TODD GRAVELINE

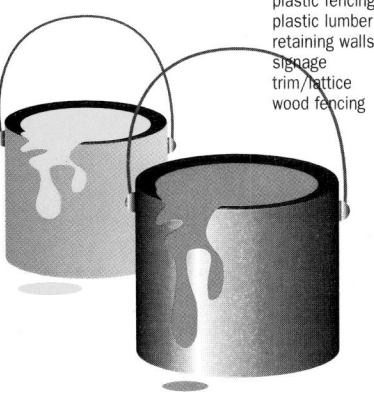

7

Appliances

Manufacturer	Cooktops	Dishwashers	Disposers	Exhaust vents/range hoods	Hot water dispensers	Microwave ovens	Ovens	Ranges	Refrigerators/freezers	Trash compactors	Washers/dryers	Water filtration systems/dispensers	Wine storage	Local dealer/distributor	Factory-direct	Circle No.
Abbaka				■										■		
Admiral	■	■				■	■	■		■						
AEG/Andi-Co Appliances	■	■				■	■	■						■	■	
Air Conditioning and Refrigeration Institute									■							
Amana Refrigeration	■	■		■		■	■	■	12	■						117
American Gas Assn.	■						■	■								
Ametek/(Plymouth Products Div.)												■		■		
Arctic Metal Products	■													■	■	
Asko		■									■			■		
Assn. of Home Appliance Manufacturers	■	■	■	■		■	■	■	■	■	■			■		
Breezaire													■	■		
Broan Mfg. Co.				■						■				■		
Brown Stove Works	■			■			■	■						■	■	
Bruner Corp.												■		■	■	
Cervitor Kitchens									■				■		■	
Creda	■	■		■				■			■			■		
Cuno												■		■		
Dacor	■			■		■	■							■		
Deflect-O-Corp.				■										■		
Dwyer Products Corp.									■						■	
DYNASTY Range	■			■			■	■						■	■	
Elan Major Appliances	■			■				■						■		
Electronic Cooking Systems	■													■		
Elkay Mfg. Co.					■									■		
Elmira Stove Works	■					■	■	■	■					■		
Everpure												■		■		
Fantech				■										■		
FiveStar	■			■				■						■		
Franke/Kitchen Systems Div.			■	■								■		■		
Frigidaire Home Products	■	■	■	■		■	■	■	12	■	■			■	■	115
Gaggenau MSA Corp.	■	■		■			■							■		
Garland Commercial Industries	■			■			■	■						■		
Gas Research Institute	■	■			■			■								
GE Appliances	■	■	■			■	■	■	12	■	■	10		■	■	116
General Ecology														■	■	301
Gibson/(A Brand of Frigidaire Co.)		■						■	■	■	■			■		
Groen/(A Dover Industries Co.)							■							■		
Heartland Appliances							■	■	■					■		
Home Ventilating Institute				■												

> **31% of new-home shoppers want a washer and dryer near the master bedroom.**
>
> *Source: What Today's Home Buyers Want/NAHB and Fulton Research*

See Manufacturer Index (beige pages at the back of this issue) for address and phone information.   Numbers in red indicate page number for additional product information.

Manufacturer	Cooktops	Dishwashers	Disposers	Exhaust vents/range hoods	Hot water dispensers	Microwave ovens	Ovens	Ranges	Refrigerators/freezers	Trash compactors	Washers/dryers	Water filtration systems/dispensers	Wine storage	Local dealer/distributor	Factory-direct	Circle No.
Honeywell/Home & Building Control												■		■		
Hotpoint Appliances	■	■	■	■		■	■	■		■				■	■	
Imperial Cal Products				■										■		
Imperial Range Hoods				■										■	■	
In-Sink-Erator Div./Emerson Electric Co.			■		10									■		304
International Energy Systems												■		■	■	
Jenn-Air	■	■	■	■		■	■	■	12	■	■			■	■	112, 287
Kanalflakt				■											■	
King Refrigerator Corp.	■	■	■	■	■	■	■	■	■					■		
Kitchen Aid/(A Brand of Whirlpool Corp.)	■	■	■	■	■	■	■	■	12	■	■			■		114
Lasky				■											■	
Magic Chef	■	■				■	■	■	■							
Marvel Industries									■				■	■		
Masco Corp.	■					■	■	■			■			■	■	
Maytag	■	■	■			■	■	■	■		■			■		
Miele Appliances	■	■		■			■				■			■		
Modern/Aire Ventilating				■										■		
North Star Water Conditioning												■		■		
NuTone				■										■	■	
Omni Corp.												■		■	■	
Pacific Sauna & Steam													■		■	
Panasonic				■										■		
Pro-Flo Products					■					10				■	■	306
Rainsoft Water Conditioning Co.												■		■		
Rangaire & Co.				■										■	■	
Regency VSA Appliances	10	■				■								■	■	302
Renato Specialty Products						■								■	■	
Richlund Sales		■							■					■	■	
Rinnai America Corp.	■													■		
Rohl Corp.	■	■	■			■	■	■	■	■				■		
Roper Department/Whirlpool Corp.		■				■	■	■		■				■		
Russell Range	■			■				■						■		
Scotsman Ice Systems									■					■		
Sears Contract Sales/Sears, Roebuck	11	10	■	■	■	■	■	■	■	■	■		■	■		109, 303
Sharp Electronics Corp.						■								■		
Sinkmaster/Anaheim Mfg. Co.			■		■									■		
Solar Survival Architecture													■	■	■	
Sub-Zero Freezer Co.									■					■		
Tamarack Technologies				■										■	■	
Tappan/(A Brand of Frigidaire Co.)	■	■		■		■	■	■						■	■	
Thermador	11			■		■	■	■						■		110
U-Line Corp.									■				■	■		
Universal Metal Industries				■										■	■	
Venmar Ventilation				■										■		
Vent-A-Hood				■										■		
Viking Range Corp.	■	■	■	■		■	■		12				■	■		113
Villagecraft Industries													■		■	
Waste King			10		■									■		300
Water Boss Intl.												■		■	■	
Whirlaway		■		■										■		
Whirlpool Corp./Whirlpool Appliance Group	11	■		■		■	■	■	■	■	■			■	■	111
White-Westinghouse/(A Brand of Frigidaire)		■					■	■	■		■					
Wolf Range Co.	■			■			■	■						■		

> **Most appliances have a life span of 10 to 20 years.**
>
> *Source: NAHB 1997 Housing Facts, Figures and Trends*

See **Manufacturer Index** (beige pages at the back of this issue) for address and phone information.   Numbers in red indicate page number for additional product information.

WASTE KING MAKES A SPLASH

Waste King's brand new Gourmet Series disposers come with new faster permanent magnet motors and some of the longest IN-HOME warranties offered anywhere. With it's fast and easy installation, the Waste King Gourmet line-up completes any kitchen. Also available with a professional 3-Bolt mounting system. For more information call **(800) 854-3229. Circle No. 300**

SEAGULL® IV
Drinking Water Purification Systems

Superb water for drinking, cooking, beverage preparation and ice cubes. Compact, top quality. Removes bacteria, chlorine, cryptosporidia, giardia, lead, tastes & odors. Quick & easy installation. The unique feature to sell your home. Dealer inquiries welcome - contact Ron at General Ecology, Inc. 1-800-441-8166 EST, 24 hr fax 610-363-0412, www.general-ecology.com. **Circle No. 301**

REGENCY VSA APPLIANCES, LTD.

Leading the trend toward "understated elegance," Regency's line of appliances takes full advantage of European design trends to blend with modern kitchen cabinetry incorporating practical design features. Call 714-544-3530 for free brochures on Regency's Built-in ovens and cooktops in both gas and electric and stainless steel interior dishwashers. **Circle No. 302**

190° INSTANT HOT WATER...EURO-STYLE

All new European styling for America's favorite instant hot water dispenser. In-Sink-Erator's new Euro Steamin' Hot® dispenser (Model H-990W) features a graceful, rounded design in a gleaming white finish to complement today's high fashion sinks and faucets. New top-mount design simplifies installation. **Circle No. 304**

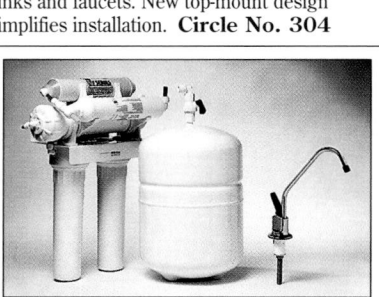

NEW REVERSE OSMOSIS SYSTEMS WITH ULTRAVIOLET

A new REVERSE OSMOSIS SYSTEM designed for use either on treated city water supply systems or non-chlorinated well systems. This system reduces mineral content of water by 96% and removes chlorine and other bad tastes to provide high-quality drinking water right at the kitchen sink. It contains a one-micron prefilter and a 4 watt ultraviolet light. Push-to-connect fittings make this system very easy to install. PRO-FLO offers other residential systems with outputs from 10 gallons per day up to 120 gallons per day. **Circle No. 306**

KENMORE APPLIANCES

Build successfully with Kenmore from Sears Contract Sales in your kitchens. It's America's most recognized appliance brand...at work today in more than one out of every two homes. For more information on how Kenmore appliances can help you sell more homes, call 1-800-359-2000. **Circle No. 303**

ROBERT H. PETERSON CO. FIRE MAGIC "GOURMET SERIES"

The gourmet barbecues sport a new sloped-front face presentation with easy-to-use control knobs and stylish good looks. The units are available in either commercial grade rust-free stainless steel, or heavy duty, welded porcelainized construction. This new styling is available as a built-in, a portable and a modular unit in the Master Chef cabinet. **Circle No. 305**

Cooktops

Sears Contract Sales: Thirty-inch radiant cooktop with downdraft venting is designed for custom built-in installations. Features four electric coil elements under sealed, scratch-resistant tempered glass. *Kenmore Radiant Cooktop. Circle no. 109.*

Thermador: Steel gas cooktop has continuous grates for a more usable cooking area, company claims. Unit can be vented with firm's downdraft ventilation system. *Steel Gas Cooktop. Circle no. 110.*

Whirlpool: Thirty-inch gas downdraft cooktop replaces company's 36-inch unit. Comes with two 10,000 Btu burners, two 9,000 LP open gas burners, and electronic ignition. *Model SC8720ED. Circle no. 111.*

Manufacturer	Product Line/Model	Gas	Electric	Full Size (width x depth, in inches)	Cutout Size (width x depth, in inches)	Depth below Top Flange (in inches)	Colors/ Finishes	Phone Number
Amana	Gas Downdraft Cooktop	■		$29^{1}/_2$ x $21^{1}/_2$	$28^{7}/_8$ x $20^{5}/_8$	—	Black, white, stainless steel	1-800-843-0304
General Electric	JP660WVWW		■	35 x 20	$33^{7}/_8$ x $19^{1}/_6$	—	Black, white, almond	1-800-626-2000
Jenn-Air	CCE 3401		■	$29^{15}/_{16}$ x $21^{1}/_2$	$28^{7}/_8$ x $20^{1}/_4$	—	Black, white	1-800-JENN-AIR
KitchenAid	KECG206S		■	36 x $21^{3}/_4$	33 x $18^{7}/_8$	—	Black, white, almond, brushed chrome, stainless steel	1-800-253-3977
Sears Contract Sales	Kenmore Radiant Cooktop		■	35 x 20	—	—	Black, white	1-800-359-2000
Thermador	Steel Gas Cooktop	■		30 x 21	$28^{5}/_8$ -$29^{3}/_8$ x $19^{1}/_8$ -$19^{7}/_8$	—	Black, white, stainless steel	1-800-656-9226
Viking	VGSU160	■		$36^{1}/_4$ x 21	$34^{3}/_8$ x $18^{5}/_8$	2	Black, white, stainless steel	1-888-845-4641
Whirlpool	SC8720ED	■		$29^{7}/_8$ x $21^{1}/_2$	$28^{7}/_8$ x $20^{15}/_{16}$	$15^{5}/_8$	Black with white porcelain burner pans	1-800-253-1301

Companies in red have product shown above.

Refrigerators

Jenn-Air: Top-mount refrigerators come in 26-, 24-, 21-, and 19-cubic-foot models. Each has a quiet compressor and sound-dampening insulation for noiseless operation. 1-800-JENN-AIR. *Circle no. 112.*

Frigidaire: Top-mount 22-cubic-foot refrigerator/freezer has spill-safe glass shelves and 4-gallon-deep adjustable door bins. *Gallery Professional Series.* 1-800-685-6005. *Circle no. 115.*

GE Appliances: Stainless-steel refrigerator has four adjustable bins, three spill-proof glass shelves, and temperature-controlled meat compartment. *Monogram refrigerator.* 1-800-626-2000. *Circle no. 116.*

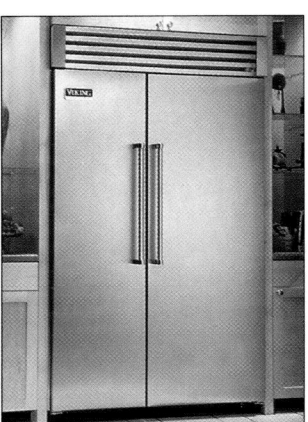

Viking: Built-in side-by-side refrigerator/freezer comes in various widths and finishes. Unit has temperature control, meat and produce drawers, and frost-free freezer. 601-455-1200. *Circle no. 113.*

KitchenAid: Built-in refrigerators have temperature control, in-door ice and water dispenser, wine rack, and stainless-steel exterior. *Model KSSP42QFS.* 1-800-422-1230. *Circle no. 114.*

Amana: Side-by-side 84-inch refrigerator has 28 cubic feet of storage space. Can be customized with ³/₄-inch cabinetry panels; ice and water dispenser optional. 1-800-843-0304. *Circle no. 117.*

Cabinetry

Manufacturer	Cabinet accessories	Custom	Modular/stock	Semi-custom	Bathroom cabinets	Entertainment centers	Kitchen cabinets	Medicine cabinets	Other room cabinets	Laminate	Medium-density fiberboard (MDF)	Metal	Thermo foil	Wood	Local dealer/distributor	Factory-direct	Circle No.
	Lines				**Types**					**Materials**					**Sales**		
Allmilmo Corp.		■		■	■		■		■					■	■	■	
ALNO Network USA	■			■	■		■	■						■			
American Cabinet	■		■		■		■	■			■			■	■	■	
American Custom Millwork		■			■		■	■						■	■	■	
Amerock Corp.	■													■			
Ampco Products			■	■	■	■	■			■			■	■	■		
Architectural Paneling		■			■		■							■			
Architectural Timber & Millwork		■			■		■							■			
Arctic Metal Products			■				■	■				■			■	■	
Areslux			■		■			■				■				■	
Aristokraft	■		■		■	■	■	■	■	■	■		■	■	■		
Bath N' Bagno		■			■						■				■		
Birchcraft Kitchens		■		■	■		■	■		■				■		■	
Bloch Industries		■		■	■		■			■	■			■	■		
Brandom Mfg. Co.			■		■		■	■		■	■			■	■		
Broan Mfg. Co.							■							■			
Bruce Cabinets	■			■	■		■	■		■				■	■		
Burgess Intl. Bath Fixtures		■		■	■					■				■			
Cabinet Restylers		■					■			■	■					■	
Canac Kitchens		■		■	■	■	■		■		■		■	■	■	■	
Canyon Creek Cabinet Co.	■		■	■	■		■	■		■				■	■		
Cardell Kitchen & Bath Cabinetry			■		■		■			■			■	■	■		
Colonial Bronze Co.	■													■			
Corsi Cabinet Co.		■		■	■		■			■	■		■	■		■	
Cortina Kitchens	■	■		■	■		■	■		■	■			■		■	
Country Homestead/Restoration Contractor		■			■		■							■	■	■	
Craft-Maid Custom Kitchens		■		■	■		■			■	■			■		■	
Crown Point Mfg.		■			■		■							■	■	■	
Crystal Cabinet Works		■		■	■	■	■	■	■	■	■		■	■	■		
Curvoflite Stairs and Millwork		■			■	■	■	■		■				■		■	
Custom Wood Products		■			■	■	■	■		■		■					
Decora'			■	■	■		17				■			■	■		123
Decora Systems		■			■					■							
Diamond Cabinets/(Schrock Cabinet Co.)			■	■	■	■	■	■		■				■	■		
The Door Company/Barber Cabinet	■	■			■	■	■	■						■			
Doug Mockett & Co.	■															■	
Downsview Kitchens			■	■	■		■			■			■	■			

See Manufacturer Index (beige pages at the back of this issue) for address and phone information.   Numbers in red indicate page number for additional product information.

continued

Manufacturer	Cabinet accessories	Custom	Modular/stock	Semi-custom	Bathroom cabinets	Entertainment centers	Kitchen cabinets	Medicine cabinets	Other room cabinets	Laminate	Medium-density fiberboard (MDF)	Metal	Thermo foil	Wood	Local dealer/distributor	Factory-direct	Circle No.
	Lines				**Types**					**Materials**					**Sales**		
Driwood Moulding Co.				■										■		■	
Dura Supreme		■		■	■		■			■	■		■	■	■	■	
Dwyer Products Corp.			■				■			■				■		■	
Eastland Industries	■	■		■	■		■	■		■	■			■	■	■	
Feeny Mfg. Co.	■													■			
Fieldstone Cabinetry	■	■	■	■			■			■	■		■	■		■	
Firma Bath Furniture		■			■								■	■	■	■	
Foremost Industries	■		■		■		■	■					■	■			
Gemini Bath & Kitchen Products		■	■				■				■			■	■		
General Marble Co.	■		■		■		■			■		■	■	■			
Gerber Plumbing Fixtures Corp.			■		■					■				■			
Grabill Cabinet Co.	■	■			■	■	■	■		■	■			■			
Grandview Products Co.	■		■	■		■	■			■	■		■	■	■	■	
GUSA/GINGER			■				■				■			■			
Hearth Kitchens	■				■		■			■	■			■	■		
Heritage Custom Kitchens		■			■	■	■			■	■			■	■		
Heritage Finishes		■					■								■	■	
Holiday Kitchens/(Mastercraft Industries)		■		■	■	■	■			■	■			■			
Home Crest Corp.	■		■	■	■		■			■	■		■	■	■	■	
Huntwood Industries		■	■	■	■		■			■	■			■	■		
IEA Intl.		■		■	■	■	■			■	■		■	■	■		
Imperial Cabinet Co.	■	■		■	■		■							■	■		
International Wood Products Assn.							■		■	■	■			■			
IRON-A-WAY	■													■			
Irpina Kitchens		■		■			■			■	■			■			
Jensen Industries			■		■			■			■			■			
Just Cabinets	■		■	■	■		■			■	■			■			
Küche Cucina		■		■	■		■			■	■		■	■	■		
Kabinart	■		■	■	■	■	■	■		■	■			■	■		
Karman Kitchens	■		■	■	■		■			■			■	■	■	■	
Kemper Distinctive Cabinetry	■				■		■							■			
Kent Moore Cabinets	■	■			■	■	■				■			■		■	
Keystone Shower Door/KSD Industries							■							■			
Kinzee Industries			■	■	■		■			■			■	■	■		
Kitchen Cabinet Manufacturers Assn.	■	■	■	■	■		■			■	■		■	■			
Kitchen Craft of Canada			■		■		■			■				■			
Kitchen Kompact			■				■			■				■			
Knape & Vogt Mfg. Co.	■													■	■		
Koch & Co.	■	■	■	■	■		■	■			■			■	■	■	
Kountry Kraft		■			■	■	■			■				■	■		
KraftMaid Cabinetry		■	■	■	■	17				■	■		■	■	■		122, 286
La Vona's Unique Hardware/Malibu Art Tile	■													■	■		
Leigh/(A Harrow Company)		■			■		■							■	■		
LesCare Kitchens		■	■	■	■	■				■	■			■	■	■	
LIFESPEC Cabinet Systems			■	■			■			■						■	
M.L. Condon Co.	■	■		■			■							■	■		789
Markus Cabinet Mfg. Co.			■		■	■	■			■	■			■	■		
Marsh Furniture Co.		■			■					■	■		■	■	■		
Masco Corp.	■	■	■	■	■	■	■	■		■				■		■	
MasterCraft		■	■		■	■	■							■		■	
Medallion Kitchens of Minnesota	■	■	■	■	■	■	■			■			■	■	■		
Mepla	■													■			
Merillat Industries	■		■	■	■	■	■		■	■			■	■			

See Manufacturer Index (beige pages at the back of this issue) for address and phone information.　　Numbers in red indicate page number for additional product information.

Manufacturer	Cabinet accessories	Custom	Modular/stock	Semi-custom	Bathroom cabinets	Entertainment centers	Kitchen cabinets	Medicine cabinets	Other room cabinets	Laminate	Medium-density fiberboard (MDF)	Metal	Thermo foil	Wood	Local dealer/distributor	Factory-direct	Circle No.
	Lines				**Types**					**Materials**					**Sales**		
Mid Continent Cabinetry/(A Div. of Norcraft)	■		■		■	■	■	■	■	■		■	■		■	■	288
Millbrook Custom Kitchens		■	■	■	■		■			■				■	■		
Mouser Custom Cabinetry		■			■		■				■			■	■		
National Products	■													■	■		
NHB Industries	■				■		■	■		■	■			■	■	■	
NuTone							■			■	■			■	■		
The October Co.	■													■	■		
Pace Industries			■		■			■		■				■	■		
Paris Kitchens		■	■		■	■	■		■				■	■			
Particleboard/MDF Institute		■			■	■	■										
Paul Decorative Products		■					■		■					■			
Pivitol Suspension Seating	■														■		
PL Bath Products	■		■		■		■							■			
Plain & Fancy Custom Cabinetry		■		■	■		■	■		■	■		■				
Plato Woodwork	■	■			■		■	■		■	■		■				
Ply Gem Mfg.	■													■			
Plywood Tropics USA				■	■		■			■	■			■	■		
Poggenpohl US	■	■			■		■							■			
Prestige			■	■	■		■						■	■			
Prime Wood Products	■													■	■		
PrimeWood			■	■										■			
Quaker Maid	■	■		■	■		■	■		■	■			■	■		
Quality Cabinets			■		■	■	■			■				■	■	■	
Raywal Kitchens	■			■			■	■		■	■	■	■	■	■		
Rich Maid Kabinetry		■		■	■		■			■			■				
Riviera Cabinets		■		■	■		■	■		■	■		■	■			
Robern	■		■	■	■		■							■			
Rosebud Mfg.			■				■			■			■	■		■	
Rutt Custom Cabinetry	■	■			■		■	■					■	■			
Rynone Mfg. Corp.		■	■		■	■	■	■	■	■			■	■	■		
Schrock Cabinet Co.	■	■	■	■	■		■	■		■			■	■	■		
Schrock Handcrafted Cabinetry			■	■	■		■	■					■	■	■		
Schroll's Kitchen Krafts		■	■	■	■		■	■		■			■	■			
Sea Gull Lighting Prods							■								■		
Sherle Wagner Intl.							■					■					
SieMatic Corp.		16			■	■	■		■	■	■		■	■	■	■	310
Simplex Access Controls/Ilco Unican Group	■																
Smedbo	■														■		
Snaidero Intl.				■	■					■	■			■		■	
Sonoma Woodworks				■	■			■		■						■	
Space-Metrics			■		■		■			■					■	■	
St. Thomas Creations			■		■			■					■	■	■		
Star-Beka Küchen		■		■	■		■			■	■			■		■	
Starmark	■	■	■	■	■		■			■	■	■		■	■		
Suncrest Cabinets		■	■	■	■	■				■	■			■		■	
Superior Wood Products	■	■			■	■	■	■						■	■	■	
Swedish Building Systems & Components				■		■						■		■	■		
TDS					■						■			■	■	■	
Texas Kiln Products		■			■		■							■		■	
Timberlake Cabinet Co.	17		■		■		■	■		■			■	■	■		119
Triangle Pacific Corp.	■		■		■		■	■		■			■	■	■	■	
TriPac Cabinets/(A Div. of Triangle Pacific)	■		■		■		■	■		■			■	■	■	■	
Ultra Craft Co./An Alside Co.	■			■	■	■	■	■		■		■		■			

See Manufacturer Index (beige pages at the back of this issue) for address and phone information.   Numbers in red indicate page number for additional product information.   continued

Cabinetry

Manufacturer	Lines				Types					Materials					Sales		Circle No.
	Cabinet accessories	Custom	Modular/stock	Semi-custom	Bathroom cabinets	Entertainment centers	Kitchen cabinets	Medicine cabinets	Other room cabinets	Laminate	Medium-density fiberboard (MDF)	Metal	Thermo foil	Wood	Local dealer/distributor	Factory-direct	
Ultra Hardware Products	■														■		
Universal-Rundle Corp./(A Nortek Co.)	■		■		■			■					■		■	■	
Vance Industries	■														■		
Villagecraft Industries		■														■	
Watercolors		■	■	■	■			■		■		■		■	■		
Wellborn Cabinet			■	■	■		■	■		■	■			■	■		
Western Cabinet & Millwork			■		■		■				■			■	■	■	
Wood-Mode		■		■	■	■	■	■		■	■			■	■		
Woodfold-Marco Mfg.	■														■		
WoodMaster Designs		■			■		■			■	■			■	■		
Woodpro Cabinetry	■	■	■	■	■			■		■				■	■		
The Woods Quality Cabinetry Co.		■			■	■	■	■	■		■			■	■	■	
WoodStar Cabinets/(Texwood Industries)		■			■		■			■				■	■	■	
Woodwork Institute of California		■	■	■	■	■	■		■	■	■		■	■			
Yorktowne/(An Elkay Co.)	■	17	■	■	■	■	■	■		■	■		■	■	■	■	120
Zaca			■					■							■		

See Manufacturer Index (beige pages at the back of this issue) for address and phone information.   Numbers in red indicate page number for additional product information.

Cabinetry

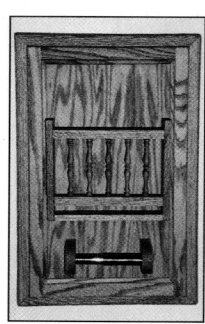

HIDE-A-ROLL CABINET
The Complete **In Wall** Toilet Paper Storage Cabinet. Stores up to 8 rolls. Made of solid oak – ready to stain or paint to your decor. Installs quickly and easily. Saves bathroom space for other items. FAX: (812) 477-2599.
Circle No. 309

SieMatic Corporation
The SieMatic Kitchen Book is a 152-page, large-format publication filled with hundreds of exciting kitchen design ideas. Rich, colorful, full-page and double-page photographs feature the full line of SieMatic's internationally known cabinets and accessories. 800-765-5266. Outside the U.S., call 215-244-6800. $19.95.
Circle No. 310

M. L. CONDON COMPANY
Lumber, mouldings, millwork and more! FREE catalog features over 40 lumber species photographed in full color...marine and architectural plywood...stock and custom mouldings, millwork, paneling, decking, more. We can duplicate any moulding — just FAX us the profile. Write M.L. Condon Co., 280 Ferris Ave, White Plains, NY 10603. Phone (914) 946-4111; FAX (914) 946-3779. **Circle No. 789**

Cabinets

Timberlake: Line of cabinet accessories includes tilt-out storage tray, pull-down cookbook rack, recycling center, and cutting-board tray with tilt-down drawer front for concealing knife storage. 1-800-895-8391. *Circle no. 119.*

Yorktowne: Stock cabinets come in 12-inch-deep base and top bookcase units for a custom built-in look. Available in maple, cherry, hickory, and oak, with 16 different door styles. *Library System Components.* 717-244-4011. *Circle no. 120.*

Amera: Contemporary cabinet-door style has a flat front with rounded corners and edges. Doors come in maple, cherry, hickory, and oak, with a choice of finishes ranging from pale tones to blue and green stains. *Sienna.* 517-263-0771. *Circle no. 121.*

KraftMaid: Pine cabinets come in various colors and finishes. Factory-produced indentations in the cabinets replicate the look of antique, distressed woods. 216-632-5333. *Circle no. 122.*

Decora: Shaker-inspired wood cabinetry has simple lines and classic details. Specialty options and decorative pulls and knobs create a custom look. Choice of 32 door styles and 12 hand-rubbed finishes. *Harmony Collection.* 812-634-2288. *Circle no. 123.*

Computer Software

Manufacturer	Accounting	Design (CAD)	Estimating	Integrated	Inventory management	Job costing	Marketing/sales/lead tracking	Purchase orders	Scheduling/project mgmt.	Service management	DOS	Mac	OS/400	UNIX	Windows	Local dealer/distributor	Factory-direct	Circle No.
	Products → **Sales**																	
	Programs										**Operating Systems**					**Sales**		
A-Systems Corp.	■		■	■	22						■				■	■		323
Aareas By Design							■				■	■			■	■	■	
Abacus Accounting Systems	■		■	■	■	■	■	■	■		■				■	■	■	
Abracadata		22	■		■			■			■	■			■	■	■	321
ACAD-Plus		■									■				■		■	
AEC Software									21			■			■	■	■	314
Add-Vantage Software			■		■			■			■	■			■	■		
American Computer Software	■			■	■			■			■				■	■		
The American Contractor	■		■	■	■		■		■		■				■		■	
Anasys	■		■		■	■	■				■						■	
Argos Systems		■	■	■		■	■							■	■		■	
Armor Systems	■			■	■						■			■			■	
ART		22				■									■		■	325
Auto-Graph Computer Designing Systems		■													■		■	
Autodesk		■		■		■					■	■	■	■	■	■	■	
AutoSight		■									■				■		■	
Ballantine & Co.			■		■			■			■				■	■	■	
Berryvale Software		■	■	■	■						■				■		■	
Best Estimate		■			■	■					■				■		■	
Bristol Information Systems	■			■	■			■			■				■	■	■	
Budgetrac	23		■		■						■				■	■		331
Builder Software Tools	■		■	■	■	■	■	■	■	■	■				■		■	
Builders CAD		21	■	■			■	■						■	■	■	■	311
Builders Software Enterprises	■		■	23	■	■					■				■		■	330
BUILDSOFT	■		■	21	■			■							■			313
BuildWare Data Systems	■				■			■			■				■			
Cabnetware		■	■	■				■			■				■		■	
CADD Services		■	■								■					■	■	
Cadkey		■	■								■					■	■	
CADKIT		■	■	■		■					■				■	■	■	
CadQuest		■	■	■	■	■									■	■		
Cadsoft Intl.		■	■	■	■	■		■			■	■		■	■	■	■	
CADworks		■									■				■			
Calculated Industries			■												■			
Chief Architect by ART		22			■	■									■	■	■	325
CMR Publishing/Const. Mgmt. Resources					■				■		■				■		■	
Comet Construction Software	■		■	■	■				■		■						■	

See Manufacturer Index (beige pages at the back of this issue) for address and phone information.   Numbers in red indicate page number for additional product information.

	Products										Operating Systems					Sales		
Manufacturer	Accounting	Design (CAD)	Estimating	Integrated	Inventory management	Job costing	Marketing/sales/lead tracking	Purchase orders	Scheduling/project mgmt.	Service management	DOS	Mac	OS/400	UNIX	Windows	Local dealer/distributor	Factory-direct	Circle No.
Comprotex		■			■	■		■			■				■		■	
Compu-Share	■														■	■	■	
Computer Presentation Systems				■		22	■	■	■		■				■	■	■	322
Computerized Micro Solutions (CMS)	■	■	■			■		■			■				■	■	■	
Computers for Tracts							■				■				■			
Comtronic Systems	■														■		■	
Construction Data Control (CDCI)	■	■	■	22	■	■	■		■		■				■			324
Constructive Computing Co.	■		■	■	■	■		■	■		■				■		■	
Contractors Software Group	■		■	■		■		■	■						■	■	■	
Corel Corp.		■													■	■		
Craftsman Book Co.			21								■	■			■	■	■	319
DACIS Systems		■	■	■		■					■			■	■			
DASI Software	■		■	■	■	■					■				■	■	■	
Data Automation Services Intl.	■		■	■	■	■					■				■	■	■	
Data-Basics	■			■		■		■	■		■			■	■			
Dataline Corp.	■	■	■		■	■		■						■	■			
Davis Technologies								■		■	■	■			■			
Deal Builder						22									■	■	■	326
Deneb	■		■		■	■	■	■		■	■			■	■			
Design & Construction Resources		■	■						■		■	■			■		■	
Diehl Graphsoft		21									■				■	■	■	315
Dimensions Computer Advisors	■				■			■						■	■		■	
Disano Systems Group	■		■	■	■	■	■	■	■	■	■			■	■		■	
Eagle Point Software		■	■	■	■						■	■		■	■		■	
Eclectus	■		■	■		■	■		■		■				■	■	■	
Enterprise Computer Systems	■		■	■	■	■	■	■	■		■				■		■	
Estimation		■	■					■			■				■		■	
Evolution Computing		■													■	■	■	
The FAST Management Group	■		■	■		■	■	■	■		■						■	
GEAC Computer Corp.	■	■	■	■	■	■		■	■	■				■	■			
Graphisoft US		■		■								■			■	■	■	
GTCO Corp.		■	■								■				■	■		
HMS Computer Co.						■					■	■			■	■	■	
Home Pro Systems			■	■		■	■		■		■							
HomeTech Information Systems			■	■		■									■	■	■	
Horizons Software/Quick Frame Systems		■													■	■	■	
Imagetects		■									■	■		■	■		■	
Industry Specific Software	22		■			■		■	■		■				■	■	■	328
Intersoft Systems	■			■	■	■		■		■				■	■		■	
Kitchen Computer Designer		■	■								■							
KMP Development Corp.			■	■		■			■						■			
Landmark Data Systems	■				■		■				■						■	
LandPlot Research		■													■		■	
Lantron Technologies	■		■	■		■			■						■	■	■	
LIBRA Corp.	■										■				■			
Masco Corp.		■					■								■	■	■	
The Master Builder Software By Omware	■		■	■	■	■	■	■	■	■	■				■		■	
Maxwell Systems	■					■					■		■	■	■			
MC2 Engineering Software									■		■				■	■	■	
McCosker Corp.	■		■	23	■	■		■					■		■	■		329
MICS	■		■	■	■	■					■				■			
MISG Software	■		■	■	■	■	■							■	■			
NEBS Software & Services	■										■				■		■	

See Manufacturer Index (beige pages at the back of this issue) for address and phone information.   Numbers in red indicate page number for additional product information.   continued

Computer Software

Manufacturer	Accounting	Design (CAD)	Estimating	Integrated	Inventory management	Job costing	Marketing/sales/lead tracking	Purchase orders	Scheduling/project mgmt.	Service management	DOS	Mac	OS/400	UNIX	Windows	Local dealer/distributor	Factory-direct	Circle No.
New World Graphics		■									■	■			■	■	■	
Newstar Technologies	■		■	■	■	■		■	■				■	■	■			
Northridge Systems		■													■		■	
Northwest Construction Software			■		■	■			■		■				■		■	
Open Systems	■		■	■	■	■			■		■			■	■			
Peachtree Software	■			■	■						■	■			■	■	■	
Perfect Software	■			■		■					■	■	■		■	■		
Pinnacle Technology			■								■						■	
Planit Intl.		■			■							■			■		■	
Porak Computing Services		■	■	■										■	■		■	
Primavera Systems/SureTrak Div.									■		■				■		■	
Pro-Mation, A Div. of Geac Commercial Sys.	■		■	■	■	■		■	■		■				■		■	
Prosoft	■		■	■	■	■		■	■		■				■		■	
Pulsar Softwares		■	■												■		■	
Rambow Enterprises		■		■	■				■		■				■		■	
Red Wing Business Systems	■			■	■				■		■					■		
RMK Enterprises		■									■					■		
RS Means		■	■			■			■						■			
Scalex		■	■								■	■			■	■		
Service Software										■	■				■		■	
Sigma Design		■													■			
Sirius Software	21		■	■	■	■	■	■	■		■			■	■	■		316
Sketchtech		■										■			■			
Small System Design	21		■	■	■	■		■	■		■				■	■	■	317
Softdesk Retail Products		■													■			
Softplan Systems		21	■								■						■	318
Software Constructors	■											■			■			
Source Mate Information Systems	■			■	■			■			■		■		■			
Spectra-Physics Laserplane			■												■	■	■	
SureSell						■									■			
Symbiotech	■		■	■	■	■		■							■		■	
Synapse Software	■		■		21		■	■				■			■		■	312
Third Millennium Software	■		■	■	■	■	■	■	■						■		■	
Timberline Software	■		■		■						■				■	■		
TimeSketch by AlderGraf							22								■		■	320
TSE Software Enterprises	■		■	■	■	■		■			■				■		■	
Turtle Creek Software	■		■	■		■			■		■	■					■	
University Software	■		■	■	■	■					■					■		
Versyss	■		■	■	■	■	■	■	■				■	■	■	■		
Vertigraph	■	22	■		■			■	■						■	■	■	327
ViaGraFix		■	■												■		■	
Virtus Corp.		■										■			■		■	
Visual Applications/VisualPhile		■				■									■		■	
Welcom Software Technology									■		■				■		■	
Win Estimator			■												■			
WWP Enterprises		■						■			■						■	
Xactware	■		■	■		■					■				■		■	
Yardi Systems	■		■	■		■		■			■				■		■	

See **Manufacturer Index** (beige pages at the back of this issue) for address and phone information.   Numbers in red indicate page number for additional product information.

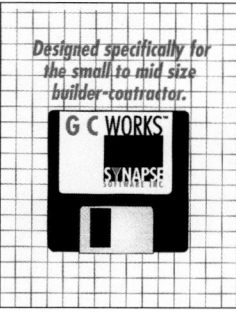

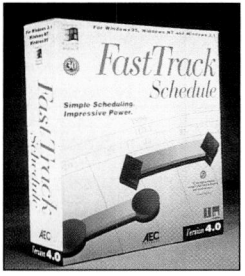

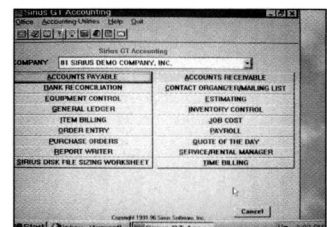

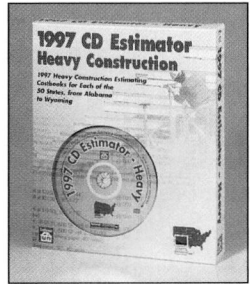

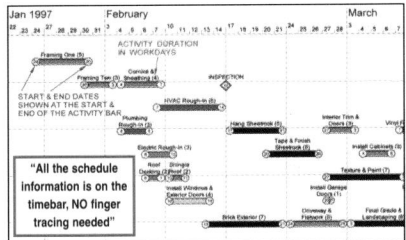

TimeSketch™ by Aldergraf, Inc.
REDEFINE PROJECT SCHEDULING
An on-screen project planning and scheduling tool with a unique graphical format. TimeSketch lets you see your project from start to finish on one page. Dates are shown at the ends of the timebar, the description and workday duration are above or below the timebar. Easy to use, clearly understood. Available for Windows 3.1/95/NT. For more information, call (800) 624-4971, (713) 467-8500 or Fax (713) 467-1062.
Circle No. 320

DESIGN YOUR OWN HOME® 3D
WALK-AROUND from Abracadata is a state-of-the-art home planning program that brings building and remodeling ideas to life for you and your clients. You can raise walls, wallpaper, lay carpet, place furniture and appliances and see it all happen in 3D. This user-friendly program has a unique automatic wall tool, a stud tool for accurate stud placement, and multiple layers for creating plumbing and electrical schematics. Available for Macintosh and Windows. For order information or catalog, call 1-800-451-4871.
Circle No. 321

SOLUTIONS FOR CONNECTIVITY
Sales Office - Construction Site - Warranty/Customer Service - Corporate Office
- **SalesBuilder** - the complete sales office system
- **DataScan** - keyboard-free prospect data entry
- **SuperSend** - sales office-corporate telecommunications
- **WarrantyWatcher** - the latest in warranty/customer service tracking
- **WalkWrite** - construction scheduling
- **SuperSync** - instant data access for field operations using a U.S. Robotics Pilot.

Computer Presentation Systems • call today (888) 635-1340 •
visit our web site: http://www.cpsusa.com
Circle No. 322

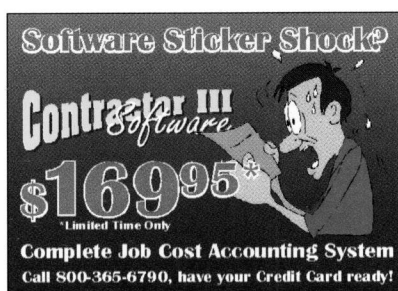

A-SYSTEMS CORPORATION
Since 1978, CONTRACTOR III has been the fully integrated job costing system to own. For a limited time, the "basics only" version is available for $169.95. As you grow, Contractor III will grow with you. Order at 800-365-6790.
Circle No. 323

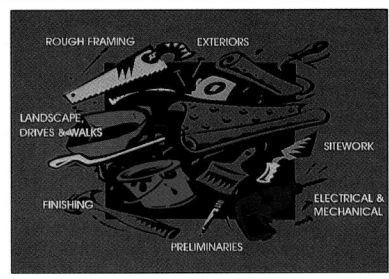

CDCI
From estimating to scheduling, purchasing and cost control, CDCI has software solutions that will fit your needs no matter what size business you run. Both our basic and advanced estimating systems are fully integrated with accounting for job budgeting, scheduling and purchasing. You get the cost control you need to make your business successful and profitable. 1-800-285-3929. www.cdci.com E-mail: sales@cdci.com
Circle No. 324

CHIEF ARCHITECT BY ART
Chief Architect proves that top quality architectural software can be easy to learn. Straight out of the box, Chief simplifies the process of creating full working drawings. Over 450,000 people worldwide prefer ART's architectural software with its full 3-D capabilities. 800-482-4433 or www.chiefarch.com
Circle No. 325

DealBuilder®7 The Only Financial Analysis Program to combine project planning with multi-phase cash, loan and equity requirements.
"Best Financial Analysis Tool I've Used."
Marc Murphy, Shea Homes

- More than $4 Billion in Transactions are Analyzed Yearly by Our Users in 30 States
- Land, Tract, & MPC Projects
- Solve for Project, Builder, Lender IRR's & NPV's. Investor IRR, Equity & Profit Splits
- First Look to Detailed Project Study
- User Defined Cost Estimating & Spending
- 47 Built-in Reports & Color Charts
- Summary & Detailed Cash Flows & Loans
- On-line Help, Input Error Checking
- Windows 3.1, Windows 95   Samples, Video

When your money is on the line, use the best!
(800) 332-5253   http://dealbuilder.com
Circle No. 326

GET IT RIGHT THE FIRST TIME
Now is the time for Bidworx takeoff and estimating. The software that recognizes not all estimates are created equally. It works the way you do. Across all trades. Under any conditions. If you need benchmarking, bid summary, time and materials or any combination, Bidworx is the right tool for taking control. Call Vertigraph, Inc. for a free demo disk. 800-989-4243.
Circle No. 327

ISS
Accounting is a pain in the...but, you know that. What you may not know is that ISS software isn't. Estimating, job costing, and accounting is affordable, flexible, and easy with ISS. And, it comes with tech. support that's so good it will knock you on your...but you may never need it. Call (800) 877-2496.   **Circle No. 328**

The McCosker Corporation

McCosker's Builder System's fully integrated project management and accounting applications combine the graphical ease-of-use of Windows 95™ and 3.x with the power and strength of the IBM AS/400. In addition to general ledger/financial and job/project cost core appplications, TMC has comprehensive home builder specific modules such as Bid Management, Order Processing, Subcontract/PO Management, Unit Sales and Inventory, Options Management, Customer Care/Warranty, Scheduling and more! Call 1-510-938-1717 for more information. **Circle No. 329**

Be the SUPER HERO for your building business and WOW your clients with leading edge technology from
BUILDERS SOFTWARE ENTERPRISES
Complete Builders System
Built by a Builder for a Builder
- Job Estimating
- Job Cost Accounting
- General Ledger/Payroll
- Purchase Order/Change Order
- Integrated Windows95 Version
Website: www.builders-software.com
E-mail: bse@iamerica.net
800-659-6410 **Circle No. 330**

BUDGETRAC SYSTEMS, INC.

Project control software from a real estate developer's perspective. Window-based modules available for contract management, contract staging, purchasing, loan draws, cost events, plus project and financial accounting. Systems starting at $5,500. (800) 556-9557.
E-mail: info@budgetrac.com
http://www.budgetrac.com
Circle No. 331

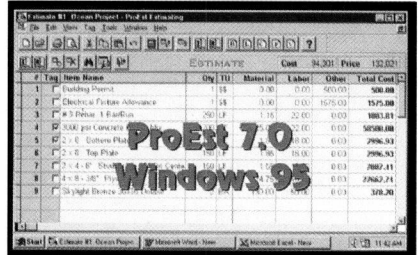

ProEST ESTIMATING FOR WINDOWS 95

The #1 choice of professional estimators worldwide! Use ProEst today and create accurate, professional estimates quickly. Create instant Bill of Materials & Labor Reports. Call for a FREE demo (800) 255-7407, (619) 578-2664 or download from our WebSite at "http://www.proest.com" today!
Circle No. 333

Countertops

Manufacturer	Ceramic tile	Cultured marble	Laminate	Marble/granite/slate/stone	Solid surfacing	Stainless steel	Wood	Local dealer/distributor	Factory-direct	Circle No.
AB Cushing Mills							■			
Advanced Technology		■						■	■	
American Marazzi Tile	■							■		
American Marble Industries/Kephaco Corp.		27						■	■	337
American Olean Tile	■			■				■		
Ampco Products		■			■			■		
Amsterdam Corp.	■							■	■	
Arctic Metal Products		■	■			■		■	■	
Arius Tile Co.	■							■		
Avonite					■			■		
Bally Block/Michigan Maple							■	■		
Bangkok Intl.								■	■	
Bloch Industries		■			■			■	■	
Block Tops					■			■	■	
Buchtal Corp. USA	■									
The Burruss Co.							■	■		
Cabinet Restylers			■						■	
Cameo Marble		■						■	■	
Cangelosi Marble & Granite				■					■	
Clifford W. Estes Co.				■				■	■	
Cold Spring Granite Co.				■				■	■	
Coni Marble Mfg.		■			■			■	■	
Continental Creative Sales				■					■	
Continental Stone Designs		■		■				■	■	
Country Homestead/Restoration Contractor							■	■	■	
Crane Plumbing/Fiat Products		■						■		
Dakota Granite				■				■	■	
Dal-Tile Corp.	■								■	
Decora Systems		■								
Decorative Laminate Products Assn.		■		■						
Designs In Tile	■								■	
DM Industries					■			■	■	
The Door Co./Barber Cabinet	■	■	■	■	■		■		■	
DuPont Co./Corian Products					■			■		
Durastone Corp.				■					■	
Eastland Industries		■	■		■		■	■	■	
Epro	■							■		

Materials homeowners prefer:

Laminate _____43%
Solid surfacing __39%
Granite _____23%
Tile _____7%
Cultured marble _7%
Wood block _____5%
Marble _____2%

Source: 1996 NKBA Trends Survey

Manufacturer	Ceramic tile	Cultured marble	Laminate	Marble/granite/slate/stone	Solid surfacing	Stainless steel	Wood	Local dealer/distributor	Factory-direct	Circle No.
Florida Tile/(A Div. of Premark)	■							■		
Forbo Arborite			■					■		
Foremost Industries		■						■		
Formica Corp.			■		■					
General Marble Co.		■						■	■	
The Georgia Marble Co.				■					■	
Georgia-Pacific Corp.			■				■	■		
Gesmar		■						■	■	
Goodwin Heart Pine Co.							■	■		
Grabill Cabinet Co.					■			■		
Hardwood Plywood & Veneer Assn.								■		
Hartson-Kennedy Cabinet Top Co.			■		■			■	■	
Hearth Kitchens			■					■		
IEA Intl.			■	■	■	■		■		
IMPO Glaztile	■								■	
International Paper Co.					■			■		
International Wood Products Assn.							■			
Italian Tile Assn.	■							■		
John Boos & Co.							27	■		335
Kentucky Millwork							■	■		
Kepcor/SSI Tiles	■							■	■	
King Refrigerator Corp.						■		■		
Kinzee Industries		■						■	■	
Koch & Co.			■					■	■	
Kuehn Bevel			■					■		
La Vona's Unique Hardware/Malibu Art Tile	■		■					■	■	
Laminated Plastics			27					■		336
Laminating Materials Assn.			■							
Latco Products	■							■	■	
Laticrete Intl.	■							■		
Laufen Ceramic Tile	■							■	■	
Laurel Co.		■						■	■	
Lodestar/Statements in Stone				■				■	■	
London Tile Co.	■							■	■	
M.L. Condon Co.							■	■	■	
Markus Cabinet Mfg. Co.							■		■	
Marvin L. Walker & Associates	■	■		■				■	■	
McIntyre Tile	■							■	■	
Micarta Laminates			■					■	■	
Michigan Maple Block Co.							27	■		338
Miracle Sealants & Abrasives	■			■				■		
MK Diamond Products	■	■		■				■		
Monarch Tile	■							■		
Nevamar, Intl. Paper Co.			■		■					
The October Co.					■			■	■	
Paris Kitchens			■					■	■	
Particleboard/MDF Institute			■				■			
Patrick Industries	■		■					■		
PermaGrain Products					■			■		
Petmal Supply Co.	■				■			■	■	
Pioneer Plastics Corp.			■					■	■	
Ply Gem Mfg.	■							■		
Porcelanite	■							■		

> 95% of shoppers say "a large" counter space in the kitchen is either desirable or essential in a new home.
>
> *Source: What Today's Home Buyers Want/NAHB and Fulton Research*

See Manufacturer Index (beige pages at the back of this issue) for address and phone information.   Numbers in red indicate page number for additional product information.   continued

Countertops

Manufacturer	Ceramic tile	Cultured marble	Laminate	Marble/granite/slate/stone	Solid surfacing	Stainless steel	Wood	Local dealer/distributor	Factory-direct	Circle No.
Premoule			■	■				■		
PrimeWood			■				■	■		
Quarry Tile Co.	■							■		
Renato Bisazza			■	■				■	■	
Rocktile Specialty Products				■					■	
Rocky Mountain Stone Co.				■				■		
Romatt Doors							■	■	■	
Rosebud Mfg.				■					■	
Rynone Mfg. Corp.		■	■	■				■	■	
Schroll's Kitchen Krafts			■				■	■		
Sherle Wagner Intl.	■			■						
Shower Shapes				■				■		
Solnhofen Natural Stone				■				■	■	
The Structural Slate Co.				■					■	
SUBA Mfg.			■					■	■	
Summitville Tiles	■							■	■	
Suncrest Cabinets				■		■		■		
Superior Wood Products						■	■		■	
Superior Wood Shelving			■						■	
The Swan Corp.					■			■		
Syntec Marble		■		■				■	■	
Terra-Green Technologies/Stoneware Tile	■							■		
Texas Kiln Products						■			■	
Texas Stone & Tile				■					■	
TFI Corp./Vanity Plus				■				■		
Tile Cera	■							■		
Tile Council of America	■							■	■	
The Tileworks	■							■	■	
Timber Products Co.			■					■	■	
Trade Commission of Spain/Tile from Spain	■							■	■	
Triangle Pacific Corp.		■	■	■				■	■	
United Panel				■				■	■	
United States Ceramic Tile Co.	■							■		
Universal Marble & Granite				■					■	
V-T Industries			■	■				■	■	
Vermont Structural Slate Co.				■					■	
Villagecraft Industries				■					■	
Walker & Zanger				■				■	■	
Westchester Marble & Granite				■				■		
Western Quarry Tile	■								■	
Wilsonart Intl.			■	■				■	■	
Woodfold-Marco Mfg.						■		■		
The Woods Co.						■		■	■	
The Woods Quality Cabinetry Co.			■	■		■		■	■	
Woodwork Institute of California		■	■	■		■				

See Manufacturer Index (beige pages at the back of this issue) for address and phone information.   Numbers in red indicate page number for additional product information.

JOHN BOOS & COMPANY

The hottest segment of the countertop market is natural maple butcher block. Perceived to be only for up-scale homes, John Boos & Company's maple tops are actually priced at a fraction of other solid surface materials. Standard 25" widths in lengths to 12' are easily installed using common woodworking tools. This 109 year old company offers widths up to 60" and lengths to 145". For more information and location of distributor nearest you, contact **John Boos & Company, 315 South First Street, P.O. Box 609, Effingham, IL 62401. E-mail johnboos@effingham.net Web: http://www.effingham.com/johnboos** Circle No. 335

LAMINATED PLASTICS, INC.

offers high pressure laminates in a variety of popular solid colors, wood grains, patterns and dimensional surfaces. Applications for the PANELYTE quality product line include: countertops, cabinets, case goods, commercial and institutional fixtures, interior doors and partitions, tables and furniture. For more information on the PANELYTE Product Line, call 1-800-631-0145. Laminated Plastics, Inc. 140 Littleton Road, Parsippany, NJ 07054. Tel: (201) 316-9595. Fax: (201) 316-6211. **Circle No. 336**

MICHIGAN MAPLE BLOCK

Solid hard maple butcher block cabinet tops add a "natural" touch of beauty in any home while contributing functionally. No maintenance required with the acrylic finish, yet safe for all food preparations. Available in widths 25", 30" & 36", lengths to 144", thickness of 1½". **Circle No. 338**

AMERICAN MARBLE INDUSTRIES

Innovative products like this edge treatment and china undermount is what we do best. Custom bath and kitchen countertops, marbleglass tubs, handicap showers and more. Manufactured in Alabaster, Onyx, Granite, marble and solid colors. New rope edging debuts this April. **Circle No. 337**

INTERIOR DOORS

Ledco: Hardwood bifold doors come in full-louver, louver-over-panel, and six-panel styles and in a variety of standard sizes with track and hardware. *Easyfit.* 1-800-626-6367. *Circle no. 168.*

Masonite: Hardboard door has a smooth finish that's primed and ready for painting. Door comes in standard and bifold sizes with an optional solid core. 1-800-446-1649. *Circle no. 169.*

Premdor: Vinyl frames on bifold doors are constructed with partial or full-length wood inserts. Prefinished units fit most standard door openings. *Vinyl Louvre Series.* 1-800-663-3667. *Circle no. 170.*

Stanley Home Decor: Raised six-panel door can be painted or stained, has interior recessed full-length mirror. Available in various widths. *Swing Mirror Door.* 203-225-5111. *Circle no. 171.*

Phoenix Moulding & Door Supply: Doors are made of MDF and engineered wood that won't warp, shrink, or expand. Available in 40 designs. *New-Tech Doors.* 714-544-6152. *Circle no. 172.*

Doors

Manufacturer	Exterior							Interior											Sales		Circle No.
	Custom	Fiberglass	Fire-rated	Sliding/patio	Steel	Storm/screen	Wood	Accordion	Bifold	Closet	Custom	French	Hardboard	Louvered	Mirrored	Moulded	Pocket	Wood	Local dealer/distributor	Factory-direct	
Acadia Windows & Doors	■		■		■														■	■	
Acan Windows			■																		
Afco Industries								■					■						■	■	
Alcoa Vinyl Windows			■																■		
Alenco			■																■		
Almetco Building Products			■																■	■	
Alside/Window Div.			■																		
Alumax Bath Enclosures								■							■				■		
Ambiance of High Point									■	■	■				■						
American Accent Homes																	■				
American Architectural Manufacturers Assn.			■	■																	
American Custom Millwork	■					■		■	■	■	■							■	■	■	
American Heritage Shutters	■					■						■						■	■	■	
American Wood Council						■												■			
Amerimax Building Products			■																■	■	
Ampco Products																		■	■		
Andersen Windows			■																■		
APC Building Products			■																■		
Architectural Paneling											■	■					■				
Arrow/Medina Group						■			■	■			■				■		■		
Arthur Cox & Sons									■	■				■		■			■	■	
Atlantic Pre-Hung Doors		■	■	■	■		■	■	■	■	■	■	■	■	■	■	■	■	■		
Atrium Door & Window Co.			■			■													■		
Beech River Mill Corp.									■	■			■							■	
Benchmark Door Systems		■	■	33				■			■								■		163
Bend Door/(A Div. of JELD-WEN)		■	■			■		■	■		■						■		■		
Bennett Industries	■					■		■	■	■	■		■				■	■	■		165
Berlinex			■																■		
Better-Bilt					■														■		
Beveled Glass Designs	■	■			■	■						■							■		
The Bilco Co.					■														■	■	
Bilt Best Windows			■																		
Bird Vinyl Products			■																■		
Blomberg Window Systems			■																	■	
Blumer & Stanton	■					■					■	■						■	■	■	
Bonneville Windows & Doors			■	■		■													■		
Bruce Alford Corp.	■					■					■	■						■	■	■	

Doors

Manufacturer	Custom	Fiberglass	Fire-rated	Sliding/patio	Steel	Storm/screen	Wood	Accordion	Bifold	Closet	Custom	French	Hardboard	Louvered	Mirrored	Moulded	Pocket	Wood	Local dealer/distributor	Factory-direct	Circle No.
	Exterior							**Interior**											**Sales**		
Buffelen Woodworking Co.	■		■				■	■		■	■						■		■		
Building Products & Nails/Div. BSTC Group							■	■				■	■						■		
Capitol Windows & Doors/(Metal Industries)			■		■			■		■		■					■		■		
Caradco			■																■		
Caradon Lock-Wood			■	■		■													■		
Carefree Windows/(CFA Window Group)			■																■		
Castlegate Entry Systems		■	■	■	■														■		
CertainTeed Windows			■																■	■	
Challenge Door/(A Div. of JELD-WEN)		■		■															■		
Chautauqua Woods Corp.	■						■				■	■					■	■	■		
Chelsea Building Products			■																■		
Classic Architectural Specialties					■														■		
Colonial Elegance										■					■				■		
Columbia Aluminum Windows & Doors			■		■			■	■						■				■		
The Combination Door Co.	■				■	■		■	■	■	■						■		■		
Comfort Line		■	■		■														■		
Comtex Industries							■				■	■					■		■		
Connoisseur & Supa Doors	■							■			■	■				■			■		
Contact Lumber Co.		■					■										■		■		
Contractors Wardrobe								■	■						■				■	■	
Country Homestead/Restoration Contractor	■																		■	■	
Craft-Bilt Mfg. Co.			■																	■	
Craftline/(A Div. of Vega Industries)			■																■		
CraftMaster								■	■			■			■	■	■		■		244
Crestline/SNE Enterprises/A PLY GEM Co.			■					■	■				■	■					■		
Cumberland Woodcraft					■															■	
Curvoflite Stairs and Millwork	■						■		■	■	■		■			■	■			■	
Custom Doors & Drawers											■	■					■			■	
David Mulder-Custom Built Circular Stairs	■										■									■	
Day Pond Woodworking	■																			■	
Dayton Technologies	■		■																	■	
Decorative Glass Intl.	■																		■		
Deines Custom Doors	■										■									■	
Delsan Industries			■																■	■	
The Door Co./Barber Cabinet											■						■				
Doorcraft/(A Div. of JELD-WEN)		■					■	■	■			■			■	■	■		■		
Driwood Moulding Co.	■						■				■	■					■			■	
DSH								■	■	■				■		■	■	■	■	■	
Duo-Temp	■		■																■	■	
Eagle Plywood & Door Manufacturers		■						■	■	■						■	■		■		
Eagle Window & Door			■																■		
Elegant Entries	■		■			■					■	■					■		■		
Elite Products Wholesale											■	■					■		■		
Elkhart Door						■													■	■	
Emco Specialties				37																	340
Engineered Profiles/North American Profiles			■																■		
Entries	■	■		■																■	
Escon Corp.	■	■	■			■						■					■		■		
Eurotec/Tilt & Turn Windows	■		■			■	■													■	
Farley Windows			■																■		
Fibertec Window Mfg.		■																	■	■	
Fibreform Wood Products						■		■									■		■		
Fillmore Thomas & Co.			■																■	■	

See Manufacturer Index (beige pages at the back of this issue) for address and phone information.   Numbers in red indicate page number for additional product information.

Products

Manufacturer	Custom	Fiberglass	Fire-rated	Sliding/patio	Steel	Storm/screen	Wood	Accordion	Bifold	Closet	Custom	French	Hardboard	Louvered	Mirrored	Moulded	Pocket	Wood	Local dealer/distributor	Factory-direct	Circle No.
	Exterior							**Interior**											**Sales**		
Forms + Surfaces																		■	■		
GAPCO			■			■													■		
Georgia-Pacific Corp.		■	■	■		■		■	■		■								■		
Gerkin Windows & Doors			■			■													■	■	
Goodwin Heart Pine Co.	■										■						■	■	■	■	
Gorell Enterprises			■		■														■		
Great Lakes Window			■																■	■	
Hardwood Plywood & Veneer Assn.															■						
Harvey Industries					■	■													■	■	
Heritage Veneered Products									■		■	■					■		■	■	
The Hess Mfg. Co.	■	■	■		■														■	■	
Holland Log Homes Mfg. Co.								■	■	■				■			■	■	■		
Homeshield Fabricated Products						■													■		
Horton Automatics				■			■												■		
Hurd Millwork Co.			■																■		
Inde-Pane	■		■	■		■														■	
Inline Fiberglass		■	■																		
Insulate Industries			■								■								■		
Insulated Steel Door Institute		■			■																
International Extrusions/(The Noecker Group)						■														■	
International Paper Co.								■					■		■				■		
International Wood Products/(JELD-WEN)	■						■				■								■		
International Wood Products Assn.	■						■	■	■				■				■				
Interplan Group/Classic Doors	■						■												■	■	
J A W Window & Door			■		■	■													■	■	
JD's Glassworks	■						■												■	■	
JELD-WEN Fiber of Iowa/(Elite Doors)		■						■	■							■			■		166,219
Jenkins Mfg./Monarch Windows			■	■		■		■	■	■	■						■	■	■		
Jessup Door Co.	■		■			■		■	■	■	■						■	■	■		
The Jordan Cos.			■			■													■	■	
Joyce Mfg.			■			■														■	
Kaylien	■	■	■								■	■			■				■	■	
Kenmore Industries	■						■													■	
Kentucky Millwork	■						■										■		■		
Kewanee Corp./Midway Tech Center			■		■														■		
Klamath Door/(A Div. of JELD-WEN)			■				■	■	■		■						■		■		
KML Windows	■						■												■		
Koch & Co.	■		■				■	■			■	■					■		■	■	
Kolbe & Kolbe Millwork Co.	■		■				■				■						■		■		
Kwik-Way Corp./Div. of Metal Industries									■	■	■			■				■			
Lamson-Taylor Custom Doors	■		■			■	■				■	■					■	■		■	
Larson Mfg.						■													■	■	
LB Plastics				■															■	■	
LE Johnson Products								■	■								■		■		
Ledco								28	■				■		■	■	■		■		168
Lincoln Wood Products			■																■		
Louisiana-Pacific Corp.		37				■	37												■		
LTL Home Products								■	■										■	■	
M.L. Condon Co.	■						■				■						■		■	■	
MacMillan Bloedel/Building Materials Mktg.							■				■						■		■		
Madawaska Doors	■		■			■	■	■	■	■					■		■	■	■	■	
Martin Door Mfg.	■				■														■	■	
Marvin Windows & Doors			38								■								■		179

See Manufacturer Index (beige pages at the back of this issue) for address and phone information.   Numbers in red indicate page number for additional product information.

continued

ENTRY DOORS

Therma-Tru: Fiberglass door resists splitting and warping. Unit can be painted. Double-paned, safety-tempered lights come in seven designs. *Classic-Craft.* 1-800-537-8827. *Circle no. 161.*

Peachtree: Line of entry doors includes four new styles: swing-out, swing-out with an operable side-light, swing-in with 10-inch sidelights, and swing-in with an integral transom. *Newport II.* 1-800-477-6544. *Circle no. 160.*

Pease: Entry door is made of 24-gauge steel with a polystyrene core that won't deteriorate. Optional tempered-glass inserts are break-resistant, company says. *Ever-Strait.* 1-800-88-DOORS. *Circle no. 162.*

Benchmark: Insulated steel door is clad in wood-grain vinyl. Matching sidelights have plastic spacers that improve energy efficiency, company says. *Legend.* 1-800-755-DOOR. *Circle no. 163.*

Weather Shield: Doors are made of a 1-inch-thick steel panel with polyurethane core and oak veneer. Multi-compression weather strip provides improved thermal protection. In eight styles, all with a vinyl bottom sweep. *Signature Series.* 1-800-477-6808. *Circle no. 164.*

Bennett Industries: Entry doors are made of medium-density fiberboard panels veneered with mahogany and are available with various glass options. *Valencia Series.* 201-947-5340. *Circle no. 165.*

Jeld-Wen: Composite door has a laminated veneer lumber frame and polystyrene core. Accepts paint or stain. *Elite Alterna.* 1-800-877-9482. *Circle no. 166.*

Stanley Door Systems: Security door has a three-point locking system. 1-800-521-2752. *Circle no. 167.*

COMPANY	MODEL	MATERIAL	DOOR HEIGHTS	DOOR WIDTHS	SIDELIGHT HEIGHTS	SIDELIGHT WIDTHS	PHONE
Benchmark	Legend	Steel	6'8", 7'0", 8'0"	2'0", 3'0"	6'8"	12", 14"	1-800-755-DOOR
Bennett Industries	Valencia Series	MDF with mahogany veneers	6'8", 7'0", 8'0"	2'0", 3'0"	—	—	201-947-5340
Jeld-Wen	Elite Alterna	Wood composite	6'7"	2'0", 3'0"	—	—	1-800-877-9482
ODL	Buckingham	Oak	6'8"	3'0"	—	—	616-772-9111
Peachtree	Newport II	Fiberglass	6'8"	3'0"	6'8"	10", 12", 14"	1-800-477-6544
Pease	Ever-Strait	Steel	6'7"	3'0"	—	—	1-800-88-DOORS
Stanley Door Systems	Security Door	Steel	6'8"	3'0"	—	—	1-800-521-2752
Therma-Tru	Classic-Craft	Fiberglass	6'8"	3'0"	6'8"	12", 14"	1-800-537-8827
Weather Shield	Signature Series	Steel	6'10", 8'10"	2'8", 3'0"	6'10", 8'0"	12"	1-800-477-6808

Companies in red have product shown above.

Doors

Manufacturer	Exterior							Interior											Sales		Circle No.
	Custom	Fiberglass	Fire-rated	Sliding/patio	Steel	Storm/screen	Wood	Accordion	Bifold	Closet	Custom	French	Hardboard	Louvered	Mirrored	Moulded	Pocket	Wood	Local dealer/distributor	Factory-direct	
The Marwin Co.								■	■					■	■	■	■	■	■		
Mason Corp.			■	■															■		
Maywood			■			■		■	■		■						■		■		
Medieval Glass Industries	■									■	■								■	■	
MGM Industries	■					■				■							■		■	■	
Milgard Windows			■			■													■	■	
The Millworks					■	■													■	■	
Missoula White Pine Sash Co.						■														■	
Modernfold							■												■		
Morgan Products	■					■		■	■	■	■						■	■	■		
Moulding Associates						■						■							■		
MW Windows/MW Manufacturers			■																■		
Nana Wall Systems						■		■									■			■	
Napco			■																■		
National Assn. of Architectural Metal Mfrs.	■		■	■																	
National Nail Corp.					■																
National Wood Window and Door Assn.	■		■	■	■	■		■	■	■	■	■			■	■	■	■			
New-Tech Doors	■		■			■		■			■			■		■	■	■	■		
Nicolai Doors						■			■		■						■	■			
Norco Windows			■			■													■	■	
Nord/(A Div. of JELD-WEN)		■	■			■				■	■						■	■			
Northeast Window and Door Assn.	■	■	■	■	■	■	■	■	■	■	■	■	■	■	■	■	■	■			
Northwest Window Works			■							■	■						■			■	
O'Keeffe's			■																		
Oakwood Classic & Custom Woodworks	■					■				■	■		■			■	■	■			
ODL			■		■	■													■		
Ohline Corp.														■						■	
The Old Wagon Factory						■															
Oldach Wood Windows & Doors		■		■		■														■	
Oregon Wooden Screen Doors	■				■	■											■		■	■	
Owens Corning			■																■	■	
Panelfold							■												■		
Peachtree Doors		■	■ 38	■															■		160,181
Pease Industries		■	■	32		■													■		162,343
Peerless Products			■		■														■	■	
Pella Corporation	■		■		■	■		■			■	■		■			■		■		
Perma-Door		■	■	■															■		
Peterson Industries								■	■						■				■	■	
PH Tech	■		■			■														■	
Philips Products		■	■	■															■		
Pinecrest	■					■		■	■	■		■					■			■	
Pollard Windows			■	■																■	
Portes Celco		■	■	■															■		
Pozzi Wood Windows/(A Div. of JELD-WEN)			■			■													■		
Premdor U.S. Holdings		■	■ 38	■		■		28	■		■	■					■	■	■		170,182
PrimeWood		■																■	■		
R & D Equipment		■																		■	
R Laflamme et Frere											■	■									
Rehau			■																■	■	
Royal Plastics Group			■	■				■					■	■						■	
RSL Woodworking Products						■													■		
Sandy Pond Hardwoods											■						■	■	■	■	
Scatton Bros. Awning Mfg.	■			■	■															■	

See Manufacturer Index (beige pages at the back of this issue) for address and phone information.   Numbers in red indicate page number for additional product information.

Manufacturer	Custom	Fiberglass	Fire-rated	Sliding/patio	Steel	Storm/screen	Wood	Accordion	Bifold	Closet	Custom	French	Hardboard	Louvered	Mirrored	Moulded	Pocket	Wood	Local dealer/distributor	Factory-direct	Circle No.
	Exterior							Interior											Sales		
Screen Manufacturers Assn.						■															
Screenex Design Center/(Riordan Group)						■										■				■	
Seal Rite Windows			■	■																■	
Sections, Inc.	■					■													■		
Semco Windows & Doors/Semling-Menke			■									■					■		■		
Silver Line Building Products			■																■	■	
Simonton Windows			■																■		
Simpson Door Co.	■		■	■		■		■			■	■					■	■	■		568
Skytech Systems	■																		■	■	
Slimfold Products/(The Dunbarton Corp.)									■					■					■		
Smith Millwork						■			■				■	■			■		■	■	
Solaris Quebec				■	■														■		
Southeastern Aluminum Products								■	■						■				■	■	
Southwest Door Co.	37					■					■	■		■		■	■	■	■	■	339
Spanish Pueblo Doors	■					■		■	■	■						■	■	■	■	■	
Spectus Systems			■									■							■	■	
Stanley Door Systems/(Stanley Works)		■	■	■	■														■		167,171
Stanley Hardware																■			■		
Starbrite/(A Div. of Vega Industries)			■																■		
Steel Door Institute					■																
Steelcraft	■		■		■														■		
Steelwood Doors					■														■	■	
Stillwater Products			■																■		
Sugarcreek Window & Door Corp.						■													■		
Summit Windows & Patio Doors/(JELD-WEN)			■																■		
Supa Doors												■								■	
Superior Hardwoods & Millwork	■					■			■		■					■	■		■	■	
Superseal Mfg. Co.			■																■	■	
Survivor Technologies			■		■														■		
Swedish Building Systems & Components			■			■										■	■	■	■		
Taylor Brothers/Chippendale Doors					37														■		851
Taylor Door/(A Div. of Masco Industries)			■	■	■														■		
Texas Kiln Products						■		■	■	■							■			■	
Therma-Tru Corp.		32	■		■														■		58,65,161
Thermal-Gard					■														■		
Thermal Industries			■																■		
Thermetic Glass			■																■	■	
Thermoplast			■																■		
Timeline Vinyl Windows			■																■		
United Window Manufacturers			■	■							■						■		■		
Vantage Products Corp.						■													■		
Vermont Timber Frames	■									■										■	
Vetter, SNE Enterprises/(A PLYGEM Co.)									■	■						■			■		
Victor Sun Control			■																■		
Viking Industries			■																■		
Vintage Wood Works						■														■	
Vinyl Building Products			■																	■	
Vinyl Lite II Window & Door Systems			■			■													■	■	
Vinyl Tech/PGT			■																■		
Vinyl View/(A Div. of Thermetic Glass)			■																■		
Vinyl Window Designs						■													■	■	
Vinyl Window & Door Institute			■																■		
Wasco Products			■																■		

See Manufacturer Index (beige pages at the back of this issue) for address and phone information.   Numbers in red indicate page number for additional product information.   continued

Doors

Manufacturer	Custom	Fiberglass	Fire-rated	Sliding/patio	Steel	Storm/screen	Wood	Accordion	Bifold	Closet	Custom	French	Hardboard	Louvered	Mirrored	Moulded	Pocket	Wood	Local dealer/distributor	Factory-direct	Circle No.
	Exterior							Interior											Sales		Circle No.
Wayne-Dalton Corp.	37		■																■	■	850
Weather Shield Windows & Doors		■	38	33	■	■						■							■		164,178
Weathervane Window Co.	■		■			■														■	
Wells Aluminum Corp.			■																		
WENCO/(A Div. of JELD-WEN)			■																■		
Western Wood Products Assn.						■											■		■		
Weyerhaeuser/Door Div.																	■		■		
Willmar Windows			■	■		■													■		
Wilmes Window Mfg. Co.					■															■	
Windsor Door		■																	■		
Windsor Window Co.-NC Plant			■			■													■		
Wing Industries								■	■	■	■	■		■			■	■	■		
Winstrom Mfg. Corp.					■														■		
Wood Factory	■				■	■					■						■			■	
Woodfold-Marco Mfg.								■		■							■	■	■		
WoodMaster Designs						■													■	■	
Woodpecker Mfg.	■					■			■	■	■	■		■			■	■	■	■	
The Woodstone Co.	■		■		■	■	■	■	■	■	■		■	■		■	■			■	
Woodwork Institute of California		■				■					■	■	■		■	■	■				
Yakima Mfg./(A Div. of JELD-WEN)								■	■										■		

See Manufacturer Index (beige pages at the back of this issue) for address and phone information.   Numbers in red indicate page number for additional product information.

SOUTHWEST DOOR CO.
Southwest Door Co. has extended its door line to include new finishes, textures and styles in an array of door designs in alder, mesquite, pine or soft maple. For a free brochure, write to: Southwest Door Co. 9280 E. Old Vail Rd., Tucson, AZ 85747 **Circle No. 339**

WOOD PATIO DOORS

LOUISIANA-PACIFIC
Cierra Grande™ French sliding patio doors provide the look of traditional French patio doors, even when there's no space for doors that swing. Energy-efficient glass and a multi-point locking system for maximum security are among the standard features. **Call (800) 299-0028, ext. 4024 for a free brochure and distributor information.**

FOREVER® MAXXCHOICES STORM DOORS
Create a one-of-a-kind storm door. Choose your 36" frame color, etched glass and handle – forty combinations available for one price. Or choose your 36" frame, brass accent glass and handle – 60 combinations for one price. Forever® MaxxChoices. Exclusively by EMCO. Call (800) 777-3626 or visit us at www.forever.com **Circle No. 340**

VINYL PATIO DOORS

LOUISIANA-PACIFIC
Louisiana-Pacific's Astoria™ vinyl windows and patio doors meet demanding energy codes and fit perfectly with both new construction and replacement. Made with a new generation of stronger, modified uPVC, they resist rust, rot, scratches and dents. Available in a wide range of sizes and styles, including a variety of custom shapes. **Call (800) 299-0028, ext. 4023 for a free brochure and distributor information.**

WAYNE-DALTON ENTRY DOORS
*Iron*wood entry doors by Wayne-Dalton offer a rich woodgrain finish, deeply embossed into the 24 gauge steel skin and stained with a beautiful oak, walnut, or mahogany finish. For the beauty of wood and the strength of steel, have the best of both worlds – choose Ironwood entry doors by Wayne-Dalton. **Circle No. 850**

CHIPPENDALE WOOD STORM/SCREEN DOORS
The touch that enhances the classic look of your home. Recapture the colonial attention to detail with our mahogany doors...for a first impression that will last a lifetime. For a free brochure of available designs, write to: Taylor Brothers, Inc., P.O. Box 11198, 905 Graves Mill Rd., Lynchburg, VA 24506. (800) 288-6767. www.taylorbrothers.com Code Dept. K7 **Circle No. 851**

PATIO DOORS

Loewen Windows: Exterior of wood sliding patio door is protected with extruded aluminum. Door has dual-pane safety glass and optional security foot lock. 1-800-245-2295. *Circle no. 180.*

Weather Shield: Patio door is accented with curved-top glass panels. Choice of oak, cherry, maple, or pine interior; available with true divided lights and snap-on grilles. *Arbor Series.* 1-800-477-6808. *Circle no. 178.*

Peachtree: Insulated door combines beveled, glue chip, and clear glass. Door is accented with brass caming; optional sidelights and transoms are available. *MH Series.* 1-800-477-6544 . *Circle no. 181.*

Marvin Windows & Doors: Wood-look extruded aluminum cladding has been added to sliding patio door line. Doors have triple-point locking system and top-hung screens. 1-800-346-5128. *Circle no. 179.*

Premdor: Vinyl patio doors won't crack, split, or warp. Doors are built with wood inserts and come prefinished in white with flat or beveled glass. *Vinyl French Door Series.* 1-800-663-3667. *Circle no. 182.*

Electrical & Lighting

Manufacturer	Lighting controls/central	Lighting controls/dimmers	Lighting, exterior	Lighting, interior	Lighting, period	Load centers	Outlets/switches/receptacles	Switch plates/covers	Wire management systems	Local dealer/distributor	Factory-direct	Circle No.
American Lantern Div./Inteletron			■	■	■					■		
American Lighting		■	■	■								
American Lighting Assn.	■	■	■	■								
American Power Products			■	■						■	■	
American Site Furniture			■		■						■	
American Tack & Hardware Co.							■			■	■	
AMX Corp.		■										
Argee Corp.			■							■	■	
Beacon Products			■							■	■	
Bend-A-Lite			■	■						■	■	
BOAM USA			■							■	■	
Brandon Industries			42								■	856
Brass Light Gallery			■	■	■					■	■	
BRK Electronics	■	■								■		
Bronzelite			■									
Calger Lighting			■	■							■	
Canaren (Palwa By Canaren)			■	■						■		
Canarm			■							■		
Carlon Electrical Products	■	■				■			■		■	
Classic Lamp Post			■		■						■	
Cooper Lighting			■	■						■	■	
Crystal Lamp Parts	■	■	■	■	■					■	■	
CSI Donner				■						■		
Danalite				■						■		
Delaware Industries/Baseway Products									■	■	■	
Delray Lighting				■						■		
Digecon Plastics Intl.			■							■	■	
Doug Mockett & Co.									■		■	
Eagle Electric Mfg. Co.	■	■	■				■	■		■		
Eclipse Lighting			■	■	■					■		
Edison Price Lighting				■						■		
Fasco Industries	■									■		
FC Lighting			■	■	■						■	
Fiskars Power Sentry							■				■	
Flos USA			■	■	■					■		
French Reflection				■						■		
GE Lighting			■	■	■							

Kitchen lighting new-home shoppers prefer:
Luminous ceiling ___54%
Recessed downlights __32%
Track ___13%

Source: Fulton Research/16th Annual National Home Shopper Survey

See Manufacturer Index (beige pages at the back of this issue) for address and phone information. Numbers in red indicate page number for additional product information. continued

Manufacturer	Lighting controls/central	Lighting controls/dimmers	Lighting, exterior	Lighting, interior	Lighting, period	Load centers	Outlets/switches/receptacles	Switch plates/covers	Wire management systems	Local dealer/distributor	Factory-direct	Circle No.
GE Lighting Systems			■									
GE Wiring Devices	■	■				■	■	■	■			
Geist							■		■	■	■	
General Marble Co.			■							■	■	
GUSA/GINGER			■	■						■		
Hafele America			■							■		
Halo Lighting/(A Brand of Cooper Lighting)		■	■							■		
Hanover Lantern/Div. of Hoffman Products		42		■						■		854
Hoglund Landscape Construction			■							■		
Holophane Lighting Co.	■	■	■	■						■	■	
Home Automation		■								■		
Honeywell/Home & Building Control		■								■		
Hubbell Lighting			■	■	■					■		
Hunter Fan Co.			■	■						■		
Idaho Wood			■	■							■	
Intelectron			■	■					■	■		
IntelliNet	■	■					■				■	
International Energy Systems		■								■	■	
Juno Lighting			■							■		
Justice Design Group			■	■						■		
K Products Group/(A Div. of Cardinal Ind.)							■			■	■	
Kenall			■	■						■		
Kichler Lighting			■	■						■		
La Vona's Unique Hardware/Malibu Art Tile			■				■			■	■	
Lectro Science/Intermark				■						■		
Leviton Mfg.		■				■	■			■		
Lighting by Hammerworks			■	■							■	
Lightolier	■	■	■	■						■		
Lightway Industries			■	■	■					■		
LiteTouch	■	■					■				■	
Liteway			■	■						■	■	
Lutron Electronics Co.	■	■					■			■	■	
Mason/Red Dot/(A Div. of LE Mason Co.)			■				■	■				
Mel Northey Co.		42	■								■	857
MH Rhodes						■				■		
Murray Electrical Products					■					■	■	
Mystica & Co.							■			■	■	
Newstamp Lighting Co.			■	■	■						■	
Niles Audio Corp.									■	■		
NuTone			■							■	■	
Omega Lighting/Div. of Thomas Lighting		■	■	■						■		
Original Cast Lighting			■	■								
OSRAM SYLVANIA			■	■	■					■		
Paige Innovations							■	■		■		
Panasonic			■	■						■		
Paragon Electric Co.	■									■		
Pass & Seymour/Legrand		■	■			42	■			■		853
Philips Lighting Co.			■	■	■					■		
Point Electric			■	■						■	■	
Precision Multiple Controls	■	■				■				■		
Prescolite	■	■	■							■		
Progress Lighting			■	42						■		855
RAB Electric Mfg. Co.		■	■							■		

> **15% of the electricity used in homes goes into lighting.**
>
> *Source: U.S. Department of Energy*

See Manufacturer Index (beige pages at the back of this issue) for address and phone information.   Numbers in red indicate page number for additional product information.

	Products									Sales		
Manufacturer	Lighting controls/central	Lighting controls/dimmers	Lighting, exterior	Lighting, interior	Lighting, period	Load centers	Outlets/switches/receptacles	Switch plates/covers	Wire management systems	Local dealer/distributor	Factory-direct	**Circle No.**
Regent Lighting Corp.			■							■		
Rejuvenation Lamp & Fixture Co.			■	■	42						■	859
Robern				■						■		
Roberts Step-Lite Systems		42	■								■	858
Rotocast/Classic Lamp Posts			■		■					■		
Roy Electric Co.			■	■	■					■	■	
Schonbek Worldwide Lighting				■	■					■		
Sea Gull Lighting Prods			■	■	■					■		
Selby Furniture Hardware Co.				■						■	■	
Sherle Wagner Intl.								■				
SNOC		■	■									
Solar Energy Industries Assn.						■						
Square D Co.						■				■		
Sunstar Lighting		■	■	■	■		■	■			■	496
Sunway Fan Co.			■							■	■	
Sure-Lites/(A Div. of Cooper Lighting)			■							■		
Swivelier			■	■						■		
Sylvan Designs			■	■						■		
Task Lighting Corp.			■	■							■	
Taymor Industries								■		■		
Tek-Tron Enterprises			■							■		
Tescom Intl.			■							■	■	
Thomas Lighting/Consumer Div.			■	■	■					■		
Thomas Lighting/Accent Division				■						■		
Tiffany Landscape Lighting			■							■	■	
TIR Systems			■	■	■					■		
Tollmark Corp.				■						■	■	
Tork	■	■								■		
Torrence Coverplates								■		■	■	
Trimblehouse Corp.			■	■	■					■		
U.S. Gaslight			■		■					■		
UNITEC	■	■	■	■						■		
US Tec							■			■	■	
WAC Lighting Co.		■	■	■						■		
Walter Absil Co.								■		■	■	
The Watt Stopper		■					■			■		
Westinghouse and Cutler-Hammer Products						■				■		
The Wiremold Co.									■			
The Wiremold Co./Brooks Electronics Div.							■		■	■		
Zaneen Lighting			■							■		

See Manufacturer Index (beige pages at the back of this issue) for address and phone information.   Numbers in red indicate page number for additional product information.

PASS & SEYMOUR/LEGRAND® TRADEMASTER® GFCI FEATURES FASTER, EASIER INSTALLATION

Pass & Seymour/Legrand® has announced an entirely new ground fault circuit interrupter (GFCI) design. Features include: ability to use side- or back-wiring for positive, easy termination of #14 and #12, solid or stranded wire; two backwire holes per termination to allow for a multitude of wiring options without sacrificing speed; longer straps for better sheet rock contact and fewer "floating" installations; and more. Available in a variety of colors, including new light almond. For more information, write: QLMS, 8350 East Evans Dr, Scottsdale, AZ 85260 or call (800) 772-4219. **Circle No. 853**

HANOVER LANTERN

Hanover Lantern designs and manufactures a comprehensive selection of high quality, heavy duty, decorative cast titanium/aluminum lighting fixtures, posts, accessories and mailbox assemblies to complement virtually any application. Whether your decorative lighting requirements are for parking lots, street lighting, complexes, residences or landscape lighting applications...call Hanover Lantern first. "We are easy to do business with." Hanover Lantern, 470 High St., Hanover, PA 17331. (717) 632-6464. Fax (717) 632-5039. **Circle No. 854**

Classic Aluminum Lighting & Mailboxes Buy Factory Direct!

Aluminum lamp posts from $178. Many styles ranging from 8' to 16'. Distinctive Pedestal Mailboxes in heavy cast aluminum.

Coordination of mailboxes, lights, and signage provides distinctive continuity for your development.

Brandon Industries
972-542-3000
Circle No. 856

Progress Lighting is the largest source for residential and commercial lighting products. With more than 2,600 products in 11 categories, Progress' reputation continues to hold strong as the #1 lighting line with both remodelers and builders. From traditional brass and crystal to contemporary designs in the latest finishes, you'll find a variety of fixtures to suit your needs. Call (864) 599-6000.
Circle No. 855

MEL-NORTHEY CO.

Antique reproductions of period light posts and luminaries in durable rust-free cast aluminum at affordable prices. America's most unique line of custom mail boxes and posts. MEL-NORTHEY COMPANY, 303 Gulf Bank, Houston, TX 77037. Call (800) 828-0302. **Circle No. 857**

ROBERTS STEP-LITE SYSTEMS®

Patented lighting system provides aesthetic lighting on interior and exterior steps, handrails and cover mouldings for commercial and residential applications. Custom Manufactured to exact dimensions, with single fixture lengths up to 20 feet and a choice of 5, 10 or 25 footcandles. **Roberts Step-Lite Systems, (800) 654-8268. Circle No. 858**

REJUVENATION LAMP & FIXTURE CO.

Established in 1977, Rejuvenation now manufactures over 250 authentic reproductions of period light fixtures and lamps from the Arts & Crafts, Victorian and Neoclassic eras. Solid brass fixtures are available in nine finishes, will accept a wide selection of shades, and can be customized to meet specific requirements. **FREE 68 page catalogue.** Call (503) 231-1900 or fax (800) LAMPFAX (526-7329). **Circle No. 859**

Engineered Lumber & Panels

Manufacturer	Finger-jointed	Glue laminated beams	I-joists	Laminated strand lumber	Laminated veneer lumber	Parallel strand lumber	Hardboard	Medium-density fiberboard (MDF)	Oriented-strand board (OSB)	Oriented waferboard	Particleboard	Plywood, hardwood	Plywood, softwood	Sheathing	Underlayment, flooring	Underlayment, roofing	Waferboard	Local dealer/distributor	Factory-direct	Circle No.
	Engineered						**Panels**											**Sales**		
AB Cushing Mills		■			■	■	■					■								
Acadia Post & Beam					■	■												■	■	
Adirondack Forest Industries			■		■	■												■		
Advanced Wood Resources (JELD-WEN)									■						■			■		
Aged Woods		■																■	■	
American Forest & Paper Assn.	■	■	■	■	■	■	■	■	■	■	■	■	■	■	■	■	■			
American Hardboard Assn.												■	■							
American Hardwoods			■		■	■														
American Wood Council	■		■		■	■	■					■	■	■						
Anthony Forest Products Co.	47																	■	■	861
APA - The Engineered Wood Assn.	■	■	■		■	■	■				■	■	■	■				■		
Atlantic Building Products									■				■	■	■	■		■		
Bangkok Intl.			■		■	■													■	
Barton Lumber Co.									■			■						■		
BB&S Treated Lumber												■	■					■		
Bingaman & Son Lumber			■		■	■													■	
Boise Cascade	■	■	■		■		■		■		■	■	■	■	■			■		
BPCO/(A Div. of EMCO)							■						■					■	■	
Brojack Lumber Co.			■		■	■												■	■	
Buehler Lumber Co.			■		■	■														
Buffalo Veneer & Plywood			■		■	■						■						■	■	
Building Products & Nails/Div. BSTC Group									■	■	■			■						
Burns, Morris & Stewart	■																	■		
Burrows Lumber			■		■	■						■	■					■		
California Redwood Assn.	■																	■		
Canadian Wood Council	■											■	■							
Cellofoam North America													■					■		
Cersosimo Lumber Co.			■		■	■														
Champion Intl. Corp.													■	■	■	■		■	■	
Chesapeake Hardwood Products											■				■			■		
Chocorua Valley Lumber Co.					■															
Coastal Lumber Co./(Treated Products Div.)												■	■					■	■	
Columbia Forest Products											■							■		
Comtex Industries	■				■	■												■		
Conner Industries						■			■		■									
Domtar Decorative Panels									■									■	■	
Downes & Reader Hardwood Co.			■		■	■	■		■	■										

See Manufacturer Index (beige pages at the back of this issue) for address and phone information. Numbers in red indicate page number for additional product information.

continued

Engineered Lumber & Panels

Products span: **Engineered** (Finger-jointed; Glue laminated beams; I-joists; Laminated strand lumber; Laminated veneer lumber; Parallel strand lumber) — **Panels** (Hardboard; Medium-density fiberboard (MDF); Oriented-strand board (OSB); Oriented waferboard; Particleboard; Plywood, hardwood; Plywood, softwood; Sheathing; Underlayment, flooring; Underlayment, roofing; Waferboard) — **Sales** (Local dealer/distributor; Factory-direct)

Manufacturer	Finger-jointed	Glue laminated beams	I-joists	Laminated strand lumber	Laminated veneer lumber	Parallel strand lumber	Hardboard	MDF	OSB	Oriented waferboard	Particleboard	Plywood, hardwood	Plywood, softwood	Sheathing	Underlayment, flooring	Underlayment, roofing	Waferboard	Local dealer/distributor	Factory-direct	Circle No.
EPS Molders Assn.													■							
Evergreen Lumber & Moulding								■												
Fen-Tech				■														■	■	
Fibreform Wood Products	■						■	■			■							■		
Fine Hardwood Veneer Assn.		■		■	■														■	
Foreign & Domestic Woods					■													■		
Forest Products Society	■	■		■	■		■	■	■	■	■			■				■		
Fort Vancouver Plywood Co.												■	■	■				■		
Fourply												■								
G/L Veneer Co.		■		■	■		■	■			■	■							■	
Georgia-Pacific Corp.	■	47		■	■		■	■			47	■	■	■	■			■		862,864
Gibco Services		■		■	■	■	■	■					■					■		
Glen Oak Lumber & Milling	■			■																
Grabill Cabinet Co.	■																			
Grace Construction Products																■		■		
Great Lake Woods		■		■	■														■	
Groleau		■		■	■													■		
HA Stiles Co.		■		■	■													■	■	
Hacker Industries															■				■	
Hardwood Distributors Assn.		■	■	■	■													■		
Hardwood Manufacturers Assn.		■		■	■															
Hardwood Plywood & Veneer Assn.		■		■	■		■	■			■									
Hardwoods Millworking		■		■	■													■		
Heritage Finishes			■															■	■	
Highland Lumber Co.	■																		■	
Homasote Co.														■	■	■		■		
Homer Wood Corp.		■		■	■														■	
Horner Flooring Co.		■		■														■	■	
Houston Woodtech								■												
Huebert Fiberboard Co.								■							■					
Huey Millwork Co.				■	■															
Hunt Plywood Co.												■		■						
Huntsville Wood Products												■								
Huntwood Industries		■	■	■														■	■	
Idaho Forest Industries	■																	■		
Industrial Energy Products							■												■	
Insulated Building Systems								■								■		■	■	
International Paper Co.							■	■			■	■	■					■		
International Wood Products Assn.		■	■	■	■	■	■	■	■	■	■	■	■	■	■	■	■	■		
JM Huber Corp.								■										■	■	
Keiver-Willard Lumber Corp.		■		■	■															
KML Windows					■													■		
L.M. Scofield Co.															■			■	■	
Laminating Materials Assn.							■	■			■									
Lewis Lumber Products		■		■	■													■		
Lewisohn Sales Co.	■		■		■														■	
Little Lumber Co.		■		■																
Louisiana-Pacific Corp.	■	■	46		47		■		47		■		47	47	47			■		
M.L. Condon Co.		■		■	■							■	■					■	■	
MacBeath Hardwood		■		■	■							■								
MacMillan Bloedel/Building Materials Mktg.	■	■	■	■	■	■	■	■			■	■		■	■	■		■		
Maple Flooring Manufacturers Assn.				■																
MaxiTile																■		■		

See Manufacturer Index (beige pages at the back of this issue) for address and phone information.

Numbers in red indicate page number for additional product information.

Manufacturer	Finger-jointed	Glue laminated beams	I-joists	Laminated strand lumber	Laminated veneer lumber	Parallel strand lumber	Hardboard	Medium-density fiberboard (MDF)	Oriented-strand board (OSB)	Oriented waterboard	Particleboard	Plywood, hardwood	Plywood, softwood	Sheathing	Underlayment, flooring	Underlayment, roofing	Waterboard	Local dealer/distributor	Factory-direct	Circle No.
	Engineered						**Panels**											**Sales**		
Medite Corp.								■										■	■	
Medply												■	■	■	■				■	
Memphis Hardwood Flooring Co.						■														
Mouldings & Millwork	■																	■		
NAC Products															■			■		
National Particleboard Assn.								■			■									
New Energy Works Timberframers		■	■																■	
Niagara Fiberboard												■						■	■	
Norbord Industries							■	■			■							■		
North American Plywood Corp.											■	■						■	■	
Northeastern Lumber Manufacturers Assn.	■																			
The Pacific Lumber Co.	■																	■		353
Pacific Wood Laminates	■				■							■	■	■	■			■		
Particleboard/MDF Institute								■							■					
Patrick Industries	■																	■		
Plum Creek/Southern Region												■	■					■		
Ply Gem Mfg.												■						■		
Plylap Industries		■			■	■						■						■	■	
Plywood Tropics USA											■	■			■			■	■	
Pope & Talbot	■																	■	■	
Potlatch Corp.						■			■		■							■		
Quality Woods		■			■													■		
Rare Earth Hardwoods												■						■	■	
Ray White Lumber Co.													■							
Rex Lumber Co.					■	■														
Rosboro Lumber Co.												■								
Roseburg Forest Products		■			■	■				■	■	■	■	■	■			■		
Rossi Corp.		■			■	■													■	
Roxco Liquidators					■	■					■	■								
Sagebrush Sales	■	■	■		■		■		■		■	■	■	■	■		■	■		
Schluter Systems															■					
SDS Lumber Co.											■									
Shelter Systems		■	■	■	■														■	
Simplex Products/(A Div. of K2)													■		■			■		
Simpson Timber Co./Panel Products Div.											■	■	■					■	■	
Snavely Forest Products	■																	■	■	
St. Croix Valley Hardwoods		■			■	■	■			■	■	■							■	
States Industries												■						■		
Structural Board Assn.									■						■			■	■	
Superior Floor Co.					■														■	
Superior Hardwoods & Millwork												■							■	
Swaner Hardwood Co.										■	■	■						■		
TEC/(A Sub. of HB Fuller Co.)																■		■		
Tecton Industries			■															■		
Temple-Inland Forest Products	■										■			■				■		
Texas Kiln Products						■													■	
Textured Forest Products												■						■	■	
Thompson Industries												■								
Timber Products Co.		■			■	■	■	■		■	■	■	■	■				■	■	
Timber Systems		■	■	■		■												■	■	
Tolleson Lumber Co.						■														
TrimJoist Corp.		■																■		
Trus Joist MacMillan		■	■	■	■	■												■		

See Manufacturer Index (beige pages at the back of this issue) for address and phone information.   Numbers in red indicate page number for additional product information.   continued

Engineered Lumber & Panels

Manufacturer	Finger-jointed	Glue laminated beams	I-joists	Laminated strand lumber	Laminated veneer lumber	Parallel strand lumber	Hardboard	Medium-density fiberboard (MDF)	Oriented-strand board (OSB)	Oriented waferboard	Particleboard	Plywood, hardwood	Plywood, softwood	Sheathing	Underlayment, flooring	Underlayment, roofing	Waferboard	Local dealer/distributor	Factory-direct	Circle No.
	Engineered						**Panels**											**Sales**		
Unadilla Laminated Products	■	■																	■	
Universal Forest Products			■								■							■		
Ward Lumber Co.			■		■													■		
Weaber	■																	■		
Western Archrib		■																■		
Western Wood Products Assn.	■																	■		
Weyerhaeuser/Oriented Strand Business									■						■	■		■		
Whittlesey Wood Products			■		■	■	■					■						■		
Willamette Industries	■	■	■		■													■		
Willamette Industries/(Sawmill Div.)								■			■	■	■	■	■	■				
Willamette Industries/Duraflake Division								■			■				■			■	■	
Windsor Mill	■																	■		
Wood Floors				■															■	
Woodcraft Supply			■	■		■	■													

See Manufacturer Index (beige pages at the back of this issue) for address and phone information.   Numbers in red indicate page number for additional product information.

Engineered Lumber & Panels

SUB-FLOORING

LOUISIANA-PACIFIC
TopNotch® T&G Flooring features L-P's patented vertical notches in the panel's tongue and ends allowing water to drain during construction, while self-spacing tongue and groove edges simplify installation. Top Notch flooring is APA® Sturd-I-Floor® rated. Available in thicknesses from 19/32" to 1-1/8".
Call (800) 299-0029, ext. 4017 for a free brochure and distributor information.

ENGINEERED WOOD

LOUISIANA-PACIFIC
L-P's Solid Start® rim board is a strong, cost-effective choice for your engineered floor system. Designed to match our LPI Joists, this engineered wood rim board is available in 1-1/8" nominal thicknesses, and depths of 9-1/2", 11-7/8", and 14" and 16". The 16' length makes it quick and easy to install. **Call (800) 299-0029, ext. 4018 for a free brochure and distributor information.**

ENGINEERED WOOD

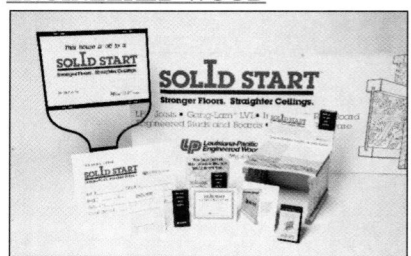

LOUISIANA-PACIFIC
Louisiana-Pacific is marketing our LPI® Joists and Gang-Lam® LVL beams with the name Solid Start®. We give you all the support you need to let home buyers know that builders who care about quality use the Solid Start system because it provides stronger floors and straighter ceilings. Solid Start promotional materials include a limited lifetime warranty, home buyers brochure, yard and lot signs, counter card displays, realtors sell sheets and national print ads. **Call (800) 299-0029, ext. 4015 for a free brochure.**

ENGINEERED WOOD

LOUISIANA-PACIFIC
Gang-Lam® LVL is available thicker, wider and longer than solid sawn lumber beams with more load carrying capacity and design freedom. By combining exterior adhesives and ultrasonically graded veneers, L-P has created a strong, engineered beam. With the shortage of large dimensional lumber, Gang-Lam LVL beams are a readily available, affordable alternative. Gang-Lam LVL is available in standard thicknesses of 1-1/2" and 3-1/2" and depths of 7-1/4" to 18". **Call (800) 299-0029, ext. 4014 for a free brochure and distributor information.**

UNDERLAYMENT

FIBERBOND®
FiberBond underlayment's smooth, durable surface is an excellent base for thin, resilient floor covering. It retains dimensional stability under high moisture conditions better than plywood, OSB and lauan underlayment. Plus, FiberBond underlayment is easy to use – 4' x 4' panels have the fastening pattern printed on the face and installation instructions, as well as a handy 800 technical assistance number printed on the back. **Call (800) 299-0028, ext. 4025 for a free brochure and distributor information.**

FIRE RETARDANTS AND PRESERVATIVES
New 12-page Sweet's catalog features *Pyro-Guard®* interior type fire retardant lumber and plywood for roof systems and other interior structural uses; *Exterior Fire-X®* FRT lumber and plywood for decks, balconies, siding and other exterior uses; and CCA/*KDAT* preservative treated lumber and plywood that's Kiln Dried After Treatment, from Hoover Treated Wood Products Inc., the USA's largest producer of fire retardant treated wood. **Circle No. 863**

ENGINEERED WOOD

LOUISIANA-PACIFIC
Louisiana-Pacific LPI® Joists are engineered to start straighter and stay straighter than solid sawn joists, and resist shrinking, twisting, splitting, warping and crowning. L-P offers six series of LPI Joists which feature strong, oriented strand board webs. The 26, 30, 36 and 56 series are made with our exclusive Gang-Lam® LVL flanges, and the 20 and 32 series are made with solid sawn lumber flanges. Depths available from 9-1/2" to 24". **Call (800) 299-0029, ext. 4013 for a free brochure and distributor information.**

THE POWER BEAM® Challenge
$3000F_b - 2.1E - 290F_v$

- Substitute for Parallam
- Substitute for LVL
- One Piece Construction
- Cambered or Noncambered
- I-Joist Depths
- Anthony WoodWorks® Sizing Software

Call (800) 221-BEAM
P.O. Box 1877 • El Dorado, AR 71731
e-mail: anthony@infogo.com
Website: http://www.anthonyforest.com
Circle No. 861

SHEATHING

LOUISIANA-PACIFIC
Engineered wood sheathing is designed for roof, wall and two-layer subfloor systems in residential and commercial constructions. These APA Span Rated panels cut, nail and staple easily, with no special tools required. Available in thickness from 3/8" to 1-1/8". **Call (800) 299-0029, ext. 4019 for a free brochure and distributor information.**

ENGINEERED LUMBER
In roof or floor systems, beams or headers, engineered lumber products from G-P deliver greater strength and load capacities and more predictable performance than dimension lumber. Unlike traditional lumber that can split, shrink, warp and twist, Wood I Beam™ joists are dimensionally stable, and allow for longer clear spans, which means fewer support beams. Call 1-800-BUILD G-P (284-5347) for details. **Circle No. 862**

G-P *PLUS*™ STURD-I-FLOOR®
G-P *Plus*™, the new name for G-P Rated Plywood Sturd-I-Floor, has been improved to surpass APA standards and is backed by a 10-year limited commercial warranty. G-P Plus, panels feature a full sanded face and no corelaps in the crossband under the face providing a smoother surface for direct application of vinyl tile and hardwood flooring (install in accordance with the APA design/construction guide form No. E30). Call 1-800-BUILD G-P (284-5347) for details. **Circle No. 864**

Equipment & Trucks

Manufacturer	Forklifts	Site buildings/trailers	Trucks	Vehicle equipment/accessories	Construction lighting	Dust control equipment	Fall protection equipment	Ladders	Lifts	Paint spraying equipment	Portable generators	Safety equipment	Scaffolding	Sheet metal equipment	Shop vacuums	Surface protection	Local dealer/distributor	Factory-direct	Circle No.
	Heavy			**Light**													**Sales**		
AC Products																■	■		
Advanced Design Products													■				■		
Alltrade								■									■		
Alum-a-Pole Corp.													50				■		868
AM General Corp.			■														■		
American Honda Motor Co.											■						■		
American Isuzu Motors			■														■		
American Roof							■										■		
Barwalt Tool Co./(Precision Tile Spacer Co.)										■							■		
Better Built Co.				■													■	■	
Bon Tool Co.								■					■				■		
Campbell Hausfeld										■							■		
Cargotec	■																■	■	
Carlisle Plastics																■	■	■	
Case Corp.	■																■		
Caterpillar	■																■		
Chevrolet Motor Div./GM Corp.			■														■		
Clark Material Handling Co.	■		■														■	■	
Clarke Industries															■		■		
Creative Building Products													■				■	■	
Cronkhite Industries		■															■		
CrossTread Industries				■													■		
Curtain Wall Co.					50													■	790
Deere & Co./(John Deere Industrial Equip.)	■																■		
Dodge Div. of Chrysler Corp.			■														■		
Dust Door/Arch Guard						■												■	
Falcon Mfg.							■						■				■	■	
Fein Power Tools															■		■		
Ford Motor Co.			■														■		
Fostoria Industries/General Products Div.					■												■	■	
Gehl Co.	■																■		
Generac Corp.											■							■	
The Genie Co.															■		■	■	
Genie Industries									■								■		
GMC Truck			■														■		
Graco										■							■		
Harrington Hoists									■								■		
Hodge Mfg. Co.			■			■											■		
Hyster Co.	■																■		
Isuzu Truck of America			■														■		
Jet Equipment & Tools									■					■	■		■		
Kargo King/(A Div. of Kiefer Built)		■															■		

See Manufacturer Index (beige pages at the back of this issue) for address and phone information.   Numbers in red indicate page number for additional product information.

Manufacturer	Heavy			Light													Sales		Circle No.
	Forklifts	Site buildings/trailers	Trucks	Vehicle equipment/accessories	Construction lighting	Dust control equipment	Fall protection equipment	Ladders	Lifts	Paint spraying equipment	Portable generators	Safety equipment	Scaffolding	Sheet metal equipment	Shop vacuums	Surface protection	Local dealer/distributor	Factory-direct	
Keller Ladders								●									●		
Kiefer Built			●														●	●	
Knaack Mfg. Co.			●														●		
Knudson Mfg.													●				●	●	
Komatsu Forklift (USA)	●								●								●	●	
Lectro Science/Intermark					●												●		
Louisville Ladder Corp.								●									●		
Makita USA										●					●		●		
Mayville Engineering Co.									●								●		
Melroe Co./Bobcat			●														●	●	
Milwaukee Electric Tool Corp.															●		●		
Mitsubishi Caterpillar Forklift	●																●		
Mitsubishi Fuso Truck of America			●														●		
Murray-Black Co.											●						●		
National Truck Equipment Assn.			●	●													●		
OSRAM SYLVANIA					●												●		
Plastival		●															●	●	
Poly-Tak Protection Systems																●	●		
Pro Tect Associates																●	●	●	
Pro Tecta Industries																●	●	●	
Proctor Products Co.							●										●		
Protective Products Intl.																50	●	●	866
Quikspray										●							●	●	
Rack-Strap			●														●		
Reading Body Works			●														●		
Ruger Equipment	●								●								●	●	
Rustgo-Nelson King							●				●						●	●	
Ryobi America Corp.															●				
Sellick Equipment	●																●		
Shur-Co.			●														●	●	
Spyder	●		●														●	●	
Surface Shields																●	●		
Sweepster			●															●	
System One Modular Truck Equipment			50														●	●	867
Tapco Products/(A Tapco Intl. Corp.)														●			●		
TCM Forklift Trucks	●																●	●	
Teledyne Specialty Equipment	●																●	●	
Toyota Motor Sales, USA	●		●														●		
Trac Rac			50														●		869
USTC	●																●		
Valeo												●					●		
Van Mark Products Corp.														●			●		
Vermeer Mfg.			●								●						●		
VIC Intl. Corp.						●											●	●	
Wallboard Tool Co.								●	●			●					●		
Warner Tentnology Corp.		●																●	
Wells Cargo		●															●		
Werner Co.								●					●				●		
Williams-Scotsman		●															●	●	
Willson Safety Products												●					●		
Winco											●						●	●	
Wing Enterprises								●									●	●	
Yale Materials Handling Corp.	●																●		

See Manufacturer Index (beige pages at the back of this issue) for address and phone information.   Numbers in red indicate page number for additional product information.   continued

Protective Products
Surface Protection Solutions

TRIM PROTECTION from PROTECTIVE PRODUCTS is ideal for masking and protecting door thresholds and clad trim to eliminate damage from mortar, stucco and jobsite dirt and grime. Trim Protection is a tough, abrasion-resistant PVC tape with a specially formulated adhesive that prevents "duct tape syndrome." For info on the full line of PROTECTIVE PRODUCTS call 24 hrs: (800) 789-6633. www.protectiveproducts.com
Circle No. 866

Alum-A-Pole Scaffolding System, Pro-Trim DuroBend™ Double Matte Finish Bendable Solid Vinyl Coil and Extruded Window/Door Trim Sets.
Call 1-800-421-ALUM today for a more Professional and Profitable tomorrow.

Circle No. 868

Tired of wimpy, low-end racks?
GET A REAL RACK!
NEW
Patented Made in the USA
TracRac

TracRac's Easy To Install
◆ Fits any pickup truck, installs in under 1 hour
◆ Mounts with no drilling, bolting or clamping
TracRac SLIDES
◆ Racks & accessories slide to adjust
◆ Cargo holder – even toolboxes – can slide back to tailgate
TracRac's Built To Take A Beating
◆ Rugged anodized aluminum – no rust!
◆ Lightweight (77 lbs.) but **mighty** (1000 lb. capacity)

Call us for free brochure: 1-800-501-1587
Circle No. 869

CONTROL DUST

THE PATENTED
Curtain-Wall
Dust Catcher

- 1 Minute Set-up
- No screwing to ceiling or wall
- Cloth Curtain & Aluminum Frame adjust to 9' high x 12' wide
- $169 each - we pay shipping to 48 states - VISA/MC

Money back Guarantee
Free Brochure **(800) 424-8251**

Circle No. 790

SYSTEM ONE MODULAR TRUCK EQUIPMENT
…quality equipment for professional contractors. System One Modular Truck Equipment is a heavy duty, high tech, aluminum alloy truck rack that is actually 3 systems in one. Overhead cargo is transported on tough rubber wear strips and secured safely with ratchet tie-downs; interior cargo is secured using cargo anchors that slide in the patented Pick-Up Trak™; tools, tool boxes and equipment are efficiently organized with over 30 accessories that mount in recessed T-slots. Call for a free brochure (800) 627-9783. **Circle No. 867**

Faucets & Fixtures

Manufacturer	Accessible products	Bath accessories	Bathtubs	Faucets, bar	Faucets, bath	Faucets, kitchen	Fittings	Hot tubs/spas	Lavatories	Saunas/steam rooms	Shower bases	Shower doors	Shower heads	Shower/tub surrounds	Sinks, kitchen	Toilets/bidets	Whirlpool tubs	Local dealer/distributor	Factory-direct	Circle No.
ABT Building Products Corp./ABTco														■				■		
Accurate Industries Steambath and Sauna		■								■		■						■		
Acme Brick Co./IBP Grid System														■				■	■	
Allied Brass Mfg. Co.		■																■		
Almico Plastics			■														■	■		
Almost Heaven								■		■							■		■	
Alro Plumbing Specialty Co.						■												■		
Alsons Corp.		■											■					■		
Alumax Bath Enclosures												■						■		
Am-Finn Sauna Co.										■									■	
Amerec Products										■								■		
American Faucet & Coatings Corp.		■		■	■	■	■						■						■	
American Marble Industries/Kephaco Corp.		■							■		■			■	■		■	■		
American Olean Tile		■																■		
American Shower and Bath/(Masco Corp.)		■							■					■		■		■		
American Shower Door												■						■	■	
American Standard	■	■	■	■	■	■		58	■	■				■	57		■	■		143,198
American Whirlpool			■					■									■	■		
Americh Corp.			■						■								■	■		
Aqua Glass Corp./(A Div. of Masco)	■		■		■			■	■	■			■				■	■		399
Aqua Plunge/Aqua Plunge Div.							■										■	■	■	
Aquatic Industries	■		■					■	■	■	■		■	■			■	■		
Areslux		■			■														■	
Around The Corner		■	■	■	■				■							■		■		
Artistic Brass/Div. of Masco Corp. of Indiana		■		■	■	■							■					■		
Astracast				■		■									■			■		
Avonite															■	■		■		
B&K Industries		■		■	■	■	■						■					■		
Baja Products							■										■	■	■	
Baker Mfg. Corp.		■					■										■	■	■	
Baldwin Hardware Corp.		■																■		
Barclay Products	■	53	■	■	■	■	■	58					■		■	■				115,196
Basco Co.												■						■		
Bates & Bates									■						■			■		
Bath Ease	■		■										■			■		■	■	
Bath N' Bagno		■																■		
Bath-Tec/Builder Sales		■			■				■				■			60			■	875
Bathcraft		■															■	■		
Bathlex		■						■		■			■				■		■	
Belanger Plumbing Accessories	■			■	■	■	■									■				
Billco Corp.						■													■	
Blanco America			■		■										■			■		

See Manufacturer Index (beige pages at the back of this issue) for address and phone information.   Numbers in red indicate page number for additional product information.

continued

Faucets & Fixtures

Manufacturer	Accessible products	Bath accessories	Bathtubs	Faucets, bar	Faucets, bath	Faucets, kitchen	Fittings	Hot tubs/spas	Lavatories	Saunas/steam rooms	Shower bases	Shower doors	Shower heads	Shower/tub surrounds	Sinks, kitchen	Toilets/bidets	Whirlpool tubs	Local dealer/distributor	Factory-direct	Circle No.
Boehm Acrilicrafts		■																	■	
Brass Accents by Urfic		■																■	■	
Brass Craft Mfg./(A Div. of Masco Corp.)						■			■											
Briggs Industries			■	■	■	55	■		■		■			57	■					132,141
The Broadway Collection		■		■	■	■	■				■							■	■	
Burgess Intl. Bath Fixtures	■		■						■						■					
Byron's Spa																■	■	■	■	
Cal Crystal Unlimited		■		■	■	■												■		
Caldera Spas & Baths			■					■								■		■		
California Acrylic Industries/Cal Spas			■					■		■								■		
Cameo Marble			■					■	■			■				■	■	■		
Cast Iron Soil Pipe Institute							■													
Cedarbrook Sauna										■									■	
Central Brass	■			■	■	■	■		■									■		
Century Shower Door												■						■		
Chicago Faucets	■			■	■	■	■											■		
Chronomite Labs													■							
Clarke Products		■								■			■	■			■			
Colonial Bronze Co.		■																■		
Concinnity/(A Div. of IW Industries)		■		■	■	■	■		■									■	■	
Coni Marble Mfg.		■								■		■	■		■	■	■	■		
Continental Stone Designs			■					■		■	■			■		■		■		
Contractors Wardrobe										■	■					■		■	■	
Crane Plumbing/Fiat Products	■		■					■	■	■	■			■	■	■		■		
CSI Donner		■																■		
Dec-Har Designs		■																■	■	
Delta Faucet Co.	■	■		■	■	■				■								■		
DM Industries			■					■		■	■	■	■			■		■	■	
Duschqueen											■	■						■	■	
Easy Heat		■																■		
Eljer Plumbingware	■	■	■	■	■	■	■		■		■			57	■			■		144
Elkay Mfg. Co.				■		■									■			■		
Elkhart Door												■						■	■	
Euromix Sales		■		■	■	■												■		
Faucet Express				■	■														■	
Federal Home Products														■				■		
Fiberez Bathware	■	■	■								■					■	■	■		
Fiberglass Access	■	■	■					■		■	■	■				■	■	■		
Fiberglass Systems	■	■	■							■	■					■		■		
Finlandia Harvia Sauna Products										61								■	■	882
Finnleo Saunas										■										
Florestone Products Co.	■		■							■	■		■			■		■		
Fluidmaster														■				■		
Foremost Industries		■	■	■	■				■					■				■		
Franke/Kitchen Systems Div.					55									■				■		128
Franklin Brass Mfg. Co.	■	■																■		
FV America	■	■			■	■			■									■		
Geberit Mfg.		61												■				■	■	884
Gemini Bath & Kitchen Products	■		■	■	■	■		■			■		■			■		■	■	
The Georgia Marble Co.								■										■		
Gerber Plumbing Fixtures Corp.	■			■	■	55	■		■		■			57				■		133,145
Gesmar			■					■		■			■			■	■	■	■	
Green Street Details		■																■	■	

See Manufacturer Index (beige pages at the back of this issue) for address and phone information.   Numbers in red indicate page number for additional product information.

continued

PEDESTAL LAVATORIES

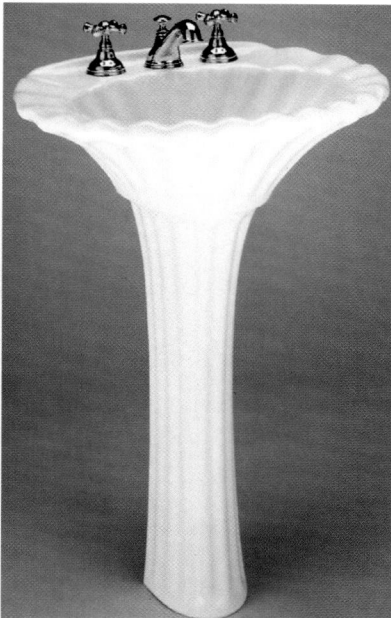

Barclay: Sculpted flutes around the pedestal lavatory column extend to the outside and inside of the bowl. Unit has a narrow rim and wide-spread-faucet holes. *Conch.* 1-800-446-9700. *Circle no. 115.*

Porcher: Pedestal lavatory has wide side decks and undersink towel bars. Unit can be customized with hand painting. *Sapho.* 1-800-359-3261. *Circle no. 114.*

American China: Pedestal lavatory is 34 inches high. Unit is part of a line that includes drop-in sink, toilet, and bath accessories. *Estate Collection.* 1-800-359-3261. *Circle no. 116.*

COMPANY	MODEL	DIMENSIONS (IN INCHES, W x D)	COLORS	FAUCET DRILLING	PHONE
Absolute	Castelli	44 x 22½	white	single hole	1-800-359-3261
American China	Estate Collection	26¾ x 19¾	white, various colors	single hole, 4", or 8"	1-800-359-3261
Barclay	Conch	23 x 18	white	4" or 8"	1-800-446-9700
Crane Plumbing	Corona	24 x 19	white, bone	4" or 8"	847-864-9777
Gerber	La Rive	25 x 21	white, various colors	4" or 8"	847-675-6570
Kohler	Ellington	24⅛ x 19	white, various colors	single hole, 4", or 8"	1-800-4Kohler
Porcher	Sapho	25⁹⁄₁₆ x 20½	white, more than 100 colors, metal finishes	single hole	1-800-359-3261
Rohl/Allia	1445	25⅝ x 20⅛	white, various colors	single hole or 8"	714-557-1933
Santile	Darling	23½ x 19½	white, nine special-order finishes	single hole or 3"	404-416-6224

Companies in red have product shown above.

Faucets & Fixtures

Manufacturer	Accessible products	Bath accessories	Bathtubs	Faucets, bar	Faucets, bath	Faucets, kitchen	Fittings	Hot tubs/spas	Lavatories	Saunas/steam rooms	Shower bases	Shower doors	Shower heads	Shower/tub surrounds	Sinks, kitchen	Toilets/bidets	Whirlpool tubs	Local dealer/distributor	Factory-direct	Circle No.
GROHE/(A Sub. of Friedrich Grohe)	■	■		■	■	55	■				■							■		130
GUSA/GINGER	■	■																■		
Hansa America			■	■	■						■							■		
Hansgrohe	■		■	■	■						■							■		
Harden Industries	■	■		■	■	■	■				■							■		
Harney Mfg.	■	■				■					■							■		
Harrington Brass Works	■	■		■	■	■	■				■							■		
Hastings Tile & Il Bagno Collection		■		■	■			■	■		■	■						■		
Herrco Enterprises			■	■	■													■		
Hindley Mfg. Co.	■																	■		
House of Ceramics		■	■		■		■		■		■				■	■	■			
Hydro Systems		■								■						■	■			
Indiana Brass				■	■	■					■							■		
Inova					■									■				■	■	
International Paper Co.								■					■	■				■		
Italbrass Corp.		■																■		
Jacuzzi Whirlpool Bath		■		■				■	■		■	■					60	■		878
Jado Bathroom & Hardware Mfg. Corp.		■		■	■	■	■				■							■		
Jason Intl.		■	■		■			■	■			■				■		■		439
Just Mfg. Co.	■			■	■	■	■		■					■				■		
Kallista	■	■	■	■	■	■	■		■		■	■				■	■	■		
KBI Industries				■							■								■	
Keystone Shower Door/KSD Industries										■								■		
Kindred Industries															■			■		
Kit Industries	■																	■	■	
Kohler Co.	■	■	■	■	■	■	■	58	■	■	■	■	■	■		57	■	■		140,197
Kolson	■	■	■	■	■	■	■		■		■	■	■		■	■				
Kroin	■	■		■	■	■	■		■		■		■					■		
KWC/(A Brand of Rohl Corp.)		■		■	■	■												■		
Lasco Bathware/(A Div. of Tomkins Ind.)	■		■														■	■		241
Laurel Co.													■					■	■	
Lenape Products		■																■	■	
Leonard Valve Co.				■									■					■		
Liette Intl.		■	■	■				■							■			■		
Lifetime Faucets			■	■	■													■	■	
Lyons Industries	■	■	■								■	■					■	■		
MAAX/Div. Acrylica, Premium	■		■								■	■	■	■			■	■		
The Majestic Shower Co.		■										■						■	■	
Mansfield Plumbing Products			■			■	■	■	■					■	■	■		■		
Marathon Spa & Bath			■						■								■	■		
Masco Corp.	■		■	■	■	■	■		■		■		■	■				■		
Melard Mfg. Corp.	■	■																		
Memry Corp.	■	■															■	■		
Microphor/(Commercial Products Div.)															■				■	
Miller Studio		■																■	■	
Mirolin Industries			■							■	■	■	■				■	■		
Mister Miser																	61	■	■	881
Modular Hardware	■	■																■	■	
Moen	■	■		■	■	55					■		■					■		129
Mr. Steam/Warmatowel/(Div. of Sussman)								■										■		
MTI Whirlpools			■							■					■		■	■		
Myro		■																■	■	
Myson		■																■		

See Manufacturer Index (beige pages at the back of this issue) for address and phone information.   Numbers in red indicate page number for additional product information.

continued

KITCHEN FAUCETS

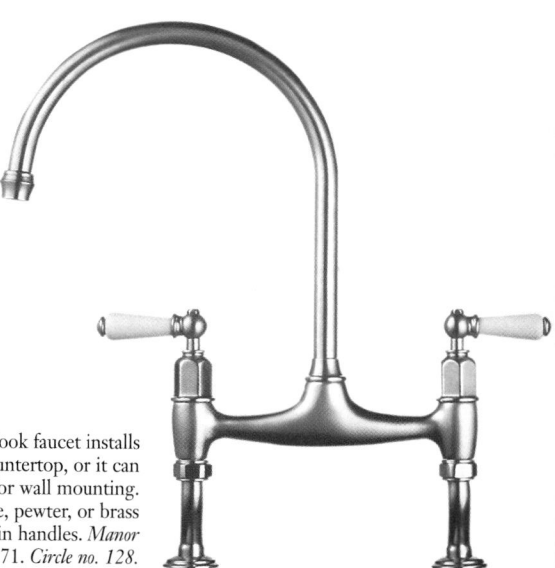

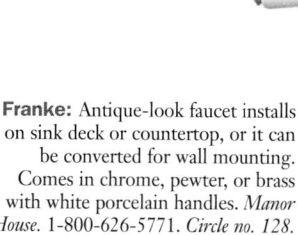

Franke: Antique-look faucet installs on sink deck or countertop, or it can be converted for wall mounting. Comes in chrome, pewter, or brass with white porcelain handles. *Manor House.* 1-800-626-5771. *Circle no. 128.*

Grohe America: Kitchen faucet has arched spout, solid brass construction, powder-coat color finish, and color-accented handle options. *Classic Line.* 708-582-7711. *Circle no. 130.*

US Brass: Pull-out spray faucet extends to 24 inches. Installs on any standard 8-inch-center, three-hole kitchen sink. *Valley.* 214-407-2600. *Circle no. 131.*

Briggs: Solid-brass faucet has a ceramic disk to prevent leaks and extend faucet life, acrylic handles, and choice of polished brass or chrome detailing. *Model 9610.* 813-878-0178. *Circle no. 132.*

Moen: Single bolt and concealed self-sealing gasket make kitchen faucet easy to install. Unit has loop-style handle and hose spray. *Monticello.* 1-800-553-6636. *Circle no. 129.*

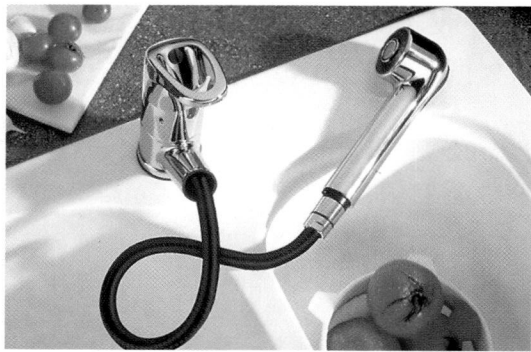

Gerber: Faucet is designed with friction-resistant ceramic disks for use in hard-water areas. Pull-out model is equipped with spring-loaded return. *Hardwater Faucets.* 847-675-6570. *Circle no. 133.*

Faucets & Fixtures

Manufacturer	Accessible products	Bath accessories	Bathtubs	Faucets, bar	Faucets, bath	Faucets, kitchen	Fittings	Hot tubs/spas	Lavatories	Saunas/steam rooms	Shower bases	Shower doors	Shower heads	Shower/tub surrounds	Sinks, kitchen	Toilets/bidets	Whirlpool tubs	Local dealer/distributor	Factory-direct	Circle No.
National Bathing Products	■		■						■		■						■	■		
National Fiber Glass Products			■					■	■		■						■	■		
National Spa and Pool Institute							■	■										■		
NIBCO						■												■		
Novi American			■						■	■		■				■	■	■		
Oasis Industries			■													■		■		
Oberon Products/TCT																		■		
Omnia Industries		■																■		
Ondine from Interbath	■	■			■		■						■				■	■	■	
Opella	■	■		61	■	■												■		880
Pacific Sauna & Steam										■								■	■	
Parker Hannifin Corp.						■												■	■	
Paul Decorative Products		■		■	■	■			■		■							■		
Pearl Baths			■													■		■		
Peerless Faucet Co./(A Div. of Masco Corp.)				■	■	■												■		
Peterson Industries												■						■	■	
Phoenix Products				■	■	■					■							■		
Plaskolite													■					■		
Plastic Creations			■														■		■	
Plumb Pak Corp.				■	■	■												■		
Plumb Shop		■					■											■		
Plumbing Manufacturers Institute	■	■	■	■	■	■	■	■	■	■	■	■	■	■	■	■	■			
Powers Process Controls	■				■													■		
Prairie Home Products	■						■			■								■		
Price Pfister		■		■	60	■												■		870
Rapetti Faucets/(A Div. of George Blotcher)				■	■	■												■		
Raphael/(A Nortek Co.)		■		■									■		■			■		
Re-Bath Corp.										■		■						■		
Reflections USA/Long Island Glass & Mirror												■						■	■	
Regency Bath Products	■		■						■		■					■	■	■	■	
Reid S Watson & Associates		■		■	■	■			■		■							■	■	
Reon		■									■							■	■	
Republic Stainless Steel Sinks				■											■			■		
Resources Conservation		■											■						■	
Rio Plastics								■									■	■	■	
Robern								■										■		
Robert Mfg. Co.							■											■		
Rohl Corp.	■	■		■	■	■			■						■	■		■		
Roma Steam Baths										■								■		
Royal Baths Mfg.			■						■		■					■	■	■	■	
The Rubinet Faucet Co.		■		■	■	■							■					■		
S & J Products							■											■		
SafeTek Intl.	■	■								■		■	■					■	■	
Sanderson Plumbing Products	■	■													■			■		
Santile Intl. Corp.		■			■				■						■			■		
Sauna Craft										■								■		
Sears Contract Sales/Sears, Roebuck			■		■												■	■		
SEPCO Industries		■		■	■	■												■		
Sherle Wagner Intl.		■			■				■				■		■			■		
Shower Shapes	■									■								■		
Showerite Div./Universal-Rundle Corp.										■	■		■					■		
Sibes Brass/ISEO Locks		■																■		
Silcraft Corp.	■	■	■							■							■		■	

See Manufacturer Index (beige pages at the back of this issue) for address and phone information.   Numbers in red indicate page number for additional product information.   continued

TOILETS

Briggs: Siphon-wash toilet uses 1.6 gallons per flush and adjusts for 10- and 12-inch rough-ins. Flush valve and seat are sold separately. *Manhattan.* 813-878-0178. *Circle no. 141.*

Kohler: One-piece toilet has large trapway for effective bowl cleaning. Unit is 22³⁄₄ inches high and comes in various colors. *Rialto Lite.* 1-800-4Kohler. *Circle no. 140.*

Toto Kiki: One-piece toilet has round, chrome-finished flush button on top of tank and a 1.6-gallon siphon-jet gravity flush. *Prominence.* 1-800-938-1541. *Circle no. 142.*

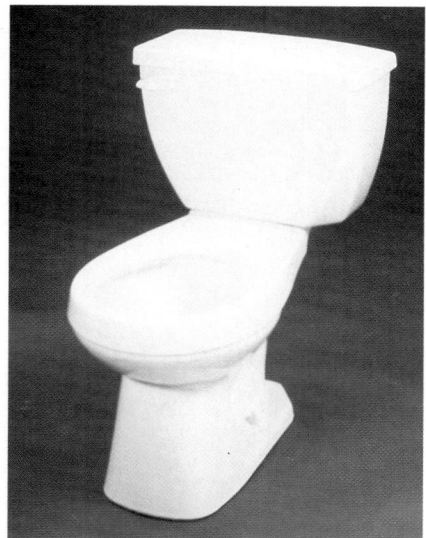

American Standard: One-piece toilet has an elongated seat that can be removed for easy cleaning. Available with side-mounted push button. *Lexington.* 1-800-524-9797. *Circle no. 143.*

Eljer: Low-profile toilet is designed with terrace-styled tank lid. Vitreous-china one-piece unit uses a 1.6-gallon siphon flush. *Aspen.* 214-407-2600. *Circle no. 144.*

Gerber: Toilet trapway has been expanded to improve waste removal. Vitreous-china model comes in several standard colors. *Aqua-Saver.* 847-675-6570. *Circle no. 145.*

BATH SINKS

Kohler: Ceramic-bowl sink is designed to sit on top of a counter. Choice of three shapes in five textured glazes and three high-gloss glazes. *Vessels.* 1-800-4Kohler. *Circle no. 197.*

Toto Kiki: Bath basins come in frosted, clear, or soda glass in red, blue, or green. Can be used as single units with standard countertops or as part of a modular system. *Cera.* 1-800-938-1541. *Circle no. 195.*

American Standard: Three neutral colors have been added to line of bath and kitchen fixtures. Shades include soft white, green, and blue. 1-800-524-9797. *Circle no. 198.*

Barclay: Bath console has vitreous china top and legs. Unit is 36 inches wide and comes with widespread-faucet drillings. *Versailles.* 1-800-446-9700. *Circle no. 196.*

Swan: Vanity top and bowl are made of solid-surface material with integral backsplash. Bowl measures 13 inches deep and 20 inches wide. Vanities come in five sizes. *Swanstone.* 314-231-8148. *Circle no. 199.*

Faucets & Fixtures

Manufacturer	Accessible products	Bath accessories	Bathtubs	Faucets, bar	Faucets, bath	Faucets, kitchen	Fittings	Hot tubs/spas	Lavatories	Saunas/steam rooms	Shower bases	Shower doors	Shower heads	Shower/tub surrounds	Sinks, kitchen	Toilets/bidets	Whirlpool tubs	Local dealer/distributor	Factory-direct	Circle No.
Sioux Chief Mfg.							■											■		
Sloan Flushmate/(A Div. of Sloan Valve Co.)																■		■		
Smedbo		■																■		
Snorkel Stove Co.								■										■	■	
The Soft Bathtub Co.			■														60	■	■	877
Southeastern Aluminum Products												■						■	■	
Southland Spa & Sauna					■	■	■	■									■	■	■	
Speakman Co./Mfg. Division	■	■		■	■	■	■						■						■	
Splash-Ender		■																■	■	
Spring Ram America					■									■				■	■	
St. Thomas Classics	■	■	■						■							■		■		
St. Thomas Creations	■	■	■	■	■		■		■			■				■	■	■		
Steamist		■	■				■			■		■						■		
Sterling Plumbing Group	■	■	■	■	■		■		■		■	■	60	60	■			■		871,873,874
Strom Plumbing By Sign Of The Crab		■	■		■	■	■		■			■	■	■				■	■	
Studor	■																			
Sunrise Specialty		61	■	■	■	■			■			■			■	■		■	■	885
The Swan Corp.		■						58		■		■	■					■		199
Swedish Building Systems & Components										■								■	■	
SwimEx Systems							■								■		■	■	■	
Swirl-way Collections/Mansfield Plumbing		■							■						■		■	■		
Symmons Industries	■			■	■								■					■		
Syntec Marble		■							■			■		■	■			■		
Taymor Industries	■	■																■		
Technically Unique Bathing Systems	■		■															■	■	
Teledyne Water Pik													■						■	
TFI Corp./Vanity Plus									■									■		
ThermaSol										■								■		
Tile Redi											■							■	■	
The TonJon Co.		■																■		
Toto Kiki	■	■			■		■		58							57		■		142,195
TUB-MASTER								■		■	■	■						■		
Tubco Whirlpools			■														■	■		
Union Brass Mfg. Co.				■	■	■												■		
Universal Plastics		■											■					■		
Universal-Rundle Corp./(A Nortek Co.)	■		■	■	■	■	■		■		■	■	■	■	■	■	■	■		
US Brass	■		■		■	55	■											■		131
Valentina Ratti Creations USA		■																■	■	
Vance Industries				■		■									■			■		
Vanguard Industries							■											■		
Ward Mfg.							■											■		
Watercolors	■	■	■	■	■			■				■	■		■			■	■	
Waterline Products Co.		■					■		■			■		■				■		
Watertech							■											■	■	
Waxman Industries		■		■	■	■	■						■					■	■	
Wesaunard		■																■	■	
Westendorf Whirlpool			■						■				■				■	■	■	
Whirljet Systems																	■	■	■	
Wilsonart International									■					■	■			■	■	
Wirsbo Co.						60												■		876
Wolverine Brass		■		■	■		■						■						■	
Woodpro Cabinetry		■																■		
Work Right Products											■							■	■	

See Manufacturer Index (beige pages at the back of this issue) for address and phone information.   Numbers in red indicate page number for additional product information.

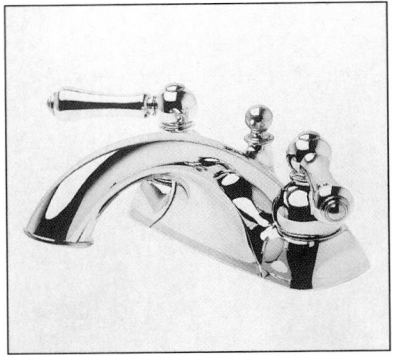

PRICE PFISTER GEORGETOWN

Get the right combination with Price Pfister's new Georgetown center set lavatory faucet. Price Pfister brings traditional looks home with greater styling and value, and includes the Pforever Seal™, the ceramic disc valve that never leaks. Guaranteed. 1-800-PFaucet. **Circle No. 870**

STERLING PLUMBING

Sterling, a Kohler company, introduces Kitchen Classics composites sinks. Made of VIKRELL™ material, they're resistant to scratching, chipping and staining. Available in various colors, they feature offset bowls – perfect for larger pots and utensils. Limited lifetime warranty. Call 1-800-STERLING. **Circle No. 873**

WIRSBO AQUAPEX

Wirsbo's trifold brochure describes the benefits of AQUAPEX™ Professional Plumbing Systems to builders. It highlights the 25 year proven history of AQUAPEX™ tubing, along with its corrosion resistance, non-toxic formula, dependable ProPEX™ Fitting System and 25 year warranty. The brochure explains why AQUAPEX™ is a plumbing system you can trust. 1-(800)-321-4739. www.wirsbo.com **Circle No. 876**

STERLING PLUMBING GROUP

Sterling Plumbing Group, a Kohler company, introduces the Polar Professional Series of stainless steel sinks. Designed exclusively for professional plumbing contractors and perfect for new construction, the Polar Professional Series - available in the most popular sizes and configurations - offers quality, style and value. Each sink in the Series is backed by Sterling's limited lifetime warranty when installed by a licensed plumbing contractor. For further information, call toll-free 1-800-STERLING. **Circle No. 871**

STERLING PLUMBING'S DEVONSHIRE COLLECTION

The Devonshire Collection is one of the newest additions to the full line of plumbing products from Sterling, A Kohler Company. Made of Grade A Vitreous China, this elegant line including a drop-in lavatory features a durable, glass-like surface and a high-gloss, scratch resistant finish.

1-800-STERLING. Circle No. 874

INTERNATIONAL CUSHIONED PRODUCTS, INC.

THE SOFT BATHTUB is a revolutionary, fully cushioned bathtub that comes in 5 sizes, in any color and with an optional whirlpool system. It's incredibly comfortable, safe, easy to clean and install, energy efficient, quiet and has a ten year warranty. 1-800-TUB-SOFT. **Circle No. 877**

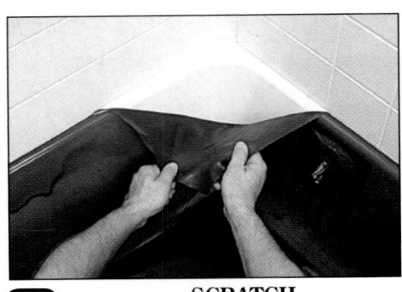

Protective Products
Surface Protection Solutions

SCRATCH PROTECTION

from Protective Products will protect tubs, whirlpools and shower stalls against costly scratches, and eliminate the cleaning of jobsite dirt and grime. The water-based protective coating is easily applied and hardens to a durable, tight "protective skin" and simply peels off when the job is done. For info and a free brochure on PROTECTIVE PRODUCTS' full line of Surface Protection Solutions, CALL 24 hrs: (800) 789-6633. www.protectiveproducts.com **Circle No. 872**

BATH-TEC WHIRLPOOL BATH

Bath-Tec manufactures a complete line of quality acrylic whirlpool baths, soaking tubs and shower bases. Many sizes, shapes, colors available including unique designs (heart shapes, oriental soakers, oversize models) and waterfall tub faucets sets. Contact our factory for product information. (972) 646-5279. **Circle No. 875**

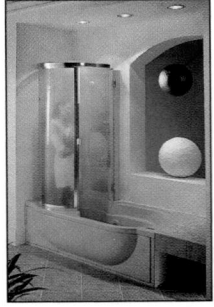

JACUZZI WHIRLPOOL BATH BUILDER

Jacuzzi Whirlpool Bath unveils the J-Stream Tower™, a full-size whirlpool bath, shower enclosure and steam bath in one innovative design. Available in five- and six-foot lengths, bathers are treated to the patented PowerPro® jet system, an adjustable overhead/hand-held shower and soothing steam from the SteamPro 120®. (800) 678-6889. www.jacuzzi.com **Circle No. 878**

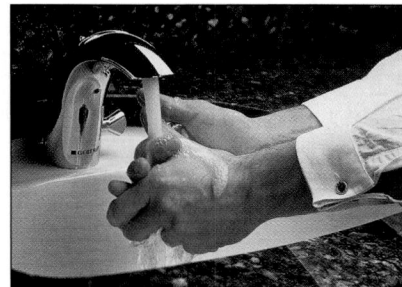

PRO TECT LIQUID MASK

Pro Tect Liquid Mask forms a "latex glove" over hard-to-cover surfaces, providing 7 mil.-protection for tubs, showers and other highly polished surfaces. Order today, or for a free brochure call **Pro Tect Associates Inc.** 1-800-545-0826. **Circle No. 879**

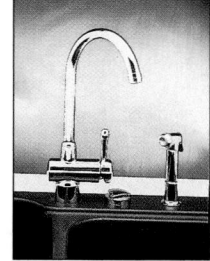

ARCADIA BAR OR KITCHEN FAUCET

Opella introduces the contemporary Arcadia, European-designed bar or kitchen faucets and accessories made of solid brass. This single-lever hot or cold cartridge faucet will provide years of dependable service, and has a 5 ½" swing-spout on the bar model and a 7 ⅜" swing-spout on the kitchen model. The Arcadia is offered in six finishes including Chrome, Brushed Chrome, White, Black, Almond, and Gold. Opella, Inc. 4062 Kingston Court, Marietta, GA 30067, (800) 969-0339. **Circle No. 880**

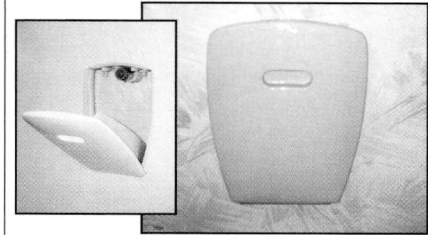

PROTECTIVE SKIN FOR TUBS, WHIRLPOOLS, SHOWER STALLS

Scratch Shield is a water-based coating that protects high gloss surfaces from dirt, stains, abrasions and paint during construction or remodeling. Easily applied by brushing or spraying, the coating dries to form a tough, durable protective skin that peels cleanly and easily upon removal. For more information about Surface Shields and our full line of protective products (Carpet, Floor, Window and Trim Shield), call 800-91-FLOOR. **Circle No. 883**

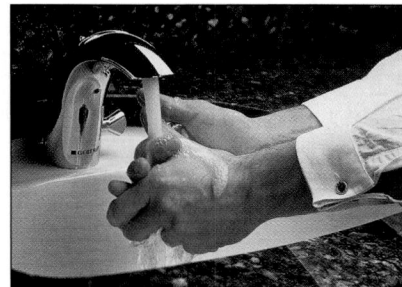

GEBERIT ELECTRONIC FAUCETS

The right choice for any new construction or renovation project. All components are conveniently designed inside the faucet – above the countertop. Access shroud on the spout provides quick and easy maintenance. Optional temperature control knob also available. Battery-operated. Geberit Manufacturing, Inc., P.O. Box 2008 (46361-8008), 1100 Boone Dr., Michigan City, IN 46360 (219) 879-4466. **Toll-free: (800) 225-7217,** Fax: (219) 872-8003 **Circle No. 884**

SUNRISE SPECIALTY

Shown here is the complete Victorian bath by Sunrise Specialty, including their #801 cast iron Clawfoot Tub, #400 Three Headed Shower, #700 vitreous china pedestal lavatory with #121 widespread faucet, and #901 pullchain commode featuring a 1.5 gallon flush, oak tank and seat, and solid copper tank liner. Send for their free full color catalog featuring a complete selection of antique style clawfoot tubs, showers, faucets and accessories. **Circle No. 885**

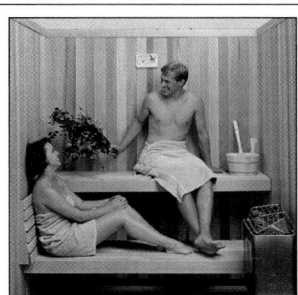

FINLANDIA SAUNA PRODUCTS

Known as the cadillac of the sauna industry, Finlandia offers quality which is unmatched. From the best heater on the market, to the highest quality, clear softwoods available. 2" x 2" bench tops, full 3/4" paneling, and the only sauna door on the market with solid fir rails (other doors are finger jointed with laminated skin). **(800) 354-3342.** **Fax (503) 684-1120.** **Circle No. 882**

Fireplaces

Manufacturer	Chimney systems	Direct-vent	Doors	Freestanding	Gas-fired	Gas logs	Heat-circulating	Inserts	Masonry	Pellet-burning	Stoves	Vent-free	Wood-burning	Zero-clearance	Local dealer/distributor	Factory-direct	Circle No.
	Products														**Sales**		
Acme Brick Co.								■							■	■	
Aladdin Steel Products		■		■	■			■		■	■	■	■		■	■	
American Energy Systems		■	■	■		■	■	■	■	■		■	■		■		
American Metal Products	■														■	■	
Architectural Paneling			■														
Arriscraft Corp.								■							■		
Benchmark Door Systems	■	■													■		
Blaze King Industries		■		■	■			■			■			■		■	
The Brick Institute of America								■				■					
Centurion Products								■							■	■	
Concrete Designs								■								■	
Country Flame		■	■	■			■	■	■	■		■			■		
Country Stoves			■				■			■		■	■	■	■		
Cultured Stone®/Stone Products Corp.							65								■		889
Deflect-O-Corp.	■														■		
Dietmeyer, Ward & Stroud													■		■	■	
The Earth Stove			■	■				■		■		■				■	
Electro Industries								■								■	
Empire Comfort Systems				■	■							65			■		891
Exhausto	■														■	■	
Fireplace Manufacturers	■	■	■		■	■	■	■			■	■	■	■	■	■	
Fireplace Xtrordinair/Mfg. by Travis Indus.		■		■	■		■	■	■	■	■		■	■	■		
Fuego Flame Fireplace Mfg.				■			■	■				■	■	■		■	
Gas Research Institute				■	■												
GFP Intl.												■			■		
Hargrove Mfg. Corp.						■						■			■		
Hart & Cooley	■														■		
Hearth Products Assn.	■	■	■	■	■	■	■	■		■	■	■	■		■		
Heat-N-Glo Fireplace Products	■	65	■	■	■	■	■	■			■		■	■	■		146,888
Heatilator	■	65	■	■	■	■	■	■			■		■	■	■		890
Heatmaster Gas Logs				■		■						■			■	■	
Hicks Waterstoves & Solar Systems													■		■	■	
Hunter Energy And Technologies		■		■	■		■	■						■	■		
I-XL Industries								■							■		
Isokern Fireplaces/Earthcore Industries	■			■				■			■	■	■	■	■	■	
Jotul USA		■		■	■			■			■		■		■		
Juca Super-Fireplace			■	■	■		■	■			■		■	■	■	■	

63% of new homes include at least one fireplace; surprisingly, fireplaces are more common in the South and West than in the Northeast and Midwest.

Source: What Today's Home Buyers Want/ NAHB and Fulton Research

Manufacturer	Chimney systems	Direct-vent	Doors	Freestanding	Gas-fired	Gas logs	Heat-circulating	Inserts	Masonry	Pellet-burning	Stoves	Vent-free	Wood-burning	Zero-clearance	Local dealer/distributor	Factory-direct	Circle No.
Kozy Heat/(A Div. of Hussong Mfg. Co.)		■	■	■			■						■	■	■		
The Majestic Products Co.	■	■	■	■	■	■	■				■		■	■	■		
Malm Fireplaces				■	■	■							■		■		
Marco Fireplaces		■		■	■	■							■	■	■		
Marell Industries	■															■	
Martin Fireplaces/Div. of Martin Industries		■	■	■	■	■	■	■			■	■	■	■	■		265
Minnesota Hearth Products						■					■				■		
Napoleon Fireplaces (Wolf Steel)		■	■	■	■	■	■	■			■		■	■	■	■	
National Concrete Masonry Assn.	■																
National Steelcrafters of Oregon			■					■		■	■						
NHC Hearthstone Stoves		■	■									■			■		
The Northern Roof Tile Sales Co.	■														■		
Old Carolina Brick Co.			■						■						■	■	
Osburn Mfg.		■		■	■			■			■		■	■	■		
Pacific Clay Brick Products									■						■		
Pacific Energy Woodstoves (1986)		■		■	■		■	■			■		■	■	■		
Petmal Supply Co.			■				■								■	■	
Prairie Home Products				■									■		■		
Pyro Industries		■		■	■		■			■	■					■	
Readybuilt Products Co.			■		■											■	
Real Brick Products									■						■	■	
Rinnai America Corp.					■							■			■		
Robert H. Peterson Co.					■										■		
RSF Energy		■		■	■		■	■					■	■	■		
Ruegg Fireplaces			■			■							■	■	■	■	
Rustic Crafts Co.			■												■		
Security Chimneys		■		■		■	■						■	■	■		
Sioux Chief Mfg.				■											■		
Southeastern Metals Mfg. Co./SEMCO			■												■		
Suburban Mfg. Co.								■		■					■	■	
Superior Clay Corp.	■							■							■		
Superior Fireplace Co.	■	65	■	■	■	■	■	■	■			■	■	■	■		148,887
Temco Fireplace Products			■	■	■		■					■	■	■	■		147
Tempcast 2000 Masonary Heater Mfg.													■			■	
Thermo-Rite Mfg. Co.		■			■	■	■								■	■	
Travis Industries		■		■	■		■	■	■	■	■		■	■	■		
Tulikivi U.S.			■						■				■		■		
Vermont Castings		■		■	■	■	■				■	■	■	■	■	■	
Whitacre-Greer									■				■		■	■	
Wilkening Fireplace Co.			■			■	■						■	■	■	■	
Williams Furnace Co.		■		■	■	■					■				■		
Wood-Aire Fireplace Systems		■											■				

See Manufacturer Index (beige pages at the back of this issue) for address and phone information.   Numbers in red indicate page number for additional product information.

DIRECT-VENT FIREPLACES

Temco: Forty-inch-wide opening on direct-vent fireplace is accented with extruded aluminum trim finished to look like anodized brass and brass-finished canopy. Features mesh fire screen and brick-look liner. *Masterworks 280. 1-800-986-5225. Circle no. 147.*

Heat-N-Glo: Fireplace has a sealed combustion chamber with top or rear venting. Choice of remote controls, blowers, and brass trim package. *Corner-TR. 1-800-669-HEAT. Circle no. 146.*

Superior: Top-vent fireplace is available with choice of natural or propane gas and millivolt or electronic ignition. Includes several factory-installed options. *DVT-33T. 1-800-238-5876. Circle no. 148.*

COMPANY	MODEL	HEIGHT (IN INCHES)	FRONT WIDTH (IN INCHES)	DEPTH (IN INCHES)	BTU INPUT (IN THOUSANDS)	PHONE
Heat-N-Glo	Corner-TR	41	$40\frac{1}{2}$	$24\frac{1}{4}$	28-40	1-800-669-HEAT
Heatilator	GC300FL Series	$37\frac{11}{16}$	40	24	36	1-800-843-2848
Majestic	DVR33	$28\frac{3}{8}$	33	$11\frac{1}{2}$	20	1-800-525-1898
Martin	DaVinci DV3	$41\frac{1}{6}$	35	$20\frac{3}{4}$	25-28	1-800-227-1055
Napoleon	3200B	33	$37\frac{1}{4}$	17	24-30	1-800-461-5581
Security Chimneys	PINS33	$36\frac{1}{2}$	40	$22\frac{1}{2}$	32	1-800-875-3131
Selkirk Metalbestos	TDV-27	$33\frac{3}{4}$	$36\frac{9}{16}$	14	19-27.5	1-800-992-8368
Superior	DVT-33T	$31\frac{1}{4}$	36	$15\frac{1}{2}$	19	1-800-238-5876
Temco	Masterworks 280	$36\frac{1}{2}$	$43\frac{1}{2}$	$21\frac{3}{4}$	28	1-800-986-5225
Vermont Castings	DV40	$39\frac{1}{2}$	40	$18\frac{1}{8}$	27-40	1-800-861-0953

Companies in red have product shown above.

DV-5000 TOP DIRECT-VENT BY SUPERIOR

Unlimited versatility! That's what you get from the new Direct-Vent gas fireplace from Superior! Installation flexibility with its compact top direct-vent design and endless opportunities for customization with its wide array of options...peeled bark oak logs, brass louvers, hoods, arches and more! Available in two heat-circulating models, with decorative louvers or the clean faced unit. Both operate at 19,000 Btu's input, in natural gas or propane models. Call Superior Fireplace Co. at (800) 731-8101. **Circle No. 887**

CULTURED STONE®

New 1997 full-color 56 page catalog contains swatch and application photos of more than 78 stone building products; it features new colors, new textures, and new trim pieces. Cultured Stone® looks and feels like stone yet costs a fraction of the price. (800) 644-4487.
Stone Products Corp.
Circle No. 889

HEATILATOR, INC.

Known as the first name in fireplaces, HEATILATOR manufactures a full line of quality gas and woodburning fireplaces and inserts along with a multitude of optional accessories. Call today for a FREE catalog. Add value to your home, add a HEATILATOR. 1-800-843-2848. We can now be found at http://www.heatilator.com
Circle No. 890

EMPIRE® HEARTH VENT-FREE ZERO CLEARANCE CERTIFIED GAS FIREPLACE

This 32,000 Btu vent-free fireplace is 99.9% efficient, heats without electricity and is available either with manual or thermostat controls. Includes ODS pilot and auto shut-off controls, accessory mantels, and automatic blower. Made in USA and A.G.A. design certified. **Circle No. 891**

MODEL 6000XLS DIRECT VENT

Heat-N-Glo's Model 6000XLS campfire fireplace offers the most realistic logs and fire on the market. It creates the natural look and feel of a traditional campfire right in your home. The 6000XLS offers maximum heat output and true heating efficiency. So if maximum heat output and a brilliant fire are priorities, take a look at Model 6000XLS. 1-800-669-4328. **Circle No. 888**

Flooring

Manufacturer	Carpet	Ceramic tile	Granite	Laminate	Linoleum	Marble	Rubber	Setting material	Slate/other stone	Solid surfacing	Vinyl sheet	Vinyl tile	Wood	Local dealer/distributor	Factory-direct	Circle No.
AB Cushing Mills													■	■		
Abet Inc.			■						■					■	■	
Acadia Post & Beam													■	■	■	
Action Floor Systems													■	■		
AE Gombert Lumber Co.													■	■		
Aged Woods													■	■	■	
AJ Stairs													■	■	■	
American Floor Products Co.						■						■		■	■	
American Marazzi Tile		■												■		
American Olean Tile		■			■		■	■						■		
American Wood Council													■			
Amsterdam Corp.		■												■	■	
Ancient Venetian Floor Co.				■										■	■	
Anderson Hardwood Floors													■			
Arius Tile Co.		■												■		
Armstrong World Industries											■	■				
Avonite									■					■		
Azrock Industries												■				
Bangkok Intl.													■		■	
Bearden Brothers Carpet	■														■	
BHK of America				■										■	■	
BiWood Flooring													■			
Boa-Franc													■	■		
Boen Hardwood Flooring													■	■		
Boiardi Products Corp.		■	■		■			■							■	
Bruce Floors			■											■		
Bruce Hardwood Floors													69	■		192,614
Buchtal Corp. USA		■														
Building Products & Nails/Div. BSTC Group											■			■		
Building Stone Institute								■								
Burke Industries						■								■	■	
The Burruss Co.													■	■	■	
C-Cure Corp.						■								■		
Cameo Carpets	■									■					■	
Canital Granite			■											■		
Carlisle Restoration Lumber													■		■	
The Carpet and Rug Institute	73															902

> 34% of new-home shoppers prefer ceramic tile in the entry foyer; 32% prefer finished hardwood, 18% prefer marble, and 7% prefer slate.
>
> *Source: What Today's Home Buyers Want/NAHB and Fulton Research*

Manufacturer	Carpet	Ceramic tile	Granite	Laminate	Linoleum	Marble	Rubber	Setting material	Slate/other stone	Solid surfacing	Vinyl sheet	Vinyl tile	Wood	Local dealer/distributor	Factory-direct	Circle No.
Ceilings & Interior Systems Constr. Assn.	■	■														
Ceramic Tile Distributors Assn.		■														
Cherrybark Flooring													72	■		897
Cold Spring Granite Co.			■											■	■	
Comtex Industries														■	■	
Congoleum Corp.											■	■		■		
Contact Lumber Co.														■	■	
Continental Creative Sales		■				■		■							■	
Country Homestead/Restoration Contractor													■	■	■	
Courey Intl.				■								■		■		
CPN													■	■	■	
Crossville Ceramics		■												■		
Dakota Granite			■											■	■	
Dal-Tile Corp.		■													■	
Dalton Paradise Carpet	72				■				■					■	■	900
Dean Hardwood													■	■	■	
Designs In Tile		■												■		
DeSoto Hardwood Flooring Co.													■	■		
Direct Carpet Mills of America	■													■		
Domco Industries											■	■		■		
Drain Frame		■												■		
DuPont Co./Corian Products										■				■		
E&E Consumer Products								■						■		
E.I. DuPont De Nemours & Co.	■													■		
Epro		■												■		
FLEXCO Co.							■				■	■		■		
Florida Tile/(A Div. of Premark)		■												■		53
Forbo Industries					■						■	■		■		
Foreign & Domestic Woods													■	■		
Formica Corp.										■				■		
Freudenberg Building Systems							■							■		
Fritz Industries			■			■								■		
The Georgia Marble Co.						■									■	
Georgia-Pacific Corp.				■										■	■	
Gibco Services				■										■	■	
Glass Blocks Unlimited		■													■	
Glen Oak Lumber & Milling														■		
Goodwin Heart Pine Co.													■	■	■	
Grani-Decor Tiles			■											■	■	
Greenheart-Durawoods													■	■		
Grill Works													72	■		894
Groleau													■	■		
Hardwood Manufacturers Assn.													■			
Hardwood Plywood & Veneer Assn.													■			
Hardwoods Millworking													■	■		
Harris-Tarkett				■									73	■		191,906
Hartco													■	■		
Hastings Tile & Il Bagno Collection		■				■								■		
Holland Log Homes Mfg. Co.													■	■	■	
Homer Wood Corp.													■		■	
Horner Flooring Co.													■	■	■	
House of Ceramics		■				■										
IEA Int'l		■	■			■								■	■	

50% of new-home shoppers prefer wall-to-wall carpeting in the dining room; 40% want hardwood floors.

Source: What Today's Home Buyers Want/NAHB and Fulton Research

Flooring

Manufacturer	Carpet	Ceramic tile	Granite	Laminate	Linoleum	Marble	Rubber	Setting material	Slate/other stone	Solid surfacing	Vinyl sheet	Vinyl tile	Wood	Local dealer/distributor	Factory-direct	Circle No.
	Products													**Sales**		
Image Carpets	■													■	■	
IMPO Glaztile		■													■	
Interceramic, USA		■												■		
International Hardwood Flooring													■	■		
International Paper Co.				■										■		
International Wood Products Assn.													■			
ITALGRANITI/Marketing & Trading Co.		■														
Italian Marble Ctr./Italian Trade Commission			■			■										
Italian Tile Assn.		■												■		
Italian Trade Commission, Tile Center		■														
Jackson Sawmill Co.													■	■	■	
Jamo						■								■		
Jason Industrial/Rubber Flooring Div.							■							■		
Johnson's Carpets	■									■				■	■	
Johnsonite/(A Div. of Duramax)							■							■		
Kahrs Intl.													■	■		
Kentucky Millwork													■	■		
Kentucky Wood Floors													69	■		190
Kepcor/SSI Tiles		■												■	■	
Korwall Industries													■		■	
Kraftile Co.		■												■		
L.M. Scofield Co.								■						■	■	
La Vona's Unique Hardware/Malibu Art Tile		■	■			■			■					■	■	
Laminating Materials Assn.				■												
Latco Products		■												■	■	
Laticrete Intl.		■						■						■		
Laufen Ceramic Tile		■												■	■	355
Lewisohn Sales Co.													■		■	
Liette Intl.		■												■		
London Tile Co.		■												■	■	
Lone Star Ceramics Co.		■												■		
M.L. Condon Co.													■	■	■	
MacMillan Bloedel/Building Materials Mktg.													■	■		
Mannington Mills	■	■								■	■			■	■	
Mannington Wood Floors													■	■		
Mapei Corp.								■						■		
Maple Flooring Manufacturers Assn.													■			
Marquis Carpet Mills	■														■	
Marvin L. Walker & Associates		■	■			■			■					■	■	
McIntyre Tile		■												■	■	
McShan Lumber Co.													■	■		
Memphis Hardwood Flooring Co.													■			
Mercer Products Co.							■							■		
Metropolitan Ceramics		■												■		
Milton W. Bosley Co.													■	■	■	
Miracle Sealants & Abrasives		■	■			■			■					■		
MK Diamond Products		■	■			■								■		
Monarch Tile		■												■		
Moose Creek Lumber Co.													■		■	
Mountain Lumber Co.													■		■	
NAFCO												■		■		
National Assn. of Floor Covering Distributors	■	■		■	■	■	■				■	■	■			
National Oak Flooring Manufacturers Assn.													■			

See Manufacturer Index (beige pages at the back of this issue) for address and phone information.   Numbers in red indicate page number for additional product information.

continued

Wood Flooring

Kentucky Wood Floors: Prefinished wood planks have no-wax urethane finish for glue-down installation. Available in seven species and ten colors. *Designer Collection II.* 502-451-6024. *Circle no. 190.*

Premier: Three-eighths-inch-thick hardwood floors install on, above, and below grade, and over most subfloors. Offered in cherry, maple, pecan, and walnut. *Jewels of Nature.* 214-931-1876. *Circle no. 193.*

Harris-Tarkett: Wide-plank hardwood flooring features 7 ½-inch-wide top layer. Available in natural pine, antique pine, and natural oak. *European Collection.* 1-800-842-7816. *Circle no. 191.*

Bruce Hardwood: Floating hardwood floors have three-strip-wide engineered panels. Measure 86⅝ inches long, 7 ¹¹⁄₁₆ inches wide, and ½ inch thick. *Coastal Woodlands.* 214-931-3100. *Circle no. 192.*

Robbins: Solid northern oak flooring is ¾ inch thick and 3 ¼ inches wide. Comes preassembled in 6- to 7-foot lengths. Available in five colors. *Lexington XL Plank.* 1-800-733-3309. *Circle no. 194.*

Flooring

Manufacturer	Carpet	Ceramic tile	Granite	Laminate	Linoleum	Marble	Rubber	Setting material	Slate/other stone	Solid surfacing	Vinyl sheet	Vinyl tile	Wood	Local dealer/distributor	Factory-direct	Circle No.
National Wood Flooring Assn.													■			
Oak Flooring Institute													■			
Oregon Lumber Co.													■	■	■	
The Pacific Lumber Co.													■	■		
Partee Flooring Mill													■	■	■	
Peace Flooring Co.													■	■	■	
Penn Wood Products													■	■	■	
PermaGrain Products					■							■	■	■		
Perstorp Flooring				■									■			
Petmal Supply Co.		■	■	■	■	■	■	■			■	■	■	■	■	
Pioneer Millworks													■		■	
Plancher Heritage													■	■		
Plaza Hardwood													■	■		
Ply Gem Mfg.		■			■								■			
Porcelanite		■											■			
Porcelanosa		■											■	■		
Precision Tile Spacer								■					■			
Premier Wood Floors													69	■		193
Prime Wood Products													■	■	■	
Pro Tect Associates	73	■	■	■				■					72	■	■	896,898,905
Protective Products Intl.	72	73	■	■				■		■				■	■	893,901
Quaker	■													■	■	
Quality Woods													■			
Quarry Tile Co.		■											■			
Rare Earth Hardwoods													■	■	■	
Ray White Lumber Co.													■			
RB Rubber Products							■						■	■		
RC Musson Rubber Co.							■						■			
Resilient Floor Covering Institute							■				■	■				
Ro-Tile		■											■			
Robbins Hardwood Flooring													69	■		194
Rocktile Specialty Products								■							■	
Rocky Mountain Stone Co.			■			■			■					■		
S & S Mills	■														■	400
Satin Finish Hardwood Flooring													■	■	■	
Seacoast Mills													■	■		
Seal-Dry										■			■			
Searcy Flooring													■	■		
Shaw Industries/Home Foundations Carpets	■														■	
Sherle Wagner Intl.		■			■											
Smith Millwork													■	■	■	
Solnhofen Natural Stone						■			■					■	■	
Southern Pine Council													■			
Southern Sales & Marketing Group		■													■	
Southwest Door Co.													■	■		
St. Thomas Creations		■												■		
Standard Plywoods													■	■		
The Structural Slate Co.									■						■	
Stuart Flooring Corp.													■	■		
Stylemark Carpet Mills	72					■		■					■	■	■	
Summitville Tiles		■												■	■	
Super-Tek Products								■						■	■	
Superior Floor Co.													■		■	

See Manufacturer Index (beige pages at the back of this issue) for address and phone information. Numbers in red indicate page number for additional product information.

Manufacturer	Carpet	Ceramic tile	Granite	Laminate	Linoleum	Marble	Rubber	Setting material	Slate/other stone	Solid surfacing	Vinyl sheet	Vinyl tile	Wood	Local dealer/distributor	Factory-direct	Circle No.
Superior Hardwoods & Millwork													■		■	
Swedish Building Systems & Components													■	■	■	
Tarkett					■						■					
TEC/(A Sub. of HB Fuller Co.)								73						■		903
Terra-Green Technologies/Stoneware Tile		■												■		
Texas Kiln Products													■		■	
Thistlewood Timber Frame Homes													■			
Tile Cera		■												■		
Tile Council of America		■												■	■	
The Tileworks		■												■	■	
Trade Commission of Spain/Tile from Spain		72												■	■	899
TriPac Cabinets/(A Div. of Triangle Pacific)													■	■	■	
Trojan Board/Forest Pride													■		■	
UniBoard Canada				■										■		
United Panel										■				■	■	
United States Ceramic Tile Co.		■												■		
Universal Flooring												■	■			
Universal Marble & Granite			■			■			■						■	
Vermont Structural Slate Co.									■						■	
VPI												■			■	
Wagoner Floor Safety Systems	■														■	
Walker & Zanger		■	■			■			■					■	■	
Westchester Marble & Granite		■	■			■			■					■		
Western Quarry Tile		■													■	
Western Wood Products Assn.													■	■		
Wilsonart Intl.				■						■				■	■	
Wineland Walnut													■	■	■	
Wood Component Manufacturers Assn.													■			
Wood Floors													■		■	
Woodline Mfg.													■	■		
The Woods Co.													■	■	■	
World Floor Covering Assn.	■	■	■		■	■	■	■	■		■	■	■			
WR Bonsal Co.								■						■		
Zickgraf Hardwood Co.													■	■		

See Manufacturer Index (beige pages at the back of this issue) for address and phone information.   Numbers in red indicate page number for additional product information.

CARPET PROTECTION
from Protective Products is ideal for protecting carpets and carpeted stairs during construction, remodeling or any high traffic event. The tough, clear adhesive-backed polyethylene film resists puncturing and stays in place for maximum protection. For info on PROTECTIVE PRODUCTS full line of surface protection call 24hrs: (800) 789-6633. www.protectiveproducts.com
Circle No. 893

SMART BUILDERS SAVE ON CARPET

Get Mill-Direct Savings from STYLMARK!
Pay less and receive excellent quality and service. STYLMARK offers a wide selection of carpet, vinyl and wood plus toll-free ordering and direct shipping. No minimum required. For free samples call STYLMARK Carpet Mill at

1-800-235-1079

PRO TECT RUNNER
Pro Tect Runner is the right solution for field finished hardwood floors, hard tile and marble as well as resilient floors like linoleum. This **non-adhesive, reusable** product is safe for your expensive polished surfaces due to its special slip-resistant backing. Call and order today, or for a free brochure, **Pro Tect Associates Inc.** 1-800-545-0826
Circle No. 898

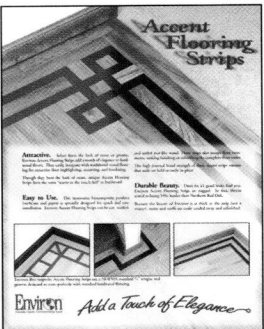

GRILL WORKS ACCENT FLOORING
Environ Accent Flooring Strips add a touch of elegance to hardwood floors. Environ has the appearance of stone and granite, yet can be installed, sanded and finished just like wood. Unfinished strips come ¾" thick, 72" long in 1½" and 2¼" widths.
Circle No. 894

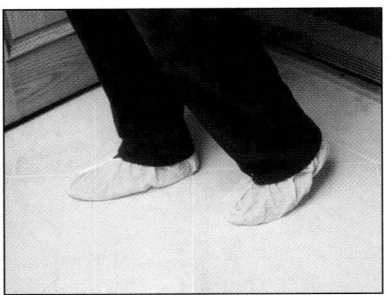

PRO TECT SHOE BOOTIES
Pro Tect Shoe Booties provide extra protection against scuffs, heel marks and foot traffic dirt at the source. They fit right over your shoes to help protect carpet, hard surface floors, and other walking areas. Order today, or for a free brochure, call **Pro Tect Associates Inc.** 1-800-545-0826. **Circle No. 896**

THE TILE OF SPAIN...A U.S. GUIDEBOOK
is now available from the Trade Commission of Spain. This full color, 50 page brochure is brimming with information and photos about Spain's vital, creative ceramic tile industry and 47 of its most prominent manufacturers with their U.S. contacts. Write or phone Trade Commission of Spain, 2655 LeJeune Road, Suite 1114, Coral Gables, FL 33134. Call (305) 446-4387 or fax: (305) 446-2602. **Circle No. 899**

ATTENTION BUILDERS!! Save your money! Don't spend another dime on costly repairs and replacements of vinyl floors and laminate counter tops. Invest in PRO TECTA FLOR or PRO TECTA TOP and virtually eliminate damage on delicate floors and counters. PRO TECTA FLOR has a reusable 30 mil plastic surface that protects against damage while the soft foam backing keeps the floor or counter top in new condition. PRO TECTA INDUSTRIES (800) 243-5434. **Circle No. 895**

CHERRYBARK
CHERRYBARK fine oak prefinished flooring is manufactured with a sprayed-on, UV cured urethane (Endura-Glo) finish. This special finish enhances the natural wood grain and clarity of the wood. Cherrybark is available in three grades and six beautiful colors to compliment your home. Call **(800) 264-8258.** **www.cherrybark.com** Circle No. 897

Circle No. 900

Protective Products
Surface Protection Solutions

HARDWOOD PROTECTION
from PROTECTIVE PRODUCTS will protect and show the natural beauty of hardwood floors without the use of adhesives. Designed specifically for hardwood floors, the non-slip vinyl covering remains in place under the heaviest foot traffic. The Seam Tape provided protects seams to create a complete, impenetrable barrier of any width. For info on PROTECTIVE PRODUCTS full line of products CALL 24hrs: (800) 789-6633. www.protectiveproducts.com **Circle No. 901**

THE CARPET & RUG INSTITUTE
New, comprehensive, **CARPET PRIMER**, with general and technical information on construction, specification, installation, maintenance and indoor air quality from the Carpet and Rug Institute, the trade association representing the carpet industry. For publications catalog or a credit card order, phone 1-800-882-8846. **Circle No. 902**

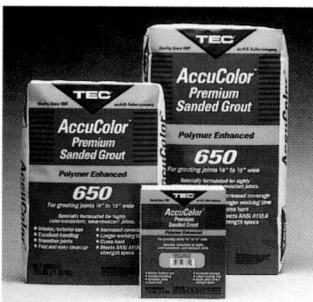

ACCUCOLOR™ GROUT BY TEC
is the first portland cement tile grout to provide consistent color by chemically-controlling the curing process. It automatically adjusts its cure to compensate for job site variables that affect grout color, including humidity, temperature, clean up technique and more. Call Customer Service at 1-800-TEC-9002 (Fax: 847-358-9510). **Circle No. 903**

SURFACE SHIELDS OFFERS AFFORDABLE CARPET AND FLOOR PROTECTION
Avoid claims - use Carpet Shield and Floor Shield, the self-adhering films which prevent damage to carpets and a variety of floor surfaces during construction, painting, remodeling, moving, home tours and other high traffic events. Easy to apply and remove even on stairs. For more information about Surface Shields and our other surface protection products (Window, Scratch & Trim Shield),call 800-91-FLOOR. **Circle No. 904**

PRO TECT FOR CARPETS
Pro Tect for **Carpets** offers surface protection for up to 45 days on all grades of carpet including industrial, commercial and residential. This 3.5 mil. self-adhering clear poly film guards against spills, dirt, and traffic and is highly resistant to tears and punctures. Call and order today, or for a free brochure, call **Pro Tect Associates Inc.** 1-800-545-0826. **Circle No. 905**

NEW TRADITIONS FROM HARRIS-TARKETT
The warmth, beauty and design versatility of pre-finished hardwood flooring are showcased in a 20-page, full-color catalog from Harris-Tarkett, Inc. Interior settings highlight the engineered plank products and the solid plank and solid parquet products. Complete satisfaction information and care and maintenance products are also explained. For more information, call toll-free 1-800-842-7816. **Circle No. 906**

GARAGE DOORS

Wayne-Dalton: Garage door has been designed to protect fingers from being pinched or crushed between closing sections. Features CFC-free polyurethane insulation and factory-installed hinges. *Thermotite.* 1-800-827-DOOR. *Circle no. 173.*

General American Door: Raised-panel steel door is offered in seven prefinished colors. Several shades, including tan, brown, blue, and gray, are made to match vinyl window exteriors. *Americana Series 7524.* 1-800-323-0813. *Circle no. 174.*

Overhead Door: Garage door has interchangeable panels made of dent- and scratch-resistant PVC material. *Renata.* 1-800-929-DOOR. *Circle no. 175.*

Amarr Garage Doors: Decorative windows come in four designs and are made of 1/8-inch frosted glass that has been tempered for safety. *DecraGlass.* 910-744-5100. *Circle no. 176.*

Clopay: Door has dent-resistant fiberglass exterior skins that can be painted or stained. Insulation options include polystyrene or polyurethane. *7000 Series.* 1-800-2CLOPAY. *Circle no. 177.*

Garage Doors & Openers

Manufacturer	Fiberglass doors	Garage-door openers	Hardboard doors	Insulated doors	Metal doors	Wood doors	Local dealer/distributor	Factory-direct	Circle No.
Amarr Garage Doors		■	■	■	■	■	■	■	176
Chamberlain Group		■					■		
Cladwood Div./Smurfit Newsprint						■	■		
Clopay Building Products Co.	74		■	■	■	■	■		177
Composite Door Industries	■						■		
Deflect-O-Corp.	■						■		
Elegant Entries						■	■	■	
Frantz/(A Div. of Wayne-Dalton Corp.)	■	■		■	■	■	■		
Garage Door Hardware Assn.		■							
General American Door Co.	■			■	74	■	■		174
The Genie Co.		■		■	■		■	■	
Holmes Garage Door	■	■	■	■	■	■	■	■	
Ideal Door		■	■				■		
International Paper Co.			■				■		
Martin Door Mfg.				■	■		■	■	
Overhead Door Corp.		■	■	■	■	76	■		175,908
Raynor Garage Doors		76		■	■		■		909
Roll-lite		■	■				■		
Sears Contract Sales/Sears, Roebuck		■					■		
Sections, Inc.						■	■		
Southwest Door Co.						■	■		
Stanley Door Systems/(Stanley Works)				■	■		■		
Taylor Door/(A Div. of Masco Industries)				■	■		■		
Wayne-Dalton Corp.	■	■	■	74	■	■	■	■	173
Western Wood Products Assn.						■	■		
Windsor Door	■	■	■	■	■	76	■		907
The Woodstone Co.						■		■	

Preferred garage location
on a 65-foot lot

Front-loaded access _____33%

Angled in rear _____28%

Turn-in garage _____20%

In rear with breezeway __12%

Rear alley access _____7%

*Source: What Today's Home Buyers Want/
NAHB and Fulton Reasearch*

See Manufacturer Index (beige pages at the back of this issue) for address and phone information.   Numbers in red indicate page number for additional product information.

A PREMIUM GARAGE DOOR WITHOUT THE PREMIUM PRICE

The Windsor Door Model 530 steel raised panel garage door is one of the best values you will find. Features like deep embossed prepainted raised steel panels, Tog-L-Loc® construction and quiet, dependable nylon rollers offer years of low maintenance, trouble-free use. Contact Windsor Door at (501) 562-1872. **Circle No. 907**

THE GARAGE DOOR THAT LOOKS RIGHT AT HOME. ANY HOME.

Welcome to a revolutionary new concept in garage doors. Where high-definition panels and precision construction provide you with the beauty and architectural style of a custom-made wood door. Innovative use of materials and the patented uni-hinge design offer much quieter operation, energy efficiency and superior durability that outperform both steel and wood. Transcend the ordinary with the Overhead Door Renata™ Collection, the incredibly beautiful, unbelievably maintenance-free garage door. **Overhead Door Corporation welcomes you home with Renata. Call 1-888-Renata-1 today. Circle No. 908**

RAYNOR GARAGE DOOR OPENER

The new Raynor FliteStar garage door opener is the strong, silent type, with a powerful 1/2 horsepower motor, an illuminated wall-mounted push button, and an "As Long As You Own Your Home" warranty. Available in Summer 1997. Call 1-800-4-RAYNOR. **Circle No. 909**

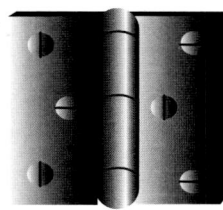

Hardware

Products — Finish: Cabinet hardware · Commercial-grade hardware · Deadbolts · Door hardware · Garage-door hardware · Hinges · Locksets · Window hardware. Rough: Bits · Blades · Fasteners. **Sales:** Local dealer/distributor · Factory-direct.

Manufacturer	Cabinet hardware	Commercial-grade hardware	Deadbolts	Door hardware	Garage-door hardware	Hinges	Locksets	Window hardware	Bits	Blades	Fasteners	Local dealer/distributor	Factory-direct	Circle No.
			Finish						Rough			Sales		
3-G's Supply Co.											■	■		
Accuride Intl.	■			■							■	■		
Ackerman Johnson Fastening Systems											■			
Acorn Mfg. Co.	■		83			■	■							914
Advanced Affiliates	■		■					■						
Air Nail Co.											■	■		
Alarm Lock Systems		■	■								■	■		
Allied Brass Mfg. Co.	■										■			
Alum-a-Pole Corp.											■	■		
American Architectural Manufacturers Assn.			■				■							
American Hardware Manufacturers Assn.		■	■	■		■	■							
American Heritage Shutters			■			■	■				■			
American Saw & Mfg. Co.									■	■	■			
American Wall Tie Co.											■			
Amerock Corp.	■		■			■	■				■			
Androck Hardware Corp.											■			
Around The Corner			■	■		■	■				■			
Arrow Lock Mfg. Co.			■	■			■				■			
Atlantic Pacific Industries	■		■			■		■			■			
Atro										■	■			
Au-ve-co Products/(Auto Vehicle Parts Co.)								■		■	■			
Auton Co.	■	■										■		
Baldwin Hardware Corp.	■	■	■	78	■	83	■				■			155,913
Barrett Mfg. Co.											■	■	■	
Bath N' Bagno	■										■			
Belwith-Keeler	■	■				■					■			
Benjamin Obdyke				■							■			
Best Lock Corp.							■					■		
Bladesmith										■	■			
Blaine Window Hardware		■	■	■				■			■		■	
Brass Accents by Urfic	■		■	■		■	■				■	■		
The Broadway Collection	■	■	■	■	■						■	■		
Building Products & Nails/Div. BSTC Group										■				
Building Products of America Corp.										■	■		■	
Cal Crystal Unlimited	■		■	■		■	■	■			■			
Cal Lock			■	■		■					■			
Carbbits									■					

See Manufacturer Index (beige pages at the back of this issue) for address and phone information.   Numbers in red indicate page number for additional product information.

continued

DOOR HARDWARE

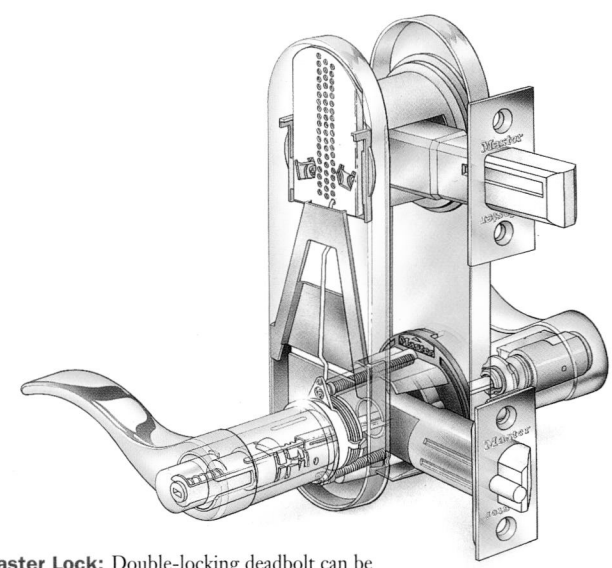

Master Lock: Double-locking deadbolt can be operated with a lever or knob. A single key unlocks both latches at once. Lock meets ADA accessibility requirements. *TwinBolt.* 414-444-2800. *Circle no. 154.*

Baldwin: Solid forged-brass locksets are designed to fit front, back, patio, and garage doors that are 1⅜ to 1¾ inches thick. Keyed entry locksets have bright brass or oil-rubbed bronze finish. *Images.* 1-800-566-1986. *Circle no. 155.*

Schlage: Security deadbolt is equipped with a pick-resistant cylinder and a steel insert bolt that extends 1 inch into the door frame. Three-piece design is easy to install, company claims. *B300.* 415-467-1100. *Circle no. 156.*

Weslock: Two-piece brass entry handle set can be ordered with a single- or double-cylinder deadbolt. Adjusts to door thicknesses from 1⅜ to 2 inches. Choice of polished or antique brass and polished or satin chrome finishes. *Savannah.* 1-800-575-BOLT. *Circle no. 157.*

Harloc: Solid zinc alloy handle set has balanced torque springs for easy opening. Available as a single or double bolt in various finishes. *Teton.* 1-800-542-7562. *Circle no. 158.*

Weiser Lock: Keyless entry system opens when a 4- to 8-digit code is entered; locks at the touch of a button. Unit comes in various styles and finishes. *Powerbolt.* 520-741-6200. *Circle no. 159.*

Hardware

Manufacturer	Cabinet hardware	Commercial-grade hardware	Deadbolts	Door hardware	Garage-door hardware	Hinges	Locksets	Window hardware	Bits	Blades	Fasteners	Local dealer/distributor	Factory-direct	Circle No.
				Finish					Rough			Sales		Circle No.
Chas O. Larson Co.	■	■					■							
CMT Tools									■		■	■		
Colonial Bronze Co.	■			■			■				■			
Concinnity/(A Div. of IW Industries)	■			■							■	■		
Cooper Tools										■				
Corbin Russwin Architectural Hardware		■	■	■		■					■			
Crawford Products											■	■	■	
The Credo Co.									■	■	■			
CSI										■	■			
D. Lawless Hardware	■	■			■	■	■				■	■		
Danish Import									■	■	■			
Dec-Har Designs	■										■	■		
Deckmaster		■												
Deflect-O-Corp.	■										■			
DeWalt Industrial Tool Co.									■	■	■			
DFS/USA/(Diversified Fastening System)									■		■	■		
Disston Co.									■	■				
The Door Company/Barber Cabinet	■													
DOORSPY/Rudolph-Desco Co.			■								■	■		
Dorchester Hardware								■			■			
Doug Mockett & Co.	■	■									■			
Duo-Fast Corp.											■	■	■	
Duschqueen					■						■	■		
E&E Consumer Products										■	■	■		
Elco Industries											■			
Emtek Products		■	■	■		■	■	■				■		
Enderes Tool Co.									■		■	■		
Engineered Profiles				■				■			■			
Entries			■	■		■						■		
Falcon Lock Co./(A Sub. of Newman Tonks)		■	■	■		■					■	■		
Faultless Lock			■	■		■					■	■		
Ferum Co.	■	■	■	■	■	■	■	■						
Fiberglass Access					■						■			
Fixrammer Fasteners Co.									■	■	■			
Forms + Surfaces	■			■								■		
Fox Valley Steel & Wire Co.											■			
Freud									■	■	■			
FSI/Scorpion Brand Products											■	■	■	
G-U Hardware		■	■	■		■	■	■			■			
Gainsborough Hardware Industries	■			■							■			
Garage Door Hardware Assn.					■									
Georgia-Pacific Corp.									■	■				
Glix Products	■	■	■	■	■	■	■	■			■			
Grabber Construction Products											■	■	■	
Grabco											■	■	■	
Grass America	■	■				■					■	■	■	
Green Street Details	■										■	■		
GRK Canada											■	■		
H.B. Ives	■	■	■	■		■	■	■			■	■		
Hafele America	■	■		■		■				■		■		
Hager Hinge Co.	■	■		■	■	■								
Hardware Technologies			■	■		■	■					■		
Harloc		■	■	78		■					■			158

> Homeowners prefer locksets with high-security features: reinforced cylinder casting, anti-pry rotating cylinder guards, all-steel latches, and a solid brass cylinder assembly.
>
> *Source:* Fenestration

See Manufacturer Index (beige pages at the back of this issue) for address and phone information.   Numbers in red indicate page number for additional product information.   continued

Hardware

Manufacturer	Cabinet hardware	Commercial-grade hardware	Deadbolts	Door hardware	Garage-door hardware	Hinges	Locksets	Window hardware	Bits	Blades	Fasteners	Local dealer/distributor	Factory-direct	Circle No.
	Finish								Rough			Sales		
Harney Mfg.			■	■			■							
HDI	■	■										■	■	
The Hess Mfg. Co.			■		■	■	■					■	■	
Hilti									■	■	■		■	
Hindley Mfg. Co.	■										■	■		
Hitachi Koki USA									■	■	■	■		
Holland Mfg. Co.											■	■		
Home Crest Corp.	■										■	■		
Hoyme Mfg.			■								■	■	■	
Huntwood Industries	■										■	■	■	
Ideal Door				■								■		
Independent Nail Co.											■			
Insteel Wire Products											■			
Interchange Brands											■	■	■	
International Staple & Machine Co.											■	■		
Italbrass Corp.	■		■	■			■					■		
ITW Buildex											■	■		
ITW Ramset/Red Head									■		■	■		
Jado Bathroom & Hardware Mfg. Corp.	■		■	■	■	■						■		
Josef Kihlberg of America											■	■		
KANT-SAG Lumber Connectors											■	■		
Kaylien			■								■	■	■	
Keystone Steel & Wire Co.											■	■		
Klein Tools									■	■	■			
Knape & Vogt Mfg. Co.	■	■									■	■	■	
Kolson	■	■	■	■	■	■	■							
Krusin Intl. Corp.				■								■	■	
Kwikset Corp./(A Sub. of Black & Decker)		■	■				■					■	■	
La Vona's Unique Hardware/Malibu Art Tile	■											■	■	
Lawrence Bros.	■	■		■		■	■					■	■	
LE Johnson Products				■		■	■					■		
Lenape Products	■											■	■	
Lighting by Hammerworks				■		■							■	
LRH Enterprises								■			■			
Ludwig Industries	■	■		■		■	■				■	■	■	
M. Green & Co.									■		■	■	■	
Macklanburg-Duncan				■										
Makita USA									■	■				
Marks USA		■	■	■			■					■		
Masco Corp.	■		■	■	■	■	■					■	■	
Master Lock Co.		78	■				■				■		■	70,154
Maze Nails											■	■		
Meister Atlanta Corp.			■											
Mepla	■		■			■					■			
Merillat Industries	■										■			
Midwest Fastener Corp.										■	■	■		
Milwaukee Electric Tool Corp.									■	■	■			
Modular Hardware			■	■							■	■		
Monterey Shelf	■													
Muro North America											■	■	■	
Mystica & Co.	■		■								■	■		
National Mfg.	■	■	■	■		■	■				■	■		
National Nail Corp.											■			

See Manufacturer Index (beige pages at the back of this issue) for address and phone information.   Numbers in red indicate page number for additional product information.

Manufacturer	Cabinet hardware	Commercial-grade hardware	Deadbolts	Door hardware	Garage-door hardware	Hinges	Locksets	Window hardware	Bits	Blades	Fasteners	Local dealer/distributor	Factory-direct	Circle No.
				Finish					**Rough**			**Sales**		**Circle No.**
The New England Lock & Hardware Co.			■	■								■		
Newman Tonks		■	■	■		■						■		
NT Falcon Lock		■		■		■						■		
NT Quality Hardware		■		■		■						■		
Oldham/United States Saw Co.									■	■		■		
Olson Saw Co.										■		■		
Omnia Industries	■	■	■	■		■	■					■		
PA Stratton & Co.											■	■	■	
Pam Fastening Technology											■	■	■	
Paul Decorative Products	■		■	■		■	■	■				■		
PDQ Industries		■	■	■		■						■		
Pease Industries		■	■		■	■						■		
Pemko Mfg. Co.		■	■	■	■		■					■	■	
Petmark Home Security Products								■				■	■	
PH Tech			■				■	■			■		■	
Philstone Fasteners	■											■		
Phoenix Lock Co.	■	■		■		■						■	■	
PMX			■											
Porter-Cable Corp.									■	■		■		
Prairie Home Products										■	■			
Preferred Engineering Products							■					■		
Preso-Matic Keyless Locks			■	■		■						■		
Primark Tool Group									■	■		■		
Primatech											■	■		
Prime-Line Products Co.	■	■		■	■		■					■		
Prudential Building Materials									■		■	■		
Quik Drive											■	■		
R. Christensen Hardware	■											■		
R & D Equipment		■		■									■	
Rawlplug Co.											■			
Renown Specialties Co.											■			
RH Tamlyn & Sons											■	■	■	
Rockford Products Corp.											■	■	■	
Ryobi America Corp.				■										
S-B Power Tool Co./(Skil Bosch)									■	■		■	■	
S & J Products											■	■		
S. Parker Hardware Mfg. Corp.	■	■	■	■	■	■	■	■				■	■	
Schlage Lock Co.		■	78	■		■						■		156
Schlegel Corp.			■			■	■					■	■	
Security Fastener Co.											■			
Selby Furniture Hardware Co.	■	■		■		■			■			■	■	
SEPCO Industries	■											■		
Sherle Wagner Intl.	■			■		■						■		
Sibes Brass/ISEO Locks	■	■	■	■			■					■		
Simpson Strong-Tie Co.											83	■		912
SIRO Design	■											■	■	
Smedbo	■			■				■				■		
Southeastern Metals Mfg. Co./SEMCO		■									■	■		
Southwest Door Co.	■			■								■		
Specialty Tools & Fasteners Distrib. Assn.											■	■		
Stanley Hardware			■		■	■	■					■		
Star Expansion Co.									■		■	■	■	
Steel & Wire Products Co.											■	■		

> Homeowners prefer polished brass locksets that resist perspiration, salt, heat, rain, and humidity.
>
> *Source:* Fenestration

See Manufacturer Index (beige pages at the back of this issue) for address and phone information.   Numbers in red indicate page number for additional product information.   continued

Manufacturer	Cabinet hardware	Commercial-grade hardware	Deadbolts	Door hardware	Garage-door hardware	Hinges	Locksets	Window hardware	Bits	Blades	Fasteners	Local dealer/distributor	Factory-direct	Circle No.
	Finish								Rough			Sales		
Steptoe & Wife Antiques							■					■	■	
Stor-A-Dor	■		■										■	
Strom Plumbing By Sign Of The Crab	■		■	■	■	■						■	■	
Swan Secure Products											■	■		
Taymor Industries	■		■	■		■						■		
TFI Corp./Avanté & TFI Hardware	■	■		■		■	■					■		
Timberlake Cabinet Co.	■											■		
TOGGLER Anchor System											■	■	■	
Tremont Nail Co.											■	■	■	
Truecraft Tools								■						
Truth Hardware			83	■	■	■					■		■	911
Ultra Hardware Products	■	■	■		■	■	■				■	■		
Unicut Corp.										■				
United Steel Products											■			
Universal Industrial Products Co.	■		■		■							■	■	
USP Lumber Connectors											■	■		
Valentina Ratti Creations USA	■											■	■	
Valli & Valli USA	■		■				■					■		
Vermont American Tool Co.									■	■		■		
VSI Fasteners											■			
Walker & Zanger	■	■										■	■	
Watercolors	■	■	■									■	■	
Weiser Lock/(A Div. of Masco Corp.)		■	78				■					■	■	159
Wen Products									■	■		■		
Weslock National		78					■					■	■	157
Westchester Marble & Granite	■	■										■		
Windsor Window Co.-NC Plant								■				■		
Woodfold-Marco Mfg.	■											■		
Woodstock Intl.											■	■		
Worthy Works	■											■		
Yale Locks & Hardware		■	■				■					■		

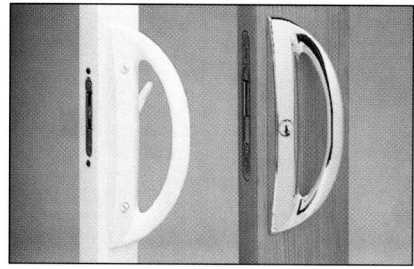

STYLINE™ PATIO DOOR HANDLE SET

Smooth flowing contour creates a unique contemporary shape complementing today's changing interior designs. The non-handed, low profile design helps to minimize interference with curtains and blinds. Designed with exterior gasket to create a superior seal for protection against air infiltration. *Truth Hardware, Owatonna, MN (800) 866-7884.* Web site: www.truth.com or E-mail: truthsal@truth.com **Circle No. 911**

STRONG-TIE® CONNECTORS

A necessary reference for builders and specifiers of wood connectors. **Introduces 12 new products.** 76-page catalog includes updated specifications, load charts, application drawings, and building code information – plus data on holdown anchorage design, and on available hanger options. **Circle No. 912**

ACORN MANUFACTURING

Acorn Manufacturing offers an array of distinctive door and cabinet hardware in nine finishes. The comprehensive selection includes reproduction pieces associated with old world and early American architecture as well as our latest southwest design. Call for information or catalogs (800) 835-0121 or fax: (800) 372-2676. **Circle No. 914**

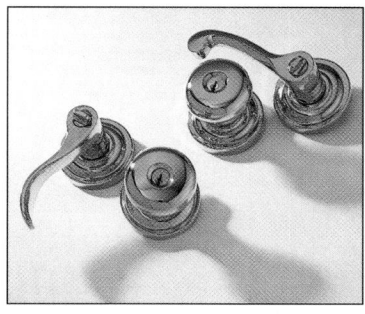

BALDWIN®

IMAGES® keyed entry locksets are easy to install and feature solid brass Baldwin quality at affordable prices. The variety of styles, the look and feel of solid brass, and The Lifetime Finish™ from Baldwin® will appeal to your customers. The Baldwin Builder program featuring the Parade of Homes and Model Home builder incentive packages will appeal to you. Call (800) 566-1986. **Circle No. 913**

HVAC

Products

Manufacturer	Air cleaners	Air conditioners	Baseboard heaters	Boilers	Dehumidifiers	Energy mgmt. systems/zone control	Fans	Furnaces	Grilles/registers	Heat exchangers	Heat pumps, electric	Heat pumps, gas-powered	Heat pumps, geothermal	Heat recovery ventilators	Humidifiers	Radiant heating	Solar energy systems	Thermostats	Ventilators	Water heaters	Local dealer/distributor	Factory-direct	Circle No.
A.O. Smith Water Products Co.																				■			
Air Conditioning and Refrigeration Institute	■	■	■	■		■	■	■		■	■	■			■	■	■	■	■	■			
Air Technology					■																■		
Air Vent							■														■		
Airmart HVAC							■														■		
Airxchange														■							■		
All American Wood Register									■												■		
Altech Energy														■							■		
Amana Refrigeration	■	■					■				■												
American ALDES Ventilation					■									88					■		■	■	916
American Energy Technologies																					■	■	
American Gas Assn.			■				■			■											■		
American Metal Products									■							■					■	■	
American Solar Energy Society (ASES)																	■						
American-Standard/Air Conditioning		■			■			■			■							■			■	■	
Arcoaire Heating & Cooling/Inter-City		■						■			■										■		
Axeman-Anderson Co.				■																	■		
BDP Co.	■	■		■		■		■			■				■			■	■		■	■	
Beacon/Morris			■																■		■		
Blaze King Industries																■						■	
Broan Mfg. Co.					■				■					■				■	■		■	■	
Browning Metal Products/(CertainTeed)					■														■		■		
Bryant	■	■		■		■		■			■				■			■	■		■	■	
Burnham Corp.			■	■												■					■		
Butler Ventamatic Corp.							■											■	■		■		
Cadet Mfg.			■				■									■							
Calorique																88					■	■	922
Canadian Geo-Solar		■						■					■			■						■	
Canarm							■												■		■		
Carrier Corp.	■	■		■		■		■			■		■		■			■	■		■	■	
Casablanca Fan Co.							■														■		
Chronomite Labs																				■	■		
Clark & Co.						■															■		
Clark United Corp.							■												■		■	■	
Classic Aire Woodvents									■												■		
Cleaver-Brooks				■																	■		
Climate Master											■		■								■	■	

See Manufacturer Index (beige pages at the back of this issue) for address and phone information.   Numbers in red indicate page number for additional product information.

Manufacturer	Air cleaners	Air conditioners	Baseboard heaters	Boilers	Dehumidifiers	Energy mgmt. systems/zone control	Fans	Furnaces	Grilles/registers	Heat exchangers	Heat pumps, electric	Heat pumps, gas-powered	Heat pumps, geothermal	Heat recovery ventilators	Humidifiers	Radiant heating	Solar energy systems	Thermostats	Ventilators	Water heaters	Local dealer/distributor	Factory-direct	Circle No.
Columbia Boiler Co.				■																	■		
Comfortmaker Heating & Cooling/Inter-City		■						■			■										■		
Conserval Systems																	■		■			■	
Continental Fan						88	■												■		■		919
Cool Attic						■												■	■		■	■	
CPN																■					■	■	
Danfoss Automatic Controls																		■			■		
Day & Night	■	■		■	■			■			■	■			■			■	■		■		
Decor Grates									■												■	■	
Deflect-O-Corp.						■			■										■		■		
Design Line			■																		■		
DRI-STEEM Humidifier Co.															■						■		
Dunham-Bush			■													■					■		
Duralast Products Corp.						■				■						■					■	■	
Easy Heat																■					■		
Electro Industries			■		■																	■	
Embassy Industries			■													■					■		
EMI Corp.		■									■										■		
Empire Comfort Systems							■									■					■		
Enerjee		■			■											■		■			■	■	
Enertel Controls					■																■		
Enerzone Systems Corp.	■				■				■		■							■			■		
Environmental Technology																■		■			■		
Exhausto																			■		■	■	
Fan America							■												■		■	■	
Fantech							■			■									■		■		
Fasco Industries			■				■		■							■		■	■		■		
Friedrich Air Conditioning Co.	■	■									■										■	■	
Frigidaire Home Products		■																			■	■	
Gas-Fired Products				■												■				■		■	
Gas Research Institute		■	■	■		■		■		■	■	■	■		■	■	■	■	■	■			
GFP Intl.								■								■					■		
Gibson/(A Brand of Frigidaire Co.)		■																			■		
Goettl Air Conditioning		■						■		■											■		
Goodman Mfg.Co.	■							■	■	■								■			■		
Grill Works									■												■		
Hamlet & Garneau			■																	■	■		
Hart & Cooley									■												■		
Harter Industries																	88				■	■	921
Heat Controller	■	■			■			■			■		■								■		
Heatway																88					■		918
Heil Heating & Cooling/Inter-City		■						■			■										■		
Heliodyne																	■				■	■	
Holdrite Brackets																				■	■		
Home Automation						■												■			■		
Home Automation Assn.						■															■		
Home Ventilating Institute/(AMCA Intl.)						■								■					■				
Honeywell/Home & Building Control	■					■													■		■		
Hoyme Mfg.																			■		■	■	
Hunter Energy and Technologies		■					■														■		
Hunter Fan Co.	■						■											■			■		
Hydronics Institute/(A Div. of GAMA)			■	■												■							
IntelliNet						■																■	

See Manufacturer Index (beige pages at the back of this issue) for address and phone information. Numbers in red indicate page number for additional product information.

continued

Products

Manufacturer	Air cleaners	Air conditioners	Baseboard heaters	Boilers	Dehumidifiers	Energy mgmt. systems/zone control	Fans	Furnaces	Grilles/registers	Heat exchangers	Heat pumps, electric	Heat pumps, gas-powered	Heat pumps, geothermal	Heat recovery ventilators	Humidifiers	Radiant heating	Solar energy systems	Thermostats	Ventilators	Water heaters	Local dealer/distributor	Factory-direct	Circle No.
International Energy Systems						■										■		■			■	■	
ISTA Energy Systems Corp.						■									■							■	
Johnson Controls						■												■			■		
Kanalflakt					■		■	■					■					■				■	
Kool-O-Matic Corp.					■													■	■		■	■	
Lectro Science/Intermark																		■			■		
Leigh/(A Harrow Co.)					■				■									■			■		
Lennox Industries	■	■	■		■		■								■			■	■	■	■		
Leslie-Locke																		■			■	■	
Litex Industries						■															■		
Luxaire/Fraser-Johnston		■					■			■											■		
Marley Electric Heating			■													■		■			■		
Masco Corp.									■												■	■	
Maxxon Corp./(formerly Gyp-Crete Corp.)																■					■		
Mid-America Building Products/(Tapco)					■														■		■		
Modern/Aire Ventilating							■														■		
Monitor Products								■												■	■		
Myson			■						■											■	■		
National Propane Gas Assn.				■			■					■									■		
Newtron Products Co.	■																				■		
Nordyne/Intertherm Heating & Air Care		■	■				■	■			■							■	■	■	■		
NORTEC Industries															■						■		
NuTone	■						■							■							■	■	
Oneida Royal Furnace/The Utica Cos.				■				■														■	
Panasonic							■												■		■		
Payne	■	■		■	■		■	■			■							■	■		■		
The Peerless Heater Co./Div. of Peerless Ind.				■																	■		
Perfection-Schwank															■						■	■	
Photocomm																	■				■	■	
PSG Limited					88													■			■	■	917
Radiant Technology			■		■											■					■	■	
Raypak				■																	■		
Rehau																■					■	■	
Research Products	■								■						■						■		
Rheem Mfg./Air Conditioning Div.		■					■			■											■		
Rheem Mfg./Water Heater Div.																				■			
Rinnai America Corp.								88								■					■		920
Runtal North America			■																		■		
Ruud Air Conditioning Div.		■					■			■											■		
Sanyo Fisher (USA) Corp.		■									■										■		
Screenex Design Center/(Riordan Group)					■																	■	
Sears Contract Sales/Sears, Roebuck		■																		■	■		
Sharp Electronics Corp.		■																			■		
Sioux Chief Mfg.															■						■		
Slant/Fin Corp.			■	■											■						■		
Solahart America																	■				■		
Solar Development																	■			■	■	■	
Solar Energy Industries Assn.							■			■						■	■		■	■	■		
Solar Survival Architecture																	■			■	■	■	
Solcan																	■					■	
Solid State Heating (SSHC)					■	■										■		■			■	■	
Southeastern Metals Mfg. Co./SEMCO																			■		■		
Southern Intl.						■															■		

Manufacturer	Air cleaners	Air conditioners	Baseboard heaters	Boilers	Dehumidifiers	Energy mgmt. systems/zone control	Fans	Furnaces	Grilles/registers	Heat exchangers	Heat pumps, electric	Heat pumps, gas-powered	Heat pumps, geothermal	Heat recovery ventilators	Humidifiers	Radiant heating	Solar energy systems	Thermostats	Ventilators	Water heaters	Local dealer/distributor	Factory-direct	Circle No.
Suburban Mfg. Co.		■						■													■	■	
Sunearth																	■			■	■	■	
Sunnyside Solar																	■						
T.H.W.S.																				■	■	■	
Tamarack Technologies						■	■		■					■					■		■	■	
Temp-Vent Corp.									■										■		■		
Tempstar Heating & Cooling/Inter-City		■						■			■										■		
Therma-Ray																■							
Therma-Stor Products/(A Div. of DEC Intl.)	■				■		■		■	■				■						■	■	■	
Thermo-Dynamics Boiler Co.				■				■												■	■		
Thermo Products		■						■														■	
Thermolec															■							■	
Thermoplus Air		■	■						■	■						■			■		■		
Tork						■															■		
The Trane Co./Unitary Products Group	■	■				■		■			■							■			■	■	
Trianco-Heatmaker				■																■	■		
Trol-A-Temp						■													■		■	■	
Unico		■								■											■		
Universal Metal Industries							■												■		■		
The Utica Cos.		■		■																	■		
Vanguard Industries																■					■		
Vent-Aire Systems									■					■					■		■	■	
Viessmann Mfg. Co. (US)				■		■														■	■		
W.H. Elevators																				■	■		
Water Furnace Intl.		■				■		■			■		■							■	■		
WeatherKing Air Conditioning		■						■			■										■		
Weil-McLain/A United Dominion Co.			■	■		■														■	■		
Western Ventilation Products																			■		■		
White-Rodgers/Emerson Electric Co.	■																	■			■		
Williams Furnace Co.								■													■		
Wirsbo Co.																■					■		
Wood Ventures							88														■		923
York Intl. Corp./Unitary Products Group	■	■				■		■			■	■	■					■			■		
ZTECH						■												■				■	

See Manufacturer Index (beige pages at the back of this issue) for address and phone information.   Numbers in red indicate page number for additional product information.

38% of new-home shoppers want electronic
air cleaners; 9% say they are essential.

Source: What Today's Home Buyers Want/NAHB and Fulton Research

80% of new homes
include central air systems.

Source: NAHB

ALDES HEAT RECOVERY VENTILATORS, 95SRD, 155SRD, 200SRD & 300DDD
exhaust stale indoor air and supply fresh outdoor air, protecting Indoor Air Quality in tightly built homes from 1100 sq. ft. up to 5000 sq. ft. (larger units available). For more information, call **American ALDES Ventilation Corp. 1-800-255-7749.** Fax: (941) 351-3442. http://www.oikos.com/aldes **Circle No. 916**

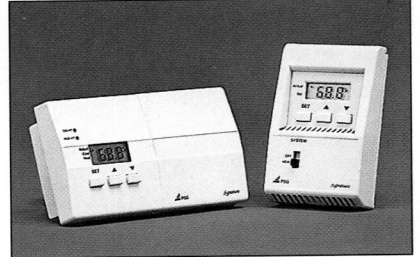

PSG LIMITED HAS THE NEW STANDARD IN DIGITAL CONTROLS
PSG Limited has a new non-programmable digital temperature control for both residential and light commercial buildings, it's called Signature Series. Room comfort is dramatically enhanced with lower energy consumption of up to 12%. Intella-Sens the custom microchip eliminates false starts and short cycling of equipment. No batteries, easy to install and easy to read. Call PSG Limited at (800) 782-8412. **Circle No. 917**

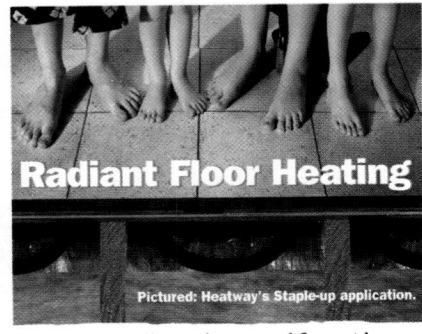

Pictured: Heatway's Staple-up application.

Enjoy warm tile, wood or carpeted floors with Heatway's UL listed floor heating products and systems. We engineer for many applications such as Slab, Thin-slab and Staple-up. Our systems offer both heating and snowmelting capability. We also offer design assistance. Call us at 1-800-255-1996 for more information.

Radiant Floors & Snowmelting
Circle No. 918

CONTINENTAL FAN MFG., Inc.
THE PROBLEM...Numerous surveys by builders and homeowners have confirmed the ineffectiveness of the typical residential bathroom exhaust system. The results are generally negative for the same reasons: too much noise and not enough air changes to eliminate humidity. THE CONCEPT... The Continental venting system addresses these flaws. By having the fan remotely mounted (in the attic or other unoccupied space), the fan noise is isolated away from the living space. This concept allows for a more powerful fan to be used without creating intrusive noise. THE SOLUTION... Remote bathroom ventilation kits utilize the AXC Series of in-line centrifugal fans. The fans incorporate a powerful backward curved fan impeller which is the quietest blade form available, yet is powerful enough for extended duct runs. Capacities are double to quadruple the CFM range of typical in-ceiling exhaust fans. **Circle No. 919**

SOLAR POOL HEATING
Hi-Tec solar heating system ktis are easy to install on any in-ground pool. EZ HEAT do-it-yourself solar systems are the lowest cost heaters for above ground pools. The Hi-Tec chlorine generator automatically sanitizes any pool. Harter Industries, Inc. (800) 566-7770, Fax: (908) 566-6977, E-mail: Harter101@aol.com **Circle No. 921**

RINNAI'S TROPIC INFRA-RED HEATER
The Tropic vent-free gas-fired heater is perfect for your mid-size to large living area, room additions. This three setting heater delivers up to 30,000 BTUs and is 99.9% energy efficient. Powered by clean burning natural or LP gas, the Tropic costs 3 - 4 times less than electricity and 1.5 - 2 times less than kerosene and is A.G.A. Design Certified. The Tropic comes with the long-standing Rinnai warranty which covers parts, labor, and shipping with absolutely no pro-rating for a **full 4 years**. Rinnai America Corporation, 1662 Lukken Industrial Drive West LaGrange, GA 30240 (800) 621-9419. **Circle No. 920**

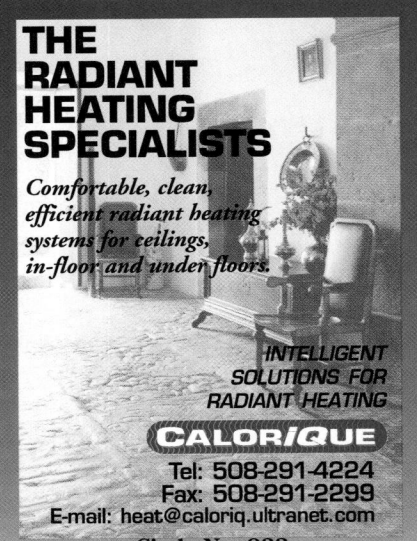

THE RADIANT HEATING SPECIALISTS
Comfortable, clean, efficient radiant heating systems for ceilings, in-floor and under floors.

INTELLIGENT SOLUTIONS FOR RADIANT HEATING

CALORIQUE
Tel: 508-291-4224
Fax: 508-291-2299
E-mail: heat@caloriq.ultranet.com
Circle No. 922

WOOD VENTURES, INC.
High quality **Wood and Brass Air Grilles** from Wood Ventures offer a distinctive finishing touch to the discriminating homeowner. Offered in a wide range of sizes and styles, these handsome and durable grilles complement any decor. Call (800) 524-5230. **Circle No. 923**

Home Technology

Manufacturer	Built-in audio	Built-in theater	Carbon monoxide detectors	Fire/smoke detectors	Fire sprinkler systems	Home automation systems	Intercoms	Security systems	Local dealer/distributor	Factory-direct	Circle No.
	Products								**Sales**		
Ademco			■			■		■	■		
AES	■								■	■	
Aiphone Intercom Systems							■	■	■		
Alpha Communications							■	■	■	■	
American Lantern Div./Inteletron							■	■			
American Power Products							■	■	■		
AMP/Building Systems Div.						■		■			
AMX Corp.						■					
Atlas/Soundolier	90	■						■			925
Audio Technology	■						■	■	■		
Auton Co.						■				■	
AVSI Automated Voice Sys./(MASTERVOICE)						■			■	■	
Bang & Olufsen of America	■	■									
Bestwood Electronics						■	■	■	■	■	
BRK Electronics			90	■				■	■		926
Broan Mfg. Co.						■		■			
Dedicated Micros								■	■		
Doorking							■	■	■	■	
DOORSPY/Rudolph-Desco Co.							■	■	■		
Enertel Controls						■		■			
Enerzone Systems Corp.						■		■	■		
Fasco Industries	■						■	■			
First Alert Professional Security Systems				■		■		■			
Ft. Knox Security								■	■		
Fyrnetics			■	■				■			
Globe Fire Sprinkler Corp.					■			■	■		
Heath Co.								■	■		
Home Automated Living						■		■	■		
Home Automation						■		■	■		
Home Automation Assn.	■	■		■	■	■	■	■			
Honeywell/Home & Building Control	■	■				■	■	■	■		
Intelecom Products						■	■			■	
IntelliNet	■			■		■		■		■	
International Energy Systems								■	■	■	
JBL Home Entertainment	■	■						■			
Leviton Mfg./Electrical Distribution						■		■			
LiteTouch						■				■	

> 68% of new-home shoppers want a home security system that's connected to a central security office.
>
> *Source: What Today's Home Buyers Want/NAHB and Fulton Research*

See Manufacturer Index (beige pages at the back of this issue) for address and phone information.   **Numbers in red indicate page number for additional product information.**

continued

Home Technology

Manufacturer	Built-in audio	Built-in theater	Carbon monoxide detectors	Fire/smoke detectors	Fire sprinkler systems	Home automation systems	Intercoms	Security systems	Local dealer/distributor	Factory-direct	Circle No.
Molex						■			■		
Multiplex Technology	■	■				■	■	■	■		
Music and Sound	■	■				■	■		■		
Napco Security Systems			■			■		■	■	■	
National Fire Protection Assn.				■							
Newtron Products Co.			■						■		
Niles Audio Corp.	■	■				■			■		
NuTone	■						■	■	■		
Pelonis/Del-Rain Corp.								■	■	■	
Petmark Home Security Products								■	■	■	
Pfanstiehl Corp.	■	■							■		
Philips Consumer Electronics Co.	■	■							■		
Pioneer Electronics (USA)	■	■							■	■	
RAB Electric Mfg. Co.								■	■		
Regent Lighting Corp.								■	■		
Snap-Trak		■							■	■	
Snif Security			■					■	■	■	
Sonance	■	■							■		
Star Sprinkler					■				■		
Systematic Irrigation Controls						■			■		
Thomas Electronics Corp.						■			■	■	
Thomson Consumer Electronics/RCA	■	■							■	■	
Tork								■	■		
UNITEC						■			■		
United Telesis Corp.						■	■			■	
V-DEC								■	■	■	
The Viking Corp.				■	■				■		

See Manufacturer Index (beige pages at the back of this issue) for address and phone information.   Numbers in red indicate page number for additional product information.

Home Technology

WHISPERTOUCH™
More than just a volume control
WhisperTouch lets you fine tune music with exquisite clarity. It adjusts volume in graceful 1-1/2 and 3dB steps. It features an elegant, nearly flush knob, decorator styling, 50 watt rating, plug-in connectors and impedance matching. Call Soundolier today: (800) 876-7337. **Circle No. 925**

BRK® ELECTRONICS:
Model CO1120B – With carbon monoxide poisoning being the leading cause of accidental deaths, a carbon monoxide detector offers peace of mind for the new home buyer. Manufactured by BRK Brands, Inc. (the #1 manufacturer of residential smoke detectors and makers of First Alert®), the CO1120B is the only unit available powered by AC with 9V battery back-up. Interconnectability with 11 other identical units provides safety throughout the home. A natural upgrade to home safety for new residential construction. **Circle No. 926**

Insulation

Manufacturer	Bats/rolls	Blown-in	Foundation	Radiant barriers	Vapor/air infiltration barriers	Water heater/pipe	Weatherstripping	Cellulose	Cotton	Fiberglass	Foam	Mineral wool	Local dealer/distributor	Factory-direct	Circle No.
	Type							**Material**					**Sales**		
3-10 Insulated Forms			■	■							■		■	■	
The 3E Group											■		■	■	
AAB Building System											■		■		
ABC Seamless Siding					■										
Acro Foam & Plastic					■									■	
Advanced Foil Systems				■									■	■	
AFM Corp.		■											■	■	
Alro Plumbing Specialty Co.						■							■		
American Accent Homes									■						
American ConForm Industries			■										■		
American Polysteel Forms			■		■								■		
American Sprayed Fibers		■						■				■	■	■	
Applegate Insulation Mfg.		■						■					■	■	
Ark-Seal Intl.		■								■	■		■	■	
Atlas Roofing Corp.											■		■		
Barrisol Stretch Ceilings					■								■		
Benjamin Obdyke					■								■		
BPCO/(A Div. of EMCO)								■					■	■	
Cellofoam North America		■									■		■		
Cellulose Insulation Manufacturers Assn.		■						■							
The Celotex Corp.					■						■		■		
Central Fiber Corp.		■						■					■	■	
CertainTeed Corp./Insulation Group	■	■								■			■	■	
Concrete Block Insulating Systems											■		■		
Consolidated Coatings Corp.											■		■	■	
Corbond Corp.											■		■		
The Dow Chemical Co.			■								■		■		151
DuPont Tyvek					■								■		
EPS Molders Assn.			■								■				
Fold-Form			■										■		
Fomo Products			■		■	■					■		■	■	
Georgia-Pacific Corp.	■							■		■	■		■		
Gossen Corp.						■							■	■	
Graham Fiberglass	■	■								■			■		
Greenwood Cotton Insulation Products	■	■						93	■				■	■	153
Guardian Fiberglass	■	■								■			■		
Hacker Industries				■										■	
Hamilton Mfg.		■	■				■						■	■	
Harvey Industries												■	■	■	
Holm Industries/Jarrow Div.						■							■		
Homasote Co.										■			■		

> **50% of new-home shoppers want adjacent kitchen and family rooms that are visually open with only a half-wall separating them.**
>
> *Source: What Today's Home Buyers Want/ NAHB and Fulton Research*

See Manufacturer Index (beige pages at the back of this issue) for address and phone information.   Numbers in red indicate page number for additional product information.   continued

Insulation

Manufacturer	Batts/rolls	Blown-in	Foundation	Radiant barriers	Vapor/air infiltration barriers	Water heater/pipe	Weatherstripping	Cellulose	Cotton	Fiberglass	Foam	Mineral wool	Local dealer/distributor	Factory-direct	Circle No.
	Type							Material					Sales		
ICE Block Building Systems			■								■		■		
Icynene		■									■			■	149
In Cide Technologies		■				■								■	
Industrial Energy Products	■			■	■			■				■		■	
Innovative Insulation			■	■	■								■	■	
Insta-Foam Products				■							■		■		
Insul-Binder		■		■			■	■		■					
Insulated Building Systems			■								■		■		
International Cellulose Corp.		■					■	■					■		
K Products Group/(A Div. of Cardinal Ind.)					■								■	■	
Kasko Industries		■	■							■				■	
Knauf Fiber Glass	■	■	■		■					■			■		
Korwall Industries											■			■	
Louisiana-Pacific Corp.		■						94					■		
Macklanburg-Duncan				■	■										
Mortite					■			■					■	■	
The Murus Co.											■			■	
Natl. Insulation & Abatement Contractors	■			■	■			■		■		■			
NEI				■									■		
North American Insulation Manufacturers	■	■								■		■			
North Carolina Foam (NCFI)				■							■			■	
NRG Barriers/The E'NRG'Y House											■		■		
Owens Corning	93	■		■	■			■		■			■	■	152,633
Palmer Industries		■		■							■		■		
ParPac		■		■		■							■		
Parsec			94	■									■	■	929
Pemko Mfg. Co.				■	■	■							■	■	
Perma R'' Products											■		■		
Plastics & Resins											■		■	■	
Polyfoam Packers Corp.											■		■	■	
Premier Building Systems			■								■		■		
Quad Lock Building Systems			■	■							■		■		
Reemay				■									■		260
Reflectix			■		■								■		
Rmax											■		■		
Safe Alternatives Sales Group		■									■		■	■	
Schlegel Corp.							■						■	■	
Schuller Intl.	■	■		■	■				93	■			■	■	150
Shelter Enterprises											■		■		
Simplex Products/(A Div. of K2)			■	■									■		
The Society of the Plastics Industry		■		■							■				
SOLEC (Solar Energy Corp.)			■										■	■	
Solid State Heating (SSHC)			■										■	■	
Sto-Cote Products				■									■	■	
Stuc-O-Flex Intl.											■		■	■	
Tenneco Building Products			■	■							■		■		
Thermoguard Co.							■						■	■	
Todol Products		■		■	■	■					■		■		
Tuff-N-Dri Waterproofing/Koch Materials Co.			■											■	
UC Industries			■								■				
WH Porter											■			■	
Winter Panel Corp.											■			■	
Woodmaster Foundations			■								■			■	

50% of new-home shoppers want four bedrooms; 40% want three.

Source: What Today's Home Buyers Want/ NAHB and Fulton Research

See Manufacturer Index (beige pages at the back of this issue) for address and phone information.   Numbers in red indicate page number for additional product information.

INSULATION

Icynene: Spray-in insulation replaces building wrap, insulation, vapor barriers, caulking, and taping. 1-800-758-7325. *Circle no. 149.*

Schuller International: Encapsulated fiberglass insulation line includes R-25 for attics and R-19 for crawl space walls and under floors. 1-800-654-3103. *Circle no. 150.*

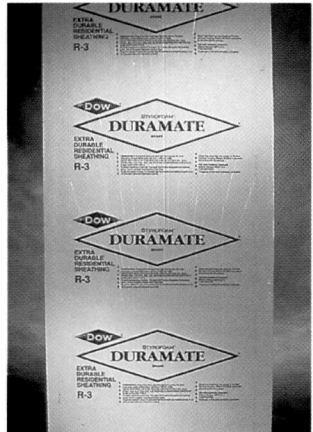

Dow Chemical: Insulation's protective facer is made of extra-durable film to maintain strength and insulation performance even when bent, soaked, or frozen. *Duramate.* 1-800-248-2436. *Circle no. 151.*

Owens Corning: Acoustic batts block noise between interior walls, ceilings, and floors. Batts measure 15 by 93 inches, are 3½ inches thick. *QuietZone.* 1-800-438-7465. *Circle no. 152.*

Greenwood Cotton Insulation: Environmentally friendly cotton batt insulation consists of recycled textiles and nontoxic binders and retardants. Loose-fill also available. 1-800-546-1332. *Circle no. 153.*

WATERPROOF UNDERLAYMENT MEMBRANES

Protect ceramic tile and natural stone installations from water, upward moisture migration and concrete cracks: inside or out. COMPOSEAL GOLD bonds direct to substrate, then tile is thin-set above GOLD. COMPOSEAL Blue Shower Pan Membrane is for thick-bed jobs. Listed by Ceramic Tile Institute, UPC, SBCCI, BOCA. Compotite (800) 221-1056.
Circle No. 928

PARSEC THERMO-BRITE RADIANT BARRIER SYSTEM

For superior energy efficiency and lower utility costs, Parsec offers the highest quality Thermo-Brite Radiant Barrier. This Low-E, durable, non-corrosive film blocks 95% of radiant heat transfer in roof/wall systems, while stopping air and moisture infiltration on the walls.
Circle No. 929

INSULATION - BLOWN-IN

LOUISIANA-PACIFIC

Made from 100% recycled newspaper, GreenStone® insulation is designed to make homes more energy efficient while increasing comfort. GreenStone is fire retardant, environmentally safe and contributes to sound control. Blown-in, it forms a tight, even seal around wiring, plumbing and framing materials in attics and walls which helps reduce heating and cooling bills. **Call (800) 299-0029, ext. 4012 for a free brochure.**

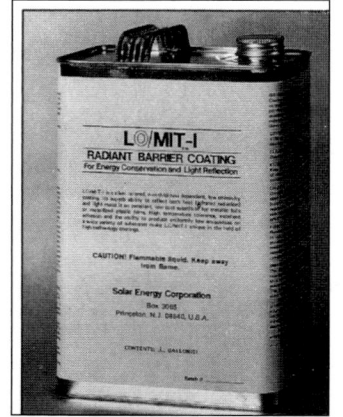

RADIANT BARRIER

LO/MIT-I is a new spray-applied radiant barrier coating for energy conservation and light reflection. It is an excellent, low cost substitute for metallic foils or metallized plastic films. **Circle No. 930**

Landscape Design

Manufacturer	Deck accessories	Drain piping	Gazebos	Lawn sprinkler systems	Mailboxes	Paving	Plastic fencing	Plastic lumber	Retaining walls	Signage	Trim/lattice	Wood fencing	Local dealer/distributor	Factory-direct	Circle No.
	Products												Sales		
AB Cushing Mills												■			
Acme Brick Co.						■							■	■	
Almost Heaven	■		■							■	■			■	
Amdega Machin Conservatories			■											■	
American ConForm Industries								■					■		
American Polysteel Forms								■					■		
Anchor Wall Systems									98				■	■	933
Arriscraft Corp.						■			■				■		
The Astrup Co.											■				
Austram	■												■		
Balcon						■			■				■	■	
Beacon Products					■					■			■	■	
Belden Brick Co.						■							■		
Bend Industries						■			■				■	■	
Bomanite Corp.						■							■		
Boral Bricks						■							■	■	
Brandon Industries					■									■	
The Brick Institute of America						■									
Brite Millwork	■										■		■		
Brochure Box Co.					■					■				■	
Brock Deck/(A Div. of CTB)	98							■		■			■	■	932
Bufftech	■		■	98	■								■	■	931
The Burruss Co.												■	■		
Burton Woodworks/(A Div. of MHJ Group)	■										■		■		
Caldera Spas & Baths		■												■	
California Acrylic Industries/Cal Spas		■												■	
California Redwood Assn.												■	■		
Cangelosi Marble & Granite						■			■					■	
Cedarbrook Sauna												■		■	
Cepco Tool	■												■	■	
Classy Glass Sunrooms			■										■	■	
Coastal Lumber Co./(Treated Products Div.)	■								■		■	■	■	■	
Concrete Designs						■								■	
Continental Industries				■									■	■	
Crane Plastics Co.							■	■					■		
Creative Building Products	■					■	■		■				■	■	
Cross Vinylattice						■				■			■	■	

See Manufacturer Index (beige pages at the back of this issue) for address and phone information.   Numbers in red indicate page number for additional product information.   continued

Manufacturer	Products												Sales		Circle No.
	Deck accessories	Drain piping	Gazebos	Lawn sprinkler systems	Mailboxes	Paving	Plastic fencing	Plastic lumber	Retaining walls	Signage	Trim/lattice	Wood fencing	Local dealer/distributor	Factory-direct	
Cultured Stone®/Stone Products Corp.						98			■				■	■	934
Cumberland Woodcraft			■											■	
Dakota Granite										■			■	■	
Daymond Building Products						■									
DEC-K-ING	■												■	■	
DecTec/(A Div. of Skyline Building Systems)	■												■	■	
Dee Sign Co.										■				■	
DuPont Co./Corian Products	■		■			■			■	■			■		
Dura Art Stone									■					■	
Earthstone Retaining Wall Systems									■				■	■	
Eldorado Stone Corp.						■			■				■	■	
Elements			■							98				■	937
Fibermesh/Div. of Synthetic Industries						■							■	■	
Flo-Well Water Management		■											■	■	
Florida Brick & Clay Co.						■							■		
Genova Products		■					■	■						■	■
The Georgia Marble Co.						■				■			■		
Georgia-Pacific Corp.								■			■		■		
Gerber Industries	■												■	■	
Glen-Gery Corp.						■							■		
Grani-Decor Tiles						■							■	■	
Greenheart-Durawoods	■												■		
Hanover Lantern/Div. of Hoffman Products				■									■		
Heritage Vinyl Products	■		■	■	■				■				■	■	936
Hoglund Landscape Construction									■				■		
I-XL Industries						■							■		
Idaho Wood				■										■	
Infiltrator Systems		■											■		
Isokern Fireplaces/Earthcore Industries									■				■	■	
Keystone Retaining Wall Systems									98				■	■	935
Kroy Building Products			■	■	■								■		
Kuny's Mfg. Co.	■												■		
London Tile Co.						■							■	■	
Lowen Sign Co.										■				■	
LWO Corp.											■	■	■		
Marell Industries				■										■	
Mel Northey Co.				■										■	
Mellco	■			■			■			■	■	■	■		
Moultrie Mfg.			■	■									■		
National Assn. of Brick Distributors						■									
National Concrete Masonry Assn.						■			■						
Old Carolina Brick Co.						■			■				■	■	
Pacific Clay Brick Products						■							■		
Paveloc Industries						■			■				■	■	
Permalatt											■		■		
Petmal Supply Co.						■			■				■	■	
Philstone Fasteners	■											■	■		
Pisa Retaining Wall Systems									■				■		
Plastics Research Corp.	■						■				■		■		
Plastival	■						■	■			■		■		
Prudential Building Materials	■						■				■		■		
PS Aluminum Products	■													■	
Quarry Tile Co.									■				■		

Outdoor features new-home buyers want:

Exterior lighting _92%
Lot with trees __85%
Deck in rear ____83%
Patio in rear ___82%

Source: What Today's Home Buyers Want/NAHB and Fulton Research

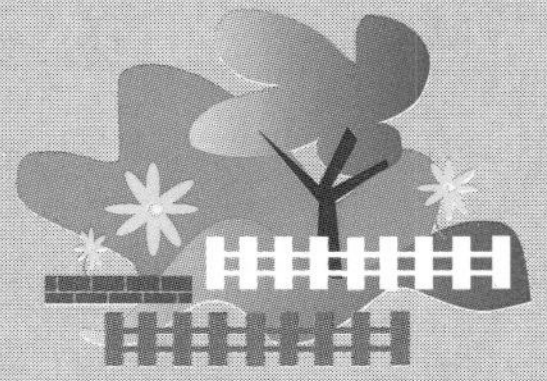

Manufacturer	Deck accessories	Drain piping	Gazebos	Lawn sprinkler systems	Mailboxes	Paving	Plastic fencing	Plastic lumber	Retaining walls	Signage	Trim/lattice	Wood fencing	Local dealer/distributor	Factory-direct	Circle No.
Re-Source Building Products	■						■	■			■		■		
Redland Brick/(Cushwa Plant)						■							■	■	
The Reinforced Earth Co.									■				■		
Renato Bisazza										■			■	■	
Risi Stone Systems/(A Div. of Rothbury Intl.)									■				■	■	
Robinson Brick Co.						■							■		
Rocktile Specialty Products						■								■	
Rockwood Retaining Walls									■				■	■	
Rotocast/Classic Lamp Posts					■									■	
Ryan Forest Products	■										■		■	■	
Scott Sign Systems										■			■		
Sever Signs & Displays										■			■	■	
Sitecraft Corp.	■													■	
Slope Block									■				■	■	
Southern Pine Council	■		■									■			
Southern Sales & Marketing Group	■											■		■	
SouthWood Corp.										■				■	
Sovebec												■	■		
Spiral Stairs of America	■													■	
Steel & Wire Products Co.							■				■	■	■		
Stone Construction Equipment						■							■		
Summitville Tiles						■							■	■	
Sunesta Products	■		■										■		
SunTuf			■										■	■	
Sweepster						■								■	
Systematic Irrigation Controls				■									■		
Thermal Industries							■	■					■		
TR Miller Mill Co.											■	■	■		
Trex Decks								■					■		
Triple Crown Fence/(A Div. of CTB)	■						■				■		■	■	
Trus Joist MacMillan									■				■		
Uni-Group USA						■			■				■	■	
USP Lumber Connectors	■												■		
Versa-Lok Retaining Wall Systems									98				■		938
Vixen Hill Mfg. Co.			■											■	
Wausau Tile						■				■				■	
Weathermatic Co.				■									■		
Western Wood Products Assn.												■	■		
Whitacre-Greer						■							■	■	

Community amenities new-home shoppers want:

Walking and jogging trails__68%

Park area_____65%

Outdoor swimming pool _________46%

Playgrounds __42%

Lake__________40%

Source: What Today's Home Buyers Want/NAHB and Fulton Research

See Manufacturer Index (beige pages at the back of this issue) for address and phone information.

Numbers in red indicate page number for additional product information.

BUFFTECH - STYLE & QUALITY
Maintenance-free vinyl fencing and railing in styles and colors to complement every design. Ornamental and privacy fences for classical and contemporary landscapes. Unique vinyl compound is safe, economical, and durable. Make a stylish statement of quality with Bufftech. 20 Year Non-Prorated Warranty.
Call (800) 333-0569. http://www.bufftech.com
Circle No. 931

CULTURED STONE®
New 1997 full-color 56 page catalog contains swatch and application photos of more than 78 stone building products; it features new colors, new textures, and new trim pieces. Cultured Stone® looks and feels like stone yet costs a fraction of the price.
(800) 644-4487. *Stone Products Corp.*
Circle No. 934

ELEMENTS, INC. CUSTOM SIGNAGE
Our **free** product catalog features a complete line of signage for builders and developers: lot markers, model home signs, entrance monuments, address plaques, brass lettering, interior displays and sandblasted redwood. Free estimates. "The Nation's #1 Provider of Signage for Builders and Developers." Call **(800) 223-2788**. Let us show you how our signage can benefit your company. **Circle No. 937**

BROCK DECK™ VINYL DECKING
BROCK DECK™ offers you an alternative to wood for residential decks. Available in white, gray and tan, this durable decking never needs paint or stain, cuts like wood and features a slip-resistant surface. BROCK DECK also offers a variety of vinyl fencing options, including privacy styles. Call (800) 488-5183 or E-mail: ctb@ctbinc.com for more details.
Circle No. 932

KEYSTONE RETAINING WALLS
The Keystone Retaining Wall System stands alone as the industry leader. Because Keystone offers great looks, easy installation, low maintenance, and durability, it delivers a superior return on investment. Keystone is the preferred choice across the United States and around the world for commercial, public and residential properties. (800) 891-9791. (612) 897-3858 fax. Internet: www.keystonewalls.com.
E-mail: keystone@keystonewalls.com
Circle No. 935

VERSA-LOK® RETAINING WALL SYSTEMS
VERSA-LOK mortarless retaining walls are unmatched in design flexibility. Unlimited varieties of curves, corners, and steps may be created using only the standard unit. Easy-to-install walls complement any environment and last a lifetime. FREE Design and Installation Guidelines. (800) 770-4525.
Circle No. 938

ANCHOR WALL SYSTEMS
Anchor Wall Systems takes you beyond the barriers of traditional retaining walls into a world of design freedom where pins, clips and mortar are things of the past. Anchor's integrated design conforms to virtually any configuration providing maintenance-free solutions for any site. Call (800) 473-4452. www.anchorwall.com   **Circle No. 933**

Vinyl Decking & Fencing

HERITAGE VINYL PRODUCTS, INC.
Teck Deck® the all-vinyl solution for deck and dock. Its patented two-piece construction uses hidden fasteners for a simple seamless installation. Maintenance-free and backed by a non-prorated Lifetime Warranty, Teck Deck® is available in four accent colors.
Circle No. 936

FOREST PRODUCTS SOCIETY
Wood Decks: Materials, Construction and Finishing contains a wealth of important information on the design, construction, finishing and maintenance of wood decks that is not available in other deck construction publications. An invaluable resource for designers, builders and remodelers.
Circle No. 787

Moulding & Millwork

Manufacturer	Columns, composite	Columns, metal	Columns, wood	Cornices	Custom millwork	Door surrounds	Gingerbread	Louvers	Mantels	Moulding, flexible	Moulding, plaster	Moulding, plastic	Moulding, veneer	Moulding, wood	Paneling	Stair parts	Stairs, attic	Stairs, circular & spiral	Stairs, pre-built	Wainscoting	Local dealer/distributor	Factory-direct	Circle No.
AB Cushing Mills		■	■	■										■	■								
ABT Building Products Corp./ABTco					■							■									■		963
Accent Millworks					105																■		943
AE Gombert Lumber Co.					■								■	■	■					■	■		
AERT					■																■	■	
AF Schwerd Mfg.			105																		■		939
Afco Industries		■																			■	■	
Aged Woods													■	■	■					■	■	■	
AJ Stairs	■			■				■	■	■				■		■	■	■	■			■	
Alum-a-Pole Corp.										■											■		
American Custom Millwork			■	■	■				■					■	■			■		■	■	■	
American Marble Industries/Kephaco Corp.									■		■										■	■	
American Wood Council		■												■									
Anderson Wood Products Co.					■									■	■					■	■		
Anthony Forest Products Co.		■						■						■							■	■	
Architectural Matters		■		■											■						■		
Architectural Ornament			■			■	■	■	■												■	■	
Architectural Paneling	■	■		■	■		■		■	■				■	■		■	■	■	■			
Architectural Reproductions	■		■							■												■	
Architectural Sculpture			■							■												■	
Architectural Timber & Millwork		■	■											■	■					■	■		
Arcways															■		106	■			■	■	949
Aristocrat Products	■		■						■													■	
Around The Corner														■							■		
Artistic Woodworking						■								■							■	■	
Atlantic Pre-Hung Doors	■					■								■							■		
B.C. Wood Specialties Group					■									■									
B-H Woodturning			■						■					■		■			■			■	
Bangkok Intl.				■										■		■						■	
Beech River Mill Corp.								■														■	
Bendix Mouldings														■							■	■	
Bennett Industries												■	■								■		
BentWood Northwest					■																	■	
Bessler Stairway (A Div. of ASI)																	105				■		946
BH Johnson Stairbuilders Co.																		■					
BiWood Flooring														■									
Black Diamond Millworks														■							■		

See Manufacturer Index (beige pages at the back of this issue) for address and phone information. Numbers in red indicate page number for additional product information.

continued

Moulding & Millwork

Manufacturer	Columns, composite	Columns, metal	Columns, wood	Cornices	Custom millwork	Door surrounds	Gingerbread	Louvers	Mantels	Moulding, flexible	Moulding, plaster	Moulding, plastic	Moulding, veneer	Moulding, wood	Paneling	Stair parts	Stairs, attic	Stairs, circular & spiral	Stairs, pre-built	Wainscoting	Local dealer/distributor	Factory-direct	Circle No.
Blainville Mouldings														■	■						■	■	
Blumer & Stanton			■	■	■	■	■							■	■						■	■	
Boen Hardwood Flooring														■							■		
Boston Design Corp.																		■				■	
Brickstone Studios									■												■	■	
Bruce Hardwood Floors														■							■		
Buffalo Veneer & Plywood													■	■							■	■	
Builders Edge		■			■		■					■								■	■	■	
Building Products & Nails/Div. BSTC Group														■									
Burns, Morris & Stewart			■							■	■									■	■		
The Burruss Co.			■													■		■			■		
Burton Woodworks/(A Div. of MHJ Group)														■							■		
Carlisle Restoration Lumber											■	■	■								■		
Caron Industries											■								■	■	■		
Carrick Turning Works														■							■		
Cast Designs & Supply			■						■	■				■						■	■		
Castings									■												■		
CDA Industries									■												■		
Chadsworth's 1.800 Columns	105	■																			■		941
Chemcrest Architectural Products	■		■	■	■	■	■	■	■		■										■		
Chesapeake Hardwood Products																				■	■		
Classic Architectural Specialties	■	■	■	■					■				■		106						■		956
Classic Cast Stone of Dallas									■													■	
Classic Mouldings	■		■						■		■										■		
Coffman Stairs																■		■			■		
Colonial Carpentry																		■	■	■	■		
Colonial Craft			■									■							■	■	■		
Colonial Elegance		■				■	■							■							■		
Columns		■																■			■		
Comtex Industries											■					■	■	■	■	■	■		
Conik Group		■																			■		
Contact Lumber Co.												■	■								■		
Contemporary Structures																		■			■	■	
Crawford's Old House Store														■							■		
Creative Building Products					■																■	■	
Cumberland Woodcraft		■	■	■		■		■				■	■	■						■		■	
Curvoflite Stairs and Millwork		■	■	■			■	■				■	■	■			■	■	■			■	
Custom Decorative Mouldings			■	■	107	■	■						■								■		957
Custom Doors & Drawers			■	■		■	■	■				■	■						■	■	■	■	
Custom Wood Turnings			■											■							■		
CW Ohio			■																		■		
David Mulder-Custom Built Circular Stairs																■		■				■	
Dean Hardwood			■			■						■	■						■	■	■	■	
Deer Park Stairbuilding/Millwork			■									■				■	■	■	■			■	
Delaware Industries/Baseway Products	■		■			■	■	■													■	■	
Dixie-Pacific Mfg. Co.	■		■											■							■		
Driwood Moulding Co.			■	■	■	■	■					■	■	■			■	■	■			■	
DuPont Co./Corian Products	■		■			■			■											■	■		
Dura Art Stone									■													■	
Duvinage Corp.																	■	■			■		
Eastern Stair Builders																		■	■	■	■		
Eastern Timber Homes			■																		■		
Elegant Entries														■						■	■	■	

Products — **Sales** — **Circle No.**

See Manufacturer Index (beige pages at the back of this issue) for address and phone information.   Numbers in red indicate page number for additional product information.

Manufacturer	Columns, composite	Columns, metal	Columns, wood	Cornices	Custom millwork	Door surrounds	Gingerbread	Louvers	Mantels	Moulding, flexible	Moulding, plaster	Moulding, plastic	Moulding, veneer	Moulding, wood	Paneling	Stair parts	Stairs, attic	Stairs, circular & spiral	Stairs, pre-built	Wainscoting	Local dealer/distributor	Factory-direct	Circle No.
Emco Specialties														■									
Entol Industries			■				■					■										■	
EPS Molders Assn.	■				■																		
Escon Corp.					■									■							■		
Executive Woodsmiths				■	■			■					■	■					■			■	
Federal Wood Products					■								■								■	■	
Felber Ornamental Plastering Corp.			■						■													■	
Ferche Millwork														■							■		
Fibreform Wood Products														■							■		
Flex Molding	■		■		■			■	■							■					■	■	
Flex Trim Industries	■		■						■				■								■	■	
FLEXCO Co.														■							■		
Foreign & Domestic Woods														■							■		
Forest Products Society														■							■		
Formglas	■	■		■		■					■											■	
Fort Smith Rim & Bow														■	■						■		
Fypon	106		■	■	■	■	■	■	■			■			■						■		950
G R Plastics/(Nu-Wood)					■		■	■	■														
George Guenzler & Sons			■													■						■	
Georgia-Pacific Corp.	■			■	■		■	■				■	■	■				■	■		■		
Gerber Industries														■							■	■	
Gibco Services		■			■		■						■	■				■	■		■		
Glen Oak Lumber & Milling														■	■						■		
Goddard Circular & Spiral Stair																■		105				■	947
Golden Log Homes/CMB Inc.								■								■							
Goodwin Heart Pine Co.				■	■			■						■	■				■		■	■	
Gossen Corp.			■						■		■			■							■		
Great Lake Woods					■		■	■			■		■	■					■		■		
HA Stiles Co.		■		■										■		■					■	■	
Hafele America														■							■		
Hardwood Distributors Assn.				■										■		■			■		■	■	
Hardwood Plywood & Veneer Assn.												■		■									
Hardwoods Millworking					■								■	■	■				■		■		
Harmonson Stairs																■		■	■			■	
Harry Wolsky Stairbuilders																■		■	■			■	
HB & G	■		■		■			■				■									■		278
Heritage Stair Co.																■		■				■	
Holiday Kitchens /(Mastercraft Industries)												■								■	■		
Holland Log Homes Mfg. Co.					■			■				■	■					■	■	■	■		
Homer Wood Corp.												■	■						■		■		
Hyde Park Fine Art of Moulding	■				■			■	■													■	
Ideal Wood Products					■									■								■	
Inova										■											■	■	
International Paper Co.														■							■		
International Wood Products Assn.		■	■	■	■									■									
The Iron Shop																		106				■	951
JD's Glassworks		■			■																■	■	
JELD-WEN of White Swan														■							■		
JMS Wood Products			■					■						■		■					■		
Kentucky Millwork			■	■	■			■						■		■		■	■		■		
Keystone Wood Products							■														■		
Keystone Wood Specialties														■							■	■	
KML Windows							■							■							■		

See Manufacturer Index (beige pages at the back of this issue) for address and phone information. Numbers in red indicate page number for additional product information. continued

Moulding & Millwork

Manufacturer	Columns, composite	Columns, metal	Columns, wood	Cornices	Custom millwork	Door surrounds	Gingerbread	Louvers	Mantels	Moulding, flexible	Moulding, plaster	Moulding, plastic	Moulding, veneer	Moulding, wood	Paneling	Stair parts	Stairs, attic	Stairs, circular & spiral	Stairs, pre-built	Wainscoting	Local dealer/distributor	Factory-direct	Circle No.
Koch & Co.																				■	■	■	
Kolbe & Kolbe Millwork Co.			■	■										■							■		
KraftMaid Cabinetry														■							■		
L.J. Smith															106						■		952
Lake Shore Stair Co.																■	■	■	■		■		
Lavi Industries																■					■	■	
Leslie-Locke		■						■													■	■	
Lianga Pacific													■	■							■		
Logcrafters Log & Timber Homes			■				■												■			■	
Lovell Lumber Co.															■						■		
LTL Home Products								■													■	■	
LWO Corp.																				■	■		
M.L. Condon Co.			■	■	■	■		■						■	■					■	■	■	
MacMillan Bloedel/Building Materials Mktg.														■							■		
Mansion Millwork/(A Div. of MHJ Group)			■	■	■										■						■		
Marell Industries	■																				■		
Markus Cabinet Mfg. Co.									■					■				■			■		
The Marwin Co.																	■				■		
Mayse Woodworking Co.				■											■							■	
McShan Lumber Co.			■	■									■	■	■			■			■		
Mellco		■			■																■		
Melton Classics	105	■	■																		■	■	944
Mid-America Building Products/(Tapco)					■			■	■				■							■	■		
Mid Continent Cabinetry//(A Div. of Norcraft)														■							■	■	
Mill River Lumber												■											
Millfab				■										■	■					■	■		
The Millwork Store	■	■	■	■	■	■	■	■	■	■				■	■			■		■	■	■	
The Millworks				■		■		■						■						■	■	■	
Milton W. Bosley Co.	■		■	■	■	■			■	■				■						■	■	■	
MIM Architecturals					■					■		■		■		■	■				■		
Missoula White Pine Sash Co.					■									■							■		
Monumental Construction and Moulding Co.		■	■					■	■	■	■										■		
Moose Creek Lumber Co.																				■		■	
Morgan Products					■			■						■							■		
Moulding Associates																	■				■		
Mouldings & Millwork												■	■								■		
Moultrie Mfg.		■																			■		
Mountain Lumber Co.														■							■	■	
Mt. Taylor Millwork														■							■		
MW Windows/MW Manufacturers					■																■		
Mylen Industries																■			■		■		
Myro									■												■	■	
National Assn. of Architectural Metal Mfrs.																■		■					
National Sash & Door Jobbers Assn.	■	■	■	■	■	■	■	■	■	■	■	■	■	■	■	■	■	■	■	■	■		
New Concept Louvers								■													■		
New-Tech Architectural Moulding		■		■						■											■		
Nicolai Doors						■															■		
NMC-Focal Point	■			■					■	■					■						■	■	
Nor-Cal Moulding Co.														■						■	■		
Northcutt Woodworks														■							■		
Oakwood Classic & Custom Woodworks			■	■				■						■	■					■	■		
The Old Wagon Factory					■																		
Oregon Lumber Co.							■								■						■	■	

See Manufacturer Index (beige pages at the back of this issue) for address and phone information. Numbers in red indicate page number for additional product information.

Manufacturer	Columns, composite	Columns, metal	Columns, wood	Cornices	Custom millwork	Door surrounds	Gingerbread	Louvers	Mantels	Moulding, flexible	Moulding, plaster	Moulding, plastic	Moulding, veneer	Moulding, wood	Paneling	Stair parts	Stairs, attic	Stairs, circular & spiral	Stairs, pre-built	Wainscoting	Local dealer/distributor	Factory-direct	Circle No.
Oregon Wooden Screen Doors					■		■															■	
Ornamental Mouldings		■			■				■	■				■							■		953
P&M Cedar Products														■					■		■		
Pacific Wood Laminates			■										■					■			■		
Pagliacco Turning & Milling	■		■		■	■								■							■	■	
Particleboard/MDF Institute														■									
Pearl Mantels									■												■		
Pemko Mfg. Co.														105							■	■	942
Penn Wood Products														■					■		■	■	
Petmal Supply Co.			■						■										■		■	■	
Piedmont Home Products													■					■					
Pinecrest						■	■															■	
Plastival										■											■	■	
Ply Gem Mfg.											■								■		■	■	
Plylap Industries					■									■							■	■	
Plywood Tropics USA														■							■	■	
Ponderosa Mouldings/(A Div. of JELD-WEN)														■							■	■	
Prefinished Millwork Corp.														■							■		
Prime Wood Products					■									■							■	■	
PrimeWood						■								■	■				■		■		
PS Aluminum Products		■																■			■		
Quality American					■						■								■		■	■	
Rainier Wood Products					■																■	■	
Rare Earth Hardwoods					■				■					■	■	■					■	■	
RAS Industries			■	■	■	■	■			■											■		
Ray White Lumber Co.														■									
Raymond Enkeboll		■							■					■	■							■	
Readybuilt Products Co.									■													■	
ResinArt Corp.										■													
Robbins Lumber							■														■		
Rocky Mountain Forest Products Corp.					■									■							■	■	
Roland Boulanger & Co.					■									■							■		
Romatt Doors					■					■	■		■						■		■	■	
Rossi Corp.										■			■									■	
RSL Woodworking Products							■			■											■		
Ryan Forest Products/(Kenora Forest Prod.)														■							■	■	
Sauder Wood Products		■			■	■				■									■		■		
Schluter Systems												■				■				■			
Sioux Veneer Panel Co.			■	■						■	■									■			
Smith Millwork			■	■						■				■						■	■		
Southern Pine Council														■	■					■			
Southern Staircase																■	105	■			■	■	940
Spiral Mfg.																■	■	■				■	
Spiral Spindles and Turning																■					■		
Spiral Stairs of America																	■	■				■	
Stair-Pak Products Co.																	106	■			■		955
Stair Parts																■					■		
Stair Works																■						■	
Staircase									■							■		■			■	■	
Staircase & Millwork Corp.																■	107	■			■	■	959
Stairways																■	105	■			■		945
Stairworld	■		■													■	■	■				■	
States Industries													■								■		

See Manufacturer Index (beige pages at the back of this issue) for address and phone information.   Numbers in red indicate page number for additional product information.   continued

Moulding & Millwork

Manufacturer	Columns, composite	Columns, metal	Columns, wood	Cornices	Custom millwork	Door surrounds	Gingerbread	Louvers	Mantels	Moulding, flexible	Moulding, plaster	Moulding, plastic	Moulding, veneer	Moulding, wood	Paneling	Stair parts	Stairs, attic	Stairs, circular & spiral	Stairs, pre-built	Wainscoting	Local dealer/distributor	Factory-direct	Circle No.
Stephan Mfg.				●									●	●							●	●	
Stepstone																		●					
Steptoe & Wife Antiques															●		●	●	●		●	●	
Stromberg's Architectural Products	●		●			●																●	
Style-Mark			●	●	●	●	●		●		●									●	●		
Sunset Moulding Co.			●	●									●							●			
Superior Aluminum Products		●																			●	●	
Superior Hardwoods & Millwork		●		●					●				●	●	●					●		●	
Superior Wood Shelving			●																			●	
Taney Corp.															●	●		●	●		●		
TDS									●														
Tecton Industries																●							
Texas Kiln Products				●					●							●						●	
TFI Corp./Cornice Div.			●																		●		
Thulman Eastern Corp.									●														
Thunderbird Moulding Co.														●								●	
Tiffany Stair Co.																●		●	●		●	●	
Timberhouse Post & Beam									●													●	
Tri-Guards								●													●		
Trojan Board/Forest Pride													●	●	●						●		
Turncraft	●	●														●					●		
Turning Point (A Div. of JELD-WEN)		●														●					●	●	
Ultra-Flex Moulding Co.										●											●		
Unity Hardwood														●									
Universal Plastics												●									●	●	
USP Lumber Connectors							●														●		
Vintage Mantle Co.									107												●	●	958
Vintage Wood Works			●	●		●	●		●					●						●	●		
Vixen Hill Mfg. Co.								●													●		
Weaber														●							●		
Werner Co.																	●				●		
Western Wood Products Assn.		●											●	●	●					●	●		
White River Hardwoods-Woodworks			●	●	●				●					●							●		
Whittlesey Wood Products												●									●		
Willamette Industries/Duraflake Division														●							●	●	
Windsor Mill													●	●							●	●	
Wisconsin Log Homes									●												●	●	
Wood Component Manufacturers Assn.				●										●		●							
Wood Factory			●	●			●		●					●		●				●		●	
Wood Floors																●							
Wood Moulding & Millwork Producers Assn		●	●	●	●	●	●					●		●						●	●		
Woodfold-Marco Mfg.														●							●		
Woodline Mfg.													●								●	●	
WoodMaster Designs			●		●				●					●							●	●	
The Woods Co.			●										●	●	●					●	●		
Woodsmiths Design & Mfg.																●		●	●		●		
Woodwork Institute of California		●	●	●	●	●	●		●			●	●	●	●			●	●	●			
Worthington Group	106	●							●													●	948
York Spiral Stair																●		●	●		●		
Yuba River Moulding & Millwork			●											●							●		
Zago Mfg.			●				●					●										●	
Zepsa Stairs																●		●	●			●	

SCHWERD MFG.

Traditional wood columns since 1860. Available from 4" to 50" diameter up to 35 feet long. Matching pilasters and 14 styles of capitals. Maintenance-free aluminum bases are available for exterior columns. Custom work done. Free catalog. Schwerd Mfg.
Circle No. 939

CAD DRAWINGS • DESIGN ASSISTANCE

"Enhance Your Reputation."

Southern Staircase

"Professionals Serving Professionals"

Call Toll Free 1-800-874-8408
Fax 1-770-664-7521
http://www.atl.mindspring.com/~stairs/

Circle No. 940

CHADSWORTH'S 1.800.COLUMNS

Unique 44-page color IDEA BOOK features an exciting collection of column projects from Classic to Contemporary for interiors and exteriors. IDEA BOOK Portfolio also includes Columns Product Portfolio. All this for $10 plus $3 p/h or Column Product Portfolio $5 with credit on first order. Wood, fiberglass, polyester. Competitive prices. Free flier. One call does it all...1.800.COLUMNS. Fax: 910.763.3191. **Circle No. 941**

PEMKO MANUFACTURING

Pemko offers a broad line of millwork sills, door bottom shoes/sweeps, kerfin, rigid and adhesive gasketing and locking astragals. New products include: water-return sills, locking astragals for outswing doors and wood astragals for 1-3/8" & 1-3/4" doors. For catalog call (800) 283-9988.
Circle No. 942

Millwork...Millwork...Millwork...

ACCENT MILLWORKS

Accent Millwork's Redwood cupolas and louvers give a home BEAUTY and DISTINCTION. Cupolas add spice to a dull roof line while providing ventilation in attics in partnership with our Redwood louvers. Four and six-sided cupolas are in stock. One-of-a-kind specials quoted. Call (800) 533-9105 for brochure. **Circle No. 943**

MELTON CLASSICS, INC.

Melton Classics proudly introduces *maintenance-free* **MarbleTex**™ synthetic stone balustrades and columns with integral color that requires no painting. Other Melton column products include:
- Redwood Classic ™
- Hardwood Classic™ Stain Grade
- DuraClassic™ Poly/Marble
- FRP Classic™ Fiberglass

Call 800-963-3060 or Fax 770-962-6988.
Circle No. 944

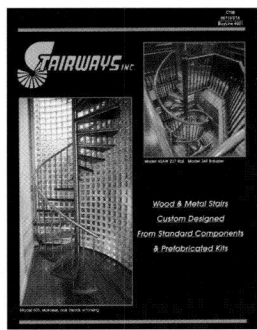

STAIRWAYS, INC.

Create a major focal point with beauty, quality and economy in a fully fabricated unit. Our stairways are built one step at a time from steel, wood, aluminum, stainless and brass. Any diameter or height, and can be installed in minutes. Also, check out our new brochure. (800) 231-0793.
Circle No. 945

MODEL 26

BESSLER STAIRWAY COMPANY

An excellent choice for the new home or as a replacement for worn-out folding attic stairs. Bessler is a *one-piece sliding stairway*...not a folding attic ladder! For a complete catalog and additional information, please contact Bessler Customer Service at (901) 360-1900, FAX (901) 795-1253 or visit our web site at www.bessler.com.
Circle No. 946

GODDARD MANUFACTURING

SPIRAL STAIRS, custom designed, handcrafted to your specifications. Choose from several different designs. Welded steel construction. All-wood classic oak stair features oak steps, handrails, and solid oak or pine center pole. Exterior stair is both practical and beautiful. Goddard MFG., Inc., Box 502, Dept. HW-B, Logan, KS 67646. (913) 689-4341. **Circle No. 947**

WORTHINGTON GROUP, LTD.

Columns and Architectural Details
Research and development has allowed Worthington to fill Builders' needs with leading products in each category. Products are strategically chosen for endurance, precision, ease of installation and price. Columns, Balustrading, Mantels, Moulding, Medallions and more. Call for our catalog. Buy direct and save. Job site delivery and technical support a phone call away. **Call- 1-800-872-1608. Circle No. 948**

ARCWAYS, INC.
For over a quarter of a century, Arcways has created premium quality staircases for discriminating builders across America. Job site delivery, installation assistance, pre-fit balustrades and shop drawings were pioneered and perfected by Arcways. Call or write for our free curved stair planning guide. It shows you how to satisfy your customers and increase your profits by designing an Arcways Curved Stair into practically any floor plan. (800) 558-5096. **Circle No. 949**

DON'T BUILD WITHOUT IT!™
Fypon, Inc. is the manufacturer of over 3,500 different millwork shapes. Cast from high density polymer in the exclusive Molded Millwork® process, they do not rot and are virtually maintenance free. Products include entrance features, brackets, balustrade systems, polymer/steel columns and posts. Contact FYPON for 124 page catalog. FYPON, Inc., 22 W. PA Ave., Stewartstown, PA 17363. 1-800-537-5349. **Circle No. 950**

THE IRONSHOP®
Since 1931, THE IRON SHOP has enjoyed a reputation for outstanding design and value in spiral stairs, making them "The Leading Manufacturer of Spiral Stair Kits™." Their superbly designed kits are available in Steel, Oak, Cast Aluminum, and Custom Welded Units. Call for a free color catalog 1-800-523-7427, ext. B07, or visit them on the Internet at http://www.theironshop.com
Circle No. 951

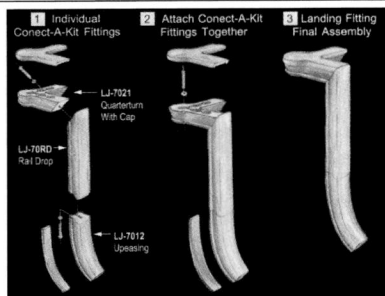

L.J. SMITH STAIR SYSTEMS
L.J. Smith introduces the patented Conect-A-Kit® method of assembling and installing handrail fittings. This unique new method will allow tremendous flexibility in the number of installation applications obtainable with each fitting. Left and right turns are made with the same fitting. No rail bolts needed. The biggest advantages of this exciting new product are time and labor savings. Videotape available.
Circle No. 952

ORNAMENTAL MOULDINGS
Ornamental® Mouldings offers a complete line of solid hardwood mouldings – traditional, architecturally correct, and beautifully designed mouldings and accessories. Specialties include dentil and embossed patterns. All are available in white hardwood, most in red oak. Custom species quoted. Accessories include carved corbels, pilasters and capitals, corner and plinth blocks, pediments and decorative trim. (800) 779-1135. **Circle No. 953**

SET YOUR HOMES APART WITH NU-WOOD
We can help you design unique entrance systems and other millwork features which will give you a marketing advantage. Contact us at 1-800-526-1278 for more information. **Circle No. 954**

STAIR-PAK ALL-WOOD SPIRALS
An elegant all-wood spiral adds a quality touch. Not only a stair, it's a fine piece of furniture. Enhance the value of your family living as you add value to your home. Make a fine investment. For information, 800/854-5100, Fax 908/688-1209. **Circle No. 955**

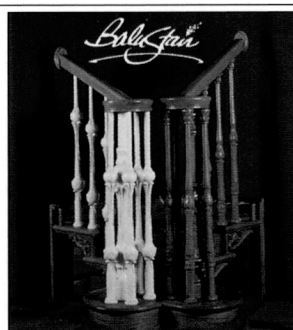

CLASSIC ARCHITECTURAL SPECIALTIES
Classic Architectural Specialties offers the broadest selection of uncommon architectural features in the U.S. Shown above, our new Balustair System featuring highly decorative poly/resin with a steel core for stain or paint. 3223 Canton St., Dallas, TX 75226. (800) 662-1221. **Circle No. 956**

CUSTOM DECORATIVE MOULDINGS

If you are replacing ornamental millwork or adding character to existing construction, CDM architectural features are the solution. Our polyurethane millwork may be installed with the factory finish or easily recoated with quality paint. CDM will not warp or rot, is impervious to insects, and is the leader with price, quality and availability. Call for free 1997 color catalog. (800) 543-0553 or (302) 349-4937. FAX: (302) 349-4816. **Circle No. 957**

VINTAGE MANTLE CO.

The Dubonnet is one of a full line of mantels that add elegance to your fireplace. Easy to assemble and manufactured from either oak or poplar, our mantels are made to fit the specifications of each individual fireplace and priced with a builder in mind. Call for a free brochure. Vintage Mantle Co. (918) 254-0800. **Circle No. 958**

ENGINEERED WOOD SIDING

LOUISIANA-PACIFIC

Louisiana-Pacific's engineered wood siding combines the look of natural cedar with enhanced performance at an affordable price. Our new formula and manufacturing process add strength and durability and our new ACI® edge coating is an L-P exclusive. Primed and ready to install in 6" and 8" widths, and in 16' lengths, L-P backs our engineered wood siding with a limited 25-year warranty. **Call (800) 299-0029, ext. 4016 for a free brochure and distributor information.**

$2433 STAIRCASE & MILLWORK DIRECT TO BUILDERS
(parts sold separate FOB Atlanta)

Supported 14 rise standard, single open 42" with solid oak treads. **100+ stock designs. Order from FREE CATALOG.** Over lay to fit your plan or custom designed to your specs. Improve marketability – increase your profits – SAVE $$$$ – premium quality, **(800) 236-1736**. **Circle No. 959**

SIDING

ABTco

UltraOak is a prefinished moulding made from a polystyrene substrate with a woodgrain design that duplicates the beauty, richness and elegance of solid oak. BUILDERS appreciate the fact that UltraOak is easier to work with than hardwood and about half the cost of real oak. ABTco's UltraOak installs like wood, but without problems such as warping, splitting or cracking. Builders who want more information on UltraOak can call 1-800-521-4250 for their nearest ABTco dealer. **Circle No. 963**

Decorative Windows & Glass

ARE YOU TIRED OF CLEAR GLASS AND BRASS??

Give your front entryway a new look, or add style and elegance to your new home with leaded stained glass. All stained glass comes with an original owner lifetime warranty against fogging & is in a tempered, sealed thermal pane unit. With 3 different sizes (Halfglass, Ovalglass, & Full glass) and 30 colors & styles to choose from, our stock items provide a wide variety. Custom designs, patterns & colors are also available. For more information, call, fax or write Campbell Stained Glass, 13 McKissic Creek Ctr., Bentonville, AR 72712. Phone/Fax: (501) 273-9139. **Circle No. 792**

PAINTS, STAINS & SEALANTS

Minwax: Water-based wood stain is offered in a range of colors including burgundy, hunter green, black, orange, red, blue, and gold. Applies with brush to interior wood surfaces; comes in quart containers. *Accents.* 1-800-526-0495. *Circle no. 183.*

Sherwin-Williams: Semi-gloss enamel finish has been added to line of stain-resistant latex wall paint. Available in more than 600 colors. *EverClean.* 1-800-336-1110. *Circle no. 186.*

Cabot Stains: Acrylic finish is made for use on trim and siding including vinyl, aluminum, brick, and masonry. Mildew-resistant formula cleans up with soap and water. *Cabot Finish.* 1-800-US-STAIN. *Circle no. 184.*

Parks: Polyurethane finish is offered in a semi-gloss formula that dries in 30 minutes. Can be applied over shellac, lacquer, and enamels; cleans up with water. *Carver Tripp Super Poly.* 1-800-225-8543. *Circle no. 185.*

Dow Corning: Water-based silicone coating covers cracks and flaws in concrete and exterior insulation finishing systems. Features matte finish that hides roller marks. *AllGuard.* 1-800-248-2481. *Circle no. 187.*

NOT PICTURED

H&C Concrete Stain: Silicone acrylic stain protects masonry and concrete surfaces. Will not peel, flake, or fade, and does not require a primer. Available in a variety of ready-mixed colors. 1-800-TO-STAIN. *Circle no. 188.*

Paints, Caulks & Adhesives

Manufacturer	Adhesives	Butyl caulks/sealants	Cleaners/strippers	Finishes/sealers	Latex caulks/sealants	Paint, exterior	Paint, interior	Paint removers/thinners	Painting tools	Polyurethane caulks/sealants	Silicone caulks/sealants	Stains/varnishes	Textured paints/finishes	Water repellents for wood	Local dealer/distributor	Factory-direct	Circle No.
The 3E Group	■		■		■									■	■	■	
Abatron	■														■	■	
ABC Seamless Siding									■								
Abilene Research & Development Corp.			■		■	■						■					
Abisko Mfg.	■							■							■		
ABT Building Products Corp./ABTco	■														■		
AC Products	■	■			■					■	■				■		
Ace Hardware Corp.			■			■	■								■		
Adhesive Technologies	■														■		
Advanced Design Products							■								■		
Afco Industries	■														■	■	
Akzo Nobel Coatings			■			■	■					■			■		
Aldon Corp.			■											■	■		
Allway Tools									■						■		
American Olean Tile	■														■		
Andek Chemical Corp.	■							■							■	■	
Basic Coatings				113								■			■		961
Benjamin Moore & Co.						■	■					■					
BiWood Flooring	■		■														
Bladesmith									■						■		
Boiardi Products Corp.	■									■	■					■	
BonaKemi USA			■								■				■		
Bondex Intl.	■												■		■	■	
Bostik/Tile & Flooring Group	■			■							■				■		
Brushtech									■						■	■	
C-Cure Corp.	■			■											■		
Capitol Adhesives	■														■		
Ceilings & Interior Systems Const. Assn.							■										
Certified Technologies		■							■						■	■	
Chemque	■									■	■				■	■	
Chemstone									■						■		
Cleform Tool Co.									■						■		
Consolidated Coatings Corp.						■	■	■							■	■	
Convenience Products	■							■							■	■	
Craft-Bilt Mfg. Co.											■				■		
Cuprinol		■										■		■	■		
Custom Building Products	■	■	■								■				■		

See Manufacturer Index (beige pages at the back of this issue) for address and phone information.   Numbers in red indicate page number for additional product information.

Paints, Caulks & Adhesives

Manufacturer	Adhesives	Butyl caulks/sealants	Cleaners/strippers	Finishes/sealers	Latex caulks/sealants	Paint, exterior	Paint, interior	Paint removers/thinners	Painting tools	Polyurethane caulks/sealants	Silicone caulks/sealants	Stains/varnishes	Textured paints/finishes	Water repellents for wood	Local dealer/distributor	Factory-direct	Circle No.
Daly's Wood Finishing Products			■	■								■		■	■	■	
Dampney Co.				■		■									■	■	
DAP	■	■	■	■	■	■	■			■	■			■	■		
Darworth Co.	■			■							■				■		
Daubert Coated Products						■											
De Neef Construction Chemicals (US)	■									■					■		
Diamondlac Corp.				■											■		
Diedrich Technologies			■											■	■	■	
Diversitech								■							■		
Dryvit Systems	■				■	■									■		
Dur-A-Flex				■					■							■	
Dutch Boy Professional Paints				■	■	■									■	■	
Dyco Paints				■	■	■	■				■	■		■	■	■	
Elmer's Products	■			■							■				■	■	
ERSystems	■	■		■						■	■					■	
Evans Adhesive	■														■		
Fabulon	■			■								■			■		
Fine Paints of Europe				■		■	■					■			■	■	
The Flecto Co.												■			■	■	
Flex Trim Industries	■														■	■	
FLEXCO Co.	■														■		
The Flood Co.			■	■											■		
Fomo Products	■									■	■				■	■	
Formica Corp.	■														■		
Franklin Intl./Const. Adhesives & Sealants	■	■		■						■	■				■	■	
Fuller-O'Brien Paints			■	■		■	■					■		■	■		
Gardner Asphalt Corp.	■			■	■										■		
GE Silicones											■				■		
Geocel Corp.	■			■					■					■	■		
Gibson-Homans Co.	■	■		■							■			■	■		
Gloucester Co.	■														■		
Grizzly Imports								■								■	
Harris Specialty Chemicals	■		■						■	■				■	■	■	
Harvey Universal/(Environmental Products)			■					■							■		
H & C Concrete Stain			■									108					188
Hilti	■															■	
Hyde & Meeks Industries								■							■	■	
Hyde Mfg.								■									
ICI Paint Stores	■	■	■	■	■	■	■	■		■	■		■		■	■	
Illbruck										■					■	■	
In Cide Technologies				■		■	■									■	
Increte Systems/(A Div. of Inco Chemical)	■			■												■	
Insta-Foam Products	■									■					■		
Insul-Binder	■			■													
Interchange Brands	■			■						■	■				■	■	
Karnak Corp.	■	■													■		
KCI Coatings			■			■	■	■				■		■	■	■	
Klean-Strip			■					■						■	■	■	
Klein Tools									■						■		
Kop-Coat				■								■		■	■		
Kraft Tool Co.									■						■	■	
Krusin Intl. Corp.									■						■	■	
L.M. Scofield Co.										■					■	■	

See Manufacturer Index (beige pages at the back of this issue) for address and phone information. Numbers in red indicate page number for additional product information.

Manufacturer	Adhesives	Butyl caulks/sealants	Cleaners/strippers	Finishes/sealers	Latex caulks/sealants	Paint, exterior	Paint, interior	Paint removers/thinners	Painting tools	Polyurethane caulks/sealants	Silicone caulks/sealants	Stains/varnishes	Textured paints/finishes	Water repellents for wood	Local dealer/distributor	Factory-direct	Circle No.
Laticrete Intl.										■					■		
Lewisohn Sales Co.		■														■	
Loctite Corp./North American Group	■									■					■		
Macco Adhesives	■			■						■					■		
Macklanburg-Duncan	■	■			■			■		■			■		■		
Mapei Corp.	■														■		
Martin-Senour			■	■	■	■				■	■		■		■		
Master Bond	■									■						■	
McGrevor Coatings			■	■		■	■		■	■	■		■		■	■	
Minwax Co.			■									108			■	■	183
Miracle Adhesives/(Div. of Pratt & Lambert)	■	■			■					■					■		
Miracle Sealants & Abrasives			■	■											■		
Multi-Seal Pacific Corp.			■					■						■	■		
Myro	■									■					■	■	
National Assn. of Floor Covering Distributors	■																
National Paint and Coatings Assn.			■		■	■				■	■	■					
Newborn Brothers Co.									■						■		
Norfield Industries									■						■	■	
Northern Paint Canada			■	■		■	■	■		■	■		■		■	■	
Norton Co.								■							■		
NPC Sealants	■	■			■				■	■					■		
Ohio Sealants	■				■				■	■					■		
Old Masters			■	■				■				■		■	■		
Olympic Paints and Stains						■	■					■			■		
Omaha Industrial Tools									■						■	■	
Orcon Corp.									■						■		
Oregon Research & Development Corp.				■		■	■							■	■		
Osmose Wood Preserving			■	■								■		■	■	■	
Palmer Industries				■		■	■							■	■		
Palmer Products Corp.	■														■	■	
Pam Fastening Technology	■														■	■	
Parex				■		■						■			■		
Parks Corp.			■	108			■	■		■					■	■	185
Patrick Ind.	■														■		
Penofin-Performance Coatings				■											■		
Perma-Chink Systems				■	■												
PL Adhesives & Sealants/ChemRex	■	■			■			■	113	■					■	■	960
Plasti-Kote Co.			■	■		■				■							
Plastics & Resins			■			■							■	■	■	■	
Portable Products									■							■	
PPG Industries			■	■		■	■					■			■		
Prairie Home Products							■										
Pratt & Lambert				■		■	■						■				
Pro/Cote				■		■	■								■		
Proko Industries				■	■	■	■						■		■		
ProSoCo.			■	■				■			■				■		
Radiator Specialty Co.					■						■				■	■	
RC Musson Rubber Co.	■														■		
Red Devil	■	■			■			■	■	■					■	■	
RHH Foam Systems										■					■		
Safe Alternatives Sales Group							■						■				
Samax Enterprises			■				■								■		
Samuel Cabot (Cabot Stains)			■	■		■		■				■		■	■	■	

See Manufacturer Index (beige pages at the back of this issue) for address and phone information.   Numbers in red indicate page number for additional product information.   continued

Paints, Caulks & Adhesives

Manufacturer	Adhesives	Butyl caulks/sealants	Cleaners/strippers	Finishes/sealers	Latex caulks/sealants	Paint, exterior	Paint, interior	Paint removers/thinners	Painting tools	Polyurethane caulks/sealants	Silicone caulks/sealants	Stains/varnishes	Textured paints/finishes	Water repellents for wood	Local dealer/distributor	Factory-direct	Circle No.
Sansher Corp.			■				■								■		
Sashco Sealants	■			■											■	■	
Sheffield Bronze Paint Corp.			■		■	■	■								■		
The Sherwin-Williams Co.			■	■	108		■				■	■	■				186
Simpson Strong-Tie Co.	■														■		
The Society of the Plastics Industry									■						■		
Sonneborn/ChemRex	■			■						■	■				■		
Specialty Tools & Fasteners Distrib. Assn.									■						■		
Standard Tar Products Co.			■			■	■					■		■	■	■	
Stanley Tools									■						■	■	
Steel & Wire Products Co.	■	■		■					■	■					■		
STO Finish Systems/(A Div. of STO Corp.)	■		■			■	■								■		
Stuc-O-Flex Intl.	■			■									■		■	■	
Super-Tek Products	■		■	■							■		■		■	■	
Surebond	■	■	■	■						■	■			■	■		
Synthetic Surfaces	■								■							■	
TACC Intl.	■	■		■					■	■					■	■	
Tarheel Wood Treating Co.	■										■	■		■	■		
TEC/(A Sub. of HB Fuller Co.)	■			■											■		
Thomas Waterproof Coatings Co.				■											■		
Todol Products	■								■						■		
Trend Coatings			■		■		■								■	■	
Tufco											■						
United Gilsonite Laboratories (UGL)			■	■	■		■				■	■	■		■		
Unwallpaper Co.									■							■	
US Sky/(A Div. of Stora Enterprises Co.)											■					■	
W.J. Ruscoe Co.	■														■		
Wagner Spray Tech Corp.									■						■		
Wagoner Floor Safety Systems			■	■												■	
Wall Firma				■											■	■	
Wallboard Tool Co.									■						■		
Welco Mfg. Co.									■		■		■			■	
Werner Co.									■						■		
White Lightning Products	■			■						■					■	■	
William Zinsser & Co.			■	■		■	■	■				■			■		
Wolman Wood Care Products				■								■		■	■		
Wood-Kote Products			■	■				■				■			■	■	
Woodcraft Supply				■					■			■					
Xypex Chemical Corp.				■													
Yenkin Majestic			■	■	■	■	■		■			■	■		■		
Z-Brick Brands	■	■		■						■		■		■	■	■	

See Manufacturer Index (beige pages at the back of this issue) for address and phone information. Numbers in red indicate page number for additional product information.

PRO TECT MIRACLE COVER

Pro Tect Miracle Cover is a water-based silicone rubber solution that seals a multitude of surfaces with just one coat. It offers maximum water repellence for wood, concrete, masonry, plastic, asphalt, metal, concrete brick, rubber, canvas and more. Guaranteed for up to 20 years to substantially prolong the life of any porous surface. **Pro Tect Associates Inc.** 1-800-545-0826. **Circle No. 960**

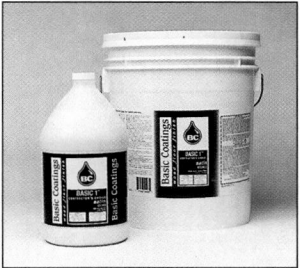

WOOD FLOOR FINISH SYSTEMS BY BASIC COATINGS

Basic 1, by Basic Coatings, is a single component wood floor finishing system designed specifically for the new construction market. This revolutionary wood floor finish combines all the benefits of both water based and solvent based systems by offering easy application, low odor and quick dry times. Basic 1 reduces job time while containing costs. For more information on this and other quality Basic Coatings wood floor finishes, call 800-247-5471. **Circle No. 961**

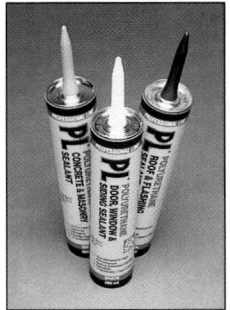

PROFESSIONAL GRADE PL® POLYURETHANE SEALANTS

PL® has introduced a new job-specific line which includes PL® Polyurethane Roof & Flashing Sealant, Concrete and Masonry Sealant, and Door, Window & Siding Sealant. It's paintable, sandable and waterproof, and has tremendous adhesion and flexibility. For more information, call (800) 433-9517. **Circle No. 962**

Plumbing Supplies

Manufacturer	ABS	Cast iron	Cement	Copper	CPVC	Flexible gas pipe	Plumbing accessories	Polybutylene	Polyethylene pipe/fittings	PVC	Local dealer/distributor	Factory-direct	Circle No.
Accurate Industries Steambath and Sauna							■				■		
Alro Plumbing Specialty Co.		■		■							■		
American Wall Tie Co.							■						
Anchortek							■				■		
Aqua-Flo							■				■	■	
B&K Industries							■				■		
BF Goodrich					■							■	
Brass Craft Mfg./(A Div. of Masco Corp.)				■			■	■		■			
Brushtech							■				■	■	
Cast Iron Soil Pipe Institute		■					■						
Cerro Copper Products				■									
CertainTeed Corp. Pipe & Plastics Group										■	■		
Charlotte Pipe and Foundry Co.	■	■		■						■	■		
Cresline Plastic Pipe				■					■	■	■		
Drain Frame							■				■		
Dura-Line Corp.									■				
Enerjee							■				■	■	
Fluidmaster							■				■		
Genova Products				■			■	■	■	■	■		
Hindley Mfg. Co.							■				■		
Holdrite Brackets							■				■		
Hoyme Mfg.							■				■	■	
La-Co Industries							■				■		
Lasco Fluid Distribution Products				■						■	■		
Leonard Valve Co.							■				■		
Mansfield Plumbing Products							■				■	■	
Melard Mfg. Corp.							■						
NIBCO			■	■						■	■		
Parker Hannifin Corp.										■	■	■	
Plastic Pipe & Fittings Assn.	■			■				■	■	■			
Plastic Tubing									■		■	■	
Plumb Pak Corp.							■				■		
Plumb Shop		■		■			■						
Plumbing Manufacturers Institute	■	■	■	■	■	■	■			■			
Prairie Home Products			■	■			■	■			■		
Radiator Specialty Co.							■				■	■	
Robert Mfg. Co.							■				■		

> Male home shoppers are willing to commute an average of 35 minutes and 25 miles to get the type of house they want; female home shoppers will travel 30 minutes and 20 miles.
>
> *Source: What Today's Home Buyers Want/NAHB and Fulton Research*

See Manufacturer Index (beige pages at the back of this issue) for address and phone information.   Numbers in red indicate page number for additional product information.

114

Manufacturer	ABS	Cast iron	Cement	Copper	CPVC	Flexible gas pipe	Plumbing accessories	Polybutylene	Polyethylene pipe/fittings	PVC	Local dealer/distributor	Factory-direct	Circle No.
	Products										**Sales**		
Sinkmaster/Anaheim Mfg. Co.							■						
Sioux Chief Mfg.				■			■	■			■		
Strom Plumbing By Sign Of The Crab							■				■	■	
Tile Redi							■				■	■	
Titeflex Corp.						■					■		
US Brass							■	■	■	■	■		
Vanguard Industries					■	■	■			■	■		
W.H. Elevators							■				■		
Ward Mfg.		■				■					■		
Water Furnace Intl.									■		■		
Waterline Products Co.				■	■			■			■		
Waxman Industries		■	■	■	■		■			■	■	■	
Wolverine Brass	■		■	■	■	■	■	■		■	■	■	

Roofing

GAF: Laminated asphalt shingles look like cedar shakes. Oversized shingles have a UL Class A fire-resistance rating, are color blended for natural shadow effects, and come in six colors. *Grand Sequoia.* 201-628-3000. *Circle no. 134.*

Slate/Select: Tiles made of cement reinforced with glass fiber resemble slate, and they meet ASTM standards for cement roofing. Tiles are fireproof, rot resistant, freeze-thaw resistant, and impact resistant, company says. 972-276-2000. *Circle no. 137.*

Scandinavian Roofing Systems: Tiles resemble clay but are made of 24-gauge galvanized steel. PVC coating and fluorocarbon paint protect and finish tiles. Material can be applied over existing roofing. *Norman Tile.* 516-863-1333. *Circle no. 135.*

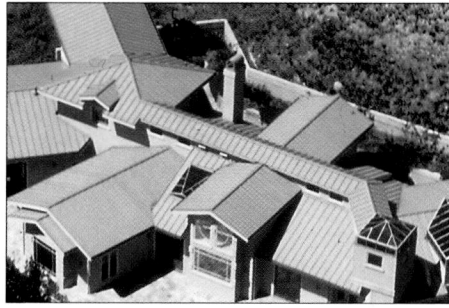

Custom-Bilt: Custom-made standing seam roof panels are of steel coated with Zincalume. Panels come in 16 colors; company can create any custom color with paint it claims resists fading, salt spray, acid rain, and ultraviolet rays. 1-800-826-7813. *Circle no. 136.*

Buckingham Virginia Slate: Natural slate comes in a blue/black color blend and has a high mica content for a bright shine. Hand-shaped shingles are $3/16$ inch thick; additional sizes are available. 804-581-1131. *Circle no. 138.*

Roofing

Manufacturer	Asphalt roll	Asphalt shingles	Built-up	Cedar	Coatings	Fiber cement	Fiberglass shingles	Flashing	Gable vents	Ice and water barriers	Metal systems	Modified bitumen	Ridge vents	Simulated slate	Slate	Soffits/other vents	Tile, ceramic/clay	Tile, concrete	Local dealer/distributor	Factory-direct	Circle No.
The 3E Group					■														■	■	
ABT Building Products Corp./ABTco								■								■			■		
ADO Products																■			■	■	
Air Vent									■				■			■			■		
ALCO - NVC				■	■	■				■	■								■		
Alcoa Building Products/Vital Statistics								■			■					■			■		
All Steel Homes											■									■	
Alsco							■			■									■		
American Cemwood Corp.					■									■					■		
American Stone-Mix				■	■														■		
Amerimax Building Products											■								■	■	
Amerimax Home Products							■									■			■		
Andek Chemical Corp.					■														■	■	
ATAS Intl.							■				■			■		■			■		
Atlas Roofing Corp.	■	■					■			■	■								■		
Benjamin Obdyke							■				■	■				■			■		
Berger Building Products Corp.							■					■				■			■		
Bethlehem Steel											■										
BHP Steel Building Products USA											■								■	■	
Bird Roofing Division	■	■	■				■			■	■								■		
Boral Lifetile																		■	■		
BPCO/(A Div. of EMCO)	■	■	■		■	■	■			■									■		
Browning Metal Products/(CertainTeed)						■	■				■			■					■		
Builders Edge						■	■				■			■					■	■	
Butler Ventamatic Corp.							■				■			■					■		
California Shake Corp.					■									■					■		
Canplas Industries							■									■			■		
Carlisle Engineered Metals											■					■				■	
Carter Holt Harvey Roofing											■									■	
Cedar Plus				■															■		
Cedar Shake & Shingle Bureau				■																	
Celadon																	■				
Cellofoam North America														■					■		
Cellwood Products/(A Div. of Stolle Corp.)							■					■							■		
The Celotex Corp.	■	■	■		■		■	■		■		■	■						■		
CertainTeed Corp./Roofing Products Group		■					■			■									■		396
Clark United Corp.					■						■					■			■	■	

Roofing

Manufacturer	Asphalt roll	Asphalt shingles	Built-up	Cedar	Coatings	Fiber cement	Fiberglass shingles	Flashing	Gable vents	Ice and water barriers	Metal systems	Modified bitumen	Ridge vents	Simulated slate	Slate	Soffits/other vents	Tile, ceramic/clay	Tile, concrete	Local dealer/distributor	Factory-direct	Circle No.
Classic Products											■		■						■		
Cobra Ventilation Products/GAF Materials		■							■	■	■		■			■			■		
Conik Group									■										■		
Consolidated Coatings Corp.	■		■		■						■	■							■	■	
Cool Attic									■				■			■			■	■	
Cor-A-Vent													121			■			■		966
Creative Building Products									■										■	■	
Curveline											■									■	
Custom-Bilt Metals								■			116									■	136
CW Ohio									■										■		
DEC-K-ING			■																■	■	
DecTec/(A Div. of Skyline Building Systems)			■																■	■	
Dura-Loc Roofing Systems											■		■						■	■	
Duradek/Ensurco Duradek (US)			■																■	■	
Dyco Paints			■																■	■	
Eastside Machine Co.											■								■		
Elk Corp.		■					■												■		
Englert											■								■	■	
EPS Molders Assn.		■																			
ERSystems					■			■				■								■	
Eternit						■								■					■		
Evergreen Slate Co.															■				■	■	
Fasco Industries									■										■		
FireFree/Quantum Roofing Materials						■						■							■		
Follansbee Steel											■								■		
GAF Materials Corp.	■		■		■		■			■	■	■							■		134
Gardner Asphalt Corp.			■		■														■		
Genova Products									■										■	■	
Georgia-Pacific Corp.	■	■	■			■	■	■	■			■				■			■		
Gerard Roofing Technologies			■						■				■						■	■	
Gibson-Homans Co.			■		■														■		
Green River			■																■		
Gregg Shakes											■									■	
GS Roofing Co.	■	■					■					■							■		
Harvey Industries		■					■					■							■	■	
The Hess Mfg. Co.											■								■	■	
Homeshield Fabricated Products								■								■			■		
Huebert Fiberboard Co.												■							■		
IKO Mfg.	■	■	■				■					■							■		
Insul-Binder																■			■		
Insul-Tray																■			■		
ITW Buildex					■														■		
James Hardie Building Products						■													■		
Joyce Mfg.											■									■	
KANT-SAG Lumber Connectors													■			■			■		
Karnak Corp.		■			■	■			■	■									■		
KenTech Plastics								■											■		
Klauer Mfg. Co.					■							■							■		
Knudson Mfg.											■								■	■	
Leigh/(A Harrow Co.)													■			■			■		
Leslie-Locke									■				■			■			■	■	
Louisiana-Pacific Corp.						121													■		
Ludowici Roof Tile																	■			■	

See Manufacturer Index (beige pages at the back of this issue) for address and phone information.   Numbers in red indicate page number for additional product information.

Products

Manufacturer	Asphalt roll	Asphalt shingles	Built-up	Cedar	Coatings	Fiber cement	Fiberglass shingles	Flashing	Gable vents	Ice and water barriers	Metal systems	Modified bitumen	Ridge vents	Simulated slate	Slate	Soffits/other vents	Tile, ceramic/clay	Tile, concrete	Local dealer/distributor	Factory-direct	Circle No.
Macklanburg-Duncan					■																
MacMillan Bloedel/Building Materials Mktg.					■														■		
MAIBEC Industries				■															■		
Majestic Forest Products Corp.					■														■		
Masco Corp.		■																	■	■	
Mason Corp.											■								■		
MaxiTile					■		■							■					■		
Met-Tile										121									■	■	967
Metal Sales Mfg. Corp.								■			■								■	■	
MFM Building Products Corp.	■		■					■		■	■	■							■		
Mid-America Building Products Corp.									■				■			■			■		
Monier									■				■					■	■		
NEI	■		■						■		■								■		
New Concept Louvers									■										■		
The Northern Roof Tile Sales Co.					■								■	■	■		■		■		
Nuline Industries											■								■	■	
O'Hagin's											■								■	■	
O'Keeffe's								■													
Ondura Corp.											■								■		
Oregon Research & Development Corp.				■						■						■			■		
Owens Corning	■	■				■					■								■	■	377,633
Palmer Industries					■				■										■		
Perma R" Products		■																	■		
Petmal Supply Co.													■						■	■	
Plastics & Resins					■														■	■	
Proko Industries					■														■		
Prudential Building Materials					■			■		■		■				■			■		
Republic Powdered Metals					■																
Resin Technology Co.					■																
Revere Copper Products											■										
RH Tamlyn & Sons								■								■			■	■	
Ro-Tile					■														■		
Roofing Industry Education Institute		■	■	■	■	■	■	■	■	■	■	■	■	■	■	■	■		■		
Sagebrush Sales	■																		■		
Sammamish Woodworks									■										■	■	
The Scandinavian Profiling Systems											116								■	■	135
Schuller Intl.	■		■	■				■				■	■		■				■	■	
Scott Cedar				■															■		
Shakertown Corp.				■															■		
Sheet Metal Mfg. Co.								■			■								■		
Slate/Select					116															■	137,537
The Society of the Plastics Industry					■																
SOLEC (Solar Energy Corp.)					■														■	■	
Sonneborn/ChemRex					■														■		
Southeastern Metals Mfg. Co./SEMCO								■	■		■		■			■			■		
Steel Tile Co.											■		■						■	■	
Stillwater Products											■								■	■	
Stirling Building Products/(Marley Roof Tile)																		■	■	■	
The Structural Slate Co.															■					■	
Stuc-O-Flex Intl.					■														■	■	
Style-Mark																■			■		
SunTuf							■												■	■	
Supradur Mfg. Co.					■														■		

Roofing

Manufacturer	Asphalt roll	Asphalt shingles	Built-up	Cedar	Coatings	Fiber cement	Fiberglass shingles	Flashing	Gable vents	Ice and water barriers	Metal systems	Modified bitumen	Ridge vents	Simulated slate	Slate	Soffits/other vents	Tile, ceramic/clay	Tile, concrete	Local dealer/distributor	Factory-direct	Circle No.
Swedish Building Systems & Components										■									■	■	
Symbold/Tropic Top Artificial Thatch										■										■	
Tamark Mfg./Life Pine Products			■																■	■	
Tamko Roofing Products	■	■	■		■		■	■		■	■								■		
Tarheel Wood Treating Co.				■															■		
Tegola USA										■									■		
Tile Master Roofing Systems										■									■		
Tri-Ply	■		■		■			■			■								■	■	
Trimline Roof Ventilation Systems													■								
Tropic Top										121										■	965
Tuff/Kote Co.					■						■								■		
U.S. Steel											■										
Universal Marble & Granite															■					■	
US Tile Co.																	■		■		
Vande Hey-Raleigh Architectural Roof Tile								■				■		■			■	■	■		
Vermont Structural Slate Co.															■					■	
VicWest Steel, US Operations											■								■	■	
Vincent Metals								■			■								■	■	
W P Hickman Co.								■												■	
Wall Firma					■	■													■	■	
Waterline Products Co.								■											■		
Weirton Steel Corp.											■									■	
Westile																		■	■		
Wheeling Corrugating Co.											■								■		
Zappone Mfg.											■								■	■	
Zion Services Corp.																■					

See Manufacturer Index (beige pages at the back of this issue) for address and phone information.   Numbers in red indicate page number for additional product information.

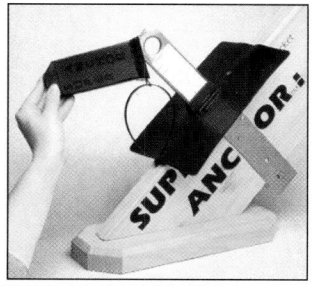

AMERICAN ROOF INC.

SUPER ANCHOR™ (U.S. Patent No. 5,370,202). Use Super Anchors as a primary component of your company's fall protection plan. Use them on every project! Provides simple, easy-to-install, anchorage points for your Framers, Roofers, Siders, Painters, Plumbers, Gutter Installers and more. Complies with OSHA Regulation. [1926.502 (d) (15)] **American Roof, Inc.** 21808 N.E. 175th Woodinville, WA 98072. **Call: (206) 488-8868 or Fax us at (360) 668-1717. After 4/30/97, our phone number will be (425) 488-8868.** **Circle No. 964**

TROPIC TOP ARTIFICIAL THATCH

At last, the demand has been met for a thatch that is virtually indestructible. Tropic Top™, a lightweight metal shingle, colorfast, 100% fireproof, installs as easily as ordinary roof shingles, and has the appearance of natural thatch without any of the disadvantages. TROPIC TOP, 2028-3 Eastbourne Way, Orlando, FL 32812. (407) 273-0069. **Circle No. 965**

VENT SYSTEMS

COR-A-VENT® is the one solution for all your ridge vent applications. With over 25 years of job proven experience and a simple straightforward design, Cor-A-Vent is the vent of choice by quality homebuilders nationwide. Instructions, technical specs., drawings and other information is available by calling (800) 837-8368 or visit our web site at "www.cor-a-vent.com". **Circle No. 966**

SOLAR ROOF VENTILATOR

NEW! Low-profile, easy to install solar-powered roof ventilator fan with a self-contained, non-breakable solar panel. No wiring necessary. The specially designed low-voltage DC motor and 5-blade fan provides for whisper quiet operation. Reduces attic heat and humidity. Also available in gable vent model. **Int'l Energy Systems Corp.,** Box 588, Barrington, IL 60011. (800) 927-0419. Fax: (847) 381-3997. **Circle No. 968**

PROTECT YOUR ROOF... JUST ADD RAIN

Shingle Shield™ protects your roof against moss, fungus and algae naturally, with rainwater. When it rains, **Shingle Shield**™ releases zinc oxide, a safe and effective natural compound which keeps moss, fungus, and algae away from your roof. **Shingle Shield**™ is easy to install and comes with a full 20-year manufacturer's warranty. **Circle No. 969**

CEMENT FIBER SHAKES

LOUISIANA-PACIFIC

Louisiana-Pacific's Nature Guard® cement fiber shakes have the classic taper, natural texture and tones of cedar shakes, with the added benefit of a Class A fire-rating. Made with a blend of renewable and recycled resources, they're an excellent alternative for re-roofing applications, as well as for new construction. Available in four colors. **Call (800) 299-0029, ext. 4011 for a free brochure.**

MET-TILE

Roofing features an exclusive, environmentally friendly coating for high performance and long life. Tile-look panels provide beautiful appearance plus protection against hurricanes (230+ mph wind rating), fires, earthquakes, pest infestation and rot. Weight: 125 lb. per square. Eight designer colors. (800) 899-0311; fax (909) 947-1510 Website: http://www.met-tile.com/roof. **Circle No. 967**

Room Enclosures

Manufacturer	Greenhouses	Passive solar systems	Porch enclosures	Storm/screen enclosures	Sunrooms	Swimming pool enclosures	Local dealer/distributor	Factory-direct	Circle No.
	Products						**Sales**		
AAA Aluminum Products			■	■		■		■	
Abundant Energy	■	■			■	■		■	
ALUMET Building Products		■	■	■	124			■	973
Amdega Machin Conservatories	■		■		■	■		■	
American Bldg. Prods./Hindman			■	■			■		
Artistic Enclosures			■	■	■			■	
Avis America		■						■	
BC Greenhouse Builders	■				■		■	■	
Brady Rooms					■		■	■	
Carolina Solar Structures	■		■	■	■	■	■	■	
Circle Redmont	■	■			■			■	
Classic Post & Beam Homes					■			■	
Classy Glass Sunrooms	■	■	■	124	■	■	■	■	972
Columbia Mfg. Co.					■	■		■	
Commonwealth Solar Rooms	■		■		■	■	■		
Contemporary Structures					■		■	■	
Craft-Bilt Mfg. Co.			■	■	■			■	
Creative Structures	■		■		■	■		■	
Duo-Gard Industries	■		■		■	■		■	
Dura-Bilt Products			■	■	■				
Evergreen Systems Sunrooms		■			■	■	■	■	
Florian Greenhouse	■	■			■	■	■	■	
Folding Shutter Corp.				■			■	■	
Four Seasons Sunrooms	■	■	■	■	■	■	■	■	
Garden Rooms by Coleman			■	■	■			■	
Gothic Arch Greenhouses	■							■	
Hardwoods Millworking		■					■		
Hartford Conservatories			■		■		■	■	974
Harvey Industries			■	■			■	■	
The Hess Mfg. Co.			■	■	■		■	■	
Holland Log Homes Mfg. Co.					■		■	■	
Houses & Barns by John Libby						■			
International Extrusions			■	■				■	
JA Nearing Co.	■				■	■	■	■	
Joyce Mfg.			■	■	■	■		■	
Legacy Timber Frames			■		■			■	
Lindal Cedar Homes/Sunrooms					■		■		

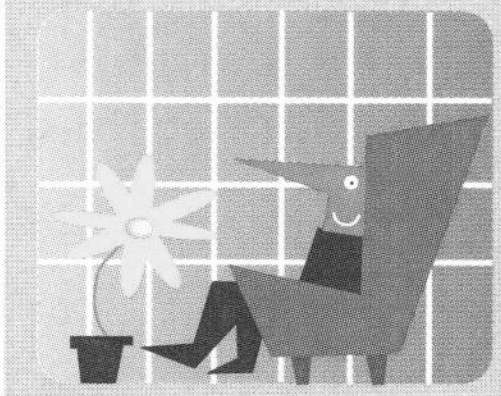

Manufacturer	Products: Greenhouses	Products: Passive solar systems	Products: Porch enclosures	Products: Storm/screen enclosures	Products: Sunrooms	Products: Swimming pool enclosures	Sales: Local dealer/distributor	Sales: Factory-direct	Circle No.
Mason Corp.			■	■	■		■		
National Mfg.			■	■			■		
National Spa and Pool Institute						■			
New England Glass Enclosures	■				■	■	■	■	
Omega Sunspaces	■	■	■		■			■	
Ondura Corp.	■		■				■		
Quality Fencing & Supply			124				■	■	971
Reynolds Metals Co.	■						■	■	
Royalston Oak Timber Frames					■	■		■	
Scatton Bros. Awning Mfg.			■	■	■			■	
Screen Manufacturers Assn.				■					
Screen Tight			■	■			■		
Screenex Design Center/(Riordan Group)				■				■	
Simpson Strong-Tie Co.	■						■		
SkyQuest	■	■	■	■	■	■		■	
Skytech Systems	■		■		■	■	■	■	
Solar Survival Architecture		■					■	■	
Southern Sales & Marketing Group	■							■	
Sun Room Co.	■				■	■	■	■	
Sunbilt Solar Products by Sussman	■	■	■	■	■	■	■	■	
Sundance Supply	■	■	■	■	■	■		■	
Sunshine Rooms	■		■		■	■	■	■	
SunTuf	■		■		■	■	■	■	
Superior Aluminum Products						■	■	■	
Thermal-Gard			■		■		■		
Thermal Industries			■	■	■		■		
Timberhouse Post & Beam	■		■		■	■		■	
Unicel					■		■	■	
US Sky/(A Div. of Stora Enterprises Co.)	■	■	■		■	■		■	
Vegetable Factory	■	■	■	■	■	■		■	
Vinyl Tech/PGT			■		■				
Vixen Hill Mfg. Co.			■					■	
Westview Products	■				■	■	■	■	
Window Saver Co.				■				■	

44% of new-home shoppers want a sunroom.

Source: What Today's Home Buyers Want/NAHB and Fulton Research

See Manufacturer Index (beige pages at the back of this issue) for address and phone information.

Numbers in red indicate page number for additional product information.

VINYL PORCH POST "FOAM FILLED"

Our posts are architecturally tested and withstood a 2000 lb. compressive load with no apparent damage. The length is 8'8" and boxed for UPS-able shipments. The entire post is filled with high density foam for strength. Colors are white, ivory or gray. Shipped Factory Direct. For more information call: (800) 633-7093. **Circle No. 971**

CLASSY GLASS STRUCTURES:
"Nature-ally" improve your bottom line. Lifetime NO-LEAK Warranty. Classy Glass can do the job that no one else can do! Our custom manufactured products offer the finest quality, and an unlimited choice of configuration; finish; size; color. Dealerships/ Factory Installation available. Contractor Discounts. Residential/Commercial. **Fax (214) 219-0348; CALL (214) 221-0445.** **Circle No. 972**

ALUMET ECLIPSE SUNROOMS

These custom, fully insulated sunrooms feature a tempered, 3/16" safety glass roof or reinforced solid roof panels with an R30 rating. Fully tempered, curved-glass front eaves are also available. Electrical raceways are U.L. Listed and the entire sunroom is backed by a 10-year limited warranty. Call 800-827-6045 or visit the Internet at **alumet.com.** **Circle No. 973**

HARTFORD CONSERVATORIES, INC.

Hartford Conservatories, Inc. offers more than a decade of experience designing and manufacturing quality hardwood conservatories. Our modular kits are easy to install, versatile, cost-effective, and offer numerous design features and options. Call for a free color brochure, price list or to inquire about how you can earn significant profits as a Hartford Conservatories dealer. (800) 963-8700. **Circle No. 974**

Siding & Accessories

Manufacturer	Aluminum	Awnings	Brick/masonry	Exterior insulation finishing systems	Fiber cement	Gutter guards	Hardboard	Oriented-strand board (OSB)	Rain carrying systems	Shutters	Siding accessories	Simulated stone veneer	Soffits/fascias	Steel	Stone	Stucco	Trim	Vinyl	Wood	Local dealer/distributor	Factory-direct	Circle No.
AAA Aluminum Products		■																		■	■	
AB Cushing Mills					■						■						■		■			
ABC Seamless Siding									■		■	131										979
ABT Building Products Corp./ABTco		■		■		■			■	■	■						■	133		■		95
AC Shutters										■												
AE Gombert Lumber Co.																			■	■		
Alcoa Building Products/Vital Statistics	■								■	■	130	■					■	133		■		98,977
Alsco	■								■	■	■						■			■		
Alside/Siding Div.	■								■	■	132	■					■	■		■	■	986
Alum-a-Pole Corp.																	■			■		
American Accent Homes				■																■		
American Bldg. Prods./Hindman		■																		■		
American Hardboard Assn.							■													■		
American Heritage Shutters										■										■		
American Roof-Brite					■															■	■	
Amerimax Building Products	■	■											■	■	■	■	■			■	■	
Amerimax Home Products						■			■				■							■		
Anchor Industries		■																		■		
Anthony Forest Products Co.																			■	■	■	
Appalachian Log Structures																			■	■		
Armor Bond Building Products											■							■		■		
Arriscraft Corp.			■												■					■		
Ashland-Davis Co.									■		■							■		■		
The Astrup Co.		■																		■		
ATAS Intl.	■												■	■		■				■		
Atlas Roofing Corp.				■																■		
Beech River Mill Corp.										■											■	
Belden Brick Co.			■																	■		
Bemis Mfg. Co./Rain Master Div.									■											■		
Bend Industries			■																	■	■	
Benjamin Obdyke	132				■				■		■									■		987
Bennett Lumber Products																			■	■		
Berger Building Products Corp.									■	■	■						■			■		
Bird Roofing Division								■												■		
Bird Vinyl Products									■	■	■							■		■		
Blumer & Stanton									■							■				■	■	
Boral Bricks			131																	■	■	983
The Brick Institute of America			■																			

See Manufacturer Index (beige pages at the back of this issue) for address and phone information.   Numbers in red indicate page number for additional product information.

continued

Siding & Accessories

Manufacturer	Aluminum	Awnings	Brick/masonry	Exterior insulation finishing systems	Fiber cement	Gutter guards	Hardboard	Oriented-strand board (OSB)	Rain carrying systems	Shutters	Siding accessories	Simulated stone veneer	Soffits/fascias	Steel	Stone	Stucco	Trim	Vinyl	Wood	Local dealer/distributor	Factory-direct	Circle No.
Builders Edge								■	■		■					■	■			■	■	
C-Cure Corp.			■													■				■		
California Redwood Assn.																			■	■		
Canada Brick			■																	■		
Canexel/(A Div. of ABT Building Products)						■														■	■	
Cardiff Industries		■							■												■	
Carlisle Engineered Metals													■	■							■	
Cedar Plus																		■		■		
Cedar Shake & Shingle Bureau																		■				
Cedar Valley Shingle Systems																		■		■		
Cellofoam North America				■																■		
Cellwood Products/(A Div. of Stolle Corp.)									■											■		
Centurion Products			■											■						■	■	
CertainTeed Siding									130		■					■	■			■		976
Chemcrest Architectural Products									■								■					
Colonial Clapboards																			■		■	
Conik Group									■											■		
Conserval Systems	■																				■	
Craft-Bilt Mfg. Co.		■																			■	
Crane Plastics Co.						■														■		
Creative Building Products						■			■								■			■	■	
Cultured Stone®/Stone Products Corp.			■									■			131					■		981
Curveline													■	■							■	
Custom-Bilt Metals	■					■				■											■	
Custom Decorative Mouldings									■											■		
Delaware Industries/Baseway Products																■				■	■	
Dryvit Systems			129																	■		59
Dura Art Stone															■						■	
Dura-Bilt Products		■																				
Eastside Machine Co.								■		■	■										■	992
Eide Industries		■																			■	
EIFS Industry Member Assn.				■																		
Eldorado Stone Corp.		■										■								■	■	
Engineered Profiles/North American Profiles																		■		■		
Englert	■								■				■			■	■			■	■	
EPS Molders Assn.				■						■												
F.C.P.				■																■		
Flex Molding										■										■	■	
Folding Shutter Corp.		■								■										■	■	
Forest Products Society																			■			
Fypon									■											■		
G R Plastics/(Nu-Wood)									■		■									■		
General Shale Brick			■																	■	■	
Genova Products						■			■											■	■	
Gentek Building Products	■							■		■		■					■	■		■		
Georgia-Pacific Corp.					132			■	■		■	■					■	132	■	■		993
Girardin Moulding									■											■		
Glen-Gery Corp.			■																	■		
Glen Raven Mills/Custom Fabrics Div.		■																		■		
Gossen Corp.																■				■	■	
Graham Products															■					■	■	
Green River																			■			
GSW Thermoplastics Co.									■											■	■	

See Manufacturer Index (beige pages at the back of this issue) for address and phone information.   Numbers in red indicate page number for additional product information.

Manufacturer	Aluminum	Awnings	Brick/masonry	Exterior insulation finishing systems	Fiber cement	Gutter guards	Hardboard	Oriented-strand board (OSB)	Rain carrying systems	Shutters	Siding accessories	Simulated stone veneer	Soffits/fascias	Steel	Stone	Stucco	Trim	Vinyl	Wood	Local dealer/distributor	Factory-direct	Circle No.
Gutter Armor	■					■			■												■	
Harris Specialty Chemicals				■																■	■	
Harvey Industries																		■	■	■	■	
Heartland Building Products									■		■							■		■		
Highland Lumber Co.																			■	■	■	
Holland Log Homes Mfg. Co.																■			■	■	■	
Homeshield Fabricated Products									■		■		■							■		
I-XL Industries			■																	■		
International Institute for Lath and Plaster				■												■				■	■	
International Paper Co.						■				■	■									■		
Jackson Sawmill Co.																			■	■	■	
James Hardie Building Products					■						■									■		60
Kasko Industries			■	■									■							■		
KenTech Plastics		■								■	■									■		
Klauer Mfg. Co.									■				■							■		
Knudson Mfg.											131									■	■	978
LaHabra Stucco				■												■				■		
Lavalley Lumber																		■	■	■	■	
Leigh/(A Harrow Co.)													■							■		
Louisiana-Pacific Corp.								■					■							■		
MacMillan Bloedel/Building Materials Mktg.	■				■					■	■						■	■		■		
Mason Corp.	■	■																		■		
Masonite							■			■	■									■		
Master Shield Building Products Co.										■	■						■			■		
Max Products				■						■	■					■				■		
MaxiTile					■					■	■					■				■		
McShan Lumber Co.																			■	■		
Metal Sales Mfg. Corp.	■										■			■						■	■	
Mid-America Building Products/(Tapco)									■	■	■									■		
The Millwork Store										■	■									■	■	
Miracle Sealants & Abrasives			■																	■		
Mitten Vinyl										■	■						■	■		■		
Moose Creek Lumber Co.																			■	■	■	
Nailite Intl.		■								■	■									■	■	
Napco	■										■							133		■		92
NASSA																		■			■	
National Assn. of Brick Distributors			■																			
National Concrete Masonry Assn.			■																			
National Mfg.		■																		■		
New Concept Louvers	■									131										■		980
Niagara Fiberboard											■									■	■	
Niles Building Products												■			■	■				■		
Norandex											■										■	
Ohline Corp.										■											■	
Old Carolina Brick Co.			■																	■	■	
Old Town Lumber Co.																			■	■		
Owens Corning									■		■							133		■	■	91,633
P&M Cedar Products																			■	■		
Pacific Clay Brick Products			■																	■		
The Pacific Lumber Co.																			■	■		
Pacific Wood Laminates													■				■			■		
Panneaux Thermo Briques			■																	■	■	
Parex				■																■		

Siding & Accessories

Manufacturer	Aluminum	Awnings	Brick/masonry	Exterior insulation finishing systems	Fiber cement	Gutter guards	Hardboard	Oriented-strand board (OSB)	Rain carrying systems	Shutters	Siding accessories	Simulated stone veneer	Soffits/fascias	Steel	Stone	Stucco	Trim	Vinyl	Wood	Local dealer/distributor	Factory-direct	Circle No.
Perma R" Products			■																	■		
Permalatt										■										■		
PH Chadbourne & Co.																			■	■		
Plastmo						■			■									■		■	■	
Plylap Industries										■	■									■	■	
Polyfoam Packers Corp.			■																	■	■	
Preswitt Mfg.			■													■				■	■	
Pro Tect Associates									■											■	■	
Protective Products Intl.																■				■	■	
Prudential Building Materials									■											■		
PS Aluminum Products		■							■												■	
Quality Fencing & Supply																		■		■	■	
Rainhandler									■											■	■	
Ray White Lumber Co.																			■			
Real Brick Products			■	■																■	■	
Redland Brick/(Cushwa Plant)			■																	■	■	
Reynolds Metals Co.	■							■	■	■			■	■			■	■		■	■	
RH Tamlyn & Sons					■								■							■	■	
Richwood Building Products											■									■	■	
Ro-Tile			■																	■		
Robbins Lumber																			■			
Robinson Brick Co.			■																	■		
Rocktile Specialty Products			■																		■	
Roll-A-Way Storm & Security Shutters										■										■	■	
Rollex Corp.	■								■				■	■				■		■		
Royal Building Products											■		■					■		■		
Royal Plastics Group											■		■				■	■			■	
The Scandinavian Profiling Systems													■							■	■	
Scatton Bros. Awning Mfg.		■																			■	
Scott Cedar																			■	■		
Seacoast Mills																			■	■		
Senergy/(Harris Specialty Chemicals)				■																■		
Shakertown Corp.																			131	■		334
Sheet Metal Mfg. Co.						■			■				■				■			■		
Shutters, Inc.										■										■		
Simplex Products/(A Div. of K2)				■																■		
Skookum Lumber Co.																			129	■		58
The Society of the Plastics Industry				■																■		
Southeastern Metals Mfg. Co./SEMCO											■			■						■		
Southern Pine Council																			■	■		
Sovebec																			■	■		
Steel Tile Co.		■										■								■	■	
Stillwater Products													■							■	■	
STO Finish Systems/(A Div. of STO Corp.)				■												■				■		
Structural Board Assn.								■												■	■	
Stuc-O-Flex Intl.				■												131				■	■	985
Style-Mark										■	■			■				■		■		
Sunesta Products		■																		■		
Supradur Mfg. Co.					■															■		
Tamark Mfg./Life Pine Products																			■	■	■	
Tapco Products/(A Tapco Intl. Corp.)																				■		
TEC/(A Sub. of HB Fuller Co.)				132																■		988
Temple-Inland Forest Products					132								■				132			■	■	989, 990

See Manufacturer Index (beige pages at the back of this issue) for address and phone information. Numbers in red indicate page number for additional product information. continued

SIDING

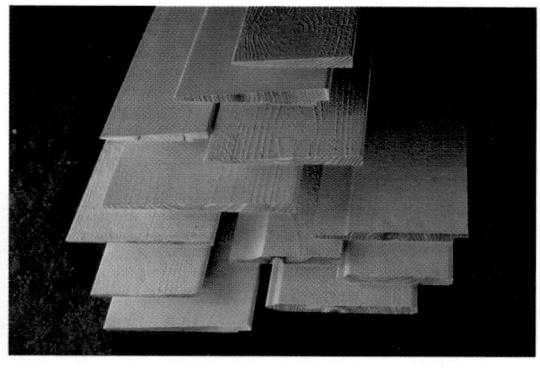

Skookum Lumber: Western red cedar siding is available with factory-applied oil-base primer on front, back, and edges. Choice of bevel or channel patterns. *StepSaver.* 206-352-7633. *Circle no. 58.*

Acme Brick: Brick is available in earth shades of charcoal, gray, and umber. Line also includes Southwest-inspired red, white, and pink. *Olde Towne.* 817-390-2409. *Circle no. 56.*

Dryvit: Exterior finishing system uses an acrylic-cement compound that resembles brick or stone. Applies with trowel and template. Comes in 12 colors and a range of patterns. *Ultra-Tex.* 1-800-556-7752. *Circle no. 59.*

Roseburg Forest Products: Premium grade plywood siding panels are 4 feet wide and 8-, 9-, or 10-feet long. Come in various grooved shiplap patterns or ungrooved patterns with square or shiplap edges. *Breckenridge.* 541-679-3311. *Circle no. 57.*

James Hardie: Stucco profile has been added to fiber-cement siding line. Recommended for walls, porches, and gable ends. Sheets are 4 feet wide and 8-, 9-, or 10-feet long. Hardipanel. 1-800-9-HARDIE. *Circle no. 60.*

Siding & Accessories

Manufacturer	Aluminum	Awnings	Brick/masonry	Exterior insulation finishing systems	Fiber cement	Gutter guards	Hardboard	Oriented-strand board (OSB)	Rain carrying systems	Shutters	Siding accessories	Simulated stone veneer	Soffits/fascias	Steel	Stone	Stucco	Trim	Vinyl	Wood	Local dealer/distributor	Factory-direct	Circle No.
TIPLOK									131											■	■	984
TR Miller Mill Co.																			■	■		
United Panel				■								■	■							■	■	
United States Seamless									132	132	■	■									■	979,991
Van Mark Products Corp.										■										■		
Vantage Products Corp.										■										■		
Variform										■	■						■			■		
Vermont Structural Slate Co.															■						■	
Vincent Metals									■			■								■	■	
Vinyl Lite II Window & Door Systems																	■	■		■	■	
VIPCO/Crane Plastics				■						■	■							■		■		93
Vixen Hill Mfg. Co.										■											■	
Vytec Corp.											■						■	■		■		
Walker & Zanger															■					■	■	
Ward Log Homes																			■		■	
Waterloov Gutter Protection Systems Co.						130			■											■	■	975
WD Cowls																				■		
Westchester Marble & Granite															■					■		
Western Red Cedar Lumber Assn.																			■	■		
Western Wood Products Assn.																			■	■		
Wheeling Corrugating Co.														■						■		
Whitacre-Greer			■																	■	■	
Wind-Lock Corp.				■																■		
Windsor Mill											■						■			■		
Wisconsin Log Homes																			■	■	■	
Wolverine Vinyl Siding										■	■						■	133		■		94,470
Yost Mfg. & Supply									■											■	■	

See Manufacturer Index (beige pages at the back of this issue) for address and phone information.   Numbers in red indicate page number for additional product information.

Siding & Accessories

WATERLOOV® GUTTER PROTECTION SYSTEM
Increase profits! The Ultimate Solution to Clogged Gutters. One person installation on all types of roof systems; new or retrofit, residential or commercial, single or multiple dwellings. Protects against debris, birds, ice and snow. Many HOT dealership territories are available nationally. Call: 1-800-841-7246.
Circle No. 975

EXTERIOR COLOR SELECTION MADE SIMPLE
CertainTeed's New StyleGuide™ makes the color selection process easy while creating profitable selling opportunities. This 100-page, mix-and-match guide helps your customers choose siding, trim and roofing colors. Includes suggested color combinations, full color idea section, home style color selector, and product/color availability. For more details and ordering information call 800-233-8990.
Circle No. 976

ALCOA BUILDING PRODUCTS
Combine one of the most trusted names in the industry with one of the broadest selections of exterior building products available and you have all you need to make your next building or remodeling project a complete success. Alcoa, a leading manufacturer of quality building products for over 30 years, now brings you its full line of vinyl siding, soffit and designer accessories in this new "ProGuide '97" catalog. For more information call (800) 962-6973. **Circle No. 977**

NEW IMPROVED 1770A 5" GUTTER MACHINE
LITTLE OR NO ADJUSTMENT NECESSARY
☆ 26 GAUGE STEEL
☆ .027 & .032" ALUMINUM
☆ 16 OZ. COPPER
✓ Powered Skate for best results
✓ NEW Swiveling cradles &uprights
✓ Transports easily without material in machine

From KNUDSON The INDUSTRY LEADER!

KNUDSON GUTTER MACHINES

On-site seamless gutter machines save up to 50% in labor and materials. Contractors expand remodeling potential, increase profits, and control product quality and delivery. With over 30 years experience producing rollforming equipment, KNUDSON has the model to meet your roof panel, gutter, siding, and framing component needs!
CALL TODAY!

Call 1-800-548-2622
Circle No. 978

SEAMLESS STEEL SIDING

If you're a business owner and would like to understand what the "niche" in niche marketing is, discover ABC Seamless. We are the world's largest seamless siding company. We assign you a territory. We give you an exclusive product. Great products generate customer referrals and better sales. We give you business support. Honesty and integrity in the franchisor and all company representatives. Our duck is a terrific marketing tool. **Call 800-732-6577 or www.abcseamless.com Circle No. 979**

CUSTOM LOUVERS

New Concept Louvers are specifically designed to match any vinyl, steel, or aluminum siding **(over 400 colors)** and never need painting. Available in many stock sizes, or can be custom made to **any size or shape.** When you want a custom look or have special requirements, rely on us! **Circle No. 980**

CULTURED STONE®

New 1997 full-color 56 page catalog contains swatch and application photos of more than 78 stone building products; it features new colors, new textures, and new trim pieces. Cultured Stone® looks and feels like stone yet costs a fraction of the price.
(800) 644-4487. *Stone Products Corp.*
Circle No. 981

CRAFTMASTER®

CraftMaster's new Colonist 8-ft. Smooth door design meets today's trend toward higher ceilings and painted interior doors. Carry Colonist Smooth's elegant look throughout the home with 6'8", 7' and 8' heights. Also available in bi-fold sizes. CraftMaster®. Doing More with Doors.
Circle No. 982

More options than anyone.

Nothing improves the exterior of a home like brick. And no one has a wider selection than Boral. To find the distributor nearest you, call 1-800-5-BORAL-5. We'll help you build a home that's appreciated by everyone who sees it.

Circle No. 983

BORAL BRICKS
A SOLID DECISION™

SHAKERTOWN

Shakertown cedar shingle panels give any home a touch of elegance. Made from high quality cedar, the panels are quick and easy to apply. The offset end-joints on 2 course panels create a seamless appearance. Fancy Cuts decorative shingle panels are also available. Visit us on the web at www.clarkegroup.com/Shakertown
(800) 426-8970. Circle No. 334

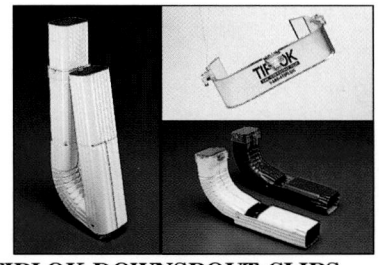

TIPLOK DOWNSPOUT CLIPS

Designed and patented as a practical solution to downspout extension pipes that get in the way during construction, and later when homeowners are mowing, gardening or landscaping. They snap on, can handle any length extension, are clear acrylic so they match any color pipe, come in two sizes - 3" & 4", can be imprinted with your company name/logo. Pre-assembled Tip-Up elbows sold separately. Let TIPLOK Downspout Clips be the "Signature Piece" for all your gutter and downspout installations! Toll-free (888)-4TIPLOK, FAX 608-836-8450, E-Mail: SIEDLECKI@MSN.COM **Circle No. 984**

STUC-O-FLEX INTERNATIONAL, INC.

Stuc-O-Flex Exterior Insulated Systems with Elastomeric Acrylic Finish provide opportunities in wall cladding performance unprecedented in stucco or brittle acrylic coatings. R-values to 6.5 per inch in a warranted system with unlimited design potential, offering extraordinary resistance against cracks and water intrusion. Stuc-O-Flex International, Inc., 17639 NE 67th Ct., Redmond, WA 98052, (800) 305-1045. **Circle No. 985**

NEW! CHARTER OAK™ REINFORCED SOFFIT

Look for it soon…the only reinforced vinyl soffit on the market. Exclusive TriBeam™ one-piece reinforcement provides almost five times the rigidity of other vinyl soffit. That means easy installations and lasting quality, even on porch ceilings and extended over-hangs. Invisible venting. 13 low-gloss colors. For new construction and remodeling. **ALSIDE, INC. (800) 922-6009. Circle No. 986**

ROLL VENT 2®

Roll Vent 2, a new patented ridge vent, offers the compression resistance of sectional products. Its in-board fabric prevents weather and insect infiltration. Its unique interlock design makes Roll Vent 2 faster and easier to install than sectional ridge vents; with no waste or scrap. Each roll comes with 2-1/2" galvanized nails and end caps. For information, contact Benjamin Obdyke Incorporated at 800-346-7655. **Circle No. 987**

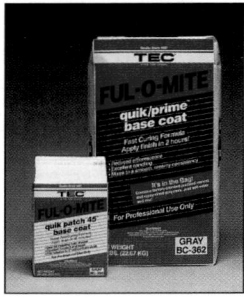

NEW BASE COATS SAVE TIME AND MONEY

Reduce labor, scaffolding and weather-related costs with two new fsat setting base coats from TEC Incorporated, manufacturer of the FUL-O-MITE® EIF system since 1976. **QuikPatch** sets in 45 minutes and **Quik/Prime** is ready for finish in two hours. Call Customer Service at 1-800-TEC-9002 (Fax: 847-358-9510). **Circle No. 988**

TEMPLE-INLAND TRIMCRAFT™

Nothing delivers the consistency and performance needed for exterior fascia and trim like TrimCraft™, Temple-Inland's engineered wood trim. Factory primed. 3/4-inch thick. Standard 16-foot length with reversible smooth/cedar finish. Available ploughed. Call (800) 231-6060. www.templeinland.com **Circle No. 989**

TEMPLE-INLAND HARDBOARD SIDING

From lap to panels, Temple-Inland offers the performance and economy you count on with 100% wood-fiber hardboard siding. Saves time, material. Use conventional tools. Factory primed for painting ease, durability. Call (800) 231-6060. www.templeinland.com **Circle No. 990**

SEAMLESS STEEL SIDING

United States Seamless was Ranked #1 Seamless Steel Siding Franchise in Entrepreneurs "BEST of the BEST" March '97 issue. Nationwide franchiser of seamless steel siding, and gutters, offering protected territories. Financing available. Call Dave Hedman (701) 241-8888, www.usseamless.com **Circle No. 991**

GUTTER MACHINE

EMCO's seamless gutter machines are the most user friendly machines ever built. Our Eagle's 14 fully driven roller stations produce quality gutter at 36 feet per minute. Distributorships & financing available. Also available; seamless siding machines and standing seam roof machines. Call Dave Hedman (701) 235-EMCO, E-mail info@eastsidemachine.com **Circle No. 992**

HARDBOARD

PRIMETRIM®

PrimeTrim exterior and interior trim from Georgia-Pacific is a precision engineered, all wood composite with a factory primed face and 2 edges. Highly resistant to rot and decay, PrimeTrim requires re-painting less often than traditional wood trim, and has no knots, finger joints or defects. PrimeTrim comes in 16' lengths, and is available in a smooth or textured surface. Call 1-800-BUILD G-P (284-5347) for details. **Circle No. 993**

CLASSIC SELECT™ PREMIUM LAP SIDING

Classic Select™ siding is a premium-grade lap siding which gives the dramatic shadow lines of old fashioned lumber siding but holds paint longer, resists rot, lasts longer and costs less. Pre-primed with a smooth or wood-grain textured face, in standard 192" lengths, nominal 6" and 8" widths, and 5/8" thickness. Paired with PrimeTrim®, we can now offer a complete exterior package with warranty. Call 1-800-BUILD G-P (284-5347) for details. **Circle No. 994**

VINYL SIDING

Wolverine: Vinyl trim panel with double $6\frac{1}{2}$-inch exposure imitates cedar shakes. Panels come in 32-inch length and can be applied over plywood or wood composite sheathing. Available in various colors. *Restoration.* 1-800-521-9020. *Circle no. 94.*

ABT Building Materials: Vinyl siding has the look of low-gloss, painted wood-grain. Positive locking system installs securely. *Harbor Ridge.* 1-800-265-9829. *Circle no. 95.*

Owens Corning: Vinyl siding is available in four profiles and 10 colors. Accessories include J-channels, soffit, and trim. *Transitions.* 1-800-GET-PINK. *Circle no. 91.*

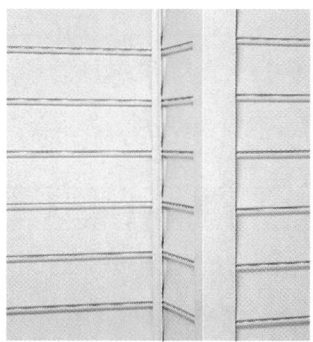

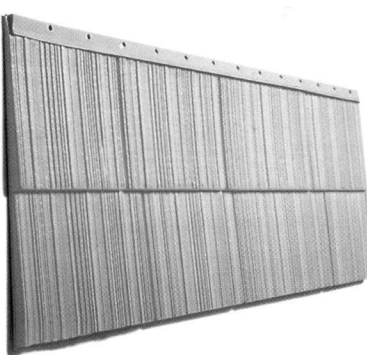

Napco: Vinyl siding features UV inhibitor that reduces the effects of sun exposure. In triple 3-inch, double 4-inch, and beaded 6.5-inch profiles. *American '76 Collection.* 412-898-1511. *Circle no. 92.*

Vipco: Vinyl shake siding imitates hand-painted cedar. Panels formed in double 5-inch profile. Come in white, gray, and ivory. *New Englander Perfection.* 1-800-366-8472. *Circle no. 93.*

Alcoa: Siding color won't chip, flake, or peel, company says. Available in double 4-inch, double 4-inch dutch lap, and 5-inch dutch lap profiles. Accessories include door surrounds, shutters, window mantels, and panels. *Mill Creek.* 1-800-952-5973. *Circle no. 98.*

Specialty Products

Manufacturer	Accessible products	Basement waterproofing systems	Bird control systems	Built-in ironing boards	Central vacuum systems	Closet/storage systems	Decorative metalwork	Elevators/dumbwaiters	Radon abatement products	Renovation & period specialties	Rolling ladders/library equipment	Wall beds	Local dealer/distributor	Factory-direct	Circle No.
	Products												**Sales**		
The 3E Group								■					■	■	
Access Industries	■							■					■		
Accessible Designs/Adjustable Systems	■												■	■	
Aid-O-Maid								■						■	
Aiphone Intercom Systems	■												■		
ALCO - NVC		■											■		
Aqua-Lock Waterproofing Materials		■											■	■	
Architectural Reproductions										■				■	
Around The Corner										■			■		
Assn. for Safe & Accessible Products	■														
Austram								■					■		
Auton Co.	■							■						■	
Barrisol Stretch Ceilings	■									■				■	
Basement De-Watering Systems		■							■					■	
Basement Systems		■												■	
Bath Ease	■												■	■	
Beam Industries					■									■	
Bird-X			■											■	
Blaine Window Hardware										■				■	
Boccia		■											■	■	
Broan Mfg. Co.				■	■								■		
Builders Edge						■							■	■	
C&H Roofing/Country Cottage Roof						■								■	
California Closet Co.						■							■	■	
Cast Designs & Supply										■				■	
Ceilings & Interior Systems Const. Assn.						■									
Cemcolift	■							■					■		
Central Vac Intl.					■									■	
CertainTeed Corp. Pipe & Plastics Group		■							■				■		
Cervitor Kitchens	■													■	
Cheney/(A Div. of Access Industries)	■							■					■		
Chimney King			■			■							■	■	
Classic Architectural Specialties										■			■		
Closet Maid						■							■		
Concord Elevator	■							■					■		
Cosella-Dorken Products		■											■		
D. Lawless Hardware										■				■	

> 35% of new-home shoppers want a central vacuum.
>
> *Source: What Today's Home Buyers Want/NAHB and Fulton Research*

See Manufacturer Index (beige pages at the back of this issue) for address and phone information.   Numbers in red indicate page number for additional product information.

Manufacturer	Accessible products	Basement waterproofing systems	Bird control systems	Built-in ironing boards	Central vacuum systems	Closet/storage systems	Decorative metalwork	Elevators/dumbwaiters	Radon abatement products	Renovation & period specialties	Rolling ladders/library equipment	Wall beds	Local dealer/distributor	Factory-direct	Circle No.
De Neef Construction Chemicals (US)		■											■		
Decor Grates							■			■			■	■	
Decora Systems						■					■				
Delaware Industries/Baseway Products										■			■	■	
Designs In Tile										■			■		
Driwood Moulding Co.										■			■		
Duralast Products Corp.								■					■	■	
Electrolux					■								■		
The Eureka Co.					■								■		
Falcon Mfg.	■												■	■	
Fan America									■				■		
Fasco Industries				■	■								■		
Feeny Mfg. Co.	■			■									■		
Fiberglass Access	■												■		
Flinchbaugh Co.	■							■					■		
Garaventa	■							■					■		
Gardner Asphalt Corp.		■											■		
Gemini Bath & Kitchen Products	■												■	■	
Grace Construction Products		■											■		
GUSA/GINGER	■												■		
Hacker Industries										■				■	
Hafele America	■				■						■		■	■	
Harney Mfg.	■														
Harris Specialty Chemicals		■											■	■	
HB & G				■									■		
Health-Mor					■								■		
Herrco Enterprises	■												■		
Honeywell/Home & Building Control	■				■								■		
Houses & Barns by John Libby/Barn Masters										■					
Inclinator Co. of America								■					■		
Increte Systems/(A Div. of Inco Chemical)	■													■	
Industries Trovac					■								■		
Innovative Insulation									■				■	■	
Insul-Tray									■				■		
Insulated Building Systems		■							■				■	■	
Interchange Brands									■				■	■	
IRON-A-WAY				■									■		
Karnak Corp.		■											■		
Knape & Vogt Mfg. Co.						■							■	■	
Lavi Industries							■						■	■	
Lee/Rowan Co./Building Products Div.						■							■	■	
Leviton Mfg./Electrical Distribution	■												■		
LIFESPEC Cabinet Systems	■													■	
Lighting by Hammerworks										■				■	
Ludwig Industries							■						■	■	
Lundia Shelving & Storage Systems						■							■	■	
M.D. Mfg. Co.					137								■	■	751,998
MAAX/Div. Acrylica, Premium	■												■		
Macklanburg-Duncan							■								
Mansfield Plumbing Products	■												■	■	
Matot, Inc.								138					■	■	995
Melard Mfg. Corp.	■														
Memry Corp.	■												■	■	

> 48% of new-home shoppers want an exhaust fan in the bathroom; 45% want a linen closet.
>
> *Source: What Today's Home Buyers Want/NAHB and Fulton Research*

See Manufacturer Index (beige pages at the back of this issue) for address and phone information.   Numbers in red indicate page number for additional product information.

continued

Specialty Products

Manufacturer	Accessible products	Basement waterproofing systems	Bird control systems	Built-in ironing boards	Central vacuum systems	Closet/storage systems	Decorative metalwork	Elevators/dumbwaiters	Radon abatement products	Renovation & period specialties	Rolling ladders/library equipment	Wall beds	Local dealer/distributor	Factory-direct	Circle No.
Mid Continent Cabinetry/(A Div. of Norcraft)	■												■	■	
Miller Mfg.						■							■	■	
The Millworks										■			■	■	
MIM Architecturals										■			■		
Modular Hardware	■												■	■	
Music and Sound					■								■		
National Products			■										■	■	
Nixalite of America			■											■	
The Northern Roof Tile Sales Co.										■			■		
NuTone				■	■								■	■	
The October Co.						■	■						■	■	
Old Carolina Brick Co.										■			■	■	
Oregon Research & Development Corp.		■											■		
Parsec									■				■	■	
Particleboard/MDF Institute						■									
Pemko Mfg. Co.	■												■	■	
Plastics & Resins									■				■	■	
Poly-Tak Protection Systems										■			■		
Poly-Wall Intl.		■												■	
Power Access Corp.	■												■		
Putnam Rolling Ladder Co.											■		■		
Quad Lock Building Systems		■											■		
Reflectix									■				■		
Reon	■												■	■	
Rev-A-Shelf						■									
S. Parker Hardware Mfg. Corp.						■				■			■	■	
S&S Wood Specialties						■							■	■	
SafeTek Intl.	■												■	■	
Schluter Systems	■						■								
Schulte Corp.						■							■	■	
Scott Sign Systems	■									■			■	■	
Seton Name Plate Co.	■													■	
Shower Shapes	■												■		
Sico North America												■	■	■	
Silcraft Corp.	■													■	
Simplex Access Controls/Ilco Unican Group	■														
Smart Central Vacuums					■								■		
Space-Metrics						■							■	■	
Steptoe & Wife Antiques							■			■			■	■	
Strom Plumbing By Sign Of The Crab							■			■			■	■	
Style-Mark										■			■		
Sun Nuclear Corp.									■					■	
Surebond		■											■		
Syntec Marble	■												■	■	
Temp-Vent Corp.									■				■		
Thomas Waterproof Coatings Co.		■							■				■	■	
TUB-MASTER	■												■		
Tuff-N-Dri Waterproofing/Koch Materials Co.		137												■	996
United House Wrecking										■				■	
VACUFLO—H-P Products					138								■	■	750
Vanguard Plastics Ltd.						■									
Vent-A-Hood					■								■		
Villagecraft Industries								■			■			■	

See Manufacturer Index (beige pages at the back of this issue) for address and phone information.   Numbers in red indicate page number for additional product information.

Manufacturer	Accessible products	Basement waterproofing systems	Bird control systems	Built-in ironing boards	Central vacuum systems	Closet/storage systems	Decorative metalwork	Elevators/dumbwaiters	Radon abatement products	Renovation & period specialties	Rolling ladders/library equipment	Wall beds	Local dealer/distributor	Factory-direct	Circle No.
Wall Firma	■						■						■	■	
Waupaca Elevator Co.								137					■	■	997
Welco Mfg. Co.	■													■	
White Home Products					■								■	■	
Windquest Cos.					■								■		
Wood Factory							■							■	
Woodwork Institute of California					■										
WR Meadows Inc.	■												■		

See Manufacturer Index (beige pages at the back of this issue) for address and phone information.   Numbers in red indicate page number for additional product information.

Specialty Products

FREE TUFF-N-DRI® BASEMENT WATERPROOFING GUIDE
Learn how TUFF-N-DRI® Exterior Foundation Waterproofing System on the outside guarantees a dry, cozy basement inside with a 10-year transferable warranty. TUFF-N-DRI, 800 Irving Wick Dr., Heath, OH 43056. **800-DRY-BSMT.**
Home page: http://www.tuff-n-dri.com
Circle No. 996

Building? Remodeling?
If so, consider planning for the future by installing a Waupaca Elevator that is designed to fit your decor. A Waupaca Elevator means comfort, convenience, mobility, and safety. DON'T BE CAUGHT UNABLE TO REMAIN IN YOUR HOME IN CASE OF ACCIDENT, ILLNESS AND/OR AGE. Our custom capabilities assure there is an elevator to fit your needs. For further information contact:
Waupaca Elevator Co.
138 S. Oborn St., P.O. Box 246
Waupaca, WI 54981
Tel: 1-800-238-8739
Circle No. 997

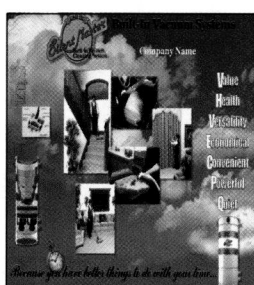

TOP-OF-THE-LINE SILENT MASTER BUILT-IN VACUUMS
by M.D. Manufacturing will generate satisfied clients who will thank you with more referrals! Over 50 powerful units to choose from backed by 35 years experience. Patented noise suppression, micro-fine filtration, extra-large capacity and superior cleaning power have made Silent Master your best choice. Call for free video. 1-800-525-2055.
www.builtinvacuum.com **Circle No. 998**

ELEMENTS, INC.
There is no substitute for the best. Dramatically enhance your development's image with custom brass letters and logos. They lend sophistication and elegance to your entrance monument thereby increasing sales. Call **(800) 223-2788** for free estimates and catalog. Offered by Elements, Inc. "The Nation's #1 Provider of Signage for Builders and Developers." **Circle No. 999**

FOR DEEP PENETRATION BEHIND ENEMY LINES
Stealth is the first central vacuum power-brush with microcomputer space-age technology to protect your client's investments. No other powerbrush outcleans, outlasts, outsells, outperforms this top-of-the-line package! Fully integrated inlet-to-brush quality for the discriminating buyer. Call for your free video! (800) 525-2055 www.builtinvacuum.com by M.D. Manufacturing **Circle No. 751**

LANDSCAPE DESIGN

BETTER THAN WOOD! BETTER THAN VINYL!
Tuff-Bilt™ lattice is made of fiberglass-reinforced plastic. Molded in one piece. Won't separate. Easy to saw and nail. *Maintenance-free.* Available in 3 styles: Classic Diamond (shown), Privacy Diamond and Privacy Square, and available in 6 colors. Plastics Research Corporation (800) 879-7723. Lifetime warranty. **Circle No. 754**

MATOT, INC.
Matot's Residential Elevators provide affordable solutions for building convenience and increasing personal mobility within your home. If you're looking for an affordable investment, built with quality craftsmanship that will last a lifetime, select a Matot Elevator for your home. For more information about our drum, traction or hydraulic elevators, call 1-800-MATOT-32 for engineering assistance or our product catalog. **Circle No. 995**

SIDING

NAILITE SIDING: THE BEAUTIFUL, DURABLE & AFFORDABLE SIDING ALTERNATIVE.
Send for Nailite's new, *free* 8-page color catalog that showcases all of Nailite's authentic-looking exterior panels: Performance- Plus™ Cedar, Hand-Split Shake, Hand-Laid Brick and Hand-Cut Stone. All of Nailite's low-maintenance products are available in a variety of finishes and ideal for whole house applications or as accents. Phone: (305) 620-6200. FAX: (305) 623-8227. **Circle No. 788**

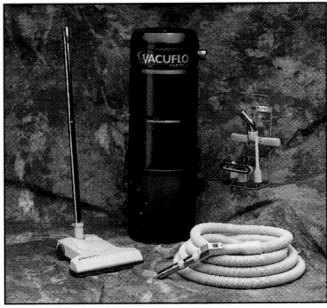

VACUFLO® ENHANCES VALUE OF HOMES
VACUFLO® Built In Central Vacuum Systems with True Cyclonic Cleaning Action provide cleaner, healthier homes. A complete product lineup offers an easy way to enhance the value of your homes. Add whole-house cleaning convenience up to 18,000 square feet, at an affordable price. For information, call 1-800-822-8356. **Circle No. 750**

EXTERIOR VINYL WITH A LIFETIME WARRANTY?
Yes! We're so confident in our VersaDek Ultra that we've given it a **Lifetime Warranty!** VersaDek exterior vinyls are waterproof, slip-resistant and have a Class I Fire Rating. Made from high quality PVC, they resist UV light, mildew and chemicals. **VersaDek installs easily in one step** and is attractive and cost-effective. VersaDek is the answer to all your needs for decks, balconies, walkways and more! (800) 497-DECK (3325). **Circle No. 753**

FORT KNOX

Vault Door 5000

SECURITY PRODUCTS
The Fort Knox vault door meets the same exacting standards as our famous line of safes. It's designed for easy installation in concrete or block to provide a walk-in security vault. Features heavy reinforced steel, 26 one inch locking bolts, electronic lock, inside release and lifetime warranty. **Call (800) 821-5216. Circle No. 752**

Structural Systems

Manufacturer	Concrete block systems	Concrete forms	Concrete & masonry repair products	Foam blocks	Log homes	Masonry products	Modular homes	Panelized building systems	Poured-concrete systems	Pre-cast concrete systems	Steel columns & beams	Steel studs, lightweight	Structural insulated panels (SIPs)	Timber frame homes	Trusses, floor	Trusses, roof	Wall panels	Local dealer/distributor	Factory-direct	Circle No.
3-10 Insulated Forms		■		■					■								■	■	■	
AAB Building System		140		140					■									■		624
Acadia Post & Beam														■				■	■	
Acme Brick Co.						■												■	■	
Acorn/(A Div. of DHI)							■							■					■	
Active Homes Corp.							■	■												
Advanced Building Systems							■												■	
Advanced Framing Systems											■							■		
AFM Corp.		■		■			■	■					■				■		■	
Air Lock Log Co.					■														■	
Aldon Corp.			■															■		
Algonquin Log Homes					■														■	
ALH Building Systems							■												■	
All Steel Homes											■	■							■	
ALUMET Building Products											■								■	
American ConForm Industries		■		■					■									■		
American Polysteel Forms		■		■														■		
American Stone-Mix						■												■		
American Technocrete Corp.									■										■	
American Wood Council													■	■	■					
Angeles Metal Systems											■				■	■	■	■	■	
Anthony Forest Products Co.			■															■	■	
Appalachian Log Structures					147													■		799
Architectural Timber & Millwork														■	■	■		■		
Arriscraft Corp.						■												■		
ATAS International																	■	■		
Avis America							■												■	
Barden Homes							■							■	■	■		■		
Beaver Mountain Log Homes					■									■				■	■	
Belden Brick Co.						■												■		
Bend Industries	■					■												■	■	
Bilco Brick						■												■	■	
Black Creek Timber Framing Co.													■	■					■	
Boiardi Products Corp.						■													■	
Bon Tool Co.		■				■												■		
The Brick Institute of America						■														
Bullock & Co.			■															■		

See Manufacturer Index (beige pages at the back of this issue) for address and phone information.   Numbers in red indicate page number for additional product information.   continued

STRUCTURAL MATERIALS

AAB Building System: Polystyrene blocks stack and interlock without tools to make concrete forms for foundations and walls. Eliminate need for air and vapor barriers. *Blue Maxx.* 1-800-293-3210. *Circle no. 624.*

◀ **Trus Joist MacMillan:** Ready-to-assemble roof trusses made of laminated strand lumber create a 200-square-foot living area. Components are predrilled and precut. *Spacemaker 3.* 1-800-338-0515. *Circle no. 625.*

Insteel: Polystyrene panels are set between welded wire mesh. They fit over slab-embedded steel dowels and fasten at seams and corners. *3-D Panel System.* 1-800-545-3181. *Circle no. 626.*

ThermaSteel: Composite panel for interior and exterior walls, roofs, and floors is made of insulating material molded into a steel frame. Includes built-in sheathing and vapor barrier. 540-633-5001. *Circle no. 627.*

Amoco Foam Products: New plastic coating strengthens insulating 3/8-inch-thick polystyrene sheathing. Board is available in 4-x 8-foot and 4-x 9-foot sizes. *Plygood.* 1-800-241-4402. *Circle no. 628.*

Structural Systems

Manufacturer	Concrete block systems	Concrete forms	Concrete & masonry repair products	Foam blocks	Log homes	Masonry products	Modular homes	Panelized building systems	Poured-concrete systems	Pre-cast concrete systems	Steel columns & beams	Steel studs, lightweight	Structural insulated panels (SIPs)	Timber frame homes	Trusses, floor	Trusses, roof	Wall panels	Local dealer/distributor	Factory-direct	Circle No.
C-Cure Corp.						■												■		
California Acrylic Industries/Cal Spas							■												■	
Canada Brick						■												■		
Canadian Cedar Log					■													■		
Cardinal Homes							■												■	
Carlisle Engineered Metals												■					■		■	
The Cascade Joinery														■		■			■	
Cellofoam North America				■									■					■		
Centurion Products						■												■	■	
CertainTeed Corp. Pipe & Plastics Group	■					■												■		
Chelsea Modular Homes							■												■	
Chemque		■																■	■	
The Chestnut Ridge Beamery														■					■	
Circle Redmont						■				■							■		■	
Classic Post & Beam Homes					■									■					■	
Cleform Tool Co.		■				■												■		
Cobblecrete	■																		■	
Cobra Tools						■												■		
Colonial Carpentry														■					■	
Concrete Block Insulating Systems						■												■		
Concrete Designs						■				■									■	
Consolidated Coatings Corp.			■															■	■	
Contemporary Structures								■						■				■	■	
Cottage Steel Industries								■				■				■		■		
Country Homestead/Restoration Contractor														■				■	■	
Craft-Bilt Mfg. Co.								■					■				■		■	
Crest Homes Corp./(A Div. of Schult Homes)							■												■	
Crockett Log and Timber Frame Homes					■			■						■					■	
Cronkhite Industries						■												■		
Cultured Stone®/Stone Products Corp.						■												■		
Customized Structures							■	■											■	
David Howard														■					■	
Day Pond Woodworking														■					■	
Deck House/(A Div. of DHI)								■						■					■	
Deltec Homes								■										■	■	
Deluxe Homes of PA							■												■	
Doucette Log Building					■									■					■	
Dynamic Homes							■												■	
E&E Consumer Products															■			■	■	
Earthstone Retaining Wall Systems										■								■	■	
Eastern Timber Homes														■					■	
Eldorado Stone Corp.						■												■	■	
ENER-GRID Building Systems									■				■					■		
Enercept													■					■	■	
Englert																	■	■	■	
EPS Molders Assn.	■			■			■	■	■								■			
Excalibur Steel Structures											■	■						■	■	
Fero Corp.		■				■												■	■	
Fibermesh/Div. of Synthetic Industries									■	■			■					■	■	
Firstday Cottage																■			■	
Fischer SIPS								■					■					■	■	
Foam Laminates of Vermont								■					■				■		■	
Fold-Form	■	■							■									■		

See Manufacturer Index (beige pages at the back of this issue) for address and phone information.   Numbers in red indicate page number for additional product information.   continued

Structural Systems

Manufacturer	Concrete block systems	Concrete forms	Concrete & masonry repair products	Foam blocks	Log homes	Masonry products	Modular homes	Panelized building systems	Poured-concrete systems	Pre-cast concrete systems	Steel columns & beams	Steel studs, lightweight	Structural insulated panels (SIPs)	Timber frame homes	Trusses, floor	Trusses, roof	Wall panels	Local dealer/distributor	Factory-direct	Circle No.
Forest Products Society														■	■					
The Future Home Technology							■											■		
Garland Homes					■													■	■	
Gastineau Log Homes					■													■	■	
General Housing Corp.							■											■		
General Shale Brick						■												■	■	
The Georgia Marble Co.						■													■	
Glen-Gery Corp.						■												■		
Golden Log Homes/CMB					■															
Grace Construction Products	■					■												■		
Graham Products																	■	■	■	
Graham Timber Frame														■				■		
Green Mountain Precision Frames														■	■	■		■		
Hardwick Post & Beam Corp.													■	■				■	■	
Harris Specialty Chemicals	■					■												■	■	
Hebel Southeast										■								■		
HL Stud Corp.												■			■			■	■	
Holdrite Brackets												■						■		
Holland Log Homes Mfg. Co.					■		■						■					■	■	
Honest Abe Log Homes					■													■	■	
Houses & Barns by John Libby/Barn Masters														■						
Hugh Lofting Timber Framing													■	■		■		■		
Husky Panel Systems													■					■	■	
I-XL Industries						■												■		
ICE Block Building Systems				■					■									■		
In Cide Technologies						■													■	
Insteel Construction Systems							140	■										■		626
Insulated Building Systems				■			■	■		■						■		■		
Insulspan								■											■	
International Homes of Cedar					■													■		
Isokern Fireplaces/Earthcore Industries						■				■								■	■	
J-Deck Building Systems								■				■				■		■		
Jamo						■												■		
Joyce Mfg.							■												■	
Kasko Industries				■					■										■	
Keystone Retaining Wall Systems	■																	■	■	
Knudson Mfg.											■							■	■	
Kondor Post and Beam														■				■	■	
Korwall Industries								■					■			■			■	
Kraft Tool Co.			■															■	■	
Kuhns Bros. Log Homes					■														■	
LaCrosse Canada										■	■									
Laurentian Log Homes					■													■		
LC Andrew Maine Cedar Log Homes					■		■							■		■		■		
Legacy Timber Frames														■					■	
Lehigh Portland Cement Co.			■															■		
Lindal Cedar Homes/Sunrooms					147									■				■		801
Lite-Form Intl.		■																■	■	
Log Cabin Homes					■	■	■											■	■	
Logcrafters Log & Timber Homes					■									■	■	■			■	
Macco Adhesives		■																■		
Macklanburg-Duncan		■																		
Mandish Research Intl.		■																	■	

See Manufacturer Index (beige pages at the back of this issue) for address and phone information.   Numbers in red indicate page number for additional product information.

Manufacturer	Concrete block systems	Concrete forms	Concrete & masonry repair products	Foam blocks	Log homes	Masonry products	Modular homes	Panelized building systems	Poured-concrete systems	Pre-cast concrete systems	Steel columns & beams	Steel studs, lightweight	Structural insulated panels (SIPs)	Timber frame homes	Trusses, floor	Trusses, roof	Wall panels	Local dealer/distributor	Factory-direct	Circle No.
Maxito Industries		■																	■	
Metal Sales Mfg. Corp.																	■	■	■	
Mitek Industries															■	■		■		
MK Diamond Products	■		■															■		
Modulex							■											■	■	
Moose Creek Lumber Co.				■															■	
Mountain Top Timber Frames													■	■					■	
Mountaineer Log Homes					■														■	
Muncy Building Enterprises/(A DKM Co.)							■											■		
The Murus Co.							■						■			■		■		
National Assn. of Architectural Metal Mfrs.											■									
National Assn. of Brick Distributors						■														
National Concrete Masonry Assn.	■					■														
National Gypsum Co.											■							■		
Nationwide Homes							146											■		796
New Dimension Homes													■							
New Energy Works Timberframers													■	■					■	
New England Homes							146											■		795
Niles Building Products											■					■		■		
Nomix Corp.			■															■		
Normerica Building Systems								■						■				■		
North American Housing Corp.							146												■	798
North American Plywood Corp.		■																■	■	
Oak Post & Beam														■				■		
Oakbridge Timber Framing														■				■		
Old Carolina Brick Co.						■												■	■	
Old Virginia Hand Hewn Log Homes					■														■	
Oregon Dome/Design Pacific							146													794
Pacific Clay Brick Products						■												■		
Pacific Post & Beam														■		■		■		
Pacific Wood Laminates		■																■		
Package Pavement Co.			■															■	■	
Patriot Log Home					■													■		
Pendu Mfg.					■														■	
Perma R" Products				■				■					■				■	■		
Petmal Supply Co.						■												■	■	
Philstone Fasteners						■												■		
Pine Grove Post & Beam Builders					■									■					■	
Pioneer Millworks														■					■	
Pitcairn-Ferguson & Associates														■					■	
PL Adhesives & Sealants/ChemRex			■															■	■	
Polyfoam Packers Corp.							■											■	■	
Portland Cement Assn.									145											755
Post & Beam														■					■	
Premier Building Systems													■						■	
ProSoCo			■															■		
Quad Lock Building Systems		■							■									■		
Quality Fencing & Supply				■														■	■	
The Quikrete Cos.			■			■												■	■	
Rapid River Rustic					■													■	■	
Rastra Technologies	■	■																■		
Real Brick Products						■												■	■	
Real Log Homes Pre-Cut Log Products					■													■		

See Manufacturer Index (beige pages at the back of this issue) for address and phone information. Numbers in red indicate page number for additional product information. continued

Structural Systems

Products   Sales

Manufacturer	Concrete block systems	Concrete forms	Concrete & masonry repair products	Foam blocks	Log homes	Masonry products	Modular homes	Panelized building systems	Poured-concrete systems	Pre-cast concrete systems	Steel columns & beams	Steel studs, lightweight	Structural insulated panels (SIPs)	Timber frame homes	Trusses, floor	Trusses, roof	Wall panels	Local dealer/distributor	Factory-direct	Circle No.
Reddi-Form									■									■		
The Reinforced Earth Co.	■																	■		
RH Tamlyn & Sons			■															■	■	
Riverbend Timber Framing													■	■		■			■	
Robinson Brick Co.						■												■		
Rocktile Specialty Products						■													■	
Romatt Doors																	■	■	■	
Royal Plastics Group							■	■										■		
Royalston Oak Timber Frames								■					■	■		■		■		
S B													■					■		
Shelter Systems								■						■	■	■		■		
Showcase Homes							146											■	■	800
Simplex Industries							■												■	
Simpson Strong-Tie Co.		■																■		
Slope Block									■									■	■	
Snap-Trak																	■	■	■	
Sonneborn/ChemRex		■																■		
Southeastern Metals Mfg. Co./SEMCO			■								■							■		
Southern Pine Council															■	■				
Southland Log Homes					■													■	■	
Sparfil Intl.	■																		■	
Stanley Tools						■												■	■	
Steel & Wire Products Co.						■												■		
Stepstone						■														
Sterling Building Systems								■											■	
STO Finish Systems/(A Div. of STO Corp.)								■										■		
Structural Board Assn.								■					■					■	■	
Structural Insulated Panel Assn.													■						■	
Sunset Structures														■				■	■	
Surebond						■												■		
Swedish Building Systems & Components								■		■							■	■	■	
T.T. Frames/Thompson Timber Frames								■					■	■	■	■		■		
Tempcast 2000 Masonary Heater Mfg.				■															■	
Texas Timber Frames								■					■	■		■			■	
Thistlewood Timber Frame Homes														■						
Timber Systems																■		■	■	
Timberhouse Post & Beam								■					■	■		■			■	
Toby Eaton Timber Frame Builders				■	■	■							■	■					■	
Tohickon Timber Frames														■						
Town & Country Cedar Homes					■	■												■		
Trenwyth Industries						■												■	■	
TrimJoist Corp.															■			■		
True North Log Homes					■													■	■	
Trus Joist MacMillan		■											■		140			■		625
Truswal Systems Corp.															■	■		■		
Tussey Mountain Log Homes					■												■		■	
U.S. Steel											■	■			■	■				756
Unarco Material Handling											■							■		
Unibuilt Industries							■											■		
Unimast												■	■	■				■	■	
United Gilsonite Laboratories (UGL)		■				■												■		
United Panel																	■	■	■	
Vermont Stresskin Panel													■					■	■	

See Manufacturer Index (beige pages at the back of this issue) for address and phone information.   Numbers in red indicate page number for additional product information.

Manufacturer	Concrete block systems	Concrete forms	Concrete & masonry repair products	Foam blocks	Log homes	Masonry products	Modular homes	Panelized building systems	Poured-concrete systems	Pre-cast concrete systems	Steel columns & beams	Steel studs, lightweight	Structural insulated panels (SIPs)	Timber frame homes	Trusses, floor	Trusses, roof	Wall panels	Local dealer/distributor	Factory-direct	Circle No.
Vermont Timber Frames														■		■			■	
Wall Firma				■														■	■	
Wall Ties and Forms									■									■	■	
Ward Log Homes					■														■	
Wausau Homes						147	■						■	■	■	■	■		■	803
Weirton Steel Corp.											■								■	
Welco Mfg. Co.				■															■	
Westchester Modular Homes							■												■	
Western Forms	■								■									■	■	
Wesure Weld								■										■		
WH Porter							■					■				■			■	
Whitacre-Greer				■														■	■	
Winter Panel Corp.							■					■				■			■	
Wisconsin Log Homes					■													■	■	
Wood Truss Council of America															■	■				
Woodkrest Custom Homes														■					■	
Woodmaster Foundations							■										■		■	
WR Bonsal Co.		■		■														■		
WR Meadows, Inc.		■																■		
Wurster Traditional Timber Building					■									■				■	■	

See Manufacturer Index (beige pages at the back of this issue) for address and phone information.   Numbers in red indicate page number for additional product information.

Structural Systems

BUILDING CONCRETE HOMES
5-part video training series from Portland Cement Association helps you master the skills to build beautiful, marketable homes with Insulating Concrete Forms. Homes with the energy efficiency, durability and sound proofing advantages of concrete. 78 minutes. Only $89.95 plus shipping. Call (800) 868-6733 and ask for VC500. http://www.portcement.org
Circle No. 755

U.S. STEEL – AISI
Steel, the consistent choice for framing – consistent price and consistent quality. The American Iron and Steel Institute is your source for information on steel framing. For construction and design publications, construction directories or simply to get answers to technical questions about steel framing, call 1-800-79-STEEL or visit the AISI web site at www.steel.org
Circle No. 756

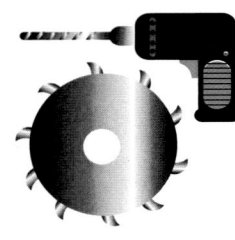

Tools / Electric & Pneumatic

Manufacturer	Accessories	Auto-feed screwdrivers	Circular saws	Compound miter saws	Drills/drivers	Drills/drivers, cordless	Jig saws	Masonry saws	Miter saws	Planers	Plate joiners	Radial saws	Reciprocating saws	Routers	Sanders	Table saws	Pneumatic accessories	Pneumatic tools	Portable compressors	Local dealer/distributor	Factory-direct	Circle No.
																Electric		**Pneumatic**		**Sales**	
3-G's Supply Co.																		■		■		
Adhesive Technologies																		■		■		
AIM Tools & Accessories	■																			■		
Air Nail Co.																	■	■		■		
Alden Corp.	■																			■		
American Design & Engineering						■														■	■	
American Saw & Mfg. Co.	■																			■		
American Tool Cos.	■																					
Atlas Copco Berema	■			■			■										■	■		■	■	
Atro																		■		■		
Au-ve-co Products/(Auto Vehicle Parts Co.)	■																			■		
Bon Tool Co.		■	■	■			■	■										■		■		
BonaKemi USA														■						■		
Campbell Hausfeld																	■	■	■			
Century Drill and Tool Co.	■																			■		
Chicago Pneumatic Tool Co.																		■		■		
Clarke Industries														■						■		
Cobra Tools	■																			■		
Cooper Tools		■															■	■				
The Credo Co.	■																			■		
Danaher Tool Group	■																					
Danair																	■	■		■		
Delta Intl. Machinery Corp.			■					■	150			■	■	■						■		758
DeWalt Industrial Tool Co.	■		■	■	■		■	■	■				■	■						■		
Diamant Boart							■	■	■											■		
Diversitech					■															■		
Dremel						■								■						■		
Duo-Fast Corp.																	■	■		■	■	
Enderes Tool Co.	■																			■	■	
Essex Silver-Line Corp.														■						■	■	
Fein Power Tools			■		■		■						■	■				■		■		
Felker								■												■		
Freud			■	■	■	■	■		■	■			■	■	■					■		
FSI/Scorpion Brand Products		■															■			■	■	
Generac Corp.																			■	■		
Georgia-Pacific Corp.																	■	■	■	■		
Grabber Construction Products			■																	■	■	

Products

Manufacturer	Accessories	Auto-feed screwdrivers	Circular saws	Compound miter saws	Drills/drivers	Drills/drivers, cordless	Jig saws	Masonry saws	Miter saws	Planers	Plate joiners	Radial saws	Reciprocating saws	Routers	Sanders	Table saws	Pneumatic accessories	Pneumatic tools	Portable compressors	Local dealer/distributor	Factory-direct	Circle No.
	Electric																Pneumatic			Sales		
Grizzly Imports	■	■	■	■	■	■	■		■	■		■	■	■	■		■	■	■		■	
Hilti	■			■			■										■	■	■		■	
Hitachi Koki USA	■		■	■	■	■	■						■	■			■	■	■	■		
Houses & Barns by John Libby/Barn Masters		■								■			■									
Indco																	■		■	■		
Ingersoll-Rand Co./Tool & Hoist Div.																■	■	■	■			
Insul-Binder																■						
Interchange Brands																■	■	■	■	■		
International Staple & Machine Co.																	■			■		
International Staple, Nail and Tool Assn.																■		■				
Jepson Power Tools	■		■		■		■	■	■			■	■	■						■		
Jet Equipment & Tools						■						■	■				■	■		■		
Josef Kihlberg of America																■				■		
Kett Tool Co.		■															■			■		
Klein Tools	■			■			■													■		
Kraft Tool Co.																			■	■	■	
Kuny's Mfg. Co.	■																			■		
Land, Air & Sea Tool Corp.	■																			■	■	
LRH Enterprises	■																			■		
Magna Professional Tools/(Primark)	■																			■		
Makita USA	■		■	■	■		■	■	■			■	■	■	■	■	■		■			
Maze Nails																■				■		
Mega Industries	■																■			■	■	
Metabo Corp.	■			■										■						■		
Milwaukee Electric Tool Corp.	■		■	■	■	■	■		■			■	■	■	■					■		
MK Diamond Products								■												■		
MK Morse Co.	■																			■		
Muro North America	■	■														■				■	■	
Newborn Brothers Co.																	■			■		
Nitto Kohki USA																■	■			■		
Norfield Industries	150	■	■	■	■	■	■		■	■							■	■		■	■	759
Norton Co.	■															■				■		
Norton Construction Products		■		■			■												■	■		
Oldham/United States Saw Co.	■																			■		
Omaha Industrial Tools	■																■	■	■	■		
Pam Fastening Technology		■						■								■	■		■	■		
Panasonic				■																■		
Parker Hannifin Corp.																	■	■	■	■		
Partner Industrial Products							■													■		
Paslode, an Illinois Tool Works Co.																	■			■		
Pendu Mfg.		■																			■	
Porter-Cable Corp.	■		■	■	■	■	■		■	■		■	■	■		■	■		■			
Power Tool Institute	■		■	■	■	■	■	■		■			■	■	■							
Power Tool Specialists	■			■	■		■		■	■				■	■		■		■			
Prazi USA	■		■	■																■		
Primark Tool Group	■		■		■	■	■													■	■	
Primatech														■		■	■	■		■		
Prudential Building Materials																■	■	■	■	■		
Quik Drive				■												■				■		
Rhino Tool Co.																	■	■		■		
Roto Zip Tool Corp.	■											■								■		
Rousseau Co.	155																		■		■	764
RSI	■																			■		

continued

Products

Manufacturer	Accessories	Auto-feed screwdrivers	Circular saws	Compound miter saws	Drills/drivers	Drills/drivers, cordless	Jig saws	Masonry saws	Miter saws	Planers	Plate joiners	Radial saws	Reciprocating saws	Routers	Sanders	Table saws	Pneumatic accessories	Pneumatic tools	Portable compressors	Local dealer/distributor	Factory-direct	Circle No.
				Electric													**Pneumatic**			**Sales**		
Ryobi America Corp.		■	■	■	■	■		■		■		■	■	■	■							
S-B Power Tool Co./(Skil Bosch)	■		■		■	■	■	■					■	■	■	■	■		■		■	
Senco Products		■															■	■	■	■		
Sioux Tools	■		■		■	■									■		■	■		■		
SK Hand Tool Corp.																						
Specialty Tools & Fasteners Distrib. Assn.	■	■	■	■	■	■	■	■	■	■	■	■	■	■	■	■						
Spotnails/(A Div. of Peace Industries)																	■	■				
Stanley-Bostitch																	■	■		■		
Steel & Wire Products Co.																	■	■		■		
Swan Secure Products																	■			■		
Target							■													■		
Tarheel Wood Treating Co.																	■	■	■	■		
Thomas Industries																		■	■			
Tridelta Industries	■																				■	
Trimtramp				■					■						■					■		
Trojan Mfg.	■			■					■						■					■	■	
Van Mark Products Corp.															■					■		
Vermont American Tool Co.	■																			■		
VIC Intl. Corp.													■							■	■	
Wen Products	■		■		■		■								■					■		
Woodstock Intl.	■																	■		■		

See Manufacturer Index (beige pages at the back of this issue) for address and phone information.   Numbers in red indicate page number for additional product information.

Tools/Electric & Pneumatic

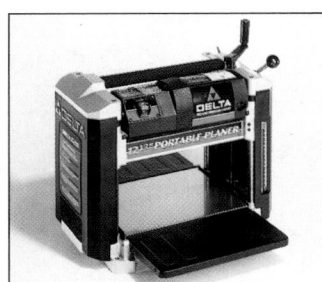

DELTA 12½" PORTABLE PLANER - MODEL 22-560
Delta's 12½" Portable Planer features an exclusive cutterhead snipe control lock that stabilizes the cutterhead for superior snipe control. Patented cutterhead adjustment system raises and lowers raises on four precision ground columns. Quick-change knife system for fast, accurate knife changing. Includes stock roller, adjustable infeed and outfeed tables, and carrying handles. **Circle No. 758**

THE MOST COMPLETE RESOURCE FOR **UNIQUE TOOLS FOR DOOR HARDWARE INSTALLATION**
Norfield Industries, a leader in prehung door machinery for over 35 years, offers a full line of industrial woodworking tools & supplies, specializing in unique tools for prehung door hardware installation. Call for a free catalog (a $10.00 value). 1-800-824-6242.
Circle No. 759

MARTEK® Professional Drill Bit Sharpener. Use the power of any standard electric drill to return high speed steel, carbon steel, masonry and other carbide tipped drill bits to the original manufacturer's specifications. Unit re-grinds dull and broken bits from 3/32" - 1/2" and produces point angles from 80° - 130°. Comes complete with grinding wheels, dressing stick, base plate and carry case. Saves time and money. Easy to use. Full one-year warranty. Satisfaction guaranteed. Just $79.95 (+$5.00 s/h) **(800) 410-5278. Circle No. 760**

Tools / Hand

Manufacturer	Hammers	Levels	Levels, laser	Measuring devices	Planers	Saws	Screwdrivers	Staplers	Tile cutting tools	Tool boxes	Tool pouches/aprons	Wrenches	Local dealer/distributor	Factory-direct	Circle No.
Akro-Mils										■			■	■	
Alltrade	■	■		■		■	■	■		■	■	■	■		
Allway Tools			■		■								■		
American Design & Engineering			■										■	■	
American Saw & Mfg. Co.					■								■		
American Tool Cos.					■	■									
Armstrong World Industries								■					■		
Arrow Fastener Co.			■					■					■		
Atro								■					■		
Better Built Co.										■			■	■	
Bon Tool Co.	■	■	■	■		■			■	■	■		■		
Calculated Industries				■											
Cementex Products					■	■						■	■	■	
Cepco Tool												■	■	■	
CJ Enterprises			■										■	■	
Cleform Tool Co.	■								■		■		■		
CMT Tools				■	■								■	■	
Cobra Tools						■					■	■	■		
Cooper Tools	■			■		■	153					■			618
The Credo Co.						■							■		
Danaher Tool Group	■			■		■	■					■			
Dasco Pro		■		■									■	■	
David White		■		■									■		
Desa Intl.							■								
Diamant Boart									■				■		
Digitool Corp.			■										■	■	
Diversitech						■						■	■		
Duo-Fast Corp.							■						■	■	
Empire Level Mfg. Corp.		■		■									■	■	
Enderes Tool Co.						■							■	■	
Evergreen Slate Co.	■												■	■	
EWC/Tool Div.		■		■									■	■	
Fein Power Tools					■	■							■		
Felker									■				■		
First Choice Tool Co.												■	■		
Frame Master		■		■									■	■	
Freud		■		■		■							■		

See Manufacturer Index (beige pages at the back of this issue) for address and phone information.   Numbers in red indicate page number for additional product information.

continued

50% of home shoppers prefer a brand-new home, 30% want a custom home built on their own lot, and 12% want an existing home.

Source: What Today's Home Buyers Want/ NAHB and Fulton Research

Manufacturer	Hammers	Levels	Levels, laser	Measuring devices	Planers	Saws	Screwdrivers	Staplers	Tile cutting tools	Tool boxes	Tool pouches/aprons	Wrenches	Local dealer/distributor	Factory-direct	Circle No.
Garland Mfg. Co.	■												■	■	
General Tools Mfg. Co.		■		■		■	■						■		
Grizzly Imports		■		■	■									■	
Hempe Mfg. Co.				■		■	■						■		
Hodge Mfg. Co.									■				■		
Interchange Brands								■					■	■	
International Staple & Machine Co.								■					■		
International Tool Boxes										■			■		
Jepson Power Tools						■							■		
Jet Equipment & Tools				■	■	■	■						■		
K Products Group//(A Div. of Cardinal Ind.)		■											■	■	
Kennedy Mfg. Co.										■			■		
Klein Tools	■	■		■		■	■			■	■	■	■		
Knaack Mfg. Co.										■			■		
Kraft Tool Co.	■	■							■	■	■		■	■	
Laser Alignment		■													
Laser Tools Co.		■											■	■	
Laseraim Technologies/Laseraim Tools Div.		■											■	■	
Lectro Science/Intermark							■					■	■		
LeveLite Technology		■	■										■		
LS Starrett Co.		■		■	■								■		
Macklanburg-Duncan		■		■											
Magna Professional Tools/(A Div. of Primark)						■							■		
Makita USA									■						
Malco Tools/(A Div. of Malco Products)	■	■										■	■		
Marshalltown Trowel Co.	■	■				155							■		762
Mayhew Steel Products						■							■		
The Millennium Group						■							■	■	
Milwaukee Electric Tool Corp.	■					■	■		■				■		
MK Diamond Products									■				■		
MK Morse Co.						■							■		
Norfield Industries	■				■							■	■	■	
Norton Construction Products						■			■				■	■	
Occidental Leather											■		■		
Omaha Industrial Tools	■	■		■		■	■					■	■		
Orcon Corp.						155							■		763
Pam Fastening Technology								■					■	■	
Partner Industrial Products						■							■		
Pentax Corp.		■	155	155									■		765, 766
Pinpoint Laser Systems		■	■										■	■	
Plano Molding Co.										■				■	
Plumb/It Level Corp.		■											■	■	
Portable Products										■				■	
Prairie Home Products						■	■						■		
Prazi USA						■							■		
Primark Tool Group		■				■	■						■	■	
Radiator Specialty Co.	■	■		■		■	■					■	■	■	
Reading Body Works										■			■		
Red Devil						■							■	■	
Rotocast/Classic Lamp Posts										■			■	■	
Scalex				■									■		
Sioux Chief Mfg.						■	■						■		
SK Hand Tool Corp.	■						■					■	■		

12.6% of the total sales price on big-volume builders' homes comes from options and upgrades.

Source: BUILDER/Market Probe Intl.

See Manufacturer Index (beige pages at the back of this issue) for address and phone information. Numbers in red indicate page number for additional product information.

continued

HAND TOOLS

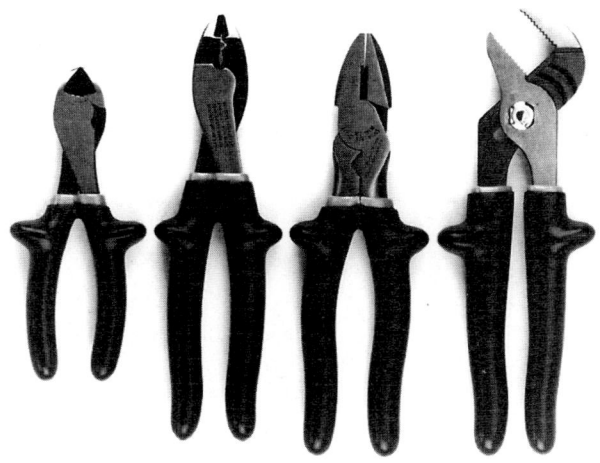

Thomas & Betts: Two-layer insulated handle on tools protects against electrical shocks up to 1,000 volts. Series includes screwdriver, pliers, and nut driver. *T&B Electrician's Supplies.* 901-682-7766. *Circle no. 621.*

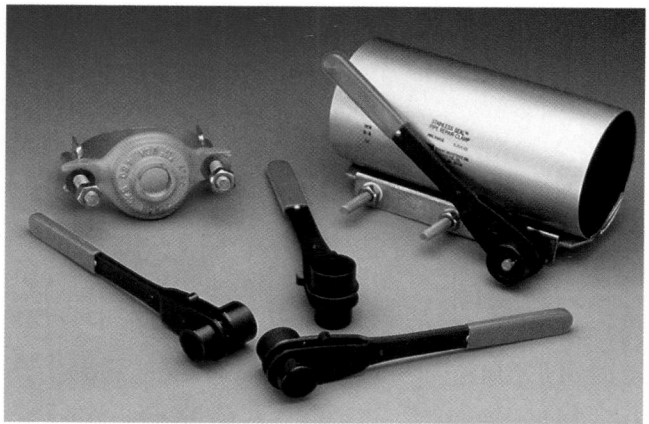

CooperTools: Screwdriver tips are vapor blasted to eliminate chipping. Choice of 10 sets in roll-up storage pouch. *1500/200 Series.* 919-387-0099. *Circle no. 618.*

Lowell: Ratcheting wrenches are equipped with two sockets and reverse control. Each unit is 18 inches long and weighs 2 pounds. *Double Shot.* 1-800-456-9355. *Circle no. 622.*

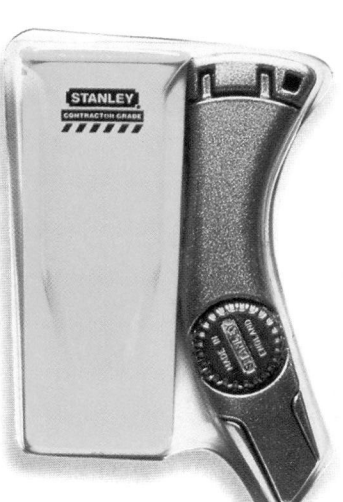

Stanley: Utility knife has brass knob that unscrews to reveal storage compartment for five blades. Available with carrying case that hooks onto belt. *Contractor Grade.* 1-800-648-7654. *Circle no. 619.*

Vaughan: Steel hammer has a plug of rubber and hickory in the striking head to dampen shock waves. Available in curved- and straight-claw styles. *Steel Eagle.* 815-648-2446. *Circle no. 620.*

Hyde Tools: Caulk gun is designed for use with all 9-inch/10-ounce cartridges. Features contoured squeeze trigger and powder-coated barrel. *Smooth Rod #46415.* 508-764-4344. *Circle no. 623.*

Tools / Hand

Manufacturer	Hammers	Levels	Levels, laser	Measuring devices	Planers	Saws	Screwdrivers	Staplers	Tile cutting tools	Tool boxes	Tool pouches/aprons	Wrenches	Local dealer/distributor	Factory-direct	Circle No.
Sokkia Corp.	■	■		■									■		
Solo						■							■	■	
Sonin		■		■											
Specialty Tools & Fasteners Distrib. Assn.	■	■	■	■	■	■	■	■			■		■		
Spectra-Physics Laserplane		■	155	■									■	■	761
Spotnails/(A Div. of Peace Industries)								■					■		
Stanley-Bostitch								■					■		
Stanley Consumer Fastening								■						■	
Stanley Tools	■	■		■	■					■	■		■	■	619
Storehorse										■			■		
Strikemaster Canada	■												■		
Super Pouch											■			■	
Superior Tile Cutter									■				■	■	
Superior Tool Co.												■	■	■	
Swanson Tool Co.				■									■		
Takagi Tools	■					■	■						■		
Truecraft Tools	■			■		■						■	■		
Unicut Corp.				■											
US Tape Co.				■									■		
Vaughan & Bushnell Mfg. Co.	153												■		620
Vermont American Tool Co.						■	■						■		
VIC International Corp.									■				■	■	
Wagner Electronic Products				■									■		
Wagner Spray Tech Corp.							■						■		
Wallboard Tool Co.	■	■		■		■							■		
Waterloo Industries										■			■		
Wen Products						■	■							■	
Wing Enterprises									■				■	■	
Z N R Concept				■									■		
Zircon		■	155										■	■	767, 768

66% of products used in big-volume builders' model homes are nationally known brands.

Source: BUILDER/ Market Probe Intl.

See Manufacturer Index (beige pages at the back of this issue) for address and phone information.   Numbers in red indicate page number for additional product information.

LASERPLANE LEVELING SYSTEMS.
Spectra-Physics Laserplane's new generation of self-leveled Laserplane™ Leveling Systems are designed and manufactured in the U.S.A. Both transmitter and receiver have been redesigned with more features and extended range. New model prices (starting at just $995) are the same as the drastically reduced 1993 prices, but have more value. Spectra-Physics Laserplane, Inc. 5475 Kellenburger Road, Dayton, OH 45424-1099. (800) 538-7800. **Circle No. 761**

MARSHALLTOWN TROWEL
MARSHALLTOWN has expanded its product catalog by 20 pages. A complete spectrum of tools from premium professional quality to homeowner quality, it covers over 1,200 products – trowels and related hand tools for brick/blocklaying, concrete finishing, plaster/drywall, EIFS, and tiling. Marshalltown Trowel Company, P.O. Box 738, Marshalltown, IA 50158. Phone: 515/753-0127. Fax: 515/753-9227. http://www.marshalltown.com. **Circle No. 762**

ROUSSEAU CO.
Portable Workstation: Complete stock support and fence systems for tablesaw, mitersaw and router. Lightweight guaranteed contractor duty components allow quick set up and breakdown for any location. Rousseau Co. 1-800-635-3416. Fax 1-509-758-4991.
Circle No. 764

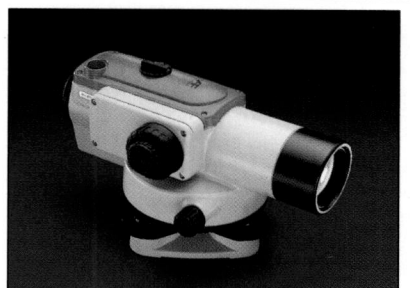

THE WORLD'S FIRST AUTO-FOCUS AUTOMATIC LEVELS
PENTAX AFL-320, AFL-280 and AFL-240 utilize auto-focus technology which provides real benefits to the user by decreasing operation time and reducing eye fatique. Focusing is far faster than manual operation. These 32x, 28x and 24x models also feature water proof construction and lifetime warranty. Pentax Instruments: (303) 643-0351, or fax: (303) 643-0253. **Circle No. 766**

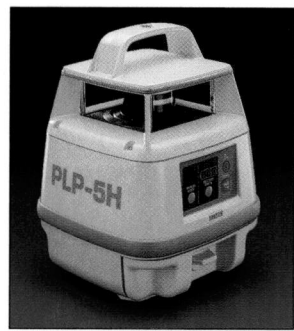

PENTAX ADDS NEW LASER SYSTEMS TO PRODUCT LINEUP
Pentax has introduced several new laser systems that cover all builder applications starting at $675. Pentax's line has lasers from low cost horizontal and vertical, visible beam systems to fully automatic self-leveling systems. They are easy to use and have Pentax's proven reliability. Pentax instruments: 1-800-729-1419. E-mail: mchambers@pentax.com **Circle No. 765**

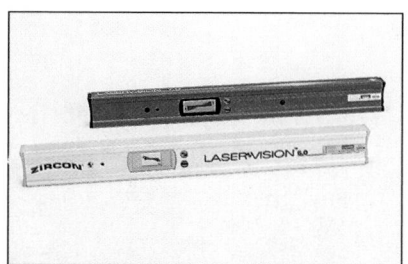

ZIRCON LaserVision™ 6.0 & 7.0
Precision electronic laser level is vastly superior to bubble levels. Saves time, money and costly errors. Recalibrate to factory precision every time used. Single-user operation for pinpoint accuracy to 300 feet. Memorizes custom angles and includes pre-set standard slopes – starting at under $200. Zircon Corporation, 1580 Dell Avenue. P.O. Box 1477, Campbell, CA 95008-6918. 1-800-245-9265 **Circle No. 767**

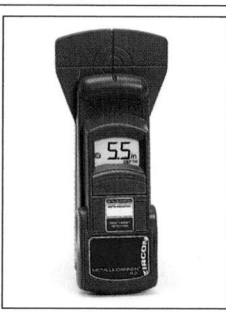

ZIRCON MetalliScanner™ 6.0
Deep scanning metal locator finds rebar and metallic pipes, conduit or studs before drilling or cutting. Pinpoints exact location *and depth* of covered metal – through solid concrete up to half foot thick. Differentiates between steel and copper (or any magnetic vs. nonmagnetic metal) – under $120. Zircon Corporation, 1580 Dell Avenue, P.O. Box 1477, Campbell, CA 95008-6918. 1-800-245-9265 **Circle No. 768**

PRO TECT DRAPE

Pro Tect Drape will allow you to mask an entire room in minutes, eliminating the need for drop cloths and tape. This pre-taped plastic masking drape covers doors, windows, appliances or any large object in one continuous application. Order today, or for a free brochure call **Pro Tect Associates Inc.** 1-800-545-0826. **Circle No. 770**

NATIONAL GYPSUM FLEXIBLE WALLBOARD

New Gold Bond® ¼" High Flex gypsum wallboard saves you time and money on the curves. For tight radius construction such as curved walls, stairways, arches and columns, High Flex eliminates the usual on-the-job scoring, wetting and plaster finishing of standard drywall. Now you can access our Internet home page at http://www.national-gypsum.com **Circle No. 772**

TEMPLE-INLAND STRETCH 54®

Stretch 54™ is the original extra-wide gypsum wallboard from Temple-Inland. Manufactured 54 inches wide, it eliminates gap-filler boards in 9-foot walls. Saves time, labor. Available in 1/2-inch thick in 12-, 14- and 16- lengths. Call (800) 231-6060. www.templeinland.com **Circle No. 774**

DENS-SHIELD® TILE BACKER

Dens-Shield® tile backer provides a superior substrate for interior tile applications – lightweight, easy-to-install and stops water at the surface protecting your wall cavity. Its proprietary treated core is reinforced by embedded glass mats for strength and then a heat-cured acrylic coating is added as water barrier. Various sizes, 20-year warranty. Call 1-800-BUILD G-P (284-5347) for details. www.gp.com **Circle No. 771**

TIN CEILINGS

Pressed-Tin for walls and ceilings. Styles range from Art-Deco to Victorian. They come in sheets 2' x 4' for easy installation. The designs are 6", 12" and 24" repeat patterns. The material is Tin-Plated Steel and is excellent for paint retention. Cornice is also available in 4' lengths; Widths vary from 2" to 9". This type of ceiling is for both commercial and residential application. We ship anywhere. Free Catalogs: Chelsea Decorative Metal Co., 9603 Moonlight Dr., Dept. B, Houston, Texas 77096. (713) 721-9200. www.TheTinman.com **Circle No. 773**

PREST-ON® DRYWALL CLIPS

Save 'lotsa' lumber, time and energy Drywaller applied and fire rated. Prest-on's also reduce corner cracking due to "truss uplift." Call (800) 323-1813 for details. **Circle No. 775**

Walls, Ceilings & Finishes

Manufacturer	Ceiling tile, acoustic	Ceiling tile, metal	Ceramic tile	Cultured marble	Drywall	Fabric-coated panels	Granite/slate/other stone	Mirrors	Paneling, board	Paneling, sheet	Plaster	Predecorated gypsum	Tile backerboard	Local dealer/distributor	Factory-direct	Circle No.
				Products										**Sales**		
AA Abbingdon Affiliates		■												■		
ABT Building Products Corp./ABTco									■					■		
AE Gombert Lumber Co.									■					■		
Afco Industries					■				■		■			■	■	
Aged Woods								■	■					■	■	
American Hardboard Assn.									■							
American Marazzi Tile			■											■		
American Marble Industries/Kephaco Corp.				■										■	■	
American Olean Tile			■										■	■		
Amsterdam Corp.			■										■	■	■	
Architectural Reproductions				■										■		
Architectural Sculpture												■		■		
Arius Tile Co.			■											■		
Armstrong World Industries	■															
Assn. of the Wall & Ceiling Industries Intl.	■	■			■						■					
Barrisol Stretch Ceilings	■													■		
Boiardi Products Corp.			■											■		
BPCO/(A Div. of EMCO)	■													■	■	
Buchtal Corp. USA			■													
Building Products & Nails/Div. BSTC Group									■							
Cameo Marble				■										■	■	
Canexel/(A Div. of ABT Building Products)									■					■	■	
Cangelosi Marble & Granite			■				■							■		
Carlisle Restoration Lumber								■						■		
Carolina Mirror Co.								■						■	■	
Ceilings & Interior Systems Const. Assn.	■	■			■						■					
The Celotex Corp.	■				■									■		
Ceramic Tile Distributors Assn.			■													
Chelsea Decorative Metal Co.		156													■	773
Chemcrest Architectural Products						■								■		
Chesapeake Hardwood Products								■	■					■		
Chicago Metallic		■														
Classic Architectural Specialties		■												■		
Continental Stone Designs				■										■	■	
Country Homestead/Restoration Contractor									■					■	■	
CSI Donner								■						■		
Cultured Stone®/Stone Products Corp.							■							■		

61% of new-home shoppers want cathedral ceilings in the living room; 44% want them in the family room; and 42% want them in the master bedroom.

Source: What Today's Home Buyers Want/NAHB and Fulton Research

See Manufacturer Index (beige pages at the back of this issue) for address and phone information.   Numbers in red indicate page number for additional product information.

continued

Walls, Ceilings & Finishes

Manufacturer	Ceiling tile, acoustic	Ceiling tile, metal	Ceramic tile	Cultured marble	Drywall	Fabric-coated panels	Granite/slate/other stone	Mirrors	Paneling, board	Paneling, sheet	Plaster	Predecorated gypsum	Tile backerboard	Local dealer/distributor	Factory-direct	Circle No.
Custom Building Products													■	■		
Dal-Tile Corp.			■												■	
Dean Hardwood									■					■	■	
Designs In Tile			■												■	
Diversitech						■								■		
Domtar Gypsum					■							■		■		
Douglas Drywall Co.					■											
Eagle Plywood & Door Manufacturers										■						
Entol Industries	■													■		
Epro			■											■		
Eternit													■	■		
F.C.P.													■	■		
Fiberglass Access						■								■		
Flexi-Wall Systems					■	■					■	■			■	
Florida Tile/(A Div. of Premark)			■											■		
Formglas					■										■	
Forms + Surfaces		■													■	
French Reflection								■						■		
Georgia-Pacific Corp.					■				■	■		156		■		771
Gibco Services					■	■			■	■				■		
Gilded Mirrors								■							■	
Giles & Kendall									■					■	■	
Goodwin Heart Pine Co.									■	■				■	■	
Graham Products							■							■	■	
Grani-Decor Tiles							■							■	■	
Gypsum Assn.					■											
Hardwood Plywood & Veneer Assn.									■							
Hardwoods Millworking									■					■		
Holland Log Homes Mfg. Co.									■					■	■	
House of Ceramics			■												■	
Hunter Douglas Architectural Products		■													■	
Hyde & Meeks Industries				■										■	■	
Hyde Park Fine Art of Moulding											■			■	■	
Illbruck	■								■					■	■	
Interceramic, USA			■											■		
International Cellulose Corp.	■														■	
International Institute for Lath and Plaster											■			■	■	
Italian Marble Ctr./Italian Trade Commission				■												
Italian Tile Assn.			■											■		
Italian Trade Commission, Tile Center			■											■		
Jackson Sawmill Co.									■						■	
James Hardie Building Products													■	■		
James Hardie Gypsum					■							■		■		
Jamo												■		■		
JJ Barker									■					■		
Kaylien									■					■	■	
Kentucky Millwork									■					■		
LaHabra Stucco											■			■		
Laminating Materials Assn.									■					■		
Latco Products			■											■	■	
Laticrete Intl.			■										■	■		
Laurel Co.				■										■	■	
Liette Intl.			■											■		

50% of new-home shoppers want a skylight in the bathroom; 46% want one in the kitchen.

Source: What Today's Home Buyers Want/NAHB and Fulton Research

Manufacturer	Ceiling tile, acoustic	Ceiling tile, metal	Ceramic tile	Cultured marble	Drywall	Fabric-coated panels	Granite/slate/other stone	Mirrors	Paneling, board	Paneling, sheet	Plaster	Predecorated gypsum	Tile backerboard	Local dealer/distributor	Factory-direct	Circle No.
London Tile Co.			■											■	■	
Lone Star Ceramics Co.			■													
Louisiana-Pacific Corp.					■									■		
LWO Corp.									■	■				■		
M.L. Condon Co.									■					■	■	
MacMillan Bloedel/Building Materials Mktg.									■	■				■		
Marlite									■	■				■	■	
Materials Marketing Corp.			■											■	■	
McIntyre Tile			■											■	■	
McShan Lumber Co.									■					■		
Miracle Sealants & Abrasives			■											■		
Mirrex Corp.								■							■	
Monarch Tile			■											■		
Monumental Construction and Moulding Co.												■			■	
National Gypsum Co.			156								■	■	■	■		772
Niagara Fiberboard					■									■	■	
Niles Building Products									■					■		
North American Assn. of Mirror Mfrs.								■								
Petmal Supply Co.			■			■								■	■	
Pinecrest		■													■	
Ply Gem Mfg.			■						■	■				■		
Plywood Tropics USA										■				■	■	
Porcelanite			■											■		
Prest-on Co.					156									■		775
Proko Industries									■					■		
Prudential Building Materials	■	■												■		
Quality American									■					■	■	
Quarry Tile Co.			■											■		
Ray White Lumber Co.									■							
Renato Bisazza							■							■	■	
Ro-Tile			■	■										■		
Rocktile Specialty Products							■								■	
Romatt Doors									■	■				■	■	
Sagebrush Sales									■					■		
Santile Intl. Corp.								■						■		
Shakertown Corp.									■					■		
Shanker Industries	■	■							■					■		
Sherle Wagner Intl.			■													
Sioux Veneer Panel Co.									■	■				■		
Snap-Trak					■									■	■	
Solnhofen Natural Stone							■							■	■	
Sound Concepts Canada				■	■									■	■	
States Industries									■					■		
Steptoe & Wife Antiques		■												■	■	
STO Finish Systems/(A Div. of STO Corp.)											■			■		
Stromberg's Architectural Products					■										■	
The Structural Slate Co.							■								■	
Summitville Tiles			■											■	■	
Super-Tek Products													■	■	■	
Superior Hardwoods & Millwork									■						■	
Surebond							■							■		
Tarheel Wood Treating Co.					■									■		
Temple-Inland Forest Products					■	■				156				■		774

See Manufacturer Index (beige pages at the back of this issue) for address and phone information.   Numbers in red indicate page number for additional product information.   continued

Walls, Ceilings & Finishes

Manufacturer	Ceiling tile, acoustic	Ceiling tile, metal	Ceramic tile	Cultured marble	Drywall	Fabric-coated panels	Granite/slate/other stone	Mirrors	Paneling, board	Paneling, sheet	Plaster	Predecorated gypsum	Tile backerboard	Local dealer/distributor	Factory-direct	Circle No.
Terra-Green Technologies/Stoneware Tile			■											■		
Tile Cera			■											■		
Tile Council of America			■										■	■	■	
Tile Showcase			■				■							■		
The Tileworks			■											■	■	
The TonJon Co.						■								■		
Trade Commission of Spain/Tile from Spain			■											■	■	
United States Ceramic Tile Co.			■											■		
United States Gypsum Co.					■						■	■				
USG Interiors	■	■														
Valentina Ratti Creations USA								■						■	■	
Virginia Mirror Co.								■						■		
Walker & Zanger			■											■	■	
WD Cowls									■							
Welco Mfg. Co.				■						■					■	
Westchester Marble & Granite			■				■							■		
Western Quarry Tile			■												■	
Western Red Cedar Lumber Assn.									■							
Western Wood Products Assn.							■		■					■		
Whittlesey Wood Products							■							■		
Windsor Mill									■					■		
Woodwork Institute of California							■		■							
Z-Brick Brands			■											■	■	

See Manufacturer Index (beige pages at the back of this issue) for address and phone information.   Numbers in red indicate page number for additional product information.

Windows & Glass

Manufacturer	Decorative glass	Glass block	Impact-resistant glass	Shading systems	Aluminum/aluminum-clad	Combination materials	Composite, wood	Fiberglass	Vinyl/vinyl-clad	Wood	Awning	Bay/bow	Casement	Cellar/basement	Circle top	Custom	Double-hung	Single-hung	Skylights/roof	Sliding horizontal	Local dealer/distributor	Factory-direct	Circle No.
	Glass				**Composition**						**Style**										**Sales**		
Abundant Energy				■														■			■		
Acadia Windows & Doors										■	■	■	■	■	■	■		■			■	■	
Acan Windows										■	■	■				■	■	■			■		
Acme Brick Co./IBP Grid System		■		■													■				■	■	
Acro Extrusion Corp.										■	■	■	■			■	■				■	■	
AFG Industries	■		■																			■	
Alcoa Vinyl Windows										■	■	■	■	■	■	■	■				■	■	
Alenco				■						■	■	■	■			■	■				■		
Almetco Building Products				■						■	■	■	■	■	■	■	■	■		■	■	■	
Alside/Window Div.										■	■	■	■	■	■	■	■			■			
ALUMET Building Products										■												■	
Ambiance of High Point	■																						
American Architectural Manufacturers Assn.					■	■	■	■		■	■	■	■	■	■	■	■	■		■	■		
American Skylites																			■		■		
Amerimax Building Products										■	■	■	■		■	■	■				■	■	
Andersen Windows								■		■	■	■	■	■	*167*	■	■			■	■		6,101
APC Building Products										■	■	■	■				■	■			■	■	
Apollo Windows/(A Div. of Sun Windows)			■	■	■	■				■	■	■	■	■	■	■	■			■	■	■	
Artisan Glass Works	■																					■	
Atrium Door & Window Co.									■	■	■		■			■		■		■	■	■	
Bautex Window Automation				■																	■	■	
Bay World Intl.									■	■			■								■		
Baylite/Div. of Bay Mills	■																					■	
Berlinex										■	■	■	■		■	■	■				■	■	
Better-Bilt				■						■		■	■		■	■	■				■		
Beveled Glass Designs	■																				■		
Beveled Glass Works	■								■				■		■	■						■	
Bilt Best Windows				■						■		■											
Bird Vinyl Products										■	■	■	■		■	■	■	■		■	■		
Bloc-Ease Corp.		■	■																		■	■	
Blomberg Window Systems				■			■			■	■	■	■		■	■	■			■		■	
Blumer & Stanton										■			■		■	■	■				■	■	
Bonneville Windows & Doors				■						■	■	■	■	■	■	■	■			■	■		
Bristolite Skylights				■															■				
Bruce Alford Corp.	■																				■	■	
Capitol Windows & Doors/(Metal Industries)				■						■	■	■	■		■	■	■	■		■	■		
Caradco				■				■ *162*		■	■	■			■	*167*	■	■		■	■		246,629,632

WOOD & WOOD-CLAD WINDOWS

Semco: Double-hung wood window has foam insulation in sill envelope; enhances thermal performance, company claims. Available with various dual-sealed glazing options. *DCS double hung window.* 1-800-333-2206. *Circle no. 630.*

Caradco: Wood windows have new tilt-assist feature that allows bottom sash to tilt inward for easy cleaning. Available on all clad and primed double-hung windows. *Tilt-Assist.* 1-800-238-1866. *Circle no. 629.*

Pozzi: Line of wood windows can be left in natural wood state, primed, or wrapped in four aluminum-clad colors. Also available in 27 colors. 1-800-821-1016. *Circle no. 631.*

COMPANY	STYLE	MATERIALS				U-VALUE (AA)	R-VALUE (AA)	GLAZING OPTIONS					PHONE
		ALUMINUM-CLAD	PRIMED WOOD	VINYL-CLAD	WOOD			ARGON-FILLED	INSULATED	LOW-E	TEMPERED	TINTED	
Andersen	Tilt double-hung	x			x	.31	4.30	x	x	x	x	x	1-800-426-4261
Caradco	Clad casement double-hung	x			x	.53	1.89	x	x	x	x	x	1-800-238-1866
Hurd	Casement		x		x	.26	3.90	x	x	x		x	1-800-433-4873
Kolbe & Kolbe	Double-hung		x		x	.38	2.63	x	x	x			715-842-5666
Lincoln Windows	Casement	x	x		x	.49	2.04	x	x	x	x	x	715-536-2461
Peachtree	Tilt double-hung	x			x	.36	2.78	x	x	x			1-800-477-6544
Pella Corporation	Tilt double-hung	x	x		x	.53	1.90	x	x	x			1-800-84-PELLA
Pozzi	Double-hung	x	x		x	—	—	x	x	x	x	x	1-800-821-1016
Semco	Double-hung	x			x	.26	3.85	x	x	x			1-800-333-2206
Vetter	Casement	x	x		x	.48	2.08	x	x	x		x	1-800-VETTER2
Weather Shield	Casement	x	x	x	x	.22	4.54	x	x	x	x	x	1-800-477-6808

Companies in red have product shown above.

Windows & Glass

Manufacturer	Glass: Decorative glass	Glass block	Impact-resistant glass	Shading systems	Composition: Aluminum/aluminum-clad	Combination materials	Composite, wood	Fiberglass	Vinyl/vinyl-clad	Wood	Style: Awning	Bay/bow	Casement	Cellar/basement	Circle top	Custom	Double-hung	Single-hung	Skylights/roof	Sliding horizontal	Sales: Local dealer/distributor	Factory-direct	Circle No.
Caradon Lock-Wood					■			■	■	■	■	■	■			■	■		■		■		
Cardiff Industries			■																			■	
Carefree Windows/(CFA Window Group)			■		■			■			■	■	■	■	■	■	■		■		■		
Castec Window Shading			■																		■	■	
CertainTeed Windows								■			■	■	■	■	■	■	■			■	■	■	9
Chautauqua Woods Corp.	■																				■		
Chelsea Building Products								■			■	■	■	■	■	■			■		■		
Circle Redmont		■			■													■			■		
Classy Glass Sunrooms					■													■					
Columbia Aluminum Windows & Doors		■			■		■	■			■	■	■	■		■							
Columbia Mfg. Co.					■			■	■									■			■		
Comfort Line								■	■		■	■	■		■	■	■		■		■		
Courtaulds Performance Films			■																		■		
Craft-Bilt Mfg. Co.			■														■	■			■		
Craftline/(A Div. of Vega Industries)			■		■			■	■	■			■		■	■	■	■			■		
Creative Structures								■	■	■							■				■		
Crestline/SNE Enterprises/A PLY GEM Co.					■	■		■	■		■	■	■			■					■		
CW Ohio					■			■	■						■	■					■		
Dayton Technologies								■			■	■	■	■		■	■					■	784
Decorative Glass Intl.	■																				■		
Delsan Industries								■			■	■	■	■	■	■	■			■	■		
Downes & Reader Hardwood Co.																	■						
Duo-Gard Industries			■	■	■	■		■					■			■		■			■		
Duo-Temp								■			■	■	■	■	■	■	■		■	■	■		
Dura Art Stone		■																			■		
Duratherm Window Corp.							■		■		■		■		■	■		■			■		
Duschqueen	■																				■	■	
Eagle Window & Door					■					■	■	167				■	■				■		103
EFCO Corp.					■								■		■	■	■				■		
Elite Products Wholesale	■																				■		
Engineered Profiles								■			■	■	■	■	■	■	■		■	■			
Eurotec/Tilt & Turn Windows									■				■			■					■		
Farley Windows								■			■	■	■		■	■	■	■			■		
FEN-Tech	■							■					■			■	■				■	■	
Fibertec Window Mfg.						■	■				■	■	■	■		■	■		■		■		
Fillmore Thomas & Co.					■				■		■		■			■	■				■		
GAPCO					■			■					■			■					■		
General Aluminum Corp.					■								■	■		■		■	■	■	■		
Georgia-Pacific Corp.							168	■			■		■	■			■	■			■		780
Gerkin Windows & Doors					■			■			■	■	■	■	■	■	■	■		■	■	■	
Glass Block Designs		■																			■		
Glass Blocks Unlimited		■																				■	
Gorell Enterprises								■			■	■	■		■	■	■	■		■	■		786
Great Lakes Window								■			■	■	■	■	■	■	■	■		■	■	■	
H Window Co.					■	■	■	■			■	■	■		■	■					■		
The Hess Mfg. Co.	■							■			■	■	■	■	■	■	■	■		■	■	■	
Hi Pro Intl.					■	■												■			■	■	
Homeshield Fabricated Products					■											■		■					
Hurd Millwork Co.					■			■		■			■			■	■			■	■		472,556
Hy-Lite Block Windows		■			■			■			■		■			■					■		
Inde-Pane	■																					■	
Inline Fiberglass							■				■	■	■	■		■			■				
Insuladome Skylights						■													■		■		

See Manufacturer Index (beige pages at the back of this issue) for address and phone information.   Numbers in red indicate page number for additional product information.   continued

Windows & Glass

Manufacturer	Decorative glass	Glass block	Impact-resistant glass	Shading systems	Aluminum/aluminum-clad	Combination materials	Composite, wood	Fiberglass	Vinyl/vinyl-clad	Wood	Awning	Bay/bow	Casement	Cellar/basement	Circle top	Custom	Double-hung	Single-hung	Skylights/roof	Sliding horizontal	Local dealer/distributor	Factory-direct	Circle No.
	Glass				**Composition**						**Style**										**Sales**		Circle No.
Insulate Industries								■			■	■	■		■	■		■	■	■	■		
J A W Window & Door			■					■			■	■	■	■	■	■		■		■	■		
Jancik Arts	■																					■	
JD's Glassworks	■							■							■	■					■	■	
JELD-WEN of Oregon								■					■								■	■	
Jenkins Mfg./Monarch Windows					■			■			■	■	■		■	■	■				■		
The JJJ Specialty Co.					■			■			■	■	■		■					■	■		
The Jordan Cos.					■		168								■	■	■		■	■	■	■	781
Joyce Mfg.					■						■						■	■	■				
Kenergy/(A Div. of SNE Enterprises)					■				■									■					
Kensington Windows								■			■	■	■		■	■	■			■	■		
Kentucky Millwork								■					■	■	■	■					■		
Kewanee Corp./Midway Tech Center					■									■							■		
Keystone Wood Products								■					■								■		
KML Windows	■				■			■	■		■	■	■		■	■	■				■		
Kolbe & Kolbe Millwork Co.					■			■			■	■	■		■	167	■	■		■	■		100
Laticrete Intl.		■																			■		
LB Plastics								■			■	■	■		■	■	■			■	■	■	
Leslie-Locke					■														■		■	■	
Lincoln Wood Products					■			■			■	■	■		■	■	■				■		
Lindal Cedar Homes/Sunrooms							■	■			■	■	■		■	■	■	■	■		■		
Loewen Windows					■			■			■	■	■	■	■	■	■			■	■		
Louisiana-Pacific Corp.					■		168	168	■		■	■		■	■	■	■			■	■		
MacMillan Bloedel/Building Materials Mktg.								■								■					■		
Major Industries					■														■		■	■	
Malta Wood Windows & Doors					■			■			■	■	■		■	■	■			■	■		
Marvin Windows & Doors					■	■	■	■			■	■	■		■	■	■			■	■		99
Mason Corp.					■			■			■				■	■	■			■	■		
Mayer Equity		■																					
Medieval Glass Industries	■																				■	■	
MGM Industries								■	■			■			■	■	■			■	■	■	
Milgard Windows			■	■		■		■	■		■	■	■		■	■	■			■	■	■	
Missoula White Pine Sash Co.								■		■	■	■	■			■				■	■		
MW Windows/MW Manufacturers								■			■	■	■		■	■	■			■	■		
Napco								■			■	■	■		■	■	■			■			
National Mfg.			■					■			■	■	■				■			■	■		
National Products	■																				■	■	
National Wood Window and Door Assn.	■		■		■		■	■	■		■	■	■	■	■	■	■				■	■	
New England Glass Enclosures																			■		■	■	
New Morning Windows			■	■	■			■			■		■		■	■	■	■			■		
Norco Windows					■			■			■	■	■		■	■	■			■	■		
Northeast Window and Door Assn.	■		■	■	■	■	■	■			■	■	■	■	■	■	■					■	
Northwest Window Works									■		■	■	■	■	■	■	■			■		■	
O'Keeffe's																			■				
ODL					■			■	■										■		■		102
Oldach Wood Windows & Doors					■			■			■	■	■		■	■	■			■		■	
Omniglass						■	■				■	■	■		■	■					■		
Owens Corning							■				■	■	■	■	■	■				■	■	■	
Peachtree Doors					■					■			■		■	■					■		245
Peerless Products		■			■			■			■	■	■		■	■	■			■	■	■	
Pella Corporation		■	■						■	■	■	■	■		■	■	■			■	■		
PH Tech								■	■		■	■	■		■	■	■	■				■	
Phifer Wire Products			■																		■	■	

See Manufacturer Index (beige pages at the back of this issue) for address and phone information.

Numbers in red indicate page number for additional product information.

Products

Manufacturer	Glass				Composition						Style										Sales		Circle No.
	Decorative glass	Glass block	Impact-resistant glass	Shading systems	Aluminum/aluminum-clad	Combination materials	Composite, wood	Fiberglass	Vinyl/vinyl-clad	Wood	Awning	Bay/bow	Casement	Cellar/basement	Circle top	Custom	Double-hung	Single-hung	Skylights/roof	Sliding horizontal	Local dealer/distributor	Factory-direct	
Philips Products				■				■			■	■	■	■		■	■			■	■		
Pittsburgh Corning Corp.		■																			■		
Plasteco				■															■			■	
Pollard Windows							■	■		■	■	■	■	■	■	■	■			■		■	
Polytronix		■		■																		■	
Portal				■							■	■	■	■	■	■	■	■	■			■	
Pozzi Wood Windows (A Div. of JELD-WEN)				■					162		■	■	■		■	■	■	■			■		631
PPG Industries			■																■				
R Laflamme et Frere							■	■		■	■	■	■	■	■	■	■		■				
RBP Custom Glass/D & S Insulated Glass	■																				■		
Rehau								■			■	■	■		■		■	■		■	■		
Repla				■				■			■	■	■	■	■	■	■	■	■	■	■		
Reynolds Metals Co.				■				■			■	■	■	■	■	■	■		■		■		
Roto Frank of America			■		■														■		■	■	
Royal Plastics Group								■			■	■	■		■	■	■		■		■		
Screen Manufacturers Assn.				■																			
Screen Tight				■															■		■		
Screenex Design Center/(Riordan Group)				■																		■	
Seal Rite Windows				■				■	■		■	■	■	■	■	■	■		■		■		
Semco Windows & Doors/Semling-Menke				■					■		■	■	■	■	■	■	162	■		■	■		630
Sholton Glass Block Systems		■											■							■	■		
Sierra Pacific Windows				■				■	■		■	■	■		■				■		■		
Silver Line Building Products				■			168				■	■	■	■	■	■	■		■		■	■	777
Simonton Windows									■		■	■	■		■		■		■		■		
SkyQuest			■																			■	
Skytech Systems																			■		■	■	
Solaris Quebec								■			■	■	■		■		■		■		■	■	
SOLATUBE Intl.				■															■			■	
Somfy Systems			■																		■		
Southwest Door Co.							■					■									■		
Spectus Systems								■			■	■	■		■	■	■		■		■	■	
Starbrite/(A Div. of Vega Industries)								■			■	■	■		■	■	■		■		■		
Stillwater Products										■											■	■	
Sugarcreek Window & Door Corp.				■				■			■	■	■		■		■				■		
Summit Windows & Patio Doors/(JELD-WEN)				■				■	■		■	■	■	■	■	■	■	■		■	■		
Sun-Tek Industries				■					■										■		■		
Sun Tunnel Skylights																			■		■	■	
Sun Windows			■	■				■	■		■	■	■		■	■	■		■		■	■	
Sunbilt Solar Products by Sussman			■	■							■		■			■	■		■			■	
Sunburst Skylights																			■		■	■	
Sunesta Products				■																	■		
SunTuf																			■		■	■	
Superior Hardwoods & Millwork	■																					■	
Superseal Mfg. Co.								■			■	■	■		■	■	■			■	■		
Survivor Technologies								■			■	■	■		■	■	■				■		
Swedish Building Systems & Components				■					■				■								■	■	
TAM Industries				■															■		■		
Thermal-Gard	■							■			■	■	■		■	■	■		■		■		
Thermal Industries	■							■			■	■	■		■	■	■		■		■		
Thermetic Glass								■			■	■	■		■	■	■		■		■		
Thermo-Vu Sunlite Industries			■													■			■		■		
Thermolock Mfg. Co.								■			■	■	■		■	■	■		■		■	■	
Thermoplast							■				■	■	■		■	■	■			■		■	

See Manufacturer Index (beige pages at the back of this issue) for address and phone information.   Numbers in red indicate page number for additional product information.

continued

Windows & Glass

Manufacturer	Glass				Composition						Style										Sales		Circle No.
	Decorative glass	Glass block	Impact-resistant glass	Shading systems	Aluminum/aluminum-clad	Combination materials	Composite, wood	Fiberglass	Vinyl/vinyl-clad	Wood	Awning	Bay/bow	Casement	Cellar/basement	Circle top	Custom	Double-hung	Single-hung	Skylights/roof	Sliding horizontal	Local dealer/distributor	Factory-direct	
Thornton Art Glass	■																						
Timeline Vinyl Windows		■						168			■	■	■	■	■	■	■	■		■	■		779
TRACO				■					■		■	■	■	■	■	■	■			■	■	■	
Tru-Vex Glass Co.	■																					■	
Tubular Skylight																			■		■	■	
Unicel			■	■									■						■		■	■	
United Window Manufacturers							■	■	■	■			■			■	■			■			
US Sky//(A Div. of Stora Enterprises Co.)			■	■															■			■	
Velux-America				■															■				
Ventana Plastics Co.							■						■		■	■		■					
Ventarama Skylight Corp.																			■				
Vetter, SNE Enterprises//(A PLYGEM Co.)				■			■	■			■	■	■		■	■	■			■	■		547
Victor Sun Control				■			■				■									■	■		
Viking Industries				■			■				■	■	■		■	■	■			■	■		
Vinyl Building Products									■		■	■	■		■	■	■	■		■	■	■	
Vinyl Lite II Window & Door Systems	■								■		■	■	■	■	■	■	■	■		■	■	■	
Vinyl Tech/PGT								■	■		■	■	■			■	■			■			
Vinyl View//(A Div. of Thermetic Glass)									■		■	■	■	■	■	■	■	■		■	■		
Vinyl Window Designs								■	■		■	■	■	■	■	■	■	■		■	■	■	
Vinyl Window & Door Institute									■		■	■	■	■	■	■	■		■	■			
Vynex Corp.									■		■	■	■	■		■	■			■	■	■	
Wasco Products							■	■											■	■			
Weather Shield Mfg.									■		■	■	■	■	■	■	■	■	■	■	■	■	81,268,269,270
Weathervane Window Co.		■							■		■	■	■	■	■	■	■			■	■	■	
Weck Glass/Glashaus		168																				■	778
WENCO//(A Div. of JELD-WEN)				■		■	■	■	■	■	■	■	■	■	■	■	■	■		■	■	■	226
Western Forms									■							■				■	■	■	
Westview Products									■							■			■		■	■	
Wheatbelt				■																	■	■	
Willmar Windows							■	■	■		■	■	■	■	■	■	■	■		■	■	■	
Wilmes Window Mfg. Co.								■	■				■			■	■					■	
Window Quilt/Northern Cross Industries				■																	■	■	
Windsor Window Co.-NC Plant						■	■	■	■		■	■	■		■	■	■				■		550
Winstrom Mfg. Corp.								■	■		■	■	■							■	■		
The Woodstone Co.							■				■	■	■		■	■	■	■	■		■	■	
Woodwork Institute of California							■					■	■		■	■	■	■		■			

See Manufacturer Index (beige pages at the back of this issue) for address and phone information.   Numbers in red indicate page number for additional product information.

79% of new-home shoppers
want double-pane windows.

*Source: What Today's Home Buyers Want/
NAHB and Fulton Research*

64% of new-home shoppers want
bay windows and 55% want skylights.

*Source: What Today's Home Buyers Want/
NAHB and Fulton Research*

DECORATIVE WINDOWS

Andersen: Window patterns imitate the geometric stained glass designs of Frank Lloyd Wright. Available in a range of patterns including Colonnade, Prairie Rhythm, Wichita, and Eucalyptus. *Art Glass Series.* 1-800-426-4261. *Circle no. 101.*

Kolbe & Kolbe Millwork: Octagonal, circle, round-top, gothic, and oval windows are set with ⅞-inch-thick triple insulating decorative glass. Also available with optional grille patterns. *Decorative Series.* 1-800-955-8177. *Circle no. 100.*

ODL: Fixed window has translucent center pane of leaded glass panels with glue chip and beveled glass in four designs. Available in four sizes, all framed with primed wood and exterior brick moulding. *Statement Glass Windows.* 1-800-253-3900. *Circle no. 102.*

Caradco: Decorative glass for transoms is set between panes of insulated glass. Frames have wood interiors and wood or aluminum-clad exteriors. Choice of three clear glass patterns trimmed with beveled glass accents and brass caming. *Decorative Glass Collection.* 1-800-238-1866. *Circle no. 632.*

NOT PICTURED

Eagle Window and Door: Two glass options have been added to line of decorative windows. Patterns have colored caming accents and are set between panes of dual-sealed insulated glass. Available with extruded aluminum-clad and all-wood windows. *Decorelle.* 1-800-453-3633. *Circle no. 103.*

PRO TECT FOR WINDOWS

Pro Tect for **Windows** is an ideal masking solution for protecting against over-sprays, mortar stains, muriatic acid and more. The clear film shows off finished surfaces while it protects for up to 45 days without leaving a residue. Call and order today, or for a free brochure, **Pro Tect Associates Inc.** 1-800-545-0826. **Circle No. 776**

WOOD WINDOWS

LOUISIANA-PACIFIC

Louisiana-Pacific has introduced a new generation of aluminum-clad wood windows and patio doors – the Cierra Grande™ line. New energy-saving glass that combines a low-e coating, warm-edge spacer and argon gas. Upgraded design features include one-piece composite sills on double-hung and glider styles., and factory-applied nail fins on all models. **Call (800) 299-0028, ext. 4021 for a free brochure and distributor information.**

TIMELINE VINYL WINDOWS & DOORS

Utilizing the latest in state-of-the-art machining, fabrication and glazing technologies, Timeline brings the ultimate in performance, quality and reliability. The complete line is available in standard or custom sizes making them the ideal for any new construction or remodeling project. Call toll-free 888-TLVINYL for more information. **Circle No. 779**

SERIES 1000 DOUBLE HUNG WINDOWS

Silver Line's Series 1000 Double Hung window provides traditional style with all of the performance expected from today's technologically advanced windows. Clean, simple sightlines, color coordinated hardware, beveled exterior profiles and specially contoured grilles offer the details of classic craftsmanship. Innovative engineering has combined all of this with the performance and convenience of maintenance free vinyl construction to create an extraordinary new construction window value. For more info, call (800) 234-4228. **Circle No. 777**

VINYL WINDOWS

LOUISIANA-PACIFIC

Introducing Astoria™Pro vinyl windows: built for beauty, energy savings, and easy maintenance. The multi-cavity construction, 3/4" double-insulating glass and a new low-conductive "warm-edge" glass spacer help reduce heat and cold transfer. Available with high-performance low-e Energywise™ glass. AstoriaPro windows come in a wide range of standard sizes and shapes. **Call (800) 299-0028, ext. 4020 for a free brochure and distributor information.**

GRAND VIEW™ VINYL WINDOWS

New Construction Series™ of uPVC windows and patio doors from Georgia-Pacific features single-hung, double-hung, casement, bay, bow and garden windows, hinged and sliding patio doors. Maintenance-free and durable. Double weatherstripping and unique insulated glass spacer systems for maximum energy efficiency. Variety of snap-on interior and exterior installation trims. Lifetime limited warranty. Call 1-800-BUILD G-P (284-5347) for details. www.gp.com **Circle No. 780**

WOOD/VINYL WINDOWS

LOUISIANA-PACIFIC

L-P's new line of Arlington™ double-hung windows combine the benefits of wood and vinyl. A welded, multicavity vinyl sash and frame on the outside is joined with a natural wood interior. Easy-to-operate tilt latches allow easy cleaning. Integral nail fin, standard sizes and economical pricing for new construction. **Call (800) 299-0028, ext. 4022 for a free brochure and distributor information.**

BLOKUP FOR GLASS BLOCK

A new silicone installation system which uses aluminum separators for spacing and wind load protection. Because mortar is eliminated, job completion is faster at lower costs by workers who do not have masonry skills. Includes catalog of WECK Glass Block. (815) 356-8440. www.glashaus.com **Circle No. 778**

JORDAN WINDOWS AND DOORS

Jordan products are value engineered to provide maximum energy efficiency without compromising on beauty. Now available in vinyl and aluminum, Jordan offers the variety of windows and patio doors to meet today's builders' ever changing needs. For information, call 800/888-8848 (Eastern U.S.), 800/388-5717 (Western U.S.). **Circle No. 781**

The decision to remodel my home wasn't easy. But the

planned chaos will soon pass and I will enjoy the light. The moon. The stars.

my life is ready for a change

And the beauty of my new windows. On this I am adamant. On this

Weather Shield
Windows & Doors

WEATHER SHIELD
MFG. INC.
MEDFORD

I won't compromise. On this I am sure.

i need more room

i need more light

(800) 477-6808 ext 979

www.weathershield.com

i need more me

Special Plans Section

Plan Number	Page	Square Footage	Width	Depth	Bedrooms	Bathrooms	Foundation	Landscape	Deck	Customization	Quote One®	Materials List	Price
2665	196	3450	108'	64'	5	3½	Basement			X		X	D
2668	197	2460	52'	42'	4	2½	Basement	X		X	X	X	B
2683	197	4008	92'	32'8"	4	2½	Basement	X	X	X	X	X	D
2774	174	2335	59'6"	46'	4	2½	Basement	X	X	X	X	X	B
2776	183	2008	61'4"	38'	3	2½	Basement	X	X	X	X	X	B
2822	193	1714	54'8"	54'	2	2	Basement	X		X	X	X	A
2864	181	1387	49'8"	52'	2	2	Basement	X	X	X	X	X	A
2878	181	1521	51'4"	52'4"	3	2	Basement	X	X	X	X	X	B
2920	193	3715	97'	102'8"	3	2½ + ½	Basement	X	X	X	X	X	D
2922	194	3505	110'7"	66'11"	3	2½	Slab			X	X	X	D
2946	175	2925	74'	46'	4	2½ + ½	Basement	X	X	X	X	X	C
2947	182	1830	75'	43'5"	3	2	Basement	X	X	X	X	X	B
2970	185	3722	67'	66'	5	3½	Basement	X		X	X	X	D
2973	185	2496	70'	44'5"	4	2½	Basement	X		X	X	X	B
3325	175	2707	63'6"	48'	4	2½	Basement	X	X	X	X	X	C
3340	180	1611	58'	52'6"	3	2	Basement	X		X	X	X	B
3380	196	4553	97'	74'4"	5	3½ + ½	Basement			X	X	X	E
3403	192	2900	77'8"	62'	4	4	Slab	X		X	X	X	C
3431	195	1907	61'6"	67'4"	3	2½	Slab			X	X	X	B
3433	195	2350	92'7"	79'	3	2½	Slab	X		X	X	X	C
3457	184	2224	48'	58'	3	2½	Basement	X		X	X	X	B
3458	191	2342	62'	41'	4	2½	Basement	X	X	X	X	X	C

Plan Number	Page	Square Footage	Width	Depth	Bedrooms	Bathrooms	Foundation	Landscape	Deck	Customization	Quote One®	Materials List	Price
3461	180	2002	64'	44'	4	2½	Basement	X		X	X	X	B
3463	184	2240	36'	63'	3	2½	Slab	X				X	C
3475	194	3286	77'4"	74'8"	3	3½	Slab	X		X	X	X	D
3558	189	2931	69'4"	66'	3	2½ + ½	Basement	X	X	X	X	X	C
3600	182	2258	68'	64'	2	2½	Basement	X		X	X	X	C
3603	189	2520	70'	67'4"	3	2½	Slab	X		X	X	X	C
3639	192	2808	75'6"	62'6"	3	2½	Slab	X		X	X	X	C
9204	191	1911	56'	58'	3	2	Basement				X	X	D
9206	188	1999	52'	47'4"	4	2½	Basement				X	X	C
9242	174	2594	56'	48'	4	2½	Basement				X	X	E
9251	188	2353	54'	50'	4	2½	Basement				X	X	D
9362	190	2172	76'	46'	3	3	Basement				X	X	C
9375	190	2456	66'	68'	3	2½	Basement				X	X	E
9606	177	1831	66'4"	50'4"	3	2½	Base/Crwl				X	X	C
9621	178	1778	48'4"	51'10"	3	2½	Base/Crwl				X	X	C
9632	178	2321	56'8"	54'4"	4	3	Base/Crwl				X	X	D
9645	179	1898	59'	64'	3	2½	Base/Crwl				X	X	C
9673	177	2161	76'4"	74'2"	3	2½	Crwlspace				X	X	D
9690	183	1663	59'4"	56'6"	3	2½	Crwlspace				X	X	C
9702	179	2188	87'	57'	3	2½	Crwlspace				X	X	D
9712	176	2436	93'10"	62'	4	3½	Crwlspace				X	X	D
9723	176	2658	92'	57'8"	4	3½	Crwlspace				X	X	D

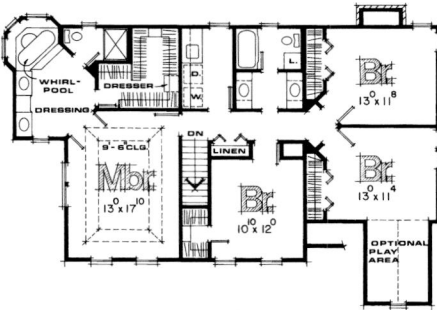

DESIGN 9242

First Floor: 1,322 square feet
Second Floor: 1,272 square feet
Total: 2,594 square feet

Farmhouse Luxury

Luxury from the wraparound covered front porch to the bright sun room at the rear. A sunken family room with fireplace serves everyday casual gatherings, while the more formal living and dining rooms are reserved for special occasions. Upstairs are four bedrooms—one a lovely master suite with French doors to the master bath. *Design by Design Basics, Inc.*

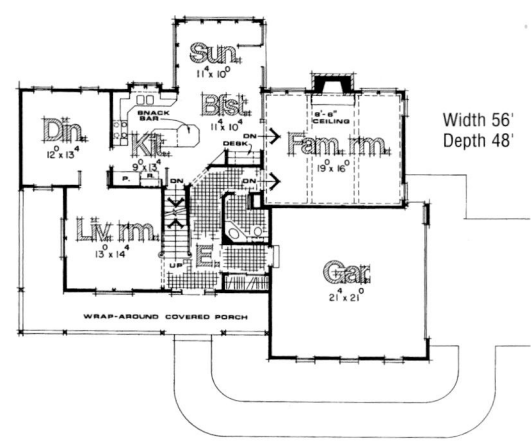

Width 56'
Depth 48'

DESIGN 2774

First Floor: 1,366 square feet
Second Floor: 969 square feet
Total: 2,335 square feet
Third-Floor Attic: 969 square feet

Picture-Perfect Farmhouse

Paint a picture of perfection with this down-home farmhouse, capturing the essence of hospitality. The spacious living room and adjoining dining room work with the U-shaped kitchen for both formal and informal entertaining. The second floor holds three family bedrooms—or, if you prefer, two and a study—and an enhanced master suite. The third-floor attic may be completed as needs arise. *Design by Home Planners.*

This home, as shown in the photograph, may differ from the actual blueprints. For more detailed information, please check the floor plans carefully.

Photo by Carl Socolow

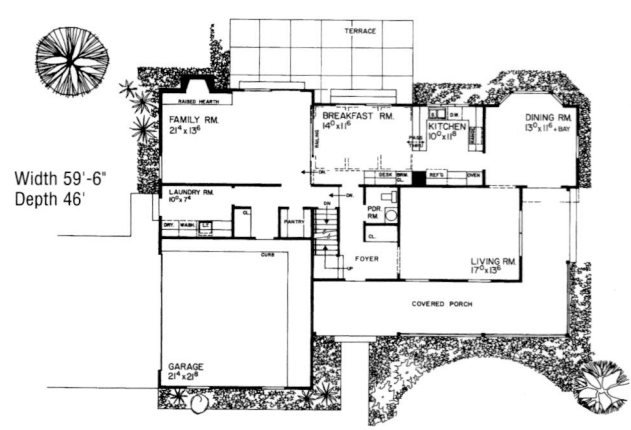

Width 59'-6"
Depth 46'

DESIGN 3325

First Floor: 1,595 square feet
Second Floor: 1,112 square feet
Total: 2,707 square feet

Create-A-Farmhouse

Details that include horizontal clapboard siding, varying roof planes and finely detailed window treatments set a distinctly farmhouse tone for this two-story beauty. Combined living and dining rooms function exceptionally well together and are complemented by a family room with raised-hearth fireplace. Four bedrooms on the second floor include three family bedrooms and a master suite with separate shower and whirlpool tub.
Design by Home Planners.

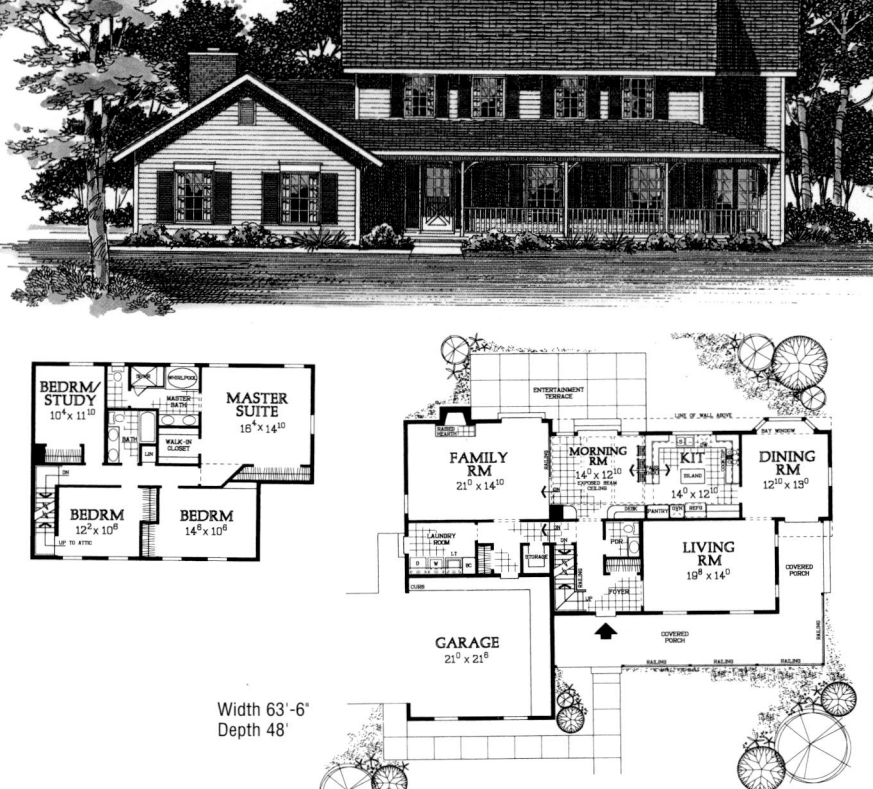

Width 63'-6"
Depth 48'

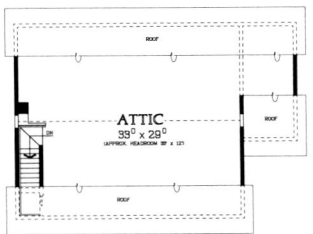

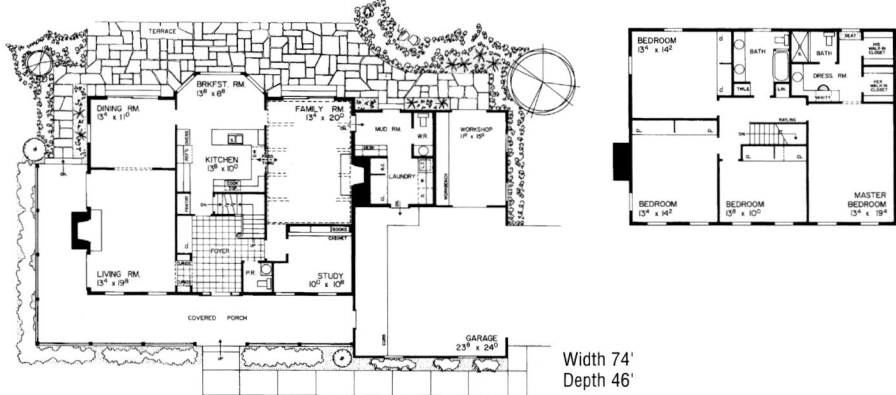

Width 74'
Depth 46'

DESIGN 2946

First Floor: 1,581 square feet
Second Floor: 1,344 square feet
Total: 2,925 square feet

All-American Country

What better way to gather with friends and family than on a wraparound porch or rear terrace? Inside, a fireplace provides a focus for the formal living room. A connecting dining room supplies passage to the rear terrace. The family room is sized comfortably to house even the largest casual gatherings. A mud room, a laundry room and a large workshop complete the first floor. Upstairs, three family bedrooms and a shared bath are joined by the master suite with His and Hers walk-in closets.
Design by Home Planners.

This home, as shown in the photograph, may differ from the actual blueprints. For more detailed information, please check the floor plans carefully.

Photo by Andrew D. Lautman

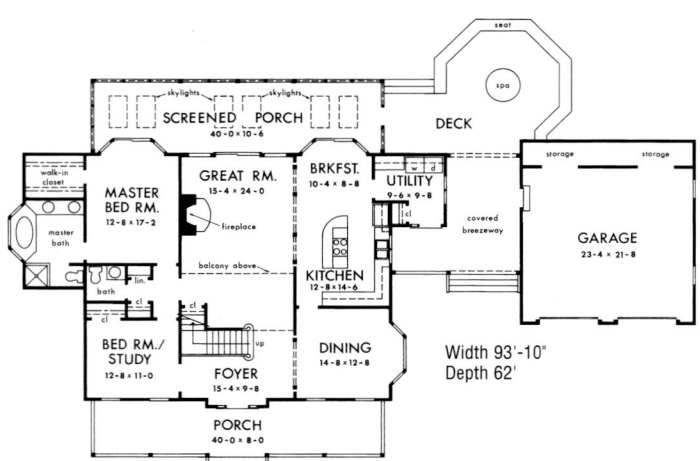

DESIGN 9712
First Floor: 1,766 square feet
Second Floor: 670 square feet
Total: 2,436 square feet

Outdoor Amenities

The covered front porch, rear screened porch and adjoining open deck that grace the outside of this country design add plenty of livability to a fine interior. The large great room with fireplace is the center of the home and is attached to a cozy breakfast room and kitchen. Formal dining takes place at the front of the plan. The master suite is on the first floor for privacy, as is a lovely bedroom or guest room. Two family bedrooms share a loft overlooking the great room. Each has its own skylit bath and dormer window. *Design by Donald A. Gardner Architects, Inc.*

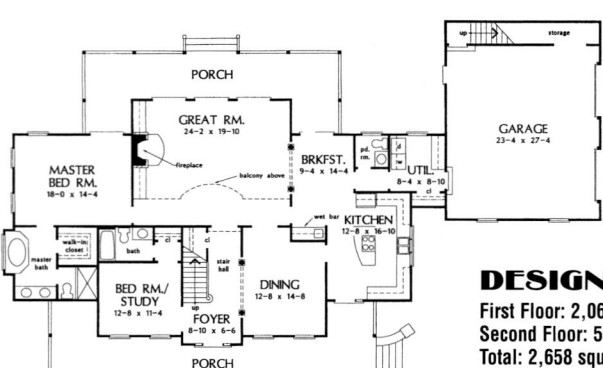

Width 93'-10"
Depth 62'

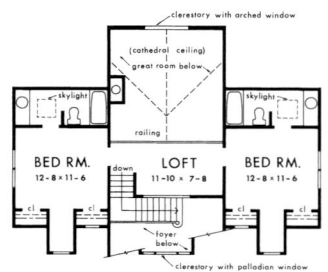

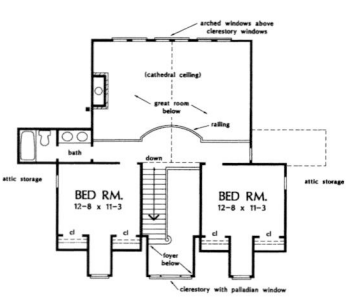

Wide-Open Spaces

The foyer of this grand country plan enjoys natural light from a Palladian clerestory window, and leads to a living area crowned with a cathedral ceiling. The gourmet kitchen includes a morning room with private access to the rear covered porch. The secluded master suite boasts a windowed garden tub and private access to the rear porch. Two family bedrooms share a balcony hall with an overlook to the great room. *Design by Donald A. Gardner Architects, Inc.*

DESIGN 9723
First Floor: 2,064 square feet
Second Floor: 594 square feet
Total: 2,658 square feet

Width 92'
Depth 57'-8"

Deck With Spa

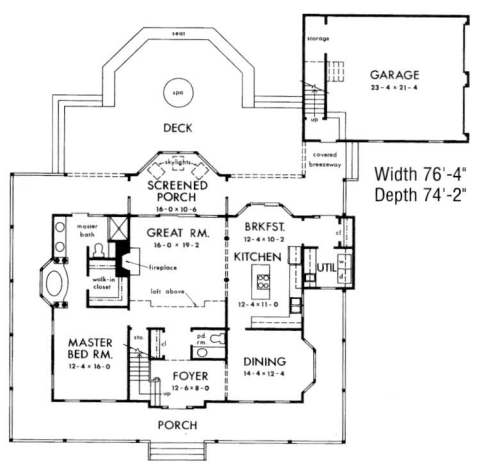

This three-bedroom, one-story farmhouse offers special features in an up-to-date plan. The generous great room with fireplace opens to a covered porch and a carefully designed deck with seating and a spa location. A kitchen with an island counter serves the breakfast and dining rooms. Located on the first floor for convenience, the master bedroom offers a large walk-in closet and a spacious master bath with a double basin vanity, a whirlpool tub and a shower. The second floor includes two family bedrooms and a shared bath. *Design by Donald A. Gardner Architects, Inc.*

DESIGN 96...

First Floor: 1,526 square feet
Second Floor: 635 square feet
Total: 2,161 square feet

Width 76'-4"
Depth 74'-2"

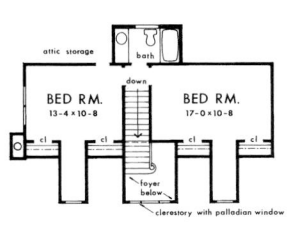

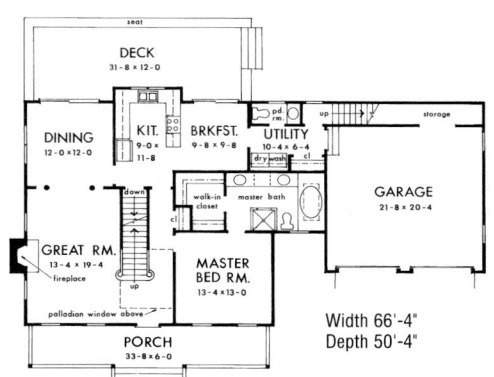

Width 66'-4"
Depth 50'-4"

DESIGN 9606

First Floor: 1,289 square feet
Second Floor: 542 square feet
Total: 1,831 square feet

Cozy Country Cottage

This cozy cottage offers both an unfinished basement and a bonus room for growth as needed. The two-story foyer features a Palladian window in a clerestory dormer above. A great room with a fireplace is enhanced by a formal dining room. Just beyond are the U-shaped kitchen and attached breakfast room. The master suite is on the first floor for privacy and accessibility and touts a bath with whirlpool tub and double-bowl vanity. The second floor contains two bedrooms, a full bath and plenty of storage. Please specify basement or crawlspace foundation when ordering. *Design by Donald A. Gardner Architects, Inc.*

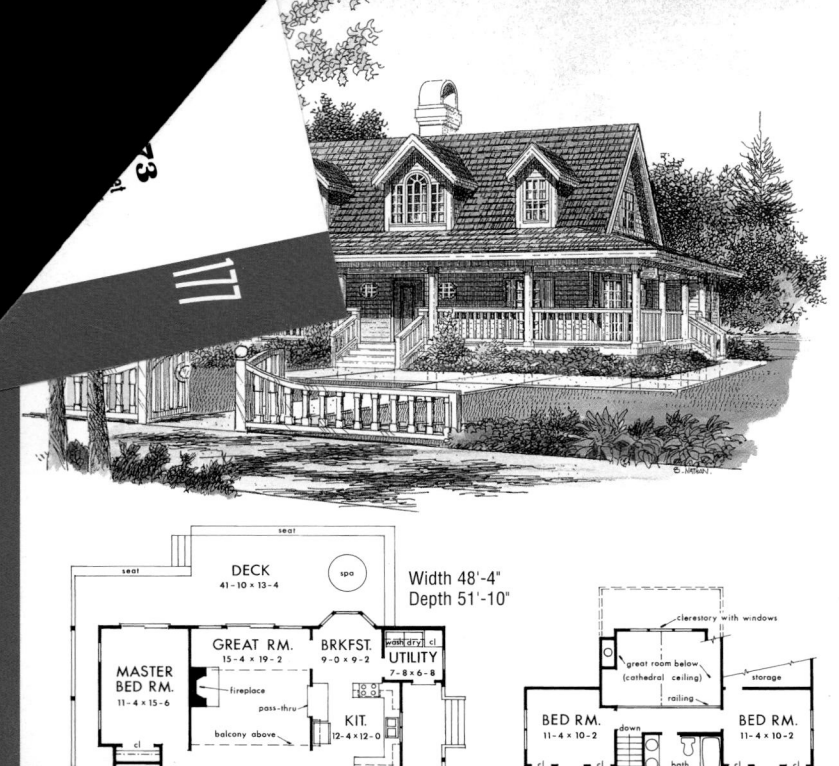

DESIGN 9621

First Floor: 1,325 square feet
Second Floor: 453 square feet
Total: 1,778 square feet

Compact And Comfortable

This compact design has all the amenities available in larger designs with little wasted space. The spacious great room has a fireplace, a cathedral ceiling and clerestory windows. A second-level balcony overlooks this area. A dining room and a casual breakfast area serve the U-shaped kitchen (a utility room is a handy addition). Besides the generous master suite, there are two family bedrooms located on the second floor. Please specify basement or crawlspace foundation when ordering. *Design by Donald A. Gardner Architects, Inc.*

Width 48'-4"
Depth 51'-10"

Rear Elevation

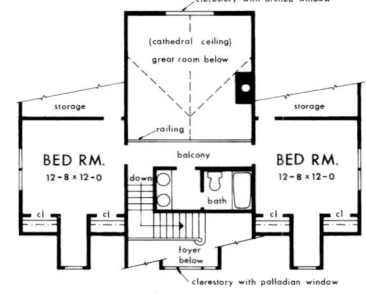

DESIGN 9632

First Floor: 1,756 square feet
Second Floor: 565 square feet
Total: 2,321 square feet

Southern Original

A wraparound covered porch at the front and sides of this Southern beauty, and an open deck at the back, provide plenty of outdoor living space. The great room features a fireplace, cathedral ceiling and clerestory with an arched window. The island kitchen has an attached, skylit breakfast room with bay window. The master suite also has a bay window, plus a host of other amenities you'll appreciate. Two family bedrooms share a full bath on the second floor. Please specify basement or crawlspace foundation when ordering. *Design by Donald A. Gardner Architects, Inc.*

Width 56'-8"
Depth 54'-4"

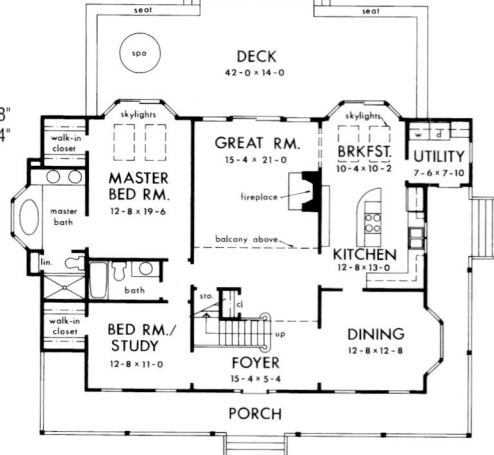

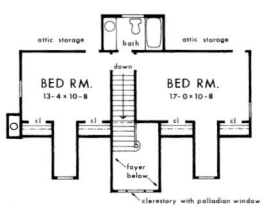

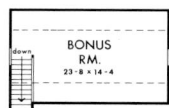

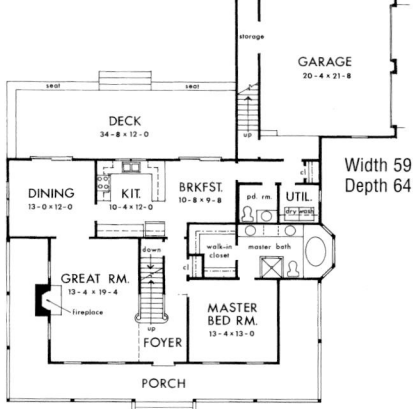

DESIGN 9645

First Floor: 1,356 square feet
Second Floor: 542 square feet
Total: 1,898 square feet

Width 59'
Depth 64'

Palladian Window And Dormers

The welcoming charm of this two-story farmhouse is due in large part to its many windows, the wrapping porch and the lovely Palladian window and dormers. The first floor features nine-foot ceilings in the great room, dining room and master suite. A practical kitchen connects to a light-filled breakfast room. The second floor provides two additional bedrooms, a full bath and plenty of storage space. Please specify basement or crawlspace foundation when ordering. *Design by Donald A. Gardner Architects, Inc.*

DESIGN 9702

First Floor: 1,618 square feet
Second Floor: 570 square feet
Total: 2,188 square feet

Screened Rear Porch

A wraparound covered porch, an open deck with spa and seating, and a screened porch enhance the impressive character of this three-bedroom home. The entrance foyer and great room have sloped ceilings and Palladian window clerestories for natural light. All other first-floor rooms have nine-foot ceilings. A generous master bedroom contains plenty of closet space as well as an extravagant master bath. Two family bedrooms on the second floor share a full bath. Bonus room over the garage allows for expansion. *Design by Donald A. Gardner Architects, Inc.*

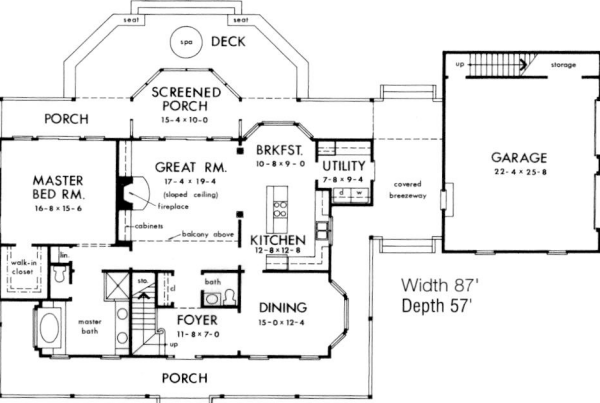

Width 87'
Depth 57'

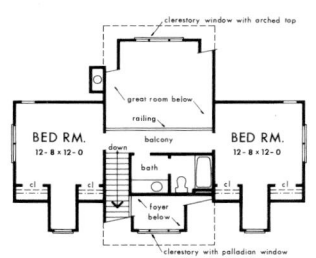

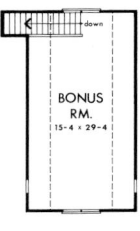

Width 58'
Depth 52'-6"

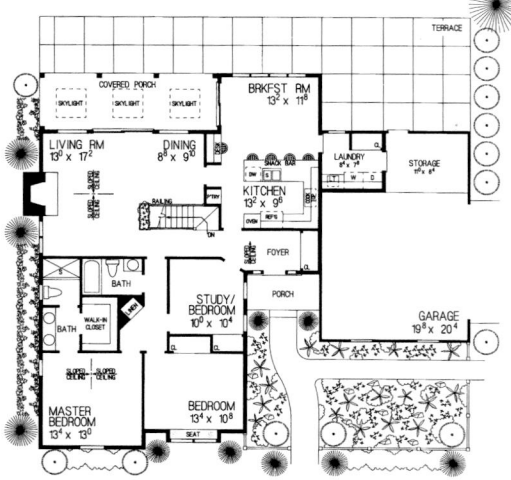

DESIGN 3340
Square Footage: 1,611

A Home For All Seasons

Imagine this charming traditional framed in fall leaves, or blanketed in winter snow, or enhanced with a riot of spring or summer flowers. Overlooking the rear terrace, the living room and dining room combine to create a wall of glass with unobstructed views. An adjacent kitchen features a built-in planning desk and snack bar that separates it from the sunny breakfast room. Clustered sleeping quarters include two family bedrooms (or make one a study) and a grand master bedroom with sloped ceiling and fine bath. *Design by Home Planners.*

DESIGN 3461
First Floor: 1,391 square feet
Second Floor: 611 square feet
Total: 2,002 square feet

High-Class Country Style

A Palladian window set in a dormer lends a classic twist to this 1½-story farmhouse. The two-story foyer draws on natural light and a pair of columns that frame the living room for a comfortable, yet elegant mood. The dining room furthers the elegance and is complemented by an L-shaped kitchen with attached family room. The master suite benefits from a bay window and impressive master bath with whirlpool tub. Three family bedrooms and a full bath share the second floor. Note the workshop area in the garage. *Design by Home Planners.*

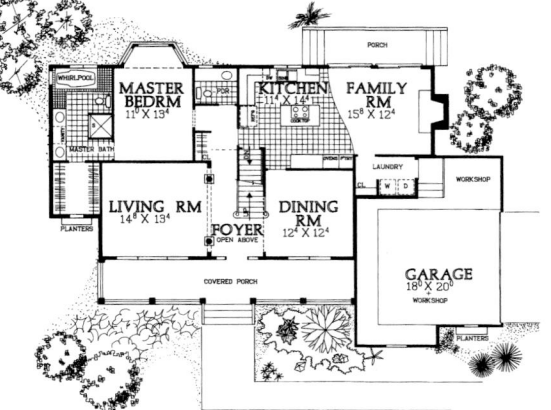

Width 64'
Depth 44'

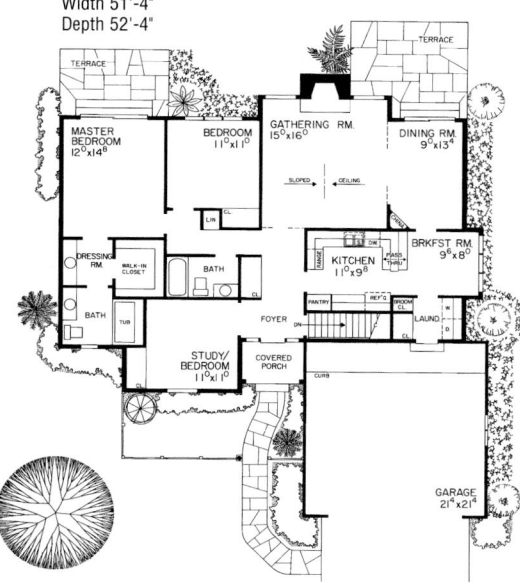

Width 51'-4"
Depth 52'-4"

This home, as shown in the photograph, may differ from the actual blueprints. For more detailed information, please check the floor plans carefully.

Photo by Andrew D. Lautman

DESIGN 2878
Square Footage: 1,521

A Traditional Story

It's difficult to believe that such great livability could be contained in less than 1,600 square feet! But this traditionally styled home is efficiently designed to make optimum use of a compact floor plan. Located to the back of the plan is a spacious gathering room, warmed by a cheerful fireplace. An adjacent dining room opens onto the rear terrace for dining al fresco. A U-shaped kitchen is close to the formal dining room for convenience. Two secondary bedrooms—or one and a study—share a full bath. The comfortable master bath is graced with a large walk-in closet, a dressing area and a private bath. *Design by Home Planners.*

DESIGN 2864
Square Footage: 1,387

Narrow-Lot Plan

Projecting the garage to the front of this house helps to reduce lot size and screen the interior from street noise. The entry leads to a giant-sized gathering room with fireplace and space for formal dining. Nearby is a study, or close it off and make it an additional bedroom. The galley-style kitchen has a pass-through snack bar to the gathering room. The two main bedrooms include a family bedroom to the front that uses a skylit bath. The master contains a dressing room and a full bath with a skylight. Sliding glass doors from the master bedroom lead to the rear terrace. *Design by Home Planners*

Width 49'-8"
Depth 52'

DESIGN 3600
Square Footage: 2,258

County Design With Three Or Four Bedrooms

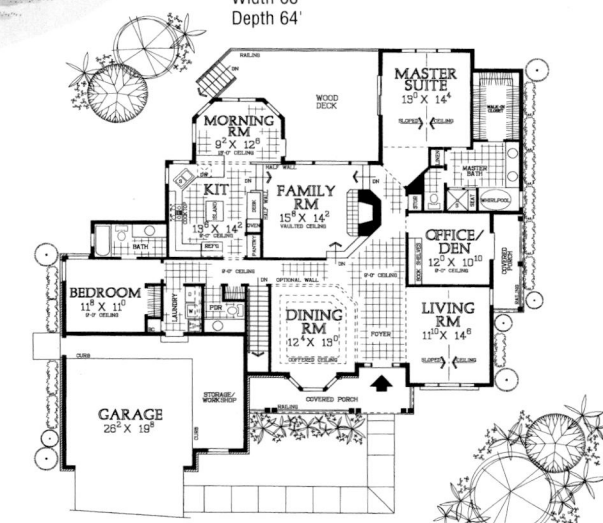

Width 68'
Depth 64'

This home is impossible to resist! Three gables, a railed front porch and a large Palladian window at the living room are enhanced by horizontal siding and brick. The floor plan includes both formal spaces for entertaining and casual areas for the family to relax. The family room is particularly appealing with access to a rear deck and welcoming hearth. The master suite is to the right of the plan and has a walk-in closet and fine bath. One family bedroom is on the other side of the home and also has a private bath. Note the light-filled morning room just off the kitchen. *Design by Home Planners.*

And The Winner Is…

Our most popular design, this home was planned with you in mind. Enjoy casual meals in the sunny breakfast room, served by a uniquely shaped galley-style kitchen. Here, the snack bar is shared with the spacious gathering room with fireplace. A dining room with terrace access is situated for formal dinners. The large master bedroom is enhanced with sliding glass doors to the terrace, a sloped ceiling and a luxurious master bath. Two additional bedrooms—one doubles as a study—are located at the front of the home. *Design by Home Planners.*

Photo by Andrew D. Lautman

This home, as shown in the photograph, may differ from the actual blueprints. For more detailed information, please check the floor plans carefully.

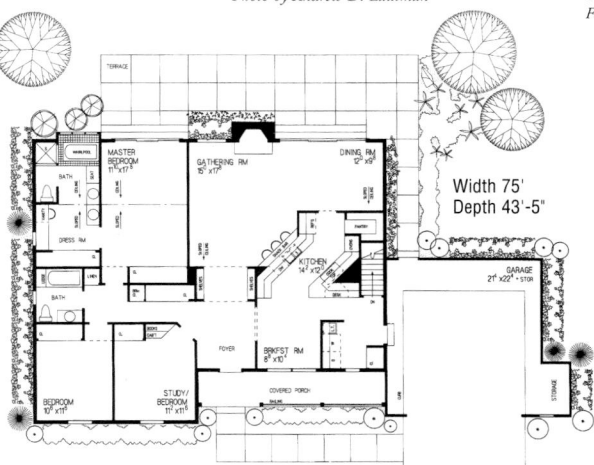

Width 75'
Depth 43'-5"

DESIGN 2947
Square Footage: 1,830

DESIGN 2776

First Floor: 1,134 square feet
Second Floor: 874 square feet
Total: 2,008 square feet

New England Country Charm

Board-and-batten siding delivers all the country charm of a New England farmhouse. Beyond the covered front porch lie a corner living room and attached dining room with bay window. A fire blazing merrily in the sunken family room welcomes casual relaxation (use the sliding glass doors in good weather to access the rear terrace). The second floor houses two family bedrooms, a full bath and a master suite to pamper royalty. A powder room and laundry on the first floor are convenient touches to a most gracious home. *Design by Home Planners.*

Width 61'-4"
Depth 38'

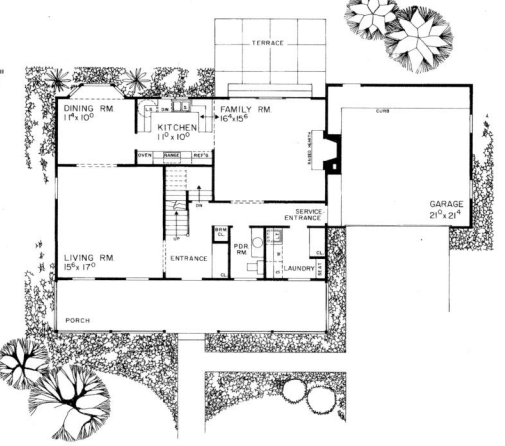

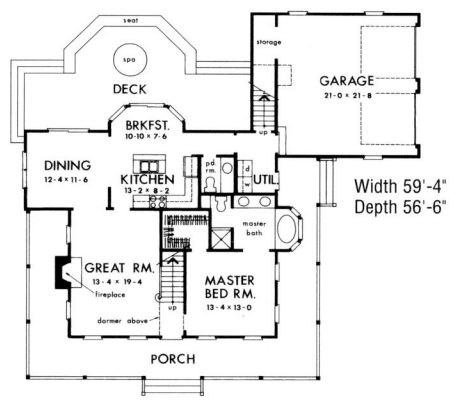

Width 59'-4"
Depth 56'-6"

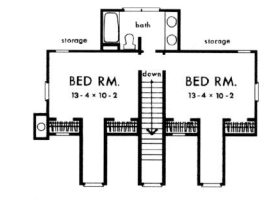

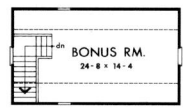

DESIGN 9690

First Floor: 1,145 square feet
Second Floor: 518 square feet
Total: 1,663 square feet

Country Pride

This plan packs a lot of livability into less than 2,000 square feet. A wrap-around porch welcomes visitors to the home. Inside lies an enormous great room with fireplace. Just beyond, to the rear of the home, the breakfast and dining rooms feature sliding glass doors to a large deck with room for a spa. The master bedroom contains a walk-in closet and an airy bath with a whirlpool spa set in a bay window. The second floor holds two bedrooms and a bath. Note the bonus space over the garage for office space, storage, or whatever! *Design by Donald A. Gardner Architects, Inc.*

The Sky's The Limit

Fine family living couples with European style in this volume plan. The tiled foyer leads to a stately living room with sliding glass doors to the terrace. Columns separate it from the formal dining room. For casual living, look no further than the family room/breakfast room combination. On the second floor, the master bedroom draws attention by offering a fireplace, access to a deck and a most exclusive bath. A smart addition, the study niche in the hallway shares the outside deck. Two family bedrooms and a bath are included on the upper level. *Design by Home Planners.*

DESIGN 3463

First Floor: 1,163 square feet
Second Floor: 1,077 square feet
Total: 2,240 square feet

DESIGN 3457

First Floor: 1,252 square feet
Second Floor: 972 square feet
Total: 2,224 square feet

Grand Gables

Gables, gables everywhere—and a cool stucco facade with multi-paned windows add up to a great exterior. For family living, this plan scores big. The family room focuses on a fireplace and enjoys direct access to a covered porch. The breakfast room allows plenty of space for casual meals while a formal dining room serves guests and holiday functions. Upstairs, the master suite affords retreat with a private bath. A private balcony adds to the appeal. The two secondary bedrooms share a full hall bath with double vanity. *Design by Home Planners.*

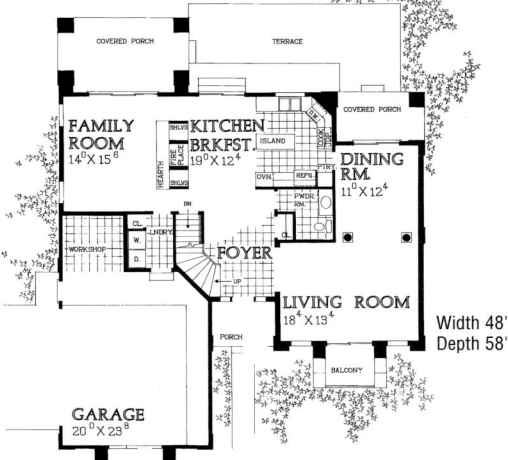

DESIGN 2973

First Floor: 1,269 square feet
Second Floor: 1,227 square feet
Total: 2,496 square feet

Victorian Drama

A circle-head window takes center stage over the front covered porch of this dramatic Victorian treasure. Enter the first-floor study and settle into your favorite easy chair. Family gatherings and conversation may be enjoyed by the fireplace in the cozy family room. A U-shaped kitchen is centered between the breakfast room and the formal dining room to easily serve both. Completing the first floor is a formal living room, a powder room and a mud room. The second floor contains an indulgent master suite, plus three family bedrooms sharing a full bath. *Design by Home Planners.*

This home, as shown in the photograph, may differ from the actual blueprints. For more detailed information, please check the floor plans carefully.

Photo by Andrew D. Lautman

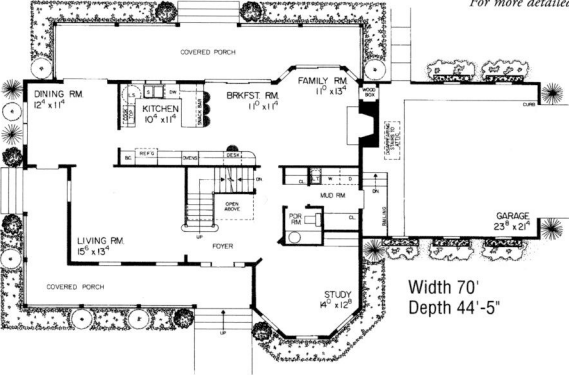

Width 70'
Depth 44'-5"

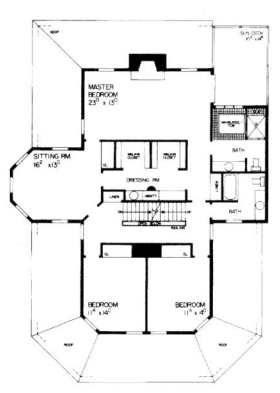

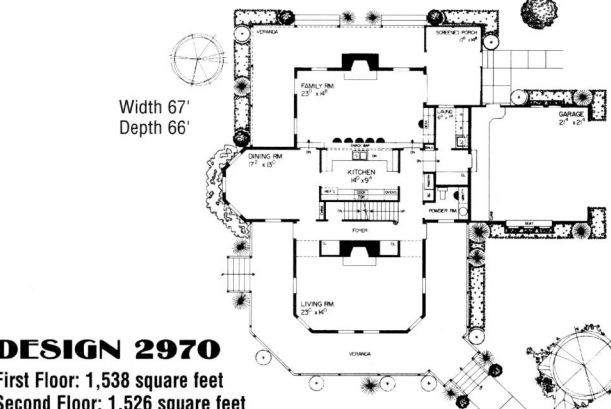

Width 67'
Depth 66'

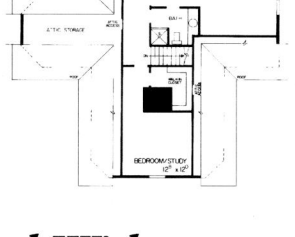

DESIGN 2970

First Floor: 1,538 square feet
Second Floor: 1,526 square feet
Third Floor: 658 square feet
Total: 3,722 square feet

Iced With Gingerbread Trim

This charming Victorian is reminiscent of a time when letter writing was an art. However, the floor plan moves it quickly into the present. The central hub of the first floor is the kitchen that efficiently serves the dining room, family room and living room. A powder room and handy laundry complete the lower-level plan. Two family bedrooms are located on the second floor. They share a full bath. The master suite is stunning and pampering with a sitting room, bath with separate shower and tub, and twin walk-in closets. The third floor offers two more bedrooms or one and a study, plus another bath. *Design by Home Planners.*

Building a new home is like creating a new life. And in

that life, I want to make sure that what I feel and what I see reflects as

soon all will be **new** and yet

much of me as possible. I will seek it in every room. Every corner. Every

view. So when the discussion turns to windows, there will be no discussion.

There's more to see in a Weather Shield window™

Weather Shield
Windows & Doors

i must admit i never

thought about windows

DESIGN 9206

First Floor: 1,421 square feet
Second Floor: 578 square feet
Total: 1,999 square feet

Stylish Practicality

Growing families will love this unique plan which combines all the essentials with an abundance of stylish touches. The living areas include a spacious great room with high ceilings, windows overlooking the back yard, a through fireplace to the kitchen and access to the outdoors. A dining room with hutch space serves formal dinners. The hearth kitchen features a bay-windowed breakfast area. The master suite with whirlpool and walk-in closet is found downstairs, while three family bedrooms are upstairs. *Design by Design Basics, Inc.*

This home, as shown in the photograph, may differ from the actual blueprints. For more detailed information, please check the floor plans carefully.

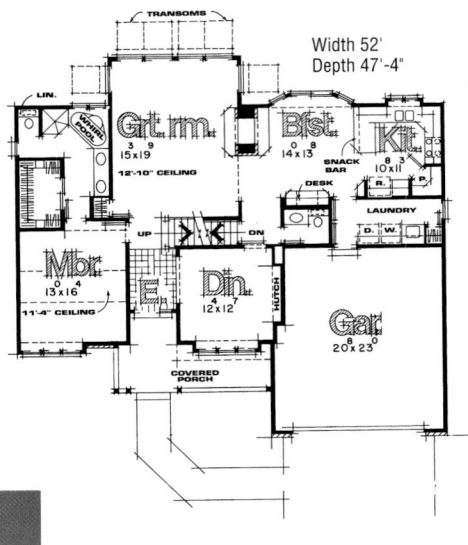

Width 52'
Depth 47'-4"

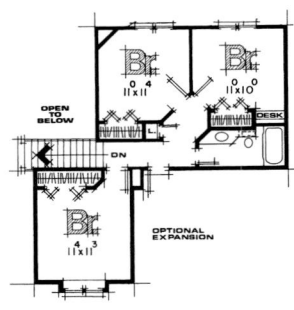

Photo by Design Basics, Inc. Built by Overholsor Builders

DESIGN 9251

First Floor: 1,653 square feet
Second Floor: 700 square feet
Total: 2,353 square feet

Victorian Touches

Beautiful arches and elaborate detail give this home unmis-takable elegance. Note the formal dining room with bay window, visible from the entry hall. The large great room has a fireplace and a wall of windows to the rear deck. A hearth room, with bookcase, adjoins the kitchen area. The master suite, on the first floor, features His and Hers wardrobes, a large whirlpool tub and double lavatories. Upstairs quarters share a full bath with compartmented sinks. Note the lovely plant shelf on the second-floor overlook. *Design by Design Basics.*

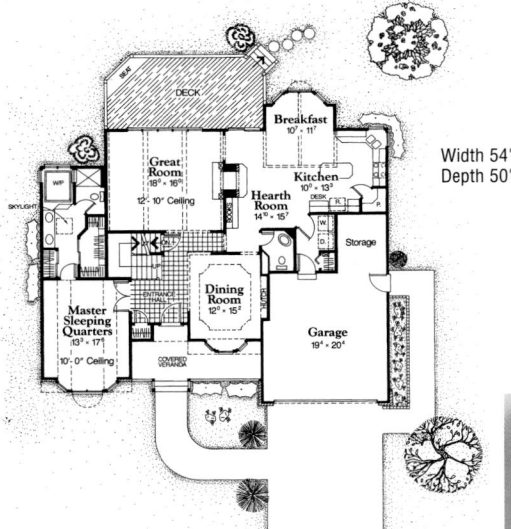

Width 54'
Depth 50'

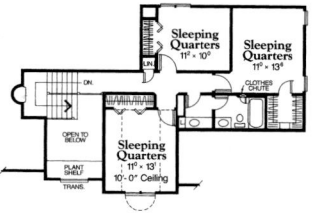

Photo by Design Basics, Inc. Built by Kendel Homes   *This home, as shown in the photograph, may differ from the actual blueprints. For more detailed information, please check the floor plans carefully.*

DESIGN 3603

Square Footage: 2,520

Echoes Of European Style

Europe's culture inspires the best in fine arts. The influence is obvious in this gracious one-story. The entry opens to formal areas well suited to entertaining—a bay-windowed living room on the right and a dining room with a niche on the left. A large family room opens to a rear-covered patio and patio retreat. The island kitchen is joined by a sun-drenched morning room for casual meals. The secluded master suite maintains a slope ceiling and lavish bath with a whirlpool tub. On the other side of the home, two family bedrooms share a full bath. A two-car garage with workshop or storage space connects to the home via a laundry area. *Design by Home Planners.*

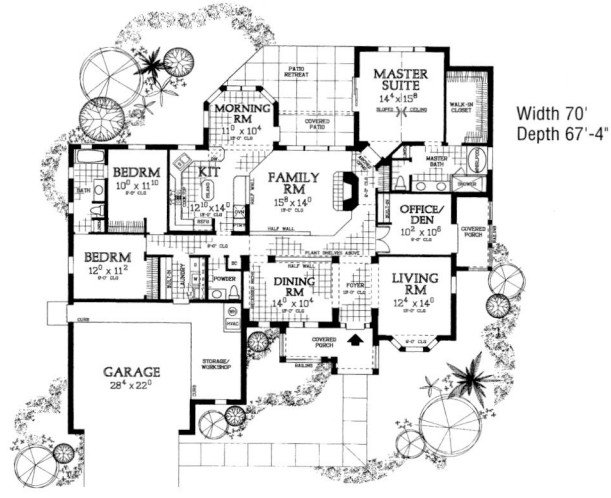

Width 70'
Depth 67'-4"

DESIGN 3558

First Floor: 2,328 square feet
Second Floor: 603 square feet
Total: 2,931 square feet

Enveloped In European Charm

Sophisticated living combined with European charm makes this stucco home one of our most popular. An elegant formal living room and dining room are ideal for entertaining as is the stunning conversation room. The large island kitchen is connected to the dining room via a butler's pantry. A library provides space for quieter pursuits. The spacious master suite includes a bath with walk-in closet, dual vanities and whirlpool tub. Two large bedrooms and a full bath are found on the second floor. *Design by Home Planners.*

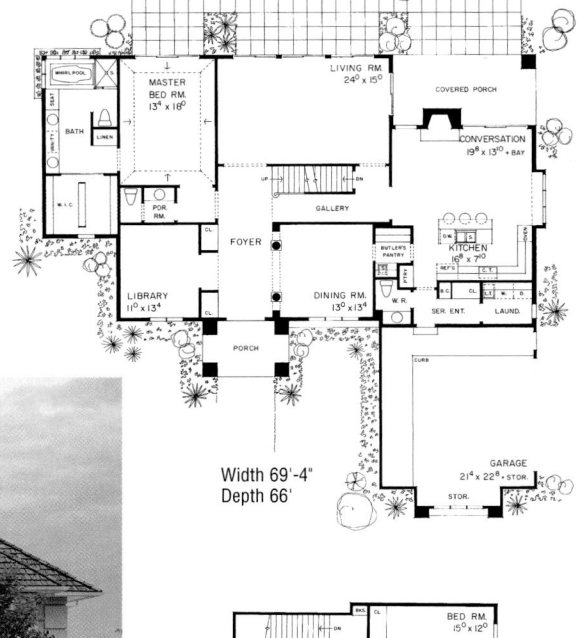

Width 69'-4"
Depth 66'

This home, as shown in the photograph, may differ from the actual blueprints.
For more detailed information, please check the floor plans carefully.

Photo by Bob Greenspan

DESIGN 9375
Square Footage: 2,456

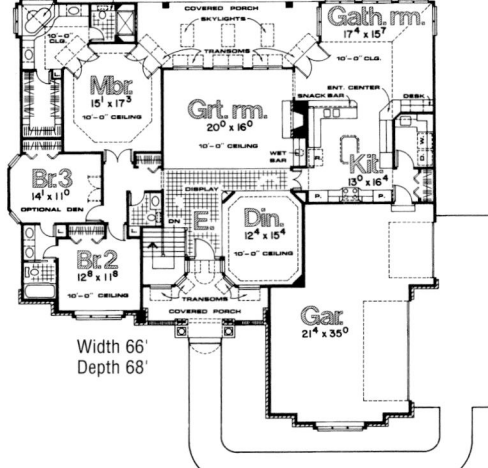

Width 66'
Depth 68'

© design basics inc. 1992

Volume Views

Tapered columns at the entry create a majestic front elevation. Inside, an open great room features a wet bar, a fireplace, tall windows and access to a covered porch with skylights. A wide kitchen is placed conveniently to serve the gathering room and dining room. Double doors lead to the master suite which includes such luxuries as a ten-foot ceiling, a whirlpool tub, a walk-in closet and dual sinks. Two secondary bedrooms share a full bath. If you choose, one of these bedrooms could be used as a den. Note the skylit covered porch to the rear of the plan. *Design by Design Basics, Inc.*

DESIGN 9362
Square Footage: 2,172

One-Story Convenience

This one-story home, with grand rooflines, holds a most interesting floor plan. The great room to the rear complements a front-facing living room. The formal dining room sits just across the hall from the living room and is also easily accessible from the kitchen. A bedroom with a full bath at this end of the house works well as an office or guest bedroom. Two additional bedrooms are to the right of the plan: a master suite with a grand bath and one family bedroom with bath. *Design by Design Basics, Inc.*

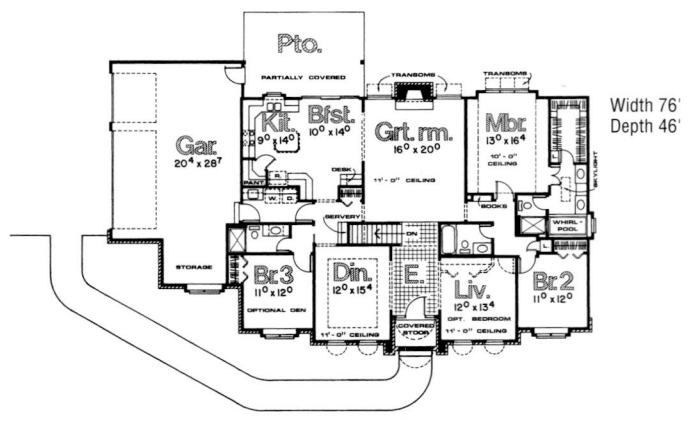

Width 76'
Depth 46'

DESIGN 9204
Square Footage: 1,911

Optional Elevation

This sophisticated three-bedroom, brick ranch with Palladian entry is a welcome addition to any neighborhood. Off the entry are the dining room, with twelve-foot detailed ceiling, and the enormous great room, which shares a through-fireplace with the well-planned kitchen. The private master suite features a detailed ceiling, corner windows, whirlpool tub and giant walk-in closet. Two family bedrooms are placed on the other side of the plan to ensure peace and quiet. An alternate elevation is available at no extra cost. *Design by Design Basics, Inc.*

Width 56'
Depth 58'

Alternate Elevation

Width 62'
Depth 41'

DESIGN 3458
First Floor: 1,617 square feet
Second Floor: 725 square feet
Total: 2,342 square feet

Eye-Catching Gables

Our "House of Five Gables" is as captivating as its 18th-Century cousins with an even better floor plan. It incorporates four bedrooms and both formal and informal living areas. The spacious family room has a high ceiling and a dramatic view of the balcony. In the U-shaped kitchen, a snack bar caters to quick meals-on-the-run. The basement allows additional space for a hobby room, recreational space or guest bedrooms. Note the workshop in the garage. *Design by Home Planners.*

DESIGN 3639

First Floor: 2,137 square feet
Second Floor: 671 square feet
Total: 2,808 square feet

Floridian In A Grand Style

If first impressions really make the most important statements—this home makes it in grand style. Inside, formal living areas grab attention with a dining room and an elegant living room that opens to an outdoor entertainment lanai. The family room—with fireplace—features open views to the kitchen and breakfast nook. The laundry room is fully functional with a laundry tub and broom closet. On the left side of the plan, the master suite has a private bath and lanai. A large den could double as a study. Two bedrooms and a full bath are located upstairs. *Design by Home Planners.*

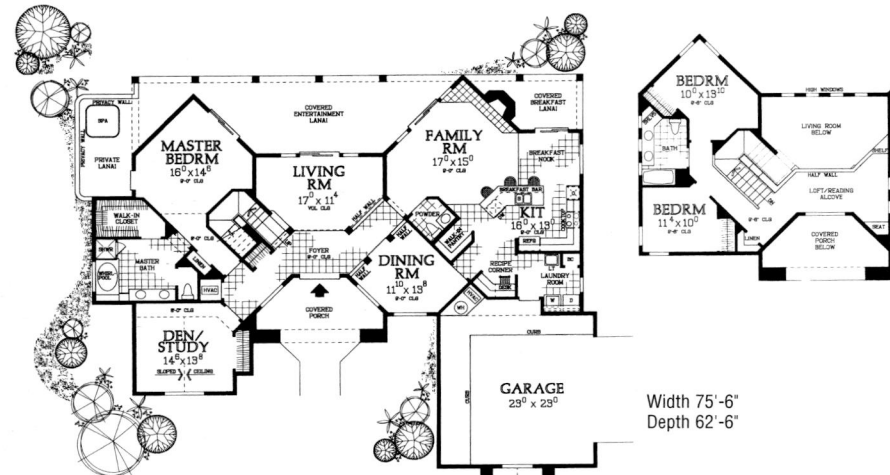

Width 75'-6"
Depth 62'-6"

DESIGN 3403

First Floor: 2,240 square feet
Second Floor: 660 square feet
Total: 2,900 square feet

California Contemporary

There's something alluring about the California lifestyle—captured perfectly in this ultra-modern contemporary. Formal living areas are concentrated in the center of the plan—the kitchen and family room work together to provide more casual space. An optional guest bedroom or den and the master suite are located to the left of the plan. The second floor holds two bedrooms and a full bath. Each of these bedrooms has a private vanity and a walk-in closet. The curved balcony on the second floor overlooks the entry and the living room. *Design by Home Planners.*

Width 77'-8"
Depth 62'

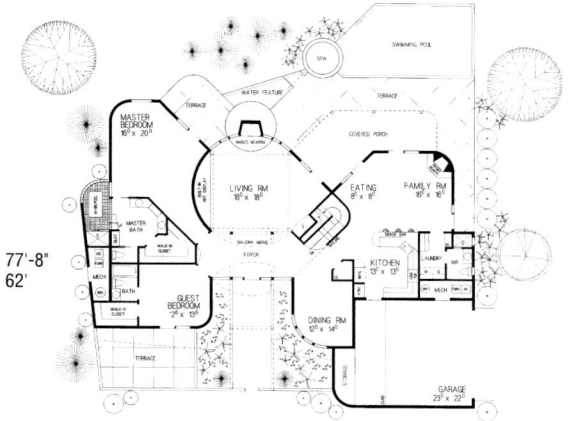

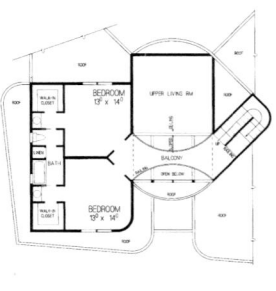

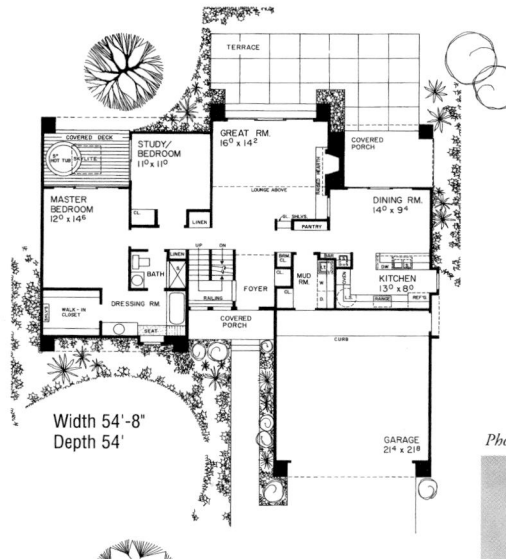

Width 54'-8"
Depth 54'

DESIGN 2822

First Floor: 1,363 square feet
Second Floor: 351 square feet
Total: 1,714 square feet

Excellent Empty-Nester

Flexibility and livability are the hallmarks of this affordable plan, just made for small families and empty-nesters. Basically a one-story with second-floor possibilities, the home can be nearly anything you want it to be. Use the upstairs for a lounge, a guest room, a hobby room—the possibilities are endless. Downstairs, a little space goes a long way. The great room has a fireplace and sliding glass doors to the terrace. The dining room, adjacent to the convenient kitchen has a covered dining porch. Two bedrooms (make one a study) open to a deck. *Design by Home Planners.*

Photo by Andrew D. Lautman

This home, as shown in the photograph, may differ from the actual blueprints. For more detailed information, please check the floor plans carefully.

DESIGN 2920

First Floor: 3,067 square feet
Second Floor: 648 square feet
Total: 3,715 square feet

Best-Selling Contemporary

The clean, bold lines and great floor plan of this design have made it one of our most popular contemporaries to date. A fireplace opens up to both the living room and country kitchen. The first-floor master bedroom is snuggled away from traffic and features a dressing room, a whirlpool tub, a shower and a spacious walk-in closet. Two additional bedrooms and a full bath are on the second floor. The cheerful sun room adds 296 square feet to the total. *Design by Home Planners.*

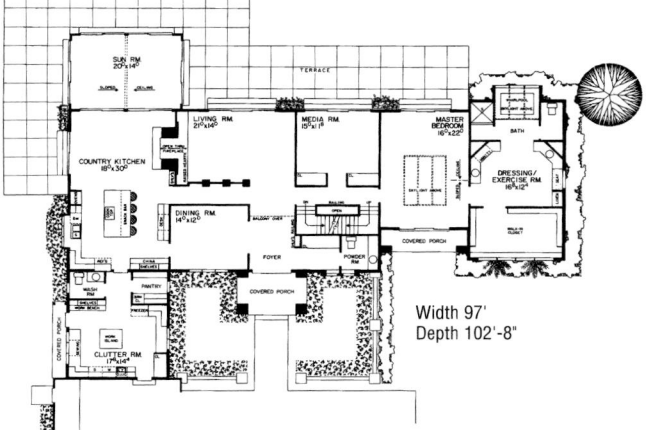

Width 97'
Depth 102'-8"

This home, as shown in the photograph, may differ from the actual blueprints. For more detailed information, please check the floor plans carefully.

Photo by Bob Greenspan

DESIGN 3475
Square Footage: 3,286

Unique Spanish Styling

The elements of Spanish styling make this home a standout—tiled roof, wide overhangs, varying roof planes. In the sunken living room, a curved, raised-hearth fireplace acts as a focal point. The U-shaped kitchen is efficient and connects to the nook and family room with a snack bar. Opposite the formal living room is the dining room, overlooking the garden courtyard. Bedrooms enjoy separation with the master suite on one side of the plan and family bedrooms on the other. A cozy den or study has a private patio and powder room. *Design by Home Planners.*

Width 77'-4"
Depth 74'-8"

DESIGN 2922
Square Footage: 3,505

Spanish Magnifico!

Drawn directly from Spanish styling, this home hums with the feeling of the Old West. It's loaded with custom features. The gathering room connects to a quiet study with warming fireplace. The dining room is also connected to the gathering room and opens to a private eating terrace. The country-style kitchen has both a morning room and a sitting room with fireplace. The master suite is of real interest. It features a fireplace with an alcove, an enormous dressing area with walk-in closets, a skylit whirlpool tub and a private terrace. *Design by Home Planners.*

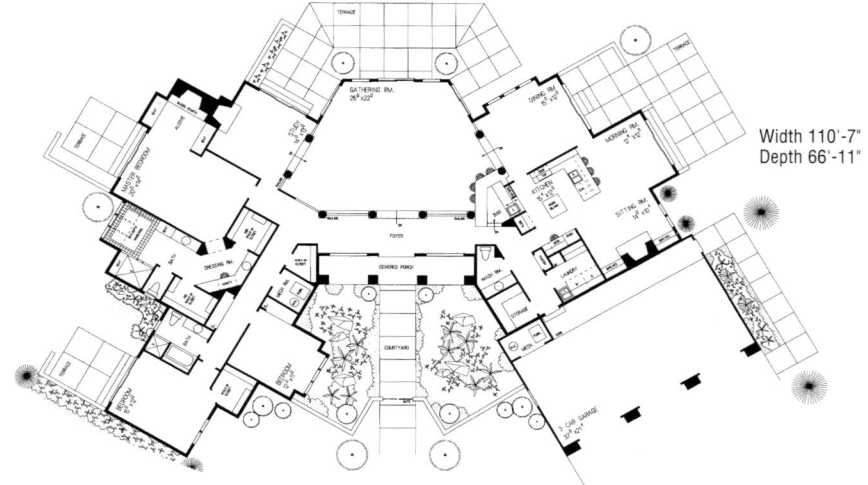

Width 110'-7"
Depth 66'-11"

DESIGN 3431

Square Footage: 1,907

Old-Style Courtyard

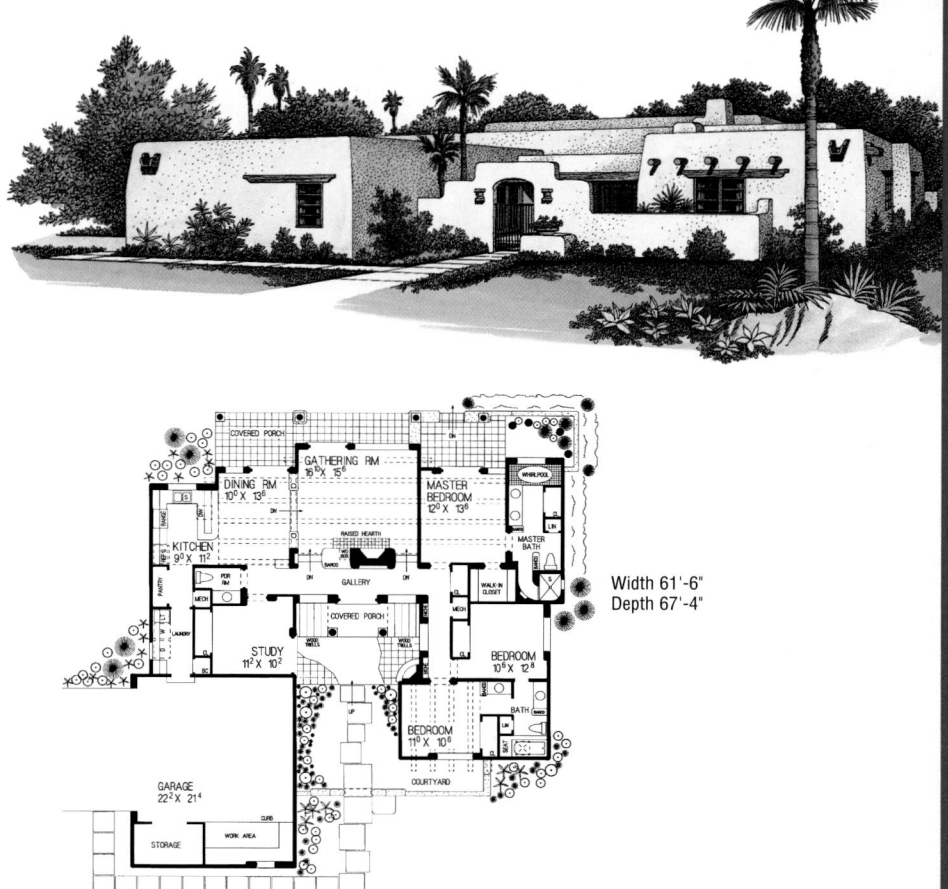

The original Santa Fe homes often featured a courtyard area, protected from noise and weather. Our design mimics this winsome feature and adds some interior touches you'll like. A gallery directs traffic to a work zone on the left and a sleeping zone on the right. Straight ahead is a sunken gathering room with beam ceiling and raised-hearth fireplace. The covered rear porch is accessible from the dining room, gathering room, and secluded master bedroom. The master bath features a whirlpool tub, a separate shower, and lots of closet space. Two family bedrooms share a compartmented bath. *Design by Home Planners.*

Width 61'-6"
Depth 67'-4"

DESIGN 3433

Square Footage: 2,350

Santa Fe Signature

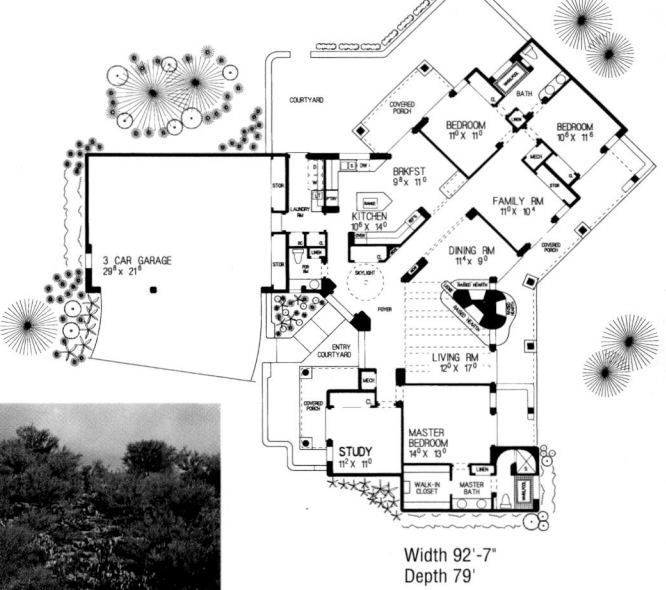

This exquisite one-story home exudes a Santa Fe style that places it in a class of its own. A grand entrance leads through a courtyard to a foyer with skylight and powder room. Turn right to the master suite with a deluxe bath and study close by. Two more family bedrooms are placed quietly in the far wing of the house. Fireplaces in the living room, dining room, and on the covered porch create interesting angles in theses areas. A small family room complements the more formal spaces. A three-car garage adds convenient storage areas to the mix. *Design by Home Planners.*

Width 92'-7"
Depth 79'

Photo by Bob Greenspan

This home, as shown in the photograph, may differ from the actual blueprints. For more detailed information, please check the floor plans carefully.

DESIGN 3380
First Floor: 3,350 square feet
Second Floor: 1,203 square feet
Total: 4,553 square feet

Azure Seas Or Massive Trees

Details for this design will put you in mind of a Mediterranean villa, but it fits well into almost any setting. An elegant foyer is flanked by a baronial dining room and distinguished library. A huge step-down gathering room is graced by a fireplace and columns. The master bedroom, on the first floor, provides unsurpassed luxury. Twin walk-in closets, a dressing room, and an inviting whirlpool tub embellish the master bath. Four family bedrooms and two full baths are contained on the second floor. *Design by Home Planners.*

Width 97'
Depth 74'-4"

Option to guest wing
First floor
688 sq. ft.

Option to guest wing
Second floor
162 sq. ft.

Width 108'
Depth 64'

DESIGN 2665
First Floor: 1,992 square feet
Second Floor: 1,458 square feet
Total: 3,450 square feet

George Washington Slept Here

The origin (you might have guessed) of this house is Washington's Mount Vernon. We've updated the floor plan to make it even more comfortable. A keeping room, dining room, breakfast room and formal living room, all on the first floor, allow space for gatherings. Four bedrooms—one a gracious master suite—and two full baths are found on the second floor. One wing accommodates guest quarters with a full bath, lounge area and upstairs studio. The other wing contains a garage with a storage/hobby room situated above. Optional uses are also provided for the guest suite and studio. *Design by Home Planners.*

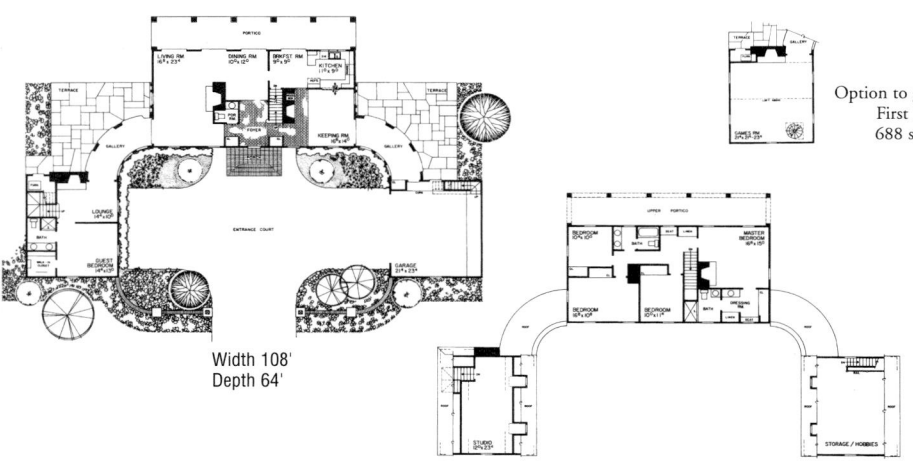

DESIGN 2668

First Floor: 1,206 square feet
Second Floor: 1,254 square feet
Total: 2,460 square feet

Gracious Southern Manor

This grand mini-manor has the demeanor of Southern mansions of the past. The grand foyer leads to a library on the right and a welcoming country kitchen on the left. The formal dining room has built-in china cabinets and is open to the hearth-warmed great room. Upstairs, three family bedrooms share a full bath. The master bedroom offers room to stretch and is high-lighted by a walk-in closet and a pampering bath. Note storage space in the two-car garage. *Design by Home Planners.*

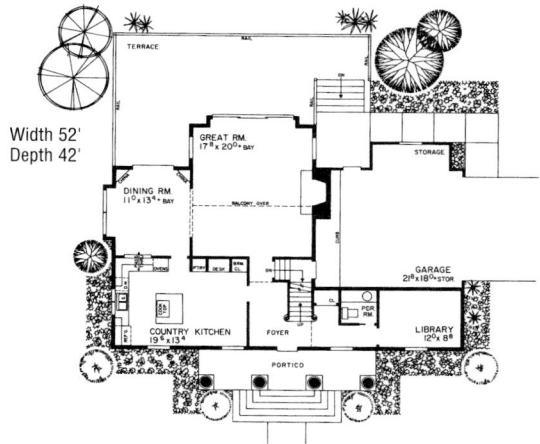

Width 52'
Depth 42'

This home, as shown in the photograph, may differ from the actual blueprints. For more detailed information, please check the floor plans carefully.

Photo by Laszlo Regos

DESIGN 2683

First Floor: 2,126 square feet
Second Floor: 1,882 square feet
Total: 4,008 square feet

Revolutionary Design

With roots in the 18th Century, this Georgian is sophisticated and easy to live in. The hearth-warmed gathering room fills one wing and accommodates formal entertaining as handily as it does family affairs. Both the study and dining room also have fireplaces and flank the foyer. The kitchen connects to a sunny breakfast room. On the second floor, three family bedrooms and a full bath are complemented by a royal master suite. Its luxuries include a fireplace, a sunken lounge and a dressing room with huge walk-in closet. *Design by Home Planners.*

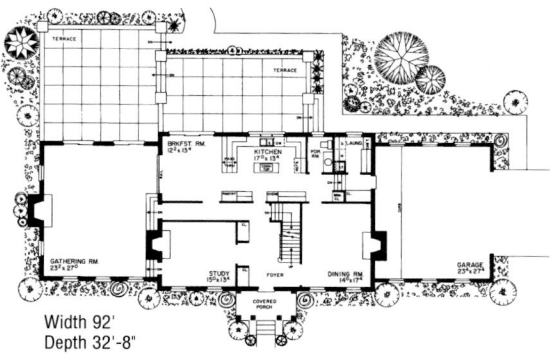

Width 92'
Depth 32'-8"

Blueprint Order Information

Many of the plans shown on the preceding pages are available with some important extras to make building easier and enhance the look and livability of the home. Please refer to pages 172-173 for products and services available for each plan.

MATERIALS LIST

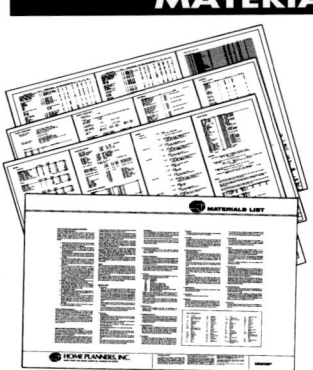

invaluable in planning and estimating the cost of your new home. This comprehensive list outlines the quantity, type, and size of material needed to build your house (with the exception of mechanical system items). Included are:

- Framing lumber;
- Roofing and sheet metal;
- Windows and doors;
- Exterior sheathing material and trim;
- Masonry, veneer, and fireplace materials;
- Tile and floor materials;
- Kitchen and bath cabinetry;
- Interior drywall and trim;
- Rough and finish hardware;
- Many more items.

(Note: Because of differing local codes, building methods, and availability of materials, our Materials Lists do not include mechanical materials. To obtain necessary take-offs and recommendations, consult heating, plumbing, and electrical contractors. Materials Lists are not sold separately from the Blueprint Package.) For many of the designs in our portfolio, we offer a customized materials take-off that is

This handy list helps you or your builder cost out materials and serves as a ready reference sheet when you are compiling bids. It also provides a cross-check against the materials specified by your builder and helps coordinate the substitution of items you may need to meet local codes.

QUOTE ONE®

This new service helps you estimate the cost of building the designs in this issue. Quote One® system is available in two separate stages: The Summary Cost Report and the Materials Cost Report. The Summary Cost Report shows the total cost per square foot for your chosen home in your zip-code area and then breaks that cost down into ten categories showing the costs for building materials, labor and installation. The total cost for the report (including three grades: Budget, Standard and Custom) is just $19.95 for one home; and additionals are only $14.95. These reports allow you to evaluate your building budget and compare the costs of building a variety of homes in your area.

The Materials Cost Report furnishes an even more detailed report. The material and installation (labor + equipment) cost is shown for each of

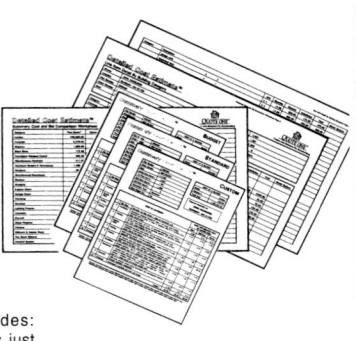

over 1,000 line items provided in the Standard grade. Space is allowed for additional estimates from contractors and subcontractors. This invaluable tool is available for a price of $110 ($120 for a schedule E plan) which includes the price of a materials list.

To order these invaluable reports, use the order form on page 199 or call **800-521-6797 or 520/297-8200.**

The Home Customizer® Package

The Home Customizer® includes everything needed to make custom changes to your favorite Home Planners design: Instruction Book with samples; Architectural Scale and Clear Work Film; Erasable Marker and Tape; 1/4"-Scale Furniture Cutouts; Reproducible Sepias; Study Blueprints; Copyright Release; Referral Letter to the design professional in your area who is trained in modifying Home Planners designs. For more complete information, call Home Planners at 1-800-521-6797.

Specification Outline

This valuable, non-plan specific, 16-page document is critical to building your house correctly. Designed to be filled in by you or your builder, this book lists 166 stages or items crucial to the building process. It provides a comprehensive review of the construction process and helps in making choices of materials. When combined with the blueprints, a signed contract, and a schedule, it becomes a legal document and record for the building of your home.

Landscape and Deck Packages

Many of our plans have matching or complementary Landscape and Deck Design Packages to help you. These are professionally developed plans that allow you to install or build custom touches for your new home. Please call 1-800-521-6797 for more detailed information.

Price Schedule

Below are the prices for the cost of one-, four- or eight-set blueprint packages or the cost of a reproducible sepia. Additional prices are shown for identical and reverse blueprint sets, as well as a useful materials list. Refer to pages 172-173 for price codes for each plan.

House Blueprint Price Schedule
(Prices guaranteed through December 31, 1998)

Price Code	1-set Building Package	4-set Building Package	8-set Building Package	1-set Reproducible Sepias	Home Customizer® Package
A	$350	$395	$455	$555	$605
B	$390	$435	$495	$615	$665
C	$430	$475	$535	$675	$725
D	$470	$515	$575	$735	$785
E	$590	$635	$695	$795	$845

Materials Lists (Available only for plans from those designers listed below):
Home Planners Designs ....$50 each
Design Basics Designs ....$75 each
Donald Gardner Designs ....$50 each

Please add $10 for Schedule E plans.

To order: Fill in and send the order form on page 199—or call us toll free 800/521-6797 or 520/297-8200.

Quote One® available for many plans.

Additional Identical Blueprints in same order...$50 per set
Reverse Blueprints (mirror image)..$50 per set
Specification Outlines ....$10 each

Before You Order . . .

Before filling out the coupon at right or calling us on our Toll-Free Blueprint Hotline, you may want to learn more about our services and products. Here's some information you will find helpful.

Quick Turnaround
We process every blueprint order from our office within 48 hours. Because of this quick turnaround, we won't send a formal notice acknowledging receipt of your order.

Our Exchange Policy
Since blueprints are printed in response to your order, we cannot honor requests for refunds. However, we will exchange your entire first order for an equal number of blueprints at a price of $50 for the first set and $10 for each additional set; $70 total exchange fee for 4 sets; $100 total exchange fee for 8 sets . . . *plus* the difference in cost if exchanging for a design in a higher price bracket or *less* the difference in cost if exchanging for a design in lower price bracket. One exchange is allowed within a year of purchase date. **(Sepias are not exchangeable.)** All sets from the first order must be returned before the exchange can take place. Please add $18 for postage and handling via ground service; $30 via Second Day Air; $40 via Next Day Air.

About Reverse Blueprints
If you want to build in reverse of the plan as shown, we will include an extra set of reverse blueprints (mirror image) for an additional fee of $50. Although lettering and dimensions will appear backward, reverses will be a useful aid if you decide to flop the plan.

Architectural and Engineering Seals
Some cities and states are now requiring that a licensed architect or engineer review and "seal" a blueprint, or officially approve it, prior to construction due to concerns over energy costs, safety and other factors. Prior to application for a building permit or the start of actual construction, we strongly advise that you consult your local building official who can tell you if such a review is required.

Local Building Codes and Zoning Requirements
At the time of creation, our plans are drawn to specifications published by the Building Officials and Code Administrators (BOCA) International, Inc.; the Southern Building Code Congress (SBCCI) International, Inc.; the International Conference of Building Officials; or the Council of American Building Officials (CABO). Our plans are designed to meet or exceed national building standards. Because of the great differences in geography and climate throughout the United States and Canada, each state, county and municipality has its own building codes, zone requirements,

ordinances and building regulations. Your plan may need to be modified to comply with local requirements regarding snow loads, energy codes, soil and seismic conditions and a wide range of other matters. In addition, you may need to obtain permits or inspections from local governments before and in the course of construction. Prior to using blueprints ordered from us, we strongly advise that you consult a licensed architect or engineer—and speak with your local building official—before applying for any permit or beginning construction. We authorize the use of our blueprints on the express condition that you strictly comply with all local building codes, zoning requirements and other applicable laws, regulations, ordinances and requirements. Notice: Plans for homes to be built in Nevada must be re-drawn by a Nevada-registered professional. Consult your building official for more information on this subject.

Foundation and Exterior Wall Changes
Most of our plans are drawn with either a full or partial basement foundation. Depending on your specific climate or regional building practices, you may wish to change this basement to a slab or crawl-space. Most professional contractors and builders can easily adapt your plans to alternate foundation types. Likewise, most can easily change 2x4 wall construction to 2x6, or vice versa.

Disclaimer
We and the designers we work with have put substantial care and effort into the creation of our blueprints. However, because we cannot provide on-site consultation, supervision and control over actual construction, and because of the great variance in local building requirements, building practices and soil, seismic, weather and other conditions, WE CANNOT MAKE ANY WARRANTY, EXPRESS OR IMPLIED, WITH RESPECT TO THE CONTENT OR USE OF OUR BLUEPRINTS, INCLUDING BUT NOT LIMITED TO ANY WARRANTY OF MERCHANTABILITY OR OF FITNESS FOR A PARTICULAR PURPOSE.

Terms and Conditions
These designs are protected under the terms of United States Copyright Law and may not be copied or reproduced in any way, by any means, unless you have purchased Sepias or Reproducibles which clearly indicate your right to copy or reproduce. We authorize the use of your chosen design as an aid in the construction of one single-family home only. You may not use this design to build a second or multiple dwellings without purchasing another blueprint or blueprints or paying additional design fees.

BLUEPRINTS ARE NOT RETURNABLE

ORDER FORM

HOME PLANNERS, A Division of Hanley-Wood, Inc.
3275 W. INA RD., SUITE 110
TUCSON, AZ 85741

THE BASIC BLUEPRINT PACKAGE
Rush me the following (please refer to the Price Schedule on page 198):

_____ Set(s) of blueprints for plan number(s) _____. $_____

_____ Set(s) of sepias for plan number(s) _____. $_____

_____ Additional identical blueprints in same order @ $50 per set. $_____

_____ Reverse blueprints @ $50 per set. $_____

_____ Materials List: $50; $75 Design Basics plans. Add $10 for a Schedule E plan. $_____

_____ **Quote One®** Summary Cost Report @ $19.95 for 1, $14.95 for each additional, for plans _____. $_____
Building location: City _____ Zip Code _____

_____ **Quote One®** Materials Cost Report @110 Schedule A-D; $120 Schedule E for plan _____. $_____
(Must be purchased with Blueprints set.)

_____ Specifications Outline @ $10 each. $_____

POSTAGE AND HANDLING	1-3 sets	4 or more sets
Carrier Delivery (requires street address - No P.O. Boxes)		
● Regular Service (Allow 4-6 days delivery)	❑ $15.00	❑ $18.00
● Priority (Allow 2-3 days delivery)	❑ $20.00	❑ $30.00
● Express (Allow 1 day delivery)	❑ $30.00	❑ $40.00
CERTIFIED MAIL (requires signature) If no street address available. Allow 4-6 days delivery.	❑ $20.00	❑ $30.00
OVERSEAS AIR MAIL DELIVERY Note: All delivery times are from date Blueprint Package is shipped.	Phone, Fax or Mail for quote	

POSTAGE (From box above) $_____
SUB-TOTAL $_____
SALES TAX (AZ, CA, DC, IL, MI, MN, NY & WA residents, please add appropriate state and local sales tax.) $_____
TOTAL (Sub-total and tax) $_____

YOUR ADDRESS (please print)
Name _____
Street _____
City _____ State _____ ZIP _____
Daytime telephone number (_____) _____

FOR CREDIT CARD ORDERS ONLY
Please fill in the information below:

Credit card number _____

Exp. Date: Month/Year _____

Check one ❑ Visa ❑ MasterCard ❑ Discover Card

Signature _____

Please check appropriate box:
❑ Licensed Builder-Contractor
❑ Homeowner

TO ORDER:
800/521-6797 or 520/297-8200

Order Form Key

TB52

Product Index

Product Index

Product Index

Manufacturer Index

A

A.O. Smith Water Products Co.
(A Div. of A.O. Smith Corp.)
HVAC
600 E. John Carpenter Fwy., Suite 200
Irving, TX 75062
Phone: 214-719-5900
Fax: 214-719-5960

A-Systems Corp.
Computer Software
339 E. 3900 St.,
Suite 101
Salt Lake City, UT 84107-1677
Phone: 801-265-0600
1-800-365-6790
Fax: 801-265-0691

AA Abbingdon Affiliates
Walls, Ceilings & Finishes
2149-51 Utica Ave., Dept BU
Brooklyn, NY 11234
Phone: 718-258-8333
Fax: 718-338-2739

AAA Aluminum Products
Room Enclosures; Siding & Accessories
1710 Gilmore Ave.
Burnaby, BC V5C 4T3
Canada
Phone: 604-298-7241

AAB Building System
Insulation; Structural Systems
840 Division St.
Cobourg, ON K9A 4J9
Canada
Phone: 905-373-0004
1-800-293-3210
Fax: 905-373-8301
Internet:
http://www.bluemaxxaab.com

Aareas By Design
Computer Software
1120 Finch Ave. W., Suite 305
Toronto, ON M3J 3H7
Canada
Phone: 416-661-2244
Fax: 416-661-1568
Internet:
http://www.aareas.com

AB Cushing Mills
Countertops; Engineered Lumber & Panels; Flooring; Landscape Design; Moulding & Millwork; Siding & Accessories
7103-30 St. S.E.,
Box 39, Station T
Calgary, AB T2H 2G7
Canada
Phone: 403-279-8800
Fax: 403-279-0077

Abacus Accounting Systems
Computer Software
#488, 9707-110 St.
Edmonton, AB T5K 2L9
Canada
Phone: 403-488-8100
1-800-992-0616
Fax: 403-482-1855
Internet: http://www.abacus-group.com

Abatron
Paints, Caulks & Adhesives
5501 95th Ave.
Kenosha, WI 53144
Phone: 414-653-2000
1-800-445-1754
Fax: 414-653-2019
Internet:
http://www.abatron.com

Abbaka
Appliances
1500 A Burke Ave.
San Francisco, CA 94124
Phone: 415-648-7210
1-800-548-3932
Fax: 415-648-6557

ABC Seamless Siding
Insulation; Paints, Caulks & Adhesives; Siding & Accessories
3001 Fiechtner Dr.
Fargo, ND 58103
Phone: 701-293-5952
1-800-732-6577
Fax: 701-293-3107
Internet:
http://www.abcseamless.com

Abet
Flooring
60 W. Sheffield Ave.
Englewood, NJ 07631
Phone: 201-541-0700
1-800-228-ABET
Fax: 201-541-0701

Abilene Research & Development Corp.
Paints, Caulks & Adhesives
PO Box 294
Hewlett, NY 11557
Phone: 516-791-6943
Fax: 516-791-6948

Abisko Mfg.
Paints, Caulks & Adhesives
50 Mural St.
Richmond Hill, ON L4B 1E4 Canada
Phone: 905-731-5141
1-800-567-4447
Fax: 905-731-7774
Internet:
http://www.abisko.com

Abracadata
Computer Software
PO Box 2440
Eugene, OR 97402-0144
Phone: 541-342-3030
1-800-451-4871
Fax: 541-683-1925
Internet:
http://www.abracadata.com

ABT Building Products/ABTco
Faucets & Fixtures; Moulding & Millwork; Paints, Caulks & Adhesives; Roofing; Siding & Accessories; Walls, Ceilings & Finishes
3250 W. Big Beaver Rd.
Troy, MI 48084
Phone: 810-649-3300
1-800-521-4250
Fax: 810-649-3139
Internet:
http://www.abtco.com

ABTco Exterior Products Group
Faucets & Fixtures; Moulding & Millwork; Paints, Caulks & Adhesives; Roofing; Siding & Accessories; Walls, Ceilings & Finishes
10115 Kincey Ave.
Huntersville, NC 28078
Phone: 1-800-566-2282
Fax: 704-875-1680

Abundant Energy
Room Enclosures; Windows
PO Box 307
Pine Island, NY 10969
Phone: 914-258-4022
1-800-426-4859

AC Products
Equipment & Trucks; Paints, Caulks & Adhesives
172 E. La Jolla St.
Placentia, CA 92670
Phone: 1-800-238-4204
Fax: 714-666-8309

AC Shutters
Siding & Accessories
3531 E. 80th St.
Cleveland, OH 44105
Phone: 216-441-9400
Fax: 216-441-9410
E-mail:
acshutters@aol.com

ACAD-Plus
Computer Software
9601 Jones Rd., No. 250
Houston, TX 77065
Phone: 713-890-3300
Fax: 713-890-3332

Acadia Post & Beam
Engineered Lumber & Panels; Flooring; Structural Systems
PO Box 217,
Port Williams
Kings County, NS
B0P 1T0 Canada
Phone: 902-542-2298
Fax: 902-542-1912

Acadia Windows & Doors
Doors; Windows
9611 Pulaski Park Dr.
Baltimore, MD 21220
Phone: 410-780-9600
1-800-638-6084
Fax: 410-780-9608

Acan Windows
Doors; Windows
131 Caldari Rd., Unit 3
Concord, ON L4K 3Z9
Canada
Phone: 905-669-5308, ext. 206
1-800-565-0403
Fax: 905-669-3846

Accent Millworks
Moulding & Millwork
285 N. Amboy Rd.
Conneaut, OH 44030
Phone: 216-593-6775
1-800-533-9105
Fax: 216-593-6927

Access Industries
Specialty Products
4001 E. 138th St.
Grandview, MO 64030
Phone: 816-763-3100
1-800-925-3100
Fax: 816-763-0780

Accessible Designs Adjustable Systems
Specialty Products
94 N. Columbus Rd.
Athens, OH 45701
Phone: 614-593-5240
Fax: 614-593-5451

Accurate Industries Steambath and Sauna
Specialty Products
Faucets & Fixtures; Plumbing Supplies
6225 W. Belmont Ave.
Chicago, IL 60634
Phone: 312-889-2144
1-800-977-8326
Fax: 312-889-5636

Accuride Intl.
Hardware
12311 Shoemaker Ave.
Santa Fe Springs, CA 90670
Phone: 562-903-0200
Fax: 562-903-0208

Ace Hardware Corp.
Paints, Caulks & Adhesives
2200 Kensington Ct.
Oak Brook, IL 60521
Phone: 630-990-1240
Fax: 630-990-9707

Ackerman Johnson Fastening Systems
Hardware
136 Official Rd.
Addison, IL 60101
Phone: 708-543-2797
1-800-543-2797
Fax: 708-543-7014

Acme Brick Co.
Fireplaces; Landscape Design; Structural Systems
PO Box 425
Fort Worth, TX 76101
Phone: 817-332-4101
1-800-433-5650, ext. 365
Fax: 817-390-2409
Internet:
http://www.acmebrick.com

Acme Brick Co./ IBP Grid System
Faucets & Fixtures; Windows
PO Box 425
Fort Worth, TX 76101
Phone: 817-332-4101
1-800-433-5650, ext. 365
Fax: 817-390-2409
Internet:
http://www.acmebrick.com

Acorn (A Division of DHI)
Structural Systems
930 Main St.
Acton, MA 01720
Phone: 617-259-9450
1-800-727-3325
Fax: 508-263-4159
Internet:
http://www.acorns.com

Acorn Mfg. Co.
Hardware
457 School St.
Mansfield, MA 02048
Phone: 1-800-835-0121
Fax: 508-339-0104

Acro Extrusion Corp.
Windows
PO Box 9410
Wilmington, DE 19808
Phone: 302-762-4476
1-800-441-3859
Fax: 302-762-1043

Acro Foam & Plastic
Insulation
8527 Coronet Rd.
Edmonton, AB T6E 4N7
Canada
Phone: 403-469-6865
Fax: 403-469-9061

Action Floor Systems
Flooring
PO Box 469, 2775 Hwy. 51
Mercer, WI 54547
Phone: 715-476-3512
1-800-746-3512
Fax: 715-476-3585

Active Homes Corp.
Structural Systems
7938 S. Van Dyke Rd.,
PO Box 127
Marlette, MI 48453
Phone: 517-635-3532
Fax: 517-635-3327

Add-Vantage Software
Computer Software
PO Box 173
Medway, MA 02053
Phone: 1-800-768-5636
Fax: 508-533-6817

Ademco
Home Technology
165 Eileen Way
Syosset, NY 11791
Phone: 516-921-6704
1-800-645-7568
Fax: 516-921-6809

Adhesive Technologies
Paints, Caulks & Adhesives; Tools/Electric & Pneumatic
3 Merrill Industrial Dr.
Hampton, NH 03842
Phone: 603-926-1616
1-800-544-1021
Fax: 603-926-1780

Adirondack Forest Industries
Engineered Lumber & Panels
7178 Fishhouse Rd.
Galway, NY 12074
Phone: 518-883-5680
Fax: 518-883-8988

Admiral
Appliances
1 Dependability Sq.
Newton, IA 50208
Phone: 515-792-7000
Fax: 515-791-8793

ADO Products
Roofing
PO Box 236,
21800 129th Ave. N.
Rogers, MN 55374
Phone: 612-428-7802
1-800-666-8191
Fax: 612-428-7806

Advanced Affiliates
Hardware
96-12 43rd Ave.
Corona, NY 11368
Phone: 718-335-3566
Fax: 718-565-1444

Advanced Building Systems
Structural Systems
PO Box 327
Paulding, OH 45879
Phone: 419-399-4412
1-800-342-3448
Fax: 419-399-4361

Advanced Design Products
Equipment & Trucks; Paints, Caulks & Adhesives
2919 Industrial Park Dr.
Finksburg, MD 21048
Phone: 410-833-8814
1-800-743-8815
Fax: 410-833-8817

Advanced Foil Systems
Insulation
820 S. Rockefeller, Suite A
Ontario, CA 91761
Phone: 909-390-5125
1-800-421-5947
Fax: 909-390-5127

Advanced Framing Systems
Structural Systems
1118 W. Spring St.
Monroe, GA 30655
Phone: 404-267-2520
1-800-633-8600
Fax: 404-267-2529

Advanced Technology
Countertops
311 Regional Rd. S.
Greensboro, NC 27409
Phone: 910-668-0488
1-800-849-1320
Fax: 910-668-0713

Advanced Wood Resources (A Division of JELD-WEN)
Engineered Lumber & Panels
34363 Lake Creek Dr.
Brownsville, OR 97327
Phone: 1-800-877-9482

AE Gombert Lumber Co.
Flooring; Moulding & Millwork; Siding & Accessories; Walls, Ceilings & Finishes
81 Island St., PO Box 58
North Tonawanda, NY 14120-0058
Phone: 716-692-4500

AEC Software
Computer Software
22611-113 Markey Ct.
Sterling, VA 20166-6903
Phone: 703-450-1980
1-800-346-9413
Fax: 703-450-9786
Internet: http://www.aecsoft.com

AEG/Andi-Co.
Appliances
65 Campus Plaza
Edison, NJ 08837
Phone: 908-225-8837
1-800-344-0043
Fax: 908-225-8839

AERT
Moulding & Millwork
HC 10 Box 116
Junction, TX 76849-9301
Phone: 915-446-3430
Fax: 915-446-3864

AES
Home Technology
22 Parsons Dr.
Swampscott, MA 01907
Phone: 617-592-4966
Fax: 617-581-2164

AF Schwerd Mfg.
Moulding & Millwork
3215 McClure Ave.
Pittsburgh, PA 15212
Phone: 412-766-6322
Fax: 412-766-2262

Afco Industries
Doors; Moulding & Millwork; Paints, Caulks & Adhesives; Walls, Ceilings & Finishes
615 E. 40th St.
Holland, MI 49423
Phone: 616-392-1826
1-800-253-4644
Fax: 616-392-8641

AFG Industries
Windows
PO Box 929,
1400 Lincoln St.
Kingsport, TN 37660
Phone: 423-229-7200
1-800-251-0441
Fax: 423-229-7459

AFM Corp.
Insulation; Structural Systems
24000 W. Hwy. 7,
PO Box 246
Excelsior, MN 55331
Phone: 612-474-0809
1-800-255-0176
Fax: 612-474-2074

Aged Woods
Engineered Lumber & Panels; Flooring; Moulding & Millwork; Walls, Ceilings & Finishes
2331 E. Market St.
York, PA 17402
Phone: 1-800-233-9307
Fax: 717-840-1468

Aid-O-Maid
Specialty Products
PO Box 3
Waco, TX 76703
Phone: 817-752-8702

AIM Tools & Accessories
Tools/Electric & Pneumatic
91 Niagara St.
Toronto, ON M5V 1C3
Canada
Phone: 416-504-9455
Fax: 416-504-9456

Aiphone Intercom Systems
Home Technology; Specialty Products
1700 130th Ave. N.W.
Bellevue, WA 98005
Phone: 206-455-0510
Fax: 206-455-0071
Internet: http://www.aiphone.com

Air Conditioning and Refrigeration Institute
Appliances; HVAC
4301 N. Fairfax Dr.,
Suite 425
Arlington, VA 22203
Phone: 703-524-8800

Air Lock Log Co.
Structural Systems
PO Box 2506
Las Vegas, NM 87701
Phone: 505-425-8880
Fax: 505-425-7636

Air Nail Co.
Hardware; Tools/Electric & Pneumatic
5335 Reisner Way
South Gate, CA 90280
Phone: 213-563-0233
1-800-479-6455 (CA)
1-800-782-8857
Fax: 213-563-0325

Air Technology
HVAC
7014 Coventry
Fort Mill, SC 29715
Phone: 803-548-4800
1-800-822-8040
Fax: 803-548-7493

Air Vent
HVAC; Roofing
3000 W. Commerce
Dallas, TX 75212
Phone: 1-800-247-8368
Fax: 1-800-635-7006

Airmart HVAC
HVAC
PO Box 41524,
230 Sandalwood Pkwy.
Brampton, ON L6Z 4R1
Canada
Phone: 905-678-7787
1-800-561-0749
Fax: 905-678-7571

Airxchange
HVAC
401 VFW. Dr.
Rockland, MA 02370
Phone: 617-871-4816
Fax: 617-871-3029

AJ Stairs
Flooring; Moulding & Millwork
1095 Towbin Ave.
Lakewood, NJ 08701
Phone: 908-905-8500
1-800-425-7824
Fax: 908-905-8558

Akro-Mils
Tools/Hand
1293 S. Main St.
Akron, OH 44301
Phone: 330-253-5592
1-800-253-2467
Fax: 330-253-9801

Akzo Nobel Coatings
Paints, Caulks & Adhesives
PO Box 7062,
1845 Maxwell
Troy, MI 48007
Phone: 810-637-0400
1-800-833-7288 (US)
1-800-663-6273 (Canada)
Fax: 810-649-6529

Aladdin Light Lift
3111 Stage Post Dr.
Suite 106
Memphis, TN 38133
Phone: 901-385-0456
Fax: 901-385-0533

Aladdin Steel Products
Fireplaces
401 N. Wynne St.
Colville, WA 99114
Phone: 509-684-3745
1-800-234-2508
Fax: 509-684-2138

Alarm Lock Systems
Hardware
345 Bayview Ave.
Amityville, NY 11701
Phone: 516-789-4871
1-800-ALA-LOCK
Fax: 516-789-3383

Alcan Building Products
(See Gentek Building Products)

Alcatel Canada Wire
250 Ferrand Dr.
North York, ON
M3C 3J4 Canada
Phone: 416-424-5000
Fax: 416-424-1008

ALCO-NVC
Roofing; Specialty Products
580 St. Jean,
PO Box 14001
Detroit, MI 48214
Phone: 313-823-7500
1-800-323-0029
Fax: 313-331-4726

Alcoa Building Products Vital Statistics
Roofing; Siding & Accessories
PO Box 57
Sidney, OH 45365
Phone: 1-800-962-6973
Internet: http://www.sweets.com

Alcoa Vinyl Windows
Doors; Windows
725 Pleasant Valley Dr.
Springboro, OH 45066
Phone: 513-746-0488
1-800-238-1866
Fax: 217-893-3695

Alden Corp.
Tools/Electric & Pneumatic
Munson Rd.
Wolcott, CT 06716
Phone: 203-879-4889
1-800-832-5336
Fax: 203-879-5556

Aldon Corp.
Paints, Caulks & Adhesives; Structural Systems
6426 Hwy. 93 S.
Whitefish, MT 59937
Phone: 406-862-6050
Fax: 1-800-332-9329
Internet: http://www.aldonchem.com

Alenco
Doors; Windows
615 Carson
Bryan, TX 77801
Phone: 409-779-7770
Fax: 409-822-3259

Algonquin Log Homes
Structural Systems
RR 1
Norland, ON K0M 2L0
Canada
Phone: 705-454-2311
Fax: 705-454-2312

ALH Building Systems
Structural Systems
I69 & US 224,
PO Box 408
Markle, IN 46770
Phone: 219-758-2141
Fax: 219-758-2177

All American Wood Register
HVAC
239 E. Main St.
Cary, IL 60013
Phone: 847-639-0393
Fax: 847-639-0157

All Steel Homes
Roofing; Structural Systems
2626 Gribble St.
North Little Rock, AR 72114
Phone: 501-945-8092
1-800-278-0888
Fax: 501-945-3303

Allied Brass Mfg. Co.
Faucets & Fixtures; Hardware
149 Wooster St.
New York, NY 10012
Phone: 212-674-1597
Fax: 212-353-0837

Allmilmo Corp.
Cabinetry
70 Clinton Rd.,
PO Box 629
Fairfield, NJ 07004
Phone: 201-227-2502
Fax: 201-227-2875

Alltrade
Equipment & Trucks; Tools/Hand
1431 Via Plata
Long Beach, CA 90810
Phone: 310-522-9008
1-800-368-6653
Fax: 310-522-9066

Allway Tools
Paints, Caulks & Adhesives; Tools/Hand
1255 Seabury Ave.
Bronx, NY 10462
Phone: 718-792-3636
1-800-422-5592
Fax: 718-823-9640
E-mail: allwaytool@aol.com

Almetco Building Products
Doors; Windows
620 Audley Blvd., Annacis Business Park
Delta, BC V3M 5P2
Canada
Phone: 604-526-0828
Fax: 604-526-6392

Almico Plastics
Faucets & Fixtures
91 Cornelia St. W.
Smith Falls, ON
K7A 4T6 Canada
Phone: 613-284-8230
1-800-333-2564
Fax: 613-284-8235

Almost Heaven
Faucets & Fixtures; Landscape Design
Rt. 5 BM
Renick, WV 24966
Phone: 304-497-3163
Fax: 304-497-2698
Internet: http://www.vmirror.com/heaven/

ALNO Network USA
Cabinetry
1 Design Center Pl.,
Suite 643
Boston, MA 02210
Phone: 617-482-2566
Fax: 617-482-2744

Alpha Communications
Home Technology
89-D Cabot Ct.
Hauppauge, NY 11788
Phone: 516-434-8080
1-800-666-41-800
Fax: 516-434-8334
Internet: http://www.alpha-comm.com

Alro Plumbing Specialty Co.
Faucets & Fixtures; Insulation; Plumbing Supplies
396 Flushing Ave.
Brooklyn, NY 11205
Phone: 718-875-5166
Fax: 718-858-3351
E-mail: alro@attmail.com

Alsco
Roofing; Siding & Accessories
3101 Poplarwood Ct.,
Suite 200
Raleigh, NC 27604
Phone: 919-876-9333
1-800-231-9333
Fax: 919-876-7885

Alside Siding Div.
Siding & Accessories
PO Box 2010
Akron, OH 44309
Phone: 1-800-922-6009
Fax: 330-922-2175
Internet: http://www.alside.com

Alside Window Div.
Doors; Windows
PO Box 2010
Akron, OH 44309
Phone: 1-800-922-6009
Fax: 330-922-2175
Internet: http://www.alside.com

Alsons Corp.
Faucets & Fixtures
42 Union St.
Hillsdale, MI 49242
Phone: 517-439-1411
1-800-421-0001
Fax: 1-800-769-2744

Altech Energy
HVAC
7009 Raywood Rd.
Madison, WI 53713
Phone: 608-221-4499
1-800-627-4499
Fax: 608-221-2824

Alum-a-Pole Corp.
Equipment & Trucks; Hardware; Moulding & Millwork; Siding & Accessories
1011 Capouse Ave.
Scranton, PA 18509
Phone: 717-969-2299
1-800-421-2586
Fax: 717-969-2531

Alumax Bath Enclosures
Doors; Faucets & Fixtures
1617 N. Washington
Magnolia, AR 71753
Phone: 501-234-4260
1-800-551-0208
Fax: 501-234-3181
Internet: http://www.infogo.com/alumax/alumax.html

ALUMET Building Products
Room Enclosures; Structural Systems; Windows
227 Town East Blvd.,
PO Box 850163
Mesquite, TX 75185
Phone: 214-285-8811
1-800-827-6045
Fax: 214-882-8813

Am-Finn Sauna Co.
Faucets & Fixtures
PO Box 810
Valley Forge, PA 19482
Phone: 610-983-3212
1-800-237-2862

AM General Corp.
Equipment & Trucks
105 N. Niles Ave.
South Bend, IN 46617
Phone: 1-800-REAL-4WD
Fax: 219-284-2933

Amana Refrigeration
Appliances; HVAC
2800 220th Trail,
PO Box 8901
Amana, IA 52204
Phone: 319-622-5511
1-800-843-0304
Fax: 319-622-2180

Amarr Garage Doors
Garage Doors & Openers
PO Box 288
Winston-Salem, NC 27102-0288
Phone: 910-744-5100
Fax: 910-744-0895
Internet:
http://www.amarr.com

Ambiance of High Point
Doors; Windows
2149 Brevard,
PO Box 528
High Point, NC 27261
Phone: 910-889-4551
1-800-440-8476
Fax: 910-889-7006

Amdega Machin Conservatories
Landscape Design; Room Enclosures
PO Box 7
Glenview, IL 60025
Phone: 1-800-922-0110

Amerec Products
Faucets & Fixtures
1700 136th Pl. N.W.
Bellevue, WA 98005
Phone: 206-643-7500
1-800-331-0349
Fax: 206-643-2124
Internet:
http://www.amerec.com

American Accent Homes
Doors; Insulation; Siding & Accessories
PO Box 131
Kannapolis, NC 28082
Phone: 1-800-737-1992
Fax: 704-938-8877

American ALDES Ventilation
HVAC
4537 Northgate Ct.
Sarasota, FL 34234-2124
Phone: 941-351-3441
1-800-255-7749
Fax: 941-351-3442
Internet:
http://www.oikos.com/aldes

American Architectural Manufacturers Assn.
Doors; Hardware; Windows
1540 E. Dundee Rd.,
Suite 310
Palatine, IL 60067-8316
Phone: 708-202-1350
Fax: 708-202-1480
Internet:
http://www.aamanet.org

American Bldg. Prods./Hindman
Room Enclosures; Siding & Accessories
PO Box 1808
Centralia, IL 62801
Phone: 618-532-4761
1-800-851-0865
Fax: 618-532-4763

American Cabinet
Cabinetry
1655 Amity Rd.,
PO Box 640
Conway, AR 72032
Phone: 1-800-643-8035
Fax: 501-329-2517

American Cemwood Corp.
Roofing
PO Box C
Albany, OR 97321-7716
Phone: 503-928-6397
1-800-367-3471
Fax: 503-928-8110

American Computer Software
Computer Software
6911 Mangrove Ln.
Madison, WI 53713
Phone: 608-221-9449
1-800-527-9449
Fax: 608-221-9422
Internet:
http://www.acsoftware.com

American ConForm Industries
Insulation; Landscape Design; Structural Systems
1820 S. Santa Fe
Santa Ana, CA 92705
Phone: 714-662-1100
1-800-CONFORM
Fax: 714-662-0405

The American Contractor
Computer Software
933 Larkin Valley Rd.
Watsonville, CA 95076
Phone: 408-724-9878
1-800-333-8435
Fax: 408-724-5391
Internet:
http://www.amercon.com

American Custom Millwork
Cabinetry; Doors; Moulding & Millwork
3904 Newton Rd.,
PO Box 3608
Albany, GA 31706
Phone: 912-888-3303
Fax: 912-888-9245

American Design & Engineering
Tools/Electric & Pneumatic; Tools/Hand
900 Third St., No. 123E
St. Paul Park, MN 55075
Phone: 612-459-7400
1-800-441-1388
Fax: 612-459-5616

American Energy Systems
Fireplaces
50 Academy Ln.
Hutchinson, MN 55350
Phone: 320-587-6565
1-800-495-3196
Fax: 320-587-8872

American Energy Technologies
HVAC
PO Box 1865
Green Cove Springs, FL 32043
Phone: 904-284-0552
1-800-874-2190
Fax: 904-284-0006

American Faucet & Coatings Corp.
Faucets & Fixtures
1260 Liberty Way E.
Vista, CA 92083
Phone: 619-598-5895
Fax: 619-598-0321

American Floor Products Co.
Flooring
PO Box 1467
Rockville, MD 20849
Phone: 301-762-8600
1-800-342-0424
Fax: 301-762-1937

American Forest & Paper Assn.
Engineered Lumber & Panels
1111 19th St. N.W.,
Suite 800
Washington, DC 20036
Phone: 202-463-2700

American Gas Assn.
Appliances; HVAC
1515 Wilson Blvd.
Arlington, VA 22209
Phone: 703-841-8400

American Hardboard Assn.
Engineered Lumber & Panels; Siding & Accessories; Walls, Ceilings & Finishes
1210 W. Northwest Hwy.
Palatine, IL 60067-3607
Phone: 708-934-8800
Fax: 708-934-8803

American Hardware Manufacturers Assn.
Hardware
801 N. Plaza Dr.
Schaumburg, IL 60173
Phone: 847-605-1025
Fax: 847-605-1093
Internet:
http://www.ahma.org

American Hardwoods
Engineered Lumber & Panels
12430 S.W. Herman Rd.
Tualatin, OR 97062
Phone: 503-692-4000
1-800-547-3401
Fax: 503-692-0618

American Heritage Shutters
Doors; Hardware; Siding & Accessories
2345 Dunn Ave.
Memphis, TN 38114
Phone: 901-743-2800
1-800-541-1186
Fax: 901-744-8356

American Honda Motor Co.
Equipment & Trucks
4475 River Green Pkwy.
Duluth, GA 30136-2565
Phone: 770-497-6000
Fax: 770-497-6008

American Institute of Timber Construction
7012 S. Revere Pkwy.,
Suite 140
Englewood, CO 80112
Phone: 303-792-9559
Fax: 303-792-0669

American Isuzu Motors
Equipment & Trucks
13181 Crossroads Pkwy.
N., Fourth Fl.
City of Industry, CA 91746
Phone: 310-699-0500
Fax: 310-692-7135

American Lantern Div. Inteletron
Electrical & Lighting; Home Technology
21021 Corsair Blvd.
Hayward, CA 94545
Phone: 510-732-6790
1-800-556-2387
Fax: 510-732-6910

American Lighting
Electrical & Lighting
5211D W. Market St.,
Suite 803
Greensboro, NC 27265
Phone: 1-800-741-0571

American Lighting Assn.
Electrical & Lighting
World Trade Center,
PO Box 420288
Dallas, TX 75342-0288
Phone: 214-698-9898
1-800-605-4448
Fax: 214-698-9899

American Marazzi Tile
Countertops; Flooring; Walls, Ceilings & Finishes
359 Clay Rd.
Sunnyvale, TX 75182
Phone: 972-226-0110
Fax: 972-226-5629

American Marble Industries Kephaco Corp.
Countertops; Faucets & Fixtures; Moulding & Millwork; Walls, Ceilings & Finishes
2700 Atlantic Blvd. N.W.
Canton, OH 44705
Phone: 330-453-8437
1-800-288-4095
Fax: 330-453-4913

American Metal Products
Fireplaces; HVAC
8601 Hacks Cross Rd.
Olive Branch, MS 38654
Phone: 601-895-4250
1-800-423-4270
Fax: 1-800-626-3825

American Olean Tile
Countertops; Faucets & Fixtures; Flooring; Paints, Caulks & Adhesives; Walls, Ceilings & Finishes
7834 CF Hawn Fwy.
Dallas, TX 75217
Phone: 214-398-1411
Fax: 215-822-7300
Internet:
http://www.aotile.com

American Polysteel Forms
Insulation; Landscape Design; Structural Systems
5150 F Edith N.E.
Albuquerque, NM 87107
Phone: 505-345-8153
1-800-977-3676
Fax: 505-345-8154
Internet:
www.ni.net/polysteel.com

American Power Products
Electrical & Lighting; Home Technology
14040 Central Ave.,
Bldg. 200
Chino, CA 91710
Phone: 714-590-2626
1-800-533-2929
Fax: 714-591-6778

American Roof
Equipment & Trucks
21808 N.W. 175th
Woodinville, WA 98072
Phone: 206-488-8868
Fax: 360-668-1717

American Roof-Brite
Siding & Accessories
4492 Acworth Ind. Dr.,
Suite 102
Acworth, GA 30101
Phone: 770-966-1080
1-800-476-9271
Fax: 770-975-4647

American Saw & Mfg. Co.
Hardware; Tools/Electric & Pneumatic; Tools/Hand
301 Chestnut St.
East Longmeadow, MA 01028
Phone: 413-525-3961
1-800-628-3030
Fax: 1-800-223-7906

American Shower and Bath
(A Div. of Masco Corp.)
Faucets & Fixtures
693 S. Ct. St.
Lapeer, MI 48446-2552
Phone: 810-664-8501
Fax: 810-664-8670

American Shower Door
Faucets & Fixtures
6920 E. Slauson Ave.
City of Commerce, CA 90040
Phone: 213-726-2478
1-800-421-2333
1-800-327-4141 (CA)
Fax: 213-726-7469

American Site Furniture
Electrical & Lighting
PO Box 158,
56 Winthrop St.
Concord, MA 01742
Phone: 508-371-3080
1-800-366-3080
Fax: 508-369-4472

American Skylites
Windows
7451 Dogwood Park
Ft. Worth, TX 76118
Phone: 817-589-7199
1-800-772-7401
Fax: 817-589-5959

American Solar Energy Society (ASES)
HVAC
2400 Central Ave., Suite G1
Boulder, CO 80301
Phone: 303-443-3130
Internet:
http://www.ases.org/solar

American Sprayed Fibers
Insulation
1550 E. 91st Dr.
Merrillville, IN 46410
Phone: 219-769-0180
1-800-824-2997
Fax: 219-736-6126

American Standard
Faucets & Fixtures
1 Centennial Plaza
Piscataway, NJ 08855
Phone: 908-980-2400
Fax: 908-980-3335

American-Standard Air Conditioning
HVAC
PO Box 9010
Tyler, TX 75711

American Stone-Mix
Roofing; Structural Systems
8320 Bellona Ave.
Baltimore, MD 21204
Phone: 410-296-6770
1-800-445-8250
Fax: 410-494-0897

American Tack & Hardware Co.
Electrical & Lighting
25 Robert Pitt Dr.
Monsey, NY 10952
Phone: 914-352-2400
E-mail: amertac.com

American Technocrete Corp.
Structural Systems
3518 Cahuenga Blvd. W.,
Suite 200
Los Angeles, CA 90068
Phone: 213-874-2427
1-800-624-9255
Fax: 213-874-4338

American Tool Cos.
Tools/Electric & Pneumatic; Tools/Hand
8400 Lakeview Pkwy.,
Suite 400
Kenosha, WI 53142
Phone: 414-947-2440
Fax: 414-947-2441

American Wall Tie Co.
Hardware; Plumbing Supplies
2711 Lake
Chicago, IL 60612
Phone: 312-533-1728
Fax: 312-533-1730

American Whirlpool
Faucets & Fixtures
3050 N. 29th Ct.
Hollywood, FL 33020
Phone: 305-921-4400
1-800-327-1394
Fax: 305-921-4519

American Wood Council
American Forest &
Paper Assn.
Doors; Engineered Lumber
& Panels; Flooring;
Moulding & Millwork;
Structural Systems
1111 19th St., N.W.
Washington, DC 20036
Phone: 202-463-2769
Fax: 202-463-2791

American Wood
Preservers Institute
1945 Old Gallows Rd.,
Suite 150
Vienna, VA 22182-3931
Phone: 703-893-4005
Fax: 703-893-8492
Internet:
http://www.awpi.org

American Woodmark
(See Timberlake Cabinet)

Americh Corp.
Faucets & Fixtures
13208 Saticoy St.
N. Hollywood, CA
91605-3404
Phone: 818-982-1711
1-800-453-1463
Fax: 818-982-2764
Internet:
http://www.americh.com

AmeriGas
460 N. Gulph Rd.
King of Prussia, PA 19406
Phone: 610-768-7678
1-800-826-5825

Amerimax Building
Products
Doors; Roofing; Siding &
Accessories; Windows
14651 Dallas Pkwy.,
Suite 330
Dallas, TX 75240
Phone: 972-701-4900
1-800-227-3940
Fax: 972-701-4960

Amerimax Home
Products
Roofing; Siding &
Accessories
450 Richardson Dr.,
PO Box 4515
Lancaster, PA 17604
Phone: 717-299-3711
1-800-347-2586
Fax: 717-293-0908

Amerock Corp.
Cabinets; Hardware
PO Box 7018
Rockford, IL 61125-7018
Phone: 815-969-6308
Fax: 815-969-6138
Internet:
http://www.amerock.com

Ametek
(Plymouth Products Div.)
Appliances
PO Box 1047,
502 Indiana Ave.
Sheboygan, WI 53082
Phone: 414-457-9435
1-800-222-7558
Fax: 414-457-6652

AMP
Building Systems Div.
Home Technology
MS 210-01,
PO Box 3608
Harrisburg, PA 17105
Phone: 717-558-6255
1-800-321-2343
Fax: 717-558-6224

Ampco Products
Cabinetry; Countertops;
Doors
7795 W. 20th Ave.
Hialeah, FL 33014-3227
Phone: 305-821-5700
Fax: 305-557-0764
Internet:
http://www.ampco.com

Amsterdam Corp.
Countertops; Flooring;
Walls, Ceilings & Finishes
150 E. 58th St.
New York, NY 10155
Phone: 212-644-1350
Fax: 212-935-6291

AMX Corp.
Electrical & Lighting;
Home Technology
11995 Forestgate Dr.
Dallas, TX 75243
Phone: 214-644-3048
1-800-222-0193
Fax: 214-907-2053

Anaheim Mfg. Co.
(See Waste King)

Anasys
Computer Software
2515 N. 124th St.
Brookfield, WI 53005
Phone: 414-784-6665
Fax: 414-784-5154

Anchor Industries
Siding & Accessories
1100 Burch Dr.
PO Box 3477
Evansville, IN 47733
Phone: 812-867-2421
1-800-255-5552
Fax: 812-867-1429
Internet: http://www.
anchorinc.com

Anchor Wall Systems
Landscape Design
6101 Baker Rd.,
Suite 201
Minnetonka, MN 55345
Phone: 612-933-8855
1-800-473-4452
Fax: 612-933-8833
Internet:
http://www.anchorwall.com/

Anchortek
Plumbing Supplies
2320 24th Ave. N.E.
Calgary, AB T2E 7N9
Canada
Phone: 403-250-3030
Fax: 403-250-3054

Ancient Venetian
Floor Co.
Flooring
1516 Edison St.
Dallas, TX 75207
Phone: 214-741-4555
Fax: 214-741-4147

Andek Chemical Corp.
Paints, Caulks &
Adhesives; Roofing
PO Box 392, 850 Glen Ave.
Moorestown, NJ 08057
Phone: 609-786-6900
1-800-1-800-2844
Fax: 609-786-0580

Andersen Windows
Doors; Windows
100 Fourth Ave. N.
Bayport, MN 55003
Phone: 612-439-5150
1-800-426-4261
Fax: 612-439-7364
Internet: http://www.
andersencorp.com

Anderson Hardwood
Floors
Flooring
Old Laurens Rd.,
PO Box 1155
Clinton, SC 29325
Phone: 803-833-6250
Fax: 803-833-6664

Anderson Wood
Products Co.
Moulding & Millwork
1381 Beech St.
Louisville, KY 40211
Phone: 502-778-5591
Fax: 502-778-5599

Androck Hardware
Corp.
Hardware
711 19th St.
Rockford, IL 61104
Phone: 815-229-1144
1-800-397-2658
Fax: 815-229-1895

Angeles Metal Systems
Structural Systems
4817 E. Sheila St.
Los Angeles, CA 90040
Phone: 213-268-1777
Fax: 213-268-8996

Anthony Forest
Products Co.
Engineered Lumber &
Panels; Moulding &
Millwork; Siding &
Accessories; Structural
Systems
PO Box 1877,
309 N. Washington
El Dorado, AR 71730
Phone: 501-862-5594
1-800-221-2326
Fax: 501-862-6502

APA-The Engineered
Wood Assn.
Engineered Lumber
& Panels
7011 S. 19th St.
Tacoma, WA 98466-5399
Phone: 206-565-6600
Fax: 206-565-7265
Internet:
http://www.apawood.org

APC Building Products
Doors; Windows
PO Box 1869
Welcome, NC 27374
Phone: 910-764-6465
1-888-764-6465
Fax: 910-764-1017

Apollo Windows
(A Div. of Sun Windows)
Windows
PO Box 1329,
1515 E. 18th St.
Owensboro, KY 42302
Phone: 502-686-8352
1-800-328-1151
Fax: 502-926-6452

Appalachian Log
Structures
Siding & Accessories;
Structural Systems
PO Box 614
Ripley, WV 25271
Phone: 304-372-6410
1-800-458-9990
Fax: 304-372-3154
Internet:
http://www.applog.com

Applegate Insulation
Mfg.
Insulation
1000 Highview Dr.
Webberville, MI 48892
Phone: 517-521-3545
1-800-627-7536
Fax: 517-521-3597

Aqua-Flo
Plumbing Supplies
PO Box 1807
Carson City, NV 89702
Phone: 702-884-4242
1-800-854-3215
Fax: 702-243-1777

Aqua Glass Corp.
(A Div. of Masco)
Faucets & Fixtures
PO Box 412,
Industrial Park
Adamsville, TN 38310
Phone: 901-632-0911
1-800-238-3940
Fax: 901-632-4232

Aqua-Lock
Waterproofing Materials
Specialty Products
1851 S. Church
Jonesboro, AR 72401
Phone: 501-935-0755
1-800-752-2558

Aqua Plunge
Aqua Plunge Div.
Faucets & Fixtures
6101 49th St. S.
Muscatine, IA 52761
Phone: 319-263-6642
1-800-553-9664
Fax: 319-263-8358

Aquatic Industries
Faucets & Fixtures
PO Box 889
Leander, TX 78646-0889
Phone: 512-259-2255
Fax: 512-259-3633

ArchiCAD
(See Graphisoft US)

Architectural Matters
Moulding & Millwork
18754 Parthenia, No. 3
Northridge, CA 91324
Phone: 818-349-4282
Fax: 818-349-9223

Architectural Ornament
Moulding & Millwork
216 Rivermede Rd., Unit 7
Concord, ON L4K 3M6
Canada
Phone: 905-738-9459
1-800-567-3554
Fax: 905-738-6734
E-mail:
archorn@accessv.com

Architectural Paneling
Cabinetry; Doors;
Fireplaces; Moulding &
Millwork
979 Third Ave., Suite 919
New York, NY 10022
Phone: 212-371-9632
Fax: 212-759-0276

Architectural
Reproductions
Moulding & Millwork;
Specialty Products; Walls,
Ceilings & Finishes
525 N. Tillamook
Portland, OR 97227
Phone: 503-284-8007
Fax: 503-281-6926

Architectural Sculpture
Moulding & Millwork;
Walls, Ceilings & Finishes
242 Lafayette St.
New York, NY 10012
Phone: 212-431-5873
Fax: 212-431-7161

Architectural Timber &
Millwork
Cabinetry; Moulding &
Millwork; Structural
Systems
35 Mount Warner Rd.,
PO Box 719
Hadley, MA 01035
Phone: 413-586-3045
Fax: 413-586-3046

Arcoaire Heating &
Cooling Products
Inter-City Products
Corp. (USA)
HVAC
650 Heil-Quaker Ave.
Lewisburg, TN 37091
Phone: 615-359-3511
Fax: 615-270-4166
Internet: http://www.
arcoaire.com/arcoaire

Arctic Metal Products
Appliances; Cabinetry;
Countertops
507 Wortman Ave.
Brooklyn, NY 11208
Phone: 718-257-5277
Fax: 718-257-5452

Arcways
Moulding & Millwork
1076 Ehlers Rd.
Neenah, WI 54957
Phone: 414-725-2667
1-800-558-5096
Fax: 414-725-2053

Areslux
Cabinetry; Faucets &
Fixtures
8229 N.W. 66 St.
Miami, FL 33166
Phone: 305-592-6448
1-800-523-1564
Fax: 305-477-5155

Argee Corp.
Electrical & Lighting
9550 Pathway St.
Santee, CA 92071-4169
Phone: 619-449-5050
Fax: 619-449-8392

Argos Systems
Computer Software
19 Crosby Dr.
Bedford, MA 01730
Phone: 617-271-9111
Fax: 617-271-9393

Aristech/Acrylic Sheet
7350 Empire Dr.
Florence, KY 41042
Phone: 1-800-354-9858
Fax: 606-283-6497

Aristocrat Products
Moulding & Millwork
8215 Roswell Rd.,
Bldg. 600
Atlanta, GA 30350
Phone: 770-913-1272
Fax: 770-391-9067

Aristokraft
Cabinetry
PO Box 420,
1 Aristokraft Sq.
Jasper, IN 47547-0420
Phone: 812-482-2527
Fax: 812-482-1763
Internet: http://www.
aristokraft.com

Arius Tile Co.
Countertops; Flooring;
Walls, Ceilings & Finishes
PO Box 5497
Santa Fe, NM 87502
Phone: 505-988-8966
1-800-36-ARIUS
Fax: 505-989-8280

Ark-Seal Intl.
Insulation
2190 S. Kalamath
Denver, CO 80223
Phone: 303-934-7772
1-800-525-8992
Fax: 303-934-5240

Armor Bond Building
Products
Siding & Accessories
PO Box 369
Sardis, MS 38666
Phone: 601-487-3031
1-800-752-8026

Armor Systems
Computer Software
1626 W. Airport Blvd.
Sanford, FL 32773-4814
Phone: 407-323-9787
Fax: 407-330-0442

Armstrong World
Industries
Flooring; Tools/Hand;
Walls, Ceilings & Finishes
PO Box 3001
Lancaster, PA 17604
Phone: 717-397-0611
1-800-233-3823

Armstrong World
Industries
Installation Products
Div.
PO Box 3001,
313 W. Liberty St.
Lancaster, PA 17604
Phone: 717-397-0611
1-800-233-3823

Around The Corner
*Faucets & Fixtures;
Hardware; Moulding &
Millwork; Specialty
Products*
550 Elizabeth St.
Waukesha, WI 53186
Phone: 414-542-0685
1-800-445-3780

Arriscraft Corp.
*Fireplaces; Landscape
Design; Siding &
Accessories; Structural
Systems*
875 Speedsville Rd.,
PO Box 3190
Cambridge, ON
N3H 4S8 Canada
Phone: 1-800-265-8123

Arrow Fastener Co.
Tools/Hand
271 Mayhill St.
Saddle Brook, NJ 07662
Phone: 201-843-6900
Fax: 201-843-3911

Arrow Lock Mfg. Co.
Hardware
103-00 Foster Ave.
Brooklyn, NY 11236
Phone: 718-257-4700
1-800-233-0478
Fax: 718-927-1753

Arrow/Medina Group
Doors
4200 Roger B Chaffee,
Memorial Dr.
Grand Rapids, MI 49548
Phone: 616-531-5440
1-800-444-5440
Fax: 616-531-3547

ART
Computer Software
3731 N. Ramsey Rd.,
Suite 150
Couer d'Alene, ID 83814
Phone: 208-664-4204
1-800-482-4433
Fax: 208-664-1316
Internet:
http://www.chiefarch.com

Arthur Cox & Sons
Doors
18311 E. Railroad St.
Industry, CA 91748
Phone: 818-965-1565
1-800-456-5656
Fax: 818-965-7507

Artisan Glass Works
Windows
5700 Bellona Ave.
Baltimore, MD 21212
Phone: 410-435-0300
Fax: 410-435-0344

**Artistic Brass
Div. of Masco Corp. of
Indiana**
Faucets & Fixtures
55 E. 111th St.
Indianapolis, IN 46280
Phone: 317-848-0991
1-800-251-2390
Fax: 1-800-551-1508

Artistic Enclosures
Room Enclosures
5 Willow St. Industrial Pk.
Fleetwood, PA 19522
Phone: 610-944-8585
1-800-944-8599
Fax: 610-944-8120

Artistic Woodworking
Moulding & Millwork
Rt. 2, Box 40B
Imperial, NE 69033
Phone: 308-882-4873
1-800-621-3992
Fax: 308-882-5507

Ashland-Davis Co.
Siding & Accessories
17199 Laurel Park Dr. N.
Livonia, MI 48152
Phone: 313-953-1300
1-800-231-1614
Fax: 313-953-0852

Asko
Appliances
PO Box 851805
Richardson, TX 75085
Phone: 214-644-8595
Fax: 214-644-8593

**Assn. for Safe &
Accessible Products**
Specialty Products
1511 K St., N.W.,
Suite 600
Washington, DC 20005
Phone: 202-347-8200
Fax: 202-393-5043
E-mail: asapdc@aol.com

**Assn. of Home
Appliance Manufacturers**
Appliances
20 N. Wacker Dr.
Chicago, IL 60606-2806
Phone: 312-984-5800
Fax: 312-984-5823

**Assn. of the Wall &
Ceiling Industries Intl.**
Walls, Ceilings & Finishes
307 E. Annandale Rd.,
Suite 200
Falls Church, VA 22042
Phone: 703-534-8300
Fax: 703-534-8307
Internet:
http://www.awci.org

Astracast
Faucets & Fixtures
2761 Golfview Dr.
Naperville, IL 60563
Phone: 708-983-4200
1-800-276-7726
Fax: 708-983-4662

The Astrup Co.
*Landscape Design; Siding
& Accessories*
2937 W. 25th St.
Cleveland, OH 44113
Phone: 216-696-2820
Fax: 216-696-0977

ATAS Intl.
*Roofing; Siding &
Accessories; Structural
Systems*
6612 Snowdrift Rd.
Allentown, PA 18106
Phone: 610-395-8445
Fax: 610-395-9342
Internet:
http://www.atas.com

**Atlantic Building
Products**
*Engineered Lumber
& Panels*
PO Box 1287
Lakeville, MA 02347
Phone: 508-947-5000
Fax: 508-946-4771

**Atlantic Pacific
Industries**
Hardware
4223-25 W. Jefferson
Blvd.
Los Angeles, CA 90016
Phone: 213-766-9075
Fax: 213-766-8866

Atlantic Pre-Hung Doors
*Doors; Moulding
& Millwork*
PO Box 1258,
143 Conant St.
West Concord, MA 01742
Phone: 508-369-5600

Atlas Copco Berema
Tools/Electric & Pneumatic
161 Lower Westfield Rd.
Holyoke, MA 01040
Phone: 413-746-0020
Fax: 413-746-5383

Atlas Roofing Corp.
*Insulation; Roofing; Siding
& Accessories*
1775 The Exchange,
Suite 160
Atlanta, GA 30339
Phone: 770-933-4463
1-800-933-1476
Fax: 770-952-3170

Atlas/Soundolier
Home Technology
1859 Intertech Dr.
Fenton, MO 63026
Phone: 314-349-3110
1-800-876-7337
Fax: 314-349-1251

**Atrium Door &
Window Co.**
Doors; Windows
9001 Ambassador Row
Dallas, TX 75247
Phone: 214-634-9663
1-800-935-2000
Fax: 214-637-6724

Atro
*Hardware; Tools/Electric
& Pneumatic; Tools/Hand*
PO Box 629
Butler, PA 16003
Phone: 412-287-7711
Fax: 412-287-2811

**Au-ve-co Products
(Auto Vehicle Parts Co.)**
*Hardware; Tools/Electric
& Pneumatic*
7 Sperti Dr.
Covington, KY 41017
Phone: 606-341-6450
1-800-354-9816
Fax: 606-331-5590

Audio Technology
Home Technology
9884 Monroe Dr.
Dallas, TX 75220
Phone: 214-351-2191
1-800-666-2191
Fax: 214-351-2194

Austram
*Landscape Design;
Specialty Products*
1400 E. Geer St.
Durham, NC 27704-5039
Phone: 919-688-1288
Fax: 919-688-0880

**Auto-Graph Computer
Designing Systems**
Computer Software
699 Perimeter Dr., Suite 300
Lexington, KY 40517
Phone: 606-269-8585
1-800-234-5089
Fax: 606-269-9821

Autodesk
Computer Software
111 McInnis Pkwy.
San Rafael, CA 94903
Phone: 415-507-5000
1-800-964-6432
Fax: 415-507-3100
Internet:
http://www.autodesk.com

Auton Co.
*Hardware; Home
Technology; Specialty
Products*
PO Box 801960
Valencia, CA 91380-1960
Phone: 805-257-9282
Fax: 805-295-5638
Internet:
http://www.auton.com

AutoSight
Computer Software
PO Box 362086
Melbourne, FL 32936-2086
Phone: 407-242-5865
Fax: 407-255-1052

Avanté Hardware
(See TFI Corp.)

Avis America
*Room Enclosures;
Structural Systems*
PO Box 420
Avis, PA 17721
Phone: 717-753-3700
1-800-AVIS AMERICA
Fax: 717-753-3291
Internet:
http://www.avisamerica.com

Avonite
*Countertops; Faucets &
Fixtures; Flooring*
1945 S. Hwy. 304
Belen, NM 87002
Phone: 505-864-3800
1-800-428-6648
Fax: 505-864-7790
Internet:
http://www.avonite.com

**AVSI Automated Voice
Systems
(MASTERVOICE)**
Home Technology
17059 El Cajon Ave.
Yorba Linda, CA 92686
Phone: 714-524-4488
Fax: 714-996-1127
Internet:
http://www.mastervoice.com

Axeman-Anderson Co.
HVAC
300 E. Mountain Ave.
South Williamsport, PA
17701
Phone: 717-326-9114
Fax: 717-326-2152

Azrock Industries
Flooring
PO Box 696060
San Antonio, TX 78269
Phone: 210-558-6400
Fax: 210-558-6614

B

B.C. Wood Specialties
Moulding & Millwork
Unit 5, 15355 102A Ave.
Surrey, BC V3R 7K1
Canada
Phone: 604-583-8786

B-H Woodturning
Moulding & Millwork
810 Derwent Way,
Annacis Business Park
Delta, BC V3M 5R1
Canada
Phone: 604-540-6232
Fax: 604-540-6101

B&K Industries
*Faucets & Fixtures;
Plumbing Supplies*
2600 Elmhurst Rd.
Elk Grove Village, IL
60007
Phone: 847-773-8585
1-800-782-2385
Fax: 847-773-0330

Baja Products
Faucets & Fixtures
4065 N. Romero Rd.
Tucson, AZ 85705
Phone: 520-887-1154
1-800-845-2252
Fax: 520-888-5711

Baker Mfg. Corp.
Faucets & Fixtures
4300-D LB McLeod Rd.
Orlando, FL 32811
Phone: 407-649-3371
Fax: 407-246-0471

Balcon
Landscape Design
PO Box 3388,
2630 Conway Rd.
Crofton, MD 21114
Phone: 301-721-1900
Fax: 301-793-0657

Baldwin Hardware Corp.
*Faucets & Fixtures;
Hardware*
841 E. Wyomissing Blvd.,
PO Box 15048
Reading, PA 19612
Phone: 610-777-7811
1-800-959-3568 (West)
1-800-437-7448 (East)
Fax: 610-775-5564

Ballantine & Co.
Computer Software
PO Box 805, 1 River Rd.
Carlisle, MA 01741-0805
Phone: 508-369-1772
1-800-536-6677
Fax: 508-369-9179
Internet:
http://ballantine-inc.com

**Bally Block/Michigan
Maple**
Countertops
30 S. Seventh St.
Bally, PA 19503
Phone: 610-845-7511
Fax: 610-845-7726

**Bang & Olufsen of
America**
Home Technology
1200 Business Center Dr.
Mount Prospect, IL 60056
Phone: 847-299-9380
1-800-323-0378
Fax: 847-699-1475

Bangkok Intl.
*Countertops; Engineered
Lumber & Panels;
Flooring; Moulding
& Millwork*
4562 Worth St.
Philadelphia, PA 19124
Phone: 215-537-5800
Fax: 215-743-3179

Barclay Products
Faucets & Fixtures
4000 Porett Dr.
Gurnee, IL 60031
Phone: 847-244-1234
1-800-446-9700
Fax: 847-244-1259

Barden Homes
Structural Systems
PO Box 210
Homer, NY 13077
Phone: 607-749-2641
Fax: 607-749-3868

Barrett Mfg. Co.
Hardware
4124 W. Parker
Chicago, IL 60639-2112
Phone: 312-772-0785
1-800-621-7522
Fax: 312-772-9619

Barrisol Stretch Ceilings
*Insulation; Specialty
Products; Walls, Ceilings
& Finishes*
1340 Depot St.,
Suite 110
Cleveland, OH 44116
Phone: 216-331-0485
Fax: 216-331-2232

Barton Lumber Co.
*Engineered Lumber
& Panels*
245 Province Rd.
Barnstead, NH 03218
Phone: 603-435-6880
1-800-894-6850
Fax: 603-435-7714

**Barwalt Tool Co.
(Div. of Precision Tile
Spacer Co.)**
Equipment & Trucks
E. 5255 Seltice Way
Post Falls, ID 83854
Phone: 208-765-3187
1-800-423-5243
Fax: 208-664-6041

Basco Co.
Faucets & Fixtures
7201 Snider Rd.
Mason, OH 45040
Phone: 513-573-1900
1-800-543-1938
Fax: 513-573-1919

**Basement De-Watering
Systems**
Specialty Products
162 E. Chestnut St.
Canton, IL 61520
Phone: 309-647-0331
1-800-331-2943
Fax: 309-647-0498

Basement Systems
Specialty Products
55 Sperry Ave.
Stratford, CT 06497
Phone: 203-377-3302
1-800-541-0487
Fax: 203-386-9907

Basic Coatings
Paints, Caulks & Adhesives
2124 Valley Dr.
Des Moines, IA 50321
Phone: 515-288-0231
1-800-247-5471
Fax: 515-288-0615

Bates & Bates
Faucets & Fixtures
3699 Industry Ave.
Lakewood, CA 90712
Phone: 310-595-8824
1-800-726-7680
Fax: 310-988-0764
Internet:
http://www.batesincs.com

Bath Ease
Faucets & Fixtures;
Specialty Products
3815 Darston St.
Palm Harbor, FL 34685
Phone: 813-786-2604
Fax: 813-786-2604

Bath N'Bagno
Cabinetry; Faucets &
Fixtures; Hardware
365 Central Ave.
Scarsdale, NY 10583
Phone: 914-723-1010
Fax: 914-723-4750

Bath-Tec
Builder Sales
Faucets & Fixtures
PO Box 1118
Ennis, TX 75120
Phone: 972-646-5279
1-800-526-3301
Fax: 972-646-5688

Bathcraft
Faucets & Fixtures
PO Box 1106, 1610
James P Rodgers Dr.
Valdosta, GA 31603
Phone: 912-333-0805
Fax: 912-245-0994

Bathlex
Faucets & Fixtures
63 Howden Rd., Unit C
Scarborough, ON
M1R 3C7 Canada
Phone: 416-288-1655
Fax: 416-755-1085

Bautex Window
Automation
Windows
10860 Alder Cir.
Dallas, TX 75238
Phone: 214-343-1610
1-800-422-8839
Fax: 214-343-2252

Bay World Intl.
Windows
395 Reed St.
Mansfield, OH 44903
Phone: 419-525-2222
1-888-767-0010
Fax: 419-522-8768

Baylite
Div. of Bay Mills
Windows
7299 David Hunting Dr.
Mississauga, ON
L5S 1W3 Canada
Phone: 905-672-2255
1-800-265-9848
Fax: 905-672-2256

BB&S Treated Lumber
Engineered Lumber
& Panels
Devil's Foot Rd.,
PO Box 982
Davisville, RI 02854
Phone: 401-884-0701
Fax: 401-295-9733

BC Greenhouse Builders
Room Enclosures
7425 Hedley Ave.
Burnaby, BC V5E 2R1
Canada
Phone: 604-433-4220
Fax: 604-433-1285

BDP Co.
HVAC
7310 W. Morris St.
Indianapolis, IN 46231
Phone: 317-240-5341

Beacon/Morris
HVAC
260 N. Elm St.
Westfield, MA 01085
Phone: 413-568-9571
Fax: 413-568-2969

Beacon Products
Electrical & Lighting;
Landscape Design
6503-E 19th St. E.
Sarasota, FL 34243
Phone: 941-755-6694
Fax: 941-751-5535

Beam Industries
Specialty Products
1700 W. Second St.,
PO Box 189
Webster City, IA 50595
Phone: 515-832-4620
1-800-369-BEAM
Fax: 515-832-6659

Bearden Brothers Carpet
Flooring
4109 S. Dixie Hwy.
Dalton, GA 30721
Phone: 1-800-433-0074
Fax: 706-277-1754

Beaver Mountain Log
Homes
Structural Systems
RD 1, PO Box 32
Hancock, NY 13783
Phone: 607-467-2700
Fax: 607-467-2715

Beech River Mill Corp.
Doors; Moulding &
Millwork; Siding &
Accessories
30 Rt. 16 B
Center Ossipee, NH
03814
Phone: 603-539-2636
Fax: 603-539-2636

Belanger Plumbing
Accessories
Faucets & Fixtures
6445 Blvd. de
Maissoneuve O
Montreal, PQ H4B 2Z1
Canada
Phone: 514-489-8431
1-800-361-5960
Fax: 514-489-5579

Belden Brick Co.
Landscape Design; Siding
& Accessories; Structural
Systems
700 W. Tuscarawas St.
Canton, OH 44702
Phone: 330-456-0031
Fax: 330-456-2694
Internet:
http://www.beldenbrick.com

Belwith-Keeler
Hardware
4300 Gerald R Ford Fwy.,
PO Box 127
Grandville, MI 49468
Phone: 616-531-8213
1-800-453-3537
Fax: 616-531-8515

Bemis Mfg. Co.
Rain Master Div.
Siding & Accessories
300 Mill St., PO Box 901
Sheboygan Falls, WI
53085
Phone: 414-467-4621
1-800-558-7651
Fax: 414-467-8573

Benchmark Door
Systems
(A Div. of General
Products Co.)
Doors; Fireplaces
PO Box 7387
Fredericksburg, VA
22404-7387
Phone: 540-898-5700
1-800-755-DOOR
Fax: 540-898-5802
Internet:
http://www.benchmark.
hw.net

Bend-A-Lite
Electrical & Lighting
6292 Windlass Cir.
Boynton Beach, FL 33437
Phone: 407-738-5300
1-800-353-9636
Fax: 407-738-5055
Internet:
http://www.bendalite.com

Bend Door
(A Div. of JELD-WEN)
Doors
62845 Boyd Acres Rd.,
PO Box 5248
Bend, OR 97708-5248
Phone: 1-800-877-9482

Bend Industries
Landscape Design; Siding
& Accessories; Structural
Systems
11412 W. Brown Deer Rd.
Milwaukee, WI 53224
Phone: 414-362-7000
Fax: 414-362-7009

Bendix Mouldings
Moulding & Millwork
37 Ramland Rd., S.
Orangeburg, NY 10962
Phone: 914-365-1111
1-800-526-0240
Fax: 1-800-423-6349

Benjamin Moore & Co.
Paints, Caulks & Adhesives
51 Chestnut Ridge Rd.
Montvale, NJ 07645
Phone: 201-573-9600

Benjamin Obdyke
Hardware; Insulation;
Roofing; Siding &
Accessories
65 Steamboat Dr.
Warminster, PA 18974
Phone: 215-672-7200
1-800-346-7655
Fax: 215-672-3731

Bennett Industries
Doors; Moulding &
Millwork
1530 Palisade Ave.
Fort Lee, NJ 07024
Phone: 201-947-5340
Fax: 201-947-3908

Bennett Lumber
Products
Siding & Accessories
PO Box 49
Princeton, ID 83857
Phone: 208-875-1321
Fax: 208-875-0191

BentWood Northwest
Moulding & Millwork
940 Greenwood St.,
PO Box 113
Junction City, OR 97448
Phone: 503-998-6738
Fax: 503-998-8925

Berger Building
Products Corp.
Roofing; Siding &
Accessories
805 Pennsylvania Blvd.
Feasterville, PA 19053
Phone: 215-355-1200
1-800-523-8852
Fax: 215-355-7738

Berlinex
Doors; Windows
4350-68 Ave.
Edmonton, AB T6B 2P3
Canada
Phone: 403-440-3888
1-800-667-5908
Fax: 403-465-2278

Berryvale Software
Computer Software
HC 69, Box 79
Cornish, ME 04020
Phone: 207-625-8272
Fax: 207-625-3738
Internet: http://www.
berryvalesoftware.com

Bessler Stairway
(A Div. of ASI)
American Machine
Works
Moulding & Millwork
3807 Lamar Ave.
Memphis, TN 38118
Phone: 901-360-1900
Fax: 901-795-1253

Best Estimate
Computer Software
740 Broadview Ave.
Toronto, ON M4K-2P1
Canada
Phone: 416-463-1108
Fax: 416-463-9550

Best Lock Corp.
Hardware
6161 E. 75th St.,
PO Box 50444
Indianapolis, IN 46250
Phone: 317-849-2250
Fax: 317-595-7620

Bestwood Electronics
Home Technology
1521 Pemberton Ave.
North Vancouver, BC
V7P 2S3 Canada
Phone: 604-987-6828
Fax: 604-987-2005

Bethlehem Steel
Roofing
Eighth and Eaton
Bethlehem, PA 18016
Phone: 610-694-2424
1-800-352-5700, ext. 400

Better-Bilt
Doors; Windows
PO Box 5700
Norcross, GA 30091
Phone: 770-497-2000
1-800-477-6544
Fax: 770-497-2437

Better Built Co.
Equipment & Trucks;
Tools/Hand
8811 Grow Dr.
Pensacola, FL 32514
Phone: 904-478-3298
1-800-366-8269
Fax: 904-484-9990

Beveled Glass Designs
Larry Robertson
Associates
Doors; Windows
3185 N. Shadeland
Indianapolis, IN 46226
Phone: 317-353-0472
1-800-428-5746
Fax: 317-547-1926

Beveled Glass Works
Windows
23852 Pacific Coast Hwy.,
Suite 351
Malibu, CA 90265
Phone: 310-457-5252
1-800-421-0518
Fax: 310-457-5591

BF Goodrich
Plumbing Supplies
9911 Brecksville Rd.
Cleveland, OH 44141
Phone: 216-447-5000
1-800-331-1144
Fax: 216-447-5750

BH Johnson
Stairbuilders Co.
Moulding & Millwork
6525 Industrial Way
Alpharetta, GA 30201
Phone: 770-475-8965
Fax: 770-664-7450

BHK of America
Flooring
PO Box 37, 3 Bond St.
Central Valley, NY 10917
Phone: 914-928-6200
1-800-724-4212
Fax: 914-928-2287

BHP Steel Building
Products USA, formerly
ASC Pacific
Roofing
2110 Enterprise Blvd.
W. Sacramento, CA
95691-3493
Phone: 916-372-6851
1-800-726-2727
Fax: 916-372-7606

Bilco Brick
Structural Systems
PO Box 430
Lancaster, TX 75146
Phone: 972-227-3380
1-800-487-3380
Fax: 972-227-3384
E-mail: bbilco@airmail.net

The Bilco Co.
Doors
PO Box 1203
New Haven, CT 06505
Phone: 203-934-6363
Fax: 203-933-8478

Billco Corp.
Faucets & Fixtures
PO Box 429,
246 E. Adele Ct.
Villa Park, IL 60181
Phone: 708-279-6300
Fax: 708-279-6303

Bilt Best Windows
Doors; Windows
175 10th St.
Ste. Genevieve, MO
63670
Phone: 314-883-3571
Fax: 314-883-2858

Bingaman & Son
Lumber
Engineered Lumber
& Panels
PO Box 247
Kreamer, PA 17833
Phone: 717-374-1108
Fax: 717-374-5342

Birchcraft Kitchens
Cabinetry
1612 Thorn St.
Reading, PA 19601
Phone: 610-375-4391
Fax: 610-375-2762

Bird Roofing Div.
Roofing; Siding &
Accessories
1077 Pleasant St.
Norwood, MA 02062
Phone: 617-551-0656
1-800-BIRD-INC
Fax: 617-762-6586

Bird Vinyl Products
Doors; Siding &
Accessories; Windows
1010 Withrow Ct.
Bardstown, KY 40004
Phone: 502-348-9231
1-800-626-1524
Fax: 502-348-4986

Bird-X
Specialty Products
300 N. Elizabeth St.
Chicago, IL 60607
Phone: 312-226-2473
Fax: 312-226-2480
E-mail:
BIRDXINC@AOL.COM

BiWood Flooring
Flooring; Moulding &
Millwork; Paints, Caulks
& Adhesives
PO Box 17276,
5744 Nanjack Cir.
Memphis, TN 38187-0276
Phone: 901-795-3567
1-800-977-9663
Fax: 901-795-5348
E-mail:
biwoodmphs@aol.com

Black & Decker
(See DeWalt Industrial Tool; Kwikset Corp.; Price Pfister)

Black Creek Timber Framing Co.
Structural Systems
RR 1
Stevensville, ON L0S 1S0
Canada
Phone: 416-382-2290

Black Diamond Millworks
Moulding & Millwork
PO Box 15307
Boise, ID 83715
Phone: 208-345-5520
Fax: 208-338-1547

Bladesmith
Hardware; Paints, Caulks & Adhesives
2 Lee Blvd.
Malvern, PA 19355
Phone: 610-296-2855
1-800-527-3343
Fax: 610-296-7911

Blaine Window Hardware
Hardware; Specialty Products
17319 Blaine Dr.
Hagerstown, MD 21740
Phone: 301-797-6500
1-800-678-1919
Fax: 301-797-2510

Blainville Mouldings
Moulding & Millwork
444 22nd Ave.
Blainville, PQ J7C 4L8
Canada
Phone: 514-430-3600
1-800-363-6367
Fax: 514-430-2286

Blanco America
Faucets & Fixtures
1001 Lower Landing Rd.,
Suite 607
Blackwood, NJ 08012
Phone: 609-228-3500
1-800-451-5782
Fax: 609-228-7956

Blaze King Industries
Fireplaces; HVAC
PO Box 367
400 W. Whitman Dr.
College Place, WA
99324-0367
Phone: 509-522-2730
1-800-456-8818
Fax: 509-522-1701

Bloc-Ease Corp.
Windows
35 Vankirk Dr., Unit 9
Brampton, ON L7A 1A5
Canada
Phone: 905-456-8891
1-800-565-5807
Fax: 905-456-8903

Bloch Industries
Cabinetry; Countertops
140 Commerce Dr.
Rochester, NY
14623-3590
Phone: 716-334-9600
Fax: 716-334-9634

Block Tops
Countertops
4770 E. Wesley Dr.
Anaheim, CA 92807
Phone: 714-779-0475
Fax: 714-779-2284

Blomberg Window Systems
Doors; Windows
PO Box 22485,
1453 Blair Ave.
Sacramento, CA 95822
Phone: 916-428-8060
Fax: 916-422-1967

Blumer & Stanton
Doors; Moulding & Millwork; Siding & Accessories; Windows
5112 Georgia Ave.
West Palm Beach, FL
33405
Phone: 407-585-2525
1-800-330-2526
Fax: 407-585-2709

Boa-Franc
Flooring
1255 98th St.
St. Georges, Beauce, PQ
G5Y 8J5 Canada
Phone: 418-227-1181
Fax: 418-227-1188
Internet: http://www.boa-franc.com

BOAM USA
Electrical & Lighting
1200 Woodruff Rd., G-16
Greenville, SC 29607
Phone: 864-627-0473
Fax: 864-627-0573

Boccia
Specialty Products
168 Broadway
Garden City Park, NY
11040
Phone: 516-747-7727
Fax: 516-747-7448

Boehm Acrilicrafts
Faucets & Fixtures
1434 10th Ct.
Lake Park, FL 33403
Phone: 561-881-3020
Fax: 561-881-4430

Boen Hardwood Flooring
Flooring; Moulding & Millwork
Rt. 2 - Hollie Dr.,
Bowles Industrial Park
Martinsville, VA 24112
Phone: 703-638-3700
Fax: 703-638-3066

Boiardi Products Corp.
Flooring; Paints, Caulks & Adhesives; Structural Systems; Walls, Ceilings & Finishes
453 Main St.
Little Falls, NJ 07424
Phone: 201-256-1100
1-800-352-8668
Fax: 201-256-5744

Boise Cascade
Engineered Lumber & Panels
1111 W. Jefferson St.
Boise, ID 83702
Phone: 208-384-6321
1-800-458-4631
Fax: 208-384-6099
Internet:
http://www.bc.com

Bomanite Corp.
Landscape Design
PO Box 599
Madera, CA 93639-0599
Phone: 209-673-2411
Fax: 209-673-8246
Internet:
http://www.bomanite.com

Bon Tool Co.
Equipment & Trucks; Structural Systems; Tools/Electric & Pneumatic; Tools/Hand
4430 Gibsonia Rd.
Gibsonia, PA 15044
Phone: 412-443-7080
1-800-444-7060
Fax: 412-443-7090

BonaKemi USA
Paints, Caulks & Adhesives; Tools/Electric & Pneumatic
14805 E. Moncrieff Pl.
Aurora, CO 80011-1207
Phone: 303-371-1411
1-800-872-5515
Fax: 303-371-6958
Internet:
http://www.bonakemi.com

Bondex Intl.
Paints, Caulks & Adhesives
3616 Scarlet Oak Blvd.
St. Louis, MO 63122
Phone: 314-225-5001
1-800-225-7522
Fax: 314-225-4159

Bonneville Windows & Doors
Doors; Windows
274 Duchesnay St.
Ste-Marie-du-Beauce, PQ
G6E 3C2 Canada
Phone: 418-387-7723
Fax: 418-387-2078

Boral Bricks
Landscape Design; Siding & Accessories
500 N. Ridge Rd.,
Suite 300
Atlanta, GA 30350
Phone: 770-645-4500
Fax: 770-645-2888
Internet:
http://www.boralbricks.com

Boral Lifetile
Roofing
4685 MacArthur Blvd.,
Suite 300
Newport Beach, CA
92660
Phone: 714-263-2780
Fax: 714-263-2788
Internet:
http://www.lifetile.com

Bostik Tile & Flooring Group
Paints, Caulks & Adhesives
Boston St.
Middleton, MA 01949
Phone: 508-777-0100
1-800-726-7845
Fax: 508-750-7212

Boston Design Corp.
Moulding & Millwork
100 Magazine St.
Boston, MA 02119
Phone: 617-442-6118
1-800-225-5584
Fax: 617-442-9633

BPCO
(A Div. of EMCO)
Engineered Lumber & Panels; Insulation; Roofing; Walls, Ceilings & Finishes
9500 St. Patrick
La Salle, PQ H8R 1R9
Canada
Phone: 514-364-0161
1-800-567-BPCO
Fax: 514-364-9029

Brady Rooms
Room Enclosures
97 Webster St.
Worcester, MA 01603
Phone: 508-755-9580
1-888-88-BRADY
Fax: 508-755-1284
Internet:
http://www.bradyrooms.com

Brandom Mfg. Co.
Cabinetry
211 Campus Dr.
Keene, TX 76059-2340
Phone: 817-645-8841
1-800-366-1-8001
Fax: 817-556-2801

Brandon Industries
Electrical & Lighting; Landscape Design
1601 W. Wilmeth Rd.
McKinney, TX 75069
Phone: 214-542-3000
Fax: 214-542-1015

Brass Accents by Urfic
Faucets & Fixtures; Hardware
1000 S. Broadway,
PO Box 110
Salem, OH 44460
Phone: 216-332-9500
Fax: 216-337-8775

Brass Craft Mfg.
(A Div. of Masco Corp.)
Faucets & Fixtures; Plumbing Supplies
39600 Orchard Hill Pl.
Novi, MI 48376
Phone: 810-305-6000
Fax: 810-305-6011

Brass Light Gallery
Electrical & Lighting
131 S. First St.
Milwaukee, WI 53204
Phone: 414-271-8300
Fax: 414-271-7755

Breezaire
Appliances
8610 Production Ave.
San Diego, CA 92121
Phone: 619-566-7465
Fax: 619-566-1943

The Brick Institute of America
Fireplaces; Landscape Design; Siding & Accessories; Structural Systems
11490 Commerce Park Dr.
Reston, VA 20191-1525
Phone: 703-620-0100
Fax: 703-620-3928
Internet:
http://www.brickinst.org

Brickstone Studios
Moulding & Millwork
2108 S. 38th St.
Lincoln, NE 68506
Phone: 402-488-8033
1-800-449-6599
Fax: 402-488-5440

Briggs Industries
Faucets & Fixtures
4350 W. Cypress St.
Tampa, FL 33607
Phone: 813-878-0178
Fax: 813-874-1394

Bristol Information Systems
Computer Software
PO Box 74184
Houston, TX 77274-1084
Phone: 281-242-0010
1-800-984-8600
Fax: 281-242-9309
E-mail: jwise@hal-pc.org

Bristolite Skylites
Windows
401 E. Goetz Ave.
Santa Ana, CA 92707
Phone: 714-540-8950
1-800-854-8618
Fax: 714-540-5415

Brite Millwork
Landscape Design
641 Hardwick Rd.
Bolton, ON L7E 5R2
Canada
Phone: 905-857-6021
1-800-265-6021
Fax: 905-857-3211

BRK Electronics
Electrical & Lighting; Home Technology
3901 Liberty St. Rd.
Aurora, IL 60504-8122
Phone: 708-851-7330
Fax: 708-851-7452

The Broadway Collection
Faucets & Fixtures; Hardware
1010 W. Santa Fe,
PO Box 1210
Olathe, KS 66051-1210
Phone: 913-782-6244
1-800-766-1966
Fax: 913-782-0647

Broan Mfg. Co.
Appliances; Cabinetry; HVAC; Home Technology; Specialty Products
926 W. State St.,
PO Box 140
Hartford, WI 53027
Phone: 414-673-4340
1-800-445-6057
Fax: 1-800-356-5862

Brochure Box Co.
Landscape Design
1621 S.E. 28th Ter.
Cape Coral, FL 33904
Phone: 813-945-7997
1-800-654-3753
Fax: 813-945-4621
Internet:
http://www.brochurebox.com

Brock Deck
(A Div. of CTB Inc.)
Landscape Design
State Rd. 15 N.,
PO Box 2000
Milford, IN 46542-2000
Phone: 219-658-9442
1-800-365-3625
Fax: 219-658-4133

Brojack Lumber Co.
Engineered Lumber & Panels
RD 1, Box 482
Olyphant, PA 18447
Phone: 717-586-2281
Fax: 717-586-4627

Bronzelite
Electrical & Lighting
PO Box 606
San Marcos, TX 78667
Phone: 512-392-5821
Fax: 512-753-1122

Brown Stove Works
Appliances
PO Box 2490
Cleveland, TN 37320
Phone: 423-476-6544
1-800-251-7485
Fax: 423-476-6599

Browning Metal Products
(A CertainTeed Co.)
HVAC; Roofing
4805 N. Prospect Rd.
Peoria Heights, IL 61614
Phone: 309-682-1015
1-800-841-8970
Fax: 1-800-548-3718

Bruce Alford Corp.
Doors; Windows
2720 Bryan
Fort Worth, TX 76104
Phone: 817-921-3683
Fax: 1-800-933-7906

Bruce Cabinets
Cabinetry
16803 Dallas Pkwy.
Dallas, TX 75248-6196
Phone: 214-931-3000
1-800-527-5903
Fax: 1-800-535-6512

Bruce Floors
Flooring
16803 Dallas Pkwy.
Dallas, TX 75248-6196
Phone: 214-887-2100
1-800-722-4647
Fax: 214-887-2234
Internet: http://www.brucefloors.com

Bruce Hardwood Floors
Flooring; Moulding & Millwork
16803 Dallas Pkwy.
Dallas, TX 75248-6196
Phone: 214-881-2100
1-800-722-4647
214-887-2234
Internet: http://www.brucehardwoodfloors.com

Bruner Corp.
Appliances
500 W. Oklahoma Ave.
Milwaukee, WI 53207
Phone: 414-747-3700
1-800-5-BRUNER
Fax: 414-747-3812

Brushtech
Paints, Caulks &
Adhesives; Plumbing
Supplies
PO Box 1130
Plattsburgh, NY 12901
Phone: 518-563-8420
Fax: 518-563-0581

Bryant
HVAC
PO Box 70
Indianapolis, IN 46206
Phone: 317-243-0851
1-800-468-7253
Fax: 317-240-5182

Buchtal Corp. USA
Countertops; Flooring;
Walls, Ceilings & Finishes
1325 Northmeadow
Pkwy., Suite 114
Roswell, GA 30076
Phone: 404-442-5500
Fax: 404-442-5502

Budgetrac
Computer Software
16700 N.W. 79th St.,
Suite 203
Redmond, WA 98052
Phone: 206-644-4100
1-800-879-3023

Buehler Lumber Co.
Engineered Lumber &
Panels
260 W. Main St.
Ridgway, PA 15853
Phone: 814-776-1121
1-800-421-3403
Fax: 814-772-0222

Buffalo Veneer &
Plywood
Engineered Lumber &
Panels; Moulding &
Millwork
501 Sixth Ave. N.W.
Buffalo, MN 55313
Phone: 612-473-0606
Fax: 612-473-9418

Buffelen
Woodworking Co.
Doors
1901 Taylor Way
Tacoma, WA 98421
Phone: 206-627-1191
1-800-423-8810
Fax: 206-383-2060

Bufftech
Landscape Design
2525 Walden Ave.
Buffalo, NY 14225
Phone: 716-685-1600
1-800-333-0569
Fax: 716-685-1172

Builder Software Tools
Computer Software
830 Penllyn Pike
Blue Bell, PA 19422
Phone: 215-542-5800
Fax: 215-654-7607

Builders CAD
Computer Software
11121 Sun Center Dr.,
Suite F
Rancho Cordova, CA
95670
Phone: 1-800-330-5671
Fax: 916-635-3630
E-mail: jimb@calweb.com

Builders Edge
Moulding & Millwork;
Roofing; Siding &
Accessories; Specialty
Products
PO Box 7739
Pittsburgh, PA 15215
Phone: 412-782-4880
1-800-969-7245
Fax: 412-782-3314

Builders Software
Enterprises
Computer Software
1619 W. Division
Suite H
Arlington, TX 76012
Phone: 817-265-3433
Fax: 817-265-2966
Internet:
http://www.builders-
software.com

Building Products &
Nails
Div. BSTC Group
Doors; Engineered Lumber
& Panels; Flooring;
Hardware; Moulding &
Millwork; Walls, Ceilings
& Finishes
75 Union Ave.
Rutherford, NJ 07070
Phone: 201-939-1200
Fax: 201-939-1720

Building Products of
America Corp.
Hardware
430 W. Merrick Rd.
Valley Stream, NY 11580
Phone: 516-568-0222
1-800-253-4738
Fax: 516-568-0709

Building Stone Institute
Flooring
PO Box 507
Purdys, NY 10578
Phone: 914-232-5725
Fax: 914-232-5259

Buildsoft
Computer Software
PO Box 13893
Research Triangle Park,
NC 27709
Phone: 919-941-6269
1-800-999-8322
Fax: 919-941-0339
Internet:
http://www.buildsoft.com

BuildWare Data Systems
Computer Software
770 Old Roswell Pl.,
Suite J300
Roswell, GA 30076
Phone: 770-641-1786
1-800-582-8185
Fax: 770-641-9183

Bullock & Company
Structural Systems
RR 3
Creemore, ON L0M 1G0
Canada
Phone: 705-466-2505
Fax: 705-466-3577

Burgess Intl. Bath
Fixtures
Cabinetry; Faucets &
Fixtures
7010 Metroplex
Romulus, MI 48174
Phone: 313-721-1101
1-800-837-0092
Fax: 313-721-2101

Burke Industries
Flooring
2250 S. 10th St.
San Jose, CA 95112-4197
Phone: 408-297-3500
1-800-669-7010
Fax: 408-280-0699

Burnham Corp.
HVAC
PO Box 3079
Lancaster, PA 17604
Phone: 717-397-4701
Fax: 717-293-5827
Internet:
http://www.burnham.com

Burns, Morris & Stewart
Engineered Lumber
& Panels; Moulding
& Millwork
PO Box 631247
Nacogdoches, TX 75963
Phone: 409-569-8211
Fax: 409-569-1967

Burrows Lumber
Engineered Lumber
& Panels
80 Fennell St.
Winnipeg, MB R3T 3M4
Canada
Phone: 204-925-6200
Fax: 204-284-0120

The Burruss Co.
Countertops; Flooring;
Landscape Design;
Moulding & Millwork
PO Box 6, 103 Maddox St.
Brookneal, VA 24528-2907
Phone: 804-376-2666
1-800-334-2495
Fax: 804-376-3698

Burton Woodworks
(A Div. of MHJ Group)
Landscape Design;
Moulding & Millwork
4290 Alatex Rd.
Montgomery, AL 36108
Phone: 334-281-0097
1-800-423-6589
Fax: 334-281-0575

Butler Ventamatic Corp.
HVAC; Roofing
Wolters Industrial Park
Mineral Wells, TX
76067-0728
Phone: 817-325-7887
1-800-433-1626
Fax: 817-325-9311
Internet:
http://www.bvc.com

Byron's Spa
Faucets & Fixtures
Rt. 1 Box 378A
Wildwood, GA 30757
Phone: 404-820-1385
1-800-843-1562
Fax: 404-820-2231

C

C-Cure Corp.
Flooring; Paints, Caulks
& Adhesives; Siding &
Accessories; Structural
Systems
16225 Park 10 Pl., Suite 850
Houston, TX 77084
Phone: 713-492-5123
1-800-895-2874
Fax: 713-697-1622

C&H Roofing
Country Cottage Roof
Specialty Products
PO Box 2105
Lake City, FL 32056
Phone: 904-755-1102
1-800-327-8115
Fax: 904-755-2353

Cabinet Restylers
Cabinetry; Countertops
471 US Rt. 250 E.
Ashland, OH 44805
Phone: 419-289-6139
1-800-544-7331
Fax: 419-281-4884

Cabnetware
Computer Software
35355 County Rd. 31
Davis, CA 95616
Phone: 916-756-7543
Fax: 916-756-5928

CADD Services
Computer Software
Rt. 2, PO Box 99
Weyers Cave, VA 24486
Phone: 703-234-8923

Cadet Mfg.
HVAC
PO Box 1675
Vancouver, WA 98668
Phone: 360-693-2505
1-800-442-2338
Fax: 360-694-8848

Cadkey
Computer Software
4 Griffin Rd. N.
Windsor, CT 06095-1511
Phone: 203-298-8888
Fax: 203-298-6404

CADKIT
Computer Software
12136 W. Bayaud Ave.
Denver, CO 80228
Phone: 303-987-2376
Fax: 303-987-9530

CadQuest
Computer Software
300 N. Corporate Dr.,
Suite 270
Brookfield, WI 53045
Phone: 414-792-9345
Fax: 414-792-9370
E-mail:
hemmer@rrgroup.com

Cadsoft Intl.
Computer Software
192 Nicklin Rd.
Guelph, ON N1H 7L5
Canada
Phone: 519-836-3990
1-800-983-4300
Fax: 519-823-8821

CADworks
Computer Software
222 Third St., Suite 2300
Cambridge, MA 02142
Phone: 617-868-6003
1-800-545-4223
Fax: 617-354-3057

Cal Crystal Unlimited
Faucets & Fixtures;
Hardware
PO Box 286
Walnut Creek, CA 94596
Phone: 510-846-7607
1-800-966-9994
Fax: 510-846-7043

Cal Lock
Hardware
14837 Proctor Ave., A
La Puente, CA 91746
Phone: 818-961-5811
1-800-227-9388
Fax: 818-961-6680

Calculated Industries
Computer Software;
Tools/Hand
4840 Hytech Dr.
Carson City, NV 89706
Phone: 702-885-4900
1-800-854-8075
Fax: 702-885-4949

Caldera Spas & Baths
Faucets & Fixtures;
Landscape Design
1080 W. Bradley Ave.
El Cajon, CA 92020
Phone: 619-562-5120
1-800-669-1881
Fax: 619-562-7806

Calger Lighting
Electrical & Lighting
200 Lexington Ave.,
Suite 801
New York, NY 10016
Phone: 212-689-9511
Fax: 212-779-0721

California Acrylic
Industries
Cal Spas
Faucets & Fixtures;
Landscape Design;
Structural Systems
1462 E. Ninth St.
Pomona, CA 91766
Phone: 909-623-8781
1-800-822-SPAS
Fax: 909-620-4673
Internet: www.cal-
spa/calspas/

California Closet Co.
Specialty Products
3385 Robertson Pl.
Los Angeles, CA 90034
Phone: 818-705-2300
Fax: 310-287-0125
E-mail: motv8id@aol.com

California Redwood
Assn.
Engineered Lumber &
Panels; Landscape Design;
Siding & Accessories
405 Enfrente Dr., Suite 200
Novato, CA 94949
Phone: 415-382-0662
Fax: 415-382-8531

California Shake Corp.
Roofing
PO Box 2165,
5355 N. Vincent Ave.
Irwindale, CA 91706
Phone: 818-812-9085
Fax: 818-969-7124

Calorique
HVAC
2380 Cranberry Hwy.
West Wareham, MA
02576
Phone: 508-291-4224
Fax: 508-291-2299
E-mail:
heat@caloriq.ultranet.com

Cameo Carpets
Flooring
PO Box 1923
Dalton, GA 30722
Phone: 706-259-7825
1-800-343-7466
Fax: 706-259-7869

Cameo Marble
Countertops; Faucets
& Fixtures; Walls, Ceilings
& Finishes
540 Central Ct.
New Albany, IN 47150
Phone: 812-944-5055
Fax: 812-944-5236

Campbell Hausfeld
Equipment & Trucks;
Tools/Electric & Pneumatic
100 Production Dr.
Harrison, OH 45030
Phone: 513-367-4811
1-800-543-6400
Fax: 513-367-3176

Canac Kitchens
Cabinetry
360 John St.
Thornhill, ON L3T 3M9
Canada
Phone: 905-881-2153
1-800-CANAC-4U
Fax: 905-881-2392

Canada Brick
Siding & Accessories;
Structural Systems
2121 Britannia Rd. W.,
PO Box 668
Streetsville, ON
L5M 2C3 Canada
Phone: 905-821-8800
1-800-724-2947
Fax: 905-821-4554
Internet:
http://www.canadabrick.com

Canadian Cedar Log
Structural Systems
3801-19th St., N.W.
Calgary, AB T2E 6S8
Canada
Phone: 403-291-6465
1-800-346-9291
Fax: 403-291-7061
Internet:
http://www.cancedarlog.ca

Canadian Geo-Solar
HVAC
Box 249, 640 Gartshore St.
Fergus, ON N1M 2W8
Canada
Phone: 519-843-3393
1-800-GEO-SOLR
Fax: 519-843-6944
E-mail:
GEOSOLAR@SENTEX.
NET

Canadian Wood Council
Engineered Lumber & Panels
1730 St. Laurent Blvd.,
Suite 350
Ottawa, ON K1G 5L1
Canada
Phone: 613-247-7077
1-800-463-5091
Fax: 613-247-7856
Internet:
http://www.cwc.ca

**Canaren
(Palwa By Canaren)**
Electrical & Lighting
255 Wildcat Rd.
North York, ON M3J 2S3
Canada
Phone: 416-650-0309
1-800-361-3699
Fax: 416-650-0248

Canarm
*Electrical & Lighting;
HVAC*
PO Box 287
Syracuse, NY 13206
Phone: 315-463-4535
1-800-267-4427
Fax: 613-342-8437

**Canexel
(A Div. of ABT Building
Products Canada)**
*Siding & Accessories; Walls,
Ceilings & Finishes*
CP 1020
Gatineau, PQ J8P 6K2
Canada
Phone: 819-643-7282
Fax: 819-643-7281

**Cangelosi Marble &
Granite**
*Countertops; Landscape
Design; Walls, Ceilings &
Finishes*
14021 S. Gessner
Missouri City, TX 77489
Phone: 281-499-7521
Fax: 281-499-5315

Canital Granite
Flooring
100 Hoka St.
Winnipeg, MB R2C 3N2
Canada
Phone: 204-224-2286
1-800-665-0045
Fax: 204-222-8602

Canplas Industries
Roofing
31 Patterson Rd.
Barrie, ON L4M 4V3
Canada
Phone: 705-726-3361
1-800-461-5300
Fax: 705-726-8991

**Canyon Creek
Cabinet Co.**
Cabinetry
8330 212th St. S.E.
Woodinville, WA 98072
Phone: 206-481-6860
1-800-228-1830
Fax: 206-668-1434
Internet:
http://www.canyoncreek.
com

Capitol Adhesives
Paints, Caulks & Adhesives
PO Box 2023
Dalton, GA 30722-2023
Phone: 706-277-6241
1-800-831-8381
Fax: 706-277-5753

**Capitol Windows &
Doors
(A Div. of Metal
Industries)**
Doors; Windows
4314 Rt. 209 E.
Elizabethville, PA 17023
Phone: 717-362-8196
Fax: 717-362-4012

Caradco
Doors; Windows
PO Box 920,
201 Evans Rd.
Rantoul, IL 61866
Phone: 217-893-4444
1-800-238-1866
Fax: 217-893-3695
Internet:
http://www.caradco.com

**Caradon Doors and
Windows Group**
(See Better-Bilt; Peachtree
Doors)

Caradon Lock-Wood
Doors; Windows
PO Box 160
Scoudouc, NB E0A 1N0
Canada
Phone: 506-532-4463
Fax: 506-532-1430
Internet:
http://www.lockwood.ca/
lockwood

Carbbits
Hardware
751 Clemson Rd.
Columbia, SC 29223
Phone: 1-800-247-1485

**Cardell Kitchen & Bath
Cabinetry**
Cabinetry
3215 N. PanAm Expwy.,
PO Box 200850
San Antonio, TX 78220
Phone: 210-225-0290
Fax: 210-223-4439

Cardiff Industries
*Siding & Accessories;
Windows*
2428 N. Rose St.
Franklin Park, IL 60131
Phone: 847-455-3702
1-800-445-5807
Fax: 847-455-3255

Cardinal Homes
Structural Systems
PO Box 10 Hwy. 15
Wylliesburg, VA 23976
Phone: 804-735-8111
Fax: 804-735-8824

**Carefree Windows
(A CFA Window
Group Co.)**
Doors; Windows
1023 Reynolds Rd.
Charlotte, MI 48813
Phone: 517-543-0430
1-800-968-7847
Fax: 517-543-1707

Cargotec
Equipment & Trucks
307 Broadway
Swanton, OH 43558
Phone: 419-825-2331
Fax: 419-826-8439

**Carlisle Engineered
Metals**
*Roofing; Siding &
Accessories; Structural
Systems*
PO Box 968
Stafford, TX 77497-0968
Phone: 713-495-0244
1-800-669-9324
Fax: 713-495-3646

Carlisle Plastics
Equipment & Trucks
1401 W. 94th St.
Minneapolis, MN 55431
Phone: 612-884-7281
1-800-873-3941
Fax: 612-884-6438

**Carlisle Restoration
Lumber**
*Flooring; Moulding &
Millwork; Walls, Ceilings
& Finishes*
HCR 32 Box 556C
Stoddard, NH 03464
Phone: 603-446-3937
1-800-595-9663
Fax: 603-446-3540

**Carlon Electrical
Products**
Electrical & Lighting
25701 Science Park Dr.
Cleveland, OH 44122
Phone: 216-831-4000
1-800-972-3462
Fax: 216-831-5579

Carolina Mirror Co.
Walls, Ceilings & Finishes
PO Box 548,
201 Elkin Hwy.
North Wilkesboro, NC
28659
Phone: 910-838-2151
Fax: 910-838-9734

**Carolina Solar Structures
(A Div. Of Bob
Thompson Builders)**
Room Enclosures
8 Loop Rd.
Arden, NC 28704
Phone: 704-684-9900
1-800-241-9560
Fax: 704-684-9977
Internet:
http://www.supplysite.
com/carolina-solar/

Caron Industries
Moulding & Millwork
CP 100
Montmagny, PQ
G5V 3S3 Canada
Phone: 418-248-0255
Fax: 418-248-0982
E-mail:
caronind@quebectei.com

**The Carpet and Rug
Institute**
Flooring
PO Box 2048
Dalton, GA 30722-2048
Phone: 706-278-3176
Fax: 706-278-8835

Carrick Turning Works
Moulding & Millwork
PO Box 1868,
Prospect St. Ext
High Point, NC 27261
Phone: 910-475-2111
Fax: 910-475-8111

Carrier Corp.
HVAC
7310 W. Morris St.
Indianapolis, IN 46231
Phone: 317-243-0851
1-800-4-CARRIER
Fax: 317-240-5253

**Carter Holt Harvey
Roofing**
Roofing
827 Ave. H E., Suite 211
Arlington, TX 76011
Phone: 817-695-1090
1-800-258-9740
Fax: 817-695-1098

Casablanca Fan Co.
HVAC
450 N. Baldwin Park Blvd.
City of Industry, CA
91746
Phone: 818-369-6441
1-800-759-3267
Fax: 818-369-9010

The Cascade Joinery
Structural Systems
1336 E. Hemmi Rd.
Everson, WA 98247
Phone: 360-398-8013
Fax: 360-398-7209

J.I. Case
(See Case Corp.)

Case Corp.
Equipment & Trucks
700 State St.
Racine, WI 53404
Phone: 414-636-6011
Fax: 414-636-7809

Cast Designs & Supply
*Moulding & Millwork;
Specialty Products*
2543 Hwy. 64 W.,
PO Box 962
Shelbyville, TN 37160
Phone: 615-685-0536
1-800-257-2182
Fax: 615-685-0990

**Cast Iron Soil Pipe
Institute**
*Faucets & Fixtures;
Plumbing Supplies*
5959 Shallowford Rd.,
Suite 419
Chattanooga, TN 37421
Phone: 615-892-0137
Fax: 615-892-0817

Castec Window Shading
Windows
7531 Coldwater
Canyon Ave.
North Hollywood, CA
91605
Phone: 818-503-8300
1-800-828-2500
Fax: 1-800-932-2232

Castings
Moulding & Millwork
151 Dekalb Industrial Way
Decatur, GA 30030-2201
Phone: 404-371-8108
Fax: 404-371-8108, ext. 19

Castlegate Entry Systems
Doors
911 E. Jefferson
Pittsburg, KS 66762
Phone: 316-231-8200
1-800-835-0364
Fax: 316-231-8239

Caterpillar
Equipment & Trucks
100 N.W. Adams St.
Peoria, IL 61629
Phone: 309-675-1000

CDA Industries
Moulding & Millwork
1430 Birchmount Rd.
Scarborough, ON
M1P 2E8 Canada
Phone: 416-752-2301
Fax: 416-752-9653

CDCI
(See Construction Data
Control)

Cedar Plus
*Roofing; Siding &
Accessories*
PO Box 515
Sumas, WA 98295
Phone: 1-800-963-3388
Fax: 604-820-3084

**Cedar Shake & Shingle
Bureau**
*Roofing; Siding &
Accessories*
515 116th Ave., N.W.,
Suite 275
Bellevue, WA 98004
Phone: 206-453-1323
Fax: 206-455-1314

**Cedar Valley Shingle
Systems**
Siding & Accessories
943 San Felipe Rd.
Hollister, CA 95023
Phone: 408-636-8110
1-800-521-9523
Fax: 408-636-9035

Cedarbrook Sauna
*Faucets & Fixtures;
Landscape Design*
21326 Hwy. 9
Woodinville, WA 98072
Phone: 509-782-2447
1-800-426-3929
Fax: 509-782-3680

**Ceilings & Interior
Systems Construction
Assn.**
*Flooring; Paints, Caulks &
Adhesives; Specialty
Products; Walls, Ceilings &
Finishes*
1500 Lincoln Hwy.,
Suite 202
St. Charles, IL 60174
Phone: 630-584-1919
1-800-524-7228
Fax: 630-584-2003
Internet:
http://ourworld.compuserve.
com/homepage/CISCA

Celadon
Roofing
PO Box 860
Valley Forge, PA 19482
Phone: 1-800-782-8777
(contractors)
1-800-699-9988
(architects/builders)

**Cellofoam North
America**
*Engineered Lumber &
Panels; Insulation; Roofing;
Siding & Accessories;
Structural Systems*
PO Box 406,
1961 Industrial Blvd.
Conyers, GA 30207
Phone: 770-483-4491
1-800-241-3634
Fax: 770-929-3608

**Cellulose Insulation
Manufacturers Assn.**
Insulation
136 S. Keowee St.
Dayton, OH 45402
Phone: 513-222-2462
Fax: 513-222-5794
Internet:
ah803@dayton.wright.edu

**Cellwood Products
(A Div. of Stolle Corp.)**
*Roofing; Siding &
Accessories*
100 Cellwood Pl.
Gaffney, SC 29340-4722
Phone: 803-489-8136
1-800-476-8136
Fax: 803-489-8146

The Celotex Corp.
*Insulation; Roofing; Walls,
Ceilings & Finishes*
4010 Boy Scout Blvd.
Tampa, FL 33607
Phone: 813-873-1700
Fax: 813-873-4103

Cemcolift
Specialty Products
PO Box 368,
5191 Stump Rd.
Plumsteadville, PA 18949
Phone: 215-766-0900
1-800-962-3626
Fax: 215-766-0610

Cementex Products
Tools/Hand
PO Box 1533,
Ellis St. at W. Broad
Burlington, NJ 08016
Phone: 1-800-654-1292

Central Brass
Faucets & Fixtures
2950 E. 55th St.
Cleveland, OH 44127
Phone: 216-883-0220
1-800-321-8630
Fax: 1-800-338-9414

Central Fiber Corp.
Insulation
4814 Fiber Ln.
Wellsville, KS 66092
Phone: 913-883-4600
1-800-654-6117
Fax: 913-883-4429

Central Vac Intl.
Specialty Products
200 Kalamath St.
Denver, CO 80223
Phone: 303-573-7308
1-800-666-3133
Fax: 303-573-7310

Centurion Products
*Fireplaces; Siding &
Accessories; Structural
Systems*
1325 Sixth Ave. N.
Nashville, TN 37208
Phone: 615-256-6694
1-888-237-8762
Fax: 615-726-1795
E-mail:
centurion0@aol.com

**Century Drill and
Tool Co.**
*Tools/Electric &
Pneumatic*
PO Box 12767
Green Bay, WI 54307
Phone: 414-339-8700
1-800-621-4776
Fax: 1-800-621-4774

Century Shower Door
Faucets & Fixtures
250 Lackawanna Ave.
West Paterson, NJ 07424
Phone: 201-785-4250
1-800-524-2578

Cepco Tool
*Landscape Design;
Tools/Hand*
PO Box 153
Spencer, NY 14883
Phone: 607-589-4313
Fax: 607-589-4313
Internet:
http://www.hobbymall.
com/CEPCO

CeramaSeal
(See Bostik)

**Ceramic Tile
Distributors Assn.**
*Flooring; Walls, Ceilings &
Finishes*
800 Roosevelt Rd.,
Bldg. C, Suite 20
Glen Ellyn, IL 60137
Phone: 708-545-9415
Fax: 708-790-3095

Cerro Copper Products
Plumbing Supplies
PO Box 66800
St. Louis, MO 63166
Phone: 618-337-6000

Cersosimo Lumber Co.
*Engineered Lumber &
Panels*
R.F.D. 6, PO Box 9
Brattleboro, VT 05301
Phone: 802-254-4508
Fax: 802-254-5691

**CertainTeed Corp.
Insulation Group**
Insulation
PO Box 860
Valley Forge, PA 19482
Phone: 610-341-7739
1-800-523-7844
Fax: 610-341-7571
Internet:
http://www.certainteed.com

**CertainTeed Corp.
Pipe & Plastics Group
Form-A-Drain**
*Plumbing Supplies;
Specialty Products;
Structural Systems*
PO Box 860,
750 E. Swedesford Rd.
Valley Forge, PA 19482
Phone: 610-341-6950
Fax: 610-341-6837
Internet:
http://www.certainteed.com

**CertainTeed Corp.
Roofing Products Group**
Roofing
PO Box 860
Valley Forge, PA 19482
Phone: 1-800-233-8990
Fax: 610-341-7940
Internet:
http://www.certainteed.com

CertainTeed Siding
Siding & Accessories
PO Box 860
Valley Forge, PA 19482
Phone: 1-800-233-8990
Fax: 610-341-7940
Internet:
http://www.certainteed.com

CertainTeed Windows
Doors; Windows
PO Box 860
Valley Forge, PA 19482
Phone: 1-800-233-8990
Fax: 610-341-7940
Internet:
http://www.certainteed.com

Certified Technologies
Paints, Caulks & Adhesives
1624 Harmon Pl.,
Suite 209
Minneapolis, MN 55403
Phone: 612-338-1250
Fax: 612-338-1443

Cervitor Kitchens
*Appliances; Specialty
Products*
10775 Lower Azusa
El Monte, CA 91731
Phone: 818-443-0184
1-800-523-2666
Fax: 818-443-0400

**Chadsworth's 1.800
Columns**
Moulding & Millwork
PO Box 2618
Historic Wilmington, NC
28402
Phone: 910-763-7600
1-800-265-8667
Fax: 910-763-3191

**Challenge Door of
Indiana
(A Div. of JELD-WEN)**
Doors
200 Gerber St.,
PO Box 259
Ligonier, IN 46767-0259
Phone: 1-800-877-9482

**Challenge Door of
Oregon
(A Div. of JELD-WEN)**
Doors
31795 Hwy. 97 N.
Chiloquin, OR 97624
Phone: 1-800-877-9482

**Challenge Door of Texas
(A Div. of JELD-WEN)**
Doors
902 Hwy. 19,
PO Box 575
Sulphur Springs, TX
75483-0575
Phone: 1-800-877-9482

Chamberlain Group
Garage Doors & Openers
845 Larch Ave.
Elmhurst, IL 60126
Phone: 630-279-3600
1-800-323-2276
Fax: 630-530-6091

Champion Intl. Corp.
*Engineered Lumber &
Panels*
7785 Bay Meadows Way,
Suite 302
Jacksonville, FL 32256
Phone: 904-731-4550
1-800-874-3240
Fax: 904-419-0233

**Charlotte Pipe and
Foundry Co.**
Plumbing Supplies
2109 Randolph Rd.
Charlotte, NC 28207
Phone: 704-372-5030
1-800-438-6091
Fax: 1-800-553-1605

Chas O. Larson Co.
Hardware
PO Box E-10
Sterling, IL 61081
Phone: 815-625-0503
Fax: 815-625-8786

**Chautauqua Woods
Corp.**
Doors; Windows
134 Franklin Ave.
Dunkirk, NY 14048
Phone: 716-366-3808
Fax: 716-366-3814

**Chelsea Building
Products**
Doors; Windows
565 Cedar Way
Oakmont, PA 15139
Phone: 412-826-8077
Fax: 412-827-0113

**Chelsea Decorative
Metal Co.**
Walls, Ceilings & Finishes
9603 Moonlight Dr.,
Dept B
Houston, TX 77096
Phone: 713-721-9200
Fax: 713-776-8661
Internet:
http://www.telluscom.
com/chelsea

Chelsea Modular Homes
Structural Systems
Rt. 9W.
Marlboro, NY 12542
Phone: 914-236-3311
Fax: 914-236-4881

**Chemcrest Architectural
Products**
*Moulding & Millwork;
Siding & Accessories; Walls,
Ceilings & Finishes*
485 Watt St., Bldg. 10
Winnipeg, MB R2K 2R9
Canada
Phone: 204-669-0224
1-800-665-6653
Fax: 204-663-6183
Internet:
http://www.chemcrest.com

Chemical Specialties
1 Woodlawn Green
Suite 250
Charlotte, NC 28217
Phone: 704-522-0825
1-800-421-8661
Fax: 704-527-8232

Chemque
*Paints, Caulks &
Adhesives; Structural
Systems*
22 Melanie Dr.
Brampton, ON L6T 4K9
Canada
Phone: 905-791-5676
1-800-268-6111
Fax: 905-791-7525

ChemRex
(See PL Adhesives &
Sealants)

Chemstone
Paints, Caulks & Adhesives
1612 Remuda Ln.
San Jose, CA 95112
Phone: 408-437-9339
Fax: 408-437-3043
E-mail:
berylex@pacbell.net

**Cheney
(A Div. of Access
Industries)**
Specialty Products
4001 E. 138th St.
Grandview, MO 64030
Phone: 816-763-3100
1-800-925-3100
Fax: 816-763-4467

Cherrybark Flooring
Flooring
PO Box 151,
3153 County Farm Rd.
Hazlehurst, MS 39083
Phone: 601-894-4441
1-800-264-8258
Fax: 601-894-4443

**Chesapeake Hardwood
Products**
*Engineered Lumber &
Panels; Moulding &
Millwork; Walls, Ceilings
& Finishes*
201 W. Dexter St.
Chesapeake, VA 23324
Phone: 757-543-1601
1-800-446-8162
Fax: 757-543-4335

**The Chestnut Ridge
Beamery**
Structural Systems
RD 1, PO Box 362
Bolivar, PA 15923
Phone: 412-676-4392
Fax: 412-676-4392

**Chevrolet Motor Div.
GM Corp.**
Equipment & Trucks
30007 Van Dyke Ave.,
Mail Code: 480-205-125
Warren, MI 48090
Phone: 1-800-222-1020

Chicago Faucets
Faucets & Fixtures
2100 Clearwater Dr.
Des Plaines, IL 60018
Phone: 708-803-5000
Fax: 708-298-3101

Chicago Metallic
Walls, Ceilings & Finishes
6750 Santa Barbara Ct.
Baltimore, MD 21227
Phone: 410-796-8220

**Chicago Pneumatic
Tool Co.**
*Tools/Electric &
Pneumatic*
2200 Bleecker St.
Utica, NY 13501
Phone: 315-792-2600
Fax: 315-792-2670

Chief Architect by ART
Computer Software
3731 N. Ramsey Rd.,
Suite 150
Coeur d'Alene, ID
83814-9037
Phone: 208-664-4204
1-800-482-4433
Fax: 208-664-1316
Internet:
http://www.chiefarch.com

Chimney King
Specialty Products
PO Box 328
Gurnee, IL 60031
Phone: 847-244-8860
Fax: 847-244-7970

**Chocorua Valley
Lumber Co.**
*Engineered Lumber
& Panels*
PO Box 57, Rt. 25
South Tamworth, NH
03883-0057
Phone: 603-323-7780
Fax: 603-323-8360

Chronomite Labs
Faucets & Fixtures; HVAC
21011 S. Figueroa St.
Carson, CA 90745
Phone: 310-320-9452
1-800-447-4962
Fax: 310-320-1465

Circle Redmont
*Room Enclosures;
Structural Systems;
Windows*
2760 Business Center Blvd.
Melbourne, FL 32940
Phone: 407-259-7374
1-800-358-3888
Fax: 407-259-7237

CJ Enterprises
Tools/Hand
5045 Windsor Ave.
Edina, MN 55436
Phone: 612-929-2519

**Cladwood Div.
Smurfit Newsprint**
Garage Doors & Openers
427 Main St.
Oregon City, OR 97045
Phone: 503-650-4274
1-800-547-6633
Fax: 503-650-4519

Clairson
(See Closet Maid)

Clark & Co.
HVAC
PO Box 10
Underhill, VT 05489
Phone: 802-899-2971

**Clark Material
Handling Co.**
Equipment & Trucks
333 W. Vine St.
Lexington, KY 40507
Phone: 606-288-1200
Fax: 606-288-1522

Clark United Corp.
HVAC; Roofing
3000 W. Commerce St.
Dallas, TX 75212
Phone: 214-630-7377
1-800-527-1924
Fax: 214-630-7413

Clarke Industries
*Equipment & Trucks;
Tools/Electric &
Pneumatic*
101 S. Hanley Rd.
St. Louis, MO 63105
Phone: 314-746-2203
1-800-253-0367
Fax: 314-746-2288

Clarke Products
Faucets & Fixtures
1170 109th St.
Grand Prairie, TX 75050
Phone: 972-660-1992
Fax: 972-660-2259

Classic Aire Woodvents
HVAC
955-B N. Columbia Blvd.
Portland, OR 97217
Phone: 503-735-3755
1-800-545-8368
Fax: 503-735-3761

**Classic Architectural
Specialties**
*Doors; Moulding &
Millwork; Specialty
Products; Walls, Ceilings
& Finishes*
3223 Canton St.
Dallas, TX 75226
Phone: 214-748-1668
1-800-662-1221
Fax: 214-748-7149

**Classic Cast Stone of
Dallas**
Moulding & Millwork
3162 Miller Park Dr. N.
Garland, TX 75042-7759
Phone: 972-276-2000
Fax: 972-272-6400

Classic Lamp Post
Electrical & Lighting
3645 N.W. 67th St.
Miami, FL 33147
Phone: 305-696-1901
1-800-654-5852
Fax: 305-836-1296

Classic Mouldings
Moulding & Millwork
226 Toryork Dr.
Weston, ON M9L 1Y1
Canada
Phone: 416-745-5560
Fax: 416-745-5566

Classic Post & Beam Homes
*Room Enclosures;
Structural Systems*
PO Box 546
York, ME 03909
Phone: 207-363-8210
1-800-872-2326
Fax: 207-363-2411

Classic Products
Roofing
8510 Industry Park Dr.,
PO Box 701
Piqua, OH 45356
Phone: 513-773-9840
1-800-543-8938
Fax: 513-773-9261

Classy Glass Sunrooms
*Landscape Design; Room
Enclosures; Windows*
344 McDonnell
Lewisville, TX 75057
Phone: 214-221-0445
Fax: 214-219-0348

Cleaver-Brooks
HVAC
PO Box 421
Milwaukee, WI 53201
Phone: 414-577-3112
Fax: 414-577-2715

Cleform Tool Co.
*Paints, Caulks &
Adhesives; Structural
Systems; Tools/Hand*
4343 Easton Rd.
St. Joseph, MO 64503
Phone: 816-233-4840
1-800-253-3676
Fax: 816-233-4624
Internet:
http://www.ccp.com/~deform

Clifford W. Estes Co.
Countertops
PO Box 907
Lyndhurst, NJ 07071-0907
Phone: 201-935-2550
1-800-248-2271
Fax: 201-935-6705

Climate Master
HVAC
PO Box 25788
Oklahoma City, OK 73125
Phone: 405-745-2071
Fax: 405-745-6000

Clopay Building Products Co.
Garage Doors & Openers
312 Walnut St.,
Suite 1600
Cincinnati, OH 45202
Phone: 513-381-4800
1-800-2CLOPAY
Fax: 513-762-3519

Closet Maid
Specialty Products
720 S.W. 17th St.
Ocala, FL 32674
Phone: 904-351-6100
1-800-874-0008
Fax: 904-867-8583

CMR Publishing Construction Management Resources
Computer Software
448 S. E St.
Santa Rosa, CA 95404
Phone: 707-575-4652
1-800-551-3564
Fax: 707-575-4710

CMS
(See Computerized Micro Solutions)

CMT Tools
Hardware; Tools/Hand
310 Mears Blvd.
Oldsmar, FL 34677
Phone: 813-891-6160
1-800-531-5559
Fax: 813-891-6259

Coastal Lumber Co. (Treated Products Div.)
*Engineered Lumber &
Panels; Landscape Design*
PO Drawer 1207
Uniontown, PA 15401
Phone: 412-438-3527
Fax: 412-438-4202

Cobblecrete
Structural Systems
485 W. 2000 South
Orem, UT 84058
Phone: 801-224-6662
1-800-798-5791
Fax: 801-225-1690

Cobra Tools
*Structural Systems;
Tools/Electric &
Pneumatic; Tools/Hand*
2309 Kimarra Pl.
Lincoln, NE 68529
Phone: 402-464-2988
Fax: 402-464-3249

Cobra Ventilation Products GAF Materials Corp.
Roofing
1361 Alps Rd.
Wayne, NJ 07470
Phone: 201-628-3874
1-800-688-6654
Fax: 201-628-3640

Coffman Stairs
Moulding & Millwork
1000 Industrial Rd.
Marion, VA 24354
Phone: 540-783-7251
1-800-833-7330
Fax: 540-783-9073

Cold Spring Granite Co.
Countertops; Flooring
202 S. Third Ave.
Cold Spring, MN 56320
Phone: 320-685-3621
1-800-328-7038
Fax: 320-685-8490

Colonial Bronze Co.
*Cabinetry; Faucets &
Fixtures; Hardware*
PO Box 207
Torrington, CT 06790
Phone: 860-489-9233
Fax: 860-482-8760

Colonial Carpentry
*Moulding & Millwork;
Structural Systems*
RR 1, Box 64,
Bog Hollow Rd.
Wassaic, NY 12592
Phone: 914-373-9395
Fax: 914-373-9395

Colonial Clapboards
Siding & Accessories
46 Wendall Rd.
Shutesbury, MA 01072
Phone: 413-259-1271

Colonial Craft
Moulding & Millwork
2772 Fairview Ave. N.
St Paul, MN 55113
Phone: 1-800-727-5187
Fax: 612-631-2925

Colonial Elegance
*Doors; Moulding &
Millwork*
3800 Blvd. du
Tricentenaire
Montreal, PQ H1B 5T8
Canada
Phone: 514-640-1212
1-800-361-2030
Fax: 514-640-1744

Columbia Aluminum Windows & Doors
Doors; Windows
1600 N. Jackson
Kansas City, MO 64120
Phone: 1-800-892-8703
Fax: 816-241-5809

Columbia Boiler Co.
HVAC
PO Box 1070
Pottstown, PA 19464
Phone: 610-323-2700
Fax: 610-323-7292

Columbia Forest Products
*Engineered Lumber
& Panels*
2020 S.W. Fourth,
Suite 520
Portland, OR 97201
Phone: 503-224-5300
Fax: 503-224-5294

Columbia Mfg. Co.
Room Enclosures; Windows
3845 William St.
Burnaby, BC V5C 3J1
Canada
Phone: 604-294-5231
Fax: 604-294-5120

Columns
Moulding & Millwork
PO Box 895
Pearland, TX 77588
Phone: 281-485-3261
Fax: 281-485-1996

The Combination Door Co.
Doors
1000 Morris St.,
PO Box 1076
Fond du Lac, WI 54936
Phone: 414-922-2050
Fax: 414-922-2917

Comet Construction Software
Computer Software
2001 Montreal Rd.,
Suite 101
Tucker, GA 30084
Phone: 770-491-9303
Fax: 770-491-0039

Comfort Line
Doors; Windows
5500 Enterprise Blvd.,
PO Box 6998
Toledo, OH 43612-0998
Phone: 419-729-8520
1-800-522-4999
Fax: 419-729-8525

Comfortmaker Heating & Cooling Products Inter-City Products Corp. (USA)
HVAC
650 Heil-Quaker Ave.
Lewisburg, TN 37091
Phone: 615-359-3511
Fax: 615-270-4166
Internet: http://www.
comfortmaker.com/
comfortmaker

Commonwealth Solar Rooms
Room Enclosures
PO Box 15035,
3401 Industrial Dr.
Durham, NC 27704
Phone: 919-620-6830
1-800-870-6830
Fax: 919-620-8665

Composite Door Industries
Garage Doors & Openers
1375 Paramount Pkwy.
Batavia, IL 60510
Phone: 708-879-3448
Fax: 708-879-3485

Comprotex
Computer Software
1805 Brazoria Dr.
Mesquite, TX 75150
Phone: 972-681-4104
Internet: http://www.net
com.com/~mthall/csi.html

Compu-Share
Computer Software
5214 68th St., Suite 200
Lubbock, TX 79424
Phone: 806-794-1400
1-800-928-2456
Fax: 806-794-1110

Computer Presentation Systems
Computer Software
2680 Walnut Ave., Suite C
Tustin, CA 92780
Phone: 714-573-2168
1-800-648-6608
Fax: 714-573-2114

Computerized Micro Solutions (CMS)
Computer Software
7966 Arjons Dr.,
Suite 220B
San Diego, CA 92126
Phone: 619-578-2664
1-800-255-7407
Fax: 619-578-2688

Computers for Tracts
Computer Software
2992 E. LaPalma Ave.,
Suite D
Anaheim, CA 92806
Phone: 714-632-0510
1-800-523-9357
Fax: 714-632-0516

Comtex Industries
*Doors; Engineered Lumber
& Panels; Flooring;
Moulding & Millwork*
9999 N.W. Second Ave.,
Suite 220
Miami Shores, FL 33138
Phone: 305-751-7131
Fax: 305-756-0348

Comtronic Systems
Computer Software
205 N. Harris Ave.
Cle Elum, WA 98922
Phone: 509-674-7000
Fax: 509-674-2383
Internet:
http://www.debtmaster.com

Concinnity (A Div. of IW Industries)
*Faucets & Fixtures;
Hardware*
35 Melville Park Rd.
Melville, NY 11747
Phone: 516-293-7272
1-800-356-9993
Fax: 516-293-3630

Concord Elevator
Specialty Products
107 Alfred Kuehne Blvd.
Brampton, ON L6T 4K3
Canada
Phone: 905-791-5555
1-800-661-5112
Fax: 905-791-2222
Internet: http://www.
concordelevator.com

Concrete Block Insulating Systems
*Insulation; Structural
Systems*
Freight House Rd.
West Brookfield, MA
01585
Phone: 508-867-4241
1-800-628-8476
Fax: 508-867-5702

Concrete Designs
*Fireplaces; Landscape
Design; Structural Systems*
3650 S. Broadmont Dr.
Tucson, AZ 85713-5247
Phone: 520-624-6653
1-800-279-2278
Fax: 520-624-3420

Congoleum Corp.
Flooring
PO Box 3127
Mercerville, NJ 08619
Phone: 609-584-3000
Fax: 609-584-3518

Coni Marble Mfg.
*Countertops; Faucets &
Fixtures*
PO Box 40
Thorndale, ON
N0M 2P0 Canada
Phone: 519-461-0100
Fax: 519-461-0733

Conik Group
*Moulding & Millwork;
Roofing; Siding &
Accessories*
3260 Watt St., Unit 104
Ste-Foy, PQ G1X 4T5
Canada
Phone: 418-651-8057
Fax: 418-651-8637

Conner Industries
*Engineered Lumber &
Panels*
700 N. Tower Rd.
Alamo, TX 76177
Phone: 817-430-3555
Fax: 817-439-1610

Connoisseur & Supa Doors
Doors
PO Box 29947
San Antonio, TX 78229
Phone: 210-492-8814
1-800-477-3667
Fax: 210-492-8870

Conserval Systems
*HVAC; Siding &
Accessories*
4242 Ridge Lea Rd., Suite 1
Buffalo, NY 14226
Phone: 716-835-4903
Fax: 716-835-4904

Consolidated Coatings Corp.
*Insulation; Paints, Caulks
& Adhesives; Roofing;
Structural Systems*
2614 Pearl Rd.,
PO Box 10
Brunswick, OH 44212
Phone: 330-220-6754
1-800-321-7886
Fax: 330-220-6761

Construction Data Control (CDCI)
Computer Software
4000 De Kalb Technology
Pkwy., Suite 220
Atlanta, GA 30340
Phone: 770-457-7725
1-800-285-3929
Fax: 770-457-7686
Internet:
http://www.cdci.com

The Construction Specifications Institute
601 Madison St.
Alexandria, VA 22314
Phone: 703-684-0300
1-800-689-2900
Fax: 703-684-0465

Constructive Computing Co.
Computer Software
PO Box 2066
Kansas City, KS 66110
Phone: 913-596-2113
1-800-456-2113
Fax: 913-287-7652

Contact Lumber Co.
*Doors; Flooring; Moulding
& Millwork*
1881 S.W. Front Ave.
Portland, OR 97201
Phone: 503-228-7361
1-800-547-1038
Fax: 503-221-1340

Contech Brands
(See PL Adhesives &
Sealants)

Contemporary Structures
Moulding & Millwork; Room Enclosures; Structural Systems
1102 Center St.
Ludlow, MA 01056
Phone: 413-589-0147
Fax: 413-589-1572

Continental Creative Sales
Countertops; Flooring
100 Outwater Ln.
Garfield, NJ 07026
Phone: 201-546-9660
1-800-227-7785
Fax: 201-546-9698

Continental Fan
HVAC
2296 Kenmore Ave.
Buffalo, NY 14207
Phone: 1-800-779-4021
Fax: 1-800-779-4022

Continental Industries
Landscape Design
100 Summerlea Rd.
Brampton, ON L6T 4X3
Canada
Phone: 905-792-9330
Fax: 905-792-8996

Continental Stone Designs
Countertops; Faucets & Fixtures; Walls, Ceilings & Finishes
3043 Wiljan Ct., Suite B
Santa Rosa, CA 95407
Phone: 707-575-1130
Fax: 707-575-3934

Contractors Software Group
Computer Software
175 Mountain View Dr.
Gainesville, GA 30501
Phone: 770-534-0790
Fax: 770-534-0191
Internet: http://www.mindspring.com/~swcsg

Contractors Wardrobe
Doors; Faucets & Fixtures
26121 Ave. Hall
Valencia, CA 91355
Phone: 805-257-1177
Fax: 805-257-4907

Convenience Products
Paints, Caulks & Adhesives
866 Horan Dr.
Fenton, MO 63026
Phone: 314-349-5333
1-800-325-6180
Fax: 314-349-5335

Cool Attic
HVAC; Roofing
Wolters Industrial Park
Mineral Wells, TX 76068-0728
Phone: 817-325-7887
1-800-433-1626
Fax: 817-325-9311
Internet: http://www.bvc.com

Cooper Lighting
Electrical & Lighting
400 Busse Rd.
Elk Grove Village, IL 60007
Phone: 708-956-8400
Fax: 708-806-3980

Cooper Tools
Hardware; Tools/Electric & Pneumatic; Tools/Hand
PO Box 728
Apex, NC 27502
Phone: 919-387-0099
Fax: 1-800-423-6175

Copper Development Assn.
260 Madison Ave.
New York, NY 10016
Phone: 212-251-7200
1-800-CDA-DATA
Fax: 212-251-7234
Internet: http://www.copper.org

Cor-A-Vent
Roofing
PO Box 428
Mishawaka, IN 46546
Phone: 219-255-1910
1-800-837-8368
Fax: 219-258-6162
Internet: http://www.cor-a-vent.com

Corbin Russwin Architectural Hardware
Hardware
225 Episcopal Rd.
Berlin, CT 06037-1524
Phone: 203-225-7411
Fax: 203-828-7266

Corbond Corp.
Insulation
32404 E. Frontage Rd.
Bozeman, MT 59715
Phone: 406-586-4583
Fax: 406-586-4584

Corel Corp.
Computer Software
1600 Carling Ave.
Ottawa, ON K1Z 8R7
Canada
Phone: 613-728-8200
Fax: 613-761-9176
Internet: http://www.corel.com

Corian
(See DuPont)

Corsi Cabinet Co.
Cabinetry
6111 Churchman Bypass
Indianapolis, IN 46203
Phone: 317-786-1434
Fax: 317-786-2706

Cortina Kitchens
Cabinetry
70 Regina Rd.
Woodbridge, ON
L4L 8L6 Canada
Phone: 905-264-6464
Fax: 905-264-0664

Cosella-Dorken Products
Specialty Products
4655 Delta Way
Beamsville, ON L0R 1B4
Canada
Phone: 905-563-3255
Fax: 905-563-5582

Cottage Steel Industries
Structural Systems
3311 Bethel Rd. S.E.,
Suite 04A
Port Orchard, WA 98366
Phone: 360-871-6555
Fax: 360-895-3282

Country Flame
Fireplaces
1200 Industrial Park
Mt. Vernon, MO 65803
Phone: 417-466-7161
Fax: 417-466-3299

Country Homestead Restoration Contractor
Cabinetry; Countertops; Doors; Flooring; Structural Systems; Walls, Ceilings & Finishes
PO Box 188
Kreamer, PA 17833
Phone: 717-374-7122
Fax: 717-374-2368

Country Stoves
Fireplaces
PO Box 987
Auburn, WA 98071-0987
Phone: 206-735-1100
Fax: 206-931-1271

Courey Intl.
Flooring
4107 Cousens
Montreal, PQ H4S 1V6
Canada
Phone: 514-956-9711
Fax: 514-956-0599

Courtaulds Performance Films
Windows
PO Box 5068
Martinsville, VA 24115
Phone: 540-627-3000
1-800-345-6088
Fax: 540-627-3032
Internet: http://www.llumar.com

CPN
Flooring; HVAC
705 Moore Station,
Industrial Park
Prospect Park, PA 19076
Phone: 1-800-437-3232
Fax: 610-534-2285
Internet: http://www.cpninc.com

Craft-Bilt Mfg. Co.
Doors; Paints, Caulks & Adhesives; Room Enclosures; Siding & Accessories; Structural Systems; Windows
53 Souderton-Hatfield Pike
Souderton, PA 18964
Phone: 215-721-7700
1-800-422-8577
Fax: 215-721-9338
E-mail: richfort@aol.com

Craft-Maid Custom Kitchens
Cabinetry
501 S. Ninth St., Bldg. C
Reading, PA 19602
Phone: 610-376-8686
Fax: 610-376-6998

**Craftline
(A Div. of Vega Industries)**
Doors; Windows
1125 Ford St.
Maumee, OH 43537
Phone: 419-893-3311
1-800-283-3311
Fax: 419-893-0735

Craftmaster
Doors
1 S. Wacker Dr., Suite 3600
Chicago, IL 60606
Phone: 312-750-0900
1-800-446-1649
Fax: 601-428-1170
Internet: www.builderonline.com/~craftmaster

Craftsman Book Co.
Computer Software
6058 Corte Del Cedro
Carlsbad, CA 92009
Phone: 619-438-7828
1-800-829-8123
Fax: 619-438-0398

Crane Plastics Co.
Landscape Design; Siding & Accessories
PO Box 1047
Columbus, OH 43216
Phone: 1-800-307-7780

Crane Plumbing/Fiat Products
Countertops; Faucets & Fixtures
1235 Hartrey Ave.
Evanston, IL 60202
Phone: 847-864-9777
Fax: 847-864-7652

Crawford Products
Hardware
301 Winter St.
West Hanover, MA 02339
Phone: 617-826-8141
1-800-225-5832
Fax: 617-826-4671

Crawford's Old House Store
Moulding & Millwork
550 Elizabeth St.
Waukesha, WI 53186
Phone: 414-542-0685
1-800-556-7878

**Creative Building Products
(A Div. of Spirit of America Corp.)**
Equipment & Trucks; Landscape Design; Moulding & Millwork; Roofing; Siding & Accessories
4307 Arden Dr.
Fort Wayne, IN 46804
Phone: 219-459-0456
1-800-860-2855
Fax: 219-459-0929

Creative Structures
Room Enclosures; Windows
1765 Walnut Ln.
Quakertown, PA 18951
Phone: 215-538-2426
1-800-873-3966
Fax: 215-538-7308

Creda
Appliances
5700 W. Touhy
Niles, IL 60714-4699
Phone: 708-647-8024
1-800-99-CREDA
Fax: 708-647-6917

The Credo Co.
Hardware; Tools/Electric & Pneumatic; Tools/Hand
2765 National Way
Woodburn, OR 97071
Phone: 503-982-0100
1-800-547-9151
Fax: 503-981-2208

Cresline Plastic Pipe
Plumbing Supplies
955 Diamond Ave.
Evansville, IN 47711
Phone: 812-428-9300
Fax: 812-428-9353

**Crest Homes Corp.
(A Div. of Schult Homes)**
Structural Systems
30 Industrial Park
Milton, PA 17847
Phone: 717-742-8521
1-800-927-4567
Fax: 717-742-0351

**Crestline/SNE Enterprises
A PLY GEM Co.**
Doors; Windows
1 Wausau Ctr.,
PO Box 8007
Wausau, WI 54401
Phone: 715-845-1161
1-800-552-4111
Fax: 715-847-6520

Crockett Log and Timber Frame Homes
Structural Systems
Rt. 12, Galen Rd.
Westmoreland, NH 03467
Phone: 603-399-7725
Fax: 603-399-7132

Cronkhite Industries
Equipment & Trucks; Structural Systems
2212 Kickapoo Dr.
PO Box 877
Danville, IL 61832
Phone: 217-443-3700
Fax: 217-443-3778

Cross Vinylattice
Landscape Design
3174 Marjan Dr.
Atlanta, GA 30340
Phone: 770-451-4531
1-800-521-9878
Fax: 770-457-5125

CrossTread Industries
Equipment & Trucks
12021 W. 91st St.
Hinsdale, IL 60521
Phone: 630-850-7100
1-800-697-1746
Fax: 630-654-4114

Crossville Ceramics
Flooring
PO Box 1168,
Industrial Park
Crossville, TN 38557
Phone: 615-484-2110
Fax: 615-484-8418

Crown Point Mfg.
Cabinetry
PO Box 1560,
153 Charlestown Rd.
Claremont, NH 03743
Phone: 603-543-1218
1-800-999-4994
Fax: 1-800-370-1218

Crystal Cabinet Works
Cabinetry
1100 Crystal Dr.
Princeton, MN 55371
Phone: 612-389-4187
1-800-347-5045
Fax: 612-389-3825

Crystal Lamp Parts
Electrical & Lighting
539 W. Rosecrans Ave.
Gardena, CA 90248
Phone: 213-324-1140
1-800-252-0660
Fax: 213-324-1312

CSI
Faucets & Fixtures; Hardware
2422 E. Hintz
Arlington Hts., IL 60004
Phone: 847-253-5927
Fax: 847-253-5928

CSI Donner
Electrical & Lighting; Walls, Ceilings & Finishes
12930 Bradley Ave.
Sylmar, CA 91342
Phone: 818-367-2131
1-800-882-0116
Fax: 818-367-2558

Cumberland Woodcraft
Doors; Landscape Design; Moulding & Millwork
PO Drawer 609
Carlisle, PA 17013-0609
Phone: 717-243-0063
1-800-367-1884 (except PA)
Fax: 717-243-6502

Cuno
Appliances
400 Research Pkwy.
Meriden, CT 06450
Phone: 1-800-243-6894
Fax: 203-238-8701

Cuprinol
Paints, Caulks & Adhesives
101 Prospect Ave.
Cleveland, OH 44115
Phone: 216-566-3131
Fax: 216-566-1655
Internet: http://www.cuprinol.com

Curtain Wall Co.
Equipment & Trucks
246 Welfare Ave.
Warwick, RI 02888
Phone: 1-800-424-8251
Fax: 401-461-4008

Curveline
Roofing; Siding & Accessories
PO Box 4268
Ontario, CA 91761-8968
Phone: 909-947-6022
1-888-998-0311
Fax: 909-947-1510
E-mail: curvline@cyberg8t.com

Curvoflite Stairs and Millwork
Cabinetry; Doors; Moulding & Millwork
205 Spencer Ave.
Chelsea, MA 02150
Phone: 617-889-0007
Fax: 617-889-6339

Cushwa
(See Redland Brick)

Custom-Bilt Metals
Roofing; Siding & Accessories
4647 Pine Timbers, Rm. 134
Houston, TX 77041
Phone: 713-690-1113
Fax: 713-690-2252
E-mail: patarootoo@aol.com

Custom Building Products
Paints, Caulks & Adhesives; Walls, Ceilings & Finishes
13001 Seal Beach Blvd.
Seal Beach, CA 90740
Phone: 310-598-8808
Fax: 310-598-4008

Custom Decorative Mouldings
Moulding & Millwork; Siding & Accessories
PO Box F, Rt. 13
Greenwood, DE 19950
Phone: 302-349-4937
1-800-543-0553
Fax: 302-349-4816

Custom Doors & Drawers
Doors; Moulding & Millwork
232 St. Amaud St.
Amherstburg, ON
N9V 2Z7 Canada
Phone: 519-736-2195
Fax: 1-800-361-5149

Custom Wood Products
Cabinetry
PO Box 4500
Roanoke, VA 24015
Phone: 540-345-8821
1-800-366-2971
Fax: 540-342-7789
E-mail: cwp@roanoke.infi.net

Custom Wood Turnings
Moulding & Millwork
PO Box 338
Ivoryton, CT 06442
Phone: 860-767-3236
Fax: 860-767-3238

Customized Structures
Structural Systems
PO Box 884, Plains Rd.
Claremont, NH 03743
Phone: 603-543-1236
1-800-523-2033
Fax: 603-542-5650

CW Ohio
Moulding & Millwork; Roofing; Windows
1209 Maple Ave.
Conneaut, OH 44034
Phone: 216-593-5800
Fax: 216-593-4545

D

D. Lawless Hardware
Hardware; Specialty Products
1707 E. Main
Olney, IL 62450
Phone: 618-395-3945
Fax: 618-395-3946

DACIS Systems
Computer Software
12300 Perry Hwy., Suite 309
Wexford, PA 15090
Phone: 412-935-4924
1-800-684-1122
Fax: 412-935-5184
Internet: http://www.dacis.com

Dacor
Appliances
950 S. Raymond Ave.
Pasadena, CA 91109
Phone: 818-799-1000
Fax: 818-441-9632

Dakota Granite
Countertops; Flooring; Landscape Design
PO Box 1351
Milbank, SD 57252
Phone: 605-432-5580
1-800-843-3333
Fax: 1-800-338-5346
Fax: 605-432-6155

Dal-Tile Corp.
Countertops; Flooring; Walls, Ceilings & Finishes
7834 Hawn Fwy.
Dallas, TX 75217
Phone: 214-398-1411
1-800-933-TILE
Fax: 214-309-4109
Internet: http://daltile.com

Dalton Paradise Carpet
Flooring
PO Box 2488
Dalton, GA 30722
Phone: 706-226-9064
1-800-338-7811
Fax: 706-226-9061

Daly's Wood Finishing Products
Paints, Caulks & Adhesives
3525 Stone Way Ave. N.
Seattle, WA 98103
Phone: 206-633-4200
1-800-735-7019
Fax: 206-632-2565

Dampney Co.
Paints, Caulks & Adhesives
85 Paris St.
Everett, MA 02149-4421
Phone: 617-389-2805
1-800-537-7023
Fax: 617-380-0484

Danaher Tool Group
Tools/Electric & Pneumatic; Tools/Hand
805 Estelle Dr.
Lancaster, PA 17604-3767
Phone: 717-898-6540
1-800-234-0221
Fax: 717-898-8360
Fax: 1-800-234-0472

Danair
Tools/Electric & Pneumatic
PO Box 3898,
1150 E. Acequia
Visalia, CA 93278
Phone: 209-734-1961
1-800-232-6247
Fax: 1-800-324-1086

Danalite
Electrical & Lighting
16200 Commerce Way
Cerritos, CA 90703
Phone: 310-802-7525
1-800-446-3262
Fax: 310-802-9006

Danfoss Automatic Controls
Building Controls Div.
HVAC
7941 Corporate Dr.
Baltimore, MD 21236
Phone: 410-931-8250
Fax: 410-931-8256

Danish Import
Hardware
488 Oliver St.,
PO Box 101
Troy, MI 48012-0101
Phone: 313-362-1122

DAP
Paints, Caulks & Adhesives
855 N. Third St.,
PO Box 277
Dayton, OH 45401-0277
Phone: 513-667-4461
1-800-543-3840
Fax: 513-667-3331

Darworth Co.
Paints, Caulks & Adhesives
3 Mill Pond Ln.,
PO Box 639
Simsbury, CT 06070
Phone: 203-843-1200
1-800-624-7767
Fax: 1-800-227-6095

Dasco Pro
Tools/Hand
2215 Kishwaukee St.
Rockford, IL 61104
Phone: 815-962-3727
Fax: 815-962-4972

DASI Software
Computer Software
Hillside Center,
Hwy. 441, Suite 1305,
PO Box 1319
Alachua, FL 32615-1319
Phone: 904-462-3048
1-800-449-3274
Fax: 904-462-2581

Data Automation Services Intl.
Computer Software
PO Box 1319
Alachua, FL 32615-1319
Phone: 904-743-1500
1-800-449-3274
Fax: 904-743-0084

Data-Basics
Computer Software
11000 Cedar Rd.
Cleveland, OH 44106
Phone: 216-721-3400
1-800-837-7574
Fax: 216-721-2398

Dataline Corp.
Computer Software
43 Danbury Rd.
Wilton, CT 06897-4470
Phone: 203-762-2473
1-800-723-3676
Fax: 203-834-1173
E-mail: sales@dlcorp.com

Daubert Coated Products
Paints, Caulks & Adhesives
1 Westbrook Corp Center,
Suite 1000
Westchester, IL 60154
Phone: 708-409-5125
1-800-634-1303
Fax: 708-409-5194

David Howard
Structural Systems
PO Box 580
Walpole, NH 03608
Phone: 603-756-3434
Fax: 603-756-3436

David Mulder-Custom Built Circular Stairs
Doors; Moulding & Millwork
2310 Watkins Rd.
Battle Creek, MI 49015
Phone: 616-965-2676
Fax: 616-965-3989

David White
Tools/Hand
11711 River Ln.,
PO Box 1007
Germantown, WI 53022
Phone: 414-251-8100
1-800-732-5478
Fax: 414-251-5696

Davis Technologies
Computer Software
11862 Red Hill Ave.
Santa Ana, CA 92705
Phone: 714-832-6096
Fax: 714-832-6134
E-mail: n-davis@msn.com

Day & Night
HVAC
PO Box 70
Indianapolis, IN 46206
Phone: 317-243-0851
1-800-468-7253
Fax: 317-240-5182

Day Pond Woodworking
Doors; Structural Systems
PO Box 299, Rt. 114
Bradford, NH 03221
Phone: 603-938-2375

Daymond Building Products
Landscape Design
2441 Royal Windsor Dr.
Mississauga, ON L5J 4C7
Canada
Phone: 905-823-4423
1-800-563-3623
Fax: 905-823-0737

Dayton Technologies
Doors; Windows
351 N. Garver Rd.
Monroe, OH 45050
Phone: 513-539-4444
1-800-432-9560
Fax: 513-539-5402
Internet: http://www.daytech.com

De Neef Construction Chemicals (US)
Paints, Caulks & Adhesives; Specialty Products
18314 Mathis Rd.,
PO Box 1219
Waller, TX 77484-1219
Phone: 409-372-9185
Fax: 409-372-9897

Deal Builder
Computer Software
5521 Reseda Blvd.
No. 203
Tarzana, CA 91356
Phone: 818-774-9851
1-800-332-5253
Fax: 818-774-1716
Internet: http://www.dealbuilder.com

Dean Hardwood
Flooring; Moulding & Millwork; Walls, Ceilings & Finishes
PO Box 1595
Wilmington, NC 28402
Phone: 919-763-5409
Fax: 919-763-3748

Dec-Har Designs
Faucets & Fixtures; Hardware
520 Homestead Ave.
Mt. Vernon, NY 10550
Phone: 914-699-5550
1-800-332-4271
Fax: 914-699-0377

Dec-K-Ing
Landscape Design; Roofing
1160 Yew Ave., Suite 84
Blaine, WA 98231
Phone: 604-530-0050
1-800-804-6288
Fax: 604-530-4466

Deck House
(A Div. of DHI)
Structural Systems
930 Main St.
Acton, MA 01720
Phone: 617-259-9450
1-800-727-3325
Fax: 508-263-4159
Internet: http://www.deckhouse.com

Deckmaster
Hardware
140 High St.
Sebastopol, CA 95472
Phone: 707-824-1354
1-800-869-1375

Decor Grates
HVAC; Specialty Products
114 Bows Rd., Unit 1
Concorde, ON L4K 1J8
Canada
Phone: 905-669-1218
1-800-903-9036
Fax: 1-800-362-0923

Decora'
Cabinetry
1 Aristokraft Sq.
Jasper, IN 47547-0420
Phone: 812-634-2288
Fax: 812-634-2850

Decora Systems
Cabinetry; Countertops; Specialty Products
1332 W. McNab Rd.
Ft. Lauderdale, FL 33309
Phone: 954-971-8350
Fax: 954-971-8352

Decorative Glass Intl.
Doors; Windows
12 Stanley Ct., No. 5
Whitby, ON L1N 8P9
Canada
Phone: 1-800-445-6395
Fax: 1-800-267-4997

Decorative Laminate Products Assn.
Countertops
13924 Braddock Rd.,
Suite 100
Centreville, VA 22020
Phone: 703-222-2300
1-800-684-3572
Fax: 703-222-6180

Dectec
(A Div. of Skyline Building Systems)
Landscape Design; Roofing
4500 8A St. N.E.
Calgary, AB T2E 4J7
Canada
Phone: 403-277-0700
1-800-268-1078
Fax: 403-277-4373

Dedicated Micros
Home Technology
11515 Sunset Hills Rd.
Reston, VA 22090
Phone: 703-904-7738
1-800-UNIPLEX
Fax: 703-904-7743

Dee Sign Co.
Landscape Design
6163 Allen Rd.
Cincinnati, OH 45069
Phone: 513-779-3333
1-800-DEE-SIGN
Fax: 513-779-3344

Deer Park Stairbuilding/Millwork
Moulding & Millwork
51 Kennedy Ave.
Blue Point, NY 11715
Phone: 516-363-5008
Fax: 516-363-5292

Deere & Co.
(John Deere Industrial Equipment Co.)
Equipment & Trucks
8000 Jersey Ridge Rd.
Davenport, IA 52807
Phone: 309-765-3195
1-800-503-3373
Fax: 309-765-3358

Deflect-O-Corp.
Appliances; Fireplaces; Garage Doors & Openers; Hardware; HVAC
PO Box 50057
Indianapolis, IN 46250
Phone: 317-849-9555
1-800-428-4328
Fax: 317-841-4393

Deines Custom Doors
Doors
325 Cherry St.
Fort Collins, CO 80521
Phone: 303-482-4806
Fax: 303-482-7996

Delaware Industries Baseway Products
Electrical & Lighting; Moulding & Millwork; Siding & Accessories; Specialty Products
867 Moe Dr., Suite D
Akron, OH 44310
Phone: 330-630-9945
1-800-450-6244
Fax: 330-630-9968

Delray Lighting
Electrical & Lighting
11916 Valerio St.
North Hollywood, CA 91605
Phone: 818-982-3701
Fax: 818-982-3715

Delsan Industries
Doors; Windows
1644 Lotsie Blvd.
St. Louis, MO 63132
Phone: 314-423-5900
Fax: 314-423-5940

Delta Faucet Co.
Faucets & Fixtures
55 E. 111th St.
Indianapolis, IN 46280
Phone: 317-848-1812
1-800-345-DELTA
Fax: 317-574-5567
Internet:
http://www.deltafaucet.com/

Delta Intl. Machinery Corp.
Tools/Electric & Pneumatic
246 Alpha Dr.
Pittsburgh, PA 15238
Phone: 412-963-2495
Fax: 412-963-2868

Deltec Homes
Structural Systems
604 College St.
Asheville, NC 28801
Phone: 704-253-0483
1-800-642-2508
Fax: 704-254-1880

Deluxe Homes of PA
Structural Systems
PO Box 323,
499 W. Third St.
Berwick, PA 18603
Phone: 717-752-5914
1-800-843-7372
Fax: 717-752-1525

Deneb
Computer Software
201 Riverside Dr.,
Suite 2C
Dayton, OH 45405
Phone: 937-223-4849
1-800-952-7888
Fax: 937-223-1548
E-mail:
deneb@worldnet.att.net

Desa Intl.
Tools/Hand
PO Box 90004,
2701 Industrial Dr.
Bowling Green, KY 42102-9004
Phone: 502-781-9800
1-800-626-2237
Fax: 502-781-9400

Design & Construction Resources
Computer Software
1439 Merrimon Ave.
Asheville, NC 28804
Phone: 1-800-334-7510
Fax: 704-252-6342

Design Line
HVAC
260 N. Elm St.
Westfield, MA 01085
Phone: 413-568-9571
Fax: 413-568-9613

Designs In Tile
Countertops; Flooring; Specialty Products; Walls, Ceilings & Finishes
PO Box 358
Mt. Shasta, CA 96067
Phone: 916-926-2629
Fax: 916-926-2629

DeSoto Hardwood Flooring Co. (A Div. of The Burruss Co.)
Flooring
977 Sledge Ave.
Memphis, TN 38104
Phone: 901-774-9672
Fax: 901-774-9684

DeWalt Industrial Tool Co.
Hardware; Tools/Electric & Pneumatic
626 Hanover Pike
Hampstead, MD 21074
Phone: 1-800-4-DEWALT

DFS/USA (Diversified Fastening System)
Hardware
501 Richings St.
Charles City, IA 50616
Phone: 515-228-1162
1-800-833-6417
Fax: 515-228-6124

Diamant Boart
Tools/Electric & Pneumatic; Tools/Hand
4320 Clary Blvd.
Kansas City, MO 64130
Phone: 816-923-5040
1-800-288-5040
Fax: 816-923-7958

Diamond Cabinets (A Schrock Cabinet Co. Brand)
Cabinetry
600 S.W. Walnut St.,
Box 547
Hillsboro, OR 97123
Phone: 503-648-3104
Fax: 503-693-0328

Diamondlac Corp.
Paints, Caulks & Adhesives
12108 Mukilteo Speedway
Mukilteo, WA 98275
Phone: 206-355-9554
1-800-621-3381
Fax: 206-353-1026

Diedrich Technologies
Paints, Caulks & Adhesives
7373 S. Sixth St.
Oak Creek, WI 53154
Phone: 414-764-0058
1-800-323-3565
Fax: 414-764-6993

Diehl Graphsoft
Computer Software
10270 Old Columbia Rd.
Columbia, MD 21046
Phone: 410-290-5114
1-800-873-5084
Fax: 410-290-8050
Internet:
http://www.diehlgraphsoft.com

Dietmeyer, Ward & Stroud EnviroTech Radiant Fireplace
Fireplaces
PO Box 323
Vashon Island, WA 98070
Phone: 206-463-3722
1-800-325-3629
Fax: 206-463-6335

Digecon Plastics Intl.
Electrical & Lighting
9160 Roe St.
Pensacola, FL 32514
Phone: 904-477-5483
1-800-843-5483
Fax: 904-474-6281

Digitool Corp.
Tools/Hand
414 N. Mill St.,
PO Box 12350
Aspen, CO 81611
Phone: 303-925-8177
1-800-543-8930
Fax: 303-925-8178

Dimensions Computer Advisors
Computer Software
5500 Amelia Earhart Dr.,
Building 100
Salt Lake City, UT 84116
Phone: 801-364-5687
1-800-648-5065
Fax: 801-521-5054
Internet:
http://www.dimen.com

Direct Carpet Mills of America
Flooring
PO Box 2759
Rome, GA 30164-2759
Phone: 706-235-6009
1-800-424-1223
Fax: 706-235-1768

Disano Systems Group
Computer Software
12 Steinway Blvd., Suite 3
Etobicoke, ON
M9W 6M5 Canada
Phone: 416-798-8277
1-800-811-5473
Fax: 416-798-8216
Internet:
http://www.disano.com

Disston Co.
Hardware
7345-G W. Friendly Ave.
Greensboro, NC 27410
Phone: 910-852-9220
Fax: 910-299-0616

Diversitech
Paints, Caulks & Adhesives; Tools/Electric & Pneumatic; Tools/Hand; Walls, Ceilings & Finishes
2530 Lantrac Ct.
Decatur, GA 30035
Phone: 770-593-0900
Fax: 770-593-8600

Dixie-Pacific Mfg. Co.
Moulding & Millwork
1700 W. Grand Ave.
Gadsden, AL 35901-8202
Phone: 205-442-4513
1-800-468-5993
Fax: 205-442-4794

DM Industries
Countertops; Faucets & Fixtures
2320 N.W. 147th St.
Miami, FL 33054
Phone: 305-688-5739
1-800-VITA SPA
Fax: 305-688-9415

Dodge Div. of Chrysler Corp.
Equipment & Trucks
12000 Chrysler Dr.
Highland Park, MI 48288
Phone: 1-800-4-A-DODGE
Internet:
http://www.4adodge.com

Domco Industries
Flooring
1001 Yamaska St. E.
Farnham, PQ J2N 1J7
Canada
Phone: 514-293-3173
1-800-465-4030
Fax: 514-293-6644

Domtar Decorative Panels
Engineered Lumber & Panels
PO Box 7500
Huntsville, ON P1H 2J7
Canada
Phone: 705-789-9683
1-800-465-6643
Fax: 705-789-6270

Domtar Gypsum
Walls, Ceilings & Finishes
24 Frank Lloyd Wright
Dr., PO Box 543
Ann Arbor, MI 48106
Phone: 313-930-4752
1-800-4GYPROC
Fax: 1-800-2GYPROC

The Door Company/ Barber Cabinet
Cabinetry; Countertops; Doors; Hardware
2957 S. Collier
Indianapolis, IN 46241
Phone: 317-247-4747
Fax: 317-247-4748

Doorcraft of Alabama (A Div. of JELD-WEN)
Doors
1101 Young Dr.
Hartselle, AL 35640
Phone: 1-800-877-9482

Doorcraft of California (A Div. of JELD-WEN)
Doors
3901 Cincinnati Ave.
Rocklin, CA 95765-1303
Phone: 1-800-877-9482

Doorcraft of Indiana (A Div. of JELD-WEN)
Doors
2526 N. Western Ave.
Plymouth, IN 46563
Phone: 1-800-877-9482

Doorcraft of Iowa (A Div. of JELD-WEN)
Doors
820 Industrial Ave.
Grinnell, IA 50112
Phone: 1-800-877-9482

Doorcraft of North Carolina (A Div. of JELD-WEN)
Doors
647 Hargrave
Lexington, NC 27292
Phone: 1-800-877-9482

Doorcraft of Oregon (A Div. of JELD-WEN)
Doors
Williamson Business Park,
Suite A
31725 Hwy. 97 N.
Chiloquin, OR 97624-9702
Phone: 1-800-877-9482

Doorcraft of Pennsylvania (A Div. of JELD-WEN)
Doors
215 Packer St.
Sunbury, PA 17801-0746
Phone: 1-800-877-9482

Doorcraft of Texas (A Div. of JELD-WEN)
Doors
2201 Baker Blvd.,
PO Box 1021
Temple, TX 76503-1021
Phone: 1-800-877-9482

Doorcraft of Vermont (A Div. of JELD-WEN)
Doors
146 Pleasant St. Extension,
Dean R Brown, Jr
Industrial Park, PO Box 465
Ludlow, VT 05149-0465
Phone: 1-800-877-9482

Doorking
Home Technology
120 Glasgow Ave.
Inglewood, CA 90301
Phone: 310-645-0023
1-800-826-7493
Fax: 310-645-7431

DOORSPY/Rudolph-Desco Co.
Hardware; Home Technology
580 Sylvan Ave.,
PO Box 1245
Englewood Cliffs, NJ 07632-1245
Phone: 201-568-4920
Fax: 201-568-0971

Dorchester Hardware
Hardware
Front St.
Dorchester, NJ 08316
Phone: 609-785-1242
1-800-546-2325
Fax: 609-785-1938

Doucette Log Building
Structural Systems
RR 1
Paris, ON N3L 3E1
Canada
Phone: 1-519-753-2700
Fax: 519-753-9112

Doug Mockett & Co.
Cabinetry; Electrical & Lighting; Hardware
PO Box 3333
Manhattan Beach, CA 90266
Phone: 310-318-2491
1-800-523-1269
Fax: 1-800-235-7743

Douglas Drywall Co.
Walls, Ceilings & Finishes
151 Payne St.
Lexington, KY 40508
Phone: 606-252-0751

The Dow Chemical Co. Construction Materials
Insulation
2020 Dow Ctr.
Midland, MI 48674
Phone: 517-636-2303
1-800-232-2436
Internet:
http://www.dow.com

Downes & Reader Hardwood Co.
Engineered Lumber & Panels; Windows
PO Box 456
Stoughton, MA 02072
Phone: 617-442-8050
1-800-788-5568
Fax: 617-344-7110

Downsview Kitchens
Cabinetry
2635 Rena Rd.
Mississauga, ON
L4T 1G6 Canada
Phone: 905-677-9354

Drain Frame
Flooring; Plumbing Supplies
PO Box 1857
Fallbrook, CA 92028
Phone: 619-728-5400
1-800-729-5874
Fax: 619-723-3203

Dremel
Tools/Electric & Pneumatic
4915 21st St.
Racine, WI 53406-9989
Phone: 414-554-1390
Fax: 414-554-7654

DRI-STEEM Humidifier Co.
HVAC
14949 Technology Dr.
Eden Prairie, MN 55344-2269
Phone: 612-949-2415
1-800-328-4447
Fax: 612-949-2933
Internet:
http://www.thomasregister.com/dristeem

Driwood Moulding Co.
Cabinetry; Doors; Moulding & Millwork; Specialty Products
PO Box 1729
Florence, SC 29503-1729
Phone: 803-669-2478
Fax: 803-669-4874

Dryvit Systems
Paints, Caulks & Adhesives; Siding & Accessories
1 Energy Way
West Warwick, RI 02893
Phone: 401-822-4100
1-800-556-7752
Fax: 401-822-1980

DSH
Doors
463 Applewood Crescent
Concord, ON L4K 4J3
Canada
Phone: 905-669-9335
1-800-493-5263
Fax: 905-669-6922
Internet:
http://www.dsh-inc.com

DuPont Co.
Corian Products
Countertops; Flooring; Landscape Design; Moulding & Millwork
Barley Mill Plaza,
Pricemill Bldg.,
PO Box 80012
Wilmington, DE 19880
Phone: 1-800-4CORIAN
Fax: 302-992-2855

DuPont Tyvek
Insulation
PO Box 80-705,
Centre Rd.
Wilmington, DE 19880
Phone: 1-800-44-TYVEK
Fax: 302-999-4135

Dunham-Bush
HVAC
101 Burgess Rd.
Harrisonburg, VA 22801
Phone: 703-434-0711
Fax: 703-432-6486

Duo-Fast Corp.
Hardware; Tools/Electric & Pneumatic; Tools/Hand
3702 River Rd.
Franklin Park, IL 60131
Phone: 1-888-DUO-FAST (386-3278)

Duo-Gard Industries
Room Enclosures; Windows
40442 Koppernick Rd.
Canton, MI 48187
Phone: 313-207-9700
1-800-872-4404
Fax: 313-207-7995

Duo-Temp
Doors; Windows
PO Box 1896
Toledo, OH 43603-1896
Phone: 1-800-888-8502
Fax: 419-661-3618

Dur-A-Flex
Paints, Caulks & Adhesives
PO Box 280166
East Hartford, CT 06128-0166
Phone: 860-528-9838
1-800-253-3539
Fax: 860-528-2802

Dura Art Stone
Landscape Design; Moulding & Millwork; Siding & Accessories; Windows
11010 Live Oak
Fontana, CA 92337
Phone: 909-350-9000
1-800-821-1120
Fax: 909-350-9632

Dura-Bilt Products
Room Enclosures; Siding & Accessories
PO Box 188
Wellsburg, NY 14894
Phone: 717-596-2000
1-800-233-4251
Fax: 717-596-3296

Dura-Line Corp.
Plumbing Supplies
PO Box 1445
Middlesboro, KY 40965
Phone: 606-248-6456
1-800-RE-TUBE1
Fax: 606-248-3940

Dura-Loc Roofing Systems
Roofing
PO Box 220
Courtland, ON N0J 1E0
Canada
Phone: 519-688-2200
1-800-265-9357
Fax: 519-688-2201

Dura-Oak Cabinet Refacing Systems
863 Texas Ave.
Shreveport, LA 71101
Phone: 318-227-9610
1-800-228-7702
Fax: 318-424-8252

Dura Supreme
Cabinetry
300 Dura Dr., PO Box K
Howard Lake, MN 55349
Phone: 320-543-3872
Fax: 320-543-3310

Duradek
Ensurco Duradek (US)
Roofing
404 E. 13th Ave.
N. Kansas City, MO 64116
Phone: 816-421-5830
1-800-338-3568
Fax: 816-421-2924
Internet:
http://www.duradek.com

Duraflake
(See Willamette Industries)

Duralast Products Corp.
HVAC; Specialty Products
PO Box 15869
New Orleans, LA 70175
Phone: 504-895-2068
Fax: 504-895-2070

Durastone Corp.
Countertops
PO Box 992
Florence, AL 35631
Phone: 205-766-6066
Fax: 615-845-4152

Duratherm Window Corp.
Windows
RR 1, Box 945
North Vassalboro, ME 04962
Phone: 207-872-5558
1-800-996-5558
Fax: 207-872-6731
E-mail:
durathrm@mint.net

Duschqueen
Faucets & Fixtures; Hardware; Windows
40 Lawlins Park
Wyckoff, NJ 07281
Phone: 201-848-8081
1-800-348-8080
Fax: 1-800-348-8438

Dust Door/Arch Guard
Equipment & Trucks
524 Green St.
Boylston, MA 01505
Phone: 508-393-7166
Fax: 508-393-7166

Dutch Boy Professional Paints
Paints, Caulks & Adhesives
101 Prospect Ave.
Cleveland, OH 44115
Phone: 216-566-2929
Fax: 216-566-2771

Duvinage Corp.
Moulding & Millwork
PO Box 828
Hagerstown, MD 21741
Phone: 301-733-8255
1-800-541-2645
Fax: 301-791-7240

Dwyer Products Corp.
Appliances; Cabinetry
418 N. Calumet
Michigan City, IN 46360-5019
Phone: 219-874-5236
1-800-348-8508
Fax: 219-874-2823

Dyco Paints
Paints, Caulks & Adhesives; Roofing
5850 Ulmerton Rd.
Clearwater, FL 34620
Phone: 813-536-6560
1-800-237-8232
Fax: 813-536-0561

Dynamic Cooking Systems
10850 Portal Dr.
Los Alamitos, CA 90720
Phone: 714-220-9505
1-800-433-8466
Fax: 714-220-9668

Dynamic Homes
Structural Systems
PO Box 1137,
525 Roosevelt Ave.
Detroit Lakes, MN 56501
Phone: 218-847-2611
1-800-492-4833
Fax: 218-847-2617

DYNASTY Range
Appliances
7355 E. Slauson Ave.
City of Commerce, CA 90040
Phone: 213-728-5700
Fax: 213-728-2318

E

E&E Consumer Products
Flooring; Hardware; Structural Systems
7200 Miller Dr.
Warren, MI 48092
Phone: 1-800-854-3577
Fax: 810-978-8400

E.I. DuPont De Nemours & Co.
Flooring
403 Holiday Ave.
Dalton, GA 30720-3755
Phone: 1-800-4DUPONT
Fax: 706-275-7752

Eagle Electric Mfg. Co.
Electrical & Lighting
45-31 Court Sq.
Long Island City, NY 11101
Phone: 718-937-8000
1-800-366-6789
Fax: 718-482-0160
Fax: 1-800-329-3055

Eagle Plywood & Door Manufacturers
Doors; Walls, Ceilings & Finishes
450 Oak Tree Ave.
South Plainfield, NJ 07080
Phone: 908-668-1460
1-800-524-2657
Fax: 908-668-4317

Eagle Point Software
Computer Software
4131 Westmark Dr.
Dubuque, IA 52002-2627
Phone: 319-556-8392
1-800-678-6565
Fax: 319-556-5321
Internet:
http://www.eaglepoint.com

Eagle Window & Door
Doors; Windows
375 E. Ninth St.,
PO Box 1072
Dubuque, IA 52004-1072
Phone: 319-556-2270
1-800-453-3633
Fax: 319-556-4408
Internet:
http://www.eaglewindow.com

The Earth Stove
Fireplaces
10595 S.W. Manhasset
Tualatin, OR 97062
Phone: 503-692-3991
1-800-821-6228
Fax: 503-692-6728

Earthstone Retaining Wall Systems
Landscape Design; Structural Systems
784 Butterfield Ln.
San Marcos, CA 92069
Phone: 619-740-9370
Fax: 619-740-9399

Eastern Stair Builders
Moulding & Millwork
PO Drawer F
Laurel, MD 20725
Phone: 410-792-0200
Fax: 301-953-7913

Eastern Timber Homes
Moulding & Millwork; Structural Systems
PO Box 359
Leverett, MA 01054
Phone: 413-665-0996

Eastland Industries
Cabinetry; Countertops
PO Box 219,
Minto Industrial Park
Minto, NB E0E 1J0
Canada
Phone: 506-327-3321
Fax: 506-327-1130

Eastside Machine Co.
Roofing; Siding & Accessories
2001 First Ave. N,
PO Box 2426
Fargo, ND 58108-2426
Phone: 701-235-EMCO
Fax: 701-232-4082

Easy Heat
Faucets & Fixtures; HVAC
31977 US 20 E.
New Carlisle, IN 46552
Phone: 1-800-537-4732
Internet:
http://www.easyheat.com

Eclectus
Computer Software
2441 W. 205th St.,
Suite C200E
Torrance, CA 90501
Phone: 310-781-8030
1-800-625-5972
Fax: 310-781-8034

Eclipse Lighting
Electrical & Lighting
3123 N. Pulaski Rd.
Chicago, IL 60641
Phone: 773-481-9161
Fax: 773-481-0729
E-mail: cigcom.net

Edison Price Lighting
Electrical & Lighting
409 E. 60th St.
New York, NY 10022
Phone: 212-838-5212
Fax: 212-888-7981

EFCO Corp.
Windows
PO Box 609,
1000 County Rd.
Monett, MO 65708-0609
Phone: 417-235-3193
1-800-221-4169
Fax: 417-235-7313

Eide Industries
Siding & Accessories
16215 Piuma Ave.
Cerritos, CA 90703-1528
Phone: 562-402-8335
1-800-422-6827
Fax: 562-924-2233

EIFS Industry Member Assn.
Siding & Accessories
402 N. Fourth St., Suite 102
Yakima, WA 98901-2470
Phone: 509-457-3500
Fax: 509-457-0169

Elan Major Appliances (A Div. of Danville International Corp.)
Appliances
5730-B Brisa St.
Livermore, CA 94550
Phone: 510-371-7000
Fax: 510-371-7008

Elco Industries
Hardware
PO Box 7033
Rockford, IL 61125
Phone: 815-229-0973

Eldorado Stone Corp.
Landscape Design; Siding & Accessories; Structural Systems
PO Box 489
Carnation, WA 98014
Phone: 206-333-6722
1-800-925-1491
Fax: 206-333-4755

Electro Industries
Fireplaces; HVAC
2150 W. River St.,
PO Box 538
Monticello, MN 55362
Phone: 612-295-4434
1-800-922-4138
Fax: 612-295-4434

Electrolux
Specialty Products
2300 Windy Ridge Pkwy.,
Suite 900
Atlanta, GA 30339
Phone: 770-933-1000
1-800-243-5893
Fax: 770-933-1019

Electronic Cooking Systems
Appliances
PO Box 4678
Sunland, CA 91041
Phone: 818-365-6757
Fax: 818-352-7034

Elegant Entries
Doors; Garage Doors & Openers; Moulding & Millwork
240 Washington St.
Auburn, MA 01501
Phone: 508-832-9898
Fax: 508-832-6874

Elements
Landscape Design
4920 Otter Lake Rd.
White Bear Lake, MN 55110
Phone: 612-653-7745
1-800-223-2788
Fax: 612-653-3575

Elite Doors
(See JELD-WEN Fiber of Iowa)

Elite Products Wholesale
Doors; Windows
13221 76th Ave.
Surrey, BC V3W 2V8
Canada
Phone: 604-590-8849
1-800-663-8801
Fax: 604-590-0805

Eljer Plumbingware
Faucets & Fixtures
17120 Dallas Pkwy.
Dallas, TX 75248
Phone: 214-407-2600
Fax: 214-407-2789

Elk Corp.
Roofing
14643 Dallas Pkwy.
Suite 1000
Dallas, TX 75240
Phone: 972-851-0400
Fax: 972-851-0401

Elkay Mfg. Co.
Appliances; Faucets & Fixtures
2222 Camden Ct.
Oak Brook, IL 60521
Phone: 630-574-8484
Fax: 630-574-5012

Elkhart Door
Doors; Faucets & Fixtures
PO Box 2177,
1515 Leininger Ave.
Elkhart, IN 46515
Phone: 219-294-5428
1-800-348-7559
Fax: 219-522-1881

Elmer's Products
Paints, Caulks & Adhesives
180 E. Broad St.
Columbus, OH 43215
Phone: 614-225-4000
1-800-848-9400
Fax: 614-225-7167

Elmira Stove Works
Appliances
145 Northfield Dr.
Waterloo, ON N2L 5J3
Canada
Phone: 519-725-5500
1-800-295-8498
Fax: 519-725-5503

Embassy Industries
HVAC
300 Smith St.
Farmingdale, NY 11735
Phone: 516-694-1800
Fax: 516-694-1836

Emco Specialties
Doors; Moulding & Millwork
2121 E. Walnut
Des Moines, IA 50317
Phone: 515-265-6101
1-800-993-3626
Fax: 515-265-1489

EMI Corp.
HVAC
5780 Success Dr.
Rome, NY 13440
Phone: 315-336-3716
Fax: 1-800-232-9364

Empire Comfort Systems
Fireplaces; HVAC
918 Freeburg Ave.
Belleville, IL 62222-0529
Phone: 618-233-7420
1-800-851-3153
Fax: 618-233-7097
1-800-443-8648
Internet: propanegas.com

Empire Level Mfg. Corp.
Tools/Hand
W229 N1420 Westwood
Dr., PO Box 868
Waukesha, WI 53186
Phone: 414-521-3171
1-800-558-0722
Fax: 414-521-3164

Emtek Products
Hardware
15250 E. Stafford St.
City of Industry, CA 91744
Phone: 1-800-356-2741
Fax: 1-800-577-5771

Enderes Tool Co.
Hardware; Tools/Electric & Pneumatic; Tools/Hand
14925 Energy Way
Apple Valley, MN 55124
Phone: 612-891-1200
1-800-874-7776
Fax: 612-891-1202

ENER-GRID Building Systems
Structural Systems
6847 S. Rainbow Rd.
Buckeye, AZ 85326
Phone: 602-386-2232
Fax: 602-386-3298

Enercept
Structural Systems
3100 Ninth Ave. S.E.
Watertown, SD 57201
Phone: 605-882-2222

Enerjee
HVAC; Plumbing Supplies
32 S. Lafayette Ave.
Morrisville, PA 19067
Phone: 215-295-0557
Fax: 215-736-2328

Enertel Controls
HVAC; Home Technology
954 Montee de Liesse
St. Laurent, PQ
H4T 1W7 Canada
Phone: 514-956-1035
1-800-363-7835
Fax: 514-956-7572

Enerzone Systems Corp.
HVAC; Home Technology
4103 Pecan Orchard
Parker, TX 75002
Phone: 972-424-9808
1-888-Statnet
Fax: 972-424-8055
Internet:
http://www.enerzone.com

Engineered Profiles Div. of North American Profiles
Doors; Hardware; Siding & Accessories; Windows
7504-L 30th St. S.E.
Calgary, AB T2C 1M8
Canada
Phone: 403-279-4497
Fax: 1-800-979-4497
E-mail: epl@cadvision.com

Englert
Roofing; Siding & Accessories; Structural Systems
1200 Amboy Ave.,
PO Box 149
Perth Amboy, NJ 08862
Phone: 908-826-8614
1-800-638-2507
Fax: 908-324-3938

Ensurco Duradek (US)
(See Duradek)

Enterprise Computer Systems
Computer Software
1 Independence Pointe,
PO Box 2383
Greenville, SC 29602-2383
Phone: 864-234-7676
1-800-569-6309
Fax: 864-987-6400
Internet: http://www.ecs-inc.com

Entol Industries
Moulding & Millwork; Walls, Ceilings & Finishes
8180 N.W. 36 Ave.
Miami, FL 33147
Phone: 305-696-0900
1-800-368-6555
Fax: 305-696-1045
E-mail:
entol.ix.netcom.com

Entries
Doors; Hardware
PO Box 39153
Redford, MI 48239
Phone: 313-532-8022
1-800-735-4671
Fax: 1-800-927-2814

Environment/One Corp.
2773 Balltown Rd.
Schenectady, NY 12309
Phone: 518-346-6161
Fax: 518-346-6188

Environmental Technology
HVAC
1302 High St.
South Bend, IN 46601
Phone: 219-233-1202
1-800-234-4239
Fax: 219-233-2152
Internet:
http://eti.skyenet.net

Epro
Countertops; Flooring; Walls, Ceilings & Finishes
156 E. Broadway
Westerville, OH 43081
Phone: 614-882-6990
Fax: 614-882-4210

EPS Molders Assn.
Engineered Lumber & Panels; Insulation; Moulding & Millwork; Roofing; Siding & Accessories; Structural Systems
1926 Waukegan Rd.,
Suite 1
Glenview, IL 60025-1770
Phone: 847-657-6745
1-800-607-EPSA
Fax: 847-657-6819
Internet:
http://www.epsmolders.org

ERSystems
Paints, Caulks & Adhesives; Roofing
2950 Niagara Ln. N.
Plymouth, MN 55447
Phone: 612-550-0038
1-800-403-7747
Fax: 612-550-1237
Internet:
http://www.ersystems.com

Escon Corp.
Doors; Moulding & Millwork
2437 S. Eastern Ave.
Commerce, CA 90040
Phone: 213-721-2211
1-800-368-7850
Fax: 213-721-4104

Essex Silver-Line Corp.
Tools/Electric & Pneumatic
PO Box 40,
1118 Lakeview Ave.
Dracut, MA 01826
Phone: 508-957-2116
1-800-451-5560
Fax: 508-957-6989

Estimation
Computer Software
805-L Barkwood Ct.
Linthicum Heights, MD 21090
Phone: 410-636-4566
1-800-275-6444
Fax: 410-636-6439

Eternit
Roofing; Walls, Ceilings & Finishes
Excelsior Industrial Park,
PO Box 679
Blandon, PA 19510-0679
Phone: 610-926-0100
1-800-233-3155
Fax: 610-926-9232

The Eureka Co.
Specialty Products
1201 E. Bell St.
Bloomington, IL 61701
Phone: 309-828-2367
1-800-282-2886

Euromix Sales
Faucets & Fixtures
7714 134th St.
Surrey, BC V3W 6Y5
Canada
Phone: 604-594-2776
Fax: 604-594-6218

Eurotec Tilt & Turn Windows
Doors; Windows
1001 E. Kentucky St.
Louisville, KY 40204
Phone: 502-637-6855
Fax: 502-637-1174

Evans Adhesive
Paints, Caulks & Adhesives
925 Old Henderson Rd.
Columbus, OH 43220
Phone: 614-451-2665
1-800-888-0925
Fax: 614-451-1373

Evergreen Lumber & Moulding
Engineered Lumber & Panels
PO Box 10518
Santa Ana, CA 92711
Phone: 714-921-8088
Fax: 714-921-8087

Evergreen Slate Co.
Roofing; Tools/Hand
68 E. Potter Ave.
Granville, NY 12832
Phone: 518-642-2530
Fax: 518-642-9313

Evergreen Systems Sunrooms
Room Enclosures
PO Box 293
Beaver Dam, WI 53916
Phone: 414-485-4848
1-800-775-1237
Fax: 414-485-4949

Everpure
Appliances
660 Blackhawk Dr.
Westmont, IL 60559
Phone: 630-654-4000
1-800-323-7873
Fax: 630-654-1115
Internet:
http://www.everpure.com

Evolution Computing
Computer Software
437 S. 48th St., Suite 106
Tempe, AZ 85281
Phone: 602-967-8633
1-800-874-4028
Fax: 602-968-4325
Internet:
http://www.evcomp.com/evcomp/

EWC/Tool Div.
Tools/Hand
11750 Sutton St.
Petaluma, CA 94952
Phone: 707-664-0620
1-800-723-4404
Fax: 707-664-0691

Excalibur Steel Structures
Structural Systems
702 Conine
Waco, TX 76706
Phone: 817-662-3099
Fax: 817-662-5511

Executive Woodsmiths
Moulding & Millwork
215 Foster Ave.
Charlotte, NC 28203
Phone: 704-527-9090
1-800-951-9090

Exhausto
Fireplaces; HVAC
PO Box 720651
Atlanta, GA 30358
Phone: 770-587-3238
1-800-255-2923
Fax: 770-587-4731
Internet:
http://www.exhausto.com

F

F.C.P.
Siding & Accessories; Walls, Ceilings & Finishes
PO Box 99, Excelsior Industrial Park
Blandon, PA 19510-0099
Phone: 610-926-5533
1-888-327-0723
Fax: 610-916-4916

Fabulon
Paints, Caulks & Adhesives
75 Tonawanda St.
Buffalo, NY 14207

Falcon Lock Co. (A Sub. of Newman Tonks Co.)
Hardware
2650 Orbiter St.
Brea, CA 92621
Phone: 1-800-266-4456
Fax: 1-800-777-8229

Falcon Mfg.
Equipment & Trucks; Specialty Products
217 Adams Rd.
Kelowna, BC V1V 1J9
Canada
Phone: 250-765-2323
1-800-522-3313
Fax: 250-765-4228

Fan America
HVAC; Specialty Products
1748 Independence Blvd.,
Suite G-4
Sarasota, FL 34234
Phone: 941-359-3616
1-800-838-4074
Fax: 941-359-3523

Fantech
Appliances
1712 Northgate Blvd.
Sarasota, FL 34234
Phone: 941-351-2947
1-800-747-1762
Fax: 1-800-487-9915
E-mail: fantech@msn.com

Farley Windows
Doors; Windows
280 MacDonald Blvd.
Alexandria, ON K0C 1A0
Canada
Phone: 613-525-3065
1-800-267-9395
Fax: 613-525-1828

Fasco America
105 Industrial Park. Dr.
PO Box 2389
Muscle Shoals, AL 35662
Phone: 205-381-6364
Fax: 205-381-6659

Fasco Industries
Electrical & Lighting; HVAC; Home Technology; Roofing; Specialty Products
810 Gillespie St.,
PO Box 150
Fayetteville, NC 28302
Phone: 919-483-0421
1-800-334-4126
Fax: 1-800-255-4391

The FAST Management Group
Computer Software
15440 N.E. 95th St.,
Suite 240
Redmond, WA 98052
Phone: 206-885-9970
Fax: 206-881-7940
Internet:
http://www.tfmg.com

Faucet Express
Faucets & Fixtures
3800 W. 12th St.
Erie, PA 16505
Phone: 814-835-0200
1-800-555-3112
Fax: 814-835-1010

Faultless Lock
Hardware
20519 Walnut Dr.
Walnut, CA 91789
Phone: 909-598-7023
1-800-621-6869
Fax: 909-594-1383

FC Lighting
Electrical & Lighting
1113 N. Main St.
Lombard, IL 60148
Phone: 708-889-8100
1-800-900-1730
Fax: 708-889-8106

Federal Home Products
Faucets & Fixtures
PO Box 1010
Ruston, LA 71273-1010
Phone: 318-255-5600
1-800-637-6485
Fax: 318-255-5653

Federal Wood Products
Moulding & Millwork
409 Highland Ave.
Middletown, NY 10940
Phone: 914-342-1511
1-800-342-1514

Feeny Mfg. Co.
Cabinetry; Specialty Products
PO Box 191
Muncie, IN 47308
Phone: 317-288-8730
1-800-554-1410
Fax: 317-288-0851

Fein Power Tools
Equipment & Trucks; Tools/Electric & Pneumatic; Tools/Hand
3019 W. Carson St.
Pittsburgh, PA 15204
Phone: 412-331-2325
1-800-441-9878
Fax: 412-331-3599

Felber Ornamental Plastering Corp.
Moulding & Millwork
PO Box 57,
1000 W. Washington St.
Norristown, PA 19404
Phone: 610-275-4713
1-800-392-6896
Fax: 610-275-6636

Felker
Tools/Electric & Pneumatic; Tools/Hand
4320 Clary Blvd.
Kansas City, MO 64130
Phone: 816-923-1718
1-800-365-4003
Fax: 816-923-7958

FEN-Tech
Engineered Lumber & Panels; Windows
1510 N. Fifth St.
Superior, WI 54880
Phone: 715-392-9500
Fax: 1-888-392-9505

Ferche Millwork
Moulding & Millwork
PO Box 39,
400 Division St. N.
Rice, MN 56367
Phone: 612-393-2288
Fax: 612-393-2545

Fero Corp.
Structural Systems
15305-117 Ave.
Edmonton, AB T5M 3X4
Canada
Phone: 403-455-5098
Fax: 403-452-5969

Ferum Co.
Hardware
53 Stiles Ln.,
PO Box 698
Pine Brook, NJ 07058
Phone: 201-575-9035
1-800-633-3786
Fax: 201-575-4390

Fiberez Bathware
Faucets & Fixtures
PO Box 295
Rooseveltown, NY 13683
Phone: 1-800-463-2779
Fax: 613-933-9844

Fiberglass Access
Faucets & Fixtures; Hardware; Specialty Products; Walls, Ceilings & Finishes
PO Box 501176
Malabar, FL 32950
Phone: 407-729-1426
Fax: 407-729-1426

Fiberglass Systems
Faucets & Fixtures
4545 Enterprise
Boise, ID 83705
Phone: 208-342-6823
1-800-727-9907
Fax: 208-342-6832

**Fibermesh
Div. of Synthetic Industries**
Landscape Design; Structural Systems
4019 Industry Dr.
Chattanooga, TN 37416
Phone: 423-892-7243
Fax: 423-499-0753
Internet:
http://www.fibermesh.com

Fibertec Window Mfg.
Doors; Windows
361 Rowntree Dairy Rd.,
No. 4
Woodbridge, ON
L4L 8H1 Canada
Phone: 905-856-1600
1-800-551-4429
Fax: 905-856-1654

Fibreform Wood Products
Doors; Engineered Lumber & Panels; Moulding & Millwork
1999 Ave. of the Stars,
Suite 1830
Los Angeles, CA 90067
Phone: 310-203-5401
Fax: 310-203-5421

Fieldstone Cabinetry
Cabinetry
PO Box 109
Northwood, IA 50459
Phone: 515-324-2114
Fax: 515-324-2390

Fillmore Thomas & Co.
Doors; Windows
350 County Center St.,
PO Box 218
Lapeer, MI 48446
Phone: 810-664-2400
1-800-482-6767
Fax: 1-800-488-9911

Fine Hardwood Veneer Assn.
Engineered Lumber & Panels
260 S. First St., Suite 2
Zionsville, IN 46077
Phone: 317-873-8780
Fax: 317-873-8788

Fine Paints of Europe
Paints, Caulks & Adhesives
PO Box 419, Rt. 4 W.
Woodstock, VT 05091
Phone: 802-457-2468
1-800-332-1556
Fax: 802-457-3984

Finlandia Harvia Sauna Products
Faucets & Fixtures
14010-B S.W. 72nd Ave.
Portland, OR 97224
Phone: 503-684-8289
1-800-354-3342
Fax: 503-684-1120

Finnleo Saunas
Faucets & Fixtures
575 E. Cokato St.
Cokato, MN 55321
Phone: 612-286-5584
1-800-346-6536
Fax: 612-286-6100

FireFree/Quantum Roofing Materials
Roofing
PO Box 1094
Sumas, WA 98295
Phone: 1-800-347-3373
Fax: 604-820-3879

Fireplace Manufacturers
Fireplaces
2701 S. Harbor Blvd.
Santa Ana, CA 92704
Phone: 714-549-7782
1-800-888-2050
Fax: 714-549-8095

Fireplace Xtrordinair
Fireplaces
10850 117th Pl. N.W.
Kirkland, WA 98033
Phone: 206-827-9505
Fax: 206-827-9363

Firma Bath Furniture
Cabinetry
80 Hanlan Rd.
Woodbridge, ON
L4L 3P6 Canada
Phone: 905-851-5552
Fax: 905-851-9467

First Alert Professional Security Systems
Home Technology
172 Michael Dr.
Syosset, NY 11791
Phone: 516-921-6066
Fax: 516-921-8118

First Choice Tool Co.
Tools/Hand
PO Box 670
Sturgis, MI 49091
Phone: 616-651-7964
1-800-782-4659
Fax: 616-651-4412

Firstday Cottage
Structural Systems
PO Box 711
Walpole, NH 03608
Phone: 603-756-3434
Fax: 603-756-3434

Fischer SIPS
Structural Systems
1843 Northwestern Pkwy.
Louisville, KY 40203
Phone: 502-778-5577,
ext. 104
Fax: 502-778-5587

Fiskars Power Sentry
Electrical & Lighting
6271 Bury Dr., Suite A
Eden Prairie, MN 55346
Phone: 612-949-1100
1-800-852-4312
Fax: 612-949-2100
E-mail:
timwalsh@fiskars.com

FiveStar
Appliances
PO Box 2490
Cleveland, TN 37320
Phone: 423-476-6544
1-800-251-7485
Fax: 423-476-6599

Fixrammer Fasteners Co.
Hardware
3927-A Morris Field Dr.
Charlotte, NC 28208
Phone: 704-391-7200
1-800-820-3136
Fax: 704-399-7883

The Flecto Co.
Paints, Caulks & Adhesives
1000 45th St.
Oakland, CA 94608-3398
Phone: 510-655-2470
1-800-635-3286
Fax: 510-652-7135

Flex Molding
Moulding & Millwork; Siding & Accessories
16 E. Lafayette St.
Hackensack, NJ 07601
Phone: 201-487-8080
Fax: 201-487-6637

Flex Trim Industries
Moulding & Millwork; Paints, Caulks & Adhesives
PO Box 4227,
11479 Sixth St.
Rancho Cucamonga, CA 91730
Phone: 909-944-6665
1-800-356-9060
Fax: 1-800-874-6832

FLEXCO Co.
Flooring; Moulding & Millwork; Paints, Caulks & Adhesives
PO Box 553
Tuscumbia, AL 35674
Phone: 205-383-7474
1-800-933-3151
Fax: 205-381-0322

**Flexi-Wall Systems
(A Div. of Wall & Floor Treatments)**
Walls, Ceilings & Finishes
PO Box 89
Liberty, SC 29657
Phone: 864-843-3104
1-800-843-5394
Fax: 864-843-9318

Flinchbaugh Co.
Specialty Products
390 Eberts Ln.
York, PA 17403
Phone: 717-848-2418
1-800-326-2418
Fax: 717-843-7385

Flo-Well Water Management
Landscape Design
80 Enterprise Rd.
Hyannis, MA 02601
Phone: 508-790-3266
1-800-356-9935
Fax: 508-790-0083

The Flood Co.
Paints, Caulks & Adhesives
PO Box 2535,
1212 Barlow Rd.
Hudson, OH 44236
Phone: 216-656-3033
1-800-321-3444
Fax: 216-650-1453
Internet:
http://www.floodco.com

Florestone Products Co.
Faucets & Fixtures
2851 Falcon Dr.
Madera, CA 93637
Phone: 209-661-4171
1-800-446-8827
Fax: 209-661-2070
Internet:
http://www.florestone.com

Florian Greenhouse
Room Enclosures
64 Airport Rd.
West Milford, NJ 07480
Phone: 201-728-7800
1-800-FLORIAN
Fax: 201-728-3206

Florida Brick & Clay Co.
Landscape Design
1708 Turkey Creek Rd.
Plant City, FL 33567
Phone: 813-754-1521
Fax: 813-754-5469

**Florida Tile
(A Div. of Premark)**
Countertops; Flooring; Walls, Ceilings & Finishes
1 Sikes Blvd.
Lakeland, FL 33815
Phone: 813-687-7171
1-800-789-TILE
Fax: 941-688-4487
Internet:
http://www.fltile.com\

Flos USA
Electrical & Lighting
200 McKay Rd.
Huntington Station, NY 11746
Phone: 516-549-2745
Fax: 516-549-4220

Fluidmaster
Faucets & Fixtures; Plumbing Supplies
1800 Via Burtom
Anaheim, CA 92806
Phone: 714-774-1444
Fax: 714-774-5764

Foam Laminates of Vermont
Structural Systems
PO Box 102
Hinesburg, VT 05461
Phone: 802-453-4438
Fax: 802-453-2339

Focal Point
(See NMC-Focal Point)

Fold-Form
Insulation; Structural Systems
PO Box 774
Sioux City, IA 51102
Phone: 712-252-3704
Fax: 712-252-3259

Folding Shutter Corp.
Room Enclosures; Siding & Accessories
7089 Hemstreet Pl.
West Palm Beach, FL 33413
Phone: 407-683-4811
Fax: 407-640-8204

Follansbee Steel
Roofing
PO Box 610, State St.
Follansbee, WV 26037
Phone: 304-527-1260
1-800-624-6906
Fax: 304-527-1269

Fomo Products
Insulation; Paints, Caulks & Adhesives
2775 Barber Rd.,
PO Box 1078
Norton, OH 44203
Phone: 330-753-4585
1-800-321-5585
(outside OH)
Fax: 330-753-5199
Internet:
http://www.fomo.com

Forbo Arborite
Countertops
385 Lafleur St.
Ville LaSalle,
PQ H8R 3H7 Canada
Phone: 514-366-2710
1-800-361-8712

Forbo Industries
Flooring
Humboldt Industrial Park, PO Box 667
Hazleton, PA 18201
Phone: 717-459-0771
1-800-342-0604
Fax: 717-450-0258

Ford Motor Co.
Equipment & Trucks
300 Renaissance Ctr.
Detroit, MI 48243
Phone: 1-800-258-FORD

Foreign & Domestic Woods
Engineered Lumber & Panels; Flooring; Moulding & Millwork
PO Box 1096
McLean, VA 22101
Phone: 703-506-4690
Fax: 703-827-7761

Foremost Industries
Cabinetry; Countertops; Faucets & Fixtures
906 Murray Rd.
East Hanover, NJ 07936
Phone: 201-428-0400
Fax: 201-428-6166

**Forest Products Laboratory
USDA-Forest Service**
1 Gifford Pinchot Dr.
Madison, WI 53705-2398
Phone: 608-231-9200
Fax: 608-231-9592

Forest Products Society
Engineered Lumber & Panels; Moulding & Millwork; Siding & Accessories; Structural Systems
2801 Marshall Ct.
Madison, WI 53705
Phone: 608-231-1361
Fax: 608-231-2152

Formglas
Moulding & Millwork; Walls, Ceilings & Finishes
20 Toro Rd.
North York, ON
M3J 2A7 Canada
Phone: 416-635-8030
Fax: 416-635-6588
Internet:
http://www.formglas.com

Formica Corp.
Countertops; Flooring; Paints, Caulks & Adhesives
10155 Reading Rd.
Cincinnati, OH 45241
Phone: 513-786-3400
1-800-FORMICA
Fax: 513-786-3024

Forms + Surfaces
Doors; Hardware; Walls, Ceilings & Finishes
PO Box 5215
Santa Barbara, CA 93150
Phone: 805-684-8626
1-800-451-0410
Fax: 805-684-8620

Fort Smith Rim & Bow
Moulding & Millwork
2605 Kelley Hwy.
Fort Smith, AR 72904
Phone: 1-800-643-4568
Fax: 501-783-6043

**Fort Vancouver
Plywood Co.**
*Engineered Lumber
& Panels*
PO Box 289
Vancouver, WA 98666
Phone: 360-694-3368
1-800-367-0038
Fax: 360-694-7882

**Fostoria Industries
General Products Div.**
Equipment & Trucks
1200 N. Main St.
Fostoria, OH 44830
Phone: 419-435-9201
Fax: 419-435-0842
E-mail:
gpfostor@bright.net

Four Seasons Sunrooms
Room Enclosures
5005 Veterans Memorial
Hwy.
Holbrook, NY 11741
Phone: 1-800-FOUR
SEASONS
1-800-521-0179
Fax: 516-563-4010
Internet: http://www.four-
seasons-sunrooms.com

Fourply
*Engineered Lumber
& Panels*
PO Box 890
Grants Pass, OR 97526
Phone: 503-479-3301
1-800-547-5991
Fax: 503-479-7206

**Fox Valley Steel
& Wire Co.**
Hardware
111 N. Douglas
Hortonville, WI 54944
Phone: 414-779-4544
1-800-236-8304
Fax: 414-779-4546

Frame Master
Tools/Hand
PO Box 151
Groton, VT 05046
Phone: 802-757-3225
1-800-750-8434
Fax: 802-757-3561
Internet:
http://www.bypass.com/
~framemaster

**Franke
Kitchen Systems Div.**
*Appliances; Faucets &
Fixtures*
212 Church Rd.
North Wales, PA 19454
Phone: 1-800-626-5771
Fax: 215-661-8258
Internet:
http://www.franke.com

Franklin Brass Mfg. Co.
Faucets & Fixtures
PO Box 4887
Carson, CA 90749-4887
Phone: 310-885-3200
1-800-421-3375
Fax: 310-885-3277

**Franklin Intl.
Construction Adhesives
& Sealants**
Paints, Caulks & Adhesives
2020 Bruck St.
Columbus, OH 43207
Phone: 614-443-0241
1-800-877-4583
Fax: 614-445-1251

**Frantz
(A Div. of Wayne-Dalton
Corp.)**
Garage Doors & Openers
PO Box 1200,
301 W. Third St.
Sterling, IL 61081-8200
Phone: 815-625-0163
1-800-423-3667
Fax: 815-626-0747

French Reflection
*Electrical & Lighting;
Walls, Ceilings & Finishes*
820 S. Robertson Blvd.
Los Angeles, CA 90035
Phone: 310-659-3800
1-800-421-4404
Fax: 310-652-8494

Freud
*Hardware; Tools/Electric
& Pneumatic; Tools/Hand*
PO Box 7187, 218 Feld Ave.
High Point, NC 27264
Phone: 910-434-3171
Fax: 910-434-8333

**Freudenberg Building
Systems
Nora Rubber Flooring**
Flooring
94 Glenn St.
Lawrence, MA 01843-1022
Phone: 508-689-0530
1-800-332-NORA
Fax: 508-975-0110

**Friedrich Air
Conditioning Co.**
HVAC
PO Box 1540
San Antonio, TX 78295
Phone: 210-225-2000
Fax: 210-228-1709

**Frigidaire Home
Products
Frigidaire, Tappan &
White-Westinghouse**
Appliances; HVAC
6000 Perimeter Dr.
Dublin, OH 43017
Phone: 614-792-4100
1-800-685-6005
Fax: 614-792-4079
Internet:
http://www.frigidaire.com

Fritz Industries
Flooring
500 Sam Houston
Mesquite, TX 75149
Phone: 972-285-5471
1-800-955-1323
Fax: 972-270-0179

**FSI/Scorpion Brand
Products**
*Hardware; Tools/Electric
& Pneumatic*
48 Commerce Way
South Windsor, CT
06074
Phone: 860-289-5776
1-800-233-0461
Fax: 860-289-1063

Ft. Knox Security
Home Technology
1051 N. Industrial Park Rd.
Orem, UT 84057
Phone: 1-800-821-5216
Fax: 801-226-5493
Internet:
http://www.ftknox.com

**Fuego Flame
Fireplace Mfg.**
Fireplaces
2618 Ellington Rd.
Quincy, IL 62301
Phone: 217-223-3473
1-800-445-1867
Fax: 217-223-1642
Internet:
http://www.greene-
assoc.com/fuego

Fuller-O'Brien Paints
Paints, Caulks & Adhesives
395 Oyster Point Blvd.,
Suite 350
South San Francisco, CA
94080
Phone: 415-871-3131
1-800-421-4404
Fax: 415-871-0680

**The Future Home
Technology**
Structural Systems
33 Ralph St.
Port Jervis, NY 12771
Phone: 914-856-9033
1-800-342-8650
Fax: 914-858-2488

FV America
Faucets & Fixtures
4000 Porett Dr.
Gurnee, IL 60031
Phone: 847-244-1234
1-800-446-9700
Fax: 847-244-1259

FYPON
*Moulding & Millwork;
Siding & Accessories*
22 W. Pennsylvania Ave.
Stewartstown, PA 17363
Phone: 717-993-2593
1-800-537-5349
Fax: 717-993-3782

Fyrnetics
Home Technology
1055 Stevenson Ct.,
102W.
Roselle, IL 60172
Phone: 708-893-4592
1-800-654-7665
Fax: 708-893-9967

G

G/L Veneer Co.
*Engineered Lumber
& Panels*
2224 E. Slauson Ave.
Huntington Park, CA
90255
Phone: 213-582-5203
Fax: 213-582-9681

**G R Plastics
(Nu-Wood)**
*Moulding & Millwork;
Siding & Accessories*
PO Box 489
Goshen, IN 46527
Phone: 219-534-1192
1-800-526-1278
Fax: 219-534-0218
E-mail: nuwood2@aol.com

G-U Hardware
Hardware
11761 Rock Landing Dr.,
Suite M6
Newport News, VA 23606
Phone: 757-873-1097
Fax: 757-873-1298
Internet: http://www.g-u.
com

GAF Materials Corp.
Roofing
1361 Alps Rd.
Wayne, NJ 07470
Phone: 201-628-3000

Gaggenau MSA Corp.
Appliances
425 University Ave.
Norwood, MA 02062
Phone: 617-255-1766
Fax: 617-769-2212

**Gainsborough Hardware
Industries**
Hardware
1255 Oakbrook Dr., Suite C
Norcross, GA 30093
Phone: 770-448-9000
1-800-845-5662
Fax: 770-448-7070

GAPCO
Doors; Windows
393 Maple St.
Gallatin, TN 37066-0469
Phone: 615-452-4550
1-800-333-0111
Fax: 615-452-4550

**Garage Door Hardware
Assn.**
*Garage Doors & Openers;
Hardware*
2850 S. Ocean Blvd.,
Suite 311
Palm Beach, FL 33480
Phone: 407-533-0991
Fax: 407-533-7466

Garaventa
Specialty Products
PO Box 1769
Blaine, WA 98231
Phone: 604-594-0422
1-800-663-6556
Fax: 604-594-9915

**Garden Rooms by
Coleman**
Room Enclosures
4820 S.E. Loop 820
Fort Worth, TX 76140
Phone: 817-483-4661
Fax: 817-572-2407

Gardner Asphalt Corp.
*Paints, Caulks &
Adhesives; Roofing;
Specialty Products*
4161 E. Seventh Ave.,
PO Box 5449
Tampa, FL 33549
Phone: 813-248-2101
1-800-237-1155
Fax: 813-248-6768

**Garland Commercial
Industries**
Appliances
185 E. South St.
Freeland, PA 18224
Phone: 717-636-1000
1-800-25-RANGE
Fax: 717-636-2713

Garland Homes
Structural Systems
PO Box 12
Victor, MI 59875
Phone: 406-642-3095
Fax: 406-642-6643

Garland Mfg. Co.
Tools/Hand
PO Box 538
Saco, ME 04072-0538
Phone: 207-283-3693
Fax: 207-283-4834
Internet: http://www.
garland mfg

**Gas Appliance
Manufacturers Assn.**
PO Box 9245
Arlington, VA 22219-1245
Phone: 703-525-9565
Fax: 703-525-0718
E-mail: 102766,2232
@compuserve.com

Gas-Fired Products
HVAC
305 Doggett St.,
PO Box 36485
Charlotte, NC 28236
Phone: 704-372-3485
1-800-438-4936
Fax: 704-332-5843

Gas Research Institute
*Appliances; Fireplaces;
HVAC*
8600 W. Bryn Mawr
Chicago, IL 60631
Phone: 312-399-8249
Fax: 312-399-8170

Gastineau Log Homes
Structural Systems
New Bloomfield, MO
65063
Phone: 314-896-5122
1-800-654-9253
Fax: 314-896-5510

GE Appliances
Appliances
Appliance Park
Louisville, KY 40225
Phone: 502-452-4311
1-800-626-2000

GE Lighting
Electrical & Lighting
Nela Park
Cleveland, OH 44112
Phone: 216-266-2121
1-800-GE-LAMPS

GE Lighting Systems
Electrical & Lighting
3010 Spartanburg Hwy.
Hendersonville, NC 28739
Phone: 704-693-2000
1-800-626-2004

GE Silicones
Paints, Caulks & Adhesives
260 Hudson River Rd.
Waterford, NY 12188
Phone: 518-233-3505
1-800-255-8886

GE Wiring Devices
Electrical & Lighting
225 Service Ave.,
PO Box 1050
Warwick, RI 02886
Phone: 401-886-6200
Fax: 401-886-6250

GEAC Computer Corp.
Computer Software
45 McIntosh Dr.
Markham, ON L3R 8C7
Canada
Phone: 905-475-7733
1-800-456-1192
Fax: 905-475-7799
Internet:
http://www.geac.com/
construction

Geberit Mfg.
Faucets & Fixtures
1100 Boone Dr.
Michigan City, IN
46360-7730
Phone: 1-800-225-7217
Fax: 219-872-8003

Gehl Co.
Equipment & Trucks
143 Water St.
West Bend, WI 53095
Phone: 414-334-9461
Fax: 414-338-7517

Geist
Electrical & Lighting
PO Box 83088
Lincoln, NE 68501
Phone: 402-474-3400
1-800-432-3219
Fax: 402-474-4369

**Gemini Bath & Kitchen
Products**
*Cabinetry; Faucets &
Fixtures; Specialty Products*
3790 E. 44th St.
Tucson, AZ 85713
Phone: 520-750-8433
Fax: 520-327-1580

Generac Corp.
*Equipment & Trucks;
Tools/Electric & Pneumatic*
Hwy. 59 and Hillside Rd.
Waukesha, WI 53187
Phone: 414-544-4811
Fax: 414-544-4851

**General Aluminum
Corp.**
Windows
PO Box 819022
Dallas, TX 75381
Phone: 214-242-5271
1-800-727-0835
Fax: 1-800-937-4422

**General American
Door Co.**
Garage Doors & Openers
5050 Baseline Rd.
Montgomery, IL 60538
Phone: 708-859-3000
1-800-323-0813
Fax: 708-859-8122

General Ecology
Appliances
151 Sheree Blvd.
Exton, PA 19341
Phone: 610-363-7900
1-800-441-8166
Fax: 610-363-0412
Internet:
http://www.general-
ecology.com

General Electric
(See GE Appliances)

General Housing Corp.
Structural Systems
900 Andre St.
Bay City, MI 48706
Phone: 517-684-8078

General Marble Co.
*Cabinetry; Countertops;
Electrical & Lighting*
350 N. Generals Blvd.
Lincolnton, NC 28092
Phone: 1-800-432-4114
Fax: 704-732-5027

General Products Co.
(See Benchmark Door Systems)

General Shale Brick
Siding & Accessories;
Structural Systems
PO Box 3547
Johnson City, TN 37602
Phone: 615-282-4661
1-800-414-4661
Fax: 615-282-0491

General Tools Mfg. Co.
Tools/Hand
80 White St.
New York, NY 10013
Phone: 212-431-6100
Fax: 212-431-6499

The Genie Co.
Equipment & Trucks;
Garage Doors & Openers
22790 Lake Park Blvd.
Alliance, OH 44601
Phone: 216-821-5360
1-800-OK-GENIE
Fax: 216-829-3636

Genie Industries
Equipment & Trucks
PO Box 97030
Redmond, WA 98073
Phone: 206-881-1800
1-800-536-11-800
Fax: 206-883-3475
Internet:
http://www.genielift.com

Genova Products
Landscape Design;
Plumbing Supplies;
Roofing; Siding &
Accessories
PO Box 309,
7034 E. Court St.
Davison, MI 48423-0309
Phone: 810-744-4500
1-800-521-7488
Fax: 810-658-1815
Internet:
http://www.cris.com/
~genova/

Gentek Building Products
Siding & Accessories
29325 Chagrin Blvd.
Cleveland, OH 44122
Phone: 216-514-3500
1-800-548-4542
Fax: 216-514-3571
Internet:
http://www.gentekinc.com

Geocel Corp.
Paints, Caulks & Adhesives
53280 Marina Dr.
Elkhart, IN 46514
Phone: 219-264-0645
1-800-348-7615
Fax: 219-264-3698

George Guenzler & Sons
Moulding & Millwork
601 Colby Dr.
Waterloo, ON N2V 1A1
Canada
Phone: 519-885-2141
Fax: 519-885-3342

The Georgia Marble Co.
Countertops; Faucets &
Fixtures; Flooring;
Landscape Design;
Structural Systems
Blue Ridge Ave., PO Box 9
Nelson, GA 30151
Phone: 404-735-2591
1-800-334-0122
Fax: 404-735-4456

Georgia-Pacific Corp.
Countertops; Doors;
Engineered Lumber &
Panels; Flooring;
Hardware; Insulation;
Landscape Design;
Moulding & Millwork;
Roofing; Siding &
Accessories; Tools/Electric
& Pneumatic; Walls,
Ceilings & Finishes;
Windows
PO Box 1763
Norcross, GA 30091
Phone: 1-800-BUILD-GP

Gerard Roofing Technologies
Roofing
955 Columbia St.
Brea, CA 92821-2923
Phone: 714-529-0407
1-800-23-ROOFS
Fax: 714-529-6643
Internet:
http://www.gerardusa.com

Gerber Industries
Landscape Design;
Moulding & Millwork
1 Gerber Industrial Dr.,
PO Box 610
St. Peters, MO 63376
Phone: 314-278-5710
1-800-844-1401
Fax: 314-278-4727

Gerber Plumbing Fixtures Corp.
Cabinetry; Faucets &
Fixtures
4600 W. Touhy Ave.
Chicago, IL 60646
Phone: 847-675-6570
Fax: 1-800-5-GERBER
(except IL)

Gerkin Windows & Doors
Doors; Windows
PO Box 3203
Sioux City, IA 51102
Phone: 402-494-6000
1-800-475-5061
Fax: 402-494-6765

Gesmar
Countertops; Faucets
& Fixtures
1806 Summit Ave.,
PO Box 11205
Richmond, VA 23230
Phone: 804-358-4956
Fax: 804-358-2462

GFP Intl.
Fireplaces; HVAC
PO Box 36271
Charlotte, NC 28236
Phone: 704-372-3486
1-800-438-4936
Fax: 704-332-5843

Gibco Services
Engineered Lumber &
Panels; Flooring; Moulding
& Millwork; Walls,
Ceilings & Finishes
725 S. Adams Rd.,
Suite L-59
Birmingham, MI 48009
Phone: 810-647-3322
Fax: 810-647-8720

**Gibson
(A Brand of Frigidaire Co.)**
Appliances; HVAC
6000 Perimeter Dr.
Dublin, OH 43019
Phone: 614-792-4100
1-800-458-1445
Fax: 614-792-4079

Gibson-Homans Co.
Paints, Caulks &
Adhesives; Roofing
1755 Enterprise Pkwy.
Twinsburg, OH 44087
Phone: 216-425-3255
1-800-433-7293
Fax: 216-425-2546

Gilded Mirrors
Walls, Ceilings & Finishes
5002 US Hwy. 411 S.
Maryville, TN 37801
Phone: 423-856-3066
1-800-422-9960
Fax: 423-856-6833

Giles & Kendall
Walls, Ceilings & Finishes
PO Box 188
Huntsville, AL 35804
Phone: 205-776-2978
1-800-225-6738
Fax: 205-776-3031

Girardin Moulding
Siding & Accessories
567 Halfway House Rd.
Windsor Locks, CT 06096
Phone: 860-623-4486
1-800-221-7654
Fax: 860-627-6716

Glass Assn. of North America (GANA)
White Lakes Professional
Building,
3310 S.W. Harrison St.
Topeka, KS 66611-2279
Phone: 913-266-7013
Fax: 913-266-0272

Glass Block Designs
Windows
381 11th St.
San Francisco, CA 94103
Phone: 415-626-5770
Fax: 415-626-4352
Internet:
http://www.glassblock
designs.com

Glass Blocks Unlimited
Flooring; Windows
126 E. 16th St.
Costa Mesa, CA 92627
Phone: 714-548-8531
Fax: 714-548-1502

Glen-Gery Corp.
Landscape Design; Siding
& Accessories; Structural
Systems
1166 Spring St.,
PO Box 7001
Wyomissing, PA 19610
Phone: 610-374-4011
Fax: 610-374-3700
Internet:
http://www.glengerybrick.
com

Glen Oak Lumber & Milling
Engineered Lumber &
Panels; Flooring; Moulding
& Millwork
N2885 County F
Montello, WI 53949
Phone: 608-297-2161
1-800-242-8272, ext. 250
Fax: 608-297-7651

Glen Raven Mills
Siding & Accessories
1831 N. Park Ave.
Glen Raven, NC 27217
Phone: 910-227-6211
Fax: 910-229-4039

The Glidden Co.
(See ICI Paint Stores)

Glix Products
Hardware
93 N.W. 166 St.
Miami, FL 33169
Phone: 305-947-4851
Fax: 305-949-6620

Globe Fire Sprinkler Corp.
Home Technology
4077 Air Park Dr.
Standish, MI 48658
Phone: 517-846-4583
1-800-248-0278
Fax: 517-846-9231

Gloucester Co.
Paints, Caulks & Adhesives
PO Box 428
Franklin, MA 02038
Phone: 508-528-2200
1-800-343-4963
Fax: 508-520-3851

GM Corp.
(See Chevrolet Motor
Div.; GMC Truck)

GMC Truck
Equipment & Trucks
31 E. Judson St.
Pontiac, MI 48342
Phone: 810-745-7786
810-745-5310
1-800-GMC-TRUCK
Internet:
http://www.gmc.com

Goddard Circular & Spiral Stair
Moulding & Millwork
PO Box 502,
Dept. HW-BG
Logan, KS 67646-0502
Phone: 913-689-4341

Goettl Air Conditioning
HVAC
3830 E. Wier
Phoenix, AZ 85034
Phone: 602-275-1515
1-800-334-6494
Fax: 602-470-4275

Golden Log Homes
Moulding & Millwork;
Structural Systems
5353 W. 56th Ave.
Arvada, CO 80002-2834
Phone: 303-420-2900
1-800-678-7547
Fax: 303-420-4448

Goodman Mfg. Co.
HVAC
1501 Seamist
Houston, TX 77008
Phone: 713-861-2500

Goodwin Heart Pine Co.
Countertops; Doors;
Flooring; Moulding &
Millwork; Walls, Ceilings
& Finishes
106 S.W. 109th Pl.
Micanopy, FL 32667
Phone: 352-466-0339
1-800-336-3118
Fax: 352-466-0608
Internet:
http://www.heartpine.com/

Gorell Enterprises
Doors; Windows
1380 Wayne Ave.
Indiana, PA 15701
Phone: 412-465-1800
1-800-946-7355
Fax: 412-465-1894

Gossen Corp.
Insulation; Moulding
& Millwork; Siding &
Accessories
2030 W. Bender Rd.
Milwaukee, WI 53209
Phone: 414-228-9800
1-800-558-8984
Fax: 414-228-9077

**Gothic Arch
Greenhouses
(A Div. of TransSphere
Trading Corp.)**
Room Enclosures
PO Box 1564
Mobile, AL 36633
Phone: 205-432-7529
1-800-628-4974

Grabber Construction Products
Hardware; Tools/Electric
& Pneumatic
205 Mason Cir.
Concord, CA 94520
Phone: 510-680-0777
1-800-477-TURN
Fax: 510-687-6261

Grabco
Hardware
3950 Industrial Ave.
Rolling Meadows, IL
60008
Phone: 708-253-2501
1-800-ANC-HOR4
Fax: 708-253-3230

Grabill Cabinet Co.
Cabinetry; Countertops;
Engineered Lumber
& Panels
PO Box 40
Grabill, IN 46741
Phone: 219-627-2131
Fax: 219-627-3539

W.R. Grace & Co.
(See Grace Construction
Products)

Grace Construction Products
Engineered Lumber &
Panels; Specialty Products;
Structural Systems
62 Whittemore Ave.
Cambridge, MA 02140
Phone: 617-876-1400
Fax: 617-498-4314

Graco
Equipment & Trucks
PO Box 1441
Minneapolis, MN 55440
Phone: 612-623-6743
1-800-367-4023

Graham Fiberglass
Insulation
300 Main St.
Erin, ON N0B 1T0
Canada
Phone: 905-453-1912
1-800-265-9123
Fax: 519-833-9749

Graham Products
Siding & Accessories;
Structural Systems; Walls,
Ceilings & Finishes
104 Maple Ave.,
PO Box 2000
Inglewood, ON L0N 1K0
Canada
Phone: 905-874-3065
1-800-268-7410
Fax: 905-838-3386

Graham Timber Frame
Structural Systems
4310 Peters Rd., RR 7
Duncan, BC V9L 4W4
Canada
Phone: 604-743-5853

Grandview Products Co.
Cabinetry
PO Box 874,
1601 Superior Dr.
Parsons, KS 67357
Phone: 316-421-6950
Fax: 316-421-4211

Grani-Decor Tiles
Flooring; Landscape
Design; Walls, Ceilings
& Finishes
1040 Rue Bussiere
St. Sebastien, PQ
G0Y 1M0 Canada
Phone: 819-652-2361
Fax: 819-652-2360
Internet:
http://www.grani-
decor.com

Graphisoft US
Computer Software
235 Kansas St., Suite 200
San Francisco, CA 94103
Phone: 415-703-9777
1-800-344-3468
Fax: 415-703-9770
Internet:
http://www.graphisoft.com

Grass America
Hardware
PO Box 1019,
1202 Hwy. 66 S.
Kernersville, NC 27284
Phone: 919-996-4041
1-800-334-3512
Fax: 919-996-5149

Great Lake Woods
Engineered Lumber & Panels; Moulding & Millwork
3303 John F. Donnelly Dr.
Holland, MI 49424
Phone: 616-399-3300
Fax: 616-399-3679

Great Lakes Window
Doors; Windows
PO Box 1896
Toledo, OH 43603-1896
Phone: 419-666-5555
1-800-666-0000
Fax: 419-661-2926
Internet:
http://www.greatlakeswind
ow.com

Green Mountain Precision Frames
Structural Systems
PO Box 293
Windsor, VT 05089
Phone: 802-674-6145

Green River
Roofing; Siding & Accessories
33610 E. Broadway Ave.
Mission, BC V2V 4M4
Canada
Phone: 604-826-9531
1-800-663-8707
Fax: 604-820-3871

Green Street Details
Faucets & Fixtures; Hardware
2133 N.W. York
Portland, OR 97210
Phone: 503-222-5537
1-800-275-7855
Fax: 503-222-1034

Greenhart-Durawoods
Flooring; Landscape Design
PO Box 279
Bayville, NJ 08721
Phone: 908-269-6400
1-800-783-7220
Fax: 908-269-9797

Greenwood Cotton Insulation Products
Insulation
70 Mansell Ct., Suite 10
Roswell, GA 30076
Phone: 404-998-6888
1-800-546-1332
Fax: 404-998-3108

Gregg Shakes
Roofing
RR 3
Orillia, ON L3V 6H3
Canada
Phone: 705-325-3405
Fax: 705-325-3020
Internet:
http://www.kadis.com/
gregg/gregghtml

Grill Works
Flooring; HVAC
1609 Halbur Rd.,
PO Box 175
Marshall, MN 56258
Phone: 1-800-347-4745
Fax: 507-532-3526
E-mail:
lyonwood@starpoint.com

Grizzly Imports
Paints, Caulks & Adhesives; Tools/Electric & Pneumatic; Tools/Hand
1821 Valencia St.
Bellingham, WA 98226
Phone: 360-647-0801
1-800-541-5537
1-800-523-4777

GRK Canada
Hardware
1499 Rosslyn Rd., RR 1
Thunder Bay, ON
P7C 4T9 Canada
Phone: 807-475-9601
1-800-263-0463
Fax: 807-475-9625

Groen
(A Dover Industries Co.)
Appliances
1900 Pratt Blvd.
Elk Grove Village, IL
60007-5906
Phone: 847-439-2400
Fax: 847-439-6018

Grohe
(A Sub. of Friedrich Grohe, Germany)
Faucets & Fixtures
241 Covington Dr.
Bloomingdale, IL 60108
Phone: 708-582-7711
Fax: 708-582-7722
Internet:
http://www.grohe.com

Groleau
Engineered Lumber & Panels; Flooring
631 Notre-Dame,
CP 160
Sainte Thecle, PQ
G0X 3G0 Canada
Phone: 418-289-2015
Fax: 418-289-3276

GS Roofing Co.
Roofing
5525 MacArthur Blvd.,
Suite 900
Irving, TX 75038
Phone: 214-580-5600
1-800-666-7005
Fax: 214-580-5692

GSI
(See Heritage Vinyl Products)

GSW Thermoplastics Co.
Siding & Accessories
26 Lorena St.
Barrie, ON L4N 4P4
Canada
Phone: 705-728-7141
Fax: 705-739-0385

GTCO Corp.
Computer Software
7125 Riverwood Dr.
Columbia, MD 21046
Phone: 410-381-6688
Fax: 410-290-9065

Guardian Fiberglass
Insulation
1000 E. North St.
Albion, MI 49224
Phone: 517-629-9464
1-800-748-0035
Fax: 517-629-9535

GUSA/GINGER
Cabinetry; Electrical & Lighting; Faucets & Fixtures; Specialty Products
250-S Executive Dr.
Edgewood, NY 11717
Phone: 516-254-0400
1-800-842-4872
Fax: 516-254-0404

Gutter Armor
Siding & Accessories
2001 First Ave. N.
Fargo, ND 58102
Phone: 701-280-5940
Fax: 701-232-4082

Gypsum Assn.
Walls, Ceilings & Finishes
810 First St., N.E.,
Suite 510
Washington, DC 20002
Phone: 202-289-5440
Fax: 202-289-3707

H

H.B. Ives
Hardware
62 Barnes Park Rd. N.
Wallingford, CT 06492
Phone: 203-294-4837
Fax: 203-284-1460

H Window Co.
Windows
1324 E. Oakwood Dr.
Monticello, MN 55362
Phone: 612-295-5305
1-800-843-4929
Fax: 612-295-4656

HA Stiles Co.
Engineered Lumber & Panels; Moulding & Millwork
170 Forest St.
Westbrook, ME 04092
Phone: 207-854-8458
1-800-447-8537
Fax: 207-854-3863
Internet:
http://www.hastiles.com

Hacker Industries
Engineered Lumber & Panels; Insulation; Specialty Products
610 Newport Center Dr.,
Suite 100
Newport Beach, CA 92660
Phone: 714-645-8891
1-800-642-3455
Fax: 714-645-5144

Hafele America
Electrical & Lighting; Hardware; Moulding & Millwork; Specialty Products
3901 Cheyenne Dr.,
PO Box 4000
Archdale, NC 27263
Phone: 919-889-2322
1-800-334-1873
Fax: 919-431-3831

Hager Hinge Co.
Hardware
139 Victor St.
St. Louis, MO 63104
Phone: 314-772-4400
1-800-325-9995
Fax: 314-772-0744

Halo Lighting
(A Brand of Cooper Lighting)
Electrical & Lighting
400 Busse Rd.
Elk Grove Village, IL
60007
Phone: 708-956-8400
Fax: 708-956-1537

Hamilton Mfg.
Insulation
118 Market St.,
PO Box 1426
Twin Falls, ID 83301
Phone: 208-733-9689
1-800-777-9689
Fax: 208-733-9447

Hamlet & Garneau
HVAC
933 Michelin
Laval, PQ H7L 5B6
Canada
Phone: 514-629-1776
Fax: 514-629-1197

Hanover Lantern Div. of Hoffman Products
Electrical & Lighting; Landscape Design
470 High St.
Hanover, PA 17331
Phone: 717-632-6464
Fax: 717-632-5039

Hansa America
Faucets & Fixtures
931 W. 19th St.
Chicago, IL 60608
Phone: 312-733-0025
1-800-343-4431
Fax: 312-733-4420

Hansgrohe
Faucets & Fixtures
1465 Ventura Dr.
Cumming, GA 30130
Phone: 770-844-7414
1-800-334-0455
Fax: 770-844-0236

Harden Industries
Faucets & Fixtures
13813 S. Main St.
Los Angeles, CA 90061
Phone: 310-532-7850
1-800-877-7850
Fax: 310-532-9699

Hardware Technologies
Hardware
205 E. Blackhawk Dr.,
PO Box 219
Fort Atkinson, WI
53538-0219
Phone: 414-563-2626
Fax: 414-563-4408

Hardwick Post & Beam Corp.
Structural Systems
PO Box 225,
Fleming Rd.
Hardwick, MA 01037
Phone: 413-477-6430
Fax: 413-477-0937

Hardwood Council
PO Box 525
Oakmont, PA 15139-0525
Phone: 412-281-4980
Fax: 412-323-9334

Hardwood Distributors Assn.
Engineered Lumber & Panels; Moulding & Millwork
PO Box 988
North Tonawanda, NY
14120
Phone: 716-694-0562

Hardwood Manufacturers Assn.
Engineered Lumber & Panels; Flooring
400 Penn Center Blvd.,
Suite 530
Pittsburgh, PA 15235
Phone: 412-829-0770
1-800-373-WOOD
Fax: 412-829-0844

Hardwood Plywood & Veneer Assn.
Countertops; Doors; Engineered Lumber & Panels; Flooring; Moulding & Millwork; Walls, Ceilings & Finishes
Box 2789
Reston, VA 20195-0789
Phone: 703-435-2900
Fax: 703-435-2537
E-mail: hpva1@digex.net

Hardwoods Millworking
Engineered Lumber & Panels; Flooring; Moulding & Millwork; Room Enclosures; Walls, Ceilings & Finishes
300 Whites Creek Rd.
Confluence, PA 15424
Phone: 814-395-5474
Fax: 814-395-5474

Hargrove Mfg. Corp.
Fireplaces
207 Wellston Park Rd.
Sand Springs, OK 74063
Phone: 918-241-4166
Fax: 918-241-2212

Harloc
Hardware
501 Railroad St.
Taylorsville, KY 40071
Phone: 502-477-8822
1-800-542-7562
Fax: 502-477-8831

Harmonson Stairs
Moulding & Millwork
823 Eastgate Dr.
Mt. Laurel, NJ 08054
Phone: 609-235-7511
Fax: 609-235-6557

Harney Mfg.
Faucets & Fixtures; Hardware; Specialty Products
9610 Harney Rd.
Thonotosassa, FL 33592
Phone: 813-986-1121
Fax: 813-986-6784

Harrington Brass Works
Faucets & Fixtures
7 Pearl Ct.
Allendale, NJ 07401
Phone: 201-818-1300
Fax: 201-818-0099

Harrington Hoists
Equipment & Trucks
401 W. End Ave.
Manheim, PA 17545
Phone: 717-665-2000
1-800-233-3010
Fax: 717-665-2861
Internet:
http://www.industry.net/
harrington

Harris Specialty Chemicals (Formerly Hydrozo Thoro, Watson Bowman Acme, Selby)
Paints, Caulks & Adhesives; Siding & Accessories; Specialty Products; Structural Systems
10245 Centurion Pkwy. N.
Jacksonville, FL 32256
Phone: 904-996-6000
Fax: 904-996-6300

Harris-Tarkett
Flooring
PO Box 300,
2225 Eddie Williams Rd.
Johnson City, TN
37605-0300
Phone: 423-928-3122
1-800-842-7816
Fax: 423-928-9445

Harry Wolsky Stairbuilders
Moulding & Millwork
PO Box 421,
2280 Grand Ave.
Baldwin, Long Island, NY
11510
Phone: 516-868-2540
1-800-432-2540
Fax: 516-868-2546

Hart & Cooley
Fireplaces; HVAC
500 E. 8th St.
Holland, MI 49423
Phone: 616-392-7855
Fax: 1-800-223-8461

Hartco
Flooring
900 S. Gay, Suite 2102
Knoxville, TN 37902
Phone: 615-544-0767
1-800-4-HARTCO
Fax: 615-544-2071

Harter Industries
HVAC
PO Box 502
Holmdel, NJ 07733
Phone: 908-566-7055
1-800-566-7770
Fax: 908-566-6977
E-mail: harter101@aol.com

Hartford Conservatories
Room Enclosures
96A Commerce Way
Woburn, MA 01801
Phone: 617-937-9050
1-800-963-8700
Fax: 617-937-9025
Internet:
http://www.hartford-con.
com

Hartson-Kennedy Cabinet Top Co.
Countertops
PO Box 3095,
522 W. 22nd St.
Marion, IN 46953
Phone: 317-668-8144
1-800-388-8144
Fax: 317-662-3452

Harvey Industries
Doors; Insulation; Roofing; Room Enclosures; Siding & Accessories
43 Emerson Rd.
Waltham, MA 02154
Phone: 617-899-3500
1-800-225-5724
Fax: 617-398-7715

Harvey Universal (Environmental Products Group)
Paints, Caulks & Adhesives
1805 W. 208 St.
Torrance, CA 90501
Phone: 310-328-9000
1-800-1-800-3330
Fax: 310-328-9100

Hastings Tile & Il Bagno Collection
Faucets & Fixtures; Flooring
30 Commercial St.
Freeport, NY 11520
Phone: 516-379-3500
Fax: 516-379-3187

HB Fuller
(See TEC)

HB & G
Moulding & Millwork; Specialty Products
PO Box 589
Troy, AL 36081
Phone: 334-566-5000
1-800-264-4HBG
Fax: 334-566-4629
Internet:
http://www.builderonline.com/sponsors/hb&g

H & C Concrete Stain
Paints, Caulks & Adhesives
101 Prospect Ave., N.W.
Cleveland, OH 44115
Phone: 216-566-2000
1-800-TO-STAIN
Fax: 216-566-1832

HDI
Hardware
342 Main St.
Danbury, CT 06810
Phone: 203-743-5161
1-800-431-1904
Fax: 203-797-1528
Internet:
http://www.drawerslides.com

Health-Mor
Specialty Products
3500 Payne Ave.
Cleveland, OH 44114
Phone: 216-432-1990
1-800-344-1840
Fax: 216-432-0013

Hearth Kitchens
Cabinetry; Countertops
711 10th Ave.
Hanover, ON N4N 2P7
Canada
Phone: 519-364-1170
1-800-267-4524
Fax: 1-800-267-0058

Hearth Products Assn.
Fireplaces
1601 N. Kent St.,
Suite 1001
Arlington, VA 22209
Phone: 703-522-0086
Fax: 703-522-0548
Internet:
http://www.hearthassoc.org

Heartland Appliances
Appliances
5 Hoffman St.
Kitchener, ON
N2M 3M5 Canada
Phone: 519-743-8111
1-800-361-1517
Fax: 519-743-1665
Internet:
http://www.heartlandapp.com

Heartland Building Products
Siding & Accessories
300 Park Pl.
Booneville, MS 38829
Phone: 601-728-6261
1-800-HEART-01
Fax: 601-728-0176
Internet: http://www.heart-land.com

Heat Controller
HVAC
1900 Wellworth Ave.,
PO Box 1089
Jackson, MI 49204
Phone: 517-787-2100
Fax: 517-787-9341

Heat-N-Glo Fireplace Products
Fireplaces
6665 W. Hwy. 13
Savage, MN 55378
Phone: 612-890-8367
1-800-669-HEAT
Fax: 612-890-3525
Internet:
http://www.heatnglo.com

Heath Co.
Home Technology
455 Riverview Dr.,
PO Box 1288
Benton Harbor, MI
94023-1288
Phone: 616-925-6000
Fax: 616-925-5990

Heatilator
Fireplaces
1915 W. Saunders St.
Mt. Pleasant, IA 52641
Phone: 319-385-9211
1-800-843-2848
Fax: 1-800-248-2038

Heatmaster Gas Logs
Fireplaces
Rt. 2, Box 48, PO Box J
Angier, NC 27501
Phone: 919-639-4568
1-800-334-0258
Fax: 919-639-0101

Heatway
HVAC
3131 W. Chestnut Expwy.
Springfield, MO 65802
Phone: 417-864-6108
1-800-255-1996
Fax: 417-864-8161
Internet:
http://www.heatway.com

Hebel Southeast
Structural Systems
3340 Peachtree Rd., N.E.,
Suite 150
Atlanta, GA 30326
Phone: 404-812-7400
1-800-994-3235
Fax: 404-812-7401

Heil Heating & Cooling Products Inter-City Products Corp. (USA)
HVAC
650 Heil-Quaker Ave.
Lewisburg, TN 37091
Phone: 615-359-3511
Fax: 615-270-4166
Internet: http://www.heil-hvac.com/heil

Heliodyne
HVAC
4910 Seaport Ave.
Richmond, CA 94804
Phone: 510-237-9614
Fax: 510-237-7018

Hempe Mfg. Co.
Tools/Hand
2750 S. 163rd St.
New Berlin, WI 53151
Phone: 414-784-2710

Henderson, Black & Greene
(See HB & G)

Heritage Custom Kitchens
Cabinetry
215 Diller Ave.
New Holland, PA 17557
Phone: 717-354-4011
Fax: 717-354-4487

Heritage Finishes
Cabinetry; Engineered Lumber & Panels
131 Mineola Rd. W.
Mississauga, ON
L5G 2C4 Canada
Phone: 905-271-9176
Fax: 905-271-4263

Heritage Stair Co.
Moulding & Millwork
4852 Maple Grove Rd. S.E.
Uhrichsville, OH 44683
Phone: 614-922-3816
Fax: 614-922-0072

Heritage Veneered Products
Doors
1275 Industrial Dr.
Shawano, WI 54166
Phone: 715-526-2146
Fax: 715-526-3226

Heritage Vinyl Products
Landscape Design
Hwy. 45 Bypass,
PO Box 460
Macon, MS 39341
Phone: 601-726-4223
1-800-736-5143
E-mail: SFullen@Aol.com

Herrco Enterprises
Faucets & Fixtures; Specialty Products
1219B Greenwood Rd.
Baltimore, MD 21208
Phone: 410-486-7274
1-800-522-3678
Fax: 410-486-9091

The Hess Mfg. Co.
Doors; Hardware; Roofing; Room Enclosures; Windows
PO Box 127
Quincy, PA 17247-0127
Phone: 717-749-3141
1-800-541-6666
1-800-321-4377
Fax: 717-749-3712

Hi Pro Intl.
Windows
5049 S. National Dr.
Knoxville, TN 37914
Phone: 423-637-1711
1-800-947-0997
Fax: 423-546-9546
Internet:
http://www.hiprointl.com

Hicks Waterstoves & Solar Systems
Fireplaces
2541 S. Main St.
Mt. Airy, NC 27030
Phone: 919-789-4977
Fax: 919-789-9451

Higgins Brick Co.
1845 S. Elena Ave.
Redondo Beach, CA 90277
Phone: 213-772-2813
Fax: 310-540-0619

Highland Lumber Co.
Engineered Lumber & Panels; Siding & Accessories
34 Pine St., PO Box 650
Dixfield, ME 04224
Phone: 207-562-7277
Fax: 207-562-8141

Hilti
Hardware; Paints, Caulks & Adhesives; Tools/Electric & Pneumatic
5400 S. 122nd E Ave.
Tulsa, OK 74146
Phone: 918-252-6000
1-800-879-1-8000
Fax: 1-800-879-7000

Hindley Mfg. Co.
Faucets & Fixtures; Hardware; Plumbing Supplies
9 Havens St.
Cumberland, RI 02864
Phone: 401-722-2550
1-800-323-9031
Fax: 401-722-3083
Internet:
http://www.hindley.com

Hitachi Koki USA
Hardware; Tools/Electric & Pneumatic
3950 Steve Reynolds Blvd.
Norcross, GA 30093
Phone: 770-925-1774
1-800-706-7337
Fax: 770-564-7003

HL Stud Corp. The Carpenter's Steel Stud/Joist
Structural Systems
2000 W. Henderson Rd.,
Suite 60
Columbus, OH 43220
Phone: 614-451-8100
1-800-HLSTUDS
Fax: 614-451-6621

HMS Computer Co.
Computer Software
3422 Lakeshore Cove
Chaska, MN 55318
Phone: 612-368-7512

Hodge Mfg. Co.
Equipment & Trucks; Tools/Hand
55 Fisk Ave.
Springfield, MA 01107-1072
Phone: 413-781-6800
1-800-262-4634
Fax: 413-733-6573

Hoglund Landscape Construction
Electrical & Lighting; Landscape Design
118 Broadway, Black
Bldg., Suite 510
Fargo, ND 58102
Phone: 701-280-3149
1-800-882-8112
Fax: 701-232-9368
Internet:
http://www.specialized-ad.com/hlc\index.htm

Holdrite Brackets
HVAC; Plumbing Supplies; Structural Systems
393 Enterprise St.
San Marcos, CA 92069
Phone: 619-744-6944
1-800-321-0316
Fax: 619-744-0507

Holiday Kitchens (A Div. of Mastercraft Industries)
Cabinetry; Moulding & Millwork
120 W. Allen St.
Rice Lake, WI 54868
Phone: 715-234-8111
Fax: 715-234-6370

Holland Log Homes Mfg. Co.
Doors; Flooring; Moulding & Millwork; Room Enclosures; Siding & Accessories; Structural Systems; Walls, Ceilings & Finishes
13352 Van Buren St.
Holland, MI 49424
Phone: 616-399-9627
Fax: 616-399-8530

Holland Mfg. Co.
Hardware
PO Box 38179
Baltimore, MD 21231
Phone: 410-732-4455
Fax: 410-732-4331

Holm Industries Jarrow Div.
Insulation
315 N. Ninth St.
Saint Charles, IL 60174
Phone: 1-800-221-2205
Fax: 312-525-2166

Holmes Garage Door
Garage Doors & Openers
2601 W. Valley Hwy. N.,
PO Box 1976
Auburn, WA 98071-1976
Phone: 206-931-8900
Fax: 206-939-8508

Holophane Lighting Co.
Electrical & Lighting
250 E. Broad St.,
Suite 1400
Columbus, OH 43215
Phone: 614-345-9631
Fax: 614-349-4426

Homasote Co.
Engineered Lumber & Panels; Insulation
PO Box 7240
West Trenton, NJ
08628-0240
Phone: 609-883-3300
1-800-257-9491
Fax: 609-530-1584

Home Automated Living
Home Technology
14311 Old Columbia Pike
Burtonsville, MD 20866
Phone: 301-879-2305
1-800-935-5313
Fax: 301-384-8275
Internet: http://www.automatedliving.com

Home Automation
Electrical & Lighting; HVAC; Home Technology
2709 Ridgelake Dr.
Metairie, LA 70002
Phone: 504-833-7256
Fax: 504-833-7258

Home Automation Assn.
HVAC; Home Technology
808 17th St., N.W.,
Suite 200
Washington, DC 20006
Phone: 202-223-9669
Fax: 202-223-9569
Internet:
http://www.hometeam.com/HAA

Home Crest Corp.
Cabinetry; Hardware
1002 Eisenhower Dr. N.,
PO Box 595
Goshen, IN 46526
Phone: 219-533-9571
Fax: 1-800-737-1500
Internet:
http://www.homecrestcab.com

Home Pro Systems
Computer Software
2841 Hartland Rd.,
Suite 201
Falls Church, VA 22043
Phone: 703-560-4663
Fax: 703-560-6121

Home Ventilating Institute (A Div. of AMCA Intl.)
Appliances; HVAC
30 W. University Dr.
Arlington Heights, IL
60004-1893
Phone: 847-394-0150
Fax: 847-253-0088

Homer Wood Corp.
Engineered Lumber & Panels; Flooring; Moulding & Millwork
1026 Industrial Dr.
Titusville, PA 16354
Phone: 814-827-3855
Fax: 814-827-3629

Homeshield Fabricated Products
Doors; Roofing; Siding & Accessories; Windows
525 Dunham Rd.,
Suite 60
St. Charles, IL 60174
Phone: 630-513-4100
1-800-323-2510
Fax: 630-513-5788

HomeTech Information Systems
Computer Software
5161 River Rd.
Bethesda, MD 20816
Phone: 301-654-8380
1-800-638-8292
Fax: 301-654-0073

Honda
(See American Honda
Motor Co.)

Honest Abe Log Homes
Structural Systems
3855 Clay County Hwy.
Moss, TN 38575
Phone: 615-258-3648
1-800-231-3695
Fax: 615-258-3397

Honeywell Home & Building Control
Appliances; Electrical & Lighting; HVAC; Home Technology; Specialty Products
1985 Douglas Dr. N.
Minneapolis, MN 55422
Phone: 1-800-345-6770,
ext. 2033
Fax: 612-951-2086

The Hoover Co.
101 E. Maple St.
North Canton, OH
44720
Phone: 216-499-9200
Fax: 216-497-5808

Horizons Software Quick Frame Systems
Computer Software
1228 Starfish Ct.
Fairfield, CA 94533-7073
Phone: 707-421-9004
1-800-479-9004
Fax: 707-429-4706
E-mail: Koten@aol.com

Horner Flooring Co.
Engineered Lumber & Panels; Flooring
PO Box 380
Dollar Bay, MI 49922
Phone: 906-482-1180
Fax: 906-482-6115

Horton Automatics
Doors
4242 Baldwin Blvd.
Corpus Christi, TX 78405
Phone: 512-888-5591
1-800-531-3111
Fax: 512-888-6510

Hotpoint Appliances
Appliances
Appliance Park
Louisville, KY 40225
Phone: 502-452-4311
1-800-626-2000

House of Ceramics
Faucets & Fixtures; Flooring; Walls, Ceilings & Finishes
17 Putnam Ave.
Port Chester, NY 10573
Phone: 914-937-0833
Fax: 914-937-1964

Houses & Barns by John Libby Barn Masters
Room Enclosures; Specialty Products; Structural Systems; Tools/Electric & Pneumatic
PO Box 258H
Freeport, ME 04032
Phone: 207-865-4169
1-800-869-4169
Fax: 207-865-6169

Houston Woodtech
Engineered Lumber & Panels
12229 Almeda Rd.
Houston, TX 77045
Phone: 713-433-2433
1-800-392-1612
Fax: 713-433-2472

Hoyme Mfg.
Hardware; HVAC; Plumbing Supplies
3843 44 Ave.
Camrose, AB T4V 3T1
Canada
Phone: 403-672-6553
1-800-661-7382
Fax: 1-800-661-8065

Hubbell Lighting
Electrical & Lighting
2000 Electric Way
Christiansburg, VA
24073-2500
Phone: 540-382-6111
Fax: 540-382-1526

Huebert Fiberboard Co.
Engineered Lumber & Panels; Roofing
1545 E. Morgan St.,
PO Box 167
Boonville, MO 65233
Phone: 816-882-2704
Fax: 816-882-7991

Huey Millwork Co.
Engineered Lumber & Panels
PO Box 248
Obion, TN 38240
Phone: 901-536-6265
Fax: 901-536-5818

Hugh Lofting Timber Framing
Structural Systems
339 Lamborntown Rd.
West Grove, PA 19390
Phone: 610-444-5382
Fax: 610-869-5382
E-mail: hlofting@aol.com

Hunt Plywood Co.
Engineered Lumber & Panels
PO Box 1263
Ruston, LA 71273
Phone: 318-255-1130
Fax: 318-255-4048

Hunter Douglas Architectural Products
Walls, Ceilings & Finishes
11455 Lakefield Dr.
Duluth, GA 30136
Phone: 404-476-8803
1-800-366-4327
Fax: 404-476-5716

Hunter Energy And Technologies
Fireplaces; HVAC
PO Box 400
Orillia, ON L3V 6K1
Canada
Phone: 705-325-6111
Fax: 705-327-5658

Hunter Fan Co.
Electrical & Lighting; HVAC
2500 Frisco Ave.
Memphis, TN 38114
Phone: 901-743-1360
Fax: 901-745-9385

Huntsville Wood Products
Engineered Lumber & Panels
109 Wholesale Ave.,
PO Box 3267
Huntsville, AL 35810
Phone: 205-533-9220
Fax: 205-536-9044

Huntwood Industries
Cabinetry; Engineered Lumber & Panels; Hardware
Spokane Industrial Park,
Bldg. 26
Spokane, WA 99216
Phone: 509-924-5858
Fax: 509-928-6647

Hurd Millwork Co.
Doors; Windows
575 S. Whelen Ave.
Medford, WI 54451
Phone: 715-748-2011
1-800-433-4873
Fax: 715-748-6043
Internet:
http://www.hurd.com

Husky Panel Systems
Structural Systems
5781 Berquist Rd.
Duluth, MN 55804-9666
Phone: 218-525-2981
Fax: 218-525-2982

Hy-Lite Block Windows
Windows
101 California Ave.
Beaumont, CA 92223
Phone: 909-769-8700
1-800-827-3691
Fax: 1-800-827-4920
Internet: http://www.
hy-lite.com

Hyde & Meeks Industries
Paints, Caulks & Adhesives; Walls, Ceilings & Finishes
556 Trapelo Rd.
Belmont, MA 02178
Phone: 617-489-1590
1-800-425-9116
Fax: 617-489-3484

Hyde Mfg.
Paints, Caulks & Adhesives
54 Eastford Rd.
Southbridge, MA 01550
Phone: 1-800-USA-HYDE

Hyde Park Fine Art of Moulding
Moulding & Millwork; Walls, Ceilings & Finishes
29-16 40th Ave.
Long Island City, NY
11101
Phone: 718-706-0504
Fax: 718-706-0507

Hydro Systems
Faucets & Fixtures
50 Moreland Rd.
Simi Valley, CA 93065
Phone: 805-584-9990
Fax: 805-584-8125

Hydronics Institute (A Div. of GAMA)
HVAC
35 Russo Pl., PO Box 218
Berkeley Heights, NJ
07922
Phone: 908-464-8200
Fax: 908-464-7818

Hydrozo
(See Harris Specialty
Chemicals)

Hyster Co.
Equipment & Trucks
PO Box 847
Danville, IL 61834-0847
Phone: 217-446-4888
1-800-HYSTER1
Fax: 217-443-7494
Internet:
http://www.hyster.industry.
net

I

I-XL Industries
Fireplaces; Landscape Design; Siding & Accessories; Structural Systems
PO Box 70
Medicine Hat, AB
T1A 7E7 Canada
Phone: 403-526-5901
Fax: 403-526-7680
Internet:
http://www.ixlbrick.com

ICE Block Building Systems
Insulation; Structural Systems
570 S. Dayton Lakeview
New Carlisle, OH 45344
Phone: 513-845-8347
1-800-423-2557
Fax: 513-845-9837

ICI Paint Stores
Paints, Caulks & Adhesives
925 Euclid Ave.
Cleveland, OH 44115
Phone: 216-344-8491
1-800-984-5444
Fax: 216-344-8883

ICYNENE
Insulation
376 Watline Ave.
Mississauga, ON
L4Z 1X2 Canada
Phone: 905-890-7325
1-800-758-7325
Fax: 905-890-7784
Internet:
http://www.icynene.on.ca

Idaho Forest Industries
Engineered Lumber & Panels
2850 W. Seltice Way,
PO Box 6600
Coeur d'Alene, ID
83816-1933
Phone: 208-765-1414
Fax: 208-765-5045

Idaho Wood
Electrical & Lighting; Landscape Design
PO Box 488
Sandpoint, ID 83864
Phone: 208-263-9521
1-800-635-1100
Fax: 208-263-3102

Ideal Door
Garage Doors & Openers; Hardware
Hwy. 12 E.
PO Box 106
Baldwin, WI 54002
Phone: 715-684-3223
1-800-621-3667
Fax: 715-684-2247

Ideal Wood Products
Moulding & Millwork
225 W. Main St.
Little Falls, NY 13365
Phone: 315-823-1124
Fax: 315-823-1127

IEA Intl.
Cabinetry; Countertops; Flooring
5 Hunter Dr.
Armonk, NY 10504
Phone: 914-273-4142
Fax: 914-273-4131

IKO Mfg.
Roofing
120 Hay Rd.
Wilmington, DE 19809
Phone: 302-764-3100
1-800-441-7296
Fax: 302-764-5857

Illbruck
Paints, Caulks & Adhesives; Walls, Ceilings & Finishes
3800 Washington Ave. N.
Minneapolis, MN 55412
Phone: 1-800-662-0032
Fax: 612-521-3555

Image Carpets
Flooring
PO Box 5555
Armuchee, GA 30105
Phone: 706-235-8444
1-800-722-2504
Fax: 706-235-0386

Imagetects
Computer Software
7 W. 41st Ave., Suite 415
San Mateo, CA 94403
Phone: 408-252-5487
Fax: 415-508-8763
Internet:
http://www.imagecels.com

Imperial Cabinet Co.
Cabinetry
300 Imperial Pl.
Gaston, IN 47342
Phone: 317-358-3301
Fax: 317-358-4357

Imperial Cal Products
Appliances
17421 Daimler St.
Irvine, CA 92714
Phone: 714-757-4663
Fax: 714-757-1510

Imperial Range Hoods
Appliances
17421 Daimler St.
Irvine, CA 92714
Phone: 714-757-4663
Fax: 714-757-1510

IMPO Glaztile
Countertops; Flooring
18500 N. Creek Dr.
Tinley Park, IL 60477
Phone: 708-633-1616
Fax: 708-633-8797

In Cide Technologies
Insulation; Paints, Caulks & Adhesives; Structural Systems
50 N. 41st Ave.
Phoenix, AZ 85009
Phone: 602-233-0756
1-800-777-4569
Fax: 602-272-4864

In-Sink-Erator Div. Emerson Electronic Co.
Appliances
4700 21st St.
Racine, WI 53406-5093
Phone: 414-554-5432
1-800-558-5712
Fax: 414-554-3530

Inclinator Co. of America
Specialty Products
PO Box 1557
Harrisburg, PA 17105
Phone: 717-234-8065
Fax: 717-234-0941

Increte Systems (A Div. of Inco Chemical Co.)
Paints; Caulks & Adhesives; Specialty Products
8509 Sunstate St.
Tampa, FL 33634
Phone: 813-886-8811
1-800-752-INCO
Fax: 813-886-0188

Indco
Tools/Electric & Pneumatic
4040 Earnings Way
New Albany, IN 47150
Phone: 812-945-4383
1-800-942-4383
Fax: 1-800-942-9742

Inde-Pane
Doors; Windows
11825 JJ Joubert
Montreal, PQ H1E 7E7
Canada
Phone: 514-494-1575
1-800-567-4633
Fax: 514-494-7191

Independent Nail Co.
Hardware
30 Mozzone Blvd.
Taunton, MA 02780
Phone: 508-880-7202
1-800-443-1966
Fax: 508-880-7511

Indiana Brass
Faucets & Fixtures
800 W. Clinton St.
Frankfort, IN 46041
Phone: 317-659-3341
1-800-428-4030
Fax: 1-800-659-6034

Industrial Energy Products
Engineered Lumber & Panels; Insulation
PO Box 371
Wood Ridge, NJ 07075
Phone: 201-939-6647
Fax: 201-933-1305

Industries Trovac
Specialty Products
3220 Autoroute Laval O
Chomedey, Laval, PQ
H7T 2H6 Canada
Phone: 514-687-8700
1-800-361-9553
Fax: 514-681-0690

Industry Specific Software
Computer Software
1200 Woodruff Rd.,
Suite B-20
Greenville, SC 29607
Phone: 864-297-7086
1-800-877-2496
Fax: 864-297-7833
E-mail:
issoftware@aol.com

Infiltrator Systems
Landscape Design
4 Business Park Rd.,
PO Box 768
Old Saybrook, CT 06475
Phone: 203-388-6639
Fax: 203-388-6810

Ingersoll-Rand Co. Tool & Hoist Div.
Tools/Electric & Pneumatic
PO Box 1776
Liberty Corner, NJ 07938
Phone: 908-647-6000
Fax: 908-647-6007

Inline Fiberglass
Doors; Windows
30 Constellation Ct.
Etobicoke, ON
M4W 1K1
Canada
Phone: 416-679-1171
Internet:
http://www.inlinefiber
glass.com

Innovative Insulation
Insulation; Specialty Products
6200 W. Pioneer Pkwy.
Arlington, TX 76013
Phone: 817-446-6200
1-800-825-0123
Fax: 817-446-6222

Inova
Faucets & Fixtures; Moulding & Millwork
9 Mars Ct.,
PO Box 840
Montville, NJ 07045
Phone: 201-316-5700
1-800-544-6682
Fax: 201-316-0122

Insta-Foam Products
Insulation; Paints, Caulks & Adhesives
1500 Cedarwood Dr.
Joliet, IL 60435
Phone: 815-741-6800
1-800-1-800-FOAM
Fax: 815-741-6822
Internet: http://www.
flexibleproducts.com

Insteel Construction Systems
Structural Systems
2610 Sidney Lanier Dr.
Brunswick, GA 31525
Phone: 912-264-3772
Fax: 912-264-3774

Insteel Wire Products
Hardware
1373 Boggs Dr.
Mt. Airy, NC 27030
Phone: 919-789-7670
1-800-247-5902
Fax: 919-789-8634

Insul-Binder
Insulation; Paints, Caulks & Adhesives; Roofing; Tools/Electric & Pneumatic
2190 S. Kalamath
Denver, CO 80223
Phone: 303-934-7772
1-800-525-8992
Fax: 303-934-5240

Insul-Tray
Roofing; Specialty Products
E. 1881 Crestview Dr.
Shelton, WA 98584-9082
Phone: 360-427-5930
1-800-221-3359
Fax: 360-427-5930

Insuladome Skylights
Windows
83 Horseblock Rd.
Yaphank, NY 11980
Phone: 516-924-7890
1-800-551-4SUN
Fax: 516-924-7870

Insulate Industries
Doors; Windows
5001 D St. N.W.
Auburn, WA 98001
Phone: 206-850-9000
1-800-227-3699
Fax: 1-800-645-6253

Insulated Building Systems
Engineered Lumber & Panels; Insulation; Specialty Products; Structural Systems
22377 Cedar Green Rd.,
Suite 2B
Dulles, VA 20166
Phone: 703-450-4886
Fax: 703-450-6642

Insulated Steel Door Institute
Doors
30200 Detroit Rd.
Cleveland, OH 44145
Phone: 216-899-0010
Fax: 216-892-1404

Insulspan
Structural Systems
PO Box 120427
Nashville, TN 37212
Phone: 1-800-726-3510

Intelecom Products
Home Technology
6488 Avondale Dr.
Suite 125
Oklahoma City, OK
73116
Phone: 405-842-0163
Fax: 405-842-0162

Intelectron
Electrical & Lighting
21021 Corsair Blvd.
Hayward, CA 94545-1301
Phone: 510-732-6790
Fax: 510-732-6910

IntelliNet
Electrical & Lighting; HVAC; Home Technology
2900 Horseshoe Dr. S.
Naples, FL 34104
Phone: 941-434-5888
1-800-899-1372
Fax: 941-434-8429
E-mail:
intellinet@worldnet.att.net

Interceramic, USA
Flooring; Walls, Ceilings & Finishes
2333 S. Jupiter Rd.
Garland, TX 75041
Phone: 214-503-5500
1-800-496-8453
Fax: 214-503-5575
Internet:
http://www.interceramicusa.
com

Interchange Brands
Hardware; Paints, Caulks & Adhesives; Specialty Products; Tools/Electric & Pneumatic; Tools/Hand
PO Box 3543
Omaha, NE 68103
Phone: 402-339-4100
1-800-458-6635
Fax: 402-593-5370

International Cellulose Corp.
Insulation; Walls, Ceilings & Finishes
PO Box 450006
Houston, TX 77245
Phone: 713-433-6701
1-800-444-1252
Internet:
http://www.spray-on.com

International Energy Systems
Appliances; Electrical & Lighting; HVAC; Home Technology
PO Box 588
Barrington, IL 60011
Phone: 708-381-0203
1-800-927-0419
Fax: 708-381-3997

International Extrusions (A Div. of The Noecker Group)
Doors; Room Enclosures
5800 Venoy
Garden City, MI 48135
Phone: 313-427-8700
Fax: 313-427-8219

International Hardwood Flooring
Flooring
1818 Bannard St.
Cinnaminson, NJ 08077
Phone: 609-786-8884
Fax: 609-786-2510

International Homes of Cedar
Structural Systems
PO Box 886
Woodinville, WA 98072
Phone: 1-800-767-7674
Fax: 206-668-5562

International Institute for Lath and Plaster
Siding & Accessories; Walls, Ceilings & Finishes
820 Transfer Rd.
St. Paul, MN 55114-1406
Phone: 612-645-0208
Fax: 612-645-0209

International Paper Co.
Countertops; Doors; Engineered Lumber & Panels; Faucets & Fixtures; Flooring; Garage Doors & Openers; Moulding & Millwork; Siding & Accessories
2 Manhattanville Rd.
Purchase, NY 10577
Phone: 914-397-1500
1-800-223-1268
Fax: 914-397-1650
Internet:
http://www.ipaper.com

International Staple & Machine Co. (A Div. of Atro)
Hardware; Tools/Electric & Pneumatic; Tools/Hand
629 E. Butler Rd.
Butler, PA 16001
Phone: 412-287-7711
Fax: 412-287-2811

International Staple, Nail and Tool Assn.
Tools/Electric & Pneumatic
512 W. Burlington Ave.,
Suite 203
LaGrange, IL 60525-2245
Phone: 708-482-8138
Fax: 708-482-8186

International Tool Boxes
Tools/Hand
1175 Frontenac Rd.
Naperville, IL 60563
Phone: 630-778-8934
1-800-348-5854
Fax: 630-778-8846

International Wood Products (A Div. of JELD-WEN)
Doors
7312 Convoy Ct.
San Diego, CA 92111
Phone: 1-800-877-9482

International Wood Products Assn.
Cabinetry; Countertops; Doors; Engineered Lumber & Panels; Flooring; Moulding & Millwork
4214 King St., W.
Alexandria, VA 22302
Phone: 703-820-6696
Fax: 703-820-8550
Internet:
http://www.ihpa.org

Interplan Group/ Classic Doors
Doors
9440 Old Katy Rd.,
Suite 100
Houston, TX 77055
Phone: 713-497-8899
1-800-610-DOOR
Fax: 713-497-5227

Intersoft Systems
Computer Software
PO Box 2200, 10550
S.W. Allen Blvd., Suite 114
Beaverton, OR 97075
Phone: 503-644-3761
1-800-547-6429
Fax: 503-626-7435

Intertherm Heating & Air Care Products
(See Nordyne)

IRON-A-WAY
Cabinetry; Specialty Products
220 W. Jackson
Morton, IL 61550-1588
Phone: 309-266-7232
Fax: 309-266-5088

The Iron Shop
Moulding & Millwork
PO Box 547, 400 Reed Rd.
Broomall, PA 19008
Phone: 610-544-7100
1-800-523-7427
Fax: 610-544-7297
Internet:
http://www.theironshop.com

Irpina Kitchens
Cabinetry
114 Peelar Rd.
Concord, ON L4K 2C9
Canada
Phone: 905-738-4554
Fax: 905-738-4512

Isokern Fireplaces/ Earthcore Industries
Fireplaces; Landscape Design; Structural Systems
8917 Western Hwy.,
Suite 120
Jacksonville, FL 32256
Phone: 904-363-3417
1-800-642-2920
Fax: 904-363-3408

ISTA Energy Systems Corp.
HVAC
415 Hope Ave., PO Box 618
Roselle, NJ 07203
Phone: 908-241-8880
Fax: 908-241-7288

Isuzu Truck of America Commercial Vehicle Div.
Equipment & Trucks
2300 Pellissier Pl.
Whittier, CA 90601
Phone: 310-699-0500
Fax: 310-908-0346
Internet:
http://www.isuzu.com

Italbrass Corp.
Faucets & Fixtures; Hardware
21 Lime St.
Marblehead, MA 01945
Phone: 617-639-1992
1-800-345-ITAL
Fax: 617-639-2458

ITALGRANITI/ Marketing & Trading Co.
Flooring
650 Dundee Rd.,
Suite 275
Northbrook, IL 60062
Phone: 708-480-7407
Fax: 708-480-7417

Italian Marble Center Div. of Italian Trade Commission
Flooring; Walls, Ceilings & Finishes
1801 Ave. of the Stars,
Suite 700
Los Angeles, CA 90067
Phone: 213-879-0950
Fax: 310-203-8335

Italian Tile Assn.
Countertops; Flooring; Walls, Ceilings & Finishes
305 Madison Ave.,
Suite 3120
New York, NY 10165
Phone: 212-661-0435
Fax: 212-949-8192

Italian Trade Commission, Tile Center
Flooring; Walls, Ceilings & Finishes
499 Park Ave., Sixth Fl.
New York, NY 10022
Phone: 212-980-1500
Fax: 212-758-1050

ITW Buildex
Hardware; Roofing
1349 W. Bryn Mawr Ave.
Itasca, IL 60143
Phone: 708-595-3500
1-800-323-0720

ITW Ramset/Red Head
Hardware
1300 N. Michael Dr.
Wood Dale, IL 60191
Phone: 630-350-0370
1-800-348-3231
Fax: 630-350-7985

J

J A W Window & Door
Doors; Windows
PO Box 72
St. Francois Xavier, MB
R0H 1J0 Canada
Phone: 204-864-2094
Fax: 204-864-2203

J-Deck Building Systems
Structural Systems
2587 Harrison Rd.
Columbus, OH 43204
Phone: 614-274-7755
1-614-274-7797

JA Nearing Co.
Room Enclosures
9390 Davis Ave.
Laurel, MD 20723
Phone: 301-498-5700
1-800-323-6933
Fax: 301-497-9751

Jackson Sawmill Co.
Flooring; Siding & Accessories; Walls, Ceilings & Finishes
PO Box 368
Jackson, AL 36545
Phone: 205-246-2424
Fax: 205-246-9692

Jacuzzi Whirlpool Bath
Faucets & Fixtures
PO Drawer J, 2121 N.
California Blvd., Suite 475
Walnut Creek, CA 94596
Phone: 510-938-7070
1-800-678-6889
Fax: 510-938-3025

**Jado Bathroom &
Hardware Mfg. Corp.**
*Faucets & Fixtures;
Hardware*
PO Box 1329,
4690 Calle Quetzal
Camarillo, CA 93012
Phone: 805-482-2666
Fax: 805-484-4799

**James Hardie Building
Products**
*Roofing; Siding &
Accessories; Walls, Ceilings
& Finishes*
26300 La Alameda,
Suite 250
Mission Viejo, CA 92691
Phone: 1-800-9-HARDIE
Fax: 714-367-0185

James Hardie Gypsum
Walls, Ceilings & Finishes
12720 Gateway Dr.,
Gateway Corp Ctr.,
Bldg. 7, Suite 208
Seattle, WA 98168
Phone: 206-246-3814
Fax: 206-246-3441

Jamo
*Flooring; Structural
Systems; Walls, Ceilings
& Finishes*
8850 N.W. 79th Ave.
Miami, FL 33166
Phone: 305-885-3444
1-800-826-6852
Fax: 305-883-5591
Internet:
http://www.jamoinc.com

Jancik Arts
Windows
2630 S.W. 87th Pl.
Ocala, FL 34476
Phone: 904-237-1593

**Jason Industrial Rubber
Flooring Div.**
Flooring
340 Kaplan Dr.
Fairfield, NJ 07004-2511
Phone: 201-227-4904
Fax: 201-227-1651

Jason Intl.
Faucets & Fixtures
8328 MacArthur Dr.
North Little Rock, AR
72118
Phone: 501-771-4477
1-800-255-5766
Fax: 501-771-2333
Internet:
http://www.jasonint.com

**JBL Home
Entertainment**
Home Technology
20630 Nordhoff St.
Chatsworth, CA 91311
Phone: 818-734-1377
1-800-377-4073
Fax: 818-709-6743

JD's Glassworks
*Doors; Moulding &
Millwork; Windows*
2100 Barrett Park Dr.
N.W., Suite 501
Kennesaw, GA 30144
Phone: 770-514-8979
Fax: 770-425-0763

**JELD-WEN Fiber of
Iowa
(Elite Doors)**
Doors
250 E. Eighth St.
Dubuque, IA 52001-7049
Phone: 1-800-877-9482

JELD-WEN of Oregon
Windows
PO Box 1329
Klamath Falls, OR
97601-0268
Phone: 503-882-3451
Fax: 503-885-7406

**JELD-WEN of White
Swan**
Moulding & Millwork
3590 Wesley Rd.,
PO Box 548
White Swan, WA 98952
Phone: 509-874-2777

**Jenkins Mfg./
Monarch Windows**
Doors; Windows
PO Box 249
Anniston, AL 36202
Phone: 205-831-7000
1-800-633-2323
Fax: 1-800-261-6116

Jenn-Air
Appliances
403 W. Fourth St.
Newton, IA 50208
Phone: 1-800-JENN-AIR
Internet:
http://www.jennair.com

Jensen Industries
Cabinetry
1946 E. 46th St.
Los Angeles, CA 90058
Phone: 213-235-6800
1-800-325-8351
(outside CA)
Fax: 213-235-6878

Jepson Power Tools
*Tools/Electric &
Pneumatic; Tools/Hand*
20333 S. Western Ave.
Torrance, CA 90501
Phone: 310-320-3890
1-800-456-8665
Fax: 310-320-1318

Jessup Door Co.
Doors
300 E. Railroad St.
Dowagiac, MI 49047
Phone: 616-782-2183
1-800-826-2367
Fax: 616-782-3505

Jet Equipment & Tools
*Equipment & Trucks;
Tools/Electric &
Pneumatic; Tools/Hand*
PO Box 1349
Auburn, WA 98071-1349
Phone: 206-351-6000
1-800-274-6848
Fax: 1-800-274-6840

J.I. Case
(See Case Corp.)

JJ Barker
Walls, Ceilings & Finishes
PO Box 40
Richford, VT 05476-0040
Phone: 514-263-0222
1-800-567-2635
Fax: 514-263-9171

The JJJ Specialty Co.
Windows
113 27th Ave., N.W.
Minneapolis, MN 55418
Phone: 612-788-9688
1-800-445-6736
Fax: 612-788-2002

JM Huber Corp.
*Engineered Lumber
& Panels*
PO Box 26704
Charlotte, NC 28221
Phone: 704-547-9220
Fax: 704-547-9228

JMS Wood Products
Moulding & Millwork
8825 Shirley Ave.
Northridge, CA 91324
Phone: 818-709-8674
Fax: 818-709-8683

John Boos & Co.
Countertops
315 S. First St.
Effingham, IL 62401
Phone: 217-347-7701
Fax: 217-347-7705

John Deere
(See Deere & Co.)

Johnson Controls
HVAC
507 E. Michigan St.
Milwaukee, WI 53202
Phone: 414-274-4000
Fax: 414-247-4701

Johnson's Carpets
Flooring
3510 Corporate Dr.
Dalton, GA 30721
Phone: 706-277-2775
1-800-235-1079
Fax: 706-277-9835

**Johnsonite
(A Div. of Duramax)**
Flooring
16910 Minn Rd.
Chagrin Falls, OH 44023
Phone: 216-543-8916
1-800-899-8916
Fax: 216-543-8920

The Jordan Cos.
Doors; Windows
4661 Burbank Rd.
Memphis, TN 38118
Phone: 901-363-2121
Fax: 901-362-5051

Josef Kihlberg of America
*Hardware; Tools/Electric
& Pneumatic*
6809 Crossbow Dr.
East Syracuse, NY 13057
Phone: 315-437-4200
1-800-437-9818
Fax: 315-437-4452

Jotul USA
Fireplaces
400 Riverside St.,
PO Box 1157
Portland, ME 04104
Phone: 207-797-5912
Fax: 207-772-0523
Internet:
http://www.hearth.com/jotul

Joyce Mfg.
*Doors; Roofing; Room
Enclosures; Structural
Systems; Windows*
5400 W. 161 St.
Cleveland, OH 44142
Phone: 216-433-4343
1-800-824-7988
Fax: 216-433-0558

Juca Super-Fireplace
Fireplaces
PO Box 93
Thornton, IL 60476
Phone: 219-393-3777
1-800-348-8850

Juno Lighting
Electrical & Lighting
2001 S. Mt Prospect Rd.,
PO Box 5065
Des Plaines, IL 60017
Phone: 708-827-9880
Fax: 708-827-2925

Just Cabinets
Cabinetry
PO Box 129, Porter Rd.
Fryeburg, ME 04037
Phone: 207-935-2220
Fax: 207-935-2111

Just Mfg. Co.
Faucets & Fixtures
9233 King St.
Franklin Park, IL 60131
Phone: 847-678-5150
Fax: 847-678-6817

Justice Design Group
Electrical & Lighting
11244 Playa Ct.
Culver City, CA 90230
Phone: 310-397-8300
Fax: 310-397-7170
E-mail: sales@jdg.com

K

**K Products Group
(A Div. of Cardinal
Industries)**
*Electrical & Lighting;
Insulation; Tools/Hand*
724 Commerce St.
Aberdeen, SD 57401
Phone: 1-800-843-1660
Fax: 605-226-1203

Kabinart
Cabinetry
3650 Trousdale
Nashville, TN 37211
Phone: 615-833-1961
Fax: 615-834-8268

Kahrs Intl.
Flooring
951 Mariner's Island,
Suite 630
San Mateo, CA 94404
Phone: 415-341-8400
1-800-800-5247
Fax: 415-341-3553
Internet:
http://www.kahrs.com

Kallista
Faucets & Fixtures
2701 Merced St.
San Leandro, CA 94577
Phone: 510-895-6400
Fax: 510-895-6990
Internet:
http://www.kallistainc.com

Kanalflakt
Appliances; HVAC
50 Sheridan Rd.,
PO Box 2000
Bouctouche, NB
E0A 1G0 Canada
Phone: 506-743-9500
Fax: 506-743-9600

**KANT-SAG Lumber
Connectors
(United Steel Products
Co.)**
Hardware; Roofing
703 Rogers Dr., PO Box 80
Montgomery, MN 56069
Phone: 612-364-7333
1-800-KANT-SAG
Fax: 612-364-8762

**Kargo King
(A Div. of Kiefer Built)**
Equipment & Trucks
305 First St.
Kanawha, IA 50447
Phone: 515-762-3201
Fax: 515-762-3425

Karman Kitchens
Cabinetry
6000 S. Stratler St.
Salt Lake City, UT 84107
Phone: 801-268-3581
Fax: 801-261-0875

Karnak Corp.
*Paints, Caulks &
Adhesives; Roofing;
Specialty Products*
330 Central Ave.
Clark, NJ 07066
Phone: 908-388-0300
1-800-526-4236
Fax: 908-388-9422

Kasko Industries
*Insulation; Siding &
Accessories; Structural
Systems*
18 Turtle Creek Dr.
Tequesta, FL 33469
Phone: 561-575-1193
Fax: 561-575-1959

Kaylien
*Doors; Hardware; Walls,
Ceilings & Finishes*
PO Box 711599
Santee, CA 92072-1599
Phone: 619-448-0544
1-800-748-5627
Fax: 619-448-5196
Internet:
http://www.kayliendoors.
com

KBI Industries
Faucets & Fixtures
222 Belmont Ct.
Michigan City, IN 46360
Phone: 219-879-5000
Fax: 219-872-5556

KCI Coatings
Paints, Caulks & Adhesives
201 E. Market
PO Box 1093
Louisville, KY 40202
Phone: 502-584-0151
Fax: 502-584-1601

**Keiver-Willard Lumber
Corp.**
*Engineered Lumber
& Panels*
11-13 Graf Rd.
Newburyport, MA 01950
Phone: 508-462-7193
Fax: 508-465-6631

Keller Ladders
Equipment & Trucks
3499 N.W. 53rd St.
Ft. Lauderdale, FL 33309
Phone: 954-777-2060
1-800-333-4568
Fax: 954-777-2080

**Kemper Distinctive
Cabinetry
(A Schrock Cabinet
Co. Brand)**
Cabinetry
701 S. N. St.
Richmond, IN 47374
Phone: 317-935-2211
Fax: 1-800-222-7166

Kenall
Electrical & Lighting
1020 Lakeside Dr.
Gurnee, IL 60031
Phone: 708-360-8200
1-800-634-5013
Fax: 708-360-1781

**Kenergy
(A Div. of SNE
Enterprises)**
Windows
PO Box 8007
Wausau, WI 54402
Phone: 715-845-1161
1-800-VETTER2
Fax: 715-847-6520

Kenmore Industries
Doors
1 Thompson Sq.,
PO Box 34
Boston, MA 02129
Phone: 617-242-1711

Kennedy Mfg. Co.
Tools/Hand
520 E. Sycamore
Van Wert, OH 45891
Phone: 419-238-2442
1-800-413-8665
Fax: 419-238-5644

Kensington Windows
Windows
RD 1, 1 Kiski Valley
Industrial Park
Vandegrift, PA 15690
Phone: 412-845-8133
1-800-444-4972
Fax: 412-845-9151

Kent Moore Cabinets
Cabinetry
1460 Fountain Ave.
Bryan, TX 77801
Phone: 409-775-2906
Fax: 409-775-0519

KenTech Plastics
*Roofing; Siding
& Accessories*
1857 Calvin Dr.,
PO Box 766
Hopkinsville, KY 42241
Phone: 502-887-6600
Fax: 502-887-6619

Kentucky Millwork
*Countertops; Doors;
Flooring; Moulding &
Millwork; Walls, Ceilings
& Finishes; Windows*
PO Box 33276
Louisville, KY 40232
Phone: 502-451-3456
1-800-235-5235
Fax: 502-451-6027

Kentucky Wood Floors
Flooring
PO Box 33276
Louisville, KY 40232
Phone: 502-451-6024
1-800-235-5235
Fax: 502-451-6027

Kepcor/SSI Tiles
Countertops; Flooring
PO Box 119
Minerva, OH 44657
Phone: 330-868-6434
Fax: 330-868-6437

Kett Tool Co.
*Tools/Electric
& Pneumatic*
5055 Madison Rd.
Cincinnati, OH 45227
Phone: 513-271-0333
Fax: 513-271-5318

**Kewanee Corp./
Midway Tech Center**
Doors; Windows
4949 W. 65th St.
Chicago, IL 60638
Phone: 708-458-1171
Fax: 708-458-2456

**Keystone Retaining Wall
Systems**
*Landscape Design;
Structural Systems*
4444 W. 78th St.
Minneapolis, MN 55435
Phone: 612-897-1040
1-800-747-8971
Fax: 612-897-3858

**Keystone Shower Door
KSD Industries**
*Cabinetry; Faucets
& Fixtures*
PO Box 544, Keystone Rd.
Southampton, PA 18966
Phone: 215-464-2700
Fax: 215-355-6881

**Keystone Steel &
Wire Co.**
Hardware
7000 S.W. Adams
Peoria, IL 61641
Phone: 309-697-7020
1-800-447-6444
Fax: 309-697-7422

Keystone Wood Products
*Moulding & Millwork;
Windows*
PO Box 4606
Winter Park, FL 32793
Phone: 407-671-3303
Fax: 407-677-9793

**Keystone Wood
Specialties**
Moulding & Millwork
PO Box 10127
Lancaster, PA 17605
Phone: 717-299-6288
1-800-233-0289
Fax: 1-800-253-0805

Kichler Lighting
Electrical & Lighting
7711 E. Pleasant Valley Rd.
Independence, OH 44131
Phone: 216-573-1000
Fax: 216-573-1001

Kiefer Built
Equipment & Trucks
305 First St.
Kanawha, IA 50447
Phone: 515-762-3201
Fax: 515-762-3425

Kindred Industries
Faucets & Fixtures
PO Box 190,
1000 Kindred Rd.
Midland, ON L4R 4K9
Canada
Phone: 705-526-5427
1-800-465-5586
Fax: 705-526-8055
Internet:
http://www.kindred-
sinkware.com

King Refrigerator Corp.
Appliances; Countertops
7602 Woodhaven Blvd.
Glendale, NY 11385
Phone: 718-897-2200
Fax: 718-830-9440

Kinzee Industries
Cabinetry; Countertops
1 Paul Kohner Pl.
Elmwood Park, NJ 07407
Phone: 201-797-4700
Fax: 201-797-1360

Kit Industries
Faucets & Fixtures
1000 Taylors Ln., Unit 4
Cinnaminson, NJ 08077
Phone: 609-786-1044
1-800-526-3186
Fax: 609-786-0865

**Kitchen Aid
(A Brand of Whirlpool
Corp.)**
Appliances
2000 M-63 N,
Mail Drop 4302
Benton Harbor, MI
49022
Phone: 616-923-5000
1-800-253-3977
Fax: 616-923-3214

**Kitchen Cabinet
Manufacturers Assn.**
Cabinetry
1899 Preston White Dr.
Reston, VA 22091
Phone: 703-264-1690
Fax: 703-620-6530

**Kitchen Computer
Designer**
Computer Software
18 Atlantic Ave.,
PO Box 268
South Dennis, MA 02660
Phone: 508-385-8569
Fax: 508-385-8467

Kitchen Craft of Canada
Cabinetry
1180 Springfield Rd.
Winnipeg, MB R2C 2Z2
Canada
Phone: 204-224-3211
Fax: 204-222-7608

Kitchen Kompact
Cabinetry
PO Box 868,
911 E. 11th St.
Jeffersonville, IN 47131
Phone: 812-282-6681
Fax: 812-282-7880

**Klamath Door
(A Div. of JELD-WEN)**
Doors
3305 Lakeport Blvd.,
PO Box 1329
Klamath Falls, OR
97601-0268
Phone: 1-800-877-9482

Klauer Mfg. Co.
*Roofing; Siding &
Accessories*
PO Box 59, 1185
Roosevelt St. Extension
Dubuque, IA 52001
Phone: 319-582-7201
Fax: 319-582-2022

Klean-Strip
Paints, Caulks & Adhesives
PO Box 1879
Memphis, TN 38101
Phone: 901-775-0100
1-800-238-2672
Fax: 1-800-621-9508

Klein Tools
*Hardware; Paints, Caulks
& Adhesives; Tools/Electric
& Pneumatic; Tools/Hand*
7200 McCormick Blvd.,
PO Box 599033
Chicago, IL 60659-9033
Phone: 708-677-9500

KML Windows
*Doors; Engineered Lumber
& Panels; Moulding &
Millwork; Windows*
23 Buchanan Ct.
London, ON N5Z 4P9
Canada
Phone: 519-681-5327
Fax: 519-668-6375

**KMP Development
Corp.**
Computer Software
5505 N. Crimson Way
Boise, ID 83703
Phone: 208-368-9734
Fax: 208-368-9734

Knaack Mfg. Co.
*Equipment & Trucks;
Tools/Hand*
420 E. Terra Cotta Ave.
Crystal Lake, IL 60014
Phone: 815-459-6020
1-800-456-7865
Fax: 815-459-9097

Knape & Vogt Mfg. Co.
*Cabinetry; Hardware;
Specialty Products*
2700 Oak Industrial Dr.
N.W.
Grand Rapids, MI 49505
Phone: 616-459-3311
1-800-253-1561
Fax: 616-454-3290
Internet:
http://www.kv.com

Knauf Fiber Glass
Insulation
240 Elizabeth St.
Shelbyville, IN 46176
Phone: 317-398-4434
1-800-825-4434
Fax: 317-398-3675
Internet:
http://www.knauffiberglass.
com

Knudson Mfg.
*Equipment & Trucks;
Roofing; Siding &
Accessories; Structural
Systems*
10401 W. 120th Ave.
Broomfield, CO 80021
Phone: 303-469-2101
1-800-548-2622
Fax: 303-469-7994

Koch & Co.
*Cabinetry; Countertops;
Doors; Moulding &
Millwork*
111 N. First St.
Seneca, KS 66538
Phone: 913-336-6040
Fax: 913-336-2638

Koch Materials Co.
(See Tuff-N-Dri
Waterproofing)

Kohler Co.
Faucets & Fixtures
444 Highland Dr.
Kohler, WI 53044
Phone: 414-457-4441
1-800-4KOHLER
Fax: 414-457-1271

**Kolbe & Kolbe
Millwork Co.**
*Doors; Moulding &
Millwork; Windows*
1323 S. 11th Ave.
Wausau, WI 54401-5998
Phone: 715-842-5666
Fax: 715-845-8270

Kolson
*Faucets & Fixtures;
Hardware*
653 Middle Neck Rd.
Great Neck, NY 11023
Phone: 516-487-1224
1-800-783-1335
Fax: 516-487-1231

Komatsu Forklift (USA)
Equipment & Trucks
5595 Fresca Dr.
La Palma, CA 90623
Phone: 714-228-3877
Fax: 714-670-0229

Kondor Post and Beam
Structural Systems
RR 2, PO Box 2794
Cambridge, VT 05444
Phone: 802-644-5598
1-800-644-5598
Fax: 802-644-5598

Kool-O-Matic Corp.
HVAC
PO Box 310
Niles, MI 49120
Phone: 616-683-2600
Fax: 616-683-2318

Kop-Coat
Paints, Caulks & Adhesives
436 Seventh Ave.
Pittsburgh, PA
15219-1818
Phone: 412-227-2700
Fax: 412-227-2618

Korwall Industries
*Flooring; Insulation;
Structural Systems*
326 N. Bowen Rd.
Arlington, TX 76012
Phone: 817-277-6741
Fax: 817-277-6743

Kountry Kraft
Cabinetry
PO Box 570
Newmanstown, PA 17073
Phone: 610-589-4575
Fax: 1-800-401-0584

**Kozy Heat
(A Div. of Hussong
Mfg. Co.)**
Fireplaces
204 Industrial Park Dr.,
PO Box 577
Lakefield, MN 56150
Phone: 507-662-6641
1-800-253-4904
Fax: 507-662-6644

Kraft Tool Co.
*Paints, Caulks &
Adhesives; Structural
Systems; Tools/Electric &
Pneumatic; Tools/Hand*
8325 Hedge Lane Ter.
Shawnee, KS 66227
Phone: 816-474-4555
Fax: 816-474-9744

Kraftile Co.
Flooring
800 Kraftile Rd.
Fremont, CA 94536
Phone: 510-793-4432
Fax: 510-791-2953

Kraftmaid Cabinetry
*Cabinetry; Moulding
& Millwork*
PO Box 1055,
16052 Industrial Pkwy.
Middlefield, OH 44062
Phone: 216-632-5333
Fax: 216-632-5648
Internet:
http://www.kraftmaid.com

Kroin
Faucets & Fixtures
180 Fawcett St.
Cambridge, MA 02138
Phone: 617-492-4000
Fax: 617-492-4001

Kroy Building Products
Landscape Design
PO Box 309,
522 W. 26th St.
York, NE 68467
Phone: 402-362-6651
1-800-933-5769
Fax: 402-362-6797

Krusin Intl. Corp.
*Hardware; Paints, Caulks
& Adhesives*
113 Winnett St.
Woodstock, ON
N4S 5Z8 Canada
Phone: 519-421-2121
1-800-377-8331
Fax: 519-539-2497

Küche Cucina
Cabinetry
489 Rt. 17 S.
Paramus, NJ 07652
Phone: 201-261-5221
Fax: 201-261-0966

Kuehn Bevel
Countertops
111 Canfield Ave.
Randolph, NJ 07869
Phone: 201-584-8282
1-800-TO-BEVEL
Internet:
http://www.kuehnbevel.com

Kuhns Bros. Log Homes
Structural Systems
RD 2, PO Box 406A
Lewisburg, PA 17837
Phone: 717-568-1412
1-800-326-9614
Fax: 717-568-1187

Kuny's Mfg. Co.
*Landscape Design;
Tools/Electric & Pneumatic*
5901 44A St.
Leduc, AB T9E 7B8
Canada
Phone: 403-986-1151
Fax: 403-986-9861

**KWC
(A Brand of Rohl Corp.)**
Faucets & Fixtures
1559 Sunland Ln.
Costa Mesa, CA 92626
Phone: 714-557-1933
1-800-777-9762
Fax: 714-557-8635

**Kwik-Way Corp.
Div. of Metal Industries**
Doors
PO Box 5289
Clearwater, FL 34618
Phone: 813-447-8742
Fax: 813-442-4247

**Kwikset Corp.
(A Sub. of Black &
Decker Co.)**
Hardware
1 Park Plaza, Suite 1000
Irvine, CA 92714
Phone: 714-474-8800
1-800-327-LOCK
Fax: 714-474-8862

L

L.J. Smith
Moulding & Millwork
35280 Scio-Bowerston Rd.
Bowerston, OH 44695
Phone: 614-269-2221
Fax: 614-269-9047

L.M. Scofield Co.
*Engineered Lumber &
Panels; Flooring; Paints,
Caulks & Adhesives*
6533 Bandini Blvd.
Los Angeles, CA 90040
Phone: 213-720-3000
1-800-1-800-9900
Fax: 213-720-3030

La-Co Industries
Plumbing Supplies
1201 Pratt
Elk Grove Village, IL
60007-5746
Phone: 847-956-7600
Fax: 847-956-9885

La Vona's Unique Hardware
Malibu Art Tile
Cabinetry; Countertops; Electrical & Lighting; Flooring; Hardware
23852 Pacific Coast Hwy., Suite 116
Malibu, CA 90265
Phone: 818-706-7369
Fax: 818-706-2766

LaCrosse Canada
Structural Systems
5475 N. Service Rd.
Burlington, ON
L7C 5H7 Canada
Phone: 905-319-9800
Fax: 905-319-9804

LaHabra Stucco
Siding & Accessories; Walls, Ceilings & Finishes
1631 W. Lincoln Ave.
Anaheim, CA 92803
Phone: 714-778-2266
1-800-649-8933
Fax: 714-774-2079

Lake Shore Stair Co.
Moulding & Millwork
615 E. Park Ave.
Libertyville, IL 60048
Phone: 847-362-3262
Fax: 847-362-3349

Laminated Plastics
Countertops
140 Littleton Rd.
Parsippany, NJ 07054
Phone: 201-316-9595
1-800-631-0145
Fax: 201-316-6211

Laminating Materials Assn.
Countertops; Engineered Lumber & Panels; Flooring; Walls, Ceilings & Finishes
116 Lawrence St.
Hillsdale, NJ 07642-2730
Phone: 201-664-2700
Fax: 201-666-5665
Internet: http://www.lma.org

Lamson-Taylor Custom Doors
Doors
Tucker Rd.
S. Acworth, NH 03607
Phone: 603-835-2992
Fax: 603-835-2992

Land, Air & Sea Tool Corp.
Tools/Electric & Pneumatic
68 Starling Ln.
Naperville, IL 60565
Phone: 630-778-1085
1-800-410-5278
Fax: 630-778-1086

Landmark Data Systems
Computer Software
2629 Ridgewood Rd.
Jackson, MS 39216-4919
Phone: 601-362-0303
1-800-424-8178
Fax: 601-362-0347

LandPlot Research
Computer Software
1328 Cape St. Claire Rd.
Annapolis, MD 21401
Phone: 410-757-8871
Fax: 410-757-8134

Lantron Technologies
Computer Software
429 Catalpa Ave.
North Plainfield, NJ 07063-1815
Phone: 908-769-8930
1-800-235-6726
Fax: 908-769-1899
Internet: Compuserve 76770-2236

Larson Mfg.
Doors
2333 Eastbrook Dr.
Brookings, SD 57006
Phone: 605-692-6115
1-800-334-1328
Fax: 605-696-3445
Internet: http://www.larsondoors.com

Lasco Bathware (A Div. of Tomkins Industries)
Faucets & Fixtures
3255 E. Miraloma Ave.
Anaheim, CA 92806
Phone: 714-993-1220
1-800-877-2005
Fax: 714-572-0998

Lasco Fluid Distribution Products (A Div. of Tompkins)
Plumbing Supplies
540 Lasco St.
Brownsville, TN 38012
Phone: 901-772-3180
Fax: 901-772-0835
Internet: http://www.lascofittings.com

Laser Alignment
Tools/Hand
2850 Thornhills
Grand Rapids, MI 49546
Phone: 616-949-7430
1-800-4-LASERS
Fax: 616-949-6975

Laser Tools Co.
Tools/Hand
3520 W. 69th St.
Suite 401
Little Rock, AR 72209
Phone: 501-562-0900
1-800-598-5973
Fax: 501-562-0022

Laseraim Technologies Laseraim Tools Div.
Tools/Hand
PO Box 3548
Little Rock, AR 72203
Phone: 501-375-2227
Fax: 501-372-1445

Lasky
Appliances
23 Broderick Rd.
Burlingame, CA 94101
Phone: 415-692-1970

Latco Products
Countertops; Flooring; Walls, Ceilings & Finishes
13536 Saticoy St.
Van Nuys, CA 91402
Phone: 818-902-5424
Fax: 818-902-5434

Laticrete Intl.
Countertops; Flooring; Paints, Caulks & Adhesives; Walls, Ceilings & Finishes; Windows
1 Laticrete Park N.
Bethany, CT 06524
Phone: 203-393-0010
1-800-243-4788
Fax: 203-393-1684

Laufen Ceramic Tile
Countertops; Flooring
4942 E. 66th St. N.
Tulsa, OK 74117-1802
Phone: 918-428-3851
1-800-758-TILE
Fax: 918-428-1279
Internet: http://www.laufen.com

Laurel Co.
Countertops; Faucets & Fixtures; Walls, Ceilings & Finishes
1620 Albritton Dr., Suite 7
Kennesaw, GA 30152
Phone: 770-424-5134
Fax: 770-424-5138

Laurentian Log Homes
Structural Systems
5636 Rt. 117
Val-Morin, PQ J0T 2R0
Canada

Lavalley Lumber
Siding & Accessories
New Dam Rd., PO Box P
Sanford, ME 04073
Phone: 207-324-3350
Fax: 207-324-1339

Lavi Industries
Moulding & Millwork; Specialty Products
27810 Ave. Hopkins
Valencia, CA 91355-3409
Phone: 805-257-7800
1-800-624-6225
Fax: 805-257-4938

Lawrence Bros.
Hardware
2 First Ave.
Sterling, IL 61081
Phone: 815-625-0360
1-800-435-9568
Fax: 815-625-2759

LB Plastics
Doors; Windows
PO Box 907
Mooresville, NC 28115
Phone: 704-663-1543
1-800-752-7739
Fax: 704-664-2989

LC Andrew Maine Cedar Log Homes
Structural Systems
35 Main St.
Windham, ME 04062
Phone: 207-892-8561
1-800-427-5647
Fax: 207-892-8563

LE Johnson Products
Doors; Hardware
2100 Sterling Ave.
Elkhart, IN 46516
Phone: 219-293-5664
1-800-837-5664
Fax: 219-294-4697

Lectro Science/ Intermark
Electrical & Lighting; Equipment & Trucks; HVAC; Tools/Hand
632 Green Bay Rd.
Kenilworth, IL 60043
Phone: 708-256-6500
1-800-453-2101
Fax: 708-256-8542

Ledco
Doors
801 Commerce Cir.
Shelbyville, KY 40065
Phone: 502-633-6304
1-800-626-6367
Fax: 502-633-6461

Lee/Rowan Co. Building Products Div.
Specialty Products
900 S. Hwy. Dr.
Fenton, MO 63026
Phone: 314-343-0700
1-800-325-6150
Fax: 314-349-9618

Legacy Timber Frames
Room Enclosures; Structural Systems
691 County Rd. 70
Stillwater, NY 12170
Phone: 518-279-9108
Fax: 518-581-9219

Legrand
(See Pass & Seymour/Legrand)

Lehigh Portland Cement Co.
Structural Systems
7660 Imperial Way
Allentown, PA 18195
Phone: 610-366-4600
1-800-523-5488
Fax: 610-366-4638

Leigh (A Harrow Co.)
Cabinetry; HVAC; Roofing; Siding & Accessories
411 64th Ave.
Coopersville, MI 49404
Phone: 616-837-8141
1-800-253-0361
Fax: 616-837-7345

Lenape Products
Faucets & Fixtures; Hardware
600 Plum St.
Trenton, NJ 08638
Phone: 609-394-5376
Fax: 609-394-0929

Lennox Industries
HVAC
PO Box 799900
Dallas, TX 75379-9900
Phone: 214-497-5000

Leonard Valve Co.
Faucets & Fixtures; Plumbing Supplies
1360 Elmwood Ave.
Cranston, RI 02910-3824
Phone: 401-461-1200
Fax: 401-941-5310

LesCare Kitchens
Cabinetry
1 LesCare Dr.
Waterbury, CT 06705
Phone: 203-755-1100
Fax: 203-755-4713

Leslie-Locke
HVAC; Moulding & Millwork; Roofing; Windows
4501 Circle 75 Pkwy.
Atlanta, GA 30339
Phone: 404-953-6366
1-800-755-9392
Fax: 404-956-0663

LeveLite Technology
Tools/Hand
476 Ellis St.
Mountain View, CA 94043
Phone: 415-254-5980
1-800-453-8354
Fax: 415-254-5989
Internet: http://www.levelite.com

Leviton Mfg.
Home Technology; Electrical & Lighting; Specialty Products
59-25 Little Neck Pkwy.
Little Neck, NY 11362
Phone: 718-229-4040
Fax: 1-800-U-FAX-LEV

Lewis Lumber Products
Engineered Lumber & Panels
190 Park St.
Williamsport, PA 17701
Phone: 717-326-7471
Fax: 717-326-7474

Lewisohn Sales Co.
Engineered Lumber & Panels; Flooring; Paints, Caulks & Adhesives
4001 Dell Ave., PO Box 192
North Bergen, NJ 07047
Phone: 201-864-0300
1-800-631-3196
Fax: 201-864-1266
Internet: http://www.lewisohn.com

Lianga Pacific
Moulding & Millwork
PO Box 1355
Tacoma, WA 98401
Phone: 206-383-4761
Fax: 206-572-8427

Libbey Owens Ford Co.
811 Madison Ave.
PO Box 799
Toledo, OH 43695-0799

LIBRA Corp.
Computer Software
4001 S. 700 E., Suite 30
Salt Lake City, UT 84107-2177
Phone: 801-281-0700
1-800-453-3827
Fax: 801-284-9180

Liette Intl.
Faucets & Fixtures; Flooring; Walls, Ceilings & Finishes
243 Fleet St.
New Bern, NC 28562
Phone: 919-636-0972
Fax: 919-633-6961

LIFESPEC Cabinet Systems
Cabinetry; Specialty Products
428 N. Lamar
Oxford, MS 38655
Phone: 601-234-0330
Fax: 601-234-0288

Lifetime Faucets
Faucets & Fixtures
PO Box 2820,
301 Mid-America Blvd.
Hot Springs, AR 71913
Phone: 501-760-1140
1-800-238-7558
Fax: 501-760-1565

Lighting by Hammerworks
Electrical & Lighting; Hardware; Specialty Products
PO Box 945
Meredith, NH 03253
Phone: 603-279-7352
Fax: 603-279-7352, ext. 51

Lightolier
Electrical & Lighting
631 Airport Rd.
Fall River, MA 02720
Phone: 508-679-8131
1-800-215-1068
Fax: 508-646-3204
Internet: http://www.lightolier.com

Lightway Industries
Electrical & Lighting
25345-213 Stanford Ave.
Valencia, CA 91355
Phone: 805-257-0286
1-800-32-LIGHT
Fax: 805-257-0201

Lincoln Wood Products
Doors; Windows
701 N. State St.
Merrill, WI 54452
Phone: 715-536-2461
Fax: 715-536-7090

Lindal Cedar Homes/Sunrooms
Room Enclosures; Structural Systems; Windows
4300 S. 104th Pl.
Seattle, WA 98178
Phone: 206-725-0900
1-800-426-0536
Fax: 206-725-1615
Internet: http://www.lindal.com

Lite-Form Intl.
Structural Systems
1210 Steuben St.
Sioux City, IA 51102
Phone: 712-252-3704
1-800-551-3313
Fax: 712-252-3259
Internet: http://www.pionet.net/~liteform/index.html

LiteTouch
Electrical & Lighting; Home Technology
3550 S. 700 W.
Salt Lake City, UT 84119
Phone: 801-268-8668
Fax: 801-268-9200

Liteway
Electrical & Lighting
PO Box 700,
1119 Beaver St.
Bristol, PA 19007
Phone: 215-788-5585
Fax: 215-788-5057

Litex Industries
HVAC
2002 Ave. R
Grand Prairie, TX 75050
Phone: 214-641-3015

Little Lumber Co.
Engineered Lumber & Panels
PO Box L
Benton, PA 17814
Phone: 717-925-2101
Fax: 717-925-2475

**Loctite Corp.
North American Group**
Paints, Caulks & Adhesives
1001 Trout Brook Crossing
Rocky Hill, CT 06067
Phone: 203-571-5100
Fax: 203-571-5465

**Lodestar
Statements in Stone**
Countertops
231 E. 58th St.
New York, NY 10022
Phone: 212-755-1818
Fax: 212-755-1828

Loewen Windows
Windows
600 Lakeview Pkwy.
Vernon Hills, IL 60061
Phone: 708-362-1600
1-800-245-2295
Fax: 708-362-8022
Internet:
http://www.loewen.com

Log Cabin Homes
Structural Systems
PO Drawer 1457,
410 N. Pearl St.
Rocky Mount, NC 27802
Phone: 919-977-7785
1-800-56-CABIN
Fax: 919-985-2810
Internet:
http://www.logcabinhomes.com

Logcrafters Log & Timber Homes
Moulding & Millwork; Structural Systems
PO Box 448
St. Ignatius, MT 59865
Phone: 406-745-3482
1-800-735-4425
Fax: 406-745-3350

London Tile Co.
Countertops; Flooring; Landscape Design; Walls, Ceilings & Finishes
65 Walnut St.
New London, OH 44851
Phone: 419-929-1551
1-800-235-1551
Fax: 419-929-1552

Lone Star Ceramics Co.
Flooring; Walls, Ceilings & Finishes
2408 Fruitland,
PO Box 810215
Dallas, TX 75381-0215
Phone: 214-247-3111
1-800-256-5248
Fax: 214-247-3113

Louisiana-Pacific Corp.
Doors; Engineered Lumber & Panels; Insulation; Roofing; Siding & Accessories; Walls, Ceilings & Finishes; Windows
111 S.W. Fifth Ave.
Portland, OR 97204
Phone: 503-221-0800
1-800-547-6331
Fax: 503-796-0107

Louisville Ladder Corp.
Equipment & Trucks
1163 Algonquin Pkwy.
Louisville, KY 40208
Phone: 502-636-2811
1-800-666-2811
Fax: 502-636-1014

Lovell Lumber Co.
Moulding & Millwork
PO Box 106
Lovell, ME 04051
Phone: 207-925-6455
Fax: 207-925-6555
E-mail: lovell_1@nxi.com

Lowen Sign Co.
Landscape Design
1330 E. Fourth St.,
PO Box 1528
Hutchinson, KS 67504
Phone: 316-663-2161
1-800-545-5505
Fax: 1-800-846-4466

LRH Enterprises
Hardware; Tools/Electric & Pneumatic
6961 Valjean Ave.
Van Nuys, CA 91406
Phone: 818-782-0226
1-800-423-2544
Fax: 818-909-7602
Internet:
http://www.lrhent.com

LS Starrett Co.
Tools/Hand
PO Box 40309
Charleston, SC 29423
Phone: 803-797-2500
1-800-772-3649

LTL Home Products
Doors; Moulding & Millwork
125 Rt. 61
Schuylkill Haven, PA 17972
Phone: 717-385-5470
1-800-360-1585
Fax: 717-385-5475

Lucent Technologies
283 King George Rd.
Warren, NJ 07059
1-800-344-0223,
ext. 5101
Internet:
http://www.lucent.com/netsys/homestar

Ludowici Roof Tile
Roofing
PO Box 69
New Lexington, OH 43764
Phone: 614-342-1995
1-800-945-8453
Fax: 614-342-5229

Ludwig Industries
Hardware; Specialty Products
133 Middleton St.
Brooklyn, NY 11206
Phone: 718-387-0947
1-800-827-2312
Fax: 718-387-0824

Lundia Shelving & Storage Systems
Specialty Products
600 Capitol Way
Jacksonville, IL 62650
Phone: 217-243-8585
1-800-726-9663
Fax: 1-800-869-9663
Internet:
http://www.lundiausa.com

Lutron Electronics Co.
Electrical & Lighting
7200 Suter Rd.
Coopersburg, PA 18036
Phone: 610-282-3800
1-800-523-9466
Fax: 610-282-3090

Luxaire/Fraser-Johnston Central Environmental Systems
HVAC
Dept 232 A, PO Box 1592
York, PA 17405-1592
Phone: 717-771-6130
Fax: 717-771-6819

LWO Corp.
Landscape Design; Moulding & Millwork; Walls, Ceilings & Finishes
PO Box 17125,
3841 N. Columbia Blvd.
Portland, OR 97217-0496
Phone: 503-286-5372
Fax: 503-286-4092

Lyons Industries
Faucets & Fixtures
30,000-M-62W.
Dowagiac, MI 49047
Phone: 616-782-3404
1-800-458-9036
Fax: 616-782-5159

M

M.D. Mfg. Co.
Specialty Products
300 Wood St.
Bakersfield, CA 93307
Phone: 805-322-7608
1-800-525-2055
Fax: 805-322-9374
Internet: http://www.builtinvacuum.com

M. Green & Co.
Hardware
PO Box 3728,
2400 Jasper St.
Philadelphia, PA 19125
Phone: 215-634-6670
Fax: 215-634-7903

M.L. Condon Co.
Cabinetry; Countertops; Doors; Engineered Lumber & Panels; Flooring; Moulding & Millwork; Walls, Ceilings & Finishes
276 Ferris Ave.
White Plains, NY 10603
Phone: 914-946-4111
Fax: 914-946-3779

**MAXX
Div. Acrylica, Premium**
Faucets & Fixtures; Specialty Products
600 Rt. Cameron
Ste-Marie, PQ G6E 1B2
Canada
Phone: 418-387-4155
Fax: 418-387-3507

MacBeath Hardwood
Engineered Lumber & Panels
930 Ashby Ave.
Berkeley, CA 94710
Phone: 510-843-4390
1-800-233-0782
Fax: 510-843-9378

Macco Adhesives
Paints, Caulks & Adhesives; Structural Systems
925 Euclid Ave.
Cleveland, OH 44115
Phone: 216-334-8000
1-800-634-0015
Fax: 216-344-7365
Internet:
http://www.liquidnails.com

Macklanburg-Duncan
Hardware; Insulation; Paints, Caulks & Adhesives; Roofing; Specialty Products; Structural Systems; Tools/Hand
4041 N. Santa Fe
Oklahoma City, OK 73118
Phone: 405-528-4411
1-800-654-0007
Fax: 405-557-3541

MacMillan Bloedel
Engineered Lumber & Panels; Flooring
5895 Winward Pkwy.
Alpharetta, GA 30202
Phone: 770-740-7100

**MacMillan Bloedel
Building Materials Mktg.**
Doors; Moulding & Millwork; Roofing; Siding & Accessories; Walls, Ceilings & Finishes; Windows
925 W. Georgia St.
Vancouver, BC V6C 3L2
Canada
Phone: 604-661-8342
Fax: 604-661-8288

Madawaska Doors
Doors
PO Box 850
Bolton, ON L7E 5T5
Canada
Phone: 905-859-4622
1-800-263-2358
Fax: 905-859-4654
Internet:
http://www.madawaska-doors.com

Magic Chef
Appliances
3035 N. Shadeland Ave.
Indianapolis, IN 46226
Phone: 1-800-536-6247

**Magna Professional Tools
(A Div. of Primark)**
Tools/Electric & Pneumatic; Tools/Hand
1350 S. 15th St.
Louisville, KY 40210
Phone: 502-635-8100
1-800-242-7003
Fax: 502-635-8134

MAIBEC Industries
Roofing
660 Lenoir St.
Sainte-Foy, PQ G1X 3W3
Canada
Phone: 418-659-3323
Fax: 418-653-4354

**Majestic Forest
Products Corp.**
Roofing
PO Box 66,
16640 111th Ave.
Edmonton, AB T5J 2G9
Canada
Phone: 403-484-7113

**The Majestic
Products Co.**
Fireplaces
1000 E. Market St.
Huntington, IN 46750
Phone: 219-356-8000
1-800-525-1898
Fax: 219-356-9672
Internet: http://www.majesticproducts.com

The Majestic Shower Co.
Faucets & Fixtures
1795 Yosemite Ave.
San Francisco, CA 94124-2621
Phone: 415-822-1513
1-800-992-9342
Fax: 415-822-6532

Major Industries
Windows
PO Box 306
Wausau, WI 54402-0306
Phone: 715-842-4616
1-888-SKYCOST
Fax: 715-848-3336

Makita USA
Equipment & Trucks; Hardware; Tools/Electric & Pneumatic; Tools/Hand
14930 Northam St.
La Mirada, CA 90638
Phone: 714-522-8088
Fax: 714-522-8194

**Malco Tools
(A Div. of Malco Products)**
Tools/Hand
14080 State Hwy. 55 N.W., PO Box 400
Annandale, MN 55302
Phone: 320-274-8246
Fax: 320-274-2269
Internet:
http://www.malcotools.com

Malm Fireplaces
Fireplaces
368 Yolanda Ave.
Santa Rosa, CA 95404
Phone: 707-523-7755
Fax: 707-571-8036

**Malta Wood Windows & Doors
(A Div. of Tompkins)**
Windows
PO Box 397, 13th St.
Malta, OH 43758
Phone: 614-962-3131
1-800-727-5167
Fax: 614-962-3700

Mandish Research Intl.
Structural Systems
5055 State Rd. 46
Mims, FL 32754
Phone: 407-267-2561
Fax: 407-268-1972
E-mail: 103350.160@compuserve.com

Mannington Mills
Flooring
PO Box 30
Salem, NJ 08079-0030
Phone: 1-800-952-1857
Fax: 609-339-5948

Mannington Wood Floors
Flooring
1327 Lincoln Dr.
High Point, NC 27260
Phone: 910-884-5600
1-800-814-7355
Fax: 910-812-4975

Mansfield Plumbing Products
Faucets & Fixtures; Plumbing Supplies; Specialty Products
150 First St.
Perrysville, OH 44864
Phone: 419-938-5211
Fax: 419-938-6234

**Mansion Millwork
(A Div. of MHJ Group)**
Moulding & Millwork
4290 Alatex Rd.
Montgomery, AL 36108
Phone: 334-281-0097
1-800-423-6589
Fax: 334-281-0575

Manufactured Housing Institute
2101 Wilson Blvd.,
Suite 610
Arlington, VA 22201-3062
Phone: 703-558-0400
Fax: 703-558-0401
Internet:
http://www.mfghome.org

Mapei Corp.
Flooring; Paints, Caulks & Adhesives
1350 Lively Blvd.
Elk Grove Village, IL 60007-4912
Phone: 708-364-4470
1-800-42-MAPEI
Fax: 708-364-4586

Maple Flooring Manufacturers Assn.
Engineered Lumber & Panels; Flooring
60 Revere Dr., Suite 500
Northbrook, IL 60062
Phone: 847-480-9138
Fax: 847-480-9282
E-mail:
mfma@maplefloor.com

Marathon Spa & Bath
Faucets & Fixtures
1549 Hwy. 36 N.
Rosenberg, TX 77471
Phone: 281-342-8775
Fax: 281-342-8756

Marco Fireplaces
Fireplaces
2520 Industry Way
Lynwood, CA 90262
Phone: 213-564-3201
1-800-232-1221
Fax: 213-564-3201

Marell Industries
Fireplaces; Landscape Design; Moulding & Millwork
453 Hwy. 74 S.
Peachtree City, GA 30269-2001
Phone: 770-487-0481
1-800-864-4510
Fax: 770-487-5494

Marks USA
Hardware
5300 New Horizons Blvd.
Amityville, NY 11701-1130
Phone: 516-225-5400
1-800-526-0233
Fax: 516-225-6136
E-mail:
wjsmarks@panix.com

Markus Cabinet Mfg. Co.
Cabinetry; Countertops; Moulding & Millwork
601 S. Clinton, PO Box 95
Aviston, IL 62216
Phone: 618-228-7203
Fax: 314-436-0700

Marley Electric Heating (A Div. of Marley Electric Heating)
HVAC
470 Beauty Spot Rd. E.
Bennettsville, SC 29512
Phone: 803-479-4006
Fax: 803-479-8912

Marley Roof Tile
(See Stirling Building Products)

Marlite
Walls, Ceilings & Finishes
202 Harger St., PO Box 250
Dover, OH 44622
Phone: 330-343-6621
Fax: 330-343-7296

Marquis Carpet Mills
Flooring
2743 Hwy. 76,
PO Box 1308
Chatsworth, GA 30705
Phone: 706-695-1060
1-800-609-3100
Fax: 706-695-4787

Marsh Furniture Co.
Cabinetry
PO Box 870
High Point, NC 27261
Phone: 910-884-7363
Fax: 910-884-0883

Marshalltown Trowel Co.
Tools/Hand
PO Box 738,
104 S. Eighth Ave.
Marshalltown, IA 50158
Phone: 515-753-0127
Fax: 515-753-9227

Martin Door Mfg.
Doors; Garage Doors & Openers
2828 S. 900 W.,
PO Box 27437
Salt Lake City, UT 84127-0437
Phone: 801-973-9310
1-800-388-9310
Fax: 801-977-4222
Internet:
http://www.martindoor.com

Martin Fireplaces Div. of Martin Industries
Fireplaces
301 E. Tennessee St.
Florence, AL 35630
Phone: 205-767-0330
1-800-235-5661
Fax: 205-740-5192

Martin-Senour
Paints, Caulks & Adhesives
101 Prospect Ave., N.W.
Cleveland, OH 44115
Phone: 216-566-3105
1-800-542-8468
Fax: 216-566-2666

Marvel Industries
Appliances
PO Box 997
Richmond, IN 47375
Phone: 317-962-2521
1-800-428-6644
Fax: 317-962-2493

Marvin L. Walker & Associates
Countertops; Flooring
3045 Kingston Ct.
Norcross, GA 30071
Phone: 404-446-0030
1-800-477-7665
Fax: 404-446-6570

Marvin Windows & Doors
Doors; Windows
PO Box 100
Warroad, MN 56763
Phone: 218-386-1430
1-800-346-5128
Internet:
http://www.marvin.com

The Marwin Co.
Doors; Moulding & Millwork
PO Box 9126
Columbia, SC 29290
Phone: 803-776-2396
Fax: 803-776-5852

Masco Corp.
Appliances; Cabinetry; Computer Software; Faucets & Fixtures; Hardware; HVAC; Roofing
21001 Van Born Rd.
Taylor, MI 48180
Phone: 313-274-7400
Fax: 313-374-6666
Internet:
http://www.masco.com

Mason Corp.
Doors; Roofing; Room Enclosures; Siding & Accessories; Windows
PO Box 59226
Birmingham, AL 35259
Phone: 205-942-4100
1-800-868-4100
Fax: 205-945-4399

Mason/Red Dot (A Div. of LE Mason Co.)
Electrical & Lighting
98 Business St.
Boston, MA 02136
Phone: 617-361-1710
Fax: 617-361-6876

Masonite
Siding & Accessories
1 S. Wacker Dr., Suite 3600
Chicago, IL 60606
Phone: 312-750-0900
1-800-255-0785
Fax: 312-634-5808

Master Bond
Paints, Caulks & Adhesives
154 Hobart St.
Hackensack, NJ 07601
Phone: 201-343-8983
Fax: 201-343-2132

The Master Builder Software By Omware
Computer Software
100 Pleasant Hill Ave. N.
Sebastopol, CA 95472
Phone: 707-823-8681
1-800-726-6278
Fax: 707-823-9788

Master Lock Co.
Hardware
2600 N. 32nd St.
Milwaukee, WI 53210
Phone: 414-444-2800
Fax: 414-449-3162
Internet:
http://www.masterlock.com/

Master Shield Building Products Co.
Siding & Accessories
1202 N. Bowie Dr.
Weatherford, TX 76086
Phone: 817-596-7090
1-800-433-5524

MasterCraft
Cabinetry
3550 Odessa Way
Aurora, CO 80011
Phone: 303-375-8220
Fax: 303-375-8224

Materials Marketing Corp.
Walls, Ceilings & Finishes
120 W. Josephine
San Antonio, TX 78212
Phone: 210-731-8453
Fax: 210-733-4658

Matot
Specialty Products
2501 Van Buren
Bellwood, IL 60104-2459
Phone: 708-547-1888
1-800-369-1070
Fax: 708-547-1608

Max Products
Siding & Accessories
680 Ben Franklin Hwy.
Birdsboro, PA 19508
Phone: 610-385-7931
1-800-238-2541
Fax: 610-385-4347
Internet:
http://www.canamould.com/canamould

MaxiTile
Engineered Lumber & Panels; Roofing; Siding & Accessories
17141 Kingsview Ave.
Carson, CA 90746
Phone: 310-217-0316
1-800-338-8453
Fax: 310-515-6851

Maxito Industries
Structural Systems
207 W. Hastings St.,
Suite 610
Vancouver, BC V6B 1H7
Canada
Phone: 604-801-6788
1-800-8-MAXITO
Fax: 604-801-6788
E-mail:
maxito@deepcove.com

Maxwell Systems
Computer Software
2328 DeKalb Pike
Norristown, PA 19401
Phone: 610-277-3515
1-800-688-8226
Fax: 610-277-2081

Maxxon Corp. (formerly Gyp-Crete Corp.)
HVAC
920 Hamel Rd.
Hamel, MN 55340
Phone: 612-478-9600
1-800-356-7887
Fax: 612-478-2431
Internet:
http://www.maxxon.com

Mayer Equity
Windows
38 Kinkel St.
Westbury, NY 11590
Phone: 516-333-0101
Fax: 516-997-3793

Mayhew Steel Products
Tools/Hand
PO Box 68
Shelburne Falls, MA 01370
Phone: 413-625-6351
1-800-872-0037
Fax: 413-625-6395

Mayse Woodworking Co.
Moulding & Millwork
319 Richardson Rd.
Lansdale, PA 19446
Phone: 215-822-8307
1-888-LONGLEAF
Fax: 215-822-8307

Maytag
Appliances
1 Dependability Sq.
Newton, IA 50208
Phone: 515-792-7000
Fax: 515-791-8264

Mayville Engineering Co.
Equipment & Trucks
715 South St.
Mayville, WI 53050
Phone: 414-387-4500
Fax: 414-387-5817
Internet:
http://www.mayvl.com

Maywood
Doors
900 E. Second,
PO Box 30550
Amarillo, TX 79120
Phone: 806-374-2835
1-800-879-6299
Fax: 806-374-3821

Maze Nails
Hardware; Tools/Electric & Pneumatic
100 Church St.
Peru, IL 61354
Phone: 815-223-8290
1-800-435-5949
Fax: 815-223-7585
Internet:
http://www.mazenails.com

MC2 Engineering Software
Computer Software
8107 S.W. 72 Ave., Suite 425, PO Box 480980
Miami, FL 33143
Phone: 305-665-0100
Fax: 305-665-8035
E-mail:
mc2engsoft@compuserve.com

McCosker Corp.
Computer Software
1777 Oakland Blvd.,
Suite 201
Walnut Creek, CA 94596
Phone: 510-938-1717
1-800-771-5555
Fax: 510-938-0112

McGraw Edison NCFI
(See North Carolina Foam)

McGrevor Coatings
Paints, Caulks & Adhesives
1701 Utica Ave.
Brooklyn, NY 11234
Phone: 718-377-0505
1-800-922-9981
Fax: 718-253-4430

McIntyre Tile
Countertops; Flooring; Walls, Ceilings & Finishes
55 W. Grant St.
Healdsburg, CA 95448
Phone: 707-433-8866
Fax: 707-433-0548
Internet:
http://users.aimnet.com:8000/~tcolson/pages/mcintyre/mctile.htm

McShan Lumber Co.
Flooring; Moulding & Millwork; Siding & Accessories; Walls, Ceilings & Finishes
PO Box 27, Hwy. 82 E.
McShan, AL 35471
Phone: 205-375-6277
Fax: 205-375-2773

Medallion Kitchens of Minnesota
Cabinetry
180 Industrial Blvd.
Waconia, MN 55387
Phone: 612-442-5171
Fax: 612-442-4998

Medieval Glass Industries
Doors; Windows
Unit 2-7338 Progress Way
Delta, BC B4G 1L4
Canada
Phone: 604-940-0980
Fax: 604-940-0984

Medite Corp.
Engineered Lumber & Panels
PO Box 4040
Medford, OR 97501
Phone: 541-773-2522
Fax: 541-779-9921

Medply
Engineered Lumber & Panels
PO Box 2488
White City, OR 97503
Phone: 503-832-3142
Fax: 503-826-8022

Mega Industries
Tools/Electric & Pneumatic
3075 Ridgeway Dr.
Unit 19
Mississauga, ON L5L 5M6 Canada
Phone: 416-828-6342

Meister Atlantic Corp.
Hardware
3673 Clairmont Rd.
Atlanta, GA 30341
Phone: 404-451-9700
Fax: 404-451-5305

Mel Northey Co.
Electrical & Lighting; Landscape Design
303 Gulf Bank Rd.
Houston, TX 77037
Phone: 281-445-3485
1-800-828-0302
Fax: 281-445-7456

Melard Mfg. Corp.
Faucets & Fixtures; Plumbing Supplies; Specialty Products
153 Linden St.
Passaic, NJ 07055
Phone: 201-472-8888
Fax: 201-472-5274

Mellco
Landscape Design; Moulding & Millwork
PO Drawer C
Perry, GA 31069
Phone: 1-800-866-1414
Fax: 1-800-777-3299
Internet:
http://www.mellco.com

Melroe Co/Bobcat
Equipment & Trucks
PO Box 6019
Fargo, ND 58108-6019
Phone: 701-241-8700
Fax: 701-241-8704

Melton Classics
Moulding & Millwork
PO Box 465020
Lawrenceville, GA 30246-5020
Phone: 770-963-3060
1-800-963-3060
Fax: 770-962-6988

Memphis Hardwood Flooring Co.
Engineered Lumber & Panels; Flooring
1551 N. Thomas St.
Memphis, TN 38107
Phone: 901-526-7306
1-800-346-3010
Fax: 901-525-0059

Memry Corp.
Faucets & Fixtures; Specialty Products
57 Commerce Dr.
Brookfield, CT 06804
Phone: 203-740-7311
1-800-582-5454
Fax: 203-775-2359

Mepla
Cabinetry; Hardware
909 W. Market Center Dr.
High Point, NC 27260
Phone: 910-410-7000
1-800-45-MEPLA
Fax: 910-410-7064

Mercer Products Co.
Flooring
PO Box 1240
Eustis, FL 32727
Phone: 1-800-447-8442
Fax: 1-1800-832-5398

Merillat Industries
Cabinetry; Hardware
5353 W. US 223
Adrian, MI 49221
Phone: 517-263-0771
Fax: 517-263-3191
Internet:
http://www.merillat.com

Met-Tile
Roofing
PO Box 4268
Ontario, CA 91761
Phone: 909-947-0311
1-800-899-0311
Fax: 909-947-1510
Internet: http://www.met-tile.com/roof

Metabo Corp.
Tools/Electric & Pneumatic
1231 Wilson Dr.
West Chester, PA 19380
Phone: 215-436-5900
Fax: 1-800-638-2261

Metal Sales Mfg. Corp.
Roofing; Siding & Accessories; Structural Systems
7800 State Rd. 60
Sellersburg, IN 47172
Phone: 812-246-1935
Fax: 812-246-1862

Metropolitan Ceramics
Flooring
PO Box 9240
Canton, OH 44711
Phone: 330-484-4876
Fax: 330-484-4880

MFM Building Products Corp.
Roofing
PO Box 340
Coshocton, OH 43812
Phone: 614-622-2645
1-800-882-7663
Fax: 614-622-6161
E-mail: mfmatsota-oh.doc

MGM Industries
Doors; Windows
287 Freehill Rd.
Hendersonville, TN 37075
Phone: 615-824-6572
1-800-476-5584
Fax: 615-822-6581

MH Rhodes
Electrical & Lighting
99 Thompson Rd.
Avon, CT 06001
Phone: 860-673-3281
1-800-548-4637
Fax: 860-673-8633
Internet:
http://www.mhrhodes@juno.com

Micarta Laminates
Countertops
304 Hoover St. N.
Hampton, SC 29924
Phone: 803-943-7200

Michigan Maple Block Co.
Countertops
PO Box 245
Petoskey, MI 49770-0245
Phone: 616-347-4170
1-800-678-8459
Fax: 616-347-7975

Microphor (Commercial Products Div.)
Faucets & Fixtures
452 E. Hill Rd.
Willits, CA 95490
Phone: 707-459-5563
1-800-358-8280
Fax: 707-459-6617
E-mail:
microphr@pacific.net

MICS
Computer Software
2995 McMillan Ave., Suite 296
San Luis Obispo, CA 93401
Phone: 805-543-7000
1-800-838-MICS
Fax: 805-543-0373

Mid-America Building Products Corp. (A Tapco Intl. Corp.)
HVAC; Moulding & Millwork; Roofing; Siding & Accessories
45657 Port St.
Plymouth, MI 48170
Phone: 313-459-5151
1-800-521-8486
Fax: 313-459-3647
Internet: http://www.Tapco-Intl.com

Mid Continent Cabinetry (A Div. of Norcraft Cos.)
Cabinetry; Moulding & Millwork; Specialty Products
30 E. Plato Blvd.
St. Paul, MN 55107
Phone: 612-297-0661
Fax: 612-221-0413

Midwest Fastener Corp.
Hardware
9031 Shaver Rd.
Kalamazoo, MI 49024
Phone: 1-800-444-7313
Fax: 616-327-9798

Miele Appliances
Appliances
22 D Worlds Fair Dr.
Somerset, NJ 08873
Phone: 908-560-0899
1-800-843-7231
Fax: 908-560-9649

Milgard Windows
Doors; Windows
1010 54th Ave. E.
Tacoma, WA 98424
Phone: 1-800-MILGARD

Mill River Lumber
Moulding & Millwork
Middle Rd., PO Box 209
N. Clarendon, VT 05759
Phone: 802-775-0032
Fax: 802-747-3075

Millbrook Custom Kitchens
Cabinetry
Rt. 3581 U.S. 20
Nassau, NY 12123
Phone: 518-766-3033

The Millennium Group
Tools/Hand
121 S. Monroe St.
Waterloo, WI 53594
Phone: 414-478-2304
1-800-504-0043
Fax: 414-478-9630

Miller Mfg.
Specialty Products
165 Cascade Ct.
Rohnert Park, CA 94928
Phone: 707-584-9528
1-800-232-2177
Fax: 707-584-0850

Miller Studio
Faucets & Fixtures
PO Box 997
New Philadelphia, OH 44663
Phone: 330-339-1100
1-800-332-0050
Fax: 330-339-4379

Millfab
Moulding & Millwork
433 E. South St.
Stoughton, WI 53589
Phone: 608-873-7795
Fax: 608-873-2007

The Millwork Store
Moulding & Millwork; Siding & Accessories
Rt. 4, Box 427A
Martinsburg, WV 25401
Phone: 1-800-670-6455
Fax: 304-267-1504
Internet:
http://www.millworkstore.com

The Millworks
Doors; Moulding & Millwork; Specialty Products
Box 2987
Durango, CO 81302
Phone: 970-259-5915
1-800-933-3930
Fax: 970-259-5919
Internet:
http://www.the_millworks.com

Milton W. Bosley Co.
Flooring; Moulding & Millwork
151 Eighth Ave. N.W.
Glen Burnie, MD 21061
Phone: 410-761-7727
1-800-638-5010
Fax: 410-553-0575

Milwaukee Electric Tool Co.
Equipment & Trucks; Hardware; Tools/Electric & Pneumatic; Tools/Hand
13135 W. Lisbon Rd.
Brookfield, WI 53005
Phone: 414-781-3600
Fax: 414-781-3611

MIM Architecturals
Moulding & Millwork; Specialty Products
3223 Canton St.
Dallas, TX 75226
Phone: 214-748-1113
1-800-662-1221
Fax: 214-748-7149

Minnesota Hearth Products
Fireplaces
110 S. Main St.
Lakefield, MN 56150
Phone: 507-662-5757
Fax: 507-662-6644

Minwax Co.
Paints, Caulks & Adhesives
10 Mountainview Rd.
Upper Saddle River, NJ 07458
Phone: 201-391-0253
1-800-526-0495
Fax: 201-573-9022

Miracle Adhesives (A Div. of Pratt & Lambert)
Paints, Caulks & Adhesives
75 Tonawanda St., PO Box 1505
Buffalo, NY 14240
Phone: 716-873-2770
1-800-876-7005
Fax: 716-874-1464

Miracle Sealants & Abrasives
Countertops; Flooring; Paints, Caulks & Adhesives; Siding & Accessories; Walls, Ceilings & Finishes
12806 Schabarum Ave., Bldg. A
Irwindale, CA 91706
Phone: 818-814-8988
1-800-350-1901
Fax: 818-851-8932

Mirolin Industries
Faucets & Fixtures
60 Shorncliffe Rd.
Toronto, ON M8Z 5K1 Canada
Phone: 416-231-9030
1-800-MIROLIN
1-800-463-2236

Mirrex Corp.
Walls, Ceilings & Finishes
2025 E. Linden Ave.
Linden, NJ 07036
Phone: 908-353-3370
Fax: 908-486-2347

MISG Software
Computer Software
1760 Shadowood Ln., Suite 408
Jacksonville, FL 32207
Phone: 904-398-2244
Fax: 904-399-5945

Missoula White Pine Sash Co.
Doors; Moulding & Millwork; Windows
1301 Scott St.
Missoula, MT 59802
Phone: 406-728-4010
Fax: 406-728-3408

Mister Miser
Faucets & Fixtures
4901 N. 12th St.
Quincy, IL 62301
Phone: 217-228-6900
1-888-228-6900
Fax: 217-228-6906
Internet:
http://www.adams.net/
~mwpatern/mrmiser.htm

Mitek Industries
Structural Systems
PO Box 7359
St. Louis, MO 63177
Phone: 314-434-1200
1-800-325-8075
Fax: 314-434-5343
E-mail:
mike.a.klein@rexam.com

Mitsubishi Caterpillar Forklift
Equipment & Trucks
2011 W. Sam Houston, Pkwy. N.
Houston, TX 77043
Phone: 713-467-1234

Mitsubishi Fuso Truck of America
Equipment & Trucks
PO Box 464,
100 Center Square Rd.
Bridgeport, NJ 08014
Phone: 1-800-MIT-FUSO

Mitten Vinyl
Siding & Accessories
70 Curtis Ave., N.,
PO Box 2005
Paris, ON N3L 3T2 Canada
Phone: 519-442-6375
1-800-265-0774

MK Diamond Products
Countertops; Flooring; Structural Systems; Tools/Electric & Pneumatic; Tools/Hand
1315 Storm Pkwy.
Torrance, CA 90501
Phone: 310-539-5221
1-800-TILE-SAW
Fax: 310-539-5158

MK Morse Co.
Tools/Electric & Pneumatic; Tools/Hand
PO Box 8677
Canton, OH 44711
Phone: 330-453-8187
1-800-733-3377
Fax: 330-453-1111

Modern/Aire Ventilating
Appliances; HVAC
7319 Lankershim Blvd.
North Hollywood, CA 91605
Phone: 818-765-9870
Fax: 818-765-4916

Modernfold
Doors
1711 I Ave.
New Castle, IN 47362
Phone: 317-529-1450
1-800-869-9685
Fax: 317-521-6204
Internet:
http://www.modernfold.com

Modular Hardware
Faucets & Fixtures; Hardware; Specialty Products
8190 N. Brookshire Ct., PO Box 35398
Tucson, AZ 85740
Phone: 1-800-533-0042
Fax: 1-800-533-7942
E-mail:
modhdwe@aol.com

Modulex
Structural Systems
3090 Blvd. Wilfrid-Hamel
Quebec City, PQ
G1P 2J1 Canada

Moen
Faucets & Fixtures
25300 Al Moen Dr.
North Olmsted, OH 44070-8022
Phone: 216-962-2000
1-800-553-6636
Fax: 216-962-2770

Molex
Home Technology
2222 Wellington Ct.
Lisle, IL 60532
Phone: 708-969-4550
1-800-99MOLEX, ext. 2639
Fax: 708-512-8639
Internet:
http://www.molex.com

Monarch Tile
Countertops; Flooring; Walls, Ceilings & Finishes
834 Rickwood Rd.
Florence, AL 35630
Phone: 205-764-6181
1-800-289-8453
Fax: 205-760-8686

Monier
Roofing
1 Park Plaza, Suite 900
Irvine, CA 92714
Phone: 1-800-571-8453
Fax: 714-756-2401

Monitor Products
HVAC
PO Box 3408
Princeton, NJ 08543
Phone: 908-329-0900
1-800-524-1102
Fax: 908-329-0904
Internet: http://www.monitorproducts.com

Monterey Shelf
Hardware
PO Box 1737
Hollister, CA 95024
Phone: 408-636-3324
Fax: 408-636-3326

Monumental Construction and Moulding Co.
Moulding & Millwork; Walls, Ceilings & Finishes
1512 14th St. N. W.
Washington, DC 20005
Phone: 202-328-6262
Fax: 202-745-5802

Moose Creek Lumber Co.
Flooring; Moulding & Millwork; Siding & Accessories; Structural Systems
Rt. 4, PO Box 204
Turner, ME 04282
Phone: 207-224-7497
Fax: 207-224-7376

Morgan Products
Doors; Moulding & Millwork
PO Box 2446,
500 Park Plaza
Oshkosh, WI 54901
Phone: 1-800-766-1992

Mortite
Insulation
PO Box 431,
70 Meadowview Center
Suite 235
Kankakee, IL 60901
Phone: 815-933-3801
1-800-435-7677
Fax: 815-933-6313

Moulding Associates
Doors; Moulding & Millwork
103 N. Kirby
Garland, TX 75042
Phone: 972-487-6680
1-800-394-6680
Fax: 972-487-6584
E-mail: mai1@airmail.net

Mouldings & Millwork
Engineered Lumber & Panels; Moulding & Millwork
PO Box 2300,
4041 Bridge St.
Fair Oaks, CA 95628
Phone: 916-965-1112
1-800-824-5878
Fax: 916-965-0854

Moultrie Mfg.
Landscape Design; Moulding & Millwork
PO Box 1179
Moultrie, GA 31776
Phone: 912-985-1312
1-800-841-8674
Fax: 912-890-7245

Mountain Lumber Co.
Flooring; Moulding & Millwork
PO Box 289
Ruckersville, VA 22968
Phone: 804-985-3646
1-800-445-2671
Fax: 804-985-4105

Mountain Top Timber Frames
Structural Systems
383 Miller Rd.
Halifax, PA 17032
Phone: 717-362-3179
Fax: 717-362-3179

Mountaineer Log Homes
Structural Systems
PO Box 248
Morgantown, PA 19543
Phone: 610-286-2005
Fax: 610-286-7995

Mouser Custom Cabinetry
Cabinetry
2102 N. Hwy. 31 W.,
PO Box 2527
Elizabethtown, KY 42702
Phone: 502-737-7477
Fax: 502-737-7446

Mr. Steam/Warmatowel (A Div. of Sussman Automatic Steam Products)
Faucets & Fixtures
43-20 34th St.
Long Island City, NY 11101
Phone: 718-937-4500
1-800-767-8326
Fax: 718-472-3256
Internet:
http://www.mrsteam.com

Mt. Taylor Millwork
Moulding & Millwork
PO Box 2307
Milan, NM 87021
Phone: 505-287-9469

MTI Whirlpools
Faucets & Fixtures
670 N. Price Rd.
Sugar Hill, GA 30818
Phone: 770-271-8228
Fax: 770-271-1125

Multi-Seal Pacific Corp.
Paints, Caulks & Adhesives
1109 S. Fremont Ave.
Alhambra, CA 91803
Phone: 818-289-5659
1-800-222-6915
Fax: 818-282-8516

Multiplex Technology
Home Technology
3001 Enterprise St.
Brea, CA 92621-6213
Phone: 714-996-4100
1-800-999-5225
Fax: 714-996-4900

Muncy Building Enterprises (A DKM Co.)
Structural Systems
Rt. 442 E, PO Box 246
Muncy, PA 17756-0246
Phone: 717-546-5444
1-800-377-3562
Fax: 717-546-3823

Muro North America
Hardware; Tools/Electric & Pneumatic
7 Tilbury Ct.
Brampton, ON L6T 3T4
Canada
Phone: 905-451-7667
Fax: 905-451-7936

Murray-Black Co.
Equipment & Trucks
1837 Columbus Ave.
Springfield, OH 45501
Phone: 513-323-3609
Fax: 513-323-3044

**Murray Electrical Products
Siemens Energy & Automation**
Electrical & Lighting
PO Box 9050
Charlottesville, VA 22906
Phone: 804-974-5100
1-800-548-6405
Fax: 1-800-548-6404

The Murus Co.
Insulation; Structural Systems
PO Box 220
Mansfield, PA 16933
Phone: 717-549-2100
Fax: 717-549-2101

Music and Sound
Home Technology; Specialty Products
2861 Congressman Ln.
Dallas, TX 75220
Phone: 214-358-3196
1-800-877-6631
Fax: 214-350-1913

**MW Windows
MW Manufacturers**
Doors; Moulding & Millwork; Windows
433 N. Main St.,
PO Box 559
Rocky Mount, VA 24151
Phone: 1-800-999-8400
540-489-0392
Internet:
http://www.mwwindows.com

Mylen Industries
Moulding & Millwork
650 Washington St.
Peekskill, NY 10566
Phone: 914-739-8486
1-800-431-2155
Fax: 914-739-9744

Myro
Faucets & Fixtures; Moulding & Millwork; Paints, Caulks & Adhesives
PO Box 23954,
8440 N. 87th St.
Milwaukee, WI 53223
Phone: 414-354-3678
1-800-222-6976
Fax: 414-354-3618

Myson
Faucets & Fixtures; HVAC
20 Lincoln St.
Essex Junction, VT 05452
Phone: 802-879-1170
Fax: 802-879-8950

Mystica & Co.
Electrical & Lighting; Hardware
1265 Birchrun Rd.
Chester Springs, PA 19425
Phone: 610-469-0535
Fax: 610-469-0999
Internet:
http://www.mystica.com/mystica

N

NAC Products
Engineered Lumber & Panels
PO Box 580
Canal Fulton, OH 44614
Phone: 330-854-9622
Fax: 330-854-9620

NAFCO
Flooring
PO Box 354
Florence, AL 35630
Phone: 205-766-0234
Fax: 205-766-9220

Nailite Intl.
Siding & Accessories
1251 N.W. 165th St.
Miami, FL 33169-5871
Phone: 305-620-6200
Fax: 305-623-8227
Internet:
http://www.nailite.com

Nana Wall Systems
Doors
707 Redwood Hwy.
Mill Valley, CA 94941
Phone: 415-383-3148
1-800-873-5673
Fax: 415-383-0312

Napco
Doors; Siding & Accessories; Windows
PO Box 208
Valencia, PA 16059
Phone: 412-898-1511

Napco Security Systems
Home Technology
333 Bayview Ave.
Amityville, NY 11701
Phone: 516-842-9400
1-800-645-9445
Fax: 516-842-9137

Napoleon Fireplaces (Wolf Steel)
Fireplaces
9 Napoleon Rd., RR 1
(Hwy. 11 & 93)
Barrie, ON L4M 4Y8
Canada
Phone: 705-721-1212
Fax: 705-722-6031

NASSA
Siding & Accessories
438 Dundas St. W.
Napanee, ON K7R 2C1
Canada
Phone: 613-354-9916
Fax: 613-354-9916

National Assn. of Architectural Metal Manufacturers
Doors; Moulding & Millwork; Structural Systems
8 S. Michigan Ave.,
Suite 1000
Chicago, IL 60603
Phone: 312-332-0405
Fax: 312-580-0165

National Assn. of Brick Distributors
Landscape Design; Siding & Accessories; Structural Systems
1600 Spring Hill Rd.,
Suite 305
Vienna, VA 22182
Phone: 703-749-NABD
Fax: 703-749-6227

National Assn. of Floor Covering Distributors
Flooring; Paints, Caulks & Adhesives
401 N. Michigan Ave.
Chicago, IL 60611
Phone: 312-644-6610
Fax: 312-245-1085

National Assn. of Home Builders
1201 15th St., N.W.
Washington, DC 20005
Phone: 202-822-0200
Fax: 202-822-0559

National Assn. of Store Fixture Manufacturers
1776 N. Pine Island Rd.
Plantation, FL 33322
Phone: 954-424-1443
Fax: 954-473-8268

National Bathing Products
Faucets & Fixtures
5 Greenwood Ave.
Romeoville, IL 60446
Phone: 815-886-5900
1-800-479-2311
Fax: 815-886-5936

National Concrete Masonry Assn.
Fireplaces; Landscape Design; Siding & Accessories; Structural Systems
2302 Horse Pen Rd.
Herndon, VA 22071
Phone: 703-713-1900
Fax: 703-713-1910

National Conference of States on Building Codes & Standards (NCSBCS)
505 Huntmar Park Dr.,
Suite 210
Herndon, VA 20170
Phone: 703-437-0100
TDD: 703-481-2019
Fax: 703-481-3596

National Decorating Products Assn.
1050 North Lindbergh Blvd.
St. Louis, MO 63132
Phone: 314-991-3470
1-800-737-0107
Fax: 314-991-5039

National Fiber Glass Products
Faucets & Fixtures
5 Greenwood Ave.
Romeoville, IL 60441
Phone: 708-257-3300
Fax: 815-886-5936

National Fire Protection Assn.
Home Technology
1 Batterymarch Park,
PO Box 9101
Quincy, MA 02269-9101
Phone: 617-984-7270

National Frame Builders Assn.
4840 W. 15th St.,
Suite 1000
Lawrence, KS 66049
Phone: 913-843-2444
1-800-557-6957
Fax: 913-843-7555

National Glass Assn.
8200 Greensboro Dr.,
Third Fl.
McLean, VA 22102-3881
Phone: 703-442-4890
Fax: 703-442-0630

**National Gypsum Co.
Gold Bond Building Products**
Structural Systems; Walls, Ceilings & Finishes
2001 Rexford Rd.
Charlotte, NC 28211
Phone: 704-365-7300
1-800-NATIONAL
Fax: 704-365-7222
Internet: http://www.national-gypsum.com

National Insulation & Abatement Contractors Assn. (NIAC)
Insulation
99 Canal Center Plaza
Suite 222
Alexandria, VA 22314
Phone: 703-683-6422

National Mfg.
Hardware; Room Enclosures; Siding & Accessories; Windows
PO Box 577
Sterling, IL 61081-0577
Phone: 815-625-1320,
ext. 129
1-800-435-4672
Fax: 815-625-1333

National Mfg.
Hardware; Room Enclosures; Siding & Accessories; Windows
811 Atlantic
North Kansas City, MO 64116-3918
Phone: 816-221-8990
1-800-444-9978
Fax: 816-221-8990

National Nail Corp.
Doors; Hardware
2964 Clydon S.W.
Grand Rapids, MI 49509
Phone: 616-538-8000
1-800-968-6245
Fax: 616-531-5970

National Oak Flooring Manufacturers Assn.
Flooring
PO Box 3009
Memphis, TN 38173
Phone: 901-526-5016
Fax: 901-526-7022

National Paint and Coatings Assn.
Paints, Caulks & Adhesives
1500 Rhode Island Ave., N.W.
Washington, DC 20005
Phone: 202-462-6272
Fax: 202-462-0347
Internet:
http://www.paint.org

National Particleboard Assn.
Engineered Lumber & Panels
18928 Premiere Ct.
Gaithersburg, MD 20879-1569
Phone: 301-670-0604
Fax: 301-840-1252

National Products
Cabinetry; Specialty Products; Windows
912 Baxter Ave.
Louisville, KY 40204
Phone: 502-583-3038
1-800-228-5276
Fax: 502-584-1022
Internet: http://www.nationalproducts.com

National Propane Gas Assn.
HVAC
1600 Eisenhower Ln.,
Suite 100
Lisle, IL 60532
Phone: 708-515-0600
Fax: 708-515-8774

National Sash & Door Jobbers Assn.
Moulding & Millwork
10225 Robert Trent Jones Pkwy.
New Port Richey, FL 34655-4649
Phone: 813-372-3665
1-800-786-SASH
Fax: 813-372-2879
Internet: http://www.nsdja.com

National Spa and Pool Institute
Faucets & Fixtures; Room Enclosures
2111 Eisenhower Ave.
Alexandria, VA 22314
Phone: 703-838-0083
Fax: 703-549-0493
Internet: http://www.resourcecenter.com

National Steelcrafters of Oregon Breckwell Pellet Stoves
Fireplaces
PO Box 24910,
1875 W. Sixth St.
Eugene, OR 97402
Phone: 503-683-3210
Fax: 503-683-3961

National Terrazzo and Mosaic Assn.
3166 Des Plaines Ave.,
Suite 121
Des Plaines, IL 60018-4223
Phone: 1-800-323-9736

National Truck Equipment Assn.
Equipment & Trucks
37400 Hills Tech Dr.
Farmington Hills, MI 48331-3414
Phone: 810-489-7090
1-800-441-NTEA
Fax: 810-489-8590
Internet: http://www@ntea.com

National Wood Flooring Assn.
Flooring
233 Old Meramec Station Rd.
Manchester, MO 63021
Phone: 314-391-5161
Fax: 314-391-6137

National Wood Window and Door Assn.
Doors; Windows
1400 E. Touhy Ave.,
Suite 470
Des Plaines, IL 60018-3305
Phone: 847-299-5200
1-800-223-2301
Fax: 847-299-1286
Internet: http://www.nwwda.org

Nationwide Homes
Structural Systems
PO Box 5511
1100 Rives Rd.
Martinsville, VA 24115
Phone: 540-632-7100
Fax: 540-632-1181

NCMA
(See National Concrete Masonry Assn.)

Nebs Software & Services
Computer Software
20 Industrial Park Dr.
Nashua, NH 03062
Phone: 603-880-5100
1-800-388-4344

NEI
Insulation; Roofing
50 Pine Rd.
Brentwood, NH 03833
Phone: 603-778-8899
1-800-998-4634
Fax: 603-778-7455
Internet: http://www.nei-act.com

Nevamar, Intl. Paper Co. Decorative Products Div.
Countertops
8339 Telegraph Rd.
Odenton, MD 21113
Phone: 410-551-5000

New Concept Louvers
Moulding & Millwork; Roofing; Siding & Accessories
2940 S. State St.,
PO Box 583
Springville, UT 84663
Phone: 801-489-0614
1-800-635-6448
Fax: 801-489-0606

New Dimension Homes
Structural Systems
RR 1, Box 95
Clinton, ME 04927
Phone: 207-426-7450
Fax: 207-426-9688

New Energy Works Timberframers
Engineered Lumber & Panels; Structural Systems
1755 Pioneer Rd.
Shortsville, NY 14548
Phone: 716-289-3220
Fax: 716-289-3221

New England Glass Enclosures
Room Enclosures; Windows
7 South End Plaza
New Milford, CT 06776
Phone: 203-355-2299

New England Homes
Structural Systems
270 Ocean Rd.
Greenland, NH 03840
Phone: 603-436-8830
1-800-800-8831
Fax: 603-431-8540

The New England Lock & Hardware Co.
Hardware
46 Chestnut St.,
PO Box 544
Norwalk, CT 06854
Phone: 203-866-9283
Fax: 203-838-4837
E-mail: gsimp33775

New Morning Windows
Windows
20845 Kenbridge Ct.
Lakeville, MN 55044
Phone: 612-985-5454
Fax: 612-985-5460

New-Tech Architectural Mouldings
Moulding & Millwork
2682 Walnut Ave.
Tustin, CA 92680
Phone: 714-544-6152
1-800-8-MOLDING
Fax: 714-544-7856

New-Tech Doors
Doors
2682 Walnut Ave.
Tustin, CA 92680
Phone: 714-544-6152
1-800-622-0688
Fax: 714-544-7856

New World Graphics
Computer Software
503 S. Warminster Rd.,
Suite W6
Hatboro, PA 19040
Phone: 215-871-3100
Fax: 215-871-3101

Newborn Brothers Co.
Paints, Caulks & Adhesives; Tools/Electric & Pneumatic
8221-D Preston Ct.,
PO Box 128
Jessup, MD 20794-0128
Phone: 301-604-1500
1-800-638-3893
Fax: 301-604-7950
Internet: http://www.newborncaulkguns.com

Newman Tonks
Hardware
805 N. Buckman
Shepherdsville, KY 40165
Phone: 502-543-2281
1-800-826-5792
Fax: 502-543-3089
Internet: http://www.newmantonks.com

Newstamp Lighting Co.
Electrical & Lighting
227 Bay Rd., PO Box 189
North Easton, MA 02356
Phone: 508-238-7071
Fax: 508-230-8312

Newstar Technologies
Computer Software
120 Commerce Valley Dr. E.
Thorn Hill, ON
L3T 7R2 Canada
Phone: 905-707-4000
Fax: 905-707-4329
Internet: http://www.newstar-tech.com

Newtron Products Co.
HVAC; Home Technology
3874 Virginia Ave.
Cincinnati, OH 45227
Phone: 513-561-7373
1-800-543-9149
Fax: 513-561-3673

NHB Industries
Cabinetry
944 Crawford Dr.
Peterborough, ON
K9J 3X2 Canada
Phone: 705-749-1201
Fax: 705-749-1618

NHC Hearthstone Stoves
Fireplaces
PO Box 1069
Morrisville, VT 05661
Phone: 802-888-5232
1-800-827-8683
Fax: 802-888-7249

Niagara Fiberboard
Engineered Lumber & Panels; Siding & Accessories; Walls, Ceilings & Finishes
PO Box 520
Lockport, NY 14095
Phone: 716-434-8881
Fax: 716-434-8884

NIBCO
Faucets & Fixtures; Plumbing Supplies
500 Simpson Ave.
Elkhart, IN 46516
Phone: 219-295-3000
1-800-NIBLINE
Fax: 219-295-3307

Nicolai Doors
Doors; Moulding & Millwork
PO Box 2446
Oshkosh, WI 54903
Phone: 414-235-7170

Niles Audio Corp.
Electrical & Lighting; Home Technology
12331 S.W. 130th St.
Miami, FL 33186
Phone: 305-238-4373
1-800-289-4934
Fax: 305-238-0185

Niles Building Products
Siding & Accessories; Structural Systems; Walls, Ceilings & Finishes
1600 Hunter St.
Niles, OH 44446
Phone: 330-544-0880
1-800-323-3329
Fax: 330-544-8868

Nitto Kohki USA
Tools/Electric & Pneumatic
4525 Turnberry Dr.
Hanover Park, IL 60103
Phone: 708-924-9393
1-800-323-8828
Fax: 708-924-0303

Nixalite of America
Specialty Products
PO Box 727,
1025 16th Ave.
East Moline, IL 61244
Phone: 309-755-8771
1-800-624-1189
Fax: 1-800-624-1196
Internet: http://www.nixalite.com

NMC-Focal Point
Moulding & Millwork
3051 Olympic Industrial Dr.
Smyrna, GA 30080
Phone: 404-351-0820
1-800-662-5550
Fax: 404-352-9049

Noise Control Assn.
680 Rainier Ln.
Port Ludlow, WA 98365
Phone: 360-437-0814
Fax: 360-437-0814

Nomix Corp.
Structural Systems
411 Stillson Rd.
Fairfield, CT 06430
Phone: 203-366-5600
1-800-426-6649
Fax: 203-336-7939

Nor-Cal Moulding Co.
Moulding & Millwork
PO Box 2720,
3663 Feather River Blvd.
Marysville, CA 95901
Phone: 916-741-1046
1-800-828-8308
Fax: 916-741-1099

Norandex
Siding & Accessories
8450 S. Bedford Rd.
Macedonia, OH 44056
Phone: 216-468-2200

Norbord Industries
Engineered Lumber & Panels
1 Toronto St., Suite 500
Toronto, ON M5C 2W4
Canada
Phone: 416-365-0710
Fax: 416-365-3292

Norco Windows (A Div. of JELD-WEN)
Doors; Windows
PO Box 140
Hawkins, WI 54530
Phone: 715-585-6311
1-800-826-6793
Fax: 715-585-6357

Norcraft
(See Mid Continent Cabinetry)

Nord (A Div. of JELD-WEN)
Doors
300 W. Marine View Dr.,
PO Box 1187
Everett, WA 98206-1187
Phone: 1-800-877-9482

Nordyne Intertherm Heating & Air Care Products
HVAC
1801 Park 270 Dr.,
Sixth Fl.
St. Louis, MO 63146
Phone: 314-878-6200
Fax: 314-878-4386

Norfield Industries
Paints, Caulks & Adhesives; Tools/Electric & Pneumatic; Tools/Hand
PO Box 459
Chico, CA 95927
Phone: 916-891-0389
1-800-824-6242
Fax: 916-891-1402
Internet: Norfield@dcs-chico.com

Normerica Building Systems
Structural Systems
4160 19th Ave.
Markham, ON L6C 1M2
Canada
Phone: 416-887-9616
1-800-463-7521
Fax: 416-887-9671
Internet: http://www.normerica.com

NORTEC Industries
HVAC
PO Box 698
Ogdensburg, NY 13669
Phone: 315-425-1255
Fax: 613-822-7964

Nortek
(See Broan Mfg. Co.; Music and Sound; Universal-Rundle Corp.)

North American Assn. of Mirror Manufacturers
Walls, Ceilings & Finishes
9005 Congressional Ct.
Potomac, MD 20854-4608
Phone: 301-365-2521
Fax: 301-365-7705

North American Housing Corp.
Structural Systems
PO Box 145
Point of Rocks, MD 21777
Phone: 301-694-9100
1-800-551-8726
Fax: 301-694-7570

North American Insulation Manufacturers
Insulation
44 Canal Center Plaza,
Suite 310
Alexandria, VA 22314
Phone: 703-684-0084
Fax: 703-684-0427

North American Plywood Corp.
Engineered Lumber & Panels; Structural Systems
10309 Norwalk Blvd.
Santa Fe Springs, CA 90670-0668
Phone: 310-941-7575
1-800-421-1372
Fax: 310-944-8368

North Carolina Foam (NCFI)
Insulation
PO Box 1528,
511 Carter St.
Mt. Airy, NC 27036
Phone: 910-789-9161
Fax: 910-789-9586

North Star Water Conditioning
Appliances
PO Box 64310
St. Paul, MN 55164-4310
Phone: 612-731-7456
1-800-972-0135
Fax: 612-739-5293
Internet:
http://www.northstar.
conditioning.com

Northcutt Woodworks
Moulding & Millwork
PO Box 820
Crockett, TX 75835
Phone: 409-544-2028
1-800-256-8788
Fax: 409-544-9537

Northeast Window and Door Assn.
Doors; Windows
PO Box 15822
Philadelphia, PA 19103
Phone: 215-546-8480
Fax: 215-546-7289

Northeastern Lumber Manufacturers Assn.
Engineered Lumber & Panels
PO Box 87A
Cumberland Center, ME 04021-0687
Phone: 207-829-6901
Fax: 207-829-4293

Northern Paint Canada
Paints, Caulks & Adhesives
394 Gertrude Ave.,
PO Box 3030
Winnipeg, MB R3C 4E5
Canada
Phone: 204-958-5400
Fax: 204-453-6731

The Northern Roof Tile Sales Co.
Fireplaces; Roofing; Specialty Products
4408 Milestrip Rd.,
Suite 266
Blasdell, NY 14219
Phone: 905-627-4035
Fax: 905-627-9648
Internet:
http://www.wchat.on.ca/
commercial/nrts

Northridge Systems
Computer Software
PO Box 1275
Layton, UT 84041
Phone: 801-779-3512
1-800-204-3377
Fax: 801-779-2021

Northwest Construction Software
Computer Software
3415 N.E. 98th Ave.
Vancouver, WA 98662
Phone: 360-944-8318
1-800-368-6335
Fax: 360-254-2581
Internet: ncs@teleport.com

Northwest Window Works
Doors; Windows
3223 164th S.W., Bldg. N
Lynnwood, WA 98037
Phone: 206-743-4442
1-800-878-4442
Fax: 206-742-8820

Norton Co.
Paints, Caulks & Adhesives; Tools/Electric & Pneumatic
1 New Bond St.,
PO Box 15008
Worcester, MA 01615
Phone: 1-800-551-4415
Fax: 817-968-7400

Norton Construction Products
Tools/Electric & Pneumatic; Tools/Hand
PO Box 2898
Gainesville, GA 30503
Phone: 770-967-3954
1-800-554-8003
Fax: 1-800-443-1092

Novi American
Faucets & Fixtures
6195 Purdue Dr.,
PO Box 44649
Atlanta, GA 30336-5649
Phone: 404-344-5600
1-800-726-6684
Fax: 404-344-3185

NPC Sealants
Paints, Caulks & Adhesives
1208 S. Eighth Ave.
Maywood, IL 60153
Phone: 708-681-1040
1-800-654-1042
Fax: 708-681-1424

NRG Barriers
The E'NRG'Y House
Insulation
27 Pearl St.
Portland, ME 04101
Phone: 207-879-7117
1-800-514-1968 (ME)
Fax: 1-800-343-1331

NT Falcon Lock
Hardware
2650 Orbiter St.
Brea, CA 92821
Phone: 714-572-6008
1-800-266-4456
Fax: 714-577-5809

NT Quality Hardware
Hardware
2650 Orbiter St.
Brea, CA 92821-6265
Phone: 714-572-6008
1-800-345-8819
Fax: 714-577-5809

Nuline Industries
Roofing
4900 Ondura Dr.
Fredericksburg, VA 22407-8773
Phone: 703-898-7000
1-800-777-7663

NuTone
Appliances; Cabinetry; Electrical & Lighting; HVAC; Home Technology; Specialty Products
Madison & Red Bank Rds.
Cincinnati, OH 45227
Phone: 513-527-5100
1-800-543-8687
Fax: 1-513-527-5177
Internet:
http://www.faucet.com/
faucet/nutone/nutone.
html

O

O'Hagin's
Roofing
2661 Gravenstein Hwy.
S., Suite 107
Sebastopol, CA 95472
Phone: 707-823-4762
1-800-394-3864
Fax: 707-823-5208

O'Keeffe's
Doors; Roofing; Windows
75 Williams Ave.
San Francisco, CA 94124
Phone: 415-822-4222
Fax: 415-822-5222

Oak Flooring Institute/ National Oak Flooring Manufacturers Assn.
Flooring
PO Box 3009
Memphis, TN 38173
Phone: 901-526-5016
Fax: 901-526-7022

Oak Post & Beam
Structural Systems
PO Box 164
Princeton, MA 01541
Phone: 508-464-5418
Fax: 508-464-7785

Oakbridge Timber Framing
Structural Systems
20857 Earnest Rd.
Howard, OH 43028
Phone: 614-599-5711

Oakwood Classic & Custom Woodworks
Doors; Moulding & Millwork
517 W. Commercial St.
East Rochester, NY 14445
Phone: 716-381-6009
Fax: 716-383-8053

Oasis Industries
Faucets & Fixtures
1600 Mountain St.
Aurora, IL 60505
Phone: 630-898-3500
1-800-323-2748
Fax: 630-898-8089
Internet: http://www.
oasisbath.com

Oberon Products/TCT
Faucets & Fixtures
4260 Kearney St.
Denver, CO 80216
Phone: 303-331-0304
1-800-852-1314
Fax: 303-331-0320

Occidental Leather
Tools/Hand
60 W. Sixth St.
Santa Rosa, CA 95401
Phone: 707-522-2500
1-800-743-6914
Fax: 707-522-2508

The October Co.
Cabinetry; Countertops; Specialty Products
PO Box 71, 51 Ferry St.
Easthampton, MA 01027
Phone: 413-527-9380
1-800-628-9346
Fax: 413-527-0091

ODL
Doors; Windows
215 E. Roosevelt Ave.
Zeeland, MI 49464
Phone: 616-772-9111
Fax: 616-772-9110

Ohio Sealants
Paints, Caulks & Adhesives
7405 Production Dr.
Mentor, OH 44060
Phone: 216-255-8900
1-800-321-3578
Fax: 216-255-1008

Ohline Corp.
Doors; Siding & Accessories
1930 W. 139th St.
Gardena, CA 90249
Phone: 310-327-4630
Fax: 310-538-5742

Old Carolina Brick Co.
Fireplaces; Landscape Design; Siding & Accessories; Specialty Products; Structural Systems
475 Majolica Rd.
Salisbury, NC 28147
Phone: 704-636-8850
Fax: 704-636-0000

Old Masters
Paints, Caulks & Adhesives
1900 Albany Pl. S.
Orange City, IA 51041
Phone: 712-737-3436
1-800-747-3436
Fax: 712-737-3893

Old Town Lumber Co.
Siding & Accessories
PO Box 465
Kenduskeag, ME 04450
Phone: 207-884-8100
Fax: 207-884-8384

Old Virginia Hand Hewn Log Homes
Structural Systems
Rt. 2, Box 455A,
US Hwy. 58
Pennington Gap, VA 24277
Phone: 540-546-5647
Fax: 540-546-2403
Internet:
http://www.mounet.com/
OLD VA Log Homes

The Old Wagon Factory
Doors; Moulding & Millwork
103 Russell St., Dept.
RME95, PO Box 1427
Clarksville, VA 23927
Phone: 804-374-5787
Fax: 804-374-4646

Oldach Wood Windows & Doors
Doors; Windows
813 N. Union Blvd.
Colorado Springs, CO 80909
Phone: 719-636-5181
Fax: 719-636-9006

Oldham/United States Saw Co.
Hardware; Tools/Electric & Pneumatic
PO Box 10, 2084
Lockport-Olcott Rd.
Burt, NY 14028
Phone: 716-778-8588
1-800-828-9000
Fax: 716-778-8625

Olson Saw Co.
Hardware
16 Stony Hill Rd.
Bethel, CT 06801-1039
Phone: 203-792-8622
Fax: 203-790-9832

Olympic Paints and Stains
Paints, Caulks & Adhesives
1 PPG Plaza
Pittsburgh, PA 15272
Phone: 412-434-3900
1-800-621-2024
Fax: 412-434-3996

Omaha Industrial Tools
Paints, Caulks & Adhesives; Tools/Electric & Pneumatic; Tools/Hand
14685 Grover St.
Omaha, NE 68144-5435
Phone: 402-334-8185
1-800-228-2765
Fax: 402-334-0409
E-mail: omaha-tools@
worldnet.att.net

Omega Lighting
Div. of Thomas Lighting
Electrical & Lighting
6430 E. Slauson Ave.
Los Angeles, CA 90040
Phone: 213-726-1800
Fax: 213-728-1319

Omega Sunspaces
Room Enclosures
3852 Hawkins N.W.
Albuquerque, NM 87109
Phone: 505-344-0333
1-800-753-3034
Fax: 505-344-0641

Omni Corp.
Appliances
2500 165th St.
Hammond, IN 46320
Phone: 219-989-9800
1-800-323-8833
Fax: 219-844-0819

Omnia Industries
Faucets & Fixtures; Hardware
5 Cliffside Dr., Box 330
Cedar Grove, NJ 07009
Phone: 201-239-7272
Fax: 201-239-5960

Omniglass
Windows
1205 Sherwin Rd.
Winnipeg, MB R3H 0V1
Canada
Phone: 204-987-8522
Fax: 204-694-9336

Omware
(See The Master Builder Software By Omware)

Ondine from Interbath
Faucets & Fixtures
665 N. Baldwin Park Blvd.
City of Industry, CA 91746-1502
Phone: 818-369-1841
1-800-1-800-2132
Fax: 818-369-3316

Ondura Corp.
Roofing; Room Enclosures
4900 Ondura Dr.
Fredericksburg, VA 22401
Phone: 703-898-7000
1-800-777-7663

Oneida Royal Furnace The Utica Cos.
HVAC
PO Box 4279,
2201 Dwyer Ave.
Utica, NY 13504
Phone: 315-797-1310
Fax: 315-797-3762

Opella
Faucets & Fixtures
4062 Kingston Ct.
Marietta, GA 30067
Phone: 770-955-5155
1-800-969-0339
Fax: 770-955-5955

Open Systems
Computer Software
7626 Golden Triangle Dr.
Eden Prairie, MN 55344
Phone: 612-829-0011
1-800-328-2276
Fax: 612-829-1493
Internet: info@osas.com

Orcon Corp.
Paints, Caulks & Adhesives; Tools/Hand
1570 Atlantic St.
Union City, CA 94587
Phone: 510-489-8100
Fax: 510-489-9349
Internet:
http://www.orcon.com

Oregon Dome/ Design Pacific
Structural Systems
3215 Meadow Ln.
Eugene, OR 97402
Phone: 503-689-3443
1-800-572-8943
Fax: 503-689-9275

Oregon Lumber Co.
Flooring; Moulding & Millwork
PO Box 711
Lake Owsego, OR 97034
Phone: 1-800-824-5671
Fax: 503-635-6140

Oregon Research & Development Corp.
Snow Roof Systems
Paints, Caulks & Adhesives; Roofing; Specialty Products
1895 16th St. S.E.
Salem, OR 97302-1436
Phone: 503-588-7000
1-800-345-0809
Fax: 1-800-588-2075
Internet: http://www.
cyberhighway.net/
~snowroof

Oregon Wooden Screen Doors
Doors; Moulding & Millwork
2767 Harris St.
Eugene, OR 97405
Phone: 503-485-0279
Fax: 503-484-0353

Original Cast Lighting
Electrical & Lighting
6120 Delmar Blvd.
St. Louis, MO 63112
Phone: 314-863-1895
Fax: 314-863-3278

Ornamental Mouldings
Moulding & Millwork
PO Box 4068,
3804 Comanche Rd.
Archdale, NC 27263
Phone: 919-431-9120
1-800-779-1135
Fax: 919-431-9104

Osburn Mfg.
Fireplaces
555 Ardersier Rd.
Victoria, BC V8Z 1C8
Canada
Phone: 604-475-3800
Fax: 604-475-1028

Osmose Wood Preserving
Paints, Caulks & Adhesives
1016 Everee Inn Rd.
Griffin, GA 30224
Phone: 404-228-8434
1-800-522-9663
Fax: 404-229-5225

Osram Sylvania
Electrical & Lighting; Equipment & Trucks
100 Endicott St.
Danvers, MA 01923
Phone: 508-777-1900
1-800-544-4828
Fax: 508-750-2152

Outwater Plastics Industries
4 Passaic St.
Wood-Ridge, NJ 07075
Phone: 201-340-1040
1-800-631-8375
Fax: 1-800-888-3315
Internet: http://www.outwater.com

Outwater Plastics Industries Architectural Div.
52 Passaic St.
Wood-Ridge, NJ 07075
Phone: 201-365-2002
1-800-835-4400
Fax: 1-800-835-4403
Internet: http://www.arch-pro.com

Overhead Door Corp.
Garage Doors & Openers
6750 LBJ Fwy.,
Suite 1200
Dallas, TX 75240
Phone: 214-233-6611
1-800-929-DOOR
Fax: 214-233-0367

Owens Corning
Doors; Insulation; Roofing; Siding & Accessories; Windows
Fiberglas Tower
Toledo, OH 43659
Phone: 1-800-GET-PINK
Internet:http://www.owenscorning.com

P

P&M Cedar Products
Moulding & Millwork; Siding & Accessories
PO Box 7349
Stockton, CA 95207
Phone: 209-957-2802
Fax: 209-474-9344

PA Stratton & Co.
Hardware
PO Box 436
Milan, OH 44846-0436
Phone: 419-499-4449
Fax: 419-499-3379

Pace Industries
Cabinetry
2545 W. Polk St.
Chicago, IL 60612
Phone: 312-226-7000
Fax: 312-226-1169

Pacific Clay Brick Products
Fireplaces; Landscape Design; Siding & Accessories; Structural Systems
PO Box 549
Lake Elsinore, CA 92531-0549
Phone: 909-674-2131
Fax: 909-674-4909

Pacific Energy Woodstoves (1986)
Fireplaces
PO Box 1060
Duncan, BC V9L 3Y2
Canada
Phone: 604-748-1184
Fax: 604-748-0844

The Pacific Lumber Co.
Engineered Lumber & Panels; Flooring; Siding & Accessories
PO Box 565
Scotia, CA 95565
Phone: 707-764-8888
Fax: 707-764-4444

Pacific Post & Beam
Structural Systems
PO Box 13708
San Luis Obispo, CA 93406
Phone: 805-543-7565
Fax: 805-543-1287

Pacific Sauna & Steam
Appliances; Faucets & Fixtures
837 Arnold Dr., Suite 4
Martinez, CA 94553
Phone: 510-370-1050
1-800-232-4356
Fax: 510-370-2431

Pacific Wood Laminates
Engineered Lumber & Panels; Moulding & Millwork; Siding & Accessories; Structural Systems
819 Rail Road Ave.
Brookings, OR 97415
Phone: 541-469-4177
Fax: 541-469-6153

Package Pavement Co.
Structural Systems
Rt. 52
Stormville, NY 12582
Phone: 914-221-2224
1-800-724-8193
Fax: 914-221-0433

Pagliacco Turning & Milling
Moulding & Millwork
PO Box 225
Woodacre, CA 94973
Phone: 415-488-4333
Fax: 415-488-9372

Paige Innovations
Electrical & Lighting
12994 Keele St.
King City, ON L7B 1H8
Canada
Phone: 905-833-0983
1-800-461-1648
Fax: 905-833-4282

Palmer Industries
Insulation; Paints, Caulks & Adhesives; Roofing
10611 Old Annapolis Rd.
Frederick, MD 21701
Phone: 301-898-7848
Fax: 301-898-3312

Palmer Products Corp.
Paints, Caulks & Adhesives
PO Box 7155
Louisville, KY 40257
Phone: 502-893-3668
1-800-431-6151
Fax: 502-895-9253
Internet: http://www.mirro-mastic.com

Pam Fastening Technology
Hardware; Paints, Caulks & Adhesives; Tools/Electric & Pneumatic; Tools/Hand
PO Box 669063
Charlotte, NC 28266
Phone: 704-394-3141
Fax: 704-394-9339

Panasonic
Appliances; Electrical & Lighting; HVAC; Tools/Electric & Pneumatic
1 Panasonic Way, 4A-4
Secaucus, NJ 07094
Phone: 201-392-6442
1-800-553-0384
Fax: 201-348-7003

Panelfold
Doors
PO Box 680130
Miami, FL 33168
Phone: 305-688-3501
Fax: 305-688-0185

Panneaux Thermo Briques
Siding & Accessories
273 Gaspe, CP 160
St. Apollinaire, PQ
G0S 2E0 Canada
Phone: 418-881-2243
Fax: 418-881-2243

Paragon Electric Co.
Electrical & Lighting
606 Pkwy. Blvd.
Two Rivers, WI 54241
Phone: 414-793-1161
Fax: 414-793-3736

Parex
Paints, Caulks & Adhesives; Siding & Accessories
PO Box 189
Redan, GA 30074
Phone: 770-482-7872
1-800-LE PAREX
Fax: 770-482-6878
Internet: http://www.parex.com

Paris Kitchens
Cabinetry; Countertops
245 W. Beaver Creek Rd.,
Unit 2
Richmond Hill, ON
L4B 1L1 Canada
Phone: 905-886-5751
1-800-656-6415
Fax: 905-886-8858

Parker Hannifin Corp.
Faucets & Fixtures; Plumbing Supplies; Tools/Electric & Pneumatic
17325 Euclid Ave.
Cleveland, OH 44112
Phone: 216-531-3000
1-800-272-7537
Fax: 216-486-0618

Parks Corp.
Paints, Caulks & Adhesives
1 West St.
Fall River, MA 02720
Phone: 508-679-5938
1-800-225-8543
Fax: 508-674-8404

ParPac
Insulation
27 Main St.
West Swanzey, NH 03469
Phone: 603-357-6625
1-800-850-8505
Fax: 603-357-6621

Parsec
Insulation; Specialty Products
PO Box 551477
Dallas, TX 75355-1477
Phone: 214-341-6700
1-800-527-3454
Fax: 214-553-0983

Partee Flooring Mill
Flooring
PO Box 667
Magnolia, AR 71753
Phone: 501-234-4082
Fax: 501-234-8123

Particleboard/Medium Density Fiberboard Institute
Cabinetry; Countertops; Engineered Lumber & Panels; Moulding & Millwork; Specialty Products
18928 Premiere Ct.
Gaithersburg, MD 20879-1569
Phone: 301-670-1752
Fax: 301-840-1252
Internet: http://www.pbmdf.com

Partner Industrial Products
Tools/Electric & Pneumatic; Tools/Hand
905 W. Irving Park Rd.
Itasca, IL 60143
Phone: 1-800-323-3553
Fax: 630-773-6339

Paslode, an Illinois Tool Works, Co.
Tools/Electric & Pneumatic
888 Forest Edge Dr.
Vernon Hills, IL 60061
Phone: 847-634-1900
1-800-323-1303
Fax: 847-634-1006
Internet: http://www.paslode.com

Pass & Seymour/ Legrand
Electrical & Lighting
PO Box 4822
Syracuse, NY 13221
Phone: 315-468-6211
1-800-223-4185
Fax: 315-468-6296

Patrick Industries
Countertops; Engineered Lumber & Panels; Paints, Caulks & Adhesives
PO Box 638,
1800 S. 14th St.
Elkhart, IN 46515
Phone: 219-294-7511
Fax: 219-522-5213

Patriot Log Home
Structural Systems
15 Robert St.
Saint-Sauveur-des-Monts,
PQ J0R 1R6 Canada
Phone: 514-227-4608
Fax: 514-227-1461

Paul Decorative Products
Cabinetry; Faucets & Fixtures; Hardware
810 E. 136th St.
Bronx, NY 10454-3509
Phone: 718-402-2988
Fax: 718-402-3649
E-mail: pauldecor@aol.com

Paveloc Industries
Landscape Design
8302 S. Rt. 23
Marengo, IL 60152
Phone: 815-568-4700
1-800-590-2772
Fax: 815-568-1210

Payne
HVAC
PO Box 70
Indianapolis, IN 46206
Phone: 317-243-0851
1-800-227-4633
Fax: 317-240-5182

PDQ Industries
Hardware
2754 Creek Hill Rd.
Leola, PA 17504
Phone: 717-656-4281
1-800-441-9692
Fax: 717-656-6892

Peace Flooring Co.
Flooring
PO Box 87
Magnolia, AR 71753
Phone: 501-234-2310
1-800-234-2510
Fax: 501-234-5145

Peachtree Doors
Doors; Windows
PO Box 5700
Norcross, GA 30091
Phone: 770-497-2000
1-800-477-6544
Fax: 404-497-2437

Peachtree Software
Computer Software
1505 Pavilion Pl.
Norcross, GA 30093
Phone: 770-724-4000
1-800-247-3224
Fax: 770-724-4009
Internet: http://www.peachtree.com

Pearl Baths
Faucets & Fixtures
9224 73rd Ave. N.
Minneapolis, MN 55428
Phone: 612-424-3335
1-800-328-2531
Fax: 612-424-9808

Pearl Mantels
Moulding & Millwork
10846 E. Shelby Dr.
Collierville, TN 38017
Phone: 901-853-8237
Fax: 901-861-1057

Pease Industries
Doors; Hardware
7100 Dixie Hwy.
Fairfield, OH 45014
Phone: 513-870-3600
1-800-88-DOORS
Fax: 513-870-3602

Peerless Faucet Co. (A Div. of Masco Corp. of Indiana)
Faucets & Fixtures
55 E. 111th St.
Indianapolis, IN 46280
Phone: 317-848-1812

The Peerless Heater Co. Div. of Peerless Ind.
HVAC
231 N. Walnut St.,
PO Box 855
Boyertown, PA 19512
Phone: 610-367-2153
Fax: 610-369-3284

Peerless Products
Doors; Windows
PO Box 2469
Shawnee Mission, KS
66201
Phone: 913-344-0770
1-800-279-9999
Fax: 913-344-0715
Internet: http://www.
peerlessproducts.com

Pella Corporation
Doors; Windows
102 Main St.
Pella, IA 50219
Phone: 515-628-1000
1-800-84-PELLA
Fax: 515-628-6457
Internet:
http://www.pella.com

Pelonis/Del-Rain Corp.
Home Technology
4808 Wilton Ave.
Niagara Falls, NY 14304
Phone: 716-283-0060
1-800-428-2204
Fax: 716-283-0201

Pemko Mfg. Co.
*Hardware; Insulation;
Moulding & Millwork;
Specialty Products*
4226 Transport St.
Ventura, CA 93003
Phone: 805-642-2600
1-800-283-9988
Fax: 805-642-4109
Internet:
http://www.pemko.com/

Pendu Mfg.
*Structural Systems;
Tools/Electric & Pneumatic*
718 N. Shirk Rd.
New Holland, PA 17557
Phone: 717-354-4348
1-800-233-0471
Fax: 717-355-2148
E-mail:
pendumfg@redrose.net

Penn Wood Products
*Flooring; Moulding &
Millwork*
PO Box 180
East Berlin, PA 17316
Phone: 717-259-9551
Fax: 717-259-7560

**Penofin-Performance
Coatings**
Paints, Caulks & Adhesives
PO Box 1569, 360 Lake
Mendocino Dr.
Ukiah, CA 95482
Phone: 707-462-3023
1-800-PENOFIN
Fax: 707-462-6139
Internet:
http://www.penofin.com

Pentax Corp.
Tools/Hand
35 Inverness Dr. E.
Englewood, CO 80112
Phone: 303-799-8000
1-800-729-1419, ext. 351
Fax: 303-643-0253

Perfect Software
Computer Software
50 E. Foothill Blvd.,
First Fl.
Arcadia, CA 91006
Phone: 818-445-9700
Fax: 818-445-0381
Internet:
http://www.perfectsoft

Perfection-Schwank
HVAC
Hwy. 56, PO Box 749
Waynesboro, GA 30830
Phone: 706-554-2101
1-800-776-8459
Fax: 706-554-3933

Perma-Chink Systems
Paints, Caulks & Adhesives
1605 Prosser Rd.
Knoxville, TN 37914
Phone: 615-524-7343
1-800-548-3554
Fax: 615-523-9475

Perma-Door
Doors
631 N. First St.
West Branch, MI 48661
Phone: 517-345-5110
1-800-842-3667
Fax: 517-345-5116

Perma R" Products
*Insulation; Roofing; Siding
& Accessories; Structural
Systems*
PO Box 279
Grenada, MS 38902
Phone: 601-226-8075
1-800-647-6130
Fax: 601-226-8088

PermaGrain Products
Countertops; Flooring
4789 West Chester Pike
Newtown Square, PA 19073
Phone: 610-353-8801
Fax: 610-353-4822
Internet: http://www.
permagrain.com/home

Permalatt
*Landscape Design; Siding
& Accessories*
1810 E. Hwy. 30,
PO Box 853
Lexington, NE 68850
Phone: 308-324-2227
1-888-457-4342
Fax: 308-324-2381

Perstorp Flooring
Flooring
524 New Hope Rd.
Raleigh, NC 27610
Phone: 919-773-6000
1-800-222-1817
Fax: 919-773-6004

Peterson Industries
Doors; Faucets & Fixtures
7350 N.W. 37 Ave.
Miami, FL 33147
Phone: 305-691-7943
1-800-331-4478
Fax: 305-693-0754

Petmal Supply Co.
*Countertops; Fireplaces;
Flooring; Landscape
Design; Moulding &
Millwork; Roofing;
Structural Systems; Walls,
Ceilings & Finishes*
830 Atlantic Ave.
Baldwin, NY 11510
Phone: 516-867-4573
Fax: 516-867-4691

**Petmark Home
Security Products**
*Hardware; Home
Technology*
11 Edvac Dr., Unit 2
Brampton, ON L6S 5W5
Canada
Phone: 905-791-1240
1-800-649-9822
Fax: 905-791-1292

Pfanstiehl Corp.
Home Technology
3300 Washington St.
Waukegan, IL 60085
Phone: 847-623-1360
1-800-323-9446
Fax: 847-623-9107

PH Chadbourne & Co.
Siding & Accessories
PO Box 88
Bethel, ME 04217
Phone: 207-824-2800
Fax: 207-824-3429

PH Tech
Doors; Hardware; Windows
8650 Blvd. de la Rive-Sud
Levis, PQ G6V 6N8
Canada
Phone: 418-833-3231
Fax: 418-835-1145

Phifer Wire Products
Windows
PO Box 1700
Tuscaloosa, AL 35403
Phone: 205-345-2120
1-800-633-5955
Fax: 205-759-4450

**Philips Consumer
Electronics Co.
Home Theater Div.**
Home Technology
1 Philips Dr.
Knoxville, TN 37914
Phone: 615-521-4316
1-800-822-4788
Fax: 615-521-3242

Philips Lighting Co.
Electrical & Lighting
200 Franklin Square Dr.
Somerset, NJ 08875
Phone: 908-563-3215
Fax: 908-563-3641
Internet:
http://www.philips.com/
lighting/

Philips Products
Doors; Windows
3221 Magnum Dr.
Elkhart, IN 46516
Phone: 219-296-0000
Fax: 219-296-0147

Philstone Fasteners
*Hardware; Landscape
Design; Structural Systems*
11 Cove St.,
PO Box 41389
New Bedford, MA
02744-1389
Phone: 508-990-2054
1-800-225-9015
Fax: 508-984-5547

Phoenix Lock Co.
Hardware
321 Third Ave.
Newark, NJ 07107
Phone: 201-483-0976
Fax: 201-483-0977

Phoenix Products
Faucets & Fixtures
583 Miller Rd.
Avon Lake, OH 44012
Phone: 216-933-8100
1-800-222-6041
Fax: 216-933-6252

Photocomm
HVAC
768 Le Gray Rd.
Scottsdale, AZ 85260
Phone: 602-948-8003
1-800-844-6466
Fax: 602-951-6329

**Piedmont Home
Products**
Moulding & Millwork
PO Box 269
Ruckersville, VA 22968
Phone: 804-985-8909
1-800-622-3399
Fax: 804-985-8910

**Pine Grove Post &
Beam Builders**
Structural Systems
4 Bates Rd.
Johnson City, NY 13790
Phone: 607-754-0821

Pinecrest
*Doors; Moulding &
Millwork; Walls, Ceilings
& Finishes*
2118 Blaisdell Ave.
Minneapolis, MN 55404
Phone: 612-871-7071
1-800-443-5357
Fax: 612-871-8956

Pinnacle Technology
Computer Software
1567 Frontenac Rd.
Naperville, IL 60563
Phone: 1-800-346-4658
Fax: 312-571-5739

Pinpoint Laser Systems
Tools/Hand
Commerce Park No. 14,
3 Graf Rd.
Newburyport, MA 01950
Phone: 508-462-8056
1-800-757-5383
Fax: 508-462-3561
Internet: http://www.
ourworld.compuserve.com/
homepages/Pinpoint_
Laser_Systems

**Pioneer Electronics
(USA)**
Home Technology
2265 E. 220th St.,
PO Box 1720
Long Beach, CA 90801
Phone: 213-746-6337

Pioneer Millworks
Flooring; Structural Systems
1755 Pioneer Rd.
Shortsville, NY 14548
Phone: 716-289-3090
Fax: 716-289-3221

**Pioneer Plastics Corp.
Pionite Decorative
Laminates**
Countertops
PO Box 1014, 1 Pionite Rd.
Auburn, ME 04211-1014
Phone: 207-784-9111
1-800-746-6483
Fax: 207-784-0392

**Pisa Retaining Wall
Systems**
Landscape Design
4362 Northlake Blvd.,
Suite 111
Palm Beach Gardens, FL
33410
Phone: 1-800-626-WALL

**Pitcairn-Ferguson &
Associates**
Structural Systems
Cairnson Farm, RD 2
Box 15-1A
Kempton, PA 19529
Phone: 610-756-6602
Fax: 610-756-6849

**Pittsburgh Corning
Corp.**
Windows
800 Presque Isle Dr.
Pittsburgh, PA 15239
Phone: 412-327-6100
1-800-992-5769
Fax: 412-327-5890

**Pivotal Suspension
Seating**
Cabinetry
5581 S. 320 W.
Salt Lake City, UT
84107-5868
Phone: 801-262-7886
1-800-678-7328
Fax: 801-262-7891
Internet: http://www.
pivotal-seating.com

**PL Adhesives & Sealants
ChemRex**
*Paints, Caulks
& Adhesives; Structural
Systems*
889 Valley Park Dr.
Shakopee, MN 55379
Phone: 612-496-6000
1-800-433-9517
Fax: 612-496-6062

PL Bath Products
Cabinetry
7 Wood Ave.
Bristol, PA 19007
Phone: 1-800-488-2284
Fax: 215-826-9666

**Plain & Fancy Custom
Cabinetry**
Cabinetry
PO Box 519
Schaefferstown, PA
17088-0519
Phone: 717-949-6571
Fax: 717-949-2114

Plancher Heritage
Flooring
PO Box 280
Kedgwick, NB E0K 1C0
Canada
Phone: 506-284-2116
Fax: 506-284-2828

Planit Intl.
Computer Software
1921 Corporate Sq. Blvd.
Slidell, LA 70458
Phone: 504-649-0484
Fax: 504-649-3849

Plano Molding Co.
Tools/Hand
431 E. South St.
Plano, IL 60545
Phone: 708-552-3111
Fax: 708-552-8989

PlanTag
3111 B-18 Fortune Way
West Palm Beach, FL
33414
Phone: 407-793-2007
1-800-289-8236
Fax: 407-790-3091

Plaskolite
Faucets & Fixtures
PO Box 1497
Columbus, OH 43216
Phone: 614-294-3281
1-800-848-9124
Fax: 614-297-7287

Plasteco
Windows
PO Box 24158
Houston, TX 77229
Phone: 713-453-8696
1-800-231-6117
Fax: 713-453-8372

Plasti-Kote Co.
Paints, Caulks & Adhesives
1000 Lake Rd.
Medina, OH 44256
Phone: 216-725-4511
1-800-431-5928
Fax: 216-723-3674

Plastic Creations
Faucets & Fixtures
1023 S. Hamilton St.
Dalton, GA 30720
Phone: 706-278-7090
1-800-868-0254
Fax: 706-272-3456

**Plastic Pipe & Fittings
Assn.**
Plumbing Supplies
800 Roosevelt Rd.,
Bldg. C, Suite 20
Glen Ellyn, IL 60137-5833
Phone: 708-858-6540
Fax: 708-790-3095

Plastic Tubing
Plumbing Supplies
PO Box 878,
1935 Hwy. 24 W.
Roseboro, NC 28382
Phone: 910-525-5121
1-800-448-4784
Fax: 910-525-4934

Plastics Research Corp.
Landscape Design
3200 Robert T. Longway
Flint, MI 48506
Phone: 810-235-0400
1-800-879-7723
Fax: 810-235-0401

Plastics & Resins
Insulation; Paints, Caulks & Adhesives; Roofing; Specialty Products
PO Box 392, 850 Glen Ave.
Moorestown, NJ 08057
Phone: 609-866-7600
1-800-1-800-2844
Fax: 609-866-7603

Plastival
Equipment & Trucks; Landscape Design; Moulding & Millwork
2035 Francis-Hughes
Chomedey, Laval, PQ
H7S 2G2 Canada
Phone: 514-629-5050
Fax: 514-629-5052

Plastmo
Siding & Accessories
8246 Sandy Court, Suite B
Jessup, MD 20794
Phone: 301-776-0200
1-800-899-0992
Fax: 410-792-8047

Plato Woodworking
Cabinetry
PO Box 98
Plato, MN 55370-5419
Phone: 1-800-328-5924
Fax: 612-238-2131

Plaza Hardwood
Flooring
5 Enebro Ct.
Santa Fe, NM 87505
Phone: 505-466-7885
1-800-662-6306
Fax: 505-466-0456

Plum Creek Southern Region
Engineered Lumber & Panels
PO Box 1919
West Monroe, LA 71294
Phone: 318-362-2372
1-800-854-0247
Fax: 318-362-2272

Plumb/It Level Corp.
Tools/Hand
3045 N. Dodge Blvd.
Tucson, AZ 85716
Phone: 602-881-5777
1-800-759-9925
Fax: 602-881-5111

Plumb Pak Corp.
Faucets & Fixtures; Plumbing Supplies
1170 Main St.
Newington, CT 06111
Phone: 860-666-3348
1-800-243-0526
Fax: 860-665-0374

Plumb Shop
Faucets & Fixtures; Plumbing Supplies
39600 Orchard Hill Pl.
Novi, MI 48375-5331
Phone: 810-305-6000
Fax: 810-305-6011

Plumbing Manufacturers Institute
Faucets & Fixtures; Plumbing Supplies
800 Roosevelt Rd.,
Bldg. C, Suite 20
Glen Ellyn, IL 60137-5833
Phone: 708-858-9172
Fax: 708-790-3095

Ply Gem Mfg.
Cabinetry; Countertops; Engineered Lumber & Panels; Flooring; Moulding & Millwork; Walls, Ceilings & Finishes
201 Black Horse Pike
Haddon Heights, NJ 08035
Phone: 609-546-0704
Fax: 609-546-0539

Plylap Industries
Engineered Lumber & Panels; Moulding & Millwork; Siding & Accessories
1462-D Tanforan Ave.
Woodland, CA 95776
Phone: 916-661-0812
Fax: 916-661-0864

Plywood Tropics USA
Cabinetry; Engineered Lumber & Panels; Moulding & Millwork; Walls, Ceilings & Finishes
1 S.W. Columbia,
Suite 480
Portland, OR 97223
Phone: 503-274-0319
Fax: 503-222-3823

PMX
Hardware
20519 Walnut Dr.
Walnut, CA 91789
Phone: 909-598-7023
Fax: 909-594-1383

Poggenpohl US
Cabinetry
145 U.S. Hwy. 46 W.,
Suite 200
Wayne, NJ 07470
Phone: 201-812-8900
Fax: 201-812-9320
Internet:
http://www.poggenpohl.usa.com

Point Electric
Electrical & Lighting
PO Box 619
Nanuet, NY 10954-0619
Phone: 914-623-3471
Fax: 914-623-1861
E-mail:
swivelier@juno.com

Polaroid Corp.
575 Technology Sq.-2
Cambridge, MA 02139
Phone: 617-386-6341
Fax: 617-386-6324
Internet:
http://www.polaroid.com

Pollard Windows
Doors; Windows
1217 King Rd.
Burlington, ON L7R 3Y3
Canada
Phone: 905-634-2365
Fax: 905-333-3521

Poly-Tak Protection Systems
Equipment & Trucks; Specialty Products
5731 McFadden Ave.
Huntington Beach, CA 92649
Phone: 714-892-6128
1-800-899-0871
Fax: 714-892-7128

Poly-Wall Intl.
Specialty Products
8400 Coral Sea St. N.E.,
Suite 800
Blaine, MN 55449
Phone: 612-780-0161
1-800-846-3020
Fax: 612-780-0170

Polyfoam Packers Corp.
Insulation; Siding & Accessories; Structural Systems
2320 Foster Ave.
Wheeling, IL 60090
Phone: 847-398-0110
Fax: 847-398-0653

Polytronix
Windows
805 Alpha Dr.
Richardson, TX 75081
Phone: 214-238-7045
Fax: 214-644-0805

Ponderosa Mouldings (A Div. of JELD-WEN)
Moulding & Millwork
423 E. Antler,
PO Box 518
Redmond, OR 97756
Phone: 503-548-2171
Fax: 503-923-0135

Pope & Talbot
Engineered Lumber & Panels
1500 S.W. First Ave.
Portland, OR 97201
Phone: 503-220-2750
Fax: 503-220-2755

Porak Computing Services
Computer Software
2140 Academy Cir.,
Suite B
Colorado Springs, CO 80909-1673
Phone: 719-573-7770
Fax: 719-573-7767

Porcelanite
Countertops; Flooring; Walls, Ceilings & Finishes
PO Box 1777
Lexington, NC 27293
Phone: 910-249-3931
Fax: 910-242-5601

Porcelanosa
Flooring
1301 S. State College
Blvd., Suite E
Anaheim, CA 92806
Phone: 714-772-3183
Fax: 714-772-9851

Portable Products
Paints, Caulks & Adhesives; Tools/Hand
58 E. Plato Blvd.
St. Paul, MN 55107
Phone: 612-221-0308
1-800-688-2677
Fax: 612-221-0040

Portal
Windows
10 Tracy Dr.
Avon Industrial Park
Avon, MA 02322
Phone: 508-588-3030
1-800-966-3030
Fax: 508-580-9943

Porter-Cable Corp.
Hardware; Tools/Electric & Pneumatic
4825 Hwy. 45 N.
Jackson, TN 38302-2468
Phone: 901-668-8600
1-800-4-US-TOOL
Fax: 901-660-9616
Internet: http://www.porter-cable.com

Portes Celco
Doors
445 First Ave.,
Industrial Park
St. Romuald, PQ
G6W 5M6 Canada
Phone: 418-839-0062
1-800-463-5011 (Quebec)
Fax: 418-839-7489

Portland Cement Assn.
Structural Systems
5420 Old Orchard Rd.
Skokie, IL 60077-1083
Phone: 847-966-6200
Fax: 847-966-8389

Post & Beam
Structural Systems
Rt. 1, Box 146A
Maidsville, WV 26541
Phone: 304-328-5925

Potlach Corp.
Engineered Lumber & Panels
PO Box 3704
Spokane, WA 99220
Phone: 509-328-0930
Fax: 509-327-9409

Power Access Corp.
Specialty Products
106 Powder Mill Rd.
Collinsville, CT 06022
Phone: 860-693-0751
1-800-344-0088
Fax: 860-693-0641

Power Tool Institute
Tools/Electric & Pneumatic
1300 Sumner Ave.
Cleveland, OH 44115
Phone: 216-241-7333
Fax: 216-241-0105

Power Tool Specialists
Tools/Electric & Pneumatic
3 Craftsman Rd.
East Windsor, CT 06088
Phone: 860-654-1761
1-800-243-5114
Fax: 806-654-1937
E-mail: ptsbob@aol.com

Powers Process Controls
Faucets & Fixtures
3400 Oakton St.
Skokie, IL 60076
Phone: 708-673-6700
Fax: 708-673-9044

Pozzi Wood Windows (A Div. of JELD-WEN)
Doors; Windows
PO Box 5249
Bend, OR 97708
Phone: 503-382-4411
1-800-257-9663
Fax: 503-382-1292
Internet:
http://www.pozzi.com

PPG Industries
Paints, Caulks & Adhesives; Windows
1 PPG Pl.
Pittsburgh, PA 15272
Phone: 412-434-3131
1-800-2-GETPPG (glass)
1-800-441-9695 (paint)
Fax: 412-434-2821

Prairie Home Products
Faucets & Fixtures; Fireplaces; Hardware; Paints, Caulks & Adhesives; Plumbing Supplies; Tools/Hand
PO Box 344,
3802 Main St.
Grandview, MO 64030
Phone: 1-800-367-1568
Fax: 816-966-1277

Pratt & Lambert
Paints, Caulks & Adhesives
75 Tonawanda St.
Buffalo, NY 14207
Phone: 716-873-6000
Fax: 716-877-9646

Prazi USA
Tools/Electric & Pneumatic; Tools/Hand
118 Long Pond Rd.,
Suite G
Plymouth, MA 02360
Phone: 508-747-1490
Fax: 508-746-8655

Precision Multiple Controls
Electrical & Lighting
33 Greenwood Ave.
Midland Park, NJ 07432
Phone: 201-444-0600
Fax: 201-444-8575

Precision Tile Spacer
Flooring
E. 5255 Seltice Way
Post Falls, ID 83854
Phone: 208-765-3187
1-800-423-5243
Fax: 208-664-6041

Preferred Engineering Products
Hardware
350 Creditstone Rd.,
Unit 204
Vaughan, ON L4K 3Z2
Canada
Phone: 905-761-1214
1-800-387-5835
Fax: 905-761-1217

Prefinished Millwork Corp.
Moulding & Millwork
8001 University Ave.
Middleton, WI 53562
Phone: 608-831-2344
1-800-356-9684
Fax: 608-831-3725
E-mail: scottpmccitis.com

Premdor U.S. Holdings
Doors
1 N. Dale Mabry Hwy.,
Suite 950
Tampa, FL 33609
Phone: 813-877-2726
1-800-895-2723
Fax: 813-876-1435

Premier Building Systems
Insulation; Structural Systems
4609 70th Ave. E.
Puyallup, WA 98371
Phone: 206-926-2020
1-800-275-7086
Fax: 206-926-3992

Premier Wood Floors
Flooring
16803 Dallas Pkwy.
Dallas, TX 75248-6196
Phone: 214-887-2100
1-800-722-4647
Fax: 214-887-2234
Internet:
http://www.premier.com

Premoule
Countertops
2375, Dalton
Sainte-Foy, PQ G1P 3S3
Canada
Phone: 418-652-1422
1-800-463-5297
Fax: 1-800-667-7234
418-652-0080
Internet:
http://www.premoule.com

Prescolite
Electrical & Lighting
1251 Doolittle Dr.
San Leandro, CA 94577
Phone: 510-562-3500
Fax: 510-562-8553

Preso-Matic Keyless Locks
Hardware
237 Coastline Rd.
Sanford, FL 32771-6659
Phone: 407-324-9933
1-800-269-4234
Fax: 407-328-9977

Prest-on Co.
Walls, Ceilings & Finishes
316 N. Point Lookout
Hot Springs, AR 71913
Phone: 501-525-4683
1-800-323-1813
Fax: 501-525-4684

Prestige
Cabinetry
PO Box 340
Neodesha, KS 66757
Phone: 316-325-8500
1-800-328-4006
Fax: 316-325-8506

Preswitt Mfg.
Siding & Accessories
5721 Production Way
Langley, BC V3A 4N5
Canada
Phone: 604-533-3368
Fax: 604-533-8622
E-mail:
luckhart@unixg.ubc.ca

Price Pfister
Faucets & Fixtures
13500 Paxton St.
Pacoima, CA 91331
Phone: 818-896-1141
Fax: 818-686-4883

A HANLEY-WOOD, INC. PUBLICATION

9710

BUILDING PRODUCTS BUYER'S GUIDE Free Information

FOR FREE PRODUCT INFORMATION, CIRCLE THE CORRESPONDING NUMBER(S) BELOW

Name_____

Title_____

Company_____

Address_____

City_____ State_____ Zip_____

Telephone ( )_____ Fax ( )_____

I need fast action. Have a salesperson call on items no. _____

Signature_____ Date_____

ALL QUESTIONS MUST BE ANSWERED FOR YOUR CARD TO BE PROCESSED

A. Reason for inquiry
1 ☐ Current Job
2 ☐ Job in next six months
3 ☐ General Interest

B. Your buying/specifying responsibilities:
1 ☐ Full Responsibility
2 ☐ Specify
3 ☐ Recommend

C. Select the category which best describes your title:
1 ☐ Owner, Partner, CEO, Director
2 ☐ Architect, Designer, Engineer
3 ☐ Construction Manager or Superintendent
4 ☐ Sales and Marketing Managers
5 ☐ Other Management Personnel
6 ☐ Carpenter, Draftsman or Salesman
7 ☐ Other (Please specify)

D. Check the one category that best describes your business
1 ☐ Builder, Builder/Developer, General Contractor, Remodeler
2 ☐ Architect/Engineer/Designer
3 ☐ Product Manufacturer
4 ☐ Retail Dealer
5 ☐ Special Trade Contractor
6 ☐ Wholesale Distributor
7 ☐ Other (Please specify)

E. Is this your copy of BUILDER?
1 ☐ Yes   2 ☐ No

F. Type of construction (check all that apply)
01 ☐ Single-family, Custom
02 ☐ Single-family, Spec/Tract
03 ☐ For Sale, Townhomes
04 ☐ Multi-family (Attached), Condo/Co-op
05 ☐ Multi-family, Rental
06 ☐ Nonresidential
07 ☐ Commercial Remodeling
08 ☐ Residential Remodeling
09 ☐ Home Manufacturer
10 ☐ Other (Please describe)

H. Annual Dollar Volume of all construction/development
1 ☐ Over $10 million
2 ☐ $5 million-$10 million
3 ☐ $1 million-$4.9 million
4 ☐ Under $1 million

I. Annual number of residential units built
1 ☐ Over 500   4 ☐ 11 to 25
2 ☐ 101 to 500   5 ☐ 10 or less
3 ☐ 26 to 100

J. Do you sell from Model Homes?:
1 ☐ Yes   2 ☐ No

K. Do you have:
access to CD-ROM? 1 ☐ Yes 2 ☐ No
a modem?   3 ☐ Yes 4 ☐ No
a subscription to
an on-line service? 5 ☐ Yes 6 ☐ No

TB52RSC

(number grid 1–1000, arranged in rows of 1–40 with columns incrementing by 40)

A HANLEY-WOOD, INC. PUBLICATION

9710

BUILDING PRODUCTS BUYER'S GUIDE Free Information

FOR FREE PRODUCT INFORMATION, CIRCLE THE CORRESPONDING NUMBER(S) BELOW

Name_____

Title_____

Company_____

Address_____

City_____ State_____ Zip_____

Telephone ( )_____ Fax ( )_____

I need fast action. Have a salesperson call on items no. _____

Signature_____ Date_____

ALL QUESTIONS MUST BE ANSWERED FOR YOUR CARD TO BE PROCESSED

A. Reason for inquiry
1 ☐ Current Job
2 ☐ Job in next six months
3 ☐ General Interest

B. Your buying/specifying responsibilities:
1 ☐ Full Responsibility
2 ☐ Specify
3 ☐ Recommend

C. Select the category which best describes your title:
1 ☐ Owner, Partner, CEO, Director
2 ☐ Architect, Designer, Engineer
3 ☐ Construction Manager or Superintendent
4 ☐ Sales and Marketing Managers
5 ☐ Other Management Personnel
6 ☐ Carpenter, Draftsman or Salesman
7 ☐ Other (Please specify)

D. Check the one category that best describes your business
1 ☐ Builder, Builder/Developer, General Contractor, Remodeler
2 ☐ Architect/Engineer/Designer
3 ☐ Product Manufacturer
4 ☐ Retail Dealer
5 ☐ Special Trade Contractor
6 ☐ Wholesale Distributor
7 ☐ Other (Please specify)

E. Is this your copy of BUILDER?
1 ☐ Yes   2 ☐ No

F. Type of construction (check all that apply)
01 ☐ Single-family, Custom
02 ☐ Single-family, Spec/Tract
03 ☐ For Sale, Townhomes
04 ☐ Multi-family (Attached), Condo/Co-op
05 ☐ Multi-family, Rental
06 ☐ Nonresidential
07 ☐ Commercial Remodeling
08 ☐ Residential Remodeling
09 ☐ Home Manufacturer
10 ☐ Other (Please describe)

H. Annual Dollar Volume of all construction/development
1 ☐ Over $10 million
2 ☐ $5 million-$10 million
3 ☐ $1 million-$4.9 million
4 ☐ Under $1 million

I. Annual number of residential units built
1 ☐ Over 500   4 ☐ 11 to 25
2 ☐ 101 to 500   5 ☐ 10 or less
3 ☐ 26 to 100

J. Do you sell from Model Homes?:
1 ☐ Yes   2 ☐ No

K. Do you have:
access to CD-ROM? 1 ☐ Yes 2 ☐ No
a modem?   3 ☐ Yes 4 ☐ No
a subscription to
an on-line service? 5 ☐ Yes 6 ☐ No

TB52RSC

(number grid 1–1000, arranged in rows of 1–40 with columns incrementing by 40)

BUILDER

READER SERVICE PROCESSING CENTER
PO BOX 99465
COLLINGSWOOD NJ   08108-0622

BUILDER

READER SERVICE PROCESSING CENTER
PO BOX 99465
COLLINGSWOOD NJ   08108-0622

Primark Tool Group
Hardware; Tools/Electric & Pneumatic; Tools/Hand
1350 S. 15th St.
Louisville, KY 40210
Phone: 502-635-8100
1-800-242-7003
Fax: 1-800-833-5460

Primatech
Hardware; Tools/Electric & Pneumatic
990 St. Therese
Quebec, PQ G1N 1S9
Canada
Phone: 418-682-2127
1-800-363-1962
Fax: 418-682-0614

Primavera Systems SureTrak Div.
Computer Software
1574 W. 1700 S.
Salt Lake City, UT 84104
Phone: 801-973-1300
1-800-872-5457
Fax: 801-973-9725

Prime-Line Products Co.
Hardware
5405 N. Industrial Pkwy.
San Bernardino, CA 92407
Phone: 909-887-8118
Fax: 909-880-8968
E-mail: dcro@plp.mhs.compuserve.com

Prime Wood Products
Cabinetry; Flooring; Moulding & Millwork
4430 136th Ave.
Holland, MI 49424
Phone: 616-399-4700
Fax: 616-399-8714

PrimeWood
Cabinetry; Countertops; Doors; Moulding & Millwork
2217 N. Ninth St.
Wahpeton, ND 58075
Phone: 701-642-2727
1-800-642-8780
Fax: 701-642-2431

Pro/Cote
Paints, Caulks & Adhesives
101 Prospect Ave.
Cleveland, OH 44115
Phone: 216-566-2929
Fax: 216-566-1350

Pro-Flo Products
Appliances
30 Commerce Rd.
Cedar Grove, NJ 07009
Phone: 201-239-2400
1-800-325-1057
Fax: 201-239-5817

**Pro-Mation,
A Div. of Geac Commercial Systems Software for Contractors**
Computer Software
5242 S. College Dr., Suite 200
Salt Lake City, UT 84123
Phone: 801-261-8595
1-800-521-4562
Fax: 801-261-8599

Prosource
2458 Old Dorsett Rd.
Suite 102
Maryland Heights, MO 63043
Phone: 314-291-0000
Fax: 314-291-6674

Pro Tect Associates
Equipment & Trucks; Flooring; Siding & Accessories
1742 Harding Rd.,
PO Box 8382
Northfield, IL 60093
Phone: 708-446-8664
1-800-545-0826
Fax: 708-446-8735
Internet: http://www.builderonline.com/builder/products/guide/protect

Pro Tecta Industries
Equipment & Trucks
1217 Second St. S.
Nampa, ID 83651
Phone: 208-463-1200
1-800-243-5434
Fax: 208-463-1299

Proctor Products Co.
Equipment & Trucks
PO Box 697
Kirkland, WA 98083-0697
Phone: 206-822-9296
Fax: 206-634-2396
E-mail: proctorp@ix.netcom.com

Progress Lighting
Electrical & Lighting
PO Box 5704
Spartanburg, SC 29304
Phone: 864-599-6000
Fax: 864-599-6151

Proko Industries
Paints, Caulks & Adhesives; Roofing; Walls, Ceilings & Finishes
18601 LBJ Fwy., Suite 400
Mesquite, TX 75150
Phone: 214-681-9261
Fax: 214-279-1983

ProSoCo.
Paints, Caulks & Adhesives; Structural Systems
PO Box 171677
Kansas City, KS 66117
Phone: 913-281-2700
1-800-255-4255
Fax: 913-281-4385

Prosoft
Computer Software
107 N. Armenia Ave.
Tampa, FL 33609
Phone: 813-251-1628
Fax: 813-254-1784
Internet: http://www.prosoftinc.com

Protective Products Intl.
Equipment & Trucks; Flooring; Siding & Accessories
1205 Karl Ct., Suite 116
Wauconda, IL 60084-1089
Phone: 847-526-1380
1-800-789-6633
Fax: 1-800-880-7141
Internet: http://www.protectiveproducts.com

Prudential Building Materials
Hardware; Landscape Design; Roofing; Siding & Accessories; Tools/Electric & Pneumatic; Walls, Ceilings & Finishes
171 Milton St.
East Dedham, MA 02026
Phone: 617-329-3232
1-800-444-9585
Fax: 617-326-0752

PS Aluminum Products
Landscape Design; Moulding & Millwork; Siding & Accessories
8055 Marco-Polo Ave.
Montreal, PQ H1E 5Y8
Canada
Phone: 514-648-1100
Fax: 514-648-9335

PSG
HVAC
1225 Tunnel Rd.
Perkasie, PA 18944
Phone: 215-257-3621
1-800-782-8412
Fax: 215-257-4288

Pulsar Softwares
Computer Software
1600 Cure Labelle,
Suite 210
Laval, QC H7V 2W2
Canada
Phone: 514-973-6065
1-800-567-2030
Fax: 514-973-6066
Internet: http://www.pulsarsoft.com

Putnam Rolling Ladder Co.
Specialty Products
32 Howard St.
New York, NY 10013
Phone: 212-226-5147
Fax: 212-941-1836

Pyro Industries
Fireplaces
695 Pease Rd.
Burlington, WA 98233
Phone: 206-757-9728
Fax: 1-800-398-5382

Q

**Quad Lock Building Systems
Div. of Building Technologies**
Insulation; Specialty Products; Structural Systems
7398 132nd St.
Surrey, BC V3W 4M7
Canada
Phone: 604-590-3111

Quaker
Flooring
639 Peeples Valley Rd.,
PO Box 745
Cartersville, GA 30120
Phone: 770-382-8252
1-800-382-8252
Fax: 770-386-5891

Quaker Maid
Cabinetry
State Rt. 61, Box H
Leesport, PA 19533
Phone: 610-926-3011
Fax: 610-926-7203

Quality American
Moulding & Millwork; Walls, Ceilings & Finishes
PO Box 471,
1 Taunton Green
Taunton, MA 02780
Phone: 508-824-3358
1-800-497-3351
Fax: 508-880-5365

Quality Cabinets
Cabinetry
515 Big Stone Gap
Duncanville, TX 75137
Phone: 1-800-298-7020
Fax: 214-709-4838
Internet: http://www.qualitycabinets.com

Quality Doors
621 Hall St.
Cedar Hill, TX 75104
Phone: 972-291-2424
1-800-950-3667
Fax: 972-291-9770

Quality Fencing & Supply
Room Enclosures; Siding & Accessories; Structural Systems
622 N. Shirk Rd.
New Holland, PA 17557
Phone: 717-355-7100
1-800-633-7093
Fax: 717-355-7129

Quality Woods
Engineered Lumber & Panels; Flooring
63 Flanders Bartley Rd.
Flanders, NJ 07801
Phone: 201-584-7554
1-800-637-6525
Fax: 201-584-3875

Quarry Tile Co.
Countertops; Flooring; Landscape Design; Walls, Ceilings & Finishes
6328 Utah Ave.
Spokane, WA 99212
Phone: 509-536-2812
1-800-423-2608
Fax: 509-536-4072

Quik Drive
Hardware; Tools/Electric & Pneumatic
436 Calvert Dr.
Gallatin, TN 37066-5401
Phone: 615-230-8788
1-888-487-7845
Fax: 615-451-9806
Internet: http://www.quikdrive.com

The Quikrete Cos.
Structural Systems
2987 Clairmont Rd.,
Suite 500
Atlanta, GA 30329
Phone: 404-634-9100

Quikspray
Equipment & Trucks
PO Box 327
Port Clinton, OH 43452
Phone: 419-732-2601
Fax: 419-734-2628

R

R. Christensen Hardware
Hardware
1720 Trent Blvd.
New Bern, NC 28560
Phone: 919-637-6310
1-800-43-BRASS
Fax: 919-637-6841

R & D Equipment
Doors; Hardware
1150 Tri-View Ave.
Sioux City, IA 51102
Phone: 712-255-5205
1-800-798-5678
Fax: 712-255-8292

R Homes
1401 W. Beechcraft St.
Pocatello, ID 83204
Phone: 208-233-2289
1-800-808-2289
Fax: 208-233-2293

R Laflamme et Frere
Doors; Windows
51 rue Industriel
St. Apollinaire, PQ G0S 2E0 Canada
Phone: 418-881-3950
Fax: 418-881-2810

RAB Electric Mfg. Co.
Electrical & Lighting; Home Technology
170 Ludlow Ave.
Northvale, NJ 07647
Phone: 201-784-8600
Fax: 201-784-0077

Rack-Strap
Equipment & Trucks
808 Molalla Ave.
Oregon City, OR 97045
Phone: 503-657-0806
1-800-841-5790
Fax: 503-657-9758

Radiant Technology
HVAC
11A Farber Dr.
Bellport, NY 11713
Phone: 516-286-0900
1-800-784-0234
Fax: 516-286-0947
Internet: http://www.radiant-tech.com

Radiator Specialty Co.
Paints, Caulks & Adhesives; Plumbing Supplies; Tools/Hand
PO Box 34689
Charlotte, NC 28234
Phone: 704-377-6555
1-800-438-4532
Fax: 1-800-421-9525

Rain Master
(See Bemis Mfg. Co.)

Rainhandler
Siding & Accessories
2710 North Ave.
Bridgeport, CT 06604
Phone: 203-382-2991
1-800-942-3004
Fax: 203-382-2995
E-mail: rainhandle@aol.com

Rainier Wood Products
Moulding & Millwork
1500 Tamarack,
PO Box 277
Sweet Home, OR 97386
Phone: 541-367-6168
Fax: 541-367-5666

Rainsoft Water Conditioning Co.
Appliances
2080 E. Lunt Ave.
Elk Grove Village, IL 60007
Phone: 847-437-9400
1-800-860-7638
Fax: 847-437-1594
Internet: http://www.aquion.com

Ralph Wilson Plastics
(See Wilsonart Intl.)

Rambow Enterprises
Computer Software
15127 N.W. 24th,
Suite 152
Redmond, WA 98052
Phone: 206-881-7243
Fax: 206-881-7243

Rangaire & Co.
Appliances
PO Box 177
Cleburne, TX 76033
Phone: 817-556-6500
1-800-777-7264
Fax: 817-556-6549

**Rapetti Faucets
(A Div. of George Blotcher)**
Faucets & Fixtures
Zero High St.
Plainville, MA 02762
Phone: 508-699-9400
1-800-688-5500
Fax: 508-699-9498

**Raphael
(A Nortek Co.)**
Faucets & Fixtures
4250 N. 124th Ave.
Milwaukee, WI 53222
Phone: 414-461-5400
1-800-727-4235
Fax: 414-461-5777

Rapid River Rustic
Structural Systems
9211 CO 511, 225 RD
Rapid River, MI 49878
Phone: 906-474-6404
1-800-422-3327
Fax: 906-474-6500

Rare Earth Hardwoods
Engineered Lumber & Panels; Flooring; Moulding & Millwork
6778 E. Traverse Hwy.
Traverse City, MI 49684
Phone: 616-946-0043
1-800-968-0074
Fax: 616-946-6221
E-mail: rare.earth@traverse.com

**RAS Industries
Life-time Pre-formed Millwork**
Moulding & Millwork
12 Eighty Four Dr.
Eighty Four, PA 15330
Phone: 412-228-1395
1-800-367-1076
Fax: 1-800-367-8685

Rastra Technologies
Structural Systems
501 E. Plaza Cir.,
Suite G
Lichfield Park, AZ 85340
Phone: 602-935-3545
Fax: 602-935-3037

Rawplug Co.
Hardware
200 Petersville Rd.
New Rochelle, NY 10802
Phone: 914-235-6300

Ray White Lumber Co.
*Engineered Lumber &
Panels; Flooring; Moulding
& Millwork; Siding &
Accessories; Walls, Ceilings
& Finishes*
PO Box 7
Sparkman, AR 71763
Phone: 501-678-2277
Fax: 501-678-2522

Raymond Enkeboll
Moulding & Millwork
16506 Avalon Blvd.
Carson, CA 90746
Phone: 310-532-1400
Fax: 310-532-2042

Raynor Garage Doors
Garage Doors & Openers
1101 E. River Rd.
Dixon, IL 61021-0448
Phone: 815-288-1431
1-800-4RA-YNOR
Fax: 815-288-7142
Internet:
http://www.raynor.com

Raypak
HVAC
31111 Agoura Rd.
Westlake Village, CA
91361-4699
Phone: 818-889-1500
Fax: 818-889-4522

Raywall Kitchens
Cabinetry
68 Green Ln.
Thornhill, ON L3T 6K9
Canada
Phone: 905-889-6243
Fax: 416-733-7629

RB Rubber Products
Flooring
904 E. 10th Ave.
McMinnville, OR 97128
Phone: 503-472-4691
1-800-525-5530
Fax: 1-800-888-1183

**RBP Custom Glass
D & S Insulated Glass**
Windows
2531 Royal Ln.
Dallas, TX 75229
Phone: 214-484-8892
1-800-225-7716
Fax: 214-484-4527

RC Musson Rubber Co.
*Flooring; Paints, Caulks
& Adhesives*
1320 E. Archwood Ave.
Akron, OH 44306
Phone: 330-773-7651
1-800-321-2381
Fax: 330-773-3254

Re-Bath Corp.
Faucets & Fixtures
1055 S. Country Club
Mesa, AZ 85210
Phone: 602-844-1575
1-800-426-4573
Fax: 602-833-7199

**Re-Source Building
Products**
Landscape Design
920 Davis Rd., Suite 101
Elgin, IL 60123
Phone: 708-931-0495
Fax: 708-931-0495

Reading Body Works
*Equipment & Trucks;
Tools/Hand*
PO Box 650, Hancock
Blvd. & Gerry St.
Shillington, PA 19607
Phone: 610-775-3301
1-800-458-2226
Fax: 610-775-3261
Internet:
http://www.readingbody.
com

Readybuilt Products Co.
*Fireplaces; Moulding
& Millwork*
PO Box 4425,
1701 McHenry St.
Baltimore, MD 21223
Phone: 410-233-5833
1-800-626-2901
Fax: 410-566-7170

Real Brick Products
*Fireplaces; Siding &
Accessories; Structural
Systems*
PO Box 907
Owosso, MI 48867-0907
Phone: 517-625-6000
1-800-447-7440
Fax: 517-625-3136

**Real Log Homes
Pre-Cut Log Products**
Structural Systems
PO Box 202
Hartland, VT 05048
Phone: 802-436-2121
1-800-REAL-LOG
Fax: 802-436-2150

Red Devil
*Paints, Caulks &
Adhesives; Tools/Hand*
2400 Vauxhall Rd.
Union, NJ 07083-1933
Phone: 908-688-6900
1-800-4-A-DEVIL
Fax: 908-688-8872

Red Dot
(See Mason/Red Dot)

Red Head
(See ITW Ramset/
Red Head)

**Red Wing Business
Systems**
Computer Software
610 Main St., PO Box 19
Red Wing, MN 55066
Phone: 612-388-1106
1-800-732-9464
Fax: 612-388-7950

Reddi-Form
Structural Systems
593 Ramapo Valley Rd.
Oakland, NJ 07436
Phone: 201-405-2030
1-800-334-4303
Fax: 201-405-1987

**Redland Brick
(Cushwa Plant)**
*Landscape Design; Siding
& Accessories*
PO Box 160
Williamsport, MD
21795-0160
Phone: 301-223-7700
Fax: 301-223-6675
Internet:
http://www.redlandbrick.
com

**Redman Building
Products**
(See Alenco)

Reemay
Insulation
PO Box 511,
70 Old Hickory Blvd.
Old Hickory, TN 37138
Phone: 615-847-7000
1-800-382-8467
Fax: 615-847-7068
Internet:
http://www.reemay.com

**Reflections USA
Long Island Glass &
Mirror**
Faucets & Fixtures
65 Sea Cliff Ave.
Glen Cove, NY 11542
Phone: 516-676-1203
1-800-759-9992
Fax: 516-676-1471

Reflectix
*Insulation; Specialty
Products*
PO Box 108, 1 School St.
Markleville, IN 46056
Phone: 765-533-4332
1-800-879-3645
Fax: 765-533-2327
Internet: http://www.
reflectixinc.com

Regency Bath Products
Faucets & Fixtures
1910 Orange Tree Ln.,
Suite 350
Redlands, CA 92374
Phone: 909-307-5800
Fax: 909-307-5806

**Regency Building
Products**
3135 Richmond St.
Richmond, BC V7E 2V4
Canada
Phone: 604-271-5227
Fax: 604-271-5227

Regency VSA Appliances
Appliances
1442 Irvine Blvd.,
Suite 125
Tustin, CA 92780
Phone: 714-544-3530
Fax: 714-544-6969

Regent Lighting Corp.
*Electrical & Lighting;
Home Technology*
PO Box 2658
Burlington, NC 27216
Phone: 919-226-2411
1-800-334-6871
Fax: 919-222-8202

Rehau
Doors; HVAC; Windows
PO Box 1706
Leesburg, VA 20177
Phone: 703-777-5255
1-800-247-9445
Fax: 703-777-3053

**Reid S Watson &
Associates**
Faucets & Fixtures
500 N. Lake Ave.
Pasadena, CA 91101
Phone: 818-792-6671
Fax: 818-792-1736

The Reinforced Earth Co.
*Landscape Design;
Structural Systems*
8614 Westwood Center
Dr., Suite 1100
Vienna, VA 22182
Phone: 703-821-1175
1-800-446-5700
Fax: 703-821-1815
Internet:
http://www.recousa.com

**Rejuvenation Lamp &
Fixture Co.**
Electrical & Lighting
1100 S.E. Grand Ave.
Portland, OR 97214
Phone: 503-231-1900
Fax: 503-230-0537

Renato Bisazza
*Countertops; Landscape
Design; Walls, Ceilings
& Finishes*
8032 N.W. 66th St.
Miami, FL 33166-2728
Phone: 305-597-4099

**Renato Specialty
Products**
Appliances
2775 W. Kingsley Rd.
Garland, TX 75040
Phone: 972-864-8800
1-800-876-9731

Renown Specialties Co.
Hardware
226 Jardin Dr., Suite 2
Concord, ON L4K 1Y1
Canada
Phone: 905-669-6955
Fax: 905-669-1563

Reon
*Faucets & Fixtures;
Specialty Products*
5010 Shoreham Pl.
Suite 300
San Diego, CA 92122
Phone: 619-450-1325
1-800-776-7366
Fax: 619-455-REON

Repla
Windows
482 S. Service Rd. E.
Oakville, ON L6J 2X6
Canada
Phone: 905-844-1271
Fax: 905-844-0672
E-mail:
104202.3327@compuserve.
com

**Republic Powdered
Metals**
Roofing
PO Box 724
Medina, OH 44258
Phone: 216-225-3192
1-800-255-1136
Fax: 216-273-5061

**Republic Stainless Steel
Sinks**
Faucets & Fixtures
PO Box 1010
Ruston, LA 71273
Phone: 318-255-5600
1-800-637-6485
Fax: 318-255-5653

Research Products
HVAC
PO Box 1467
Madison, WI 53701
Phone: 608-257-8801
Fax: 608-257-4357
Internet:
http://www.resprod.com

**Resilient Floor Covering
Institute**
Flooring
966 Hungerford Dr.,
Suite 12-B
Rockville, MD 20850
Phone: 301-340-8580
Fax: 301-340-7283

Resin Technology Co.
Roofing
2270 Castle Harbor Pl.
Ontario, CA 91761
Phone: 909-947-7224
1-800-729-0795
Fax: 909-923-9617

ResinArt Corp.
Moulding & Millwork
1625 Placentia Ave.
Costa Mesa, CA 92627
Phone: 714-642-3665
1-800-258-8820
Fax: 714-642-6519
Internet:
http://www.flexmoulding.
com

Resources Conservation
Faucets & Fixtures
PO Box 71
Greenwich, CT 06386
Phone: 203-964-0600
1-800-243-2862
Fax: 203-324-9352

Rev-A-Shelf
Specialty Products
2409 Plantside Dr.
Jeffersontown, KY 40299
Phone: 502-499-5835
1-800-626-1126
Fax: 502-491-2215

Revere Copper Products
Roofing
PO Box 300
Rome, NY 13440
Phone: 315-338-2022
1-800-448-1776
1-800-962-2150 (NY)
Fax: 315-338-2224

Rex Lumber Co.
*Engineered Lumber
& Panels*
840 Main St.
Acton, MA 01720
Phone: 508-263-0055
1-800-322-1221
Fax: 508-263-9806

**Reynolds Metals Co.
(Construction Products
Div.)**
*Room Enclosures; Siding
& Accessories; Windows*
6601 W. Broad St.,
PO Box 27003
Richmond, VA 23230
Phone: 804-281-2000
Fax: 804-281-3602

RH Tamlyn & Sons
*Hardware; Roofing; Siding
& Accessories; Structural
Systems*
10406 Cash Rd.
Stafford, TX 77477-4415
Phone: 713-499-9604
1-800-334-1676
Fax: 713-499-8948

**Rheem Mfg.
Air Conditioning Div.**
HVAC
5600 Old Greenwood Rd.
Fort Smith, AR 72917
Phone: 501-646-4311
Fax: 501-648-4918

**Rheem Mfg.
Water Heater Div.**
HVAC
PO Box 244020
Montgomery, AL 36124
Phone: 334-260-1500
Fax: 334-260-1562

RHH Foam Systems
Paints, Caulks & Adhesives
PO Box 752, 6001 S.
Pennsylvania Ave.
Cudahy, WI 53110-0752
Phone: 414-744-6066
1-800-657-0702
Fax: 414-744-8227
Internet:
http://www.rhhfoamsystems.
com

Rhino Tool Co.
Tools/Electric & Pneumatic
620 Andrews Ave.,
PO Box 111
Kewanee, IL 61443
Phone: 309-853-5555
Fax: 309-856-5905

Rich Maid Kabinetry
Cabinetry
633 W. Lincoln Ave.
Myerstown, PA 17067
Phone: 717-866-2112

Richlund Sales
Appliances
75695 Hwy. 1053
Kentwood, LA 70444
Phone: 504-229-4922
Fax: 504-229-4956
Internet: http://www.
naponnet.org/rich

**Richwood Building
Products**
Siding & Accessories
315 Shorland Dr.
Richwood, KY 41094
Phone: 606-485-7444
1-800-243-0202
Fax: 606-485-9966

Rinnai America Corp.
Appliances; Fireplaces; HVAC
1662 Lukken Industrial Dr. W.
LaGrange, GA 30240
Phone: 706-884-6070
1-800-621-9419
Fax: 706-884-6099

Rio Plastics
Faucets & Fixtures
PO Box 3707
Brownsville, TX 78523
Phone: 210-831-2715
Fax: 210-831-9851

Risi Stone Systems (A Div. of Rothbury Intl.)
Landscape Design
Le Parc Office Tower,
8500 Leslie St., Suite 390
Thornhill, ON L3T 7P1
Canada
Phone: 905-882-5898
1-800-626-9255
Fax: 905-882-4556
Internet: http://www.risistone.com

Riverbend Timber Framing
Structural Systems
PO Box 26
Blissfield, MI 49228
Phone: 517-486-4355
Fax: 517-486-2056

Riviera Cabinets
Cabinetry
3860 Vermillion St.
Red Wing, MN 55981
Phone: 612-388-4721
1-800-598-4570
Fax: 1-800-822-5244

Rmax
Insulation
13524 Welch Rd.
Dallas, TX 75244-5291
Phone: 972-387-4500
1-800-527-0890
Fax: 972-387-4673

RMK Enterprises
Computer Software
PO Box 5489
Pinehurst, NC 28374
Phone: 910-295-5250
Fax: 910-295-5153

Ro-Tile
Flooring; Roofing; Siding & Accessories; Walls, Ceilings & Finishes
1615 S. Stockton St.
Lodi, CA 95240
Phone: 209-334-1380
1-800-688-1380
Fax: 209-334-3136

Robbins Hardwood Flooring
Flooring
4785 Eastern Ave.
Cincinnati, OH 45226
Phone: 513-871-8510
Fax: 513-871-8069
Internet: http://www.robbinsfloor.com

Robbins Lumber
Moulding & Millwork; Siding & Accessories
PO Box 9
Searsmont, ME 04973
Phone: 207-342-5221
1-800-287-5067 (ME)
Fax: 207-342-5201
Internet: http://www.rlco.com

Robern
Cabinetry; Electrical & Lighting; Faucets & Fixtures
7 Wood Ave.
Bristol, PA 19007
Phone: 215-826-9800
1-800-877-2376
Fax: 215-826-9633

Robert H. Peterson Co.
Fireplaces
530 Baldwin Park Blvd.
City of Industry, CA 91746
Phone: 818-369-5085
1-800-332-0240
Fax: 818-369-5979
Internet: http://www.net-dot-com.com/rhp/home.htm

Robert Mfg. Co.
Faucets & Fixtures; Plumbing Supplies
10667 Jersey Blvd.
Cucamonga, CA 91730
Phone: 909-987-4654

Roberts Step-Lite Systems
Electrical & Lighting
8413 Mantle Ave.
Oklahoma City, OK 73132
Phone: 405-728-4895
1-800-654-8268
Fax: 405-728-4878

Robinson Brick Co.
Landscape Design; Siding & Accessories; Structural Systems
1845 W. Dartmouth Ave.
Denver, CO 80110-1309
Phone: 303-783-3000
1-800-477-9002
Fax: 303-781-1818

Rockford Products Corp. (International Group)
Hardware
PO Box 6306
Rockford, IL 61125
Phone: 815-397-6000
Fax: 815-229-7155

Rocktile Specialty Products
Countertops; Flooring; Landscape Design; Siding & Accessories; Structural Systems; Walls, Ceilings & Finishes
220 S. Ave. A
Boise, ID 83702
Phone: 208-342-7700
1-800-545-7735
Fax: 208-342-7880

Rockwood Retaining Walls
Landscape Design
7200 N. Hwy. 63
Rochester, MN 55906
Phone: 507-288-8850
1-800-535-2375
Fax: 507-288-3810
Internet: http://www.retainingwall.com

Rocky Mountain Forest Products Corp.
Moulding & Millwork
667 W. Flint, PO Box 777
Laramie, WY 82070
Phone: 307-745-8924
1-800-421-3725
Fax: 307-742-2510
Internet: http://www.jacksonholenet.com/RMFP/

Rocky Mountain Stone Co.
Countertops; Flooring
4741 Pan American Fwy.
Albuquerque, NM 87109
Phone: 505-345-8518
Fax: 505-345-8510

Rohl Corp.
Appliances; Faucets & Fixtures
1559 Sunland
Costa Mesa, CA 92626
Phone: 714-557-1933
1-800-777-9762
Fax: 714-557-8635

Roland Boulanger & Co.
Moulding & Millwork
177 rue St. Louis, CP 580
Warwick, PQ JOA 1MO
Canada
Phone: 819-358-2022
Fax: 819-358-5178

Roll-A-Way Storm & Security Shutters
Siding & Accessories
10597-10601 Oak St. N.W.
St. Petersburg, FL 33716
Phone: 813-576-6044
1-800-683-9505
Fax: 813-579-9410

Roll-lite
Garage Doors & Openers
10407 Rocket Blvd.
Orlando, FL 32824-8512
Phone: 407-857-0680
Fax: 407-859-9770

Rollex Corp.
Siding & Accessories
2001 Lunt Ave.
Elk Grove Village, IL 60007
Phone: 847-437-3000
1-800-251-3300
Fax: 847-437-7561

Roma Steam Baths
Faucets & Fixtures
16802 Barker Springs, Suite 500
Houston, TX 77084
Phone: 713-578-9945
1-800-657-0656
Fax: 713-578-9948

Romatt Doors
Countertops; Moulding & Millwork; Structural Systems; Walls, Ceilings & Finishes
45 Rivalda Rd.
North York, ON M9M 2M4 Canada
Phone: 416-741-3667
1-800-268-0689
Fax: 416-741-4163

Roofing Industry Education Institute
Roofing
14 Inverness Dr., Suite H-110
Englewood, CO 80112
Phone: 303-790-7200
Fax: 303-790-9006

Roper Department Whirlpool Corp.
Appliances
2000 N. State Rt. 63
Benton Harbor, MI 49022
Phone: 616-923-5000
Fax: 616-923-2555

Rosboro Lumber Co.
Engineered Lumber & Panels
PO Box 20
Springfield, OR 97477
Phone: 503-746-8411
1-800-447-6737
Fax: 503-726-8919

Rosebud Mfg.
Cabinetry; Countertops
111 West Ctr.
Madison, SD 57042
Phone: 605-256-4561
Fax: 1-800-356-3842
E-mail: rosebud1@hcpd.com

Roseburg Forest Products
Engineered Lumber & Panels
PO Box 1088
Roseburg, OR 97470
Phone: 503-679-3311
Fax: 503-679-9543

Rossi Corp.
Engineered Lumber & Panels; Moulding & Millwork
82 Seabrook Rd.
Higganum, CT 06441
Phone: 203-345-4561
Fax: 203-345-4078

Roto Frank of America
Windows
Research Park, PO Box 599
Chester, CT 06412
Phone: 860-526-4996
1-800-243-0893
Fax: 860-526-3785
E-mail: rotofr@nai.net

Roto Zip Tool Corp.
Tools/Electric & Pneumatic
1861 Ludden Dr.
Cross Plains, WI 53528
Phone: 608-798-3737
1-800-521-1817
Fax: 608-798-3739
Internet: http://www.rotozip.com

Rotocast Classic Lamp Posts
Electrical & Lighting; Landscape Design; Tools/Hand
3645 N.W. 67th St.
Miami, FL 33147
Phone: 305-696-1901
1-800-654-5852
Fax: 305-836-1296
Internet: http://www.rotocast.com/classic

Rousseau Co.
Tools/Electric & Pneumatic
1712 13th St.
Clarkston, WA 99403
Phone: 509-758-3954
1-800-635-3416
Fax: 509-758-4991

Roxco Liquidators
Engineered Lumber & Panels
601 Third St.
Eureka, CA 95501
Phone: 707-445-0329
Fax: 707-445-8772

Roy Electric Co.
Electrical & Lighting
1054 Coney Island Ave.
Brooklyn, NY 11230
Phone: 718-434-7002
1-800-366-3347
Fax: 718-421-4678

Royal Baths Mfg.
Faucets & Fixtures
14635 Chrisman Rd.
Houston, TX 77039
Phone: 713-442-3400
1-800-826-0074
Fax: 713-442-1455

Royal Building Products
Siding & Accessories
1 Royal Gate Blvd.
Woodbridge, ON L4L 8Z7 Canada
Phone: 905-850-9700
1-800-387-2789
Fax: 1-800-461-0849

Royal Plastics Group
Doors; Siding & Accessories; Structural Systems; Windows
1 Royal Gate Blvd.
Woodbridge, ON L4L 8Z7 Canada
Phone: 905-264-0701
Fax: 905-264-0702

Royalston Oak Timber Frames
Room Enclosures; Structural Systems
N. Fitzwilliam Rd.
Royalston, MA 01331
Phone: 508-249-9633
Fax: 508-249-9633

RS Means
Computer Software
100 Construction Plaza, PO Box 800
Kingston, MA 02364
Phone: 617-585-7880
1-800-448-8182
Fax: 617-585-7466
Internet: http://www.rsmeans.com

RSF Energy
Fireplaces
2965 Tatlow Rd., PO Box 3637
Smithers, BC V0J 2N0 Canada
Phone: 604-847-4301
Fax: 604-847-4432

RSI
Tools/Electric & Pneumatic
PO Box 54
Idyllwild, CA 92549
Phone: 909-659-4635
1-800-869-9546
Fax: 909-659-9730

RSL Woodworking Products
Doors
3092 English Creek Ave.
Egg Harbor Township, NJ 08234
Phone: 609-484-1600
Fax: 609-484-0422

The Rubinet Faucet Co.
Faucets & Fixtures
91 Haist Ave.
Woodbridge, ON L4L 5V5 Canada
Phone: 905-851-6781
1-800-461-5901
Fax: 905-851-8031

Ruegg Fireplaces
Fireplaces
216 Hwy. 206, Suite 12
Somerville, NJ 08876
Phone: 908-281-9555
1-800-347-3843
Fax: 908-281-9515

Ruger Equipment
Equipment & Trucks
615 W. Fourth St., PO Box 724
Uhrichsville, OH 44683
Phone: 614-922-3000
1-800-25-RUGER
Fax: 614-922-0300
Internet: http://www.rugerequipment.com

Runtal North America
HVAC
PO Box 8278
Ward Hill, MA 01835
Phone: 508-373-1666
1-800-526-2621
Fax: 508-372-7140

Russell Range
Appliances
229 Ryan Way
South San Francisco, CA 94080
Phone: 415-873-0105
1-800-878-7877
Fax: 415-873-0970

Rustgo-Nelson King
Equipment & Trucks
PO Box 320287
Birmingham, AL 35232
Phone: 205-591-6875
1-800-448-4077
Fax: 205-591-6876

Rustic Crafts Co.
Fireplaces
PO Box 1085
Scranton, PA 18501
Phone: 717-969-1777
Fax: 717-969-2160

Rutt Custom Cabinetry
Cabinetry
PO Box 129,
1564 Main St.
Goodville, PA 17528
Phone: 717-445-6751
1-800-420-7888

Ruud Air Conditioning Div.
HVAC
PO Box 17010
Fort Smith, AR 72917
Phone: 501-646-4311
Fax: 501-648-4918

Ryan Forest Products (A Div. of Kenora Forest Products)
Landscape Design; Moulding & Millwork
165 Ryan St.
Winnipeg, MB R2R 0N9
Canada
Phone: 204-989-9600
1-800-665-0273
Fax: 204-694-7232

Rynone Mfg. Corp.
Cabinetry; Countertops
PO Box 128,
N. Thomas Ave.
Sayre, PA 18840
Phone: 717-888-5272
Fax: 717-888-1175

Ryobi America Corp.
Equipment & Trucks; Hardware; Tools/Electric & Pneumatic
5201 Pearman Dairy Rd.
Anderson, SC 29625
Phone: 803-226-6511
1-800-525-2579
Fax: 803-261-9435

S

S B
Structural Systems
PO Box 111
Friday Harbor, WA 98250
Phone: 206-378-4831

S-B Power Tool Co. (Skil Bosch)
Hardware; Tools/Electric & Pneumatic
4300 W. Peterson
Chicago, IL 60646
Phone: 312-286-7330
Fax: 312-794-7434

S & J Products
Faucets & Fixtures; Hardware
1770 W. Berteau
Chicago, IL 60613
Phone: 312-549-7983
Fax: 312-871-4070

S. Parker Hardware Mfg. Corp.
Hardware; Specialty Products
PO Box 9882, Parker Dr.
Englewood, NJ 07631
Phone: 201-569-1600
Fax: 201-569-1082
E-mail: sparker@crusoe.net

S & S Mills
Flooring
PO Box 1568
Dalton, GA 30722
Phone: 706-277-3677
1-800-241-4013
Fax: 706-277-3922

S&S Wood Specialties
Specialty Products
170 Forest St.
Westbrook, ME 04092
Phone: 207-854-8149
1-800-242-9663
Fax: 207-854-1243

Safe Alternatives Sales Group
Insulation; Paints, Caulks & Adhesives
2615 Pacific Coast Hwy.,
Suite 300
Hermosa Beach, CA 90254-2225
Phone: 310-379-0099
1-888-701-SAFE
Fax: 310-379-1466
Internet:
http://www.dxtc.com/sacusa/

Safe Tek Intl.
Faucets & Fixtures; Specialty Products
2850 Kirby Ave.
Palm Bay, FL 32905
Phone: 407-952-1300
Fax: 407-952-2766
Internet:
http://www.spacecst.net/sti

Sagebrush Sales
Engineered Lumber & Panels; Roofing; Walls, Ceilings & Finishes
PO Box 25606
Albuquerque, NM 87125
Phone: 505-877-7331
1-800-444-7990
Fax: 505-873-4777

Samax Enterprises
Paints, Caulks & Adhesives
62 Woolsey St.
Irvington, NJ 07111
Phone: 201-399-2121
1-800-545-7658
Fax: 201-399-5872

Sammamish Woodworks
Roofing
17825 N.E. 65th St.,
Suite A155
Redmond, WA 98052-0558
Phone: 206-883-0558
Fax: 206-883-0558

Samuel Cabot (Cabot Stains)
Paints, Caulks & Adhesives
100 Hale St.
Newburyport, MA 01950
Phone: 508-465-1900
1-800-US-STAIN
Fax: 508-462-0511

Sanderson Plumbing Products
Faucets & Fixtures
Tuffy Ln.
Columbus, MS 39701
Phone: 601-328-4000
1-800-647-1042
Fax: 601-329-4362

Sandy Pond Hardwoods
Doors
921-A Lancaster Pike
Quarryville, PA 17566
Phone: 717-284-5030
1-800-546-9663
Fax: 717-284-5739
Internet: http://www.
figuredhardwoods.com

Sansher Corp.
Paints, Caulks & Adhesives
8005 N. Clinton St.
Fort Wayne, IN 46825
Phone: 219-484-2000
Fax: 219-482-6780

Santile Intl. Corp.
Faucets & Fixtures; Walls, Ceilings & Finishes
6687 Jimmy Carter Blvd.
Norcross, GA 30071
Phone: 770-416-6224
Fax: 770-416-6239

Sanyo Fisher (USA) Corp.
HVAC
21350 Lassen St.,
PO Box 2329
Chatsworth, CA 91311
Phone: 818-998-7322, ext. 567
Fax: 818-701-4149

Sashco Sealants
Paints, Caulks & Adhesives
3900 E. 68th Ave.
Commerce City, CO 80022-2241
Phone: 303-286-7271
1-800-289-7290
Fax: 303-286-0400

Satin Finish Hardwood Flooring
Flooring
8 Oak St.
Weston, ON M9N 1R8
Canada
Phone: 416-241-8631
1-800-26SATIN
Fax: 416-241-8636

Sauder Wood Products
Moulding & Millwork
5575 Nordic Way
Ferndale, WA 98248
Phone: 360-384-4774

Sauna Craft
Faucets & Fixtures
115 Bowes Rd., Unit 1
Concord, ON L4K 1H7
Canada
Phone: 905-738-9443
1-800-363-8270
Fax: 905-738-2486

Scalex
Computer Software; Tools/Hand
2794 Loker Ave., Suite 105
Carlsbad, CA 92008
Phone: 619-438-5619
1-800-653-3532
Fax: 619-438-5539
Internet:
http://www.scalex.com

The Scandinavian Profiling Systems
Roofing; Siding & Accessories
5449 Maule Way
Mangonia Park, FL 33407
Phone: 407-863-1333
1-800-248-6955
Fax: 407-863-7722

Scatton Bros. Awning Mfg.
Doors; Room Enclosures; Siding & Accessories
284 Wissahickon Ave.,
PO Box 1428
North Wales, PA 19454
Phone: 215-699-9211
1-800-523-2280
Fax: 215-699-9215

Schlage Lock Co.
Hardware
2401 Bayshore Blvd.
San Francisco, CA 94134
Phone: 415-467-1100
Fax: 415-330-5626
Internet:
http://schlagelock.com/
schlage

Schlegel Corp.
Hardware; Insulation
PO Box 23197
Rochester, NY 14692
Phone: 716-427-7200
1-800-586-0354
Fax: 716-427-9993
E-mail:
bpdproducts@schlegel.com

Schluter Systems
Engineered Lumber & Panels; Moulding & Millwork; Specialty Products
194 Pleasant Ridge Rd.
Plattsburgh, NY 12901
Phone: 514-695-2100
1-800-361-3127
Fax: 514-630-0983
Internet:
http://www.schluter.com

Schonbek Worldwide Lighting
Electrical & Lighting
61 Industrial Blvd.
Plattsburgh, NY 12901
Phone: 518-563-7500
1-800-836-1892
Fax: 518-563-4228 or
1-800-443-7358
Internet:
http://www.schonbek.com

Schrock Cabinet Co.
Cabinetry
6000 Perimeter Dr.
Dublin, OH 43017
Phone: 614-792-4970
Fax: 614-792-4979

Schrock Handcrafted Cabinetry (A Schrock Cabinet Co. Brand)
Cabinetry
217 S. Oak St.
Arthur, IL 61911
Phone: 217-543-3311
Fax: 217-543-3394

Schroll's Kitchen Krafts
Cabinetry; Countertops
4691 Raycom Rd.
Dover, PA 17315
Phone: 717-292-5625
Fax: 717-292-7567

Schuller Intl.
Insulation; Roofing
PO Box 5108
Denver, CO 80217
Phone: 303-978-4900
1-800-654-3103
Fax: 303-978-2318
Internet:
http://www.schuller.com

Schulte Corp.
Specialty Products
12115 Ellington Ct.
Cincinnati, OH 45249
Phone: 513-489-9300
1-800-669-3225
Fax: 513-247-3389

Seal-Dry
3300 S. Woodrow
Little Rock, AR 72204
Phone: 501-663-3063
1-800-SEAL-DRY
Fax: 501-663-1926

Scotsman Ice Systems
Appliances
775 Corporate Woods Pkwy.
Vernon Hills, IL 60061
Phone: 708-215-4500
Fax: 708-913-9844

Scott Cedar
Roofing; Siding & Accessories
PO Box 515
Sumas, WA 98295
Phone: 1-800-963-3388
Fax: 604-820-3084

Scott Sign Systems
Landscape Design; Specialty Products
PO Box 1047
Tallevast, FL 34270-1047
Phone: 941-355-5171
1-800-237-9447
Fax: 941-351-1787
Internet:
http://www.scottsigns.com

Screen Manufacturers Assn.
Doors; Room Enclosures; Windows
2850 S. Ocean Blvd.,
Suite 114
Palm Beach, FL 33480
Phone: 561-533-0991
Fax: 561-533-0991
E-mail:
104200.266@compuserve.com

Screen Tight
Room Enclosures; Windows
407 St. James
Georgetown, SC 29440
Phone: 803-527-7658
1-800-768-7325
Fax: 803-527-6498

Screenex Design Center (Riordian Group)
Doors; HVAC; Room Enclosures; Windows
759 Zena Highwoods Rd.
Kingston, NY 12401
Phone: 914-246-3432
1-800-746-7326
Fax: 1-800-RIORDAN

SDS Lumber Co.
Engineered Lumber & Panels
PO Box 266
Bingen, WA 98605
Phone: 509-493-2155
Fax: 509-493-1149

Sea Gull Lighting Prods
Cabinetry; Electrical & Lighting
301 W. Washington St.
Riverside, NJ 08075
Phone: 609-764-0500
Fax: 609-764-0813

Seacoast Mills
Flooring; Siding & Accessories
136 Pine Rd.
Brentwood, NH 03833
Phone: 603-778-8216
Fax: 603-778-0926

Seal Rite Windows
Doors; Windows
3500 N. 44th St.
Lincoln, NE 68504
Phone: 402-464-0202
Fax: 402-467-4101

Sealant, Waterproofing & Restoration Institute
3101 Broadway, Suite 585
Kansas City, MO 64111
Phone: 816-561-8230

Sealed Insulating Glass Manufacturers Assn.
401 N. Michigan Ave.
Chicago, IL 60611-4212
Phone: 312-644-6610
Fax: 312-527-6783
E-mail: sigma@sba.com

Searcy Flooring
Flooring
PO Box 906
Searcy, AR 72145-0906
Phone: 501-268-8694
Fax: 501-279-2446

Sears Contract Sales Sears, Roebuck and Co.
Appliances; Faucets & Fixtures; Garage Doors & Openers; HVAC
3333 Beverly Rd.,
E3-381A
Hoffman Estates, IL 60179
Phone: 847-286-2994
1-800-359-2000
Fax: 847-286-1864

Sections
Doors; Garage Doors & Openers
3580 Kennebec Dr.
Eagan, MN 55122
Phone: 612-686-9911
1-888-686-9911
Fax: 612-686-9922
Internet:
http://www.sections.com

Security Chimneys
Fireplaces
2125 Monterey St.
Laval, PQ H7L 3T6
Canada
Phone: 514-973-9999
Fax: 514-687-9569

Security Fastener Co.
Hardware
3854 Industrial Way
Benicia, CA 94510
Phone: 707-746-8025
1-800-227-2424
Fax: 707-746-0347

Selby Furniture Hardware Co.
Electrical & Lighting; Hardware
321 Rider Ave.
Bronx, NY 10451
Phone: 718-993-3700
Fax: 718-993-3143

Sellick Equipment
Equipment & Trucks
PO Box 2547
Detroit, MI 48231
Phone: 519-738-2255
Fax: 519-738-3477

Semco Windows & Doors
Semling-Menke Co.
Doors; Windows
PO Box 378
Merrill, WI 54452
Phone: 715-536-9411
1-800-333-2206
Fax: 715-536-3067

Senco Products
Tools/Electric & Pneumatic
8485 Broadwell Rd.
Cincinnati, OH 45244
Phone: 513-388-2000
1-800-543-4596
Fax: 1-800-543-3299

Senergy
(A Div. of Harris Specialty Chemicals)
Siding & Accessories
1367 Elmwood Ave.
Cranston, RI 02910
Phone: 401-467-2600
1-800-221-9255
Fax: 401-941-7480

SEPCO Industries
Faucets & Fixtures; Hardware
491 Wortman Ave.
Spring Creek, NY 11208
Phone: 718-257-2800
1-800-842-7277
Fax: 718-257-2144

Service Software
Computer Software
26 Country Club Village
Pueblo, CO 81008
Phone: 1-800-583-8474
Fax: 719-542-5669

Seton Name Plate Co.
Specialty Products
PO Box 819
Branford, CT 06405
Phone: 203-488-8059
1-800-243-6624
Fax: 203-488-5973
Internet:
http://www.seton.com

Sever Signs & Displays
Landscape Design
532 Archibold St.
Winnipeg, MB R2J 0X4
Canada
Phone: 204-233-3444
1-800-665-5110
Fax: 204-231-0977

Shakertown Corp.
Roofing; Siding & Accessories; Walls, Ceilings & Finishes
PO Box 400
Winlock, WA 98596
Phone: 206-785-3501
1-800-426-8970
Fax: 206-785-3076

Shanker Industries
Walls, Ceilings & Finishes
3435 Lawson Blvd.
Oceanside, NY 11572
Phone: 516-766-4477
Fax: 516-766-6655

Sharp Electronics Corp.
Appliances; HVAC
Sharp Plaza
Mahwah, NJ 07430
Phone: 201-529-8698
Fax: 201-529-9597

Shaw Industries
Home Foundations Carpets
Flooring
1000 S. Harris St.
Dalton, GA 30722
Phone: 706-275-1711
1-800-441-7429
Fax: 706-275-1719

Sheet Metal Mfg. Co.
Roofing; Siding & Accessories
1080 Wyckoff Ave.,
PO Box 175
Ridgewood, NY 11385
Phone: 718-366-2000
Fax: 718-366-4767

Sheffield Bronze Paint Corp.
Paints, Caulks & Adhesives
PO Box 19206,
17814 S. Waterloo Rd.
Cleveland, OH 44119
Phone: 216-481-8330
Fax: 216-481-6606

Shelter Enterprises
Insulation
PO Box 618, Saratoga St.
Cohoes, NY 12047
Phone: 518-237-4101
1-800-836-0719
Fax: 518-237-0125

Shelter Systems
Engineered Lumber & Panels; Structural Systems
633 Stone Chapel Rd.
Westminster, MD 21157
Phone: 410-876-3900
Fax: 410-857-5754
Internet:
http://www.sheltersystems.com

Sherle Wagner Intl.
Cabinetry; Countertops; Electrical & Lighting; Faucets & Fixtures; Flooring; Hardware; Walls, Ceilings & Finishes
60 E. 57th St.
New York, NY 10022
Phone: 212-758-3300
Fax: 212-207-8010

The Sherwin-Williams Co.
Paints, Caulks & Adhesives
101 Prospect Ave. N.W.
Cleveland, OH 44115
Phone: 216-566-2000
1-800-336-1110

Sholton Glass Block Systems
Windows
6915 S.W. 57th Ave.,
Suite 206
Coral Gables, FL 33143
Phone: 305-667-4471
1-800-272-9400
Fax: 305-667-4419

Showcase Homes
Structural Systems
PO Box 489
Nappanee, IN 46550
Phone: 1-800-777-0745

Shower Shapes
Countertops; Faucets & Fixtures; Specialty Products
51 Cass Pl.
Goleta, CA 93117
Phone: 805-967-4739
Fax: 805-967-5896

Showerite Div.
Universal-Rundle Corp.
Faucets & Fixtures
7519 S. Greenwood
Chicago, IL 60619
Phone: 312-483-5400
1-800-925-9131
Fax: 312-483-5409

Shur-Co.
Equipment & Trucks
PO Box 713
Yankton, SD 57078
Phone: 605-665-6000
1-800-437-4172
Fax: 605-665-0501
Internet:
http://www.shurco.com

Shutters
Siding & Accessories
12213 Hwy. 173,
PO Box 407
Hebron, IL 60034
Phone: 815-648-2494
1-800-548-3336
Fax: 815-648-2518
Internet:
http://www.shuttersinc.com

Sibes Brass/
ISEO Locks
Faucets & Fixtures; Hardware
260 Lambert St., Suite K
Oxnard, CA 93030
Phone: 805-988-0232
1-800-483-4951
Fax: 805-988-9493

Sico North America
Specialty Products
7525 Cahill Rd.,
PO Box 1169
Minneapolis, MN 55440
Phone: 612-941-1700
1-800-328-6138
Fax: 612-941-6688

SieMatic Corp.
Cabinetry
2 Greenwood Sq.
3331 Street Rd.,
Suite 450
Bensalem, PA 19020
Phone: 215-244-6800
Fax: 215-244-6822

Sierra Pacific Windows
Windows
PO Box 8489
Red Bluff, CA 96089
Phone: 1-800-824-7744
1-800-729-7943
Internet: http://sierra
pacificind.com

Sigma Design
Computer Software
60 Mall Rd., Suite 300
Burlington, MA 01803
Phone: 617-270-1000
Fax: 617-270-9477

Silcraft Corp.
Faucets & Fixtures; Specialty Products
528 Hughes Dr.
Traverse City, MI 49684
Phone: 616-946-4221
1-800-678-7100
Fax: 616-946-1740

Silver Line Building Products
Doors; Windows
1 Silver Line Dr.,
PO Box 6029
North Brunswick, NJ
08902-6029
Phone: 908-937-5800
1-800-234-4228
Fax: 908-418-0190

Simonton Windows
Doors; Windows
5300 Briscoe Rd.,
PO Box 1646
Parkersburg, WV 26102
Phone: 1-800-542-9118
1-800-542-9116

Simplex Access Controls
Ilco Unican Group
Cabinetry; Specialty Products
2941 Indiana Ave.,
PO Box 4114
Winston Salem, NC
27115-4114
Phone: 910-725-1331
Fax: 1-800-346-9640

Simplex Industries
Structural Systems
Keyser Valley Industrial
Park, 1 Simplex Dr.
Scranton, PA 18504
Phone: 717-346-5113
1-800-233-4233
Fax: 717-346-3731

Simplex Products
(A Div. of K2)
Engineered Lumber & Panels; Insulation; Siding & Accessories
3000 W. Beecher
Adrian, MI 49221
Phone: 517-263-8881
Fax: 517-263-2835

Simpson Door Co.
Doors
400 Simpson Ave.
McCleary, WA 98557
Phone: 360-495-3291
1-800-952-4057
Fax: 360-495-3295
Internet:
http://www.simpson-
door.com

Simpson Strong-Tie Co.
Hardware; Paints, Caulks & Adhesives; Room Enclosures; Structural Systems
4637 Chabot Dr.,
Suite 200
Pleasanton, CA 94588
Phone: 510-460-9912
1-800-999-5099
Fax: 510-847-0694
Internet:
http://www.strongtie.com

Simpson Timber Co.
Panel Products Div.
Engineered Lumber & Panels
Third & Franklin Sts.
Shelton, WA 98584
Phone: 360-427-4905
1-800-782-9378
Fax: 360-427-4922

Single Ply Roofing Institute
175 Highland Ave.
Needham, MA 02194
Phone: 617-444-0242
Fax: 617-444-6111
Internet:
http://www.spri.org

Sinkmaster
Anaheim Mfg. Co.
Appliances; Plumbing Supplies
4240 E. La Palma Ave.
Anaheim, CA 92807
Phone: 714-524-7770
Fax: 714-996-7073

Sioux Chief Mfg.
Faucets & Fixtures; Fireplaces; HVAC; Plumbing Supplies; Tools/Hand
PO Box 397,
Old S. 71 Hwy.
Peculiar, MO 64078
Phone: 816-779-6104
1-800-821-3944
Fax: 1-800-758-5950

Sioux Tools
Tools/Electric & Pneumatic
2901 Floyd Blvd.,
PO Box 507
Sioux City, IA 51102
Phone: 712-252-0525
1-800-722-7290
Fax: 1-800-722-7236

Sioux Veneer Panel Co.
Moulding & Millwork; Walls, Ceilings & Finishes
2000 Yamhill Rd.
Boise, ID 83706
Phone: 208-344-8357
1-800-786-8357
Fax: 208-345-2759

Sirius Software
Computer Software
345 W. Second St.,
Suite 201
Dayton, OH 45402-1443
Phone: 937-228-4849
1-800-788-4849
Fax: 937-228-1159
Internet: http://www.
siriusacct.com

SIRO Design
Hardware
10301 N.W. 50th St.,
Suite 111
Sunrise, FL 33351-8009
Phone: 954-749-1155
1-800-537-7476
Fax: 954-749-9745

Sitecraft Corp.
Landscape Design
40-25 Crescent St.
Long Island City, NY
11101
Phone: 718-729-4900
1-800-221-1448
Fax: 718-482-0661

SK Hand Tool Corp.
Tools/Electric & Pneumatic; Tools/Hand
3535 W. 47th St.
Chicago, IL 60632
Phone: 312-523-1300
1-800-U-CALL-SK
Fax: 312-523-2103

Sketchtech
Computer Software
43 Main St. S.E., Suite 410
Minneapolis, MN 55414
Phone: 612-379-1435
Fax: 612-331-4962
E-mail:
haglu001@maroon.tc.umn.
edu

Skil Bosch
(See S-B Power Tool Co.)

Skookum Lumber Co.
Siding & Accessories
PO Box 1398
Olympia, WA 98507
Phone: 206-352-7633
Fax: 206-352-7638
Internet: http://www.
skookumlumber.com

Skyline Building Systems
(See DecTec)

SkyQuest
Room Enclosures; Windows
811 E. Waterman
Wichita, KS 67202
Phone: 316-262-4811
1-800-279-8568
Fax: 316-262-2653

Skytech Systems
Doors; Room Enclosures; Windows
7030 New Berwick Hwy.
Bloomsburg, PA 17815
Phone: 717-752-1111
1-800-447-4938
Fax: 717-752-3535

Slant/Fin Corp.
HVAC
100 Forest Dr.
Greenvale, NY 11548
Phone: 516-484-2600
Fax: 516-484-5921

Slate/Select
Roofing
3162 Miller Park Dr. N.
Garland, TX 75042-7759
Phone: 972-276-2000
Fax: 972-272-6400

Slimfold Products
(A Div. of the Dunbarton Corp.)
Doors
PO Box 6416
Dothan, AL 36302
Phone: 334-794-0661
1-800-633-7553
Fax: 334-793-7022
Internet:
http://www.dunbarton.com

Sloan Flushmate
(A Div. of Sloan Valve Co.)
Faucets & Fixtures
10500 Seymour Ave.
Franklin Park, IL 60131
Phone: 708-671-4300
1-800-875-9116
Fax: 708-671-6944

Slope Block
Landscape Design; Structural Systems
280 Asta Ave.
Newbury Park, CA 91320
Phone: 805-376-9924
Fax: 805-499-0864

Splash-Ender
Faucets & Fixtures
PO Box 19202
Portland, OR 97280
Phone: 503-244-2422
Fax: 503-244-1785

Spotnails
(A Div. of Peace Industries)
Tools/Electric & Pneumatic; Tools/Hand
1100 Hicks Rd.
Rolling Meadows, IL 60008
Phone: 847-259-1620
1-800-873-2239
Fax: 847-259-9236

Spring Ram America
Faucets & Fixtures
2761 Golfview Dr.
Naperville, IL 60563
Phone: 708-983-4200
Fax: 708-983-4662

Spyder
Equipment & Trucks
PO Box 266106
Houston, TX 77207
Phone: 713-641-6377
1-800-231-5916

Square D Co.
Electrical & Lighting
3201 Nicholasville Rd.,
Suite 300
Lexington, KY 40503
Phone: 1-800-392-8781

St. Croix Valley Hardwoods
Engineered Lumber & Panels
PO Box 120
Luck, WI 54853
Phone: 715-472-2131
1-800-236-7098
Fax: 715-472-2108

St. Thomas Classics
(A Div. of St. Thomas Creations)
Faucets & Fixtures
1022 W. 24th St.,
Suite 125
National City, CA 91950-6302
Phone: 619-474-9490
1-800-536-2284
Fax: 619-474-9493

St. Thomas Creations
Cabinetry; Faucets & Fixtures; Flooring
1022 W. 24th St.,
Suite 125
National City, CA 91950-6302
Phone: 619-474-9490
1-800-536-2284
Fax: 619-474-9493

Stair-Pak Products Co.
Moulding & Millwork
2575 Rt. 22
Union, NJ 07083
Phone: 908-688-1200
1-800-854-5100
Fax: 908-688-1209

Stair Parts
Moulding & Millwork
2197 Canton Rd.
Marietta, GA 30066
Phone: 770-427-0124
1-800-827-8247
Fax: 770-425-6140

Stair Works
Moulding & Millwork
PO Box 384
Fishers, IN 46038
Phone: 317-845-0022
1-800-353-0273
Fax: 317-579-0860

Staircase
Moulding & Millwork
65 Kings Trail
Buffalo, NY 14221-2608
Phone: 716-689-0155
1-800-255-5062
Fax: 716-689-4047

Staircase & Millwork Corp.
Moulding & Millwork
610 McFarland 400 Dr.
Alpharetta, GA 30201
Phone: 404-664-6664
1-800-878-9778
Fax: 404-664-6185
E-mail: mrstair@atl.mindspring.com

Stairways
Moulding & Millwork
4166 Pinemont
Houston, TX 77018
Phone: 713-680-3110
1-800-231-0793
Fax: 713-680-2571

Stairworld
Moulding & Millwork
39 Cleopatra Dr.
Ottawa, ON K2G 0B6
Canada
Phone: 613-723-5454
1-800-387-7711
Fax: 613-723-5149
Internet: http://www.stairworld.com

Standard Plywoods
Flooring
Old Laurens Rd.
Clinton, SC 29325
Phone: 803-833-6250
Fax: 803-833-6664

Standard Tar Products Co.
Paints, Caulks & Adhesives
2456 W. Cornell St.
Milwaukee, WI 53209
Phone: 414-873-7650
1-800-825-7650
Fax: 414-873-7737

Stanley-Bostitch
Tools/Electric & Pneumatic; Tools/Hand
Briggs Dr.
East Greenwich, RI 02818
Phone: 401-884-2500
1-800-556-6696
Fax: 401-885-3122

Stanley Consumer Fastening
Stanley Fastening Systems
Tools/Hand
Briggs Dr.
East Greenwich, RI 02818
Phone: 1-800-343-9329
Fax: 1-800-842-9360

Stanley Door Systems
(A Sub. of Stanley Works)
Doors; Garage Doors & Openers
1225 E. Maple Rd.
Troy, MI 48083-5600
Phone: 810-528-1400
1-800-521-2752
Fax: 810-528-1424
Internet: http://www.stanleyworks.com

Stanley Hardware
Doors; Hardware
480 Myrtle St.
New Britain, CT 06053
Phone: 860-225-5111
Fax: 860-827-5729

Stanley Home Decor
480 Myrtle St.
New Britain, CT 06053
Phone: 860-827-5724
Fax: 860-827-5135

Stanley Tools
Paints, Caulks & Adhesives; Structural Systems; Tools/Hand
600 Myrtle St.
New Britain, CT 06053
Phone: 203-225-5111
1-800-648-7654
Fax: 203-827-5926

Star-Beka Küchen
Cabinetry
489 Rt. 17 S.
Paramus, NJ 07652
Phone: 201-261-5221
1-888-STAR-BEKA
Fax: 201-261-0966

Star Expansion Co.
Hardware
Pleasant Hill Rd.
Mountainville, NY 10953
Phone: 914-534-2511
1-800-247-8274
Fax: 914-534-2510

Star Sprinkler
Home Technology
7071 S. 13th St.,
Suite 103
Oak Creek, WI 53154
Phone: 414-570-5000
1-800-558-5236
Fax: 1-800-877-1295
Internet: http://www.star-sprinkler.com

Starbrite
(A Div. of Vega Industries)
Doors; Windows
1125 Ford St.
Maumee, OH 43537
Phone: 419-893-3311
1-800-283-3311
Fax: 419-893-0735

Starmark
Cabinetry
600 E. 48th St. N.
Sioux Falls, SD 57104
Phone: 605-335-8600
Fax: 605-336-5566

States Industries
Engineered Lumber & Panels; Moulding & Millwork; Walls, Ceilings & Finishes
PO Box 7037,
29545 Enid Rd. E.
Eugene, OR 97401-0038
Phone: 1-800-626-1981
Fax: 541-689-8051
Internet: http://www.statesind.com

Steamist
Faucets & Fixtures
1 Altman Dr.
Rutherford, NJ 07070
Phone: 201-933-0700
Fax: 201-933-0746

Steel Door Institute
Doors
30200 Detroit Rd.
Cleveland, OH 44145
Phone: 216-899-0010
Fax: 216-892-1404

Steel Tile Co.
Roofing; Siding & Accessories
RR 1
Thornton, ON L0L 2N0
Canada
Phone: 705-436-1723
Fax: 705-436-6329

Steel & Wire Products Co.
Hardware; Landscape Design; Paints, Caulks & Adhesives; Structural Systems; Tools/Electric & Pneumatic
PO Box 207,
1501 W. Patapsco Ave.
Baltimore, MD 21203
Phone: 410-355-2800
Fax: 410-355-1880

Steelcraft
Doors
9017 Blue Ash Rd.
Cincinnati, OH 45242
Phone: 513-745-6400
Fax: 513-745-6657
Internet: http://www.steelcraft.com

Steelwood Doors
Doors
155 Regalcrest Ct.
Woodbridge, ON L4L 8P3 Canada
Phone: 905-851-4665
Fax: 905-851-7340

Stephan Mfg.
Moulding & Millwork
103 Neal Ave.
West Monroe, LA 71291-4917
Phone: 318-396-2875
Fax: 318-396-2881

Stepstone
Moulding & Millwork; Structural Systems
17025 S. Main St.
Gardena, CA 90248
Phone: 310-327-7474
1-800-572-9029
Fax: 310-327-0318

Steptoe & Wife Antiques
Hardware; Moulding & Millwork; Specialty Products; Walls, Ceilings & Finishes
322 Geary Ave.
Toronto, ON M6H 2C7 Canada
Phone: 416-530-4200
1-800-461-0060
Fax: 416-530-4666
Internet: http://www.steptoewife.com

Sterling Building Systems
Structural Systems
PO Box 1967
Wausau, WI 54402-1967
Phone: 715-359-7108
1-800-735-1812
Fax: 715-359-2867

Sterling Plumbing Group
Faucets & Fixtures
2900 Golf Rd.
Rolling Meadows, IL 60008
Phone: 847-734-1777
1-800-STERLING
Fax: 847-734-4767

Stillwater Products
Doors; Roofing; Siding & Accessories; Windows
400 Commerce St.
Brevard, NC 28712
Phone: 704-883-4833
1-800-326-5355
Fax: 1-800-325-5355

Stirling Building Products
(Marley Roof Tile)
Roofing
PO Box 278,
281 Alliance Rd.
Milton, ON L9T 4N9 Canada
Phone: 905-878-5531
1-800-521-5832
Fax: 905-878-8334

Sto-Cote Products
Insulation
Drawer 310
Richmond, IL 60071
Phone: 815-675-2358
1-800-435-2621
Fax: 414-279-6744
E-mail: stocote@genevaonline.com

STO Finish Systems
(A Div. of STO Corp.)
Paints, Caulks & Adhesives; Siding & Accessories; Structural Systems; Walls, Ceilings & Finishes
6175 Riverside Dr. S.W.
Atlanta, GA 30331
Phone: 404-346-3666
1-800-221-2397
Fax: 404-346-3119

Stone Construction Equipment
Landscape Design
32 E. Main St.,
PO Box 150
Honeoye, NY 14471
Phone: 716-229-5141
1-800-888-9926
Fax: 716-229-2363
Internet: http://www.stone-equip.com

Stone Products Corp./ Cultured Stone®
Fireplaces; Landscape Design; Siding & Accessories; Structural Systems; Walls, Ceilings & Finishes
PO Box 270
Napa, CA 94559
Phone: 707-255-1727
1-800-255-1727
Fax: 707-255-5572
Internet: http://www.culturedstone.com

Stor-A-Dor
Hardware
The Manse
Heath, MA 01346
Phone: 413-337-0211
Fax: 413-337-0212
E-mail: jcour31073@aol.com

Storehorse
Tools/Hand
16607 Blanco Rd., Suite 100
San Antonio, TX 78232
Phone: 210-492-8907
1-800-555-9753
Fax: 210-492-8908

Strikemaster Canada
Tools/Hand
3097 Universal Dr.
Mississauga, ON L4X 2E2 Canada
Phone: 905-625-4788
Fax: 905-625-5499

Strom Plumbing By Sign Of The Crab
Faucets & Fixtures; Hardware; Plumbing Supplies; Specialty Products
Dept RM,
3756 Omec Cir.
Rancho Cordova, CA 95742-7399
Phone: 916-638-2722
1-800-843-2722
Fax: 916-638-2725

Stromberg's Architectural Products
Moulding & Millwork; Walls, Ceilings & Finishes
PO Box 8036
Greenville, TX 75401
Phone: 903-454-8682
Fax: 903-454-3642

Structural Board Assn.
Engineered Lumber & Panels; Siding & Accessories; Structural Systems
45 Sheppard Ave. E.,
Suite 412
Willowdale, ON M2N 5W9 Canada
Phone: 416-730-9090
Fax: 416-730-9013
Internet: http://www.sba-osb.com

Structural Insulated Panel Assn.
Structural Systems
1511 K St., N.W.,
Suite 600
Washington, DC 20005
Phone: 202-347-7800
Fax: 202-393-5043
E-mail: SIPADC@aol.com

The Structural Slate Co.
Countertops; Flooring; Roofing; Walls, Ceilings & Finishes
222 E. Main St.
Pen Argyl, PA 18072
Phone: 610-863-4141
1-800-677-5283
Fax: 610-863-7016

Stuart Flooring Corp.
Flooring
PO Box 947
Stuart, VA 24171-0947
Phone: 540-694-4547
Fax: 540-694-4953
E-mail:
sfcfloor@swva.com

Stuc-O-Flex Intl.
Insulation; Paints, Caulks & Adhesives; Roofing; Siding & Accessories
17639 N.W. 67th Ct.
Redmond, WA 98052
Phone: 206-885-5085
1-800-305-1045
Fax: 206-869-0107

Studor
Faucets & Fixtures
2030 Main St.
Dunedin, FL 34698
Phone: 813-734-7750
1-800-447-4721
Fax: 813-734-7753

Style-Mark
Moulding & Millwork; Roofing; Siding & Accessories; Specialty Products
960 W. Barre
Archbold, OH 43502
Phone: 419-445-0116
1-800-446-3040
Fax: 419-445-4440

Stylemark Carpet Mills
Flooring
PO Box 2509
Dalton, GA 30722
Phone: 1-800-532-2257
Fax: 706-277-3355

Sub-Zero Freezer Co.
Appliances
4717 Hammersley Rd.
Madison, WI 53711
Phone: 608-271-2233
1-800-222-7820
Fax: 608-271-7471
Internet:
http://www.builderonline.com/sponsors/subzero

SUBA Mfg.
Countertops
921 Bayshore Rd.
Benicia, CA 94510-2990
Phone: 707-745-0358
Fax: 707-745-2985

Suburban Mfg. Co.
Fireplaces; HVAC
PO Box 399
Dayton, TN 37321
Phone: 423-775-2131
Fax: 423-775-7015

Suburban Propane
PO Box 206
Whippany, NJ 07981
Phone: 1-800-663-6642
Fax: 201-515-5976
Internet: http://www.suburbanpropane.com

Sugarcreek Window & Door Corp.
Doors; Windows
425 S. Broadway St.
Sugarcreek, OH 44681
Phone: 216-852-2416
Fax: 216-852-2490

Summit Windows & Patio Doors of Cheyenne, Wyo.
(A Div. of JELD-WEN)
Doors; Windows;
310 Cleveland Pl.
Cheyenne, WY 82007
Phone: 1-800-877-9482

Summit Windows & Patio Doors of Corsicana, Texas
(A Div. of JELD-WEN)
Doors; Windows
4000 E. Hwy., No. 31
Corsicana, TX 75110
Phone: 1-800-877-9482

Summit Windows & Patio Doors of Denver, Colo.
(A Div. of JELD-WEN)
Doors; Windows
5055 Lima St.
Denver, CO 80239
Phone: 1-800-877-9482

Summit Windows & Patio Doors of Kent, Wash.
(A Div. of JELD-WEN)
Doors; Windows
PO Box 886
Kent, WA 98035
Phone: 1-800-877-9482

Summit Windows & Patio Doors of Kingman, Ariz.
(A Div. of JELD-WEN)
Doors; Windows
4550 Mohave Airport Dr.
Kingman, AZ 86401
Phone: 1-800-877-9482

Summit Windows & Patio Doors of Lathrop, Calif.
(A Div. of JELD-WEN)
Doors; Windows
1683 E. Louise Ave.
Lathrop, CA 95330
Phone: 1-800-877-9482

Summit Windows & Patio Doors of Sandy, Utah
(A Div. of JELD-WEN)
Doors; Windows
8585 S. Sandy Pkwy.,
Suite A
Sandy, UT 84070
Phone: 1-800-877-9482

Summit Windows & Patio Doors of Stayton, Ore.
(A Div. of JELD-WEN)
Doors; Windows
2044 Deschutes Dr.
Stayton, OR 97383
Phone: 1-800-877-9482

Summit Windows & Patio Doors of Vista, Calif.
(A Div. of JELD-WEN)
Doors; Windows
2470 Ash St.
Vista, CA 92083
Phone: 1-800-877-9482

Summitville Tiles
Countertops; Flooring; Landscape Design; Walls, Ceilings & Finishes
PO Box 73
Summitville, OH 43962
Phone: 330-223-1511
Fax: 330-223-1414

Sun Industries
4204 15A St. S.W.
Calgary AB T2T 4C9
Canada
Phone: 403-243-0534
Fax: 403-243-0534

Sun Nuclear Corp.
Specialty Products
425-A Pineda Ct.
Melbourne, FL 32940
Phone: 407-254-7785
Fax: 407-259-7979

Sun Room Co.
Room Enclosures
PO Box 301
Leola, PA 17540
Phone: 717-391-7035
1-800-426-2737
Fax: 717-391-7039

Sun-Tek Industries
Windows
10303 General Dr.
Orlando, FL 32824
Phone: 407-859-2117
1-800-334-5854
Fax: 407-859-6607

Sun Tunnel Skylights
Windows
786 McGlincey Ln.
Campbell, CA 95008
Phone: 408-369-7447
1-800-369-3664
Fax: 408-369-0228

Sun Windows
Windows
1515 E. 18th St.
Owensboro, KY 42303
Phone: 502-684-0691
1-800-328-1151
Fax: 502-926-6452

Sunbilt Solar Products by Sussman
Room Enclosures; Windows
109-10 180th St.
Jamaica, NY 11433
Phone: 718-297-6040
Fax: 718-297-3090

Sunburst Skylights
Windows
1210 Industrial Way
Parksville, BC V9P 1R2
Canada
Phone: 604-248-8131
Fax: 604-248-4354

Suncrest Cabinets
Cabinetry; Countertops
110 12591 Bridgeport Rd.
Richmond, BC V6V 1J4
Canada
Phone: 604-278-3445
Fax: 604-278-0924

Sundance Supply
Room Enclosures
1678 Shattuck Ave.,
Suite 173
Berkeley, CA 94709
Phone: 510-845-0525
1-800-776-2534
Fax: 1-800-775-4479
Internet: http://www.sundancesupply.com

Sunearth
HVAC
4315 Santa Ana St.
Ontario, CA 91761
Phone: 909-605-5610
Fax: 909-605-5613
E-mail: 3670@sshare.com

Sunesta Products
Landscape Design; Siding & Accessories; Windows
11320 Distribution Ave. E.
Jacksonville, FL 32256
Phone: 904-268-8000
1-800-874-2001
Fax: 904-260-4499

Sunnyside Solar
HVAC
RD 4, Box 808,
Green River Rd.
Brattleboro, VT 05301-9202
Phone: 802-257-1482
Fax: 802-254-4670
E-mail:
sunnysde.@sover.net

Sunrise Specialty
Faucets & Fixtures
5540 Doyle St.
Emeryville, CA 94608
Phone: 510-654-1794
1-800-444-5280
Fax: 510-654-5775

Sunset Moulding Co.
Moulding & Millwork
PO Box 327
Live Oak, CA 95953
Phone: 916-695-1000
1-800-824-5888
Fax: 916-695-2560

Sunset Structures
Structural Systems
390 Sunset Dr.
Elkview, WV 25071
Phone: 304-965-6831
Fax: 304-965-6831

Sunshine Rooms
Room Enclosures
3333 N. Mead
Wichita, KS 67219
Phone: 316-838-0033
1-800-222-1598
Fax: 316-838-0839

Sunstar Lighting
Electrical & Lighting
1723A N.W. 33rd St.
Pompano Beach, FL 33064
Phone: 954-972-6136
1-800-881-7827
Fax: 954-968-8321

SunTuf
Landscape Design; Roofing; Room Enclosures; Windows
30 W. Mt. Pleasant Ave.,
Suite 201
Livingston, NJ 07039
Phone: 201-535-8222
1-800-278-6883
Fax: 201-535-6124

Sunway Fan Co.
Electrical & Lighting
3221 Garden Brook Dr.
Dallas, TX 75234
Phone: 214-241-3778
1-800-484-9096, ext. 6809
Fax: 214-484-1597

Supa Doors
Doors
6450 Camp Bullis Rd.
San Antonio, TX 78257
Phone: 210-698-8500
1-888-787-2366
Fax: 1-888-787-2329

Super Pouch
Tools/Hand
335 High St.
Metuchen, NJ 08840
Phone: 908-494-8165
1-800-888-9428
Fax: 908-494-0636

Super-Tek Products
Flooring; Paints, Caulks & Adhesives; Walls, Ceilings & Finishes
25-44 Borough Pl.
Woodside, NY 11377
Phone: 718-278-7900
Fax: 718-204-6013

Superior Aluminum Products
Moulding & Millwork; Room Enclosures
555 E. Main St., PO Box 430
Russia, OH 45363
Phone: 513-526-4065
Fax: 513-526-3904

Superior Clay Corp.
Fireplaces
PO Box 352
Uhrichsville, OH 44683
Phone: 1-800-848-6166
Fax: 614-922-6626

Superior Fireplace Co.
Fireplaces
4325 Artesia Ave.
Fullerton, CA 92633
Phone: 714-521-7302
Fax: 714-521-5223

Superior Floor Co.
Engineered Lumber & Panels; Flooring
803 Jefferson St.
Wausau, WI 54401
Phone: 715-845-2642
Fax: 715-848-1793

Superior Hardwoods & Millwork
Doors; Engineered Lumber & Panels; Flooring; Moulding & Millwork; Walls, Ceilings & Finishes; Windows
5120 Hwy. 93 S.,
PO Box 4731
Missoula, MT 59806
Phone: 406-251-2272
1-800-572-9601
Fax: 406-251-2520

Superior Tile Cutter
Tools/Hand
1566 W. 134th St.
Gardena, CA 90249
Phone: 310-324-3771
Fax: 310-324-0757

Superior Tool Co.
Tools/Hand
100 Hayes Dr., Unit C
Brooklyn Heights, OH 44131
Phone: 216-398-8600
1-800-533-3244
Fax: 216-398-8691
E-mail:
chuckm7578@aol.com

Superior Wood Products
Cabinetry; Countertops
1058 W. County Rd.
400 N.
Warsaw, IN 46580
Phone: 219-267-5879
Fax: 219-269-3488

Superior Wood Shelving
Countertops; Moulding & Millwork
PO Box 21
Glenville, NC 28736
Phone: 704-743-9040
Fax: 704-743-2020

Superseal Mfg. Co.
Doors; Windows
125 Helen St.
South Plainfield, NJ 07080
Phone: 908-561-5910
1-800-521-6704
Fax: 908-561-7885

Supradur Mfg. Co.
Roofing; Siding & Accessories
PO Box 908
Rye, NY 10580
Phone: 914-967-8230
1-800-223-1948
Fax: 914-967-8344

Sure-Lites
(A Div. of Cooper Lighting)
Electrical & Lighting
400 Busse Rd.
Elk Grove Village, IL 60007
Phone: 708-956-8400
Fax: 708-956-1537

Surebond
Paints, Caulks & Adhesives; Specialty Products; Structural Systems; Walls, Ceilings & Finishes
500 E. Remington Rd.
Schaumburg, IL 60173
Phone: 708-843-1818
Fax: 708-843-0765

SureSell
Computer Software
335 Boylston St., Suite J2
Newton, MA 02159
Phone: 617-965-9513
1-800-234-3391
Fax: 617-965-0779
Internet:
http://www.suresell.com

Surface Shields
Equipment & Trucks
13506 S. Kenton Ave.
Crestwood, IL 60445
Phone: 708-385-7340
1-800-91FLOOR
Fax: 708-597-2436

Survivor Technologies
Doors; Windows
PO Box 757,
1441 Chestnut Ave.
Hillside, NJ 07205
Phone: 1-800-733-1601
Fax: 1-800-733-1602

The Swan Corp.
Countertops; Faucets & Fixtures
1 City Centre,
Suite 2300
St. Louis, MO 63101
Phone: 1-800-325-7008
Fax: 314-231-8165

Swan Secure Products
Hardware; Tools/Electric & Pneumatic
7525 Perryman Ct.
Baltimore, MD 21226
Phone: 410-360-9100
1-800-966-2801
Fax: 410-360-2288

Swaner Hardwood Co.
Engineered Lumber & Panels
5 W. Magnolia Blvd.
Burbank, CA 91502
Phone: 213-849-6761
Fax: 818-846-3662

Swanson Tool Co.
Tools/Hand
1010 Lambrecht Rd.
Frankfort, IL 60423
Phone: 815-469-9453
Fax: 815-469-4575

Swedish Building Systems & Components Office (SWEBCO)
Cabinetry; Doors; Faucets & Fixtures; Flooring; Roofing; Structural Systems; Windows
150 N. Michigan Ave.,
Suite 1200
Chicago, IL 60601-7524
Phone: 312-781-6210
Fax: 312-346-0683

Sweepster
Equipment & Trucks; Landscape Design
2800 N. Zeeb Rd.
Dexter, MI 48130
Phone: 313-996-9116
1-800-456-7100
Fax: 313-996-9014
E-mail: sweep@sweepster.com

SwimEx Systems
Faucets & Fixtures
Rt. 136 Market St.,
PO Box 328
Warren, RI 02885
Phone: 401-245-7946
1-800-877-7946
Fax: 401-245-3160

Swirl-way Collections Mansfield Plumbing Products
Faucets & Fixtures
1505 Industrial Dr.
Henderson, TX 75652
Phone: 903-657-1436
1-800-999-1459
Fax: 903-657-3450

Swivelier
Electrical & Lighting
33 Rt. 304, PO Box 619
Nanuet, NY 10954-0619
Phone: 914-623-3471
Fax: 914-623-1861
E-mail: swivelier@juno.com

Sylvan Designs
Electrical & Lighting
8921 Quartz Ave.
Northridge, CA 91324
Phone: 818-998-6868
Fax: 818-998-7241

Symbiotech
Computer Software
1011 Stonebridge Pkwy.,
Suite 106-306
Watkinsville, GA 30677
Phone: 706-769-1549
Fax: 706-769-1678
Internet: http://www.builder software.com

Symbold Tropic Top Artificial Thatch
Roofing
2028-8 Eastborne Way
Orlando, FL 32812
Phone: 407-273-0069
Fax: 407-273-0069

Symmons Industries
Faucets & Fixtures
31 Brooks Dr.
Braintree, MA 02184-3804
Phone: 617-848-2250
1-800-796-6667
Fax: 617-843-3849
Internet: http://www.symmons.com

Synapse Software
Computer Software
1171 Titus Ave.,
Lower Level
Rochester, NY 14617
Phone: 716-467-5796
1-800-420-2521
Fax: 716-266-8437

Syntec Marble
Countertops; Faucets & Fixtures; Specialty Products
339 Industrial Dr.
Kepon, CA 95366
Phone: 209-599-6330
Fax: 209-599-6399

Synthetic Surfaces
Paints, Caulks & Adhesives
PO Box 241
Scotch Plains, NJ 07076
Phone: 908-233-6803
Fax: 908-233-6844

System One Modular Truck Equipment
Equipment & Trucks
PO Box 592
Pennington, NJ 08534
Phone: 609-466-9700
1-800-627-9783
Fax: 609-466-9779

Systematic Irrigation Controls
Home Technology; Landscape Design
PO Box 8051
Newport Beach, CA 92660
Phone: 714-347-1922
Fax: 714-347-1941

T.H.W.S.
HVAC
PO Box 38901,
1676 Cordova Rd.
Germantown, TN 38138
Phone: 901-756-7080
Fax: 901-751-8847
E-mail: thwsinc@aol.com

T.T. Frames
Structural Systems
PO Box 464
Thompson, CT 06277
Phone: 203-923-2231
Fax: 203-923-2686

TACC Intl.
Paints, Caulks & Adhesives
Air Station Industrial Park
Rockland, MA 02370
Phone: 617-878-7015
1-800-503-6991
Fax: 617-871-6727

Takagi Tools
Tools/Hand
337-A Figueroa St.
Wilmington, CA 90744
Phone: 310-513-1113
1-800-777-5538
Fax: 310-513-2199

TAM Industries
Windows
9420 16th Ave. S.W.
Seattle, WA 98106
Phone: 206-763-6868
1-800-SKY-LITE
Fax: 206-768-0327

Tamarack Technologies
Appliances; HVAC
PO Box 490
W. Wareham, MA 02576
Phone: 508-295-8103
1-800-222-5932
Fax: 508-295-8105

Tamark Mfg.
Roofing; Siding & Accessories
PO Box 1386,
508 Stella Ave.
Savannah, GA 31402
Phone: 912-232-0786
1-800-735-7663
Fax: 912-232-7826

Tamko Roofing Products
220 W. Fourth St.
Joplin, MO 64801
Phone: 417-624-6644
1-800-641-4691
Fax: 417-624-8935

Taney Corp.
Moulding & Millwork
5130 Allendale Ln.
Taneytown, MD 21787
Phone: 410-756-6671
Fax: 410-756-4103
Internet: http://www.taney.com

Tapco Products (A Tapco Intl. Corp.)
Equipment & Trucks; Siding & Accessories
45657 Port St.
Plymouth, MI 48170
Phone: 313-451-8272
1-800-521-7567
Fax: 313-451-0702

Tappan (A Brand of Frigidaire Co.)
Appliances
6000 Perimeter Dr.
Dublin, OH 43017
Phone: 614-792-4100
1-800-685-6005
Fax: 614-792-4079

Target
Tools/Electric & Pneumatic
4320 Clary Blvd.
Kansas City, MO 64130
Phone: 816-923-5040
1-800-288-5040
Fax: 1-800-825-0028

Tarheel Wood Treating Co.
Paints, Caulks & Adhesives; Roofing; Tools/Electric & Pneumatic; Walls, Ceilings & Finishes
10309 Chapel Hill Rd.,
PO Box 480
Morrisville, NC 27560
Phone: 919-467-9176
Fax: 919-467-6707

Tarkett
Flooring
PO Box 264
Parsippany, NJ 07054
Phone: 201-428-9000
1-800-FOR-TARKETT

Task Lighting Corp.
Electrical & Lighting
PO Box 1090
Kearney, NE 68848
Phone: 308-236-6707
1-800-445-6404
Fax: 308-234-9401

Taylor Brothers Chippendale Doors
Doors
PO Box 11198
Lynchburg, VA 24506
Phone: 804-237-8100
1-800-288-6767
Fax: 804-237-4227

Taylor Door (A Div. of Masco Industries)
Doors; Garage Doors & Openers
631 N. First St.,
PO Box 457
West Branch, MI 48661
Phone: 517-345-5110
1-800-248-3600
Fax: 517-345-5116

Taymor Industries
Electrical & Lighting; Faucets & Fixtures; Hardware
1586 Zephyr Ave.
Hayward, CA 94544
Phone: 510-429-0888
1-800-388-9887
Fax: 510-429-0397

TCM Forklift Trucks CIM Industrial Machinery
Equipment & Trucks
7950 Blankenship
Houston, TX 77055
Phone: 713-681-8888
Fax: 713-681-8899

TDS
Cabinetry; Moulding & Millwork
9040 Junction Dr.
Annapolis Junction, MD 20701
Phone: 410-880-0006
1-800-TDS-FACE

TEC (A Sub. of HB Fuller Co.)
Engineered Lumber & Panels; Flooring; Paints, Caulks & Adhesives; Siding & Accessories
315 S. Hicks Rd.
Palatine, IL 60067
Phone: 847-358-9500
1-800-323-7407
Fax: 847-358-9510

Technically Unique Bathing Systems
Faucets & Fixtures
7 Monroe St.
Troy, NY 12180
Phone: 518-274-BATH
Fax: 518-272-0342

Tecton Industries
Engineered Lumber & Panels; Moulding & Millwork
PO Box 587
Hines, OR 97738
Phone: 1-800-678-2312
Fax: 503-573-6474
Internet: http://www.teclam.com

Tegola USA
Roofing
PO Box 300443
Denver, CO 80203
Phone: 303-231-6025
1-800-598-8936
Fax: 303-727-6932

Tek-Tron Enterprises
Electrical & Lighting
1652 Deere Ave.
Irvine, CA 92714
Phone: 714-975-1978
Fax: 714-975-1980

Teledyne Specialty Equipment Princeton Products
Equipment & Trucks
250 E. Wilson Bridge Rd.
Worthington, OH 43085
Phone: 614-837-9096
1-800-331-5851
Fax: 614-837-2105

Teledyne Water Pik
Faucets & Fixtures
1730 E. Prospect Rd.
Fort Collins, CO 80553
Phone: 303-221-8616
1-800-825-1964
Fax: 303-221-8715

Temco Fireplace Products
Fireplaces
301 S. Perimeter Park Dr.,
Suite 227
Nashville, TN 37211
Phone: 615-831-9393
Fax: 615-831-9127

Temp-Vent Corp.
HVAC; Specialty Products
107 Cherryville Rd.
Shelby, NC 28150
Phone: 704-482-0324
1-800-525-3271
Fax: 704-482-5241

Tempcast 2000 Masonry Heater Mfg.
Fireplaces; Structural Systems
12 Winton Rd.
Toronto, ON M4N 3E3
Canada
Phone: 416-322-6084
Fax: 416-486-3624

Temple-Inland Forest Products
Engineered Lumber & Panels; Siding & Accessories; Walls, Ceilings & Finishes
303 S. Temple
Diboll, TX 75941
Phone: 409-829-1224
1-800-231-6060

Tempstar Heating & Cooling Products Inter-City Products Corp. (USA)
HVAC
650 Heil-Quaker Ave.
Lewisburg, TN 37091
Phone: 615-359-3511
Fax: 615-270-4166
Internet: http://www.tempstar.com/ TEMPSTAR

Tenneco Building Products
Insulation
2907 Log Cabin Dr.
Smyrna, GA 30080-7013
Phone: 1-800-241-4402
Fax: 404-350-1489

Terra-Green Technologies Stoneware Tile Div.
Countertops; Flooring; Walls, Ceilings & Finishes
1650 Progress Dr.
Richmond, IN 47374
Phone: 317-935-4760
Fax: 317-935-3971

Tescom Intl.
Electrical & Lighting
590 Alden Rd., Suite 206
Markham, ON L3R 8N2
Canada
Phone: 905-470-1741
Fax: 905-475-6369

Texas Kiln Products
Cabinetry; Countertops; Doors; Engineered Lumber & Panels; Moulding & Millwork
Rt. 1 Box 66
Bastrop, TX 78602
Phone: 512-303-7700
1-800-825-9158
Fax: 512-321-5907

Texas Stone & Tile
Countertops; Flooring
2683 Lombardy Ln.,
PO Box 540755
Dallas, TX 75354-0755
Phone: 214-358-4698
Fax: 214-353-9688

Texas Timber Frames
Structural Systems
7214 Eckhart
San Antonio, TX 78238
Phone: 210-647-4662
Fax: 210-647-4667

Textured Forest Products
Engineered Lumber & Panels
PO Box 125
Washougal, WA 98671
Phone: 360-835-2164
Fax: 360-835-8038

TFI Corp.
Cornice Div.
Moulding & Millwork
2812 Hegan Ln.
Chico, CA 95928
Phone: 916-891-6390
Fax: 916-893-1273

TFI Corp. &
TFI Hardware
Hardware
2812 Hegan Ln.
Chico, CA 95928
Phone: 916-891-6390
1-800-395-8797
Fax: 916-893-1273

TFI Corp.
Vanity Plus
Countertops; Faucets & Fixtures
2812 Hegan Ln.
Chico, CA 95928
Phone: 916-891-6390
Fax: 916-893-1273

Therma-Ray
HVAC
255 Resticoughe Rd.
Oromocto, NB E2V 2H1
Canada
Phone: 506-446-6879
1-800-661-4328
Fax: 506-446-6879
E-mail: kilbride@nbnet.nb.ca

Therma-Stor Products
(A Div. of DEC Intl.)
HVAC
1919 S. Stoughton Rd.,
PO Box 8050
Madison, WI 53708
Phone: 608-222-5301
1-800-533-7533
Fax: 608-222-1447

Therma-Tru Corp.
Doors
1687 Woodlands Dr.
Maumee, OH 43537
Phone: 419-891-7400
1-800-537-8827
Fax: 419-891-7411

Thermador
Appliances
5119 District Blvd.
Los Angeles, CA 90040
Phone: 213-562-8100
Fax: 213-560-1788
Internet: http://www.thermador.com/

Thermal-Gard
Doors; Room Enclosures; Windows
400 Walnut St.
Punxsutawney, PA 15767-1368
Phone: 814-938-1408
Fax: 814-938-1428

Thermal Industries
Doors; Landscape Design; Room Enclosures; Windows
301 Brushton Ave.
Pittsburgh, PA 15221
Phone: 412-244-6400
1-800-245-1540
Fax: 412-244-6496

ThermaSol
Faucets & Fixtures
2255 Union Pl.
Simi Valley, CA 93065
Phone: 805-520-2468
1-800-776-0711
Fax: 805-579-8765

Thermetic Glass
Doors; Windows
Rt. 1, Box 1A
Toluca, IL 61369
Phone: 815-452-2371
1-800-747-4774
Fax: 815-452-2374

Thermo-Dynamics Boiler Co.
HVAC
PO Box 325, Rt. 61-S
Schuylkill Haven, PA 17972
Phone: 717-385-0731
Fax: 717-385-5304

Thermo Products
HVAC
PO Box 217
North Judson, IN 46366
Phone: 219-896-2133
Fax: 219-896-2410

Thermo-Rite Mfg. Co.
Fireplaces
PO Box 1108,
1355 Evans Ave.
Akron, OH 44309
Phone: 216-633-8680
1-800-321-0313
(outside OH)
Fax: 216-633-8701

Thermo-Vu Sunlite Industries
Windows
51 Rodeo Dr.
Brentwood, NY 11717
Phone: 516-243-1000
Fax: 516-243-1004

Thermoguard Co.
Insulation
451 Charles
Billings, MT 59101
Phone: 406-252-1938
1-800-821-5310
Fax: 406-252-5019

Thermolec
HVAC
2060 Thimens Pl.
Saint Laurent, PQ H4R 1L1 Canada
Phone: 514-336-9130
Fax: 514-336-3270

Thermolock Mfg. Co.
Windows
16880 Front St.
Copemish, MI 49625
Phone: 616-378-2923
Fax: 616-378-2922

Thermoplast
Doors; Windows
3035 Blvd. le Corbusier
Laval, PQ H7L 4C3
Canada
Phone: 514-687-5115
1-800-361-9261
Fax: 514-687-5196

Thermoplus Air
HVAC
262 Scott St.
St. Jerome, PQ J7Z 1H1
Canada
Phone: 514-436-7555
Fax: 514-436-5970

Third Millennium Software
Computer Software
120-1889 Springfield Rd.
Kelowna, BC V1Y 5V5
Canada
Phone: 250-762-9065
1-800-313-0833
Fax: 250-862-3885
Internet: http://www.ibuildit.com

Thistlewood Timber Frame Homes
Flooring; Structural Systems
RR 6
Markdale, ON N0C 1H0
Canada
Phone: 519-986-3280
Fax: 519-986-4461
Internet: http://www.interlog.com/~thistle

Thomas Electronics Corp.
Home Technology
N5 W22966
Bluemound Rd.
Waukesha, WI 53186
Phone: 414-521-9451
1-800-819-5934
Fax: 414-521-9453

Thomas Industries
Tools/Electric & Pneumatic
1419 Illinois Ave.
Sheboygan, WI 53081
Phone: 414-457-4891
Fax: 414-451-4325
Internet: http://www.thomaspumps.com

Thomas Lighting Consumer Div.
Electrical & Lighting
950 Breckinridge Ln.,
Suite G50
Louisville, KY 40207
Phone: 502-894-2400
1-800-36LIGHT
Fax: 502-894-2427
Internet: http://www.thomaslighting.com

Thomas Lighting Accent Div.
Electrical & Lighting
6430 E. Slauson Blvd.
Los Angeles, CA 90040
Phone: 213-726-1800
Fax: 213-726-1319

Thomas Waterproof Coatings Co.
Paints, Caulks & Adhesives; Specialty Products
543 Whitehall St., S.W.
Atlanta, GA 30303
Phone: 404-523-0493
1-800-223-8483
Fax: 404-523-1234

Thompson Industries
Engineered Lumber & Panels
Rt. 1, Box 142
Russellville, AR 72801
Phone: 501-968-5085
Fax: 501-968-4636

Thompson Minwax Lumber Div.
825 Crossover Ln.
Memphis, TN 38117
Phone: 901-684-3031
Fax: 901-763-2096

Thomson Consumer Electronics
RCA Custom Home Theatre
Home Technology
10330 N. Meridian
INH215
Indianapolis, IN 46206
Phone: 1-800-722-6585
Fax: 317-587-6736

Thornton Art Glass
Windows
PO Box 634,
3010 Col-Lan Rd.
Lancaster, OH 43130
Phone: 614-653-8060
Fax: 614-653-8070

The 3E Group
Insulation; Paints, Caulks & Adhesives; Roofing; Specialty Products
PO Box 392
Moorestown, NJ 08057
Phone: 609-866-7600
1-800-800-2844
Fax: 609-866-7603

3-G's Supply Co.
Hardware; Tools/Electric & Pneumatic
4640 Manufacturing Rd.
Cleveland, OH 44135
Phone: 216-362-1240
1-800-421-2854
Fax: 216-362-1249

3-10 Insulated Forms
Insulation; Structural Systems
PO Box 460790
Omaha, NE 68128
Phone: 402-592-7077
1-800-468-6344
Fax: 402-592-7969

Thulman Eastern Corp.
Moulding & Millwork
9040 Junction Dr.
Annapolis Junction, MD 20701
Phone: 410-880-0006
Fax: 410-880-0009

Thunderbird Moulding Co.
Moulding & Millwork
8180 Industrial Pkwy.
Sacramento, CA 95824
Phone: 916-381-4200
Fax: 916-381-0803

Tiffany Landscape Lighting
Electrical & Lighting
118 Broadway,
Black Bldg., Suite 510
Fargo, ND 58102
Phone: 701-238-6456
1-800-882-8112
Fax: 701-232-9368
Internet: http://www.specialized-ad.com/hlc/tiff.htm

Tiffany Stair Co.
Moulding & Millwork
16601 Bruke Ln.
Huntington Beach, CA 92647
Phone: 714-848-4680
Fax: 714-848-4928

Tile Cera
Countertops; Flooring; Walls, Ceilings & Finishes
300 Arcata Blvd.
Clarksville, TN 37040
Phone: 615-645-5100
1-800-782-8453
Fax: 615-647-5974

Tile Council of America
Countertops; Flooring; Walls, Ceilings & Finishes
PO Box 1787
Clemson, SC 29633
Phone: 864-646-TILE
Fax: 864-646-2821

Tile Master Roofing Systems
Roofing
5972 Ambler Dr.
Mississauga, ON L4W 2N3 Canada
Phone: 905-624-0953
1-800-461-3805
Fax: 905-238-8141

Tile Redi
Faucets & Fixtures; Plumbing Supplies
2570 N. Powerline Rd.,
Suite 504
Pompano Beach, FL 33069
Phone: 954-971-0209
1-888-445-TILE
Fax: 954-971-0158
Internet: http://www.tileredi.com

Tile Showcase
Walls, Ceilings & Finishes
291 Arsenal St.
Watertown, MA 02172
Phone: 617-926-1100
1-800-852-0922
Fax: 617-926-9714

The Tileworks
Countertops; Flooring; Walls, Ceilings & Finishes
4140 Grand Ave.
Des Moines, IA 50312
Phone: 515-255-1300
Fax: 515-255-5124

Timber Products Co.
Countertops; Engineered Lumber & Panels
PO Box 269
Springfield, OR 97477
Phone: 503-747-4577
1-800-547-9520
Fax: 503-744-4296

Timber Systems
Engineered Lumber & Panels; Structural Systems
120 Bullock Dr.
Markham, ON L3P 1W2 Canada
Phone: 905-294-7091
Fax: 905-294-3944

Timberhouse Post & Beam
Moulding & Millwork; Room Enclosures; Structural Systems
150 Sheafman Creek Rd.
Victor, MT 59875
Phone: 406-961-3276
Fax: 406-961-4643

Timberlake Cabinet Co.
Cabinetry; Hardware
PO Box 1990
Winchester, VA 22601
Phone: 540-665-9100
1-800-895-8391
Fax: 540-665-9176

Timberline Software
Computer Software
9600 S.W. Nimbus
Beaverton, OR 97008
Phone: 503-626-6775
1-800-628-6583
Fax: 503-526-8010
Internet: http://www.timberline.com

Timeline Vinyl Windows
Doors; Windows
701 N. State St.
Merrill, WI 54452
Phone: 715-536-2461
Fax: 715-536-7090

TimeSketch by AlderGraf
Computer Software
10620 Stebbins Cir.,
Suite B
Houston, TX 77043
Phone: 713-467-8500
1-800-624-4971
Fax: 713-467-1062
E-mail: TimeSketch@aol.com

TIPLOCK
Siding & Accessories
4596 Signature Dr.
Middleton, WI 53562
Phone: 608-836-8450
1-888-4TIPLOK
Fax: 608-836-6538
E-mail: siedlecki@msn.com

TIR Systems
Electrical & Lighting
3350 Bridgeway St.
Vancouver, BC V5K 1H9
Canada
Phone: 604-294-8477
1-800-663-2036
Fax: 604-294-3733

Titeflex Corp.
Plumbing Supplies
PO Box 90054
Springfield, MA 01139
Phone: 413-739-5631
1-800-662-0208
Fax: 413-739-7325
E-mail: gastite@titeflex.com

Toby Eaton Timber Frame Builders
Structural Systems
PO Box 232,
Vittum Hill Rd.
Center Sandwich, NH 03227
Phone: 603-284-7782
1-800-499-6408

Todol Products
Insulation; Paints, Caulks & Adhesives
20 Charles St.,
PO Box 398
Natick, MA 01769
Phone: 508-651-3818
Fax: 508-651-0729

TOGGLER Anchor System
(A Div. of Mechanical Plastics Corp.)
Hardware
444 Saw Mill River Rd.,
PO Box 554
Elmsford, NY 10523
Phone: 914-347-2727
1-800-544-2552
Fax: 914-347-3634

Tohickon Timber Frames
Structural Systems
PO Box 45
Revere, PA 18953
Phone: 610-847-2777
Fax: 610-847-2390

Tolleson Lumber Co.
Engineered Lumber & Panels
PO Box E
Perry, GA 31069
Phone: 1-800-768-2150
Fax: 912-987-5773

Tollmark Corp.
Electrical & Lighting
PO Box 2295
Prescott, AZ 86302
Phone: 520-445-7323
1-800-477-7723
Fax: 520-778-9477

The TonJon Co.
Faucets & Fixtures; Walls, Ceilings & Finishes
56 S. LaSalle
Aurora, IL 60507
Phone: 708-892-9200
Fax: 708-892-3989

Tork
Electrical & Lighting; HVAC; Home Technology
1 Grove
Mount Vernon, NY 10550
Phone: 914-664-3542
Fax: 914-664-5052

Torrence Coverplates
Electrical & Lighting
865 Balsam St.
Lakewood, CO 80215
Phone: 303-232-5673
1-800-880-5673
Fax: 303-232-8909
Internet:
http://www.coverplate.com

Toto Kiki
Faucets & Fixtures
1155 Southern Rd.
Morrow, GA 30260
Phone: 770-961-7016
1-800-938-1541
Fax: 770-968-2803

Town & Country Cedar Homes
Structural Systems
4772 US 131 S.
Petoskey, MI 49770
Phone: 616-347-4360
1-800-968-3178
Fax: 616-347-7255
Internet: http://www.cedarhomes.com

Toyota Motor Sales, USA
Equipment & Trucks
19001 S. Western Ave.
Torrance, CA 90509
Phone: 1-800-331-4331
Internet:
http://www.toyota.com

TR Miller Mill Co.
Landscape Design; Siding & Accessories
PO Box 708
Brewton, AL 36427
Phone: 205-867-1227
Fax: 205-867-6882

Trac Rac
Equipment & Trucks
994 Jefferson St.
Fall River, MA 02721
Phone: 508-677-4130
1-800-501-1587
Fax: 508-677-4136

TRACO
Windows
71 Progress Ave.
Cranberry Township, PA 16066
Phone: 412-776-7000
1-800-837-7003
Fax: 1-800-776-7154

Trade Commission of Spain
Countertops; Flooring; Walls, Ceilings & Finishes
2655 LeJeune Rd.,
Suite 1114
Coral Gables, FL 33134
Phone: 305-446-4387
Fax: 305-446-2602

The Trane Co. Unitary Products Group
HVAC
6200 Troup Hwy.
Tyler, TX 75707
Internet:
http://www.trane.com

Travis Industries
Fireplaces
10850 117th Pl. N.W.
Kirkland, WA 98033
Phone: 206-827-9505
Fax: 206-827-9363

Tremont Nail Co.
Hardware
PO Box 111A, 8 Elm St.
Wareham, MA 02571
Phone: 508-295-0038
1-800-842-0560
Fax: 1-800-295-1365

Trend Coatings
Paints, Caulks & Adhesives
3110 63rd Ave. E.
Bradenton, FL 34203
Phone: 813-727-8911
1-800-632-2063
Fax: 813-727-7034

Trenwyth Industries
Structural Systems
1 Connelly Rd.,
PO Box 438
Emigsville, PA 17318
Phone: 717-767-6868
1-800-233-1924
Fax: 717-767-4023

Trex Decks
Landscape Design
20 S. Cameron
Winchester, VA 22601
Phone: 540-678-8100
1-800-BUY-TREX
Fax: 540-678-8139

Tri-Guards
Moulding & Millwork
490 Hintz Rd.
Wheeling, IL 60090
Phone: 847-537-8444
1-800-783-8445
Fax: 847-537-8507

Tri-Ply
Roofing
1250 Fourteen Mile Rd.,
Suite 103
Clawson, MI 48017
Phone: 810-288-9780
1-800-445-9856
Fax: 810-288-9788

Trianco-Heatmaker
HVAC
111 York Ave.
Randolph, MA 02368
Phone: 617-961-1660
Fax: 617-986-9907

Triangle Pacific Corp.
Cabinetry; Countertops
16803 Dallas Pkwy.
Dallas, TX 75248
Phone: 214-887-2100
1-800-722-4647
Fax: 214-887-2234

Tridelta Industries
Tools/Electric & Pneumatic
7350 Corporate Blvd.
Mentor, OH 44060
Phone: 216-255-1080
1-800-776-7350
Fax: 216-255-2831

Trimblehouse Corp.
Electrical & Lighting
4658 S. Old Peachtree Rd.
Norcross, GA 30071
Phone: 770-448-1972
1-800-241-4317
Fax: 770-447-9250

TrimJoist Corp.
Engineered Lumber & Panels; Structural Systems
PO Drawer 2286
Columbus, MS 39704
Phone: 601-327-7950
1-800-844-8281
Fax: 601-329-4610
Internet:
http://www.trimjoist.com

Trimline Roof Ventilation Systems
Roofing
705 Pennsylvania Ave. S.
Minneapolis, MN 55426
Phone: 612-540-9737
1-800-438-2920
Fax: 612-540-9209

TrimTramp
Tools/Electric & Pneumatic
151 Carlingview Dr.,
Unit 11
Etobicoke, ON
M9W 5S4 Canada
Phone: 416-798-3160
1-800-387-8746
Fax: 416-798-3162

TriPac Cabinets
(A Div. of Triangle Pacific)
Cabinetry; Flooring
16803 Dallas Pkwy.
Dallas, TX 75248
Phone: 214-931-3000
1-800-527-5903
Fax: 1-800-527-5903, ext. 434

Triple Crown Fence
(A Div. of CTB)
Landscape Design
State Rd. 15 N.,
PO Box 2000
Milford, IN 46542-2000
Phone: 219-658-9442
1-800-365-3625
Fax: 219-658-4133

Trojan Board/Forest Pride
Flooring; Moulding & Millwork
333 Archibald St.
Winnipeg, MB R2J 0W6
Canada
Phone: 204-233-7171
Fax: 204-233-7174

Trojan Mfg.
Tools/Electric & Pneumatic
9810 N. Vancouver Way
Portland, OR 97217
Phone: 503-285-2120
1-800-745-2120
Fax: 503-285-7731

Trol-A-Temp
HVAC
57 Bushes Ln.
Elmwood Park, NJ 07407-3204
Phone: 201-794-8004
1-800-TAT-TEMP
Fax: 201-794-1359
E-mail:
tatzoning@aol.com

Tropic Top
Roofing
2028-3 Eastbourne Way
Orlando, FL 32812
Phone: 407-273-0069
Fax: 407-273-0069
E-mail:
jsymbold@aol.com

Tru-Vex Glass Co.
Windows
1707 East Main
Olney, IL 62450
Phone: 618-395-7212
Fax: 618-395-3946

True North Log Homes
Structural Systems
PO Box 2169,
Winhara Rd.
Bracebridge, ON
P1L 1W1 Canada
Phone: 705-645-3096
1-800-661-1628
Fax: 705-645-4256

Truecraft Tools
Hardware; Tools/Hand
615 Pierce St.
Somerset, NJ 08875
Phone: 908-805-1800
Fax: 908-805-9736

Trus Joist MacMillan
Engineered Lumber & Panels; Landscape Design; Structural Systems
PO Box 60
Boise, ID 83706
Phone: 208-364-1200
1-800-628-3997
Fax: 208-364-1300

Truswal Systems Corp.
Structural Systems
1101 N. Great Southwest Pkwy.
Arlington, TX 76011
Phone: 817-633-5100
1-800-521-9790
Fax: 817-652-3079

Truth Hardware
Hardware
700 W. Bridge St.
Owatonna, MN 55060
Phone: 507-451-5620
1-800-866-7884
Fax: 507-451-5655
Internet:
http://www.truth.com

TSE Software Enterprises
Computer Software
209 Granite Dr.
Lakeland, FL 33809
Phone: 941-853-2086
Fax: 941-859-1765

TUB-MASTER
Faucets & Fixtures; Specialty Products
413 Virginia Dr.
Orlando, FL 32803-1892
Phone: 407-898-2881
1-800-327-1911
Fax: 407-898-3856

Tubco Whirlpools
Faucets & Fixtures
2870 Slough St.
Mississauga, ON
L4T 1G3 Canada
Phone: 905-677-3333
Fax: 905-677-4852

Tubular Skylight
Windows
5704 Clark Rd.
Sarasota, FL 34233
Phone: 941-927-8823
1-800-315-TUBE
Fax: 941-924-0500
Internet: http://www.tubular-skylight.com

Tufco
Paints, Caulks & Adhesives
PO Box 23500,
3161 Ridge Rd.
Green Bay, WI 54305
Phone: 414-336-0054
1-800-558-8145
Fax: 414-336-9041

Tuff/Kote Co.
Roofing
210 Seminary Ave.
Woodstock, IL 60098
Phone: 815-338-2006
Fax: 815-338-9105

Tuff-N-Dri Waterproofing Koch Materials Co.
Insulation; Specialty Products
800 Irving Wick Dr. W.
Heath, OH 43056
Phone: 614-788-8847
1-800-379-2768
Fax: 1-800-230-8178
Internet: http://www.tuff-n-dri.com

Tulikivi U.S.
Fireplaces
255 Ridge McIntire Rd.
Charlottesville, VA 22903
Phone: 804-977-5500
1-800-843-3473
Fax: 804-977-5164

Turncraft
Moulding & Millwork
PO Box 2429
White City, OR 97503
Phone: 503-826-2911
Fax: 503-826-1393

Turning Point
(A Div. of JELD-WEN)
Moulding & Millwork
300 W. Marine View Dr.
Everett, WA 98201-1030
Phone: 206-259-9292
Fax: 206-252-3269

Turtle Creek Software
Computer Software
Babcock Hall 201,
118 Prospect St.
Ithaca, NY 14850
Phone: 607-272-1008
Fax: 607-272-5446

Tussey Mountain Log Homes
Structural Systems
RD 1, Box 53-A
Pittsfield, PA 16340
Phone: 814-563-4648
Fax: 814-563-4977

U

U-Line Corp.
Appliances
8900 N. 55th St.
Milwaukee, WI 53223
Phone: 414-354-0300
Fax: 414-354-7905

U.S. Gaslight
Electrical & Lighting
4658 S. Old Peachtree Rd.
Norcross, GA 30071
Phone: 770-448-1972
1-800-241-4317
Fax: 770-447-9250

U.S. Steel
Roofing; Structural Systems
600 Grant St.
Pittsburgh, PA 15219
Phone: 412-433-3567
Fax: 412-433-3891

UC Industries
Insulation
3 Century Dr.
Parsippany, NJ 07054
Phone: 201-267-1605
1-800-828-7155
Fax: 201-267-1495

UFAB
(See BUILDSOFT)

UGL
(See United Gilsonite Laboratories)

Ultra Craft Co.
An Alside Co.
Cabinetry
6163 Old 421 Rd.
Liberty, NC 27298
Phone: 910-622-4281

Ultra-Flex Moulding Co.
Moulding & Millwork
207 N. Las Posas Rd.
San Marcos, CA 92069
Phone: 619-744-6579
1-800-344-5293
Fax: 619-744-7286
1-800-545-9865

Ultra Hardware Products
Cabinetry; Hardware
1777 Hylton Rd.
Pennsauken, NJ 08110
Phone: 1-800-426-6379
Fax: 609-663-1743

Unadilla Laminated Products
Engineered Lumber & Panels
32 Clifton St.
Unadilla, NY 13849
Phone: 607-369-9341
Fax: 607-369-3608

Unarco Material Handling
Structural Systems
701 16th Ave. E.,
PO Box 547
Springfield, TN 37172
Phone: 615-384-3531
1-800-862-7261
Fax: 615-382-2777

Uni-Group USA
Landscape Design
4362 Northlake Blvd.,
No. 207
Palm Beach Gardens, FL 33410
Phone: 561-626-4666
1-800-USA-1UNI
Fax: 561-627-6403
E-mail:
unigroup@siservices.net

UniBoard Canada
Flooring
3080 blvd. le Correfour,
Suite 400
Laval, PQ H7I 2R5
Canada
Phone: 514-682-5240
1-800-263-5240
Fax: 514-682-0550

Unibuilt Industries
Structural Systems
PO Box 373
Vandalia, OH 45377
Phone: 513-890-7570
1-800-777-9942
Fax: 513-890-8303

Unicel
Room Enclosures; Windows
88 Rue de Vaudreuil
Boucherville, PQ
J4B 5G4 Canada
Phone: 514-655-1580
1-800-668-1580
Fax: 514-655-0162

Unico
HVAC
4160 Meramec St.
St. Louis, MO 63116
Phone: 314-771-7007
1-800-527-0896
Fax: 314-771-6298

Unicut Corp.
Hardware; Tools/Hand
1770 W. Berteau Ave.
Chicago, IL 60613
Phone: 312-525-4210
1-800-621-1204
Fax: 312-525-7966

Unimast
Structural Systems
4825 N. Scott St.,
Suite 300
Schiller Park, IL 60176
Phone: 708-928-3400
1-800-654-7883
Fax: 708-928-1099

Union Brass Mfg. Co.
Faucets & Fixtures
2955 Lone Oak Cir.
Eagan, MN 55121
Phone: 612-454-8858
Fax: 612-454-1228

Unitary Products Group
(See York Intl. Corp.)

UNITEC
*Electrical & Lighting;
Home Technology*
Bahia de Todos Los Santos
No. 26
Col. V. Anzures, Mexico
City, DF 11300 Mexico
Phone: 011.52.5.545-1009
Fax: 011.5 2.5.531-9622

**United Gilsonite
Laboratories (UGL)**
*Paints, Caulks &
Adhesives; Structural
Systems*
PO Box 70
Scranton, PA 18501-0070
Phone: 717-344-1202
1-800-UGL-LABS
Fax: 717-969-7634

United House Wrecking
Specialty Products
535 Hope St.
Stamford, CT 06906
Phone: 203-348-5371
Fax: 203-961-9472

United Panel
*Countertops; Flooring;
Siding & Accessories;
Structural Systems*
PO Box 188,
8 Wildon Dr.
Mt. Bethel, PA 18343
Phone: 610-588-6871
1-800-933-8700
Fax: 610-588-0536

**United States Ceramic
Tile Co.**
*Countertops; Flooring;
Walls, Ceilings & Finishes*
10233 Sandyville Rd.
S.E., PO Box 338
East Sparta, OH 44626
Phone: 216-866-5531
1-800-321-0684
Fax: 216-866-5340

United States Gypsum Co.
Walls, Ceilings & Finishes
125 S. Franklin St.
Chicago, IL 60680-4124
Phone: 312-606-4000
1-800-USG4YOU
Fax: 312-606-4093

United States Saw Co.
(See Oldham/United
States Saw Co.)

United States Seamless
Siding & Accessories
2001 First Ave., N.,
Box 2426
Fargo, ND 58108-2426
Phone: 701-241-8888
Fax: 701-241-9999

United Steel Products
Hardware
PO Box 80,
703 Rogers Dr.
Montgomery, MN 56069
Phone: 612-364-7333
1-800-328-5934
Fax: 612-364-8762

United Telesis Corp.
Home Technology
6488 Avondale St., Suite 125
Oklahoma City, OK 73116
Phone: 405-842-1942
Fax: 405-842-0162

**United Window
Manufacturers**
Doors; Windows
8550 Keele St.
Concord, ON L4K 2N2
Canada
Phone: 416-738-0066
1-800-440-2714
Fax: 905-738-5748

Unity Hardwood
Moulding & Millwork
PO Box 663
Newport, NH 03773
Phone: 603-863-1420
Fax: 603-863-9132

Universal Flooring
Flooring
14800 Quorum Dr.,
Suite 110
Dallas, TX 75240
Phone: 214-387-0867
Fax: 214-387-7873

**Universal Forest
Products**
*Engineered Lumber &
Panels*
2801 E. Beltline, N.E.
Grand Rapids, MI 49505
Phone: 616-364-6161
Fax: 616-364-5558

**Universal Industrial
Products Co.
(A Div. of Core
Industries)**
Hardware
1 Coreway Dr.
Pioneer, OH 43554-0628
Phone: 419-737-2324
1-800-922-6957
Fax: 419-737-2130

**Universal Marble &
Granite**
*Countertops; Flooring;
Roofing*
1919 Halethorpe Farms Rd.
Baltimore, MD 21227
Phone: 410-247-2442
1-800-828-5611
Fax: 410-247-8043

**Universal Metal
Industries**
Appliances; HVAC
48 N. 56th St.
Phoenix, AZ 85034
Phone: 602-275-3654
1-800-875-3654
Fax: 602-267-9328

Universal Plastics
*Faucets & Fixtures;
Moulding & Millwork*
165 Front St.
Chicopee, MA 01013
Phone: 413-592-4791
Fax: 413-592-6876

**Universal-Rundle Corp.
(A Nortek Co.)**
*Cabinetry; Faucets
& Fixtures*
217 N. Mill St.
New Castle, PA 16103
Phone: 412-658-6631
1-800-955-0316
Fax: 412-658-8646

University Software
Computer Software
4801 Lynn Oaks Cir.
Dover, FL 33527
Phone: 813-754-6422
1-800-749-5995

Unwallpaper Co.
Paints, Caulks & Adhesives
PO Box 757
Silver Spring, MD 20918
Phone: 301-680-2512

Urfic
(See Brass Accents)

US Brass
*Faucets & Fixtures;
Plumbing Supplies*
17120 Dallas Pkwy.
Dallas, TX 75248
Phone: 972-407-2600
1-800-US-BRASS
Fax: 972-578-3414

**US Sky
(A Div. of Stora
Enterprises Co.)**
*Paints, Caulks &
Adhesives; Room
Enclosures; Windows*
2907 Agua Fria
Santa Fe, NM 87501
Phone: 505-471-5711
1-800-323-5017
Fax: 505-471-5437

US Tape Co.
Tools/Hand
217 River Ave.
Patchogue, NY 11772
Phone: 516-289-0500
1-800-472-8273
Fax: 516-289-0512

US Tec
Electrical & Lighting
470 S. Pearl St.
Canandaigua, NY 14424
Phone: 716-396-9680
1-800-836-2312
Fax: 716-394-7095
E-mail: ustec@aol.com

US Tile Co.
Roofing
909 W. Railroad St.
Corona, CA 91720
Phone: 909-737-0200
1-800-CLAYLIT
Fax: 909-734-9591
Internet:
http://www.ustile.com

USG
(See United States
Gypsum Co.)

USG Interiors
Walls, Ceilings & Finishes
125 S. Franklin St.
Chicago, IL 60606
Phone: 312-606-4000

USP Lumber Connectors
*Hardware; Landscape
Design; Moulding &
Millwork*
2150 Kitty Hawk Rd.
Livermore, CA 94550
Phone: 510-449-4100
1-800-227-0470
Fax: 415-373-9213

USTC
Equipment & Trucks
RD 6, Box 34-B, Rt. 30
W. & Bowman Rd.
York, PA 17404-9806
Phone: 717-792-9731
1-800-556-8280
Fax: 1-717-792-4938

The Utica Cos.
HVAC
PO Box 4729,
2201 Dwyer Ave.
Utica, NY 13504
Phone: 315-797-1310
Fax: 315-797-3762

V

V-Dec
Home Technology
7306 Driver Rd.
Berlin Heights, OH
44814
Phone: 419-588-2796
Fax: 419-588-3514

V-T Industries
Countertops
1000 Industrial Park
Holstein, IA 51025
Phone: 712-368-4381
1-800-827-1615

**VACUFLO—
H-P Products**
Specialty Products
512 W. Gorgas St.
Louisville, OH 44641
Phone: 330-875-5556
1-800-822-8356
Fax: 330-875-7584

**Valentina Ratti
Creations USA**
*Faucets & Fixtures;
Hardware; Walls, Ceilings
& Finishes*
PO Box 1301, Elf Way
Pittsboro, NC 27312
Phone: 919-542-3900
1-800-832-2987
Fax: 919-542-2727

Valeo
Equipment & Trucks
W229 N1680
Westwood Dr.
Waukesha, WI 53186
Phone: 414-547-9474
1-800-634-2704
Fax: 414-547-5270

Valli & Valli USA
Hardware
PO Box 245
Duarte, CA 91009-0245
Phone: 818-359-2569
1-800-423-7161
Fax: 818-358-0743

**Van Mark Products
Corp.**
*Equipment & Trucks;
Siding & Accessories;
Tools/Electric & Pneumatic*
24145 Industrial Park Dr.
Farmington Hills, MI
48335
Phone: 810-478-1200
1-800-VAN-MARK
Fax: 1-800-232-9987

Vance Industries
*Cabinetry; Faucets &
Fixtures*
7401 W. Wilson Ave.
Chicago, IL 60656
Phone: 708-867-6000
Fax: 708-867-5601

**Vande Hey-Raleigh
Architectural Roof Tile**
Roofing
1665 Bohm Dr.
Little Chute, WI 54140
Phone: 414-766-0156
1-800-236-8453
Fax: 414-766-0776
Internet:
http://www.arcat.com

Vanguard Industries
*Faucets & Fixtures; HVAC;
Plumbing Supplies*
831 N. Vanguard St.
McPherson, KS 67460
Phone: 316-241-6369
1-800-775-5039
Fax: 316-241-1772

Vanguard Plastics Ltd.
Specialty Products
19239 96th Ave.
Surrey, BC V4N 4C4
Canada
Phone: 1-800-663-0077
Fax: 604-888-5330

Vantage Products Corp.
Doors; Siding & Accessories
1715 Dogwood Dr.
Conyers, GA 30207
Phone: 404-483-0915
Fax: 404-483-5801

Variform
Siding & Accessories
303 W. Major,
PO Box 559
Kearney, MO 64060
Phone: 816-635-6400
1-800-1-800-2244
Fax: 816-635-6942

**Vaughn & Bushnell
Mfg. Co.**
Tools/Hand
11414 Maple Ave.
Hebron, IL 60034
Phone: 815-648-2446
Fax: 815-648-4300
Internet:
http://www.hammernet.
com

Vega Industries
(See Craftline; Starbrite)

Vegetable Factory
Room Enclosures
655 Washington Blvd.
Stamford, CT 06901
Phone: 203-324-0010
1-800-221-2550
Fax: 203-324-0520

Velux-America
Windows
PO Box 5001
Greenwood, SC 29648
Phone: 864-941-4700
1-800-283-2831
Fax: 864-941-4870
Internet:
http://www.velux.com

Venmar Ventilation
Appliances
2355 Canadien
Drummondville, PQ
J2B 8A9 Canada
Phone: 819-477-6226
1-800-567-3855
Fax: 819-475-5923

Vent-A-Hood
Appliances; Specialty Products
PO Box 830426
Richardson, TX 75083
Phone: 214-235-5201

Vent-Aire Systems
HVAC
4850 Northpark Dr.
Colorado Springs, CO
80918-3872
Phone: 719-599-9080
1-800-937-9080
Fax: 719-599-9085

Ventana Plastics Co.
Windows
6001 Enterprise Dr.
Export, PA 15632-8969
Phone: 412-325-3400
Fax: 412-327-4540
Internet:
http://www.custom.
net/sundance

Ventarama Skylight Corp.
Windows
425 Underhill Blvd.
Syosset, NY 11791
Phone: 516-364-1818
1-800-237-8096
Fax: 516-364-2066

Vermeer Mfg.
Equipment & Trucks
PO Box 200
Pella, IA 50219
Phone: 515-628-3141
1-888-VERMEER
Fax: 515-621-7734
Internet:
http://www.vermeer.com

Vermont American Tool Co.
Hardware; Tools/Electric & Pneumatic; Tools/Hand
PO Box 340
Lincolnton, NC 28093
Phone: 704-735-7464
1-800-742-3869
Fax: 1-800-442-3405
Internet: http://www.
vermontamerican.com

Vermont Castings
Fireplaces
Rt. 107, PO Box 501
Bethel, VT 05032
Phone: 802-234-2300
1-800-227-8683
Fax: 1-800-241-7140

Vermont Stresskin Panel
Structural Systems
RR 2, Box 2794
Cambridge, VT 05444
Phone: 802-644-8885
1-800-644-8885
Fax: 802-644-5598

Vermont Structural Slate Co.
Countertops; Flooring; Roofing; Siding & Accessories
3 Prospect St.
Fair Haven, VT 05743
Phone: 802-265-4933
1-800-343-1900
Fax: 802-265-3865

Vermont Timber Frames
Doors; Structural Systems
130 Bowen Rd.
Bennington, VT 05201
Phone: 802-447-8860
Fax: 802-447-8861
Internet:
http://www.vtf.com

Versa-Lok Retaining Wall Systems
Landscape Design
6348 Hwy. 36, Suite 1
Oakdale, MN 55128
Phone: 612-770-3166
1-800-770-4525
Fax: 612-770-4089
Internet:
http://www.versa-
lok.com.wall

Versyss
Computer Software
15 Crawford St.
Needham, MA 02194
Phone: 617-433-3300
1-800-899-6400

Vertigraph
Computer Software
12959 Jupiter Rd.,
Suite 252
Dallas, TX 75238
Phone: 214-340-9436
1-800-989-4243
Fax: 214-340-9437
E-mail:
76702.3340@compuserve.com

Vetter, SNE Enterprises (A Ply Gem Co.)
Doors; Windows
1 Wausau Center,
PO Box 8007
Wausau, WI 54402-8007
Phone: 715-845-1161
1-800-VETTER2
Fax: 715-847-6520

ViaGraFix
Computer Software
1 American Way
Pryor, OK 74361-8801
Phone: 918-825-7555
1-800-233-3223
Fax: 918-825-6359

VIC International Corp.
Equipment & Trucks; Tools/Electric & Pneumatic; Tools/Hand
PO Drawer 12610
Knoxville, TN 37912
Phone: 423-947-2882
1-800-423-1634
Fax: 423-947-2634
Internet:
http://www.vicintl.com

Victor Sun Control
Doors; Windows
4101 G St.
Philadelphia, PA 19124
Phone: 215-743-0800
Fax: 215-743-3164

VicWest Steel, US Operations
Roofing
900 Wessex Pl., Suite 201
Louisville, KY 40222
Phone: 502-339-7222
1-800-VIC-WEST
Fax: 502-339-8980

Viessmann Mfg. Co. (US)
HVAC
83 Vermont Ave., Bldg. 3
Warwick, RI 02888
Phone: 401-732-0667
Fax: 401-732-0590

The Viking Corp.
Home Technology
210 N. Industrial Park Rd.
Hastings, MI 49058
Phone: 616-945-9501
1-800-968-9501
Fax: 616-945-9599

Viking Industries
Doors; Windows
PO Box 20518
Portland, OR 97220
Phone: 503-667-6030
Fax: 503-669-1135

Viking Range Corp.
Appliances
111 Front St.
Greenwood, MS 38930
Phone: 601-455-1200
1-888-845-4641
Fax: 601-453-7939

Villagecraft Industries
Appliances; Cabinetry; Countertops; Specialty Products
PO Box 707
State College, PA 16804
Phone: 814-353-1777
1-800-458-9396
Fax: 814-692-4414

Vincent Metals
Roofing; Siding & Accessories
PO Box 360
Minneapolis, MN 55440
Phone: 612-378-1131
1-800-328-71-800
Fax: 612-378-6122

Vintage Mantle Co.
Moulding & Millwork
PO Box 702415
Tulsa, OK 74170
Phone: 918-254-0800
Fax: 918-250-8750

Vintage Wood Works
Doors; Moulding & Millwork
Hwy. 34 S, PO Box R
Quinlan, TX 75474
Phone: 903-356-2158
Fax: 903-356-3023
Internet: http://www.
vintagewoodworks.com

Vinyl Building Products
Doors; Windows
1 Raritan Rd.
Oakland, NJ 07436
Phone: 201-337-9151
1-800-468-4695
Fax: 201-337-7491

Vinyl Lite II Window & Door Systems (A Div. of TARA Industries)
Doors; Siding & Accessories; Windows
544 N. Highland
Aurora, IL 60506-2986
Phone: 708-844-3400
Fax: 708-844-1528

Vinyl Siding Institute Div. of the Society of the Plastics Industry
1275 K St., N.W.,
Suite 400
Washington, DC 20005
Phone: 202-371-5200
Fax: 202-371-1022

Vinyl Tech/PGT
Doors; Room Enclosures; Windows
PO Box 1529
Nokomis, FL 34274
Phone: 941-493-4858
Fax: 941-497-3655

Vinyl View (A Div. of Thermetic Glass)
Doors; Windows
Rt. 1, PO Box 1A
Toluca, IL 61369
Phone: 815-452-2371
1-800-747-4774
Fax: 815-452-2374

Vinyl Window Designs
Doors; Windows
300 Chrislea Rd.
Woodbridge, ON
L4L 8A8 Canada
Phone: 905-850-3222
1-800-668-4820
Fax: 905-850-9940

Vinyl Window & Door Institute Div. of the Society of the Plastics Industry
Doors; Windows
1275 K St., N.W.,
Suite 400
Washington, DC 20005
Phone: 202-371-5200
Fax: 202-371-1022

VIPCO/Crane Plastics
Siding & Accessories
PO Box 1058
Columbus, OH 43216
Phone: 614-443-4841
1-800-366-8472
Fax: 1-800-733-8469

Virginia Mirror Co.
Walls, Ceilings & Finishes
300 S. Moss,
PO Box 5431
Martinsville, VA 24112
Phone: 540-632-9816
1-800-826-4776
Fax: 540-632-2488

Virtus Corp.
Computer Software
118 MacKenan Dr.,
Suite 250
Cary, NC 27511
Phone: 919-467-9700
1-800-VIRTUS1

Visual Applications VisualPhile
Computer Software
2301 Burlington,
Suite 270
North Kansas City, MO 64116
Phone: 816-472-1522
1-800-798-4727
Fax: 816-472-0941
Internet:
http://www.visapp.com

Vixen Hill Mfg. Co.
Landscape Design; Moulding & Millwork; Room Enclosures; Siding & Accessories
Main St.
Elverson, PA 19520
Phone: 610-286-0909
1-800-423-2766
Fax: 610-286-2099

VPI
Flooring
3123 S. Ninth St.,
PO Box 451
Sheboygan, WI 53082
Phone: 414-458-4664
Fax: 414-458-1368

VSI Fasteners
Hardware
15901 Red Hill Ave.,
Suite 200
Tustin, CA 92680
Phone: 714-566-0550
1-800-331-8484
Fax: 714-566-0555

Vynex Corp.
Windows
135 40th St.
Pittsburgh, PA 15201
Phone: 412-681-3800
1-800-666-8969
Fax: 412-681-3817

Vytec Corp.
Siding & Accessories
25 Midpark Cres.
London, ON N6N 1A9 Canada
Phone: 519-681-7743
1-800-265-2230
Fax: 519-681-9371

W

W.H. Elevators
HVAC; Plumbing Supplies
7700 E. Waterloo
Edmond, OK 73034
Phone: 1-800-566-4430
Fax: 405-348-7103

W.J. Ruscoe Co.
Paints, Caulks & Adhesives
485 Kenmore Blvd.
Akron, OH 44301
Phone: 330-253-8148
1-800-293-8148
Fax: 330-253-2933

W P Hickman Co.
Roofing
PO Box 15005
Asheville, NC 28813
Phone: 704-274-4000
Fax: 704-274-4031
Internet:
http://www.wph.com

WAC Lighting Co.
Electrical & Lighting
PO Box 560218,
113-25 14th Ave.
College Point, NY 11356
Phone: 718-961-0695
1-800-526-2588
Fax: 1-800-526-2585
E-mail:
WACLGT@AOL.COM

Wagner Electronic Products
Tools/Hand
326 Pine Grove Rd.
Rogue River, OR 97537
Phone: 541-582-0541
1-800-634-9961
Fax: 541-582-4138
Internet:
http://www.wwwagner.com

Wagner Spray Tech Corp.
Paints, Caulks & Adhesives; Tools/Hand
1770 Fernbrook Ln.
Plymouth, MN 55447
Phone: 612-553-7000
1-800-328-8251
Fax: 612-553-7288

Wagoner Floor Safety Systems
Flooring; Paints, Caulks & Adhesives
PO Box 2784
Reno, NV 89505
Phone: 702-878-4768

Walker & Zanger
Countertops; Flooring; Hardware; Siding & Accessories; Walls, Ceilings & Finishes
31 Warren Pl.
Mt. Vernon, NY 10550
Phone: 914-667-1600
Fax: 914-667-6244

Wall Firma
Paints, Caulks & Adhesives; Roofing; Specialty Products; Structural Systems
733 E. Main St.
Monongahela, PA 15063
Phone: 412-258-6873
1-800-333-4333
Fax: 412-258-3188

Wall Ties and Forms
Structural Systems
4000 Bonner Industrial Dr.
Shawnee, KS 66226
Phone: 913-441-0073
1-800-444-9692
Fax: 913-441-0076

Wallboard Tool Co.
Equipment & Trucks; Paints, Caulks & Adhesives; Tools/Hand
1697 Seabright Ave.
Long Beach, CA 90813
Phone: 310-437-0701
1-800-433-0320
Fax: 310-437-8700

Walter Absil Co.
Electrical & Lighting
875 McCaffrey St.
St. Laurent, PQ
H4T 1N3 Canada
Phone: 514-341-4152
Fax: 514-342-9760

Ward Log Homes
Siding & Accessories;
Structural Systems
PO Box 72
Houlton, ME 04730
Phone: 207-532-6531
1-800-341-1566
Fax: 207-532-7806

Ward Lumber Co.
Engineered Lumber &
Panels
Glen Rd.
Jay, NY 12941-1054
Phone: 518-946-2214
Fax: 518-946-2188

Ward Mfg.
Faucets & Fixtures;
Plumbing Supplies
PO Box 9, 115 Gulick St.
Blossburg, PA 16912-0009
Phone: 717-638-2131
1-800-248-1028
Fax: 717-638-3410

Warner Tentnology
Corp.
Equipment & Trucks
15427 66th Ave.
Surrey, BC V3S 2A1 Canada
Phone: 604-597-8368
1-800-663-8858
Fax: 604-597-8749

Wasco Products
Doors; Windows
26 Pioneer Ave.,
PO Box 351
Sanford, ME 04073
Phone: 207-324-8060
1-800-388-0293
Fax: 207-490-1218
Internet:
http://www.wascol.com

Waste King
Appliances
4240 E. LaPalma Ave.,
PO Box 4146
Anaheim, CA 92803-4146
Phone: 714-524-7770
1-800-854-3229
Fax: 714-996-7073

Water Boss Intl.
Appliances
1699 N. Astor
Milwaukee, WI 53202
Phone: 414-224-0878
1-800-489-2677
Fax: 414-224-6055

Water Furnace Intl.
HVAC; Plumbing Supplies
9000 Conservation Way
Fort Wayne, IN 46809
Phone: 219-478-5667
1-800-222-5667
Fax: 219-478-3029
Internet:
http://www.waterfurnace.
com

Watercolors
Cabinetry; Faucets &
Fixtures; Hardware
Garrison, NY 10524
Phone: 914-424-3327
Fax: 914-424-3169

Waterline Products Co.
Faucets & Fixtures;
Plumbing Supplies; Roofing
5159 Bradco Blvd.
Mississauga, ON
L4W 2A6 Canada
Phone: 905-625-9440
1-800-361-3773
Fax: 905-625-9481

Waterloo Industries
Tools/Hand
PO Box 2095
Waterloo, IA 50704
Phone: 319-235-7131
Fax: 319-235-6849

Waterloov Gutter
Protection Systems Co.
Siding & Accessories
210 Broad St.
Red Bank, NJ 07701
Phone: 908-530-3600
1-800-841-RAIN
Fax: 908-224-0540

Watertech
Faucets & Fixtures
2507 Plymouth Rd.
Johnson City, TN 37601
Phone: 1-800-BUY-TUBS
Fax: 615-926-1470

The Watt Stopper
Electrical & Lighting
2800 De La Cruz Blvd.
Santa Clara, CA 95050
Phone: 408-988-5331
1-800-879-8585
Fax: 408-988-5373

Waupaca Elevator Co.
Specialty Products
PO Box 246
Waupaca, WI 54981
Phone: 715-258-5581
1-800-238-8739
Fax: 715-258-5004

Wausau Homes
Structural Systems
PO Box 8005
Wausau, WI 54402-8005
Phone: 715-359-7272
Fax: 715-359-2867
Internet:
http://wausauhomes.com

Wausau Tile
Landscape Design
PO Box 1520
Wausau, WI 54402-1520
Phone: 715-359-3121
1-800-388-8728
Fax: 715-355-4627

Waxman Industries
Faucets & Fixtures;
Plumbing Supplies
24460 Aurora Rd.
Bedford Heights, OH
44146
Phone: 216-439-1830
Fax: 216-439-4909

Wayne-Dalton Corp.
Doors; Garage Doors &
Openers
1 Door Dr.
Mt. Hope, OH 44660
Phone: 216-674-7015
1-800-827-DOOR
Fax: 216-674-1857

WD Cowls
Siding & Accessories; Walls,
Ceilings & Finishes
134 Montague Rd.,
PO Box 9677
North Amherst, MA
01059-9677
Phone: 413-549-1403
Fax: 413-549-0000

Weaber, Inc.
Engineered Lumber
& Panels; Moulding
& Millwork
RR 4, Box 1255
Lebanon, PA 17042
Phone: 717-867-2212
1-800-745-9663
Fax: 717-867-1711

Weather Shield Windows
& Doors
Doors; Windows
PO Box 309,
1 Weather Shield Plaza
Medford, WI 54451
Phone: 715-748-2100
1-800-477-6808
Fax: 414-289-0417
Internet:
http://www.weathershield.
com

WeatherKing Air
Conditioning
HVAC
5600 Old Greenwood Rd.
Fort Smith, AR 72917
Phone: 501-646-4311
Fax: 501-648-4918

Weathermatic Co.
Landscape Design
PO Box 180205
Dallas, TX 75218
Phone: 214-278-6131
Fax: 214-271-5710

Weathervane Window Co.
Doors; Windows
10819 120th Ave. N.W.
Kirkland, WA 98033
Phone: 206-827-9669
1-800-634-3433
Fax: 206-822-9797

Weck Glass/Glashaus
Windows
450 E. Congress Pkwy.,
Suite E
Crystal Lake, IL 60014
Phone: 815-356-8440
Fax: 815-356-8450

Weil-McLain
A United Dominion Co.
HVAC
500 Blaine St.
Michigan City, IN
46360-2388
Phone: 219-879-6561
Fax: 219-879-4025

Weirton Steel Corp.
Roofing; Structural Systems
400 Three Springs Dr.
Weirton, WV 26062
Phone: 304-797-2873
Fax: 304-797-2267
Internet:
http://www.weirton.com

Weiser Lock
(A Div. Of Masco Corp.)
Hardware
6660 S. Broadmoor Rd.
Tucson, AZ 85746
Phone: 602-741-6200
1-800-677-LOCK
Fax: 602-741-6241

Welco Mfg. Co.
Paints, Caulks &
Adhesives; Specialty
Products; Structural
Systems; Walls, Ceilings &
Finishes
1225 Ozark
North Kansas City, MO
64116
Phone: 816-471-1788
1-800-821-7352
Fax: 816-471-3439

Welcom Software
Technology
Computer Software
15995 N. Barkers
Landing, Suite 275
Houston, TX 77079
Phone: 713-558-0514
Fax: 713-584-7828

Wellborn Cabinet
Cabinetry
Rt. 1, PO Box 1210
Ashland, AL 36251
Phone: 205-354-7151
1-800-762-4475
Fax: 205-354-7022

Wells Aluminum Corp.
Doors
PO Box 67 Sale Barn Rd.
Cassville, MO 65625
Phone: 417-847-4771
Fax: 417-847-3042

Wells Cargo
Equipment & Trucks
PO Box 728-1094
Elkhart, IN 46515-0728
Phone: 219-264-9661
1-800-348-7553
Fax: 219-264-5938
Internet:
http://www.wellscargo.com

Wen Products
Hardware; Tools/Electric
& Pneumatic; Tools/Hand
1240 E. Diehl Rd.,
Suite 100
Naperville, IL 60563
Phone: 708-955-0006
1-800-462-3630
Fax: 708-955-0422

WENCO of Iowa
(A Div. of JELD-WEN)
Doors; Windows
PO Box 741
Grinnell, IA 50112
Phone: 1-800-877-9482

WENCO of Mississippi
(A Div. of JELD-WEN)
Doors; Windows
540 E. Industrial Park
Holly Springs, MS 38635
Phone: 1-800-877-9482

WENCO of North
Carolina
(A Div. of JELD-WEN)
Doors; Windows
5427 N. Sharon Amity Rd.
Charlotte, NC 28215
Phone: 1-800-877-9482

WENCO of Ohio
(A Div. of JELD-WEN)
Doors; Windows
335 Commerce Dr.
Mt. Vernon, OH 43050
Phone: 614-397-3403
1-800-877-9482
Fax: 614-397-7442

WENCO of
Pennsylvania
(A Div. of JELD-WEN)
Doors; Windows
PO Box 259
Ringtown, PA 17967
Phone: 1-800-877-9482

Werner Co.
Equipment & Trucks;
Moulding & Millwork;
Paints, Caulks & Adhesives
10900 Belmont Ave.
Franklin Park, IL 60131
Phone: 708-455-9450
Fax: 708-455-1042

Wesaunard
Faucets & Fixtures
9429 Courthouse Rd.
Spotsylvania, VA 22553
Phone: 540-582-6677
Fax: 540-582-5233

Weslock National
Hardware
13344 S. Main St.
Los Angeles, CA 90061
Phone: 310-327-2770
1-800-762-4475
Fax: 310-324-4624

Westchester Marble
& Granite
Countertops; Flooring;
Hardware; Siding &
Accessories; Walls, Ceilings
& Finishes
31 Warren Pl.
Mt. Vernon, NY 10550
Phone: 914-667-1600
1-800-634-0866
Fax: 914-668-9474
E-mail:
wzwmgny@worldnet.att.net

Westchester Modular
Homes
Structural Systems
30 Reagans Mill Rd.
Wingdale, NY 12594
Phone: 914-832-9400
1-800-832-3888
Fax: 914-832-6698

Westendorf Whirlpool
Faucets & Fixtures
PO Box 37218
Omaha, NE 68137
Phone: 402-333-0568
1-800-747-0500
Fax: 402-333-3406

Western Archrib
Engineered Lumber
& Panels
PO Box 580
Boissevain, MB R0C 0E0
Canada
Phone: 204-534-2486
Fax: 204-534-2236
E-mail:
westernarchrib@mail.
techplus.com

Western Cabinet &
Millwork
Cabinetry
PO Box 137,
15300 Woodinville-
Redmond Rd. N.W.
Woodinville, WA 98072
Phone: 206-823-4141
Fax: 206-823-7668

Western Forms
Structural Systems;
Windows
6200 Equitable Rd.
Kansas City, MO 64120
Phone: 816-241-0477
1-800-821-3870
Fax: 816-241-6877

Western Quarry Tile
Countertops; Flooring;
Walls, Ceilings & Finishes
490 E. Duarte Rd.
Monrovia, CA 91016
Phone: 818-358-2465
Fax: 818-303-0532

Western Red Cedar
Lumber Assn.
Siding & Accessories; Walls,
Ceilings & Finishes
1100-555 Burrard St.
Vancouver, BC V7X 1S7
Canada
Phone: 604-684-0266
Fax: 604-682-8641
Internet: http://www.
cofi.org/WRCLA

Western Ventilation
Products
HVAC
1430 40th Ave. N.W.
Calgary, AB T2E 6L1
Canada
Phone: 403-250-3348
Fax: 403-250-7786

Western Wood
Products Assn.
Doors; Engineered Lumber
& Panels; Flooring; Garage
Doors & Openers;
Landscape Design;
Moulding & Millwork;
Siding & Accessories; Walls,
Ceilings & Finishes
522 S.W. Fifth Ave.,
Suite 400
Portland, OR 97204
Phone: 503-224-3930
Fax: 503-224-3934

Westile
Roofing
8311 W. Carder Ct.
Littleton, CO 80125
Phone: 303-791-1700
1-800-433-8453
Fax: 303-791-9906

Westinghouse and
Cutler-Hammer
Products
Electrical & Lighting
1090 W. Thorndale Ave.
Bensenville, IL 60106
Phone: 630-595-1667
1-800-443-3342
Fax: 630-595-2574

Westview Products
Room Enclosures; Windows
PO Box 569
Dallas, OR 97338
Phone: 503-623-5174
1-800-203-7557
Fax: 503-623-3382

Wesure Weld
Structural Systems
4510-80 Ave. S.E.
Calgary, AB T2C 4H9
Canada
Phone: 403-279-2440
Fax: 403-236-8135

Weyerhaeuser Door Div.
Doors
1401 E. Fourth St.
Marshfield, WI 54449
Phone: 715-384-2141
1-800-869-3667
Fax: 715-384-3802

Weyerhaeuser Oriented Strand Business
Engineered Lumber & Panels
2000 Frontis Plaza Blvd., Suite 101
Winston-Salem, NC 27101
Phone: 910-659-2900
1-800-648-2566
Fax: 910-768-5688

WH Porter
Insulation; Structural Systems
4240 N. 136th Ave.
Holland, MI 49424
Phone: 616-399-1963
Fax: 616-399-9123

Wheatbelt
Windows
300 Industrial Rd.
Hillsboro, KS 67063
Phone: 316-947-2323
1-800-264-5171
Fax: 316-947-3053

**Wheeling Corrugating Co.
(A Div. of Wheeling Pittsburgh Steel Corp.)**
Roofing; Siding & Accessories
1134 Market St.
Wheeling, WV 26003
Phone: 304-234-2400
Fax: 304-234-2210

Whirlaway
Appliances
4240 E. LaPalma Ave., PO Box 4146
Anaheim, CA 92803
Phone: 714-524-7770
1-800-854-3229
Fax: 714-996-0572

Whirljet Systems
Faucets & Fixtures
1500 Quail St., Suite 500
Newport Beach, CA 92660
Phone: 714-751-4422
1-800-234-0576
Fax: 714-832-3476

Whirlpool Corp. Whirlpool Appliance Group
Appliances
2000 M-63
Benton Harbor, MI 49022
Phone: 616-923-5000
1-800-253-1301
Fax: 616-923-3785
Internet:
http://www.whirlpool.com/

Whitacre-Greer
Fireplaces; Landscape Design; Siding & Accessories; Structural Systems
1400 S. Mahoning Ave.
Alliance, OH 44601
Phone: 330-823-1610
1-800-WGPAVER
Fax: 330-823-5502

White Home Products
Specialty Products
PO Box 340
Smyrna, GA 30080
Phone: 404-431-0900
1-800-200-9272
Fax: 404-432-3778

White Lightning Products
Paints, Caulks & Adhesives
2375 130th Ave. N.W., Suite 103
Bellevue, WA 98005
Phone: 206-881-5770
1-800-869-4483
Fax: 206-881-5892

White River Hardwoods-Woodworks
Moulding & Millwork
1197 Happy Hollow Rd.
Fayetteville, AR 72701
Phone: 501-442-6986
1-800-558-0119
Fax: 501-442-0257
Internet: http://www.Mouldings.com

White-Rodgers Emerson Electric Co.
HVAC
9797 Reavis Rd.
St. Louis, MO 63123
Phone: 314-577-1300
Fax: 314-577-1517

White-Westinghouse (A Brand of Frigidaire Co.)
Appliances
6000 Perimeter Dr.
Dublin, OH 43017
Phone: 614-792-4100
1-800-685-6005
Fax: 614-792-4079

Whittlesey Wood Products
Engineered Lumber & Panels; Moulding & Millwork; Walls, Ceilings & Finishes
1590 N.W. 159th St.
Miami, FL 33169
Phone: 305-621-4242
1-800-225-6384
Fax: 305-621-2022

Wilkening Fireplace Co.
Fireplaces
HCR 73, PO Box 625
Walker, MN 56484
Phone: 218-547-1988
1-800-367-7976
Fax: 218-547-2848

Willamette Industries
Engineered Lumber & Panels
2730 Pacific Blvd., S.E.
Albany, OR 97321
Phone: 541-926-7771
Fax: 541-924-5296

Willamette Industries (Duraflake Div.)
Engineered Lumber & Panels; Moulding & Millwork
PO Box 428
Albany, OR 97321
Phone: 541-928-3341
Fax: 541-928-4116

Willamette Industries (Sawmill Div.)
Engineered Lumber & Panels
PO Drawer 1100
Ruston, LA 71273
Phone: 318-255-6258
Fax: 318-251-9589

William Zinsser & Co.
Paints, Caulks & Adhesives
173 Belmont Dr.
Somerset, NJ 08875
Phone: 908-469-4367
Fax: 908-563-9774

Williams Furnace Co.
Fireplaces; HVAC
225 Acacia St.
Colton, CA 92324
Phone: 909-825-0993
1-800-266-0993
Fax: 909-370-0581

Williams-Scotsman
Equipment & Trucks
8211 Town Center Dr.
White Marsh, MD 21236
Phone: 410-931-6000
1-800-782-1500
Fax: 410-931-6047
Internet:
http://www.willscot.com

Willmar Windows
Doors; Windows
PO Box 99,
RPO Elmwood
Winnipeg, MB R2L 2A5
Canada
Phone: 204-668-8230
Fax: 204-663-1072

Wilson Saftey Products
Equipment & Trucks
Second and Washington Sts., PO Box 622
Reading, PA 19603-0622
Phone: 610-376-6161
Fax: 610-371-7725

Wilmes Window Mfg. Co.
Doors; Windows
234 W. 23rd St.
Ferdinand, IN 47532
Phone: 812-367-1811
1-800-477-1811

Wilsonart Intl.
Countertops; Faucets & Fixtures; Flooring
2400 Wilson Pl.,
PO Box 6110
Temple, TX 76503-6110
Phone: 817-778-2711
1-800-433-3222
Fax: 817-770-2384
Internet: http://www.builder online.com/~wilsonart

Win Estimator
Computer Software
8209 S. 222nd St., Suite B
Kent, WA 98032
Phone: 206-395-3631
1-800-950-2374
Fax: 206-395-3634

Winco
Equipment & Trucks
225 S. Cordova Ave.
Le Center, MN 56057
Phone: 507-357-6821
1-800-733-2112
Fax: 507-357-4857

Wind-Lock Corp.
Siding & Accessories
1055 Leisz's Bridge Rd.
Leesport, PA 19533
Phone: 1-800-872-5625
Fax: 610-926-6815

Window Quilt/Northern Cross Industries
Windows
7 Technology Dr.
Brattleboro, VT 05301
Phone: 802-257-4500
1-800-257-4501
Fax: 1-800-257-9246

Window Saver Co.
Room Enclosures
177 E. Riding Dr.
Carlisle, MA 01741
Phone: 508-369-8505
1-800-321-WARM
Fax: 508-369-9759

Windquest Cos.
Specialty Products
3311 Windquest Dr.
Holland, MI 49424
Phone: 616-399-3311
1-800-562-4257
Fax: 616-399-8784

Windsor Door
Doors; Garage Doors & Openers; Hardware
5800 Scott Hamilton Dr.
Little Rock, AR 72209
Phone: 501-562-1872
Fax: 501-562-0406

Windsor Mill
Engineered Lumber & Panels; Moulding & Millwork; Siding & Accessories; Walls, Ceilings & Finishes
8711 Bell Rd.,
PO Box 39
Windsor, CA 95492
Phone: 707-546-6373
Fax: 707-838-7978

Windsor Window Co.
Doors; Windows
900 S. 19th St.
West Des Moines, IA 50265
Phone: 515-223-6660
1-800-887-0111

Windsor Window Co.-NC Plant
(See Windsor Window Co.)

Wineland Walnut
Flooring
9009 River Rd.
Chico, CA 95928
Phone: 916-345-4012
Fax: 916-345-0990

Wing Enterprises
Equipment & Trucks; Tools/Hand
1325 W. Industrial Cir.
Springville, UT 84663
Phone: 801-489-3684
1-800-453-1192
Fax: 801-489-3685

Wing Industries
Doors
PO Box 38347
Dallas, TX 75238
Phone: 214-699-9900
1-800-341-WING (except TX)
Fax: 214-470-9304

Winstrom Mfg. Corp.
Doors; Windows
70 North St.
Park Forest, IL 60466
Phone: 708-748-8200
1-800-WINSTROM
Fax: 708-748-8222

Winter Panel Corp.
Insulation; Structural Systems
74 Glen Orne Dr.
Brattleboro, VT 05301
Phone: 802-254-6529
Fax: 802-254-4999

Wire Reinforcement Institute
203 Loudoun St., S.W.
Leesburg, VA 22075
Phone: 703-779-2339
Fax: 703-779-2340

The Wiremold Co.
Electrical & Lighting
60 Woodlawn St.
West Hartford, CT 06133
Phone: 203-233-6251
1-800-243-8421
Fax: 203-231-1812

The Wiremold Co. Brooks Electronics Div.
Electrical & Lighting
13200 Townsend Rd.
Philadelphia, PA 19154
Phone: 215-969-3803
1-800-523-0130
Fax: 215-969-3858

Wirsbo Co.
Faucets & Fixtures; HVAC
5925 148th St. W.
Apple Valley, MN 55124
Phone: 612-891-2000
1-800-321-4739
Fax: 612-891-2008
Internet:
http://www.wirsbo.com

Wisconsin Log Homes
Moulding & Millwork; Siding & Accessories; Structural Systems
2390 Pamperin Rd.
Green Bay, WI 54313
Phone: 414-434-3010
1-800-678-9107
Fax: 414-434-2140

Wolf Range Co.
Appliances
19600 S. Alameda
Compton, CA 90221
Phone: 310-637-3737
1-800-366-9653
Fax: 310-637-7931

Wolman Wood Care Products
Paints, Caulks & Adhesives
1850 Koppers Bldg.,
436 Seventh Ave.
Pittsburgh, PA 15219
Phone: 1-800-556-7737
Fax: 412-227-2618

Wolverine Brass
Faucets & Fixtures; Plumbing Supplies
2951 Hwy. 501 E.
Conway, SC 29526
Phone: 803-347-3121
1-800-944-9292
Fax: 1-800-945-9292

Wolverine Vinyl Siding
Siding & Accessories
17199 Laurel Park Dr. N.
Livonia, MI 48152-2679
Phone: 313-953-1100
1-800-521-9020
Fax: 313-953-0855

Wood-Aire Fireplace Systems
Fireplaces
PO Box 88, 210 S. Main
Commerce, OK 74339
Phone: 918-675-4355
1-800-533-4264
Fax: 918-675-5455

Wood Component Manufacturers Assn. (formerly National Dimension Manufacturers Assn.)
Flooring; Moulding & Millwork
1000 Johnson Ferry Rd., Suite A-130
Marietta, GA 30068-2114
Phone: 770-565-6660

Wood Factory
Doors; Moulding & Millwork;p Specialty Products
111 Railroad St.
Navasota, TX 77868
Phone: 409-825-7233
Fax: 409-825-1791

Wood Floors
Engineered Lumber & Panels; Flooring; Moulding & Millwork
Hwy. 301 N.,
PO Box 1522
Orangeburg, SC 29116
Phone: 803-534-8478
Fax: 803-533-0051

Wood-Kote Products
Paints, Caulks & Adhesives
8000 N.E. 14th Pl.
Portland, OR 97211
Phone: 503-285-8371
Fax: 503-285-8374
Internet:
http://www.woodkote.com

Wood Machinery Manufacturers of America
1900 Arch St.
Philadelphia, PA 19103
Phone: 215-564-3484
1-800-BUY-WMMA
Fax: 215-963-9785
E-mail:
assnhqt@netaxs.com

Wood-Mode
Cabinetry
1 Second St.
Kreamer, PA 17833
Phone: 717-374-2711
Fax: 717-374-2700

Wood Moulding & Millwork Producers Assn.
Moulding & Millwork
507 First St.
Woodland, CA 95695
Phone: 916-661-9591
1-800-550-7889
Fax: 916-661-9586

Wood Truss Council of America
Structural Systems
5937 Meadowood Dr., Suite 14
Madison, WI 53711
Phone: 608-274-4849
Fax: 608-274-3329

Wood Ventures
HVAC
PO Box 563
Grass Valley, CA 95945
Phone: 916-272-4972
1-800-524-5230
Fax: 916-272-4932

Woodcraft Supply
Engineered Lumber & Panels; Paints, Caulks & Adhesives
210 Wood County Industrial Park,
PO Box 1686
Parkersburg, WV 26102
Phone: 304-428-4866
1-800-225-1153
Fax: 304-428-8271

Woodfold-Marco Mfg.
Cabinetry; Countertops; Hardware
PO Box 346
Forest Grove, OR 97116
Phone: 503-357-7181
Fax: 503-357-7185
Internet: http://www.woodfold.com

Woodkrest Custom Homes
Structural Systems
3175 Johnson Ave.
Memphis, TN 38112
Phone: 901-324-0152

Woodline Mfg.
Flooring; Moulding & Millwork
1013 Hwy. 53
Eveleth, MN 55734
Phone: 218-744-5966
Fax: 218-744-5969

WoodMaster Designs
Cabinetry; Doors; Moulding & Millwork
30489 San Antonio St.
Hayward, CA 94544
Phone: 510-487-1706
1-800-285-8551
Fax: 510-487-4239

Woodmaster Foundations
Insulation; Structural Systems
PO Box 66,
845 Dexter St.
Prescott, WI 54021
Phone: 715-262-3655
Fax: 715-262-5079
Internet: http://www.pressenter.com/~woodmstr/

Woodpecker Mfg.
Doors
1010 N. Cascade
Montrose, CO 81401
Phone: 970-249-2616
1-800-524-7055
Fax: 970-249-2392

Woodpro Cabinetry
Cabinetry; Faucets & Fixtures
PO Box 70
Cabool, MO 65689-0070
Phone: 417-962-5127
1-888-2WOODPRO
Fax: 417-962-5332

The Woods Co.
Countertops; Flooring; Moulding & Millwork
610-B Fifth Ave.
Chambersburg, PA 17201
Phone: 717-263-6524
Fax: 717-263-9346

The Woods Quality Cabinetry Co.
Cabinetry; Countertops
42 84 Dr.
Eighty Four, PA 15330
Phone: 412-228-3040
Fax: 1-800-882-84PA

Woodsmiths Design & Mfg.
Moulding & Millwork
515 Main St.
Gunter, TX 75058
Phone: 903-433-1133
Fax: 903-433-1204

WoodStar Cabinets (A Div. of Texwood Industries)
Cabinetry
PO Box 380640
Duncanville, TX 75138
Phone: 214-283-3425
Fax: 214-709-7771

Woodstock Intl.
Hardware; Tools/Electric & Pneumatic
PO Box 2309
Bellingham, WA 98227
Phone: 206-734-3482
Fax: 206-671-3053

The Woodstone Co.
Doors; Garage Doors & Openers; Windows
PO Box 223, Patch Rd.
Westminster, VT 05158
Phone: 802-722-9217
Fax: 802-722-9528
Internet: http://www.woodstone.com

Woodwork Institute of California
Cabinetry; Countertops; Doors; Moulding & Millwork; Specialty Products; Walls, Ceilings & Finishes; Windows
PO Box 980247
Sacramento, CA 95798
Phone: 916-372-9943
Fax: 916-372-9950
Internet: http://www.wicnet.org

Work Right Products
Faucets & Fixtures
4615 Work Right Cir.
Lakeport, CA 95453-9302
Phone: 707-263-0290
1-800-862-4995 (CA)
Fax: 707-263-4048

World Floor Covering Assn.
Flooring
2211 E. Howell Ave.
Anaheim, CA 92806
Phone: 714-978-6440
1-800-624-6880
Fax: 714-978-6066

Worthington Group
Moulding & Millwork
PO Box 868
Troy, AL 36081
Phone: 205-566-9607
1-800-872-1608

Worthy Works
Hardware
1220 Rock St.
Rockford, IL 61101-1437
Phone: 815-968-5858
1-800-373-5662
Fax: 815-968-5959

WR Bonsal Co.
Flooring; Structural Systems
8201 Arrowridge Blvd.,
PO Box 241148
Charlotte, NC 28224-1148
Phone: 704-525-1621
1-800-738-1621
Fax: 704-529-5261

W.R. Grace
(See Grace Construction Products)

WR Meadows
Specialty Products; Structural Systems
PO Box 543
Elgin, IL 60121
Phone: 847-683-4500
1-800-342-5976
Fax: 847-683-4544

Wurster Traditional Timber Building
Structural Systems
RD 4, PO Box 427
Montoursville, PA 17754
Phone: 717-435-2468

WWP Enterprises
Computer Software
2815 Greenbrier Rd.
Anniston, AL 36207
Phone: 205-835-9952
Fax: 205-835-9952
Internet: http://www.wwpent.com/wwpent.htm

X

Xactware
Computer Software
1426 E. 750 N
Orem, UT 84057
Phone: 1-800-424-9228
Fax: 801-224-5218
Internet: http://www.xactware.com

XYPEX Chemical Corp.
Paints, Caulks & Adhesives
13731 Mayfield Pl.
Richmond, BC V6V 2G9
Canada
Phone: 604-273-5265

Y

Yakima Mfg. (A Div. of JELD-WEN)
Doors
1123 N. Sixth Ave.,
PO Box 1427
Yakima, WA 98907-1427
Phone: 1-800-877-9482

Yale Locks & Hardware
Hardware
PO Box 25288
Charlotte, NC 28229
Phone: 704-283-2101
1-800-438-1951
Fax: 704-289-2875

Yale Materials Handling Corp.
Equipment & Trucks
15 Junction Rd.
Flemington, NJ 08822
Phone: 1-800-233-YALE

Yardi Systems
Computer Software
819 Reddick Ave.
Santa Barbara, CA 93103
Phone: 805-966-3373
1-800-866-1144
Fax: 805-963-3155
Internet: http://yardi.com

Yenkin Majestic
Paints, Caulks & Adhesives
1920 Leonard Ave.
Columbus, OH 43219
Phone: 614-253-8511
Fax: 614-253-6327

York Intl. Corp. Unitary Products Group
HVAC
Dept. 232A,
PO Box 1592
York, PA 17405-1592
Phone: 717-771-6225
Fax: 717-771-6819
Internet: http://www.york.com

York Spiral Stair
Moulding & Millwork
Dept. B, RR 1, Box 945
North Vassalboro, ME 04962
Phone: 207-872-5558
Fax: 207-872-6731

Yorktowne (An Elkay Co.) Yorktowne Cabinets
Cabinetry
100 Redco Ave.
Red Lion, PA 17356
Phone: 717-244-4011
1-800-777-0065
Fax: 717-244-5497

Yost Mfg. & Supply
Siding & Accessories
1018 Hartford Tpk.,
Rt. 85
Waterford, CT 06385
Phone: 860-447-9678
1-800-872-9678
Fax: 860-444-9678

Yuba River Moulding & Millwork
Moulding & Millwork
PO Box 1078
Yuba City, CA 95992
Phone: 916-742-2475
Fax: 916-742-7140

Z

Z-Brick Brands
Paints, Caulks & Adhesives; Walls, Ceilings & Finishes
889 Valley Park Dr.
Shakopee, MN 55379
Phone: 612-496-6016
1-800-433-9517
Fax: 612-496-6067

Z N R Concept
Tools/Hand
13667 Detroyes
Mirabel, PQ J7J 1E1
Canada
Phone: 514-437-0773
1-800-667-7773
Fax: 514-437-0804

Zaca
Cabinetry
2630 Townsgate Rd.
Westlake Village, CA 91361
Phone: 805-446-4460
Fax: 805-446-4455

Zago Mfg.
Moulding & Millwork
240 King Blvd.
Newark, NJ 07102
Phone: 201-643-6700
Fax: 201-643-4433

Zaneen Lighting
Electrical & Lighting
67 Colville Rd.
Toronto, ON M6M 2Y2
Canada
Phone: 416-247-9221
1-800-388-3382
Fax: 416-247-9319

Zappone Mfg.
Roofing
2928 N. Pittsburg
Spokane, WA 99207
Phone: 509-483-6408
1-800-285-2677
Fax: 509-483-8050

Zepsa Stairs
Moulding & Millwork
PO Box 260
Clover, SC 29710
Phone: 803-222-1212
Fax: 803-222-3153

Zickgraf Hardwood Co. Smoky Mountain Hardwood Flooring
Flooring
PO Box 1149,
137 Depot St.
Franklin, NC 28734
Phone: 704-369-9156
1-800-243-1277
Fax: 704-524-5581

Zion Services Corp.
Roofing
11300 N.W. S. River Dr.
Medley, FL 33178
Phone: 305-557-5737
1-800-772-4165
Fax: 305-557-0249

Zircon
Tools/Hand
1580 Dell Ave.
Campbell, CA 95008
Phone: 408-866-8600
1-800-245-9265
Fax: 408-866-9230

ZTECH
HVAC
2340 Gold River Rd.,
Suite E
Gold River, CA 95670
Phone: 916-635-7484
Fax: 916-635-7668